Latina/o Sexualities

Latina/o Sexualities

Probing Powers, Passions, Practices, and Policies

EDITED BY

MARYSOL ASENCIO

RUTGERS UNIVERSITY PRESS

NEW BRUNSWICK, NEW JERSEY, AND LONDON

LIBRARY OF CONGRESS CATALOGING-IN-PUBLICATION DATA

Latina/o sexualities : probing powers, passions, practices, and policies / edited by
Marysol Asencio.
        p.   cm.
    Includes bibliographical references and index.
    ISBN 978-0-8135-4599-8 (hardcover : alk. paper)
    ISBN 978-0-8135-4600-1 (pbk. : alk. paper)
        1. Hispanic American women—Sexual behavior.   2. Hispanics—Sexual behavior.
I. Asencio, Marysol, 1960–
    E184.S75L346 2010
    306.76—dc22   2008051485

A British Cataloging-in-Publication record for this book is available
from the British Library.

Visit our Web site: http://rutgerspress.rutgers.edu

Manufactured in the United States of America

CONTENTS

         JOSÉ QUIROGA AND MELANIE LÓPEZ FRANK

10   Where There's *Querer*: Knowledge Production
         and the Praxis of HIV Prevention   150
         GEORGE AYALA, JAIME CORTEZ,
         AND PATRICK "PATO" HEBERT

11   Religion/Spirituality, U.S. Latina/o Communities, and
         Sexuality Scholarship: A Thread of Current Works   173
         SALVADOR VIDAL-ORTIZ

12   Latina/o Sexualities in Motion: Latina/o Sexualities
         Research Agenda Project   188
         SUSANA PEÑA

13   Latinas, Sex Work, and Trafficking in the United States   207
         AMALIA L. CABEZAS WITH DOLORES ORTIZ
         AND SONIA VALENCIA

14   Latina *Lesbianas, BiMujeres,* and Trans Identities:
         Charting Courses in the Social Sciences   217
         LUZ CALVO AND CATRIÓNA RUEDA ESQUIBEL

15   Latina/o Transpopulations   230
         MARCIA OCHOA

16   Boundaries and Bisexuality: Reframing the Discourse
         on Latina/o Bisexualities   243
         MIGUEL MUÑOZ-LABOY AND CARMEN YON LEAU

17   Revisiting *Activos* and *Pasivos*: Toward New Cartographies
         of Latino/Latin American Male Same-Sex Desire   253
         SALVADOR VIDAL-ORTIZ, CARLOS DECENA,
         HÉCTOR CARRILLO, AND TOMÁS ALMAGUER

18   Retiring Behavioral Risk, Disease, and Deficit Models:
         Sexual Health Frameworks for Latino Gay Men and
         Other Men Who Enjoy Sex with Men   274
         GEORGE AYALA

         Epilogue: Rethinking the Maps Where
         "Latina/o" and "Sexuality" Meet   279
         CARLOS DECENA

         Notes   287
         Contributors   355
         Index   363

PREFACE

In April 2005 the editor of this volume hosted a conference entitled "Latina/o Sexualities: Breaking Silences, Creating Changes" at the University of Connecticut through the Institute for Puerto Rican and Latino Studies. In the course of planning this conference, many Latina/o scholars working on Latina/o sexualities, shared frustrations regarding the limited amount and range of empirically based research on Latina/o sexualities. In addition, there was disappointment with the lack of critical analysis of the available social and behavioral science literature to assess its validity, relevance, and applicability to Latinas and Latinos. We believe that this type of mapping and analysis is urgently needed and that Latina/o scholars and decision makers need to play a major role in such an initiative.

During this same period, Barbara Klugman at the Ford Foundation had arrived at a similar conclusion as she sought consultations from experts in Black and Latina/o sexualities. In Ford's discussions, it was clear that a concerted effort was needed to advance social and behavioral research on Latina/o sexualities. There was no current work that attempted to assess the overall field of Latina/o sexualities, a field that is slowly emerging yet remains fragmented. What was being produced, and ignored? And what contributions, if any, are there for policies and programs to address the well-being and future needs of this population regarding sexuality? In January 2006 the Ford Foundation funded a two-year project on Latina/o Sexualities, which I directed, to begin mapping the current state of knowledge and discourse, in particular within the social and behavioral sciences. It also funded a similar project on Black Sexualities, directed by Juan Battle, professor of sociology at the City University of New York.

This project brought together an advisory board of experts, which included Latina/o academics across various disciplines as well as policymakers and educators, to debate and outline a plan to systematically assess and document the state of Latina/o sexualities research. This volume contains papers that were commissioned by the Latina/o Sexualities Research Project based on themes and issues the board identified either as having sufficient scholarship available or as being important areas of exploration. All authors were asked to ascertain what had been written on a particular theme or topic and to identify gaps and future directions for research, and policy implications wherever possible. There were disciplinary differences in how authors approached this task as well as variations in the amount of social and behavioral science literature available from which to draw on particular topics. This placed a great demand on the authors' creativity. Until now, no project had addressed different areas of scholarship on Latina/o sexualities utilizing a multidisciplinary perspective. Our goal is to situate the current field of knowledge and look at the needs for future research related to the sexualities of Latinas and Latinos as well as to develop a more cohesive field.

It is important to point out that it is not our intention to present Latina/o sexualities as a unique phenomenon distinct and apart from the sexualities of other racial/ethnic groups. Rather, our goal is to recognize that under the current (and contested) system of racial/ethnic categorization, Latina/o history and social circumstances within the United States frames and influences Latina/os' sexual beliefs, attitudes, and behaviors as well as the way their sexuality is viewed by the dominant society. Our understanding of their position within U.S. society and their multiple statuses, histories, and identities both complicate and advance our knowledge about Latinas and Latinos and their sexualities. We hope that this volume creates a space to explore and discuss Latina/os and their sexualities devoid of the limitations of the prevalent literature or the narrow research models of the past.

ACKNOWLEDGMENTS

This volume would not have been possible without the support and contributions of the Ford Foundation and many exceptional individuals. The first person I would like to thank is Barbara Klugman from the Ford Foundation, who advocated strongly for the development and financial support of this project. Her steadfast belief in the need for more research, scholarship, and policy-driven projects on race, ethnicity, and sexuality was a significant catalyst for this work. I am very grateful to Dorinda Welle from the Ford Foundation, who continued the commitment to the project, as the program officer, and facilitated our abilities to pursue this work in creative ways. She has continuously been available to assist in strengthening this initiative. I am grateful to both of these women for their dedication and support as well as to the Ford Foundation for its commitment to prioritize issues of race, ethnicity, and sexuality.

The success of this project is due in large part to the engaged efforts of its advisory and editorial board: Tomás Almaguer (San Francisco State University, Calif.), George Ayala (AIDS Project Los Angeles–The David Geffen Center, Calif.), Héctor Carrillo (Northwestern University, Evanston, Ill.), Carlos Decena (Rutgers University, N.J.), Jessica Gonzalez (National Latina Institute for Reproductive Health, New York City), Gloria González-López (University of Texas at Austin), Pablo Mitchell (Oberlin College, Ohio), Monica Rodriguez (Sex Information and Education Council of the United States [SIECUS], New York City), Salvador Vidal-Ortiz (American University, Washington, D.C.), and Patricia Zavella (University of California–Santa Cruz). I would like also to thank Angela Hooton for her service to the board.

The assistance of these individuals in mapping the major areas of the field and their willingness to provide guidance on all the issues that arose during the course of the project created a strong bond among the board members. Their collegiality set the tone for the entire project, including the work with the authors in this volume, who for the last two years have been working diligently to address their areas of expertise. They did so with grace and generosity. In addition to all the contributions by the board and other authors of this collection, many academics and experts in the field provided helpful feedback: Frances Aparicio, Elizabeth Bernstein, Paisley Currah, Raquel Donoso, Pamela Erickson, Robert T. Francoeur, Deena Gonzalez, Vincent Guilamo-Ramos,

Matthew Gutmann, Eithne Luibhéid, Frances Negrón-Muntaner, Tooru Nemoto, Martin Nesvig, Mark Overmyer-Velazquez, Mark Padilla, Richard Parker, Emma Pérez, Horacio Roque Ramírez, Jesus Ramirez, Xaé Reyes, Paula Rodriguez-Rust, Ben Sifuentes-Jáuregui, Deborah Tolman, Carole Vance, and María Cecilia Zea. Although all the final decisions were outside their control, I thank them for all their hard work and thoughtful insights. I would also like to thank Mary Burke, Marisol Garcia, and Susy J. Zepeda, who as graduate students did literature searches to assist the board in evaluating particular areas of research.

This project could not have been accomplished without its core staff. Anne Theriault, the administrative assistant on the project, was an integral part of the process. She provided the management and organization that permitted us to collaborate with a significant number of scholars and researchers in the field. She also provided insightful feedback to improve our work as well as doing all the paperwork necessary to keep the project moving forward. Another person who was integral to the project was Katie Acosta. As the research assistant, she operated more as a colleague than as an assistant. Our coauthoring of the introduction to the volume reflects our collaboration at all levels. She is an emerging scholar in the field who has much to offer to its future development.

The Institute of Puerto Rican and Latino Studies (IPRLS) at the University of Connecticut, under the auspices of the Office of Multicultural and International Affairs (OMIA), housed this project. Dr. Ronald Taylor and Dr. Cathleen Love, as the vice provost and associate vice provost, enthusiastically supported the project from its inception. Dr. Guillermo Irizarry, the director of IPRLS, provided additional resources as well as encouragement and commitment to the field of Latina/o sexualities. In addition, several members of OMIA and the Office of Sponsored Research provided their active support to the project who deserve special thanks, in particular, Giselle Russo, Matt Cahill, Gianfranco Barbato, and Barbara Jolley. I am grateful to the faculty of IPRLS who accommodated this project within their work environment. I would also like to thank Christopher Petkovich at the UConn Foundation for promoting the work that we are doing and advocating on our behalf to further develop this field of study within the university.

I also hold an appointment in Human Development and Family Studies (HDFS). The faculty and staff in HDFS have been extraordinarily supportive and encouraging of my work. Their collegiality and cooperation provide a model for any academic department. I would like to thank Ron Sabatelli, who as department head has supported my involvement in this project.

Ann Gross was an integral part of preparing and copyediting this manuscript so as to develop as much consistency as possible given the diverse backgrounds and writing styles of the authors. Jane Bradley assisted with editing early versions of the work. Adi Hovav, Marilyn Campbell, and Beth Kressel at Rutgers University Press facilitated the process to publish this volume with care and in a timely manner. Sandra Barnes, coeditor of the companion *Black*

Sexualities volume, has been exceptional in providing support and feedback to this volume as well.

As we all know, any work of this type involves many sacrifices and support from family and friends who bear the burden of broken engagements, skipped vacations, and stress-filled days. I would like to thank my immediate family, in particular, Juan and Eliseo Asencio, Rick Cardenas, and Mayra and Jose Gonzalez, as well as other family and friends, Josiah L. Acosta, Thomas Blank, Anita Garey, Jane Goldman, Virginia and Gabriela Graham, Mary Kenny, Stephen Ostertag, and Nancy Sheehan for all their active support over the last two years. I would also like to take the opportunity to above all thank Margaret Hynes, without whose presence through all the ups and downs this project would have been impossible. Margaret provided not only emotional sustenance but also keen analytical, organizational, and editorial comments that strengthened the work. I give a collective thanks to the rest of my extended family and network of friends who are there for me through all the trials and tribulations of work and life.

Last but not least, I thank my colleague and friend Juan Battle, who as project director and coeditor of our sister project, the *Black Sexualities* volume, provided leadership, intellect, vision, and the drive that only he can bring to a project. I benefited and learned tremendously from our collaboration and his example. I am thankful to have gone through these two years and projects with him. He is a force of nature.

Marysol Asencio

Latina/o Sexualities

Introduction

Mapping Latina/o Sexualities
Research and Scholarship

MARYSOL ASENCIO AND KATIE ACOSTA

When you think of Latina/o sexuality, what images pop into your head? Perhaps you think of Jennifer Lopez, Ricky Martin, Salma Hayek, Shakira, or Antonio Banderas. Or maybe you just envision large booties, swiveling hips, and sweltering heat? Or do you picture brutish "macho" men and passive women on welfare who cannot or do not want to control their fertility? Do you picture men and women having healthy sexual lives or ignorant, uncaring people who reproduce children and poverty? Or do images of dark-skinned sex workers working the corners of urban streets come to mind? Given these decontextualized and pathologized images, one cannot help but wonder what the relationship between Latinas and Latinos and sexuality may really be. Who are these people? How do they express their sexualities? Why do we hold such limited and narrow stereotypical views of them in relation to sexuality? Is there such a thing as a Latina/o sexuality that is distinct and separate from white non-Latina/o sexuality?

For years, academics and activists have critiqued the oversimplification of Latina sexualities. They questioned the image of the Latina who is characterized as either the virgin who is passive, submissive, and altruistic or the whore who is promiscuous, sexually aggressive, and uncouth. Latinas have been racialized[1] and exoticized in pop culture.[2] As Patricia Hill Collins notes, these depictions produce images of women of color as sexually wild and uncivilized beings.[3] Images of Latina icons like Jennifer Lopez that build upon existing views of the Latinas' bodies have enabled the dominant society to fetishize us, reduce us to sexual objects, erase our particular racial/ethnic identities, and decontextualize our historical experiences.[4]

Scholars have also critiqued the conceptualization of Latino males' sexualities.[5] The image of the "Latin lover" who is more sexually sophisticated, has more sexual allure, and more seductive power than do other men is challenged, as is the image of the hypersexual, aggressive, brutish, "macho" Latino male.

These portrayals of hypersexuality mirror those of African American men. As Collins notes, these images reinforce racist ideologies.[6]

A contemporary example of such an oversimplification and stereotyping of Latino male sexualities is Ricky Martin, whose talent and vibrancy have aided in his gaining crossover appeal in the U.S. media industry. Despite his talent and versatility as an entertainer, the media have become preoccupied with his sexuality on and offstage. The media's particular obsession with his sexual orientation stems from his position as the "sexy Latin" pop star to so many women and men in the dominant society. By not playing out the stereotype of the Latin lover and refusing to display or discuss his conquests of women, he fuels suspicions about his sexuality. This media focus on his sexuality has obscured many other important facets of his life, such as his charitable foundation to stop the trafficking of children and his open and vocal opposition to the Iraq War.[7] Despite his complexity, Martin is most often reduced to "shake your bon bon" and "gay or not gay."

What becomes relevant for us as scholars, educators, policymakers, students, and activists in contextualizing contemporary popular media examples is how they affect others' perceptions of our sexualities and our racial identities as Latinas and Latinos. Because we are underrepresented in mainstream media, existing images come to represent us as a whole. Thus, the diversity of Latinas and Latinos as sexual beings whose lives are shaped by race, class, nationality, and immigration—among many other factors—becomes invisible.

Scholars question whether many of these constructs of Latina/o sexualities actually exist in the lived experiences of Latinas and Latinos, and if so, how and to what extent they are really manifested. There are more stereotypes about Latinas' and Latinos' sexualities than actual research on their lived experiences. Many times these stereotypes are presented with little empirical support and utilize a pathological lens in understanding Latinas and Latinos or their sexuality.

Based on the available social and behavioral research on Latina/os, the essays in this volume begin to address these issues and pose the following questions: What is the status of research on the sexualities of Latinas and Latinos? What sexualities have we ignored and why? Who are we as sexual beings outside of our sexual behaviors and risk tendencies? What are the diversities among us as a group with various histories, racial identifications, and class backgrounds? This volume is the result of our attempt to map and critique our knowledge of Latinas and Latinos and their sexualities as produced through the social and behavioral sciences. It is an attempt to claim our sexualities, to create our own dialogues, and to rethink the underlying power dynamics of our sexual lives.

Who Are These Latina/os? The Use of Panethnic Categories

The term "Hispanic" has been uniformly used by the U.S. Census since 1970, while the term "Latino" appeared for the first time in the 2000 Census.[8] These terms are often used interchangeably. Within this large imposed category, there is little distinction across individual groups or the diverse historical, social, and political contexts in which they are situated. As such, it is easy to ignore the varied national origins, cultures, socioeconomic conditions, geographic locations, official residential status (including U.S. citizenship), political histories, racial identifications, dialects, native languages other than Spanish, religious and spiritual affiliations, experiences of political or social discrimination and oppression, and migrations and transnational movements of those we label Latinas and Latinos. To further complicate this debate in the United States, "Latina/o" or "Hispanic" is also a racialized category.[9] Thus, this nonwhite status provides another lens to Latinas' and Latinos' characterizations and experiences. That is to say, their position as a nonwhite population plays a role in their experiences and in the social hierarchy.

The use of the terms Hispanic or Latina/o is problematic not simply because of the immense differences they obscure but also because there is no common agreement by scholars or activists as to what the unifying thread among the groups really is or should be. Some scholars have argued that Hispanic tends to emphasize Spanish cultural (especially linguistic) connections among these ethnic groups while deemphasizing the political relationship and racialization of Latinas and Latinos in the United States and within U.S.–Latin American relations. This privileging of the Spanish culture also minimizes the multitude of other local and imported cultures, such as indigenous and African peoples that have influenced the heritages of those we refer to as Hispanic. As such, some prefer the term Latino since they believe the unifying thread is more about the social and political relationship within the U.S. context than cultural similarities deriving from Spanish colonization. For these scholars, the term Latino is used to refer to Caribbean and Latin American heritages while sometimes excluding Spain, a European country, and including Brazil as a Latin American country. Many scholars, however, use these terms without much thought about the terms themselves but rather adapt to the common usage in their geographic locations or disciplinary literature. As you read through the chapters in this volume, keep in mind that there is an ongoing underlying discussion regarding the use and purpose of these panethnic labels and their significance in our understanding of research findings.[10]

The way in which the U.S. government officially categorizes these populations, however, frames the way much of the research is collected on Hispanics/Latinos and who is included in that category. The U.S. Census Bureau established federal guidelines to collect and present data on race and Hispanic origin as set by the Office of Management and Budget (OMB) in October 1997. The OMB defines Hispanic or Latino as "a person of Cuban, Mexican, Puerto Rican, South or Central American, or other Spanish culture or origin, regardless of race." In terms of the Census and other government data collection projects, Hispanic and Latino are synonymous and interchangeable.[11]

In this volume, we use the term Latina/o and incorporate both the political and the cultural complexity of the supra-aggregate identity. In addition, we choose to refer to this population as Latina and Latino or Latina/o (or plural Latina/os) over simply using Latino (or Latinos) because of the inherent sexism in the masculine collective. In this way, we acknowledge equally the experiences of women and men in the construction of this diverse and heterogeneous community. We do not ignore the fact that "Latina/os" is an imposed category that often serves as a secondary identity. For many, national identities such as Mexican or Puerto Rican are the preferred term for self-identification.[12] Yet the reality is that most research utilizes these supra-aggregate terms.

While we agree that when using pan-ethnic categories, one runs the risk of obfuscating differences, we also remain mindful of their utility. These pan-ethnic categories provide us with a language and a platform from which to begin to implement social and policy changes in a way that would not be possible had we focused on a single ethnic group. Still, we struggle to understand exactly what our common thread is. Is it a shared history of Spanish and Portuguese colonization and the "racial" mixing that transpired as a result? Is it shared language (in the case of Spanish), Catholic religion, and similar cultural background? Is it a shared social and political history and positioning vis-à-vis whites and the United States? Despite many of the possible or imagined commonalities, we need to recognize that there are vast differences as well.

According to the 2000 Census, Latina/os are currently the largest minority group in the United States. They also constitute one of the fastest-growing. If the Latina/o population continues to grow at its current projected rate, one in four residents of the United States will claim some Latina/o heritage in the next forty years. At the same time, the white population has been decreasing steadily as a percentage of the U.S. population.[13] The implication for sexuality research in the United States is that the growing numbers of Latinas and Latinos will also shape our overall understanding of sexualities in the present and in the future. Therefore, their absence in the sexuality research literature produced in the social and behavioral sciences has significant repercussions for knowledge production and for the creation of policy.

As researchers and scholars working on sexualities issues, we have become aware of the influences of social context in framing sexual identities, attitudes, and behaviors. Therefore, many of the differences, as well as any similarities, we may note between Latina/os and others have to be explored in terms of these differing contexts. For example, while 26 percent of the U.S. population was under age eighteen in 2000, 35 percent of Latina/os were under age eighteen. The median age for Latina/os was twenty-six years, while the median age for the entire U.S. population was thirty-five years. Latina/os are three times more likely to be living in poverty than whites, with the disparity being greater for those under age eighteen. Latina/os in the United States have the lowest educational attainments as compared to the rest of the U.S. population. Latina/os who are twenty-five years of age or older were six times more likely to have less than a ninth-grade education than non-Latina/o whites. Latina/os are also more likely to be unemployed, to be employed in low-paying occupations, and to earn less than non-Latina/o whites.[14] The lower socioeconomic conditions in which Latina/os disproportionately find themselves compared to the white population create different opportunities, challenges, and sexual contexts, as do language, (im)migration, citizenship, or residential status.

A large proportion (39 percent) of Latina/os are foreign born.[15] The great majority of Latina/os are bilingual, as compared to non-Latina/o white and African American populations, who are almost exclusively English speakers. There is also a significant number of recent (im)migrant Latina/os who are Spanish-speaking only. Thus, they may be underrepresented in research and education efforts conducted solely in English or through strategies that are not targeted to this particular population.

Such differences are not simply found between Latina/os and others but also among Latinas and Latinos. This diversity in social context is immediately evident when looking at even the most basic circumstances; in fact, the differences within this population may actually be greater than the similarities between it and other populations. Among the various U.S. Latina/o groups, the median age varies significantly: Mexican Americans have a median age of twenty-four years while Cuban Americans have a median age of forty-one years. Among the main subgroups of Latina/os, poverty rates range from 17 percent of Cuban Americans to 26 percent of Puerto Ricans. Median reported household incomes also vary, with those of Spanish descent having a median income of $53,000 and Dominicans having a median income of $28,700. Educational levels also vary: Spanish- and South American–origin populations have the highest proportion of those with at least a high school diploma (77 percent), while those of Mexican and Central American origin have the lowest (46 percent). The birthrate among Latinas likewise varies, with the highest being among Mexican Americans and the lowest among Cuban Americans. As we discuss Latina/o sexualities, we must ask which Latinas and Latinos are we researching, in terms of ethnicity, social class, racial phenotypes, age, education, language, geographic location, generation, and the like.[16] How does their social context affect their sexuality? Can we extrapolate or generalize specific findings regarding sexuality from one subgroup of Latinas and Latinos to another?

While it would be our ultimate goal to advance a larger conversation on how similarly and differently positioned Latina/o ethnic groups experience their sexual lives, at this time we simply do not have the needed research to offer such an analysis. As the chapters in this volume reiterate, there are few empirical studies that compare the sexualities of specific Latina/o ethnic groups or even include certain Latina/o nationalities to do the necessary comparative work. These complexities and gaps in research on Latina/o sexualities call for further integration of sexualities studies in Latina/o research as well as of Latina/o studies in sexuality research.

Integrating Latina/o Studies and Sexuality Research

Many Latina/o studies programs (in particular Chicano and Puerto Rican studies) came into being through student activism in order to incorporate their issues, histories, politics, and experiences into academic programs. Until then, experiences of groups such as Latinas and Latinos and African Americans were routinely rendered invisible by many researchers or analyzed with culturally deterministic frameworks that slighted structural forces or left little room for human agency. Such programs offered the possibility of new directions for research and provided a venue for hearing alternative perspectives. Latina/o studies, historically, has been concerned with issues of multiple oppressions, mostly focused on race, class, and gender. Historically, sexuality as an area of research and a focus of additional oppression has been largely ignored until recently.[17]

Conversely, within sexuality research, there are limited studies on Latina/os. Michael W. Wiederman, Carri Maynard, and Amelia Fretz found that only 7 percent of articles published in the two major journals on human sexuality during a twenty-five-year period addressed the ethnicity of participants.[18] Thus, the nationality, ethnicity, and culture of a group, as contextual experiences for understanding sexuality, were made invisible. While sexuality is one of the areas that has been minimally studied in the experiences of Latinas and Latinos, it has tremendous significance for their future and well-being in the United States. As such, these two areas of study that have been marginalized in many academic disciplines are now meeting at a critical juncture. While in this volume we primarily draw from Latina/o studies and sexualities studies, it is important to point out that there are many other academic and activist projects that inform the work of both these areas of study.

Contributions from feminist, postcolonial, race, queer, migration, and globalization studies as well as other theoretical frameworks have been incorporated in our understanding of the Latina/o experience.[19] These same intellectual projects have also informed the study of sexuality. Feminist scholars have advanced our understanding of the complex relationship of gender, sexuality, and power. Some of these scholars are directly engaged in ongoing analyses about sexualities, in particular, the role of desire and erotic pleasure in female sexualities.[20] Third world feminists interject the importance of considering the unique power and cultural dynamics of women of color in these debates.[21] These scholars have emphasized the intersections of race, sex, and gender in feminist thinking and have subsequently been instrumental in the early inceptions of queer theory. The lesbian, gay, bisexual, and transgender (LGBT) movement and queer studies have challenged scholars to become aware of and address the heteronormative lens in social science research.[22] The AIDS crisis, which led to HIV/AIDS activist movements and HIV research, propelled research on sexuality. These theoretical and empirical contributions as well as others have informed each other and advanced our knowledge so that we now speak of and understand Latina/o ethnicities, identities, genders, and sexualities as multidimensional and fluid concepts influenced by social contexts.[23] Moreover, we have become more keenly aware that sexuality, like gender, race, and socioeconomic status, provides an analytic lens to understand social organization and power. These intersectional advancements provide a theoretical and empirical backdrop for this volume. Yet we must still contend with past research and current research in which both Latina/os and sexuality are presented as unproblematic, agreed-upon concepts.

The present volume, which is informed by this research and the knowledge gathered from the scholarship in these chapters, is clearly needed to enable sexuality studies to meet the challenges and needs of the twenty-first century by further moving away from ethnocentric, pathological, and static models of the past. With globalization, migration, transnationalism, and an increasingly Latina/o and nonwhite U.S. population, this collection lays the foundation for a more dynamic and global perspective on sexualities studies. Through the work of the contributors to this volume, we can begin a more formal dialogue on the future of sexuality studies in the United States and beyond its borders as well. We hope that Latin American scholars as well as scholars from around the world will participate and contribute to this dialogue.

We have attempted to map the field of Latina/o sexualities, centering on the empirical work currently available. The contributors address the myriad issues related to Latinas and Latinos and their sexualities while not privileging any particular culture or sexual lifestyle. We recognize that Latina/os' sexual experiences are influenced by how they are racially positioned in the United States. This volume begins to carve out a separate space where Latinas and Latinos and their sexualities can be explored despite the limitations of prevalent research frameworks and the biases in the production of knowledge. While it is a challenge to dispel the popular stereotypical images of Latinas and Latinos and their sexualities from the dominant U.S. society—and even among some social and behavioral researchers—this volume begins to answer some of the questions posed in this introduction. The following is a brief overview of the chapters and their contribution to surveying Latina/o sexualities research in the United States.

Mapping Latina/o Sexualities Research

While the HIV/AIDS epidemic has created a need for social and behavioral research on Latina/o sexualities, the focus of much of this research on sexuality has been limited to and framed by particular health-related issues and specific populations of Latinas and Latinos. Thus, Latino men who have sex with men are a population for which there has been increased sexuality research because of their history within the AIDS epidemic and in HIV-risk profiles. Family planning research involving primarily heterosexual Latinas (with few heterosexual males in the samples) has also been limited both in scope and in the issues addressed. Latinas who have sex with women are usually not studied since they are invisible within the framework of either HIV-risk or pregnancy concerns. Thus, the limited sexuality research is predominantly on heterosexual Latina women (particularly adolescent and reproductive females), gay Latino men, and Latino men who have sex with men. There is very little research on lesbians or on women who have sex with women. Latino male heterosexual experiences and/or perspectives on sexuality are also underrepresented among the studies available.

The studies on HIV/AIDS, pregnancy, contraception (including condom use), and sexually transmitted infections (STIs) are the sources for information in many of the contributions to this volume. These studies, which employ a medical model of disease and risk, have created a major paradigm for our understanding of Latina/o sexuality, oftentimes restricting the questions asked and the answers offered. Since most of the research is based on risk-related concerns and disease prevention, sexual development and experiences as normative, pleasurable, and erotic are limited in most of the literature. Also, the most socioeconomically marginalized Latina/os are the focus of this at-risk, problem-oriented research. Latina/os who have more financial and social resources and are not deemed "at-risk" are not the object of studies in these frameworks. Such an unbalanced approach leads to a skewed and biased reading of Latina/o sexualities in general.

The historical marginalization of minority groups in the social sciences and in behavioral studies continues to influence contemporary understandings of Latina/o sexualities and subsequent policy and program decisions. The oversimplification of supposed "Latina/o culture" has resulted in the misrepresentations of the sex lives of Latina/os. The chapters in this volume were commissioned with the intent of avoiding the dominant model and fostering a more complex and dynamic understanding of Latina/os and sexualities.

We begin to contextualize the present state of Latina/o sexualities research through two historical papers. Ramón Gutiérrez notes that the history of Latina/o sexuality dates back to the Spanish conquest of the Americas. He points to the impact that colonialism had on the culture of indigenous peoples and in particular how colonization influenced sexuality in Mexico. Pablo Mitchell begins where Gutiérrez leaves off, exploring the history of sexuality from 1898 to the near present. These authors provide a historical context for the taken-for-granted models that have become pervasive in Latina/o sexuality research.

Several authors critique existing contemporary scholarship for limiting the discussion of Latina/o sexual behaviors to a risk model. Scholarship written within this framework often focuses on the risks of the HIV/AIDS epidemic and leads to the medicalization of Latina/os' sex lives. George Ayala the limitations of sexual health scholarship on Latino gay men. He a more nuanced understanding of sexual health that is informed dependent on the disease-prevention framework. He argues that relying solely on this framework has stifled the conversation on gay sexuality and allowed us to ignore examinations of pleasure, satisfaction, and desire. In their chapter on bisexuality, Miguel Muñoz-Laboy and Carmen Yon Leau argue that a reductionist medical framework does not allow us to understand the sexuality of Latina/os outside of their transactional sexual encounters. Instead, Muñoz-Laboy and Leau promote scholarship that explores how social boundaries and sexual rights influence bisexuality among Latinas and Latinos. Echoing the work of these scholars, in her chapter on childhood sexuality Sonya Grant Arreola critiques existing childhood sexuality studies for focusing too much on deterrence of sexual activity and sexual abuse and not enough on the healthy ways that children and adolescents experience their sexuality. She calls for a more culturally relevant research agenda to understand better the natural course of childhood sexual development. Inherent in these scholars' analyses as well as in that of others in this volume is a collective challenge to scholarship that overemphasizes the risks involved in nonconforming sexual behavior devoid of a more nuanced construction of sexual pleasure, health, and intimate relationships.

Marcia Ochoa points to the struggles against invisibility for Latina/o transgender individuals in an essay on Latina/o trans populations. She argues that scholars often collapse the experiences of sexuality and gender of nonconforming Latino men into that of Latino gay men, thus rendering their identities as transgenders, *locas*, or *vestidas* invisible. Ochoa observes that the invisibility of Latina/o transgender individuals leaves them susceptible to misrepresentation and manipulation. In her chapter on popular culture, Deborah Vargas shows the ways in which the visibility of Latina/o gays and lesbians is not always positive. Vargas notes an increase in the visibility of Latina/o gay and lesbian subjects in popular culture; however, she problematizes this popularity arguing that it does not capture the multiple and ever-shifting sexualities of Latinas and Latinos. Moreover, the stereotypes of Latinas and Latinos in popular culture can be disempowering because they are polarizing representations that serve to entertain and ridicule. Luz Calvo and Catrióna Rueda Esquibel point to the invisibility of Latina lesbians in social science research. These scholars attribute this invisibility in part to how researchers conceptualize their subjects' identities. They argue that by adopting fixed identity categories such as "lesbian," researchers exclude Latinas who are reluctant to identify as lesbians despite their choices in sexual expression. Calvo and Esquibel encourage future scholars to allow subjects to define their own identities, and they propose utilizing a more inclusive definition of lesbian in an effort to establish more visibility for these marginalized women.

In their chapter on the cultural production of knowledge, José Quiroga and Melanie López Frank are critical of the term Latina/o sexuality. They argue that concepts such as these assume differences between Latina/os and other groups. They are further critical of such terms for essentializing sexuality and not acknowledging its plurality. Similarly, in their conversation on the *activo/ pasivo* paradigm, Salvador Vidal-Ortiz, Carlos Decena, Héctor Carrillo, and Tomás Almaguer hold that this paradigm has become decontextualized by scholars, who use it to reify difference, presenting gay Latino sexual culture as static rather than in flux. They propose repositioning the activo/pasivo paradigm as one of many options available to gay Latino men and refute the oversimplification of this paradigm as the only way that gay Latino men experience sexual pleasure.

An ongoing problem in Latina/o sexuality scholarship is the limited way researchers address "culture," which views values, norms, or ethnic expression as devoid of agency, contestation, or structural constraints and as presumably adhered to by all Latinas and Latinos. In a related conceptual move, those who do not conform to this limited vision of culture are then seen to be "acculturated,".particularly if they are not predominantly Spanish speakers. This general view has produced a cultural caricature of Latinas and Latinos and their sex lives while ignoring structural forces such as poverty, racism, and discrimination, which also shape their cultural and sexual experiences in the United States.[24] Several of the scholars problematize Latina/o scholarship for not adequately exploring how intersecting oppressions influence the sex lives of Latina/os. Amalia Cabezas, Dolores Ortiz, and Sonia Valencia critique the sex work literature in the United States for not paying sufficient attention to the role that racism, undocumented status, and language barriers play in shaping how Latina/os are positioned in the industry. In their chapter on sexual health, Sandra Arévalo, Mariana Gerena, and Hortensia Amaro argue that different forms of marginalization including racism, poverty, low educational attainment, and high incarceration rates all have a significant impact on the production of sexual health disparities between Latina/os and other groups. In her review of the scholarship on Latina/o immigration and sexuality, Susana Peña questions the role that racism plays in the immigration outcomes of Latina/o subjects. She encourages us to explore how racism complicates the relationship between migration and sexuality. Interestingly, while a few scholars in this volume address the process of racialization of Latinas and Latinos, very little research incorporates race and racial phenotypes as part of the analysis of Latina/o sexualities. Even though race is rarely addressed in the research cited, it is omnipresent. It is the proverbial "elephant in the room." How racial oppression shapes the sexual experiences of Latina/o subjects is something that can not continue to be ignored and should not be separated from the larger conversation.

We have included a chapter that directly addresses Latina/o heterosexuality. Doing so allows us to challenge heteronormativity, a pervasive ideology reproduced by the institutions in our society whereby heterosexuality is seen as normal. In her chapter on heterosexuality in Latina/o communities, Gloria González-López analyzes the ways that heteronormativity reinforces heterosexuality and white supremacy in Latina/o communities via the heterosexual imaginary.[25] Laura Romo, Erum Nadeem, and Claudia Kouyoumdjian examine the types of conversations that parents have with their adolescent children regarding sexuality. These authors note that sexual attitudes and moral values are the most common topics of these conversations. Birth control and sexually transmitted infections are the least often discussed topics in Latina/o families.

We have maintained a commitment in this volume to promote scholarship with a vision toward effecting policy changes. Elena Gutiérrez's chapter, which focuses on sexual health and reproductive policies, notes a dearth in academic scholarship that explores the policy implications of research on the lives of Latina/os. She argues that the existing policy-geared research overutilizes a medicalized approach. Additionally, the other contributors were each asked to remain mindful of the policy implications of their topics and to incorporate a conversation of this issue in their chapters whenever possible.

A remarkable result of this collective survey of the literature on Latina/os and their sexualities is the realization of how limited the research across these themes actually is, given the importance of understanding this fast-growing segment of the U.S. population. There is no question of the need to support and encourage a tremendous amount of research to begin to address some basic questions that emerged in the compilation of this volume, as noted by the authors. First, there is a lack of research in many aspects of Latina/o sexualities in the U.S. context such as disability, chronic illness, sexual citizenship, romance and intimacy, race, and desire and the erotic. Second, there is very little on older, middle-class, and various ethnic subgroups of Latinas and Latinos.

Research on Latinas and Latinos in the United States has focused primarily on Mexican or Chicana/o populations, and these findings have often been misinterpreted as representative of other Latina/o groups. Moreover, research conducted in Latin America has been taken to be representative of Latinas and Latinos in the United States. Although Mexicans are clearly the majority group among Latinas and Latinos in the United States and although more research on them certainly is needed as well, each group and subgroup have their particular experiences, desires, and practices that should be understood. In addition, there is a need to encourage comparative research on Latinas and Latinos of different nationalities and social conditions.[26]

The contributors to this volume ask us to expand the boundaries of knowledge and to consider what counts as knowledge. We have incorporated an interdisciplinary and multidisciplinary array of work from academics, activists, and policymakers, all of whom bring strengths and unique perspectives to the book. George Ayala, Jaime Cortez, and Patrick Hebert, for example, remind us that knowledge should not be a static process, but a dynamic one. Their chapter synthesizes how we have envisioned the knowledge production process of this book. As much as possible, we have tried to adhere to their suggestions that knowledge is produced through partnerships with community workers and activists rather than in isolation. We hope that this book will provide emerging scholars as well as policymakers and program designers with an overview of the challenges in mapping Latina/o sexualities, and that it will ultimately inspire us all to begin filling in the academic gaps and provide knowledge that informs better policies.

1

A History of Latina/o Sexualities

RAMÓN A. GUTIÉRREZ

A history of Latina and Latino sexualities in the United States is not easy to write. The *Oxford English Dictionary* notes that the word "Latino" comes from the Spanish *latinoamericano*, which means Latin American. Most of those who now call themselves Latinas or Latinos in the United States either migrated from one of Latin America's many nations or are descended from such immigrants and here putatively were transformed in some profound ways.[1] If we were simply dealing with one set of national values, ideals, and norms about sexuality coming into contact with another, that in itself would be terrain complex and difficult to map. What complicates the story are the immense social, cultural, and historical differences that developed in Latin America over time. The differential impact of Spanish colonialism on the hemisphere's indigenous peoples compounds the task, as does the massive importation of African slaves into the area; roughly 2 million between 1500 and 1821. (The total number of slaves imported to all the American colonies—British, French, Spanish, Portuguese— was 14 million, of which 10 million went to Brazil, with 2 million more going to British and French colonies.) Today Latin American nations have mostly erased this brutal history of oppression and extermination of indigenous and African peoples from their memories by proclaiming a history of *mestizaje*, a word that in the English language translates poorly as "miscegenation." The mythology of mestizaje cheerfully celebrates the extensive biological mixing that transpired in Latin America among Spaniards, Native Americans, and Africans, producing a hybrid race—a race of mestizos and mulattoes—through sometimes legal but most often illegal and violent conjugation.[2]

The Spanish conquistadores repeatedly said that they came to the Americas primarily to convert to Christianity the many pagans they encountered. But except for some of the Spanish crown's lofty but clearly delusional pronouncements on this point, conversion of the native peoples was quite a secondary goal. What really made the passions of the enterprising conquerors boil, what made them pant and slobber, what made them engage in death-defying feats, were gold and silver. When most of them failed to find such instant wealth, they turned to the next best thing: lordship over others and the accumulation of land.

The Spaniards who came to America were largely young and single men. From the start of the Conquest, they exercised their sexual dominion over native women and men. The conquest of the Americas was a sexual conquest of Indian peoples. Indians were made objects both of desire and of derision, vessels that would reproduce a new people and that would provide the domestic labor to reproduce households, and ultimately, the profitability of a massive mercantile empire. The history of Latino and Latina sexuality thus necessarily begins with the conquest and proceeds by exploring the nexus among bodies, gender, and power. I draw most of my examples from colonial Mexico and Peru, which were the hubs of the Spanish Empire from 1500 to 1800, and from the experiences of *mexicanos* and *mexicanas* who set up residence in what became the United States or who in more recent times migrated there. Where the Mexican and Peruvian evidence is sketchy or incomplete, I draw on studies from other areas of Latin America, mainly from Argentina and Brazil. The general patterns of sexual ideology and behavior are really quite uniform across Latin America in colonial and early national times. As distinct nation-states were born in the hemisphere, different inflections were given to longer historical patterns of sexual ideology and behavior. At the end of this essay, I delve into these changes.

We moderns, living in the secularized, industrialized countries of the West, have very definite ideas about what we regard the "sexual" to be. Whether it be in defining the sexual and the asexual; what is heterosexual, homosexual, and bisexual; or pathologies that are thought of as having a sexual component, those categories come to us largely through the discourses of illness, crime, and depravity first articulated in late-nineteenth-century science. Today we deem the scientific ideas about sexuality to be "true" and "natural," or as the French philosopher Michel Foucault put it, "the truth of our being." Just how much we are still products of our historical moment is readily apparent on consulting the oldest known dictionary of the Spanish language, Sebastián de Covarrubias's 1611 *Tesoro de la lengua castellana o española*. The dictionary has no entry for the word *sexo* (sex) or *sexual* (sexual). Nor do these words appear in the 1732 *Diccionario de la lengua castellana*, prepared by the Spanish Royal Academy for King Philip V. *Sexo* first entered the Spanish language as a neologism in 1809, notes Joan Corminas in his *Diccionario crítico etimológico castellano e hispánico*. The etymology of *sexo* is the Latin *sexus*, which means "cut, divided," as into male and female organisms of the species. In colonial Spanish America, the very concepts that we now take for granted to describe the realm of the sexual simply did not then.[3]

Please do not misunderstand my point that the modern categories of the sexual did not come into existence until the end of the nineteenth century in Spanish America. My argument here is that the discourses that are used to define the body at any historical moment, to order the body into two genders, to articulate how, where, and for what end its parts could be used—be it for procreation, pleasure, or pain—are always the product of distinct warps in the distribution of power and are unique to specific historical moments. My goal here is to explore the dominant discourses that have been used in Latin America to describe the body as an erotic and reproductive site and to examine conflicting and contestatory discourses, particularly in moments of change.

Discourses of the Catholic Church

For the inhabitants of Spanish America—natives, Africans, and Europeans—the religious discourses of the Roman Catholic Church, then Spain's official state religion, provided the basic categories for the regulation of the human body and its social life. These ideas were expressed by priests and theologians in biblical exegesis and juridical pronouncements, in rituals that marked every phase of the life cycle, in confessional manuals, and in guides for the administration of the sacraments. From this vantage point, the body was imagined dualistically as composed of spirit and substance, of soul and flesh. From the very moment of its conception, the body was endowed with an eternal soul that bore the stain of Original Sin, born of human sinfulness in the Garden of Eden. At the beginning of time, or so the book of Genesis explained, Eve, the first woman whom God created by taking a rib from Adam's side, ate of the forbidden fruit and thereby transgressed the commandment of God. As a result of this original sin, Eve and her husband, Adam, were expelled from Paradise and forced to endure privations of every sort, to feel hunger and cold, to experience shame over the nakedness of their bodies, and for women, to suffer great pain giving birth.

Daily in teaching from pulpits and in confessional boxes, clerics articulated the Church's vision of a properly ordered body politic, which was to be manifested through bodily behavior. To transform its ideology into action, the Church relied on penances imposed by its disciplinary agents: local priests, judges in ecclesiastical courts, officers of the Holy Office of the Inquisition. Through coercion and through fear, the Church imposed on physical bodies the social order envisaged in the Pater Noster, "on earth as it is in heaven."

Despite the Church's enormous power to impose its vision of a proper bodily regime, other models for the body politic constantly challenged, subverted, and threatened to undermine it. Among Spanish colonists there was a secular theory of power, power that did not derive from God but that emanated from physical mastery and sheer force. This discourse of the body had its own notion of a properly ordered polity, which likewise was writ large on the human body, proscribing its own ideals about the physical body, about procreation, and about its pleasures, desires, and pains. We know of these ideas and how they were displayed in behavior primarily through the repressive apparatus of the Church, through the workings of the Inquisition, and through the ruminations of clerics who often lambasted as pagan and sinful these alternative notions. As the power of religious discourses waned with the secularization of colonial society at the end of the eighteenth century, these secular ideas were increasingly embraced by state functionaries with the goal of subordinating the Catholic Church in society and undermining the authority of the clergy. The native peoples in the Americas whom the Spaniards called Indians had their own religious discourses about the place of the body in a harmonious cosmos, as well as ideas about the sources of chaos and destruction that could wreak havoc.

Since antique times the fathers of the Catholic Church had defined humans as constituted of body and soul. To engender a child, a man and woman united in intercourse, sharing physical substance, mixing semen and ovum. Once the child was conceived and born into the world, through the sacrament of Baptism a person was reborn into Christ, began a spiritual life, and had the stain of Original Sin cleansed from its soul. As Saint Thomas Aquinas noted in the *Summa Theologica*, when a priest christened a child, it was "born again a son of God as Father, and of the Church as mother."[4] According to the Church, this act of spiritual regeneration rivaled, if not surpassed, the act of physical generation itself.

The body, though base and vile, was but a transitory vessel for the eternal soul, whose spiritual journey to God was assured only through a virtuous life sanctified by the sacraments. Clerics maintained that because of the sinful quality of the flesh, the persons whom God most favored were prepubescent children and those who had completely forsaken the flesh and the vainglories of the world for a life of virginity and chastity. Mystical marriage to Christ and a union with God was the highest state of spiritual perfection to which one could aspire. The first marriage canon of the 1563 Council of Trent made this point clear: "Whoever shall affirm that the conjugal state is to be preferred to a life of virginity or celibacy, and that it is not better or more conducive to happiness to remain in virginity or celibacy than to be married, let them be excommunicated."[5]

Theologians viewed human marriage as a less desirable state that had only been elevated to a sacrament by Christ as a *remedium peccati*, a remedy for humanity's inherently sinful state. The function of marriage was primarily the reproduction of the species and only secondarily to provide for the peaceful containment of lust and desire. Most of the prescriptive literature produced by theologians and moral philosophers during Spain's colonial period thus did not focus squarely on what we now consider sexuality. The topic surfaced only tangentially as part of larger discussions of marriage as related to the Ten Commandments. "Thou shalt not commit adultery" and "Thou shalt not covet thy neighbor's wife," or glosses on these the sixth and ninth commandments, were the points at which extensive discussion of lust, conjugal intercourse, and physical desire most often appeared.

The Church maintained that marriage was the normative institution that assured the regeneration of the species, the peaceful continuation of society, and the orderly satisfaction of bodily desires. When couples channeled their sexual desires toward the explicit aim of procreation, they fulfilled God's natural design. The two most important objectives of marriage, explained Father Clemente de Ledesma in his 1695 *Confesionario del despertador de noticias de los Santos Sacramentos*, a confessional guide for the administration of the sacraments, were procreation and the satisfaction of the *débito conjugal*, the conjugal debt that required reciprocal service between husband and wife. Intercourse was imagined as a contractual exchange. Married couples could, so to speak, request a regular servicing of the debt by their partner and were duty bound to pay it. Intercourse could be withheld only if it was requested too frequently, during periods of illness or menstruation, or during religiously motivated temporary vows of chastity. Confessional manuals contained counsel for men to avoid excessive conjugal demands and injunctions for women to be charitable and understanding in giving what was requested of them.[6]

For clerics and theologians, the line between duty and sin was a very fine one. Couples were constantly advised not to be overwhelmed by lust, thereby losing control of their rational faculties. In his *Espejo de la perfecta casada* (1693), a manual for the Christian education of married women, Fray Alonso de Herrera cautioned that an excessive display of lust in marriage was tantamount to the sin of adultery. "Engaging one's wife like an animal, inflamed by the libidinous fire of desire, is a very grave sin," he warned.[7]

Churchmen often frenzied themselves with the minutiae of marriage, prescribing precisely where and in exactly what position the conjugal act should occur. "The natural manner for intercourse as far as position is concerned," advised the seventeenth-century Spanish theologian Tomás Sánchez in his *De sancto matrimonii sacramento* (1607), is for "the man [to] lie on top and the woman on her back beneath. Because this manner is the most appropriate for the effusion of the male seed, for its reception into the female vessel." Railing in condemnation about the *mulier supra virum* (woman atop man) coital position, Sánchez continued: "This method [of intercourse] is absolutely contrary to the order of nature. . . . It is natural for the man to act and for the woman to be passive; and if the man is beneath, he becomes submissive by the very fact of his position, and the woman being above is active." Sánchez added: "Who cannot see how much nature herself abhors this mutation? Because in scholastic history it is said that the cause of the flood was that women, carried away by madness, used men improperly, the latter being beneath and the former above." Needless to say, that a man might copulate with his spouse from behind, in *more canino* (the way of dogs), was clearly sinful and way beyond what could be tolerated among humans.[8]

Engaging in sex in places other than the conjugal bed also was frowned on by priests but apparently with only modest success. It was not uncommon for spouses and even for consorts to report that they had consummated their affections "in the woods," "by the river," or in some isolated natural setting. Since most couples lived with parents, other relatives, and children in close quarters, it was usually only outside, in nature, that lovemaking (*amores*) could escape the attentive eyes of others. Santa Fe, New Mexico, resident Juana Carrillo's 1712 admission that she had enjoyed the affections of a man while "out in the fields" during the spring planting aptly characterizes the type of spaces that proved to be expedient for such consummation.[9] Provided that churches, chapels, and shrines were not desecrated by such acts, priests had little ability to do much about it, though that did not keep them from constantly fulminating against it.

The "natural" function of marital intercourse was procreation. All sexual uses of the body's organs and orifices that did not have this as their ultimate goal were "unnatural" and punishable as violations of natural law, whatever one's marital state. Masturbation, or the sin of Onan (onanism), was said to pollute the body. In the parlance of the sixteenth and seventeenth centuries such self-pleasuring caused one a sinful pollution (*polución*). Masturbation was particularly evil for men because it wasted their seed in ways incapable of reproducing human life. From studies on the erotic behavior of nuns in convents and from Inquisition cases involving ordinary women we know that this solitary pleasure was not uncommon among women.[10]

Fray Bartolomé de Alva's 1634 *Confesionario mayor* urged confessors to interrogate women penitents about masturbation: "Did you repeatedly feel your body, thinking of a man, and wanting him to sin with you? Did you do it to yourself with your hands, bringing to a conclusion your lust?" While Alva did not urge confessors to ask their women penitents if they had used objects to reach a *polución*, other clerics did. Twenty-year-old Agustina Ruiz was interrogated by representatives of the Inquisition in Mexico in 1621 because of the autoerotic fantasies that constantly caused her pollutions whenever she looked at pictures of Jesus, the Virgin Mary, and a number of other saints in church. She would become so excited, she said, when Christ would expose his genitals to her that she would immediately pleasure herself right there in the sanctuary. Ruiz admitted that she frequently masturbated "more or less three times a day for the last nine years." She told the representatives of the Inquisition that from the age of eleven she had also carnally communicated with Jesus, Mary, and a number of saints in various positions, "with her underneath them, and from the side, and her on top of them, and also with her lying facing down while they conjoin themselves with both of her dishonest parts, both vaginally and anally."[11]

Sodomy (*sodomía*), which in colonial times was defined as anal copulation with a partner of either sex, was called the "abominable crime" (*abominable delito*) and the "nefarious sin against nature" (*pecado nefando contra natura*). Father Alva in 1634 again asked confessors to query not only male penitents, but females as well. "When your husband was drunk," Alva's manual asked, "did he have sex with you where you are a woman, or sometimes did he do the disgusting sin to you? Did you restrain him?" While sodomy between a man and a woman was deemed sinful, as Alva's confessional manual attests, it was primarily among members of the same sex that it provoked the most concern and punishment. Historian Mary Elizabeth Perry has argued that the revulsion over male same-sex sodomy was "not in ejaculating nonprocreatively, nor in the use of the anus, but in requiring a male to play the passive 'female' role and in violating the physical integrity of the male recipient body."[12]

Male same-sex sodomy is fairly well documented throughout colonial Spanish America. We know of its occurrence before the Conquest among indigenous men of the nobility, among priests and warriors, and among members of lower castes. During the colonial period male same-sex sodomy is copiously recorded in civil and ecclesiastical court cases between indigenous men, between Spaniards and African slaves, between Spaniards and Indians, between and among Spaniards of every class, and particularly among priests. From this documentation we know that there was a rather lively sodomitical subculture in monasteries, in the large cities of Mexico and Brazil, and undoubtedly in other places that we have still to learn about. These men had networks of erotic partners who regularly frequented certain parks, certain streets, certain taverns, knowing that they would surely find partners to partake of the nefarious vice. Often the status differences between partners were particularly marked, as when members of the nobility and of the clergy cavorted with their African and Indian male servants. But Spanish men of the same class mingled as well, mounting each other in the manner in which husbands bedded their wives. Indeed, judicial authorities were always particularly eager to know which person had played the *hombre* (male), or insertive, role in anal intercourse, and which the *mujer* (female), or receptive, role. Religious authorities in colonial Spanish America found it particularly repugnant that men were copulating as if they were husband and wife, using the anus as the feminine part. But sodomites, or *putos* (faggots) as they were then called, engaged in a great variety of other lascivious behaviors. The 1595 Inquisition case against André de Freitas Lessa documents such variety. Admitting that he had engaged in hundreds of acts of sodomy with male partners over the course of years, de Freitas Lessa said that he had "meetings of nefarious alternatives," "nefarious assaults from the back," "union of virile members from the front," "the spilling of seed between the legs," "*punhetas*" (*punho*: hand or self-masturbation in front of others), "pollution in the hands of others," "*coxetas*" (intercuripal sex, or rubbing the penis between a partner's legs), as well as phallic exposure. It seems likely that the only thing that kept de Freitas Lessa from engaging in oral copulation, what the Church called "viperous intercourse," were the low standards of bodily hygiene at the time.[13]

Both from confessional manuals and from litigation against women for sodomy, we know that women also shared intimacies with members of their own sex. Fray Bartolomé de Alva's confession manual instructed priests to question women about such behavior: "Were you responsible for dirty words with which you provoked and excited women? When you cohabited with some woman: did you show and reveal what was bad in front of those who had not yet seen the sin?"[14] From the 1598 case against Mariana de San Miguel, who was pursued by the Mexican Inquisition for heresy, claiming she had been personally illuminated by the Holy Spirit without clerical instruction, we learn that she too had religiously inspired erotic fantasies that frequently caused her pollutions. Mariana confessed that she and another *beata* (pious woman) would often meet and when they did, "ordinarily they kissed and hugged and put her hands on the breasts and . . . she came to pollution ten or twelve times, twice in the church." Similar erotic behaviors were reported among Mexico City's *beatas* in the colonial period in a number of other instances. These pious women wore clerical garb, lived cloistered lives, and refrained from public activities. And while no one to my knowledge has yet documented the erotic dimensions of the lives of nuns in colonial Spanish America, it would be naive to surmise that women's close, intimate friendships within the convent were always of a chaste sort.[15]

Sodomy, stated the 1585 *Tercero cathecismo y exposición de la doctrina Cristiana, por sermones*, was "for man to sin with man, or with woman not in the natural way, and even above all these, to sin with beasts, such as ewes, bitches, or mares, which is the greatest abomination." Incidents of bestiality, though infrequently reported, do occasionally appear in court cases. In 1801 José Antonio Rosas, an eighteen-year-old soldier stationed at Santa Barbara, California, was found guilty of mounting his mule for other than transportation. Both he and the mule were executed and publicly incinerated, the flames believed necessary to purify their wicked flesh. In a 1770s New Mexican case involving a young Indian boy from Isleta Pueblo and a cow, charges against the boy were dismissed because the lad had not yet reached the age of reason. He did not understand the gravity of his sin, the judge opined. Repeatedly the ecclesiastical judge queried the boy about whether the cow had been standing up or lying down. The boy, having never apparently understood the question the interpreter posed, failed to answer satisfactorily. Whether being in one position or the other would have spared the cow's life will never be known, as the court docket does not detail what happened to the beast.[16]

Both the prosecution and the punishment for sodomy varied considerably in colonial Spanish America by gender, by class, and by one's erotic posture in the act. Women were usually discovered in such nefarious deeds by accident, when they were accused of other profanations, such as heresy, as in the case cited above. It is hard to know whether such tales of erotic behaviors were introduced into testimony to win convictions, as a way of underscoring the severity of the sin committed and the depravity of the person involved. Few clerical women were accused of sodomy with other women, and many fewer were punished for the sin in any way. When a man shared his posterior part with another, there too the judicial outcome varied considerably by social class. Men of the nobility, landed aristocracy, and military, because of their status and connections, routinely made the accusations and concrete evidence against them disappear, particularly if they had sinned with their servants and subordinates, as so often was the case. So too was the case with priests. Ecclesiastical authorities preferred to keep their own sins hushed up and corrected by exile and simple penances, thus retaining intact the Church's rhetorical power to denounce society's sinfulness and to correct the popular classes without being seen as having a double standard.

The *Siete partidas*, the medieval legal code that ultimately became the law of Castile and of the Spanish colonies in the New World, prescribed that the "male," or insertive, partner in sodomy would be castrated and stoned to death. In the late fifteenth century, under the rule of King Ferdinand and Queen Isabella, the punishment was changed to burning. Who actually suffered this punishment? Men of the lower classes were the ones who most often endured the brunt of sodomy laws. Their bodies were whipped and tortured, publicly shamed and derided, and ultimately burned at the stake. From the perspective of the Catholic Church the integrity of the male who had played the receptive, or "female," role had been violated. This person was thus not guilty of sin. Indeed, he had been dishonored and used for the commission of a grievous sin. If the receptive partner had only allowed himself to be mounted once—say, while intoxicated, by a man of higher status and who was much stronger—such an individual was usually dispatched with a penance and the injunction never to so sin again. But when the evidence clearly existed, as it did in Mexico City and Puebla in 1657, when 123 men were discovered to be frequently engaging in sodomy—the receptive partners even sporting such nicknames as "La Estampa" (the Print), "La Morossa" (the Slow One), and "Las Rosas" (the Roses)—the Church had to confront the fact that this was habitual and deeply entrenched sin. It was punished fully according to the letter of the law.[17]

Perhaps because clerics considered women the weaker sex in need of male supervision, or perhaps because of their own sense of priestly modesty, cases of heterosexual sodomy seemed to have provoked less sustained anxiety, as is evident from the sketchy legal archives on the matter. Women appear to have routinely engaged in *amores secos*, as sodomy was sometimes called (literally "dry loves"; i.e., "dry" in comparison to "wet" vaginal sex), as a way of maintaining their virginity while still consenting to the sexual desires of their suitors and as a common form of birth control. Juana Rodríguez of Santa Fe, New Mexico, explained in 1705 that she had been coaxed and consented to amores secos with Calletano Fajardo because he had promised her marriage, saying that she would soon enough be his wife. Unfortunately for Rodríguez, Fajardo developed amnesia soon after their lovemaking. The onset of such a memory lapse was a common strategy men employed to avoid prosecution for such seductive acts. Since they had not deflowered a maiden, which was the actionable offense before the law, this strategy usually proved successful as a way for men to avoid punishment for their behavior.[18]

According to the sixth and ninth commandments, adultery and lust were the two sins that most threatened the social order based on marriage. Adultery violated the sexual exclusivity of the sacramental bond of matrimony, created the possibility of illegitimate children, occasioned the spread of disease, and potentially could disrupt the peaceful order of life. As for the unfettered expression of lust (*lujuría*; literally, luxury or excessive desire), the first bishop of Mexico, the Franciscan friar Juan de Zumárraga, railed in his 1543 catechism, *Doctrina breve muy provechosa*, that "nothing fouls or destroys the heart of men as much as the desires and fantasy of carnality." The Jesuit priest Fray Gabino Carta explicated the topic of lust thoroughly in his *Práctica de confessores: Práctica de administrar los sacramentos, en especial el de la penitancia* (1653), a manual for the administration of the sacrament of confession. He explained that lust was the most evil emotion because it occasioned such heinous mortal sins as fornication, adultery, incest, rape (*estupro*), abduction (*rapto*), sins against nature, and sacrilege. Carta defined fornication as any sexual act outside the sacrament of marriage. He differentiated rape from abduction—the former as forced intercourse, the latter a violation compounded by the victim's abduction. Having sex with a priest or nun or having sex in sacred places were but two of the sacrileges Carta had in mind when he cautioned against excessive desire.[19]

In addition to these base-level mortal sins stemming from lujuría, Carta articulated a second layer of mortal sins caused by taking morose delight (*delectación morosa*) in one's erotic fantasies. If a person lusted vicariously watching someone else in the coital act, if one fantasized about intercourse with a particular person while masturbating, or if one took pleasure recalling erotic dreams after awakening, yet another mortal sin was committed. In short, any activity that was eroticized outside the bonds of marriage, in either fact or fancy, motivated solely by the pursuit of pleasure, was sinful. Such behavior alienated the soul from God, lowered humans to the level of animals, and endangered one's personal salvation.

When Roman Catholic missionaries arrived in the Americas, they judged the sexual behavior of the indigenous peoples particularly sinful, heinous, and clearly of demonic design. The clergy always admitted baldly, at times almost gleefully, that they had been able to repress these Indian behaviors only by resorting to force, by whipping heathens to a pulp, by burning them at the stake, and by desecrating and destroying their sacred spaces. This was the sure way to extirpate the devil from the Indian body politic, or so opined the clerics of the day. Given that these stories were largely recorded by clerical quills in judicial dockets meant to regulate and punish, it is difficult to study the integrity of indigenous thought and practice regarding the relationship between the body politic and the physical body.[20]

For many of the native inhabitants of the Americas, human sexual intercourse was essential for the promotion of fertility. It assured the regeneration necessary for the continuation of life. Intercourse was deemed a symbol of cosmic harmony because it balanced all the masculine forces of the sky above with the feminine forces of the earth below. Thus were the erotic feats of the gods that had occurred at the beginning of time memorialized and celebrated. Gods that combined all masculine and feminine potentialities into one were particularly revered. In the natural world, intercourse was everywhere, from the regenerative activities of animals to the toponyms that local inhabitants gave the earth, names that translate as Clitoris Spring, Girl's Breast Point, and Buttocks-Vagina, for example. Among humans, few boundaries other than those against incest and age constrained erotic behavior and its forms. In religious ritual, the Indians sang of erotic feats and copulated openly to awaken the earth's fertility and to assure that the gods blessed them with fecundity and peace.[21]

The nexus that existed in the indigenous world between sexual intercourse and the sacred was repugnant to Catholic clerics, who had vowed themselves to lives of chastity. European descriptions of native sexual ideology and practice thus must be read with this bias in mind. There is little doubt that the Indians were really as frisky as they were described. The ribaldry of their "orgiastic" dances, the "lewdness" of their incorporation rituals that ended in intercourse, and the naturalness with which they regarded the body and its functions are all too well documented from various points of view to be dismissed as pure figments of clerical anxiety. But did the Indians live in a state of unbridled lust, as the friars constantly complained? I think not.

The goal of the Catholic missionaries was to lead the Indians to God. To keep them on that path, priests established a regime of bodily repression. They justified what they did by telling the readers of their letters, reports, and denunciations that the Indians lived in wicked debauchery in a society devoid of rules. Anthropologists attest that every society has rules governing sexual comportment, especially about such things as incest. Thus when we read the 1660 Inquisitorial denunciation by Fray Nicolás de Chavez, who stated that when Indians staged their dances they frolicked in intercourse "fathers with daughters, brothers with sisters, and mothers with sons," we must ask: What rhetorical end did such statements play in the contestation between Indians and Spaniards over the place and meaning of biological reproduction in a well-ordered society? Priests clearly believed that intercourse could only transpire within the bonds of marriage. By describing Indian behavior as wildly incestuous, priests thus gained authorization to repress native erotic activities as they deemed fit.[22]

Clerical anxiety over the "wretched" indigenous flesh had three principal foci. First, at contact most Indian groups did not wear clothing or only scantily covered their genitals. The missionaries were clearly quite disturbed by this. Asking one indigenous man why he went about naked, the man explained to the friar, "Because I was born naked." Vast amounts of energy were spent getting the Indians to wear clothes, in the hope that by so doing they would eventually develop a European and "civilized" sense of modesty and shame toward their bodies. Second was the prohibition of indigenous religious rituals, particularly those performed by women to vivify and awaken the earth's desire, that according to the missionaries were the work of the devil, characterized by lewdness, random promiscuity, and debauchery. Third, a well-ordered Christian society required chastity before marriage, fidelity within the nuptial state, and lifelong indissoluble monogamy. Indian men and women were forced to conform, men abandoning multiple wives, and if serially married, returning to their first.

The Secular Model: The Politics and Erotics of Power

The Spanish soldiers who conquered and colonized Spanish America were propelled by dreams of fame and fortune and rarely showed concern about the salvation of their souls except when they wrote their last wills and testaments. These were largely young and single Spanish men who measured their worth through military might and their honor or their social status through the spoils of war: gold, women, tribute, land, and slaves. In a society that had been fighting Moors for some seven centuries, pushing back the boundaries of Islam on the Iberian Peninsula since the year 711, by 1492 the habits of war were well entrenched.

Indian women became the alchemists who transformed labor into gold. Because of their reproductive capacities, the sexual violence of the conquistadores in short order produced illegitimate, mixed-blood children begotten only to labor and to serve. The Spanish conquest was a sexual conquest of Indian women. Through rape and rapine, through intimidation and humiliation, the Spanish soldiers subjugated native men and women, interpreting their ability to dominate others as a testament to their virility and prowess. From a reading of the clerical chronicles of the Conquest one gleans the horrors that marked the event. Fray Francisco Zamora swore before God that he had witnessed native men stabbed and knifed to death because the Spanish soldiers wanted to take their wives. "I know for certain that the soldiers have violated them [the Indian women] often along the roads," Zamora wrote. Fray José Manuel de Equía y Leronbe said that he had heard the conquistadores shouting, as they went off to their debaucheries: "Let us go to the pueblos to fornicate with Indian women. . . . Only with lascivious treatment are Indian women conquered."[23]

Whereas the clerics who toiled in the spiritual conquest of the Americas relied on the lexicon of sin and salvation to describe the process, the Spanish soldiers explained their conquests in the language of power and honor. As conquerors of the land, confirmed by royal writ, they became men of honor with all the rights and privileges of Iberia's aristocrats. Their honor had been won by acts of bravery, cunning, and brutality. Indeed, these abilities were those they needed to lord their status over others, seizing the best fruits of the land as their own, taking whatever they wanted. In public they were feared and revered for their power and might; in private it was much the same. They were masters over their domestic dominions, protecting the honor of their households and of their womenfolk, simultaneously guarding the vergüenza (shame) of their females from assault. The ideology of honor was contradictory in that familial protection went hand in hand with the affirmation of one's own prowess and virility, manifested by assaulting the integrity of others through violent acts. The loss of honor by one man was his adversary's gain, and so the pecking order of honor was established.

A woman's shame, intimately tied to her physical purity as a virgin, was a limited asset that could only be lost or tarnished, never restored. Since a woman's honor always reflected on that of her menfolk, women were usually under the vigilant care of fathers, husbands, brothers, and sons. Female seclusion varied significantly by class. Social ideals became norms only when material resources would allow it. In the households of the lower castes, and in households where men were not often in residence, it was always much more difficult to seclude women and, obviously, much more difficult to protect them, given the requisites of daily life. In such households it was much more difficult to fend off assaults on personal and familial honor and thus more common for women of the lower classes to be deemed *sin vergüenza* (shameless) and thus more subject to random assaults.

Men were honorable if they acted with *hombría* (manliness), which was believed to arise from basic physiology. The *miembro viril* (virile member) produced masculinity and hombría. Men were legally impotent without it. An emasculated man was *manso*, meaning meek, gentle, humble, lamblike. But manso also signified a castrated animal or person. Some Spanish men even equated penis size with virility and manliness. In 1606 Gaspar Reyes found himself sick and destitute. Hoping to secure charity from the local friars, he begged for food at their residence. A certain Fray Pedro took him in and fed him lavishly with a meal, which included even wine. Reyes recalled that when he was finished eating, the friar "stuck his hand into my pants, took my virile member and wiggled it . . . and said to me, yours is small, mine is bigger." The priest then took Reyes to his cell, where he tried to use his posterior for the nefarious sin. To be buggered was a symbolic sign of defeat equated with femininity; to bugger was an assertion of dominance and masculinity. It was thus not insignificant that it was a priest who was concerned about his penis size and actively tried to sodomize Reyes. Any man who did not assert his manhood and lived a life of abstinence and purity ran the risk of being labeled tame, assumed castrated, and thereby lacking the necessary appendage of honor. Femininity and shame in women were likewise believed to be located in the *partes vergonzozas* (shameful parts).[24]

In the initial years of Spanish America's settlement, before Spanish women arrived in significant numbers and before stable families had been formed, it was not uncommon for soldiers and settlers to rape Indian women and men with impunity. Most cases of rape were not reported, much less litigated, but when they were, the accused man usually maintained that what had transpired was an act of virility, of prowess, a simple assertion of his masculinity over a willing partner who had seduced him. For after all, as one group of soldiers in the conquest of Mexico asserted in 1601, indigenous people "have no vices other than lust."[25]

By the eighteenth century, rape in New Spain was a more openly discussed fact of life. The majority of reported rape victims in the 1700s were women under the age of nineteen who did not have a strongly knit family to protect them. Most were assaulted while home alone or while out and about on errands without a male chaperon. While women of the upper classes, of Spanish and mestizo origin, were less often victims than enslaved African and indigenous women, women of all races and status were raped. Single men between the ages of twenty and thirty who lived outside tightly integrated webs of kinship—itinerant merchants, muleteers, and seasonal day laborers—were most often accused of rape.[26]

Raping a woman was considered a repugnant, antisocial crime. Men found guilty of it, however, typically received rather insignificant punishment. Exile, public shaming in the stocks, being tied to the gibbet, and monetary compensation for the woman were the ways in which most cases were resolved by the courts. In extreme cases, corporal punishment with up to two hundred lashes did occur. Nonetheless, since a man enhanced his honor through displays of virility, the greater and more permanent dishonor belonged to the raped woman and to her kinsmen who had failed to protect her honor and physical integrity.

Female rape victims were the persons who suffered most from this crime socially. They were often publicly humiliated as loose, shameless women. Their families frequently blamed the victim for inciting the passions of strangers and kin. If the rape involved incest, the victims often were removed from their homes and placed in a house for wayward women by the authorities. It was believed that such removals would thwart a father's, brother's, or uncle's incestuous desires. In such cloistered institutions, "fallen" women were isolated from contact with their families and were all but forgotten for long periods of time—some for life.[27]

Rape pitted the erotic prerogatives of masculine honor against the Catholic Church's desire to regulate society by containing the expression of lust. Thus, when church officials were faced with a report of rape, their response focused primarily on the woman's dishonor, on minimizing the public damage that her reputation might suffer. Priests usually dealt with this sin by keeping the assault as secret as possible. Clerics feared that other young men, by hearing of it, might be emboldened to similar violence. The nature of the penances that the Church imposed on rapists illustrates clearly the fundamental conflicts between ecclesiastical theory and the ideal prerogatives of masculinity that were intrinsic to the honor code. In the eyes of the Church, only the rapist was a sinner. His penance usually amounted to prayers, corporal works of mercy, and some economic compensation for the loss of a woman's virginity and shame, all of which were viewed as outward signs of contrition for the absolution of his sin. The raped woman was guilty of no sin. But according to the honor ideology, she and her family were the persons who remained defamed and dishonored until the assault was avenged. If the rapist prevailed in any blood feud that might result from the rape, his honor was enhanced by the sexual assault.

Enslaved Indian and African boys and men were also the victims of rape. But in the cultural lexicon of the Spanish colonists, such assaults were the prerogatives of conquest that had been practiced in Europe for many centuries and not deemed a crime, though most certainly a sin. Between men, such acts of violence were part of the physical rhetoric of humiliation by which conquered men were transformed symbolically into effeminates and dominated as "women." Raping defeated warriors was a supreme act of virility and prowess. Indeed, a whole class of defeated men known as *berdaches* existed in many indigenous societies in the Americas.[28]

European polemics on the meaning of the berdache in the Americas give us yet another instance where the lexicon of punishment that was part of war was radically at odds with that of sin. Since the times of the powerful city-states of Greece and the spread of Rome's empire, male rape was a fact of war, intended to show a defeated man that his status in the victor's world was that of an outsider, a foreigner, a slave, and worst, of a powerless and dependent woman. In medieval Islamic Spain there was an active commerce in young male slaves who were sold primarily to serve their masters as a "wife."

Indeed, the word berdache comes from the Arabic *bradaj*, meaning male prostitute. When the Spaniards arrived in the Americas, they found a host of men dressed as women, performing women's work, and offering receptive anal intercourse to powerful men in the communities in which they lived. From the ethnographic descriptions we know that these men had been captured in warfare and had their lives spared in order to serve and service their master's needs. When and where these berdaches were reported in the colonial period, they were always in the presence of men, carrying loads into battle, cooking their meals, and cooling their passions. Berdaches were found as temple adepts donning women's clothes, playing the feminine role, fellating and offering their posterior to powerful men in orgiastic rituals to the gods. In smaller towns and villages in which berdaches were observed, they offered hospitality to visiting dignitaries and were pimped out to young unmarried men who had not yet earned the right to consort with females.[29] Of course, all of these activities, in the eyes of clerics and theologians, were pure abomination, evidence that the Indians were addicted to the nefarious sin, to the sin against nature, sodomy. That such sinful behavior justified the Spanish conquest was clear enough. What was not was how extensively sodomy was practiced. And on this point there was considerable debate. Fray Bartolomé de Las Casas, the great defender of the Indians, found its existence marginal and insignificant, while his adversary Fray Gonzalo Fernández de Oviedo found it everywhere.

Spanish church and state officials believed that the only way in which social stability would be established in its colonies was by creating stable families. Today, we equate family (*familia*) with immediate kin and relatives. That which is within the family is intimate, within the private walls of the home, and excludes strangers. But if we focus carefully on the historical genealogy of the word *familia*, we find that in its antique meanings it was tied neither to kinship nor to a specific private space or house. Rather, what constituted family was the relationship of authority that one person exercised over another. Specifically, familia was imagined as the relationship of a master over his slaves and servants.

The etymological root of the Spanish *familia* is the Latin *familia*. Roman grammarians believed that the word entered Latin as a borrowing from the language of the neighboring Oscan tribe. In Oscan, *famel* means slave; the Latin for a slave is *famulus*. The second-century novelist Apuleius wrote that "fifteen slaves make a family, and fifteen prisoners make a jail." The Roman jurist Ulpian gave more precision to the term, explaining in the second century A.D. that "we are accustomed to call staffs of slaves families. . . . We call a family the several persons who by nature of law are placed under the authority of a single person." Family thus initially referred to the hierarchical authority relationship between people. This relationship could be based on kinship and marriage but was not limited to such situations. The family relationship is implicit in the definition of the word *pater* (father): the *paterfamilias* was the legal head of a familia, whereas a biological father was called the *genitor*. Only a man could exercise *patria potestas*—that is, the legal authority over anyone under his command—even if he himself was an unmarried man.[30]

Many of the antique meanings of familia persisted with some modifications into the seventeenth century in the Americas, undoubtedly because of the revival of Roman juridical thought in canon law and in the legal institutions of the fifteenth-century Iberian kingdoms. By the early 1600s, Sebastián de Covarrubias, in his dictionary *Tesoro de la lengua castellana o española* (1611), defined *familia* as "the people that a lord sustains within his house." Covarrubias concurred that familia was of Latin and Oscan etymology and explained that "while previously it had only meant a person's slaves," the word's contemporary meaning included "the lord and his wife, and the rest of the individuals under his command, such as children, servants, and slaves." Citing contemporary seventeenth-century usage, Covarrubias quoted the legal code known as the *Siete partidas*, which stipulated, "There is family when there are three persons governed by a lord." The 1732 *Diccionario de la lengua castellana* repeated Covarrubias's definition of familia almost verbatim.

By the seventeenth century, both in Spain and in Spanish America, familia was a jural unit based on authority relationships that were established primarily, though not exclusively, through marriage and procreation. Family was tied to a particular place, to a *casa* (house) in which the lord and his subordinates lived. The casa was a domestic realm, much as the public *real* was the king's domain. Family was thus synonymous with authority, lordship, and household.

Families were constructed through marriage, or the sacrament of matrimony, and it was through the institution of matrimony that the kings of Spain and the bishops of Spanish America hoped that the foundations of an orderly society would be built. While initially most of the Spanish men who came to the Americas did so alone, by the 1570s increasing numbers were bringing their wives. Men who were married in Spain but emigrated alone sometimes sent for their spouses after they were established. A significant number of these men also became bigamists, contracting marriages anew in Spanish America, denying that they had a wife elsewhere until clerical officials dug into the matter, usually spurred on by an abandoned wife. "Has anyone seen my husband?" these women would typically write to officials in the Americas. "His name is XYZ, a native of Andalucia, known by these nicknames, and so tall and so wide."[31] The majority of single Spanish men in the Americas were forced to turn to the local supply of women for their consorts, partners, and often for their legal brides.

Before the early 1800s, marriages were arranged by parents to advance the consolidation, protection, and expansion of familial wealth. Children could and did express their personal desires, but their opinions rarely were decisive in the selection of a mate. Starting at the Council of Elvira (ca. 300), the Catholic Church repeatedly tried to temper the power of patriarchs (paterfamilias) to expand and consolidate their wealth and cohesion by marrying off their children in calculating and economically advantageous ways. The Church opposed this practice by defining a whole set of impediments to matrimony based on concepts of incest, initially prohibiting marriage between persons related to the fourth degree of consanguinity (that is, three generations removed from the common ancestor). This prohibition was extended to the seventh degree of consanguinity at the Council of Rome in 1059. To understand how restrictive this incest law was, imagine a couple in each of six generations giving birth to two children. The consanguinity impediment to marriage eliminated 2,731 "blood" relatives of the same generation from choosing one another as mates. The intent of such consanguinity impediments was clear. As family solidarity increased, the Church tried to weaken its power by greatly expanding the consanguinity impediments or restrictions on sacramental matrimony.

The power that fathers exercised within the family over wife, children, and slaves was also a very complex and, at times, contradictory issue for the Church. The fourth commandment enjoins children to "honor thy father and mother," a scriptural injunction further elaborated in Saint Paul's Epistle to the Ephesians (5:22–6:9). Paul urges Christians to obey God as wives, children, and slaves obeyed the master of the house: "Wives, submit yourselves unto your own husbands, as unto the Lord. . . . Children, obey your parents in the Lord. . . . Servants, be obedient to them that are your masters . . . with fear and trembling . . . with good will doing service as to the Lord." According to Paul, the kingdom of heaven is governed by rules not unlike those that governed terrestrial kingdoms. But the Church also maintained a healthy skepticism about the untrammeled exercise of patriarchal power and through its theory of spiritual kinship consistently tried to limit its exercise. Biological parents were simply the earthly custodians and guardians of the children of God, or so argued clerics and theologians.

Arranged marriages remained the norm in Spanish America until the beginning of the nineteenth century, when romantic love became an equally compelling reason for choosing a particular individual as one's mate. Arranged marriages were often loveless matches, full of domestic discord, and routinely punctuated by adulterous liaisons. Married men who were unhappy often solved the problem by creating what in Spanish-speaking America is still known as the "*casa grande*" (big house), in which the legal wife and legitimate children lived, and the "*casa chica*" (small house), where the mistress and her illegitimate children resided. A form of legal separation known as "ecclesiastical divorce" was theoretically possible to dissolve particularly loveless but economically robust unions. Ecclesiastical divorces were granted only in extreme cases and then mostly to elites.[32]

Adultery was another instance where local honor codes and canon law set radically different parameters for comportment. The seduction of a woman, even if she was married, was a sign of a man's virility. A man's urge to dominate was deemed a natural impulse of the species. Adulterous women were considered shameless or *sin vergüenza*; their behavior shamed and dishonored their entire family. But adultery's greatest stigma fell on the cuckolded husband whose wife had not been restrained and kept from such dishonorable behavior. He had the right, still practiced in some honor-based societies to this day, of killing his wife, avenging her impurity, and or sending her into exile to live the rest of her days shunned, alone, and without a husband or family to provide for her. In canon law adultery was viewed very differently. In such sinful acts both male and female were equally culpable, though it was usually only the woman who suffered its social consequences. Adulterous men were urged to return home and to make a *vida mariable* (marriageable life) with their spouse. If they continued in their philandering ways but were discreet, they could, and often did, escape the attention of the authorities. Women who desecrated the matrimonial bond were usually given penances and told to refrain from such sinful behavior in the future.

Illegitimate children were the biological byproducts of philandering husbands and of young unmarried men who exploitatively sowed their seed outside marriage. The logical result was that by the early 1700s, roughly half of New Spain's population had been born outside of wedlock, a percentage that was much higher among the offspring of Indians and African slaves. In the northern Mexican mining town of Charcas, the incidence of illegitimacy among mulattoes was 65 percent in the period 1635–39 and 75 percent in 1650–54. Between the sixteenth and eighteenth centuries, roughly similar levels of illegitimacy were the norm in Peru.[33]

How those who bore the stigma of illegitimacy were viewed and treated in society has long been a topic of debate in the historiography of colonial Spanish America. The extant evidence suggests that the stain of bad birth was not very important in the day-to-day behavior of face-to-face communities. Before the law, the case was very different. Illegitimate aspirants to educational opportunities and honorific posts were often significantly hampered because they lacked a known and honorable father of pure blood. Partly in response to the desires of such men and women for upward mobility, and largely to gather extra cash from the colonies, at the end of the eighteenth century the Spanish monarchy began selling writs of legitimacy and the cleansing of stained racial pasts known as *cédulas de gracias al sacar* (certificates of purity).[34]

These cédulas de gracias al sacar point to the fact that in the second half of the eighteenth century a whole series of social, political, and economic reforms were instituted by the crown to intensify its exploitation of the colonies and to maximize its profits therefrom. These reforms, collectively known as the Bourbon Reforms, were organized to streamline the colonial bureaucracy, heighten economic development, and subordinate the power of the Catholic Church, guilds, and hereditary groups. As part of the crown's attempt to secularize society, a whole range of activities that the Church had regulated through canon law, ecclesiastical courts, and its concept of sin gradually was replaced by civil law, secular courts, and concepts of property, degeneracy, and disease. For example, in 1700, because matrimony was a sacrament, all aspects regarding the formation of marriages were under the exclusive jurisdiction of the Church; by 1800 the state had intervened, separating out those issues related to contract and property (How had the marriage been contracted? How much dowry had been exchanged? What would be the disposition of dotal property that had been brought to a marriage?) and left issues related to the nature of the sacrament to the Church (Had it been entered into of free will? Was there any coercion involved in the promise of marriage? Were there any impediments to the sacramental state such as impotence or incest?).[35]

The tempo at which secularization occurred was particularly rapid around Indian missions. As one parish after another was taken from the control of religious orders and given to secular priests, the power the Church previously had used to dictate social behavior began to weaken and to be replaced by secular discourses of criminality, medicine, and disease. Many parishes were left without priests, and once such places were devoid of overt repression, indigenous and secular ideas and behaviors about the body and desire became increasingly important.

One gets an idea of how profound the Bourbon Reforms were in transforming personal life by examining the stated motives for marriage given in New Mexico between 1693 and 1840. When the friars asked men and women why they wished to marry, the most common responses recorded between 1693 and 1790 were religious and obligational. Individuals wanted "to serve God," "to save their souls," or to put themselves "in a state of grace." The first sign of any change in the reasons for desiring marriage appeared in a 1798 record. José García of Albuquerque averred that he wanted to marry María López "because of the growing desire [voluntad] that we mutually have for each other." Voluntad had previously appeared in marital investigations but only to mean volition, as in the determination that a person's free will was being exercised. María Durán gave voluntad this meaning when she proclaimed "I marry freely and spontaneously, neither counseled nor coerced, but totally of my own volition." By the end of the eighteenth century the responses, though likewise formulaic, had begun to change radically. Juan José Ramón Gallego, a resident of Jémez, wanted to marry Juana María because, he said, "I fell in love [me enamore]." While previously love and desire would not have been deemed acceptable justifications for seeking a marital partner, after the 1770s young men and women increasingly married for reasons of love, physical attraction, sexual passion, and personal and individual likes and dislikes. We also note a fundamental change in how the Spanish word for love (amor) was used. In Spanish America during the seventeenth and eighteenth centuries, the word love appeared mainly in two ways. First, it referred very broadly to Christian love and, secondly, to illicit sexual contact. Thus when men admitted to the ecclesiastical courts that they had seduced a woman or were living in adultery, they usually said that "I happened to make love to [llegue a enamorar]" a particular woman. After about 1800, such illicit acts were referred to as illicit friendship (amistad ilicita) or illicit coitus (cópula ilicita), and love took on meanings close to those we moderns give it today.[36]

Social Transformations: The Invention of Sexuality

The Bourbon Reforms are often referred to as the second colonization of Spanish America, in that they led to the intensification of colonial exploitation, provoking the revolutionary movements for independence that swept the continent between 1807 and 1821. In this period all of Spain's colonial possessions in the Americas became independent save for Cuba and Puerto Rico. How independence may have transformed intimate personal lives is not well known or understood. The basic cultural transformation was that a colonial society that was hierarchically organized and viewed as holistic, in that everyone had a place in the body politic, came to be imagined as a society that was egalitarian and individualistic in organization. I use the word egalitarian here guardedly, because clearly to this day no former Spanish colony except Cuba has made any significant strides toward ending entrenched inequalities. What I mean here is that, at least before the law, the power of corporate groups—the Church, guilds, cattle breeders—evaporated and people came before the courts not as groups with privileges but as individuals. People began likewise to enter the marketplace to sell their labor and to profit, again, on the basis of their personal skills and as autonomous agents.[37] In my mind, the development of notions of personal autonomy and individualism were absolutely necessary for personal identities based on sexuality to emerge.

In the study of the Latina/o past, how sexuality was invented out of the set of former discourses about the body and its sinfulness is not yet entirely clear and needs further investigation. Nevertheless, I attempt to identify, if only in a cursory fashion, a number of areas where current research offers glimpses about the direction of changes wrought by modernity. As noted while discussing the transition from arranged marriages to those based on love, a new understanding of marriage emerged that saw it as an institution for the fulfillment of personal erotic desires and needs. If such motivations were recognized within marriage, one can only assume that similar sentiments pervaded the society more broadly, allowing for such expressions outside of marriage, be they through seduction, mutual desire, or even the purchase of commercialized sex. Sexual pleasure, while mostly documented among men in the colonial period, increasingly became an expectation among women as well, whether as a solitary activity, in the conjugal bed, in positions other than the missionary, and with the aid of instruments or toys of various sorts.

During the nineteenth century, largely as a result of the rise of export economies organized around commercial agriculture, large numbers of peasants migrated into central urban places, which often became the burgeoning hubs of industrialization. As extended households and broadly integrated kinship groups were disrupted and re-formed in cities, their dimensions and domains of influence became smaller and more intense. The nuclear family increasingly dominated the social life of urbanites. Within the nuclear family women had more ability to exercise their free will. Whether patriarchal power continued to reign supreme, declined as women contested male power within and outside of the home, or intensified, we do not really yet know. Hypermasculinity, what is often called *machismo*, became a frequent symbol of the authority men exercised over women, children, and subordinates, though clearly this ability to lord it over others had a long and complex historical lineage.[38]

The power of the Catholic Church to influence behavior through its discourse of sin remained, albeit substantially weakened and no longer as hegemonic as it had been during the colonial period. Spanish America's modernizing states turned to European discourses of science, and particularly to medicine, to define the normative and the aberrant in society.[39] It was then that sexuality was born as a way of talking about bodily genital difference and about particular kinds of sexual behavior that imbued individuals with personal identities based on desire as heterosexuals and homosexuals.

The word for sex (*sexo*), as we saw, did not enter the Spanish language until 1809. Etymological dictionaries of the Spanish language affirm that the word *sexo* is taken from the Latin *seco*, which means "to cut or to divide," as into male and female organisms. The word sex became particularly capacious in its meanings; it denoted both a category of person (the male sex, the female sex) most readily understood as having a physiological basis in the genitals and an act (to have sex), which was believed to be an imperative of the genitals themselves. Gender ideals were tied naturally to the genitals, and how and with which genitals one got excited (different, same, both) gave rise to the behavioral identities of heterosexual and homosexual, much later to bisexual, always recognizing asexual and autosexual as alternatives realities. What was particularly new about the invention of "sexuality" in Spanish America was that it brought together a range of biological and mental possibilities—gender, bodily differences, reproductive capacity, needs, fantasies, and desires.[40]

How exactly sexuality was constructed in Latin America during the period from 1800 to 1880, we do not know. By this later date, largely from studies about how modern medicine defined social deviants in Mexico, Argentina, and Brazil, we have come to understand the extent of class anxieties about social mixing.[41] What these three countries had in common in 1880, aside from their rapid industrialization and booming export economies, was that the nation-state was being constructed and local and regional loyalties destroyed, as large numbers of migrants and immigrants flocked to Mexico City, to Buenos Aires, and to Rio de Janeiro seeking work and pleasure. It was through a new language of sex and gender that citizen-subjects were born. The nation needed strong men—active, virile, muscular, and masculine. It was out of discussions about the gendering of the fatherland (*patria*) that statesmen, politicians, and scientists debated about how the body politic would be writ on human bodies, which bodies were healthy and led to the nation's reproduction, and which were sickly and necessary to criminalize and correct.

Heterosexuals and their opposite, homosexuals, emerged out of these discussions, thus transforming the Church's and the state's older, exclusive focus on sinful and socially disruptive behaviors and giving rise to personal sexual identities. Who was normal or abnormal presupposed a sexual identity that was either heterosexual or homosexual. Homosexuals were inverts, were men and women who had made the wrong sex-object choice. The malady of the invert was that he (most of the literature is about men) was a sexually receptive, passive man and also one who did not and could not reproduce. In Spanish America, where the nationalist slogan at the time was "To govern is to populate," homosexuals were aberrant. They inverted the natural insertive and active role of men in sexual intercourse and instead were passive pederasts. Once this inversion occurred in terms of sexual desire, it was assumed that the dress, manners, and dispositions associated with the male sex were also inverted. Transvestism and prostitution were the logical results. Much of the discourse of sexual inversion borrowed the colonial Spanish American lexicon of male sodomy. The sexual postures that were coded as hombre and mujer were now conflated with *activo* (active or insertive) and *pasivo* (passive or receptive) positions of intercourse and thus associated with masculinity and femininity, respectively. In the largely male-dominated discourse of medicine, this inversion was imagined as something learned, or as a disease, a contagion that could weaken the body politic and lead to societal ruin.

By the 1600s there already existed, in the major urban centers of Latin America, a subculture among men who had sex with other men. At the end of the nineteenth century, that subculture became much more open and much more pronounced. The clinical gaze with which we read about it was particularly obvious at Carnival. Carnival, which marked the beginning of Lent, allowed men of every status and state to invert their social and sexual worlds, dressing as women if they wanted and taking it from behind. When the merriment ended, some men remained in their new roles and never looked back. The invert subculture of many cities was marked by drag shows, transvestite displays on the grand boulevards, and men sporting female names, and even speaking a feminine language of their own. Some of the inverts even formally took other men as their husbands. One Argentine physician in Buenos Aires in the early 1900s noted that "the marriage of sexual inverts is not a rare occurrence, to be sure, but this ceremony ordinarily happens only as an act of scandalous ostentation . . . with the conventional apparatus of a real wedding: *she* dressed in white, her head adorned with orange blossoms, he in tuxedo and white gloves."[42]

Eusebio Gómez, an Argentine criminologist who studied the habits of homosexuals in Buenos Aires and reported them in *La mala vida en Buenos Aires* (1908), transcribed verbatim a letter he had received from an invert named Mysotis: "I am like this because I was born like this. Anyway, this is the way I should behave because beauty has no sex. . . . I do not do anything extraordinary: I like men and for that reason I amuse myself with them. I treat them with exquisite *savoir faire*." Mysotis went on to describe the group of homosexual men he associated with and called it a *cofradía* (confraternity). Cofradias were technically religious associations of pious women and men under the supervision of the Catholic Church, but in this case clearly without ecclesiastical sanction.[43]

Much of the medical literature on inverts in Spanish America at the beginning of the twentieth century assumed that only the passive, receptive partner was a homosexual. The insertive, active partner was characterized as a seducer, who most certainly behaved against the laws of nature but was guilty only of pushing other men to invert their sexual object choice so that seducers could use them. Active, insertive men did not invert a male's correct sexual role; they were simply acting as men should. This argument was premised on the assumption that the invert had a natural predisposition to homosexuality that could be ignited by certain environments or contact with certain persons. Gymnasiums, swimming pools, segregated high schools, military barracks, seminaries, clubs all required special vigilance, criminologists of the time advised. For it was at such sites that innate tendencies, if given the slightest push, might flourish without limit. Of course, bear in mind that the etiology of homosexuality was debated endlessly not only at the beginning of the twentieth century but throughout the entire course of the century.[44]

Is homosexuality learned or innate behavior? Whatever the answer in 1900, the solution was identical: to root it out lest others learn it; to extirpate it lest its ugly head awaken latent dispositions. To this day, attitudes toward the social acceptance of homosexuality can be largely predicated on the basis of which side of this nurture/nature divide one finds most compelling. Survey research clearly shows that when most people believe that homosexuality is biologically innate, that one is born with this orientation, and that it cannot be changed or for that matter cannot be propagated and spread, social acceptance is common and with it often come beliefs that legal protections and full cultural citizenship for homosexuals are necessary and justified. When more people believe that homosexuality is learned, social responses to it are much more negative, precisely because of feelings that it can be taught by teachers in schools and by predators in the various spaces of exclusive male or female congregation. Such an understanding of homosexuality as nurtured contagion naturally requires its eradication, suppression, and criminalization.[45]

In looking at the history of Latina and Latino sexualities over the long view, what I have tried to show is how central was the family as an institution shaping colonial understandings of the ways physical desire and passion could and should be expressed in an orderly society. Clerical discourse on the sinfulness of bodily desire—in particular and on its most evil passion, lust—occupied countless pages of printed confessional guides and sermon manuals with one goal in mind: to create stable families. For this to occur clerics had to teach old and new Christians alike about the sanctity of the matrimonial vow, its dependence on marital monogamy, and premarital chastity and marital fidelity to insure legitimate heirs to honor, fame, and property. The Spanish state endorsed or passively acquiesced in all of these church dictates until the middle of the eighteenth century, largely because it was the official patron of the Catholic Church in the Americas and by papal arrangement had defined Catholicism as the official state religion. But beginning with the Enlightenment in the early 1700s, with the rise of secular states, and with the subordination of religion to science, new discourses about the body emerged. Many of these secular discourses were rooted in older sources about the nature of power, which fit perfectly with expansionist colonial policies and the development of imperialism. Sex emerged as a discrete category in the Spanish language in 1809 out of the language of science, and it was from this language that personal identities based on sex were born.

This history of Latina/o sexualities would be much more robust, much richer in detail, more varied in geographic scope if scholars turned their attention to a number of topics. First and foremost, we know very little about African slave and ex-slave sexual ideology and comportment in the Americas. Colonial and contemporary theories of mestizaje presuppose a constant sexual mixing between dominant masters and female slaves and between persons of their own status. At the moment, these are all largely educated hunches rather than based on any sustained empirical research. The same can be said about the indigenous population of Latin America. What we know comes from a very limited perspective. Gay and lesbian scholars since the Gay Liberation movement of the 1970s in the United States have been interested in finding alternative systems of gender socialization for young girls and boys. This has led to a plethora of writing, most of it wrong-headed, on the berdache tradition, those indigenous biological males who played female roles in the aftermath of capture and enslavement. As a result, we have only a very limited understanding of indigenous sexual ideology and behavior written with a purple-colored pen. We know a great deal more about male sexual ideology, behavior, exceptions, and aberrations than we know about female, particularly when it comes to love and sex between and among women. More research is definitely needed here. Finally, our understanding of sexual identities, their genealogy, and their articulation during independence and in the period from 1800 to 1900 requires more investigation. These are some of the themes and periods that require the attention of students and scholars if we are to understand more completely the history of sexualities in Latin America and among Latinas and Latinos in the United States.

2

Making Sex Matter

Histories of Latina/o Sexualities, 1898 to 1965

PABLO MITCHELL

For a sobering view of the state of the field of the history of Latina/o sexualities, one need only type a handful of relevant keywords into any major academic database. "Latino" and "sexuality," for instance, returns a total of two citations from *America: History and Life*, which includes more than two thousand journals, as well as book reviews and dissertations. One is a 2003 essay on gay Latinos in San Francisco by Horacio Roque Ramírez, the other a 1999 essay by George Lipsitz on popular music in the 1980s and 1990s.[1] A search with "Hispanic" and "sexuality" produces similarly thin results: six citations, two of which are the essays mentioned above. The seventy-two history journals in JSTOR's database reveal much the same story, with few relevant essays for either "Latino" or "Hispanic" paired with "sexuality." Monographs on the history of Latina/o sexuality are likewise few and far between, especially for the period covered by this chapter, roughly the beginning of the twentieth century through the 1960s. The online catalog for the University of California library system, for example, produced only a handful of historical works on the subjects of Latina/os and sexuality.

While few major works have addressed the history of Latina/o sexuality, or sexualities, in the twentieth century, the topic has received some limited attention from historians. This essay is organized into two broad sections: the first surveys sexuality scholarship within Latina/o history; the second examines the place of Latina/os in the history of American sexualities. I consider Latina/o history to include the histories of people of Latin American descent in the United States, both those born in the United States and those who migrated to the country, with Mexican Americans, Puerto Ricans, Cuban Americans, Dominican Americans, and people of Central American descent as the most prominent groups. The history of American sexualities is similarly broad, covering a range of sexual activity and sexual understandings. Historians, especially historians of the twentieth century, have focused on commercial sex (specifically prostitution), same-sex sexuality, sexual violence, female reproductive control including abortion and sterilization, and the scientific and medical study of sexual behavior.

Two critical events in Latina/o history bookend this essay: the 1898 Spanish-American War and the 1965 immigration act. As occurred fifty years earlier in the aftermath of the 1846–48 Mexican-American War, Puerto Ricans and Cubans were subjected to U.S. occupation and imperial control in the wake of the American military victory over Spain in 1898. Legal U.S. citizenship for Puerto Ricans and intensified economic and political relations between the United States and Cuba led to increased migration between Puerto Rico and Cuba and the U.S. mainland. In early-twentieth-century Mexico, similar forms of American political and economic intervention, combined with the upheavals of revolution and ample jobs to the north, led hundreds of thousands of Mexicans to migrate to the United States. As a result, Latina/o communities developed throughout much of the United States in the first half of the twentieth century, and Latina/os became a significant presence in major cities in the East, Midwest, and Southwest, as well as in smaller towns and rural areas.

The passage of the Hart-Cellar Act in 1965, which serves as the end point of this survey, was also a turning point in Latina/o history, as major new migrations originated from the Dominican Republic, Cuba, and Central American nations. The act dismantled four decades of immigration policy that had explicitly favored Europeans over migrants from Asia and Latin America. Latin American newcomers benefited from new policies promoting family reunification and prioritizing those seeking jobs in high-demand fields. U.S. political concerns similarly spurred migration from countries deemed hostile to American interests, such as Cuba after the 1959 revolution. At the same time, as David G. Gutiérrez notes, "the huge and growing demand for labor in the United States during the war in Vietnam, aggressive U.S. economic policy and practices abroad, and the persistence of political and economic instability in Latin America" created strong new incentives for extralegal migration to the United States from Latin America. As a result of the 1965 legislation, the numbers of Latin American immigrants entering the country through formal channels grew from 1 million in the 1960s to 1.4 million in the 1970s to more than 4 million between 1990 and 2000. "The officially authorized and acknowledged immigrant flow was always augmented," adds Gutiérrez, "by the constant circulation into and out of U.S. territory of millions of unauthorized, 'illegal' migrants."[2]

Ending this overview in 1965 is not without its disadvantages. Major events in Latina/o history (the Chicano movement, the Young Lords Party, the Mariel boatlift) and the history of sexuality (Stonewall, HIV/AIDS) lie largely outside the range of the study. Important historical work on Latina/o sexuality is also slighted by this approach. Lawrence La Fountain-Stokes, Jennifer Nelson, Susana Peña, and Horacio Roque Ramírez have all produced important work on the more recent history of Latina/o sexuality. Given the importance of the 1965 immigration act in the history of Latina/o peoples and the rich scholarship that has already developed on the period after 1965, there will undoubtedly soon be a need for a historiographical essay that covers the more contemporary period.[3]

For the time being, however, the vitality of post-1965 studies of Latina/o sexuality should not obscure the fact that, for much of the twentieth century, Latina/o sexual practices, understandings, and politics have remained largely hidden from historians. This absence has occurred even as the field of Latina/o history has prospered. Indeed, chroniclers of the period 1898–1965 have produced many of the signature works in Latina/o history. Matters of sex and sexuality have on occasion surfaced in such works, but material in general has been scarce. Likewise, the field of the history of Latina/o sexuality is hardly comparable to, say, the fields of Latina/o labor history or the history of Latina/o political activity. Instead, discussions of sex in the Latina/o past have been limited to such topics as personal narratives based on oral history interviews, prostitution and other forms of sexual violence, sterilization and birth control research, notions of female sexual purity, and sex in popular culture.

Oral history research has produced some of the field's most thoughtful and compelling historical work. Two decades ago, *Compañeras: Latina Lesbians*, with its numerous autobiographical accounts of Latinas, was published. Several of the narratives highlight sexuality, such as the description by Julia Pérez, a *puertorriqueña* who arrived in New York City in the mid-1940s, of "María," her first love. "I loved María, I adored María," Pérez remembers, "María was my savior. . . . I was horny too!"[4] Oral history is at the center of Horacio Roque Ramírez's recent essay on Teresita la Campesina, the famed male-to-female (MTF) transgender Latina singer based in San Francisco. Based on extensive interviews with the performer, the article contains valuable biographical information about her childhood and young adulthood in midcentury Los Angeles, her early singing career as "Margarita" on L.A.'s Spanish-language radio stations, and her move north to San Francisco in 1958, where, according to the author, she was "a legend from the moment of her arrival until her death on the 12th of July, 2002." Roque Ramírez notes that "she was one of the most important personalities in [San Francisco's] queer Latino history."[5] Oral history interviews are also prominent in accounts of the life of Sylvia Rivera, described by Lawrence La Fountain-Stokes as "the Bronx-born, Venezuelan/Puerto Rican Stonewall veteran, transgender activist, and Young Lords member."[6]

The most thorough study of commercial sex among U.S. Latina/os occurs in Eileen J. Suárez Findlay's *Imposing Decency*. As part of her broader focus on racial and sexual politics, Findlay examines prostitution in Puerto Rico from the 1890s through World War I, with individual chapters focusing on prostitution in the city of Ponce in the 1890s and debates over female sex workers during the Great War. In addition to her invaluable archival research into the history of prostitution in early-twentieth-century Puerto Rico, Findlay offers a critical analysis of how race and sexuality together helped create and maintain social inequality on the island. "White women of Puerto Rico's middle and upper classes, including the early feminists," she writes, "defined their own respectability in opposition to working women's supposed inherent degeneracy," with supposed sexual deviance at the core of this distinction.[7]

Other authors have explored the relationship between sexuality and U.S. colonial rule in Puerto Rico beginning in 1898. José Flores Ramos's essay "Virgins, Whores, and Martyrs: Prostitution in the Colony, 1898–1919," for example, explores commercial sex in early-twentieth-century Puerto Rico.[8] In the first chapter of *Reproducing Empire*, Laura Briggs situates U.S. colonial policy in Puerto Rico within a broader context of "imperialism, sex, and science" through a discussion of syphilis and colonial policy regarding prostitution. In the following chapter, Briggs examines prostitution in early-twentieth-century Puerto Rico and describes how debates over prostitution helped "both Puerto Rican elites and North American colonials . . . solidify their claims to power." In later chapters, Briggs discusses birth control programs in mid-twentieth-century Puerto Rico, including the testing of the birth control pill, and politics and activism surrounding sterilization programs and theories of "culture of poverty." In addition, Briggs considers *puertorriqueña* sexuality, often denounced and demonized, to have been a pivotal site in the constitution of Puerto Rican identities and American empire.[9]

References to the participation of ethnic Mexicans in commercial sex appear in Francisco A. Rosales's *Pobre Raza*, a study of Mexican migrants and the American criminal justice system in the early twentieth century. Rosales cites arrest records involving Mexican women from throughout the Southwest and describes several antiprostitution raids in the region, including an antivice campaign in Phoenix in 1930, where "police arrested and deported a number of Mexican women." Rosales quotes one woman's complaint after being arrested and deported: "I paid my bribes to the police like everyone else," she said. "It is the Phoenix police who are to blame."[10] In my *Coyote Nation*, I cite newspaper accounts of prostitution in turn-of-the-twentieth-century New Mexico that record the involvement of Hispanas in commercial sex work and include the description of prostitutes in the Spanish-language press. A more detailed discussion of Hispana/o sexuality occurs in a chapter on rape trials in New Mexico, in which I examine several cases involving both Hispana victims and Hispanos accused of sexual assault.[11] Mark Wild's *Street Meeting*, a monograph examining racial and ethnic mingling in early-twentieth-century Los Angeles, devotes a chapter to cross-cultural sexual intimacies in L.A. Wild describes "inter-ethnoracial contact" in several settings, including prostitution and commercial sex, teen romances, and long-term adult relationships. He cites examples of prostitution in predominantly Mexican areas of downtown L.A. as well as complaints about the sex trade filed by Mexican residents with local officials. Wild also describes cross-cultural dating and marriage involving Mexican men and women.[12]

Other recent scholarship has reexamined iconic moments in Latina/o history through the lens of sexuality. Elizabeth R. Escobedo's recent essay on "*pachucas*" in

World War II Los Angeles, for instance, highlights the young women's sexual non-conformity and the threat that such practices posed to both mainstream Anglo society and members of L.A.'s Mexican American community during the era of zoot suits and the Sleepy Lagoon trial. Escobedo builds on the work of Chicana historians like Vicki Ruiz who have examined generational tensions between first-generation Mexican immigrants and their second-generation daughters. Escobedo importantly illustrates how critics, Anglo and Mexican alike, of pachucas linked sexual nonconformity with refusal either to assimilate to "American" ideals or to adopt traditional "Mexican" gender and sexual values and behaviors.[13]

Representations of Latina/os in American popular culture offer another valuable site for the study of the history of Latina/o sexuality. In *MeXicana Encounters*, Rosa Linda Fregoso places sexuality at the center of her analysis of the creation of Chicana and Mexicana social identities over the course of the twentieth century. Fregoso's analysis of early film representations of racialized Mexican sexuality is especially valuable for historians. She describes how images of Mexican women as sexually deviant "were intimately connected to . . . racial formation during the period these films were made." Fregoso also discusses Latina film stars, such as Lupe Vélez, who, she argues, presented her fans with a "subversion of traditional notions of femininity—especially her newfound sexual freedom." Vélez, Fregoso says, "openly advocated sex beyond the confines of marriage."[14] Gustavo Pérez Firmat's *Life on the Hyphen* provides an analysis of Desi Arnaz, the midcentury Cuban American singer and movie star best known for the television show *I Love Lucy* and his marriage to Lucille Ball. "Love, lust, loss, language, identity, authenticity," he says, "these are the large themes of Desi Arnaz's biography and autobiography, and the reasons he is a crucial presence in Cuban America."[15] José Limón's *Dancing with the Devil* similarly explores the erotic and the sexual in midcentury Westerns, focusing on cross-cultural desire involving Latinas in films like *High Noon*.[16] Frances Negrón-Muntaner's examination of *West Side Story* in her 2004 book, *Boricua Pop*, also foregrounds sexuality. Negrón-Muntaner's nuanced reading of the film and its cultural contexts and reverberations includes sections on Rita Moreno and on "the uncanny queerness of *West Side Story*."[17]

Methodologically, such works for the most part employ traditional forms of historical research—criminal records, newspaper accounts, film and television archives. One prominent exception is Emma Pérez's *The Decolonial Imaginary*. Like Fregoso, Pérez skillfully applies insights from critical theory and feminist studies to her subject matter. The book is a wide-ranging discussion of Chicana/o history in the twentieth century, with sexuality and desire at its core.[18]

Just as major works in Latina/o history have rarely addressed sexuality, so too has the history of American sexualities focused only sparingly on U.S. Latina/os. For instance, *Intimate Matters*, the valuable survey of sex in American history from the colonial era to the 1980s, contains just a handful of references to Latina/os. The authors cite two examples of the sexual experiences of Mexicans in the twentieth century: one is a *corrido* bemoaning the lack of sexual modesty in young Mexicanas ("The girls go about almost naked / And call *la tienda* 'estor'"); the other is a quotation from a young L.A. woman working at a dance hall describing the sexual propositions directed toward her at work. The only other references to Latina/os are two descriptions of high sterilization rates among Puerto Ricans in the mid-twentieth century.[19]

Yet among major works in American sexual history, *Intimate Matters* is one of the more inclusive in terms of Latina/os. Many works fail to address race and racial differences in any significant sense, and even those concerned with concepts such as racialized sexuality tend to focus on interactions between Anglos and African Americans. In Jennifer Terry's *An American Obsession*, a sprawling survey of the study of homosexuality and sexual difference in modern American science and medicine, Latina/o groups are invisible, without a single reference in the book's index, while African Americans are cited on more than a dozen index entries. This otherwise fine book has little to offer scholars interested in the ability of sexual discourses to structure racial hierarchies. Kevin J. Mumford's *Interzones*, an examination of sex districts in early-twentieth-century Chicago and New York, similarly includes only one reference to Latina/os: a book on taxi-dance halls from the early 1930s which observed that "Mexican, Filipino, Chinese, and Japanese men were not so freely admitted."[20]

There are, nonetheless, a number of historians of sexuality who have addressed the sexual lives of Latina/os in their work. Johanna Schoen's *Choice and Coercion*, which focuses on birth control, sterilization, and abortion in the midcentury United States, contains a lengthy section on "feminist activism and women's desire to control their contraception" in Puerto Rico. Like Laura Briggs and Eileen Findlay, Schoen is attuned to the intertwining of sexuality with U.S. imperial and racial politics in Puerto Rico. "Sexuality," she writes, "lay at the heart of American ideas about the modernization of Puerto Rico from the moment the United States took colonial possession of the island in 1898." Schoen describes the active participation of Puerto Rican women in clinical trials for the birth control pill in the 1950s. Women, according to Schoen, "took the initiative in approaching health and welfare personnel involved with the trials and requesting to join the group of participants." Schoen also discusses sterilization programs in Puerto Rico, as an example both of Puerto Rican women's attempt to control their own reproductive lives and of the abuse of sterilization programs by government officials.[21]

Stephen Robertson's *Crimes against Children*, a meticulous analysis of sex crimes committed against children in New York City from 1880 to 1960, also contains several references to Latina/os, namely Puerto Ricans in New York, who were especially visible in sex crime prosecutions after 1950. In 1951, he notes, twenty-three of the sixty-six men charged with the rape of girls between the ages of eleven and seventeen were Puerto Ricans. In 1955, 45 of the 104 charged with the same crime were Puerto Ricans. According to Robertson, Puerto Ricans were more concerned than other groups with girls' pregnancies outside of marriage and their supposedly "ruined" reputations. Though Robertson relies on seriously outdated material for evidence of Puerto Ricans' emphasis on female virginity, his data are notable. In legal proceedings involving pregnant girls and their parents between 1951 and 1955, he reports, "marriage was discussed in nine of the eighteen cases involving a pregnant Puerto Rican girl, in only two of the eleven cases involving a pregnant African-American girl, and in six of the twenty-five cases involving a pregnant white girl." Robertson also describes several criminal cases involving Puerto Ricans in some detail, such as the statutory rape charge filed in 1936 against twenty-one-year-old Ronaldo Feliciano for sexual involvement with thirteen-year-old Anacelia Lopez.[22]

Other Latina/os besides Puerto Ricans appear briefly in the book. Robertson ends his first chapter with the case of Juan Bana, a twenty-seven-year-old Mexican who was convicted of raping twenty-year-old Clara Maguire in 1911. Robertson notes that Bana would likely not have been convicted if he were not a Mexican and that such instances of interracial sexuality were uncommon in the court records. He describes a 1941 case in which six-year-old Angel Ramirez, whose background was unspecified, had been sexually assaulted by "a 33-year-old Cuban neighbor named Martin Bailey." In another case, Eddie Padilla, a janitor from Colombia, attacked an eight-year-old Anglo girl. Robertson also includes numerous references to Spanish-surnamed individuals, both victims and their parents, and criminal defendants.[23]

Mary Odem's *Delinquent Daughters*, a California-based study of adolescent female sexuality in the late nineteenth and early twentieth centuries, contains references to Latinas and their families in northern California. Odem describes the importance that Mexican families placed on female chastity as well as the role of parents in demanding that local courts punish wrongdoing. She points, for example, to the case of Carmen Hernandez, who at age fifteen became pregnant. After Hernandez's Mexican boyfriend refused to marry her or provide support for the child, Hernandez's parents encouraged police to arrest him for statutory rape.[24]

Another study of sexuality in a Western city includes a discussion of Latinas involved in prostitution. Ann R. Gabbert's essay on prostitution in turn-of-the-twentieth-century El Paso provides valuable, and rare, statistical information on Mexican sex workers in the United States. Citing census data, Gabbert concludes that 30 percent of prostitutes in El Paso were Mexicans in 1900. According to immigration records from 1908–9, she adds, "about 11 percent (39 of 358) of the aliens deported from the United States for prostitution were Mexican." After the passage of the Mann Act in 1910, she argues, the percentage jumped dramatically in the next years, resulting in Mexican women accounting for "39 percent (69 of 178) of the total debarred." Gabbert also offers individual descriptions of Mexicans involved in sex work, including a rare oral history account from a Mexican woman recorded in 1976.[25]

Eithne Luibhéid's *Entry Denied* places sexuality at the center of the history of U.S. immigration policy and border enforcement. Luibhéid's broad historical scope ranges from the exclusion of Asian women in the nineteenth century to the end of the twentieth century. The book's fourth chapter, "Looking Like a Lesbian," examines the case of Sara Harb Quiroz, who was detained while entering the United States in January 1960 because, according to Luibhéid, "an agent suspected that she was a lesbian." Weaving critical theory into her analysis of one woman's struggle against border authorities, Luibhéid "us[es] Quiroz's case to explore U.S. immigration-service constructions of homosexuality."[26]

Luibhéid is also the coeditor of *Queer Migrations*, an important collection of essays analyzing intersections of race, sex, and migration. Several of the book's authors, such as Susana Peña and Horacio Roque Ramírez, make valuable contributions to Latina/o history, although their topics fall outside the chronological scope of this survey. Another essay in the collection, by Siobhan B. Somerville, analyzes the 1952 Immigration and Nationality Act, also known as the McCarran-Walter Act. She observes that the act is "still function[ing] as the basic body of immigration law in the United States today." While Somerville does not address the effect of the law on Latina/os or migrants from Latin America, the impact of the "simultaneous disappearance of overt language of race and appearance of 'outlawed' sexual formations such as homosexuality and adultery" has been profound for Latina/os' sexual practices.[27]

While Nan Alamilla Boyd's *Wide Open Town*, a history of queer San Francisco, does not include a full discussion of queer Latina/os in the city, José Sarria is one of the five prominent oral history profiles in the book. Sarria, who was born in San Francisco of mixed Colombian and Nicaraguan heritage, was one of the most popular female impersonators in midcentury San Francisco and also ran for the city's board of supervisors in 1961. Had he won, Boyd points out, "he not only would have been the first self-identified gay man to serve on the board, but he would also have been the first Latino." Boyd includes several additional references to Latina/os in the book. She notes, for instance, that at the club Finocchio's in the 1930s the "lineup always included Asian and Latino female impersonators," and a 1940 show was "called 'Down Argentine Way,' which featured South American rhythms and dancing." She quotes from a 1960s description of the club where Latina/o performers were similarly prominent: "Juan Jose is a flamenco expert, clacking with castanets. Rene de Carlo is a lithe hula dancer in green skirt and bra. Bobby de Castro, billed as the 'Cuban King Kong,' performs a strip comedy complete with gorilla costume."[28]

Gay L.A., by Lillian Faderman and Stuart Timmons, offers further archival evidence of the significant role of Latina/os in the sexual history of California and the nation. The book begins with Chicano author John Rechy's account of a "small homosexual riot" involving mostly Latinos and African Americans that occurred outside a downtown L.A. doughnut shop in 1959 after yet another police raid. Throughout the book, the authors point to examples of gay Latino community building before 1960. In the 1950s, a bar in East Los Angeles called the Redhead "welcomed only Mexican American lesbians"; another, M&M, "catered primarily to Latinas." Individual Latinos also appear in the text, many of them as subjects of oral history interviews: for example, Rudy Ruano, a Guatemalan immigrant, recalled being entrapped by L.A.P.D. vice officers. Joanne Meyerowitz's *How Sex Changed* is similarly valuable, though most of the material in the book related to Latina/os is drawn from the late 1960s and 1970s. Meyerowitz, for instance, describes the founding of a branch of the Transvestite/ Transsexual Action Organization in Miami in 1972 that included "several Latina (Cuban and Puerto Rican) members."[29]

With such a limited pool of material, it is difficult to identify broad themes in the field. Clearly, the sexuality of Latinas—whether their presence in prostitution, attempts to control their reproductive lives, or heightened parental concern about the sexual reputation of young Latinas—is the primary focus of most of the authors mentioned here. Concepts of sexual honor and sexual shame also appear with some frequency in the literature. Notions of decency and respectability in Eileen Findlay's depiction of turn-of-the-century Ponce, for instance, have much in common with arguments of Mexican American parents against supposedly disreputable behavior by their daughters in World War II–era Los Angeles.

Such similarities notwithstanding, absence and discontinuity are the most prevalent themes here. With the exception of material directly related to their own subject matter—such as historians of early-twentieth-century prostitution in Puerto Rico, who engage other historians of Puerto Rican sexuality during the same period—authors have tended not to place their own work in conversation either with other Latina/o historians or with other historians focusing on Latina/o sexuality. As a result, there are unfortunate lapses in the field, small as it is. Discussions of sexual propriety in the twentieth-century American Southwest, for instance, seldom engage issues of honor and shame in Puerto Rico or within other locations in the Latina/o diaspora in the United States.

As this essay suggests, there are significant gaps in the twentieth-century history of Latina/o sexuality. One strategy for filling these gaps would be to follow the research trail of other historians of sexuality. Historians like Carroll Smith-Rosenberg, Lillian Faderman, Elizabeth Lapofsky Kennedy, Madeline D. Davis, and Lisa Duggan have pioneered the study of women's same-sex sexual relations. Rochella Thorpe's similarly groundbreaking essay on African American lesbians in midcentury Detroit describes a vibrant community whose social life focused on rent parties and socializing in the home rather than in bars.[30] It is conceivable that similar research could be conducted on Latina lesbians in locations throughout the country, including Detroit, which had a significant Latina/o population by the mid-twentieth century.

Same-sex relationships involving men is another potential area for further research. George Chauncey's *Gay New York* is an important book in many ways, including methodologically. Like Chauncey, other historians have successfully mined newspaper records and police reports for evidence of same-sex intimacy. Essays by David K. Johnson and Allen Drexel on gay male culture in midcentury Chicago, for instance, make no mention of Latinos, but, like Thorpe's article, they offer a roadmap of sorts for Latina/o historians interested in same-sex relationships before 1965. Peter Boag's excellent *Same-Sex Affairs* offers similar archival clues, especially in sections describing itinerant male laborers in the Pacific Northwest. Although Boag does not focus on Latinos, his careful use of government reports and criminal cases in examining the lives of transient working-class men is a valuable model for Latina/o historians whose male subjects often tend to be similarly working class and relatively mobile.[31]

Other efforts could extend the research of current historians of Latina/o sexuality into new regions and communities. Several historians, for instance, have examined prostitution in various settings such as Los Angeles and Puerto Rico. Future researchers could examine Latina/os' involvement in sex work and, most important, how the women and men involved in commercial sex understood their own sexual lives and experiences.

Such work on the history of Latina/o sexualities could have important policy implications. The limited research that does exist on Latina/o sexual histories suggests a range of sexual practices, sexual understandings, and strategies in the organization of sexual lives. Given this sexual diversity, lawmakers should approach with caution legislation and policies that privilege the lives of Latina/os in traditional patriarchal and heteronormative domestic situations.

At a most basic level, policymakers must also be attentive to the importance of archival records and historical documents in the work of historians. Reconstructing and critically analyzing the Latina/o sexual past depends on the availability of accessible and well-cataloged primary sources. The paucity of scholarship that this essay has identified reflects in part the absence of available primary sources regarding Latina/o sexuality. Delays in identifying and properly preserving the few remaining primary sources would have a devastating effect on this promising and important emerging field.

3

Latina/o Childhood Sexuality

SONYA GRANT ARREOLA

Latina/os are the fastest-growing and the largest ethnic minority group in the United States. Latina/os, with a median age of twenty-seven years in 2005, were much younger than the population as a whole at thirty-six years. Further, whereas 25 percent of the total U.S. population was under eighteen years of age, 34 percent of the Latina/o population was under age eighteen. Despite these large and growing numbers of Latina/os in the United States, research on their childhood sexuality is limited. Studying childhood sexuality among Latina/os is important, because their cultural beliefs and values may mediate the relationships between sexual experiences and various developmental, psychological, and biological health outcomes during childhood and in adulthood.[1]

Childhood sexuality is a controversial topic in the United States, as is made evident by the paucity of research on normative childhood sexual development. What research there is focuses primarily on nonnormative sexual development, such as childhood sexual abuse and negative outcomes of adolescent sexual initiation, such as unwanted pregnancy and sexually transmitted infections (STIs), described below. The existing literature on normative childhood sexuality is limited in scope and depth. In an attempt to broaden our understanding of childhood sexuality, scholars and clinicians have recently begun a discourse that explores the existing literature and calls for a wider scope of research that examines both normative and nonnormative childhood sexual development. Although this literature does not specifically address aspects of childhood sexuality unique to Latina/os, it provides a framework for understanding childhood development in which to situate Latina/o childhood sexuality.[2]

The goal of the present review is to present findings on Latina/o childhood sexuality in the context of the cultural norms that may influence that sexuality and on childhood sexual development generally. For the purposes of this review, research on "Latina/os" denotes individuals or populations referenced in the literature as Latina/o or Hispanic; the literature on "childhood" comprises research

48

conducted with children or adolescents, or both; and "sexuality" research is limited to studies primarily focused on sexual behavior or development.

Latina/o Cultural Norms

Research on Latina/o cultural norms suggests that religiosity, *familismo*, and traditional gender roles have culturally specific effects on Latina/o sexuality. Although not all identifiable cultural norms apply to all Latina/os, they portray some of the context in which sexuality develops for Latina/os.[3]

Religiosity

Religiosity is characterized by religious practice and belief, church attendance, and valuing religion and has been associated with less permissive attitudes about sex and with limited sexual experience.[4] Given that the Roman Catholic Church advocates monogamy and abstinence until marriage and prohibits birth control, it may be that religiosity associated with Roman Catholicism among Latina/os accounts for these findings. Yet not all Latina/os are Roman Catholic, and among those who identify as such, sexual behaviors are not always tied to religious imperatives.[5]

Familismo

Stemming from a collective worldview, *familismo* involves a strong identification with and attachment to one's nuclear and extended family and is associated with loyalty, reciprocity, and solidarity among family members.[6] Familismo may mediate stressors confronted by Latina/o adolescents and has been associated with decreased influence by peers to initiate sexual intercourse.[7] Familismo may also be related to the cultural value placed on being a mother, which has been associated with positive views of pregnancy and childbearing, low contraceptive use, and higher pregnancy, birth, and marriage rates.[8]

Traditional Gender Roles

It has been suggested that the stereotypical gender role for Latinos is that they are afforded more power and hold a dominant position within the family, whereas Latinas are expected to have less decision-making power and more household responsibilities than men. Expressions of these gender roles are captured in the terms machismo and *marianismo*. Machismo is a term that has at times been used in the United States to describe Latinos as controlling, possessive, sexist, and domineering and often is associated with violence against women. Machismo as an "ideology" characterizes men as poor, uneducated, violent, and oppressive and, as perpetuated in the United States, may negatively affect how Latinos develop and behave sexually.[9] In the context of men's roles in family life, however, machismo implies that the "man's responsibility is to provide for, protect, and defend his family," and that men should be "family oriented, brave, hardworking, proud, and interested in the welfare and honor of their loved ones." Interviews with Latino fathers support this positive interpretation of machismo.[10] In examining how fathers' perceptions of their daughters' virginity are shaped by regional expressions of patriarchy and masculinity and the socioeconomic segregation of inner-city barrios, protecting their daughters from a sexually dangerous society and improving the daughters' socioeconomic future were of greater concern to Latino fathers than preserving their daughters' virginity per se. This finding challenges stereotypical images and archetypes of machismo in the Latino father.[11]

Marianismo holds that Latinas should be nurturing, virtuous, self-sacrificing, and virgins until they marry—characteristics associated with the Virgin Mary and therefore to be desired.[12] When women marry and become mothers, their roles would be to protect, nurture, and sacrifice themselves for their husbands and children, as well as provide spiritual strength to family members.

It has been suggested that machismo and marianismo may dictate sexual scripts. For example, machismo may lead men to view sex as a way to prove their masculinity by determining the frequency and type of sex they have, whereas marianismo may lead Latinas to feel obligated to remain virgins until marriage and to be modest, monogamous, and deferential to men and comply with male sexual advances.[13] More recent research has found that gender role attitudes among Latina/os may vary by generation, social class, region, and ethnic group and that sexual scripts change with the level of acculturation. Nonetheless, marianismo has been associated with later initiation of sexual intercourse and with contraceptive use among Latina adolescents, especially Mexican American adolescents. Machismo, implying power to decide sexual and contraceptive behavior, has been associated with unprotected sexual behavior and multiple sexual partners.[14]

Sexual Silence

Traditionally in Latina/o cultures, sex and sexuality are not discussed. Researchers have described how a cultural emphasis on women's innocence may lead Latina/o parents to be reluctant to discuss sexuality with daughters. For some Latinas, sexual silence dictates that they should not know about or talk to men about sex because doing so implies promiscuity. Sexual silence can prevent gay Latinos from discussing their sexual preferences, instilling low self-esteem and personal shame. Sexual silence may be particularly problematic in light of studies indicating that Latina/o adolescents have greater respect for their parents' beliefs than do white adolescents, suggesting that what parents say or do not say has particular relevance for Latina/o children's and adolescents' developing sexuality. Longitudinal research with Latina/os has found that more talk from parents about beliefs and values is related to adolescents' abstaining from, or delaying, sexual involvement for about a year.[15]

It is not within the scope of the current review to examine the complexity of the cultural norms and values that influence Latina/o childhood sexuality. Rather, the cultural concepts mentioned above are intended to provide a sense of how researchers have interpreted Latina/o cultural values in their attempts to understand Latina/o sexual development in a cultural context.

Normative Childhood Sexuality

As mentioned above, very little research exists on the normative aspects of Latina/o childhood sexual development. However, research on human sexual development generally provides a point of departure. In an outline of human sexual development, John DeLamater and William Friedrich concluded that sexual development begins at conception, ends at death, and is influenced by biological maturation and aging; progression through socially defined stages of childhood, adolescence, adulthood, and later life; and interpersonal relationships. The authors argue that these forces shape the person's gender and sexual identities, sexual attitudes, and sexual behavior.[16]

In spite of the complex nature of researching childhood sexuality, normative sexual behaviors have been observed during childhood (0–7 years), including erections, vaginal lubrication in female infants, genital fondling during infancy, and rhythmic manipulation associated with adult masturbation at ages 2 ½ to 3.[17] Further, it appears that sexual play experiences (such as "playing house" or "playing doctor") are common among non–sexually abused children while very young (3–7 years), becoming progressively more secretive with increasing age (4–5 years) and growing awareness of cultural norms. During preadolescence (8–12 years), masturbation, first sexual attraction, and first sexual fantasies may begin to emerge. The biological changes—sudden enlargement and maturation of the gonads, other genitalia, and secondary sex characteristics associated with puberty or adolescence (13–19 years) lead to increased sexual interest. These biological changes may begin from as early as ten years of age to as late as fourteen, and include rises in levels of sex hormones, which may produce sexual attraction and fantasies. Many males begin masturbating between ages thirteen and fifteen, whereas the onset among females is more gradual. Social factors interact with biological changes, either facilitating or inhibiting sexual expression, as do cultural factors, as described below.[18]

However constrained the existing literature on normative childhood sexual development may be overall, the literature on the cultural norms that inform normative Latina/o childhood sexual development is even more inadequate. Scholars have noted the importance of uncovering how cultural values and norms influence childhood sexual development, in order to refrain from attributing to pathology what is normative as well as to be able to detect nonnormative sexual behaviors when they occur.[19]

Nonnormative Childhood Sexuality: Childhood Sexual Abuse

Childhood sexual abuse (CSA) has become a significant area of childhood sexuality studies. It is important to research CSA specifically among Latina/os for several reasons. As Lisa Fontes has noted, "cultural issues are relevant to CSA in three major ways: how cultural beliefs or attitudes contribute to family climates in which children can be abused; how cultural organization prohibits or hinders disclosure; and how culture plays a role in seeking or accepting social service or mental health assistance."[20] However, insufficient CSA research has been conducted that is specific to Latina/os, and existing studies that do focus on Latina/os suffer from the same limitations found among those centered in the broader U.S. population, the biggest challenge being a lack of consistent operational definitions of CSA.

Defining Childhood Sexual Abuse

To date, CSA has been used as an inclusive term encompassing phenomena that range from no physical contact to penetration, and one that varies widely in how it is measured. In general, it has been dichotomized into those who have and those who have not experienced CSA. Criteria for inclusion in the CSA category vary by:

1. upper age limit of the child, generally between twelve and eighteen years;
2. severity of abuse, ranging from no physical contact to penetration;
3. minimum age difference between the child and the abuser, from none to ten years; and
4. whether force or threat was used.[21]

Studies also vary by which of these criteria is defined in their measurement of CSA; some specify the number of times certain abusive activities must occur in order to meet the criteria. The lack of any uniform operationalization of CSA makes it difficult to compare outcomes across studies. Additionally, no theoretically or empirically based rationale is given for including any particular criteria in respective studies, which contributes to the lack of a consistent definition. The lack of theory or empiricism to guide how CSA is measured and understood leaves the operational definitions vulnerable to researcher assumptions and social or political bias. It is likely that the variability in reported prevalence of CSA is owing, in part, to the wide range of operational definitions. A theoretically and empirically based definition is sorely needed if we are to advance the field. The existing literature on CSA among Latina/os also suffers from this serious limitation.

Prevalence

Prevalence of CSA among Latina/os, much like that among non-Latina/o whites, ranges from 11 percent to 62 percent. Research comparing prevalence among

Latinas with other ethnic groups is equally inconsistent, suggesting either higher or lower CSA risk for Latinas compared to other ethnic groups. Using a representative sample, one study found that 21 percent of the Latinas reported sexual abuse (compared to 10 percent of the African American females and 10 percent of the white females). A second study concluded that Latinas are four times as vulnerable as whites to experiencing CSA. These findings would suggest that Latinas are at higher risk for CSA.[22] However, another study conducted in the Los Angeles area reported that the proportions of reported cases of CSA among Latinas and whites were lower than among African Americans. And yet another study in Los Angeles found that whites were three times (9 percent) as likely to have experienced CSA as Latinas (3 percent), suggesting that Latinas are at reduced risk for CSA. None of these studies used representative samples to make their conclusions, nor did they apply consistent definitions. Therefore, definitive conclusions cannot be made regarding the prevalence of CSA among Latinas or how Latinas compare to other ethnic groups.[23] Further research is needed to identify differences among Latinas in order to differentiate those at greatest risk.

Although it appears that sexual abuse is more commonly experienced by girls than by boys and by lesbians and gays than by heterosexuals, prevalence estimates for Latina lesbians are lacking. In a study of lifetime victimization among predominantly white lesbian/gay, bisexual, and heterosexual adults, sexual orientation was a significant predictor of CSA. Compared with heterosexual participants, lesbian, gay and bisexual participants reported more abuse. However, sexual orientation differences in sexual victimization were greater among men than among women.[24]

Efforts to explain the high incidence of HIV among gay men have led investigators to identify determinants of increased risky sexual behavior and have found that a history of CSA increases the risk for HIV among gay Latinos.[25] This has fostered interest in research on the prevalence of CSA among men who have sex with men (MSM), including gay Latino men. Significantly, the research includes excellent probability base studies with conservative definitions of CSA.

It has recently been acknowledged that abuse of boys is likely to be underreported and that the prevalence of CSA among boys, especially at an earlier age and in more severe cases, may approach that of girls. Compared to non-gay/non-bisexual men, the prevalence of CSA is higher among gay/bisexual men when comparing homosexual to heterosexual samples, as well as comparing sexual orientation in abused and nonabused samples. As high as the prevalence is among gay/bisexual men generally (17–39 percent), it is even higher among gay/bisexual Latinos. For example, in a probability survey of 2,881 adult men who have sex with men residing in San Francisco, New York, Los Angeles, and Chicago, a significantly higher proportion of Latino MSM reported sexual abuse before age 13 (22 percent) than did non-Latino MSM (11 percent). Other studies have also found that, compared to non-Latinos, CSA among Latinos is generally more severe: Latino boys are more likely to have been sexually abused by an extended family member such as a cousin or an uncle, experienced more genital fondling, been exposed to more sexually abusive behaviors, and experienced more anal abuse. It is yet unclear how machismo may contribute to the increased risk for CSA among Latinos.[26]

Disclosure

Support, especially maternal support, following disclosure of abuse is a mediating factor in the child's adjustment, with those children who received the most support faring the best emotionally after the abuse. Latina/o children are the least likely to receive support from their mothers subsequent to CSA, as compared to African American or white children. It has been hypothesized that Latina/o victims seemed to perceive a lack of support from their mothers that may contribute to their unwillingness to disclose. Regardless of how CSA is measured, when it has taken place, Latina/os are less likely to disclose such abuse than are non-Latina/o whites.[27]

Researchers have offered sociocultural reasons, such as lower levels of acculturation, for nondisclosure. Protectiveness toward girls among Latina/o families and the stigma connected to the loss of virginity may also lead these girls and their families to conceal abuse. The Latina/o cultural norm that children will always obey adults also may lead children to comply with adults' sexual advances and to maintain silence if any adult has forbidden disclosure. In addition to the taboo against discussing sex altogether (sexual silence) in Latina/o cultures, shame has been identified as a factor that may inhibit children's disclosure because of the emphasis and value placed on virginity at marriage. Fears of deportation or harassment by immigration authorities may influence whether families or even child protection workers report incidents of CSA if children or their families might be forced to return to living arrangements that could increase the risks of revictimization. Male victims may be reluctant to disclose abuse, especially by a male perpetrator, for fear that they will be considered homosexual.[28] Language barriers between families on the one hand and child protection services on the other may discourage reports to personnel who frequently cannot understand attempts to report the circumstances of an incident. Further, when disclosure is made, lack of bilingual services may leave families without the help needed to deal with the abusive situation.[29]

Psychosocial Outcomes

Research on the effects of CSA has shown increased levels of depression, suicidal behavior, sexual dysfunction, and lower self-esteem on the part of victims in adulthood. Compared to non-Latinas, Latinas who experience CSA have significantly higher levels of depression. In a study attempting to uncover the circumstances of CSA in a community sample of Latina women, more than one-third of the women also experienced revictimization, with more than 80 percent of initial incidents occurring from the age of seven.[30] Researchers attempting to explain why Latinas may have more severe psychological outcomes suggest that cultural factors may influence the manner of the abuse as well as interpretations of the abuse differently than for non-Latina whites. A study attempting to uncover the mediating variables between adult psychological sequelae and CSA in the general population has found that a relation with the offender (such as someone known to the child or a relative of the child's), young age at onset of abuse, and longer duration of abuse were directly associated with increased psychological distress in adulthood. Research on Latinas has found that the majority of the abuse experiences occurred in private locations, carried out by male perpetrators who were known to the girl (such as a family member), and a small number were later forced to marry the abuser. These and other findings that Latina/os are more likely to know the offender, be younger at the age of the abuse, and have a longer duration of abuse support the conclusion that differences in the characteristics of the abuse account for more severe psychological distress among Latina/o victims. It remains unknown how ethnicity may contribute to these differences. Other authors caution that the differences among ethnic groups' responses to CSA are outweighed by the similarities, and that differences in outcome may vary by type of sexual abuse experiences rather than by racial-ethnic factors.[31] How this pattern holds up among Latina/os remains to be studied.

Although fewer studies have been conducted with boys, a review of CSA among boys found that a history of abuse increased psychological distress (including major depression, bulimia, post-traumatic stress disorder [PTSD], and suicide attempts), substance abuse, and sexually related problems.[32]

Childhood Sexual Abuse and HIV

Abuse is strongly linked to HIV risk behavior and HIV infection. Research on the impact of CSA at earlier ages among adolescent women indicates that they are more likely to engage in numerous risky sexual behaviors (e.g., earlier initiation of consensual sex and greater number of sexual partners) upon entering adolescence. Research is needed to uncover how this pattern holds for Latinas. Probability samples of gay/bisexual men have found that those with a history of CSA were more likely to engage in unprotected anal intercourse with a nonprimary partner in the previous twelve months (21 percent) than those who had not been abused (15 percent). Research on Latina/o MSM also shows that a history of CSA is significantly related to an increased likelihood of engaging in risky sexual behaviors.[33] While the data compellingly show that CSA among Latina/os is linked to risk for HIV, we do not yet know the mechanisms by which CSA may lead to greater HIV risk or how sociocultural and contextual factors mediate this relationship.

Future Directions

A consistent theoretically and empirically based definition of CSA is needed in order to make prevalence comparisons across studies and to protect against biases that may influence the research in this area. Even so, however CSA is measured, some of the psychological and biological sequelae are strong enough to be captured. But a clear definition will allow for a finer analysis of the mediating factors that contribute to these relationships. Further research on CSA among Latina/os requires a culturally relevant, empirical model to guide future work, as well as the interventions that will protect Latina/o children. One promising area of investigation comes from the literature on dissociation related to trauma. The essential feature of dissociation is a disruption in any one or more of the usually integrated functions of consciousness, memory, identity, or perception of the environment, such that an event is processed in a way that breaks up the pieces of the event into differing states of consciousness. In general, people who have experienced CSA rely heavily on cognitive or behavioral avoidance strategies such as dissociation, presumably as a way to survive the overwhelming traumatic experience. It is likely that the ability to dissociate during traumatic situations is adaptive, especially when one lacks control over the situation. To the extent that dissociation generalizes to nonthreatening situations, however, the ability to make conscious choices about behavior is dramatically limited. Theoretically, an individual who has learned to dissociate as a way of coping with CSA may continue to dissociate during sexual situations as an adult, owing to the close match in state of arousal that triggers the body's memory of earlier episodes.

Studies of women have found a strong relationship between CSA and dissociation, especially among severe cases. A recent meta-analysis of the predictors of PTSD across different types of trauma found dissociation to be the strongest predictor, even stronger than the effects of prior trauma, prior psychological adjustment, family history of psychopathology, perceived threat during the trauma, and post-trauma social support. While this study was not exclusive to CSA and did not focus on Latina/os, its findings highlight the robust effect of dissociation on psychological outcomes such as PTSD. Although other aspects of CSA are likely also related to risky sexual behavior, dissociation may offer a framework from which to understand the link between the two.[34] The relationship between dissociation and CSA and the role of dissociation in psychopathologies, such as depression and PTSD, offer a propitious preliminary theoretical grounding for a model of the link between CSA and psychological and behavioral risk outcomes.

Nonnormative Adolescent Sexuality: Negative Outcomes of Early Sexual Initiation

One prominent area of childhood sexuality research centers on negative outcomes of adolescent sexual initiation and the demographic characteristics (such as ethnicity, economic status, level of acculturation, and gender) that predict adolescent sexual initiation. Adolescent sexual behavior is a public health concern because of associated negative outcomes. These outcomes include sexually transmitted infections (STIs), especially HIV, and unintended pregnancies. In 2000 approximately 822,000 pregnancies occurred among fifteen- to nineteen-year-old women, and in 1994 almost 80 percent of such pregnancies were unintended.[35]

Ethnicity and Economic Status

Outcomes of early sexual initiation reported in different studies vary to some extent by the upper age limit defining childhood (usually ranging between thirteen and eighteen years) and by how the outcomes are measured. For example, contraceptive use at first sex was associated with economic status and ethnicity, where the poor and Latina/os were less likely to use contraceptives than the nonpoor and non-Latina/o whites, respectively. Another study found no difference by economic status or ethnicity regarding contraceptive use when asking about respondents' most recent sexual experience.[36] Latina adolescents aged fifteen to nineteen have the highest fertility of all racial or ethnic groups, give birth at younger ages, and have more children compared to non-Latina whites. Depending on the data source and year of measurement, Latina girls are slightly less or slightly more likely to have had heterosexual intercourse as compared to non-Latina white girls.[37] Nonetheless, pregnancy rates are much higher for Latina girls than for non-Latina white girls (e.g., 163 per 1,000 for Latina girls versus 72 per 1,000 for non-Latina whites in 1995). The likelihood of unintended pregnancy is highest for Latina immigrants, followed by U.S.-born Latinas, and then non-Latina whites, suggesting an acculturation effect.[38] This pattern of fertility suggests that, compared to sexually active white adolescents, sexually active Latina adolescents may also be at higher risk for STIs, including HIV, and for pregnancy.

Acculturation

The process of acculturation (by which immigrants learn a new language and take on attitudes and values of the dominant culture) appears to have a somewhat contradictory impact on the sexual behaviors of Latina/os, especially females. In the acculturation literature generally, more-acculturated Latina/o youths are more likely to engage in risky behaviors such as smoking, alcohol use, and illicit drug use. In the United States, less-acculturated girls are less likely to have had sex than those who are more acculturated. Of those who are sexually active, the less acculturated are less likely to use birth control, and if they become pregnant, the less acculturated are more likely to have the baby. Among adult Latinas, more-acculturated women are more likely to report multiple sexual partners and are also more likely to use condoms than the less acculturated. Thus, a lower level of acculturation may be protective by slowing the rate of sexual initiation, but the impact on other sexual behaviors is not always protective.[39] Although this pattern suggests behavioral differences by degree of acculturation, the effects of acculturation on psychosocial and contextual variables related to sex have not been well examined.

Gender

Latino boys are two to three times more likely than Latina girls to have had sex. While this gender difference in sexual initiation has been acknowledged, the pattern of variables associated with this difference has not been fully explored. Research findings do suggest that Latino boys initiate sex at an earlier median age (16.5 years) than Latina girls (17.3 years). It has been argued that the gender difference in ages of initiation may result from Latina girls' reactions to more-proscriptive cultural expectations (marianismo) regarding their sexual activity, especially premarital sex. This interpretation is supported by a study on Latina sexuality that found attitudes, beliefs, and values accounted for differences between girls who initiated sex and those who did not.[40]

Research on cultural and social factors affecting the initiation of sexual intercourse among Latina mothers who were under age eighteen when they gave birth suggests that their sexual intercourse was initiated in the context of developing highly scripted relationships with their partners. The scripts included:

1. men pressure for sex (machismo) and women resist (marianismo);
2. women should be ignorant about sex but control access to intercourse (marianismo);
3. sex is never discussed (sexual silence) and thus is unexpected; and
4. contraception other than withdrawal is not used.[41]

In another study, gender role orientation significantly predicted age at first intercourse, where more-traditional young women (marianismo) were older at sexual debut. These results suggest that gender role orientation is important for delaying first intercourse. This study also indicated that, once they had become sexually active, acculturation and substance experimentation become more important influences on sexual risk taking among Latina adolescents.[42]

Psychosocial and Contextual Factors

Other studies suggest additional determinants of sexual behaviors, such as having a boy/girl friend, opportunities for sex, and unwanted sexual advances.[43] Because of the associations between all three determinants and sexual behaviors, interventions have aimed to reduce the incidence of these determinants. Less understood is the effect of teaching children how to manage, cope, or set limits around having a boy/girl friend, opportunities for sex, and unwanted sexual advances in ways that are consistent with their ages or their intentions. Further research is needed to learn how these variables influence Latina/o childhood sexuality.

Studies of Latina/o adolescents have generally focused on demographic and situational predictors of sexual initiation rather than contextual and psychosocial variables. The latter predictors of sexual initiation have not been examined specifically among Latina/os but may provide some guidance for future consideration in understanding Latina/o childhood sexual initiation. Although distal determinants such as demographic and biological factors provide some understanding of the causal pathways leading to sexual initiation, more-proximal determinants of sexual initiation such as psychosocial factors (e.g., attitudes and beliefs about oneself or others) are also important. Relative to distal determinants of initiation, psychosocial factors tend to be stronger predictors of sexual intercourse and may be more amenable to change through large-scale behavioral interventions.[44]

Future Directions

As noted above, several researchers have examined selected predictors of sexual initiation among adolescents generally and Latina/os specifically, but there remain significant gaps in our understandings of which factors affect sexual behaviors among Latina/o youths. Future research on Latina/o sexual initiation could benefit from addressing an array of such potentially important variables as psychosocial and contextual predictors that are unique to Latina/os, in addition to the culturally normative determinants of sexual behaviors. One significant gap has been the lack of a culturally relevant theoretical model to guide what research needs to be conducted, as well as the interventions and education that should be developed. A number of theoretical models of behavior may be useful if adapted to the specific cultural contexts of Latina/o youths, including the theory of reasoned action, the theory of planned behavior, and the theory of social cognition.[45] Consistent with these theories, some researchers have investigated the determinants that predict whether someone intends to refrain, and succeeds, from sexual intercourse. These include attitudinal beliefs, such as reasons to have or not to have sex; self-efficacy beliefs, such as self-efficacy to avoid sex and set sexual limits; and normative beliefs, such as peer norms regarding sex.[46] Although it is not clear how these theoretical approaches to understanding adolescent sexual initiation would apply to Latina/o adolescents, they may offer a framework for moving beyond the demographics and circumstances of Latina/os who engage in sexual behaviors.

Philosophically, the literature on early sexual initiation has developed under the premise that sex before a certain age is inherently risky because of its strong associations with STIs and unintended pregnancies. As a result, research questions aim to uncover reasons for early sexual initiation with the intention of using the findings to develop policy and interventions to restrict it. This line of investigation provides a partial understanding of adolescent sexuality. A different line of investigation is needed to uncover the various trajectories of childhood sexual development, one that includes the possibility of appropriate and healthy sexual experiences. This line of research would offer needed guidance for developing interventions directed at, for example, sex education. Indeed, although not focused on Latina/o childhood sexuality specifically, a recent review of twenty-four developmentally appropriate, randomized, controlled trials of sexual risk reduction interventions for adolescents concluded that limited information exists to identify the aspects of intervention design or content that make an intervention developmentally appropriate. The authors highlighted the importance of understanding developmental transitions during adolescence that influence sexual behavior for developing and evaluating interventions for youth and recommended that future research assess process measures of key developmental constructs, as well as risk behavior and biological outcomes.[47]

Conclusion

With the exceptions of research on adolescent sexual initiation and childhood sexual abuse, childhood sexuality has been woefully neglected as a field of study. As a result, the field of sexuality research is limited in its understanding of the child as subject learning about sexuality and capable of experiencing sexual pleasure.[48] This is no less true for the field of Latina/o childhood sexuality studies. The research on Latina/o childhood sexuality is modeled after that of childhood sexuality studies generally. As a result, the prevalence and predictors of Latina/o adolescent sexual initiation, as well as the prevalence of CSA among Latina/os, are inconsistent. Lacking is any theoretical understanding of age-appropriate sexual development and exploration in the context of Latina/o sociocultural norms.

A theoretical model of Latina/o adolescent sexual initiation (or development) is needed for guiding policy and educational efforts that would protect many young Latina/os from poor outcomes and that could also teach adolescents about positive and healthy sexual development and responsibility. It would be most effective if it went beyond the pathological approach to adolescent sexual development that focuses on uncovering adolescent sexual behaviors that predict negative outcomes toward one that includes resiliency factors that predict safe and age-appropriate sexual exploration. It should use empirical data based on experiences of a broader sample of Latina/o youths than only those who have had negative outcomes. One of the limitations in developing such a theory is the lack of empirical research on the determinants of age-appropriate sexual development and behaviors. While there are important obstacles to overcome (such as possible parental, cultural, societal, and governmental pressures to restrict sexual expression among adolescents), it is critical to develop a robust and representative theoretical model that can serve the needs of Latina/o youth as they develop sexually.

The literature on Latina/o adolescent sexual initiation lacks any discourse on homosexuals. A useful theoretical model should take into account the reality of homosexuality so that policy and educational interventions will have the tools to protect this vulnerable population. The extent that gay and lesbian Latina/o youths are forced to explore blindly their sexuality under the burden of oppressive environmental and social strictures is the degree to which risk for psychological distress, STIs, and HIV increases.

The literature on Latina/o CSA is inconclusive about the relative prevalence among Latinas, but studies of gay Latino men suggests that Latino boys are at increased risk for abuse compared to non-Latino boys. This literature also suggests that CSA leads to increased psychological distress and risk for HIV in adulthood for both men and women, though the mechanism is unknown. Again, a culturally appropriate, empirically based theoretical model is needed to help drive policy and interventions that will protect Latina/o children from sexual abuse. Such a model should differentiate consensual sex among Latina/o adolescents from forced or unwanted sex. Again, there are important and difficult restraints on considering a sexual relationship between, say, a fifteen-year-old and a twenty-year-old. It is unclear how age difference may contribute to a power differential that masks presumed consent. Nonetheless, given that some adolescents who initiate sex with adults insist that it was consensual, it is critical that we begin to put aside assumptions about adolescent sexuality (including the assumption that all sex involving an older partner and an adolescent is necessarily abusive) in favor of collecting data that will help us differentiate abusive sexuality from developmentally normative and/or healthy (or less negative) sexuality.

Overall, the state of the research on Latina/o childhood sexuality calls for the development of theory that is empirically based to guide policy, future research, and interventions that are culturally appropriate. Additionally, it calls for a broader view of childhood sexuality that includes an examination of normative sexual development among Latina/os. To the extent that it is assumed that all sex among Latina/o adolescents will lead to negative outcomes or is abusive, we undermine our ability to learn from participants what sexual development among Latina/o adolescents may entail.

4

Latina/o Parent-Adolescent Communication about Sexuality

An Interdisciplinary Literature Review

LAURA F. ROMO, ERUM NADEEM, AND CLAUDIA KOUYOUMDJIAN

Parents play a key role in the sexual socialization of adolescents, the transmission of sexual beliefs, values, and norms. Research in this area is important, given that patterns of socialization may determine adolescent sexual decision making. Currently, there is a growing interest across disciplines to understand the nature of sexuality communication in Latina/o families. This topic is meaningful to health researchers because the prevalence of sexually transmitted infections (STIs) and teenage birthrates among Latina/o youth are consistently higher than those for non-Latina/o youths,[1] yet Latina/o adolescents report less discussion with parents about sexual risk and self-protective factors, and lower levels of contraceptive use.[2] Thus, an important goal for health interventionists is to identify communication barriers that can be targeted in family-based programs aimed at reducing sexual risk behavior among Latina/o youth.

Additionally, understanding sexual socialization patterns in Latina/o families is of growing interest to developmentalists and researchers who study family processes. Like other areas of psychosocial development, adolescence entails several developmental challenges related to sexuality, such as realizing that sexual desires are normal, feeling comfortable with the choice to abstain from or engage in sexual activity, and understanding how to practice safe sex.[3] The ways in which Latina/o parents handle sexual socialization and its impact on adolescent sexual development have implications for a broader understanding of how families influence adolescent outcomes. While a prevalence of data in the health and psychology fields has been collected through survey-driven studies, researchers in humanities and social science who study culture and gender role socialization have further advanced our knowledge about Latina/o parent-adolescent communication through qualitative methodologies.

The goal of this essay is to synthesize the literatures from these multidisciplinary fields to highlight what has been learned in recent years about the nature of sexuality communication between Latina/o adolescents and their parents. Mothers as communicators are the main focus, given their prominence in studies of sexual socialization. One reason for this focus is that Latina/o adolescents report higher levels of discussion and more comfort talking about sexuality with their mothers than with their fathers.[4] Research also suggests that mother-adolescent communication in Latina/o families has more impact than father-adolescent communication in relation to minimizing risk-taking behavior in both boys and girls.[5] Other scholars point to the centrality of the mother's role in Latina/o families as a figure of authority who is highly respected and revered.[6] Hence, researchers have taken more interest in the mother-adolescent relationship. There are considerably fewer studies related to how Latina mothers communicate with their sons about these topics as opposed to their daughters. Consequently, this literature review focuses largely on sexuality communication between mothers and daughters, although research on mothers and sons is not excluded.

We define Latina/os as individuals of origin and descent from Mexico, the Caribbean, and Central and South America. The studies reviewed here mostly include Mexican, Puerto Rican, and Dominican subgroups. Although communication research on Latina/o families has increased in recent years, we still lack sufficient knowledge about any one subgroup to draw conclusions. We therefore speak generally about Latina/os as a whole, but wherever possible we specify the majority subgroup under study or the geographic region in the United States where the data were collected. In 2002 the Census Bureau estimated that Latina/os of Mexican descent tend to live mostly in the western part of the United States, with a smaller proportion living in the South; Puerto Ricans and Dominicans tend to live in the Northeast; and Central and South Americans are about equally concentrated on the West Coast, and in the Northeast and the South.[7] Knowledge about the demographic profile where the data were collected can help with generalizability. In addition, because few survey studies have been conducted solely on Latina/os, we include research conducted with multiethnic samples in which Latina/os made up at least 20 percent of the participants and where no ethnic variations existed in the trends among the variables. We also report findings from national studies with large sample sizes that provide relevant statistical comparisons between Latina/o participants and those from other ethnic groups.

In the first section, we review potential barriers to sexuality communication between Latina mothers and their adolescents and outline possible reasons these barriers exist. In the second section, we provide a comprehensive overview of what Latina mothers and their adolescents talk about and whether such communication is associated with adolescent sexual outcomes. We approach this task in two ways: by summarizing findings obtained through naturalistic methods—in-depth interviews, observation, and focus groups—to elucidate the content and process of sexuality communication; and by reporting systematic relations between communication constructs and adolescent behavior variables derived from statistical analyses of survey data. An overall analysis of these trends can shed light on the effectiveness of various communication strategies in promoting positive outcomes. The third section briefly reviews what has been learned about the understudied topic of parent-adolescent communication about homosexuality. In the final section, we summarize gaps in the literature related to sexuality communication between parents and adolescents and offer directions for future research.

Potential Barriers to Sexuality Communication between Mothers and Adolescents

Sexuality communication is awkward for most parents and adolescents, but it seems especially difficult for Latina/os. One of the most widely reported reasons is embarrassment. In a large multiethnic sample of mothers and adolescent daughters who participated in the National Longitudinal Study of Adolescent Health, for example, Latina mothers reported substantially higher levels of discomfort communicating with daughters about sexuality in comparison to Euro-American mothers.[8] For women from traditional Latina/o backgrounds, discomfort may stem from their observance of cultural norms, which dictate that proper women should be "silent" about these issues. Adherence to this value is fueled in part by gender-related ideals in Latina/o culture emphasizing that women should be chaste and naive about sex.[9] As a result, women gain little or no experience discussing these topics with family members, which contributes to their heightened sensitivity in later conversations with daughters. Limited familial communication fostered by sexual silence may also explain why some Latina mothers believe that they lack the knowledge or appropriate language to impart information.[10]

Reluctance to talk about sexuality may stem from the mother's belief that these topics are age-inappropriate, particularly for daughters. In fact, some mothers have expressed that it is unnecessary to raise these issues with daughters unless they are soon to be married. Another reason for not addressing the topic is that they believe that their daughters are receiving adequate health information from school counselors and teachers.[11] A possible third reason is that the mothers are satisfied with knowing that their daughters discuss these topics with other relatives—for example, aunts, sisters, and cousins.[12]

Infrequency or absence of discussion of sexuality topics can also stem from the adolescent's hesitation to discuss these issues. Latina girls report that they sense their mother's discomfort, which in turn makes daughters feel ashamed about asking questions.[13] Along the same lines, a parent-initiated discussion can create an uncomfortable atmosphere because it suggests to adolescents that their parents are suspicious or knowledgeable about their sexual behavior.[14] Indeed, research suggests that Latina mothers do increase discussion about sexual topics if they believe that their adolescent is sexually active or at risk of engaging in sexual activity.[15] Fears that their mothers would react negatively (become angry, administer punishment) deter some adolescents from raising the topic of sexuality, although mothers report that these fears are unfounded.[16] In light of these findings, it makes sense that openness and trust in the mother-adolescent relationship itself is found to be associated with safer sexual practices among adolescents,[17] perhaps because it facilitates more discussion about sexual topics.

These potential barriers have raised questions among health educators as to whether Latina/o parents are a useful and meaningful source of information for their adolescents. However, Latina/o adolescents assert that they want to communicate frequently and openly with their parents about sexuality.[18] Moreover, there is growing evidence that parent-adolescent sexuality communication protects adolescents against potential negative outcomes. The next section describes the various themes that mothers discuss with adolescents to accomplish this goal.

Common Themes in Sexuality Discussion and Linkages to Adolescent Sexual Behavior

Health Risks and Self-Protective Behaviors

Perhaps the area that has received the most attention in the health communication literature is the extent to which Latina/o parents and adolescents discuss health risks and related self-protective behaviors. In survey studies conducted on both coasts of the United States, a broader range or a greater number of sexual topics discussed between parents and adolescents was shown to be linked to fewer adolescent sexual episodes, increased efficacy of condom use, and more consistent contraceptive use.[19] Along these lines, pregnant and parenting teens in the West reported that they received less information about sexual topics from their parents in comparison to girls who were not parenting or expecting a child.[20] Other research suggests that both the quality of sexuality communication between Latina/o parents and adolescents and the ease with which adolescents believe that they can discuss sexual content with their parents have protective health benefits. More perceived openness, comfort, and confidence discussing sexuality has been shown to be associated with less sexual risk taking among Northeast Latina/o youths,[21] and with more condom usage among a diverse group of male adolescents that included Latina/os from the West Coast.[22]

These findings suggest that Latina/o adolescents stand to benefit from frequent discussion with their parents about a broad range of sexuality topics, particularly in relation to self-protective behaviors. Unfortunately, numerous survey studies suggest that birth control and information about STIs tend to be among the least discussed topics between Latina parents and adolescents, particularly daughters.[23] Another problem noted in the literature is that when Latina mothers do communicate to their daughters about these topics, these messages lack sufficient detail. For example, Latinas are told "don't let men touch you" or "you better not get pregnant"[24]—messages that can be confusing to girls who know little or nothing about the facts involved in sexual intercourse. In other cases, girls report that they are advised to protect themselves (to "be careful"), implying that they should engage only in safe sexual behavior, but these messages do not include explicit information about what is "safe."[25] Such limited and vague discussion surrounding sex-related topics may help explain why studies show that Latina adolescents have less conceptual knowledge about contraception and reproductive processes than do African Americans and Euro-Americans.[26]

To illustrate the importance of explicit maternal communication, consider our findings from an observational study conducted with low-income Mexican immigrant, U.S.-born Mexican American, and Central American mothers and their pregnant adolescent daughters.[27] After videotaping the mothers and daughters talking about sexuality, we later coded the extent to which the mothers provided explicit messages related to contraceptive use (e.g., "Are you going to use a condom?") and related implicit messages (e.g., "You should protect yourself"). Although these messages were few, the prevalence of explicit messages in these discussions had a positive influence on adolescent knowledge. Specifically, more maternal explicit messages about the adolescent's plans for contraceptive use were associated with the daughters having more detailed, and accurate, knowledge about how condoms work to protect against pregnancy. Importantly, this knowledge was associated with the girls reporting higher levels of confidence about condom use, and increased comfort discussing condom usage with partners. The number of implicit messages transmitted from mothers to daughters about contraceptive use had no such effect, raising questions about the value of this communication style in promoting safe sexual behavior. Overall, these findings support the need to create health education programs that help Latina mothers feel comfortable in discussing the specifics of contraceptive use, enabling them to engage in deeper discussions about these issues.

Sexual Attitudes and Values

Sexual attitudes and values tend to be among the most commonly discussed topics between Latina/o parents and adolescents.[28] A prevalent message relayed by mothers to adolescents in particular is the importance of delaying sexual activity until marriage, or at least until young adulthood.[29] These messages are targeted mainly at girls, although some boys report receiving these messages as well.[30] Much of what is communicated to girls implies that premarital sexual activity fosters a loss of self-respect, a loss of innocence, and a loss of personal capital that threatens a young woman's opportunity to find an ideal spouse.[31]

The extent to which messages about sexual values influence adolescent decision making is becoming evident, as numerous studies converge on the finding that parental attitudes and adolescent behavior are linked. For example, perceptions that their parents had conservative attitudes toward teen sexual behavior was associated with youths on the West Coast reporting less sexual experience[32] and less risky sexual behavior.[33] In a study with a majority Puerto Rican sample, intentions to have sex in the near future were negatively correlated with adolescents' beliefs that their parents would be proud of them for not having sex.[34] Later age of sexual debut as reported by low-income Mexican American women attending outpatient and community-based clinics was associated with retrospective accounts that their families expected them to abstain from sexual activity.[35] In a mixed sample of minority urban adolescents that included Latinas, mothers' talking about waiting to have sex was significantly related to girls remaining abstinent or using a condom if sexually active.[36] Similarly, through analyses of videotaped conversations, we have found that increased discussion about sexuality beliefs and values among a majority-Mexican sample of mothers and adolescents was linked to adolescents' reporting of less intimate sexual experience about one year later.[37] By and large, adolescents' knowledge of their parents' beliefs about sex can reduce the likelihood of their engaging either in early sex or in protected sexual activity, perhaps by shaping their attitudes and beliefs about sexual activity. Lending additional support are two studies showing that adolescents' perceptions about what their parents think minimizes the negative influence that sexually active peers can have on the adolescents' own behavior.[38]

The Value of Education

Education has emerged as a key topic in parent-adolescent communication about sexuality as mothers and their adolescent children discuss potential barriers that pregnant and parenting adolescents face in completing school and pursuing their academic goals.[39] In videotaped conversations, Latina mothers admonished their sons and daughters to "avoid sex, delay dating, and finish school."[40] This message was communicated about equally to sons and daughters, suggesting that education is valued for both sexes in Latina/o culture. Education and career success holds added value for women because it enables them to stay independent of men and develop egalitarian relationships.[41] Yet, in some families, messages about the value of education may conflict with traditional gender role expectations for girls. For example, although girls are strongly encouraged to finish school to become self-sufficient,[42] they are also socialized to believe that marrying a nice, responsible man is an important and valuable goal in life.[43] Thus, some Latina adolescents face the challenge of having to both resist and accept traditional gender values set by their parents.[44]

Do parental messages about education influence Latina/o adolescent sexual behavior? Parental messages may motivate Latina/o adolescents to aspire to higher academic goals and achievements, which purpose in life may in turn motivate adolescents to delay sex or engage only in safe sexual behaviors. In a study by M. L. Gilliam et al., the researchers found that later sexual debut was associated with low-income Mexican American women's reports that their parents valued education over marriage when they were growing up.[45] Mexican American adolescents who valued education and felt positive toward school were less likely to engage in early sexual activity and become pregnant, compared to adolescents who did not report these attitudes; this finding supports the notion that personal educational values are linked to sexual activity.[46] Similarly, in a majority–Puerto Rican sample, adolescents who believed that avoiding sexual activity would enhance their chances of achieving their career goals were more likely to report intentions of remaining abstinent in the three months preceding the study.[47] In two different survey studies conducted in Southern California, researchers found that adolescents with high educational expectations were less likely to engage in unprotected sexual activity.[48] Thus, parental discussions with adolescents about their academic goals can positively influence adolescent sexual decision making as well as academic outcomes.

Repercussions of Sexual Activity

Qualitative research suggests that Latina mothers warn their daughters about relationship consequences resulting from sexual activity, in addition to potential health hazards. Specifically, girls are told to remain on guard because boys are always looking for opportunities to have sex.[49] Girls are also told that boys (or men) cannot be trusted because they are known to break promises of loyalty. If a pregnancy occurs, boys (men) will disappoint and abandon them.[50] In the same vein, we too observed that mothers gave these messages to their daughters, but in addition, some Mexican immigrant mothers imparted these messages to sons. For example, mothers warned that boys should be on guard because promiscuous girls in the United States lie about their sexual experiences and thus pass on sexually transmitted diseases. It seems that messages about relationship consequences are meant to protect vulnerable adolescents, who, we found anecdotally, include sons as well as daughters, perhaps because of maternal concerns about their exposure to America's sexualized culture.[51]Whether these warnings deter adolescents from early and risky sexual behavior is unclear.

Maternal Self-Disclosure of Past Experiences

Latina mothers rely on self-disclosure of personal past experiences as a strategy for communicating their beliefs, values, and concerns. Through in-depth interviews, M. D. McKee and A. Karasz found that some Dominican and Puerto Rican mothers conveyed personal narratives of early childbearing to help their daughters avoid similar experiences of hardship.[52] In a focus group study conducted also with Dominican and Puerto Rican participants, V. Guilamo-Ramos et al. found that immigrant mothers talked about the conservative sexual culture in which they were brought up, in their criticism of the sexually permissive norms that adolescents are exposed to in the United States.[53] We too found similar narratives in our videotape data, but in addition we observed that Latina mothers talked positively about the days when they were teens and had romantic interests.[54] Whether personal narratives influence adolescent sexual behavior has not been systematically studied, but at the very least we have shown that maternal self-disclosure has been shown to be connected to adolescent reports of positive relationship quality.

Adolescents' Current Experiences Related to Dating and Sexuality

In discussions about sexuality, mothers typically seek information about the adolescents' interests and experiences related to dating and sexuality; however, these lines of inquiry are not always welcomed.[55] Although personal questions may be seen by the adolescents as intrusive, there is substantial evidence that parental knowledge regarding the adolescents' whereabouts and activities is linked to positive adolescent outcomes. M. K. Kerr and colleagues found that parental monitoring of whereabouts, friends, and activities was associated with Latina/o adolescents having fewer sexual partners.[56] In a study by E. A. Borawski et al. higher levels of parental monitoring and trust were linked to less sexual activity and higher rates of consistent condom use for Latino males.[57] Among a sample of Latina/o adolescents from San Juan, Puerto Rico, metro area schools, teens who were abstinent were more likely to report that their parents know their whereabouts and what time they get home, compared to sexually active teens.[58] Although parental monitoring is a useful strategy for protecting adolescents from negative outcomes, it is not clear from this pattern of findings whether adolescents willingly disclose information about their activities, or whether their parents actively obtain the information by questioning or in other ways.

Personal questions can be a source of contention between Latina mothers and their daughters when the topic is about dating and socializing with others.[59] Girls report that their parents set more rules and place greater restrictions on their activities in comparison to boys,[60] even on activities such as getting a job that are not obviously linked to sexuality.[61] Simply put, a girl who is well behaved (*bien educada*) is one who goes to school, returns home, and does not hang around on the streets.[62] Although many girls voice their objections to rules that limit their social freedom, there is no evidence that this conflict is detrimental to the quality of the parent-daughter relationship.[63] For example, M. Hovell et al. found that even though Latina girls reported living in more restrictive households, they were just as likely as Euro-American girls to agree with and accept their parents' rules.[64] In addition, adolescents have suggested that these rules convey to them that their parents care about them.[65]

Discussion

In summary, this collection of findings reveals that Latina mothers from different subgroups are highly similar in what and how sexuality themes are discussed with their adolescent children. This is not to say that there are no meaningful differences between Latina/o subgroups in general. Rather, we find that the socialization strategies of mothers from Mexican, Puerto Rican, and Dominican backgrounds are comparable when it comes to adolescent sexual activity. One important determination is that quite a few studies show that these strategies are linked to positive adolescent sexual behavior outcomes. Mothers who share their sexual beliefs and values, inspire their adolescents, believe in the importance of education, communicate explicitly about a range of sexual topics and self-protective behaviors, and monitor the adolescents' activities have adolescents who delay sexual behavior or engage in safe sexual behavior when they become sexually active. Moreover, communication is facilitated by trust in the mother-adolescent relationship. Sexuality communication tends to be inhibited by embarrassment on the part of mothers and adolescents, lack of knowledge about sexual topics, maternal perceptions that the topics are age- or gender-inappropriate, misperceptions about where their adolescents get their health information, and adolescent concerns about negative parental reactions. These significant findings have important implications for the design of health education and communication programs for Latina/o parents and adolescents.

Despite what is known, much remains to be learned about how parents and adolescents communicate positively about normative aspects of sexuality and its influence on healthy adolescent sexual development. For example, in addition to warnings, we observed that Latina mothers talk comfortably to their sons and daughters about romantic interests, such as when is a good age to start dating, and to older adolescents—for example, inquiring what their dates have been like.[66] Furthermore, we found that the number of open-ended questions the mothers asked about the adolescents' opinion on dating and sexuality issues far surpassed the number of questions they asked about the adolescents' whereabouts and activities, a communication style associated with an open relationship. It is possible that participants underreport positive aspects of communication in focus groups or interviews, because they assume that researchers are mostly interested in hearing about communication difficulties and barriers. This is a logical assumption, given the implications of this topic for communication training programs, and for this reason, health researchers tend to collect data from very low-income Latina/o sample populations whose adolescents are at high risk for negative sexual outcomes. Yet socioeconomic status and associated neighborhood characteristics clearly influence the types of parenting practices that parents engage in,[67] and researchers find that low-income Latina mothers living in impoverished neighborhoods are compelled to give warnings and strictly monitor their adolescents' whereabouts for safety reasons. Therefore, future studies need to include specific questions focusing exclusively on positive aspects of communication and to explore communication practices among families from a broad range of income levels.

Parent-Adolescent Communication about Homosexuality

The literature on sexual-minority youths suggests that parental communication and closeness play a key role in adolescent well-being. Gay youths who report a sense of obligation to their parents tend to engage in safer sexual practices.[68] Beyond sexual health, a close open relationship with parents appears to be vital to mental health. Among adolescents who have attempted suicide, many reported that they argued with their parents.[69] Examined from the opposite perspective, a sense of family connectedness—as described by parental care, understanding, and communication—and parental awareness of sexual orientation have been linked to lower levels of suicide ideation.[70] These findings highlight the importance of helping gay and lesbian youths develop positive relationships with their parents that include acceptance of and open communication about their sexual orientation.

Unfortunately, gay and lesbian Latina/o youths face significant barriers in communicating with their parents about their sexual preferences. As adolescents are growing up, messages at home about same-sex relationships are virtually unheard of. One reason is that such behavior may go against familial expectations that the youths will fulfill idealized gender-stereotyped roles of masculinity and femininity.[71] Perceptions of parental disapproval of homosexuality have been linked to adolescents' reporting of their families strong endorsement of traditional values (e.g., importance of religion, marriage, and children) upheld in the culture.[72] As they fail to live up to these ideals, some gay and lesbian youth become concerned about bringing shame to the family or dishonoring the family name.[73] Other concerns are linked directly to protecting parents' feelings. Research suggests that mothers may develop a sense of guilt in the coming out process, as if having gay or lesbian children signifies their failure as mothers to inculcate good morals.[74] In addition, disclosure of sexual orientation may disrupt their parents' dreams of future grandchildren.[75] Desires to protect their parents' feelings, in addition to the family reputation, can create a need for Latina/o gay and lesbian youths to live a "closeted" life through sexual silence.

For the most part, adolescent concern about parental disapproval is warranted, as Latina/o adolescents potentially face negative reactions from their parents in the coming out process.[76] Consequently, few Latina/o adolescents challenge the practice of sexual silence about homosexuality in their family households, but this may work to their benefit. That is, it allows for a slow transition in the coming out process, until all parties involved are ready to hear the news.[77] A. Hurtado found in a sample of young college women that it was not until they moved out of their parents' house and went to college that they were able to explore ideas that were not discussed or tolerated at home. It was important for these women to first secure independence before voicing these issues to their parents in a manner that was sensitive to cultural norms of sexual communication.[78]

The coming-out process is not negative for all Latina/o youth, however. Organizations and media outlets suggest that some Latina/o parents and adolescents find ways to cope positively with the challenges of coming out. As one Latina mother stated, reflecting on her own parenting experience, "My daughter did not need rejection and confusion at that time. She needed my love, understanding and guidance to help her be self confident to face society's homophobia."[79] The documentary film *De Colores*, produced and directed by D. Mosbacher, P. Barbosa, and G. Lenoir, points to a trend in which "Latino families and communities are replacing the deep roots of homophobia with the even deeper roots of love."[80] However, according to R. M. Diaz, the most that the majority of Latina/o gay and lesbian youths can truly hope for is accommodation and tolerance from their parents.[81] Acceptance and tolerance are more likely to come from mothers compared to fathers.[82] Moreover, Latina/o youths report lower levels of acceptance and tolerance from their fathers vis-à-vis coming out compared to non-Latina/o white adolescents.

To summarize, we know very little about the specific ways in which parents discuss the topic of homosexuality with their adolescents. Most of what is known has been collected through retrospective accounts, all of which suggest that such communication is extremely uncommon. When exceptions do occur and homosexuality is discussed as a hypothetical topic, parents stress heterosexuality as the ideal.[83] The literature would benefit from an understanding of how parents and adolescents face the challenges of talking about the adolescent's sexual orientation during the coming-out process.

Gaps in the Literature on Latina/o Parent-Adolescent Communication about Sexuality

It is immediately apparent that, one topic that would tremendously enhance the parent-adolescent sexuality communication field is research on father-son and father-daughter communication. Although mothers do appear to be the primary source of information about sexuality in the family context, it is certainly not the case that fathers have no role in communicating sexual values or in playing a protective role for adolescent sexual behavior. Our review of the literature has elucidated some of the explicit and some of the more subtle and nuanced ways that messages about sexual behavior are communicated between Latina mothers and their adolescent children. The same is likely true for fathers. In addition, future researchers could focus more on co-parenting relationships. Similarly, there has been relatively less attention given to sexual communication for boys than there has been for girls. This is a noteworthy trend in that it may serve unintentionally to minimize the shared responsibility of both boys and girls in preventing pregnancy and sexually transmitted infections.

A second area that is conspicuously missing from the literature is the nature of communication between pregnant and parenting adolescents and their own parents. Some researchers have evaluated Latina mother-daughter communication between pregnant and nonpregnant girls to identify factors that put adolescents at risk for pregnancy. Not surprisingly, communication is characterized as being more positive in families with a nonpregnant adolescent.[84] However, the literature on currently pregnant and parenting adolescents has focused on family structure and demographic characteristics as they predict subsequent pregnancies. With the exception of work by J. M. Contreras and colleagues and some of our recent work,[85] there has been relatively little attention given to the nature of communication processes. Further research is needed to identify characteristics of sexuality communication that may reduce the adolescent mother's risk for rapid repeated pregnancies.

Finally, we had planned to include in this review a synthesis of the literature related to the influence of acculturation on parent-adolescent communication and adolescent sexual behavior until we discovered that studies on this topic are virtually nonexistent. By acculturation, we refer to the process of immigrant Latina/o parents and adolescents adopting new values of the host culture versus maintaining traditional values from their country of origin. Acculturation in many studies is typically measured by how long the participants have lived in the United States and the primary language spoken in the home. There is a growing body of research examining how these characteristics are linked to differences in U.S. Latina/o adolescent sexual behavior,[86] with later age of sexual initiation being positively related to a preference to speak Spanish and being foreign born. However, these studies do not inform us about the nature of sexuality communication in Spanish-speaking versus English-speaking households and whether acculturation differences in communication impact adolescent sexual behavior. This gap in the literature is not trivial, given that acculturation can impact family functioning, parental socialization goals, and adolescent adherence to traditional cultural values, all of which are likely to influence how they talk about sexuality. In a retrospective study conducted with Latina/o college students, M. Raffaelli and L. L. Ontai found that Latina mothers who speak more often in English than in Spanish tend to hold egalitarian gender role beliefs with their spouses in comparison to mothers with less fluent English-speaking skills.[87] If less exposure to U.S. culture is linked to Latina mothers valuing gender-stereotyped roles, this could have implications for the type of messages that mothers give to their adolescents. More studies are needed on how communication patterns are influenced by the generational status or the predominant language spoken of the participants to better understand the impact of parental communication on adolescent sexual decision making.

Conclusion

Although findings from survey data suggest that Latina/o families talk less about sexuality than other ethnic groups do, Latina mothers and adolescents have a lot to say. By way of focus groups, open-ended interviews, observational studies, and surveys, we found that Latina mothers and adolescents talk about sexual beliefs and values, educational values, sexual topics, relationship consequences, maternal stories about their youth, and the adolescents' whereabouts and activities. While certain cultural values may contribute to low levels of communication about sexual topics between parents and adolescents (sexual silence), many Latina/o parents and their adolescent children want to break through these barriers. This examination of the topic from an interdisciplinary literature base can provide important insights into the nature of communication processes, aiding the efforts of health researchers in preventing negative adolescent sexual outcomes, and enhancing knowledge in the field about normative aspects of family processes related to gender role socialization and adolescent sexual development.

5

Sexual Health of Latina/o Populations in the United States

SANDRA ARÉVALO AND HORTENSIA AMARO

This chapter presents a critical examination of the literature related to Latina/o sexual health in the United States in order to inform researchers and public policymakers about the sexual health needs of Latina/os. We start by contrasting the World Health Organization (WHO)'s definition of sexual health and recommendations with those laid down by the U.S. surgeon general. We then present the theoretical framework of the chapter and describe the social context of Latina/os living in the United States. These sections are followed by an examination of the literature on the sexual health of Latina/os published in the last sixteen years. The literature review is organized into four major sections: adolescents, heterosexual adults, gay/lesbian/bisexual populations, and older Latina/os. We define Latina/o following the U.S. Census Bureau definition: "Hispanics or Latinos are those people who classified themselves in one of the specific Spanish, Hispanic, or Latino categories listed on the Census 2000 questionnaire—"Mexican, Mexican Am., Chicano," "Puerto Rican," or "Cuban"—as well as those who indicate that they are "other Spanish/Hispanic/Latino." Persons who selected "other Spanish/Hispanic/Latino" include people whose place of origin is Spain, one of the Spanish-speaking countries of Central or South America, or the Dominican Republic and those identifying themselves generally as Spanish, Spanish American, Hispanic, Hispano, Latino, and so on.[1] The terms Hispanic and Latina/o will be used interchangeably in this chapter. Moreover, we define gay, lesbian, bisexual, and transgender populations as those who identify with any of these categories when defining their sexual orientation.

Definition of Sexual Health and the Approach to Sexual Health in the United States

The most recent definition of sexual health offered by the WHO and that is used in this survey is: "Sexual health is a state of physical, emotional, mental and social well-being in relation to sexuality; it is not merely the absence of disease, dysfunction or infirmity. Sexual health requires a positive and respect-ful approach to sexuality and sexual relationships, as well as the possibility of having pleasurable and safe sexual experiences, free of coercion, discrimination and violence. For sexual health to be attained and maintained, the sexual rights of all persons must be respected, protected and fulfilled." The WHO then pro-poses five goals aimed at attaining sexual health:

1. the elimination of barriers to sexual health;
2. provision of sexuality education to everybody;
3. the education, training, and support of professionals in the fields of sexual health;
4. access to comprehensive sexual health care services; and 5. the promo-tion and dissemination of research and evaluation regarding sexuality and sexual health.[2]

In the United States, the *Surgeon General's Call to Action to Promote Sexual Health and Responsible Sexual Behavior* is the document that sets the agenda in the field of sexual health. In contrast to the WHO's definition of sexual health, which emphasizes the individual's physical and psychological well-being, the free and responsible expression of sexuality, and the positive worth of sexual pleasure, the *Call to Action* focuses on the avoidance of sexually transmitted infections (STIs) and unintended pregnancies. Sexual activity is perceived in the context of social and health problems; public health interventions are thus aimed at changing sexual behaviors and individual factors that influence those behaviors. The effect of other health problems on sexual life is neglected, as is the positive nature of erotic pleasure. The sexual health model in the *Call to Action* places major emphasis on the negative consequences of sexual activity and a conception of sexuality as a source of problems.[3]

Theoretical Framework for the Study of Human Sexuality

Social epidemiological studies have shown the tremendous impact of social status—more specifically, social hierarchies based on race, ethnicity, class, and gender—on the health, including the sexual health, of populations in the United States.[4] Most studies of human sexuality have centered on one specific population—white, middle-class males—and have used developmental theories and biopsychology models that emphasize individual differences and individual intrinsic traits and states. This work devotes little attention to an individual's social surroundings and none at all to cultural diversity. These studies not only have provided an incomplete spectrum of sexual behavior but also have influenced social attitudes that perpetuate structures of sexual inequality by portraying racial/ethnic minority groups' sexuality or sexual behavior, or both, as promiscuous and lacking in impulse control.[5] The almost exclusive use of developmental theories and biopsychology models in the field of sexuality needs, and is slowly experiencing, a paradigm shift toward a social theory of sexuality that takes into account social structures, social environment, and socialization, acculturation, and enculturation processes across the course of life.[6] More specifically, there is a need for empirical studies that expand our knowledge of the role that parents, family caregivers, peers, communities, and major institutions of society play in shaping sexual behaviors. Moreover, greater support to scholars and policymakers that have started to look at the effects of social oppression on the sexual lives of people is warranted.[7] We share their critique and seek to present a compilation of literature that includes a comprehensive approach to sexual health issues for Latina/os. We also aim to contribute to the growing Latina/o sexual health literature focusing on the changing significance of Latina/o sexual health in U.S. society.

The Social Context of Latina/os Living in the United States

Different forms of marginalization, such as racism, poverty, low educational attainment, lack of sexual health education, and high incarceration rates, play a significant role in the production of sexual health disparities between Latina/o and non-Latina/o groups; therefore our first goal in understanding the state of Latina/o sexual health is to determine the social context of Latina/os living in the United States.[8]

Despite the overall improvement of high school completion rates in the United States since the 1970s, this advance has been minimal among Latina/o high school students, who have higher dropout rates compared to white and black students: almost four in ten Latina/os have not graduated from high school, compared to two out of ten blacks and one out of ten whites. Lower educational attainment, in turn, negatively affects chances for employment.[9] Of Latina/os between ages fifteen and nineteen, 30 percent live below the official poverty level, compared to 27 percent of blacks and 9 percent of whites; 17 percent of Latino men in their thirties and forties live below the official poverty level, compared to the national average of 7–8 percent. Poverty and lower socioeconomic position, in turn, affect sexual health by limiting access to health care: Latino men are more likely to have no health insurance (45 percent) than blacks (31 percent), whites (17 percent), or other minority groups (21–26 percent). These factors also influence sterilization practices among couples. For instance, despite the fact that compared with a vasectomy, bilateral tubal ligation (BTL) costs three times as much, is 20 times more likely to result in major complications, and 10 to 37 times more likely to fail—and although complications are rare, mortality rates are 12 times higher with procedures that sterilize a woman than those for men—the poorest women are the most likely to have a BTL (41 percent, compared with 19 percent of those in the highest-income category), especially among Hispanic and African American couples, among whom it is

overwhelmingly the woman who becomes sterilized; moreover, the poorest men
are the least likely to have had a vasectomy (5 percent, compared with 15 percent
of better-off men).[10]

The incidence of incarceration among Latino men is also higher compared
to white men. Latinos comprised 20.2 percent of prisoners in federal and state
correctional facilities and 15 percent of inmates in local jails, while constitut-
ing only 14 percent of the overall U.S. adult population in 2005. Incarceration places men at greater risk for acquiring high-risk sexual behaviors, HIV,
and STIs mainly owing to the higher prevalence rates of sexually transmitted
diseases (STDs) in jails and prisons compared to rates in the general population. Moreover, incarceration disrupts existing relationships and changes the
sexual networks of both the incarcerated and the nonincarcerated persons; the
incarcerated partner is more vulnerable to risky sexual partnerships (which frequently are coercive), and the nonincarcerated partner is more likely to engage
in sexual practices with other nonincarcerated persons to satisfy his or her
social, sexual, and financial needs.[11]

Lack of access to health services and low quality of health services is also
evident among Latina/o groups. Data reported in the 2006 National Healthcare
Disparities Report (NHDR) from the U.S. Department of Health and Human
Services indicates that Hispanics had worse access to health care compared to
whites in five out of six core measures (83 percent) and received poorer-quality
care compared to whites in seventeen out of twenty-two core measures (77 percent). These social conditions of low educational attainment, impoverishment,
high incarceration rates, and lack of access to health services create situations
of oppression that impede and limit personal agency.[12]

Literature on the Sexual Health of Latina/o Adolescents

Data on age at first intercourse, sexual intercourse with multiple partners,
and sexual activity come from the 2007 Youth Risk Behavior Survey (YRBS),
a nationally representative study conducted every two years with a sample
of male and female students in grades 9 through 12. Although the YRBS is a
valuable tool for examining trends in youth behavior, caution must be taken
when examining the statistics on Latina/os since the YRBS is a school-based
survey; given that Latina/o high school students have a high dropout rate, the
sample may not be representative of all Latina/o youth. Dropout students are
more likely to have lower socioeconomic status, to become single parents, and
to engage in high-risk sexual behaviors. Results from the 2007 YRBS indicate
that overall 7.1 percent of all students in the United States have had *sexual
intercourse for the first time* before age thirteen. Males (10.1 percent) are more
likely than females (4.0 percent) to have engaged in sexual intercourse before
thirteen years of age. This holds true when comparing racial/ethnic groups:
white males (5.7 percent) compared to white females (3.1 percent), black males

(26.2 percent) to black females (6.9 percent), and Latino males (11.9 percent) to Latina females (4.5 percent).[13]

Overall, the survey found that 47.8 percent of all students have had sexual intercourse in their lifetime. Latina/o students (58.2 percent of females and 45.8 percent of males) were more likely to have had sexual intercourse than white students (43.6 percent and 43.7 percent for females and males, respectively), but less likely compared to African American students (60.9 percent of females and 72.6 percent of males). Similar patterns were found among students who reported *sexual intercourse with four or more people in their lifetime*: Latina/o students (20.4 percent of males and 11.3 percent of females) were more likely to report this level of sexual activity than white students (12.2 and 10.6 percent for males and females, respectively) and less likely than black students (37.6 and 18.1 percent for males and females, respectively). For currently sexually active students (the YRBS defines as "sexually active" those students who reported having had intercourse with at least one person in the three months prior to answering the survey), a third of all students in the United States are classified as sexually active. Similar to patterns of first sexual activity before age thirteen, Hispanic students have higher overall rates (39.6 percent for males and 35.3 percent and females) than white students (30.6 and 35.1 percent for males and females, respectively), but lower rates than black students (48.7 and 43.5 percent for males and females, respectively).[14]

Likewise, in 2002 the Centers for Disease Control (CDC) found that Latina teenagers accounted for 20 percent of all new HIV cases reported in the United States for young women ages thirteen through nineteen, even though they represented less than 16 percent of the U.S. population for that age group. Higher birthrates are also seen among Latina women between the ages of fifteen and nineteen, compared to white and black women of the same age group: 83 per 1,000 for Latina teens compared to 27 and 63 per 1,000 for white and black teens, respectively. Moreover, while pregnancy rates in women under twenty years of age have dropped across all ethnic groups over the past fifteen years, the decline has been smallest among Latinas (46 percent compared to 60 percent and 65 percent for black and white teens, respectively, between 1991 and 2005).[15]

Literature on Youth by Theme

For the literature on youth, we focused our search on the period 1990–2006, using the terms "Hispanic" (including "Hispanic Americans"), "sexuality" (including "sexual behavior"), and "youth" (including "adolescent"). The search was limited to English-language journal articles or reviews and to studies including thirteen- to eighteen-year-old adolescents. We excluded articles that focused on individuals eighteen to twenty-five years old, on comparisons of Latina/os in the United States to Latina/os in Latin America, or on violence in relationships. Our search yielded a total of 291 articles, from which we selected 25 that focused on the three major themes identified in this review: self-esteem, parent-child communication, and acculturation. Of this total number of articles reviewed, the majority—12—used an unrepresentative sample of respondents in their quantitative studies. Only 4 studies used a nationally representative data set, and all those studies also conducted quantitative data analyses. Two of the studies used qualitative research methods to collect their data. Both of those studies utilized an unrepresentative sample. We also used 4 studies that reviewed programs for adolescents in a number of areas related to sexual health and three literature reviews.

Self-Esteem

Researchers have demonstrated the impact of self-esteem on a number of sexual behaviors, such as early sexual initiation, condom use and contraception, unplanned pregnancy, and STIs. Among Latina/o adolescents, factors associated with high self-esteem are warm and supportive parent-child relationships, positive attitude toward life, academic motivation, and academic competence. Higher self-esteem has also been reported among bilingual students.[16] Comprehensive and abstinence-only approaches to sex education have stressed the value of high self-esteem in creating sexually healthy adolescents. However, recent research has started to question the effects of self-esteem on adolescents' sexual behaviors. In a methodologically high-level review of the literature on self-esteem and sexual behavior in adolescents over the last twenty years, Patricia Goodson, Eric R. Buhi, and Sarah C. Dunsmore stated that 62 percent of the sexual behavior findings and 72 percent of the sexual attitudinal findings in peer-reviewed articles report no significant relationships between self-esteem and sexual behavior and attitudes. Some authors also caution that an emphasis on building self-esteem as a main instrument for creating social change merely places all responsibility on individuals rather than addressing the structural factors present.[17]

Parent-Child Communication

Adolescents who experience open communication with their parents about sex are less likely to engage in unsafe sexual behavior. The quality of parent-adolescent relationships is important as well; parental values seem to be communicated more effectively if parents provide warmth and support to their teens. Teens who discuss condom use with their mothers before their first sexual intercourse are more likely to use condoms than those who did not have such discussions or had them after becoming sexual active; using condoms in their first encounter also seems to predict future condom use. Similarly, communication about sexuality with parents increases the likelihood that the adolescents will communicate with their future partners about HIV/AIDS. Although the literature on parent-child communication is relatively rich, still little is known about the dynamics of Latina/o parent-child communication related to sexuality. While some studies show no significant differences by race/ethnicity on parent-child communication about HIV, others report that Latina/o adolescents communicate less with their parents about sexuality than do white adolescents.[18]

The studies on parent-child communication among Latina/o populations show that, much like non-Latina white mothers, Hispanic mothers are the primary communicator with both male and female adolescents regarding sexual behavior and related themes; these discussions, however, seem more likely to be about HIV/AIDS and STDs than about sexual behavior, contraceptive use, or physical development. Similarly, Latina/o conversations that center on the beliefs and values of the parent regarding sexuality have better outcomes than conversations on day-to-day happenings in the adolescent's life. Some studies with Latina mother-daughter dyads have found more restricted communications: Latina mothers were unenthusiastic about communicating information beyond merely biological facts to their daughters; their communication was more moralistic and restrictive, which seemed to discourage daughters from confiding in them. This is an area of concern, especially because when Latina adolescents are able to talk to their parents, they are much less likely to get pregnant compared to those teens who communicate less with their parents.[19]

Acculturation

Conflicting results have been reported on the association between levels of acculturation and risky sexual behavior among Latina/o adolescents. Some research suggests, on the one hand, that higher acculturation levels among Latina/o adolescents seem to detach them from traditional protective behaviors—for instance, Latina/os born in the United States are more likely to engage in unsafe sexual behaviors than those born outside the United States. On the other hand, low acculturation levels among Latina/o teens have been found to be associated with lack of information about their own bodies, contraceptive options, negotiation skills, and health care resources—factors that in turn are associated with negative sexual health outcomes. Differences in acculturation levels between parents and adolescents can also have negative consequences on Latina/o adolescents' sexual health, as tensions in the parent-child relationship may decrease the possibility for open communication.[20] Moreover, more restrictive gender expectations held among some more traditional Latina/os, namely machismo and marianismo, play a role in Latina/o adolescents' sexual expectations. Such gender role expectations among some Latino adolescents include the measuring of men's masculinity by the number of sexual conquests and degree of sexual risk taking and the placing of full responsibility on women both to satisfy their male partner's sexual requests and to avoid unwanted pregnancies—all while women are expected to be ignorant about sex facts, as knowledge about sex is for the men's realm.[21] Clearly, these unbalanced power dynamics create situations where risky sexual behaviors are encouraged, limiting at the same time adolescents' autonomy and ability to enjoy their own sexuality.

Literature on Heterosexual Adult Populations

National data describing the sexual health of Latina/o populations, like the national approach on sexual health, are especially disease and problem oriented. National data sets reveal that Latina/os in the United States have higher rates of STIs, HIV infection, and AIDS cases compared to non-Latina/o whites. The latest STD Surveillance published by the CDC reported that chlamydia incidence among Latina/os was more than three times higher than among whites (459.0 and 152.1 per 100,000, respectively), while gonorrhea incidence among Latina/os was more than twice that for whites (74.8 and 35.2 per 100,000, respectively). Even more severe differences were reported for congenital syphilis, which was ten times greater among Latina/os (based on the mother's race/ethnicity) than among non-Latina/o whites (13.4 and 1.3 cases per 100,000 live births, respectively).[22]

Similarly, Latina/os have higher rates of HIV/AIDS diagnosis compared to non-Latina/o whites. Among Latino men who have sex with men (MSM), the rate of HIV/AIDS was 37.8 cases per 100,000, compared to 13.9 per 100,000 among white MSM; the rate of HIV/AIDS among Latino men injection drug users (IDU) was 12.0 per 100,000, compared to 1.7 per 100,000 for white men IDU; among women the rates were 4.8 and 1.0 per 100,000 for Latinas and whites, respectively. In addition, rates of HIV/AIDS among men and women with high-risk heterosexual contact (i.e., with persons known to have HIV/AIDS or a risk factor for HIV/AIDS) were higher among Latina/os than whites: for Latino men 10.9 per 100,000, compared to 1.1 for white men; among women, the rate for Latinas was 15.0 per 100,000, compared to 2.2 for whites. Notwithstanding the higher rates of HIV/AIDS diagnosis among Latina/os compared to whites, because incidence and prevalence of health outcomes are often presented for Latina/os as one single group, critical differences among Latina/o subgroups frequently go unnoticed, which in turn may limit preventive efforts and targeted campaigns to reduce these disparities. For instance, J. Murphy examined cumulative AIDS prevalence rates through June 1994 that showed Latina/os with higher prevalence rates (235 per 100,000) compared to whites (86 per 100,000) but lower rates compared to blacks (335 per 100,000). He performed the same calculation using Latina/o subgroups (Mexican Americans, Puerto Ricans, and other Latina/os). The results showed that Puerto Ricans had significantly higher rates of AIDS (511 per 100,000) not only compared to whites (86 per 100,000) but also compared to blacks (335 per 100,000), to Mexican Americans (136 per 100,000), and to other Latina/o groups (268 per 100,000).[23]

Factors Affecting the Sexual Health
of Adult Heterosexual Latina/os

Consistent with the national approach to sexual health, our review found that the literature on Latina/o sexual health is especially disease and problem oriented. The literature presented in this section reflects that interpretation. An extensive literature search was conducted on MEDLINE and PSYCHINFO for the years 1990–2006. The following keywords were used in the search: "sexual health," "Hispanic," "Latina women," "Latino men," "Mexican American women," "Mexican American men," "Puerto Rican women," and "Puerto Rican men." Research conducted outside the United States was excluded. Out of a total of 275 records found, 65 publications are relevant to the topic of sexual health among adult Latina/o men and women. Of these 65 publications, 44 are empirical studies that focus on factors related to sexual risk behaviors and medical problems related to reproductive health; 10 explore factors related to HIV-risk behaviors and beliefs, attitudes, and misconceptions concerning STIs and HIV infection, and social constructions of sexual health; and 11 are critical or theoretical approaches attempting to elucidate the factors underlying sexual health disparities between Latina/os and non-Latina/os.

Earlier we saw how different forms of marginalization, such as poverty and high incarceration rates, present barriers to the attainment of healthy sexuality among Latina/os. The literature has found additional barriers, namely, traditional gender role beliefs among Latina/os, the Latina/o cultural value of machismo, and fear of intimacy.[24] These themes are explored in the four sections that follow.

Sexual Health Education among Latina/os

Using data from the 1995 National Survey of Family Growth, R. E. Zambrana and colleagues found that among Puerto Rican and Mexican American women aged fifteen through forty-four years, 60 percent did not receive sex education from parents, with 21 percent of the Puerto Rican women and 38 percent of the Mexican American women reporting no sex education in schools. Studies have shown that television is the main source of knowledge about sexual health among older urban women, information that is mostly limited to modes of transmission for HIV/AIDS and STDs; friends and newspapers are the next in the list of sources. A smaller proportion of these women received their sexual health information from health professionals. Reliance on TV and print media instead of direct communication with health care specialists adds another risk for Latina women, especially when (as studies have shown) issues such as abortion and STIs including HIV/AIDS are the least mentioned in Hispanic and African American magazines. Similarly, lack of knowledge about HIV and AIDS and rare visits to health clinics are common among Latino men of all ages.[25]

Lack of sexual knowledge is especially troublesome because HIV misperceptions (for instance, beliefs that HIV is an agent of genocide; that the government is misinforming the public about HIV; that risky partners can be identified by appearance; that a partner's reported history is always accurate; and that only specific classes of people are at risk for HIV) constitute barriers against safe-sex practices. In addition, sexual health misconceptions affect Latina/os' sexual health by discouraging their use of health services and procedures like emergency contraception, amniocentesis, regular mammograms and Pap smears, and vasectomies, and in general, by limiting their access to health information on STIs and sexually related problems. Recent findings on the lower screening rates of Latina women point to differences in socioeconomic status (SES), health care coverage, and education level rather than ethnic differences.[26]

Sexual Communication and Gender Norms

Sexual communication is necessary for an individual to attain a fulfilled sexual life; among certain Latina/o couples, however, good communication is difficult and infrequent. Some of the factors related to this lack of communication are cultural upbringing, machismo, lack of education, and everyday life stress (due to, for example, immigration, poverty, and discrimination). In their study, Liani Arroyo and L. Amparo Pinzón found that sexual conversations among Latino men were related to granting their partner permission to use contraceptives or exploring whether the partner is in the mood for sex. Latina women's conversational exchanges were more focused on feelings of love, desire, permission, and trust. Greater sexual communication among Latina/o couples is associated with greater commitment to the relationship, the practice of safe sexual behaviors, and higher acculturation levels.[27]

Sexual communication with their partners seems difficult to establish particularly among Latina women with low levels of acculturation. Mexican American women with low levels of acculturation have reported that to suggest their primary partners use a condom goes against their cultural beliefs, which dictate that it is the man's responsibility to make sexual and contraceptive decisions. Moreover, the norms of *respeto* and *confianza* that should exist within a couple would be violated if the woman asked her partner to use a condom. Similarly, in another sample with undergraduate male and female students, Mexican American students with low levels of acculturation rated females who introduced condom use as higher on the promiscuous scale, compared to Mexican American students with higher levels of acculturation and white students. In a more recent qualitative study exploring the sexual health of a group of Mexican American women, Yolanda R. Dávila reported that women in her sample believed that respectable women should be ignorant of sexual matters and that it is the male's responsibility to initiate sex and to decide on the use of contraception; moreover, women in this study did not use condoms, in order to show commitment in their relationship and to keep their partner happy. Unfortunately, these norms are followed even when a woman is aware of her partner's infidelity (with other women as well as with men), placing her at a higher risk of acquiring STIs, including HIV.[28]

Not only is it worthy of note that gender norms among Latina women are affected by such factors as levels of acculturation or ethnic subgroup, it is also important to highlight that gender norm is a dynamic concept that changes with time, as Jennifer J. Frost and Anne K. Driscoll showed in their study. Using General Social Survey data for the years 1974–94, the authors found that Latina gender role attitudes changed to a more egalitarian view during this twenty-year period; moreover, they found no statistically significant differences on gender role attitudes among their sample of Latina, black, and white women. A similar trend toward more egalitarian relationships among more acculturated Latina/o couples has been observed. While men are still perceived as the ones responsible for initiating sexual behavior, women are perceived as responsible for suggesting condom use, with the couple sharing responsibility about sexual activities and contraceptive use.[29]

Some Latino men also believe that sex is the arena where they can prove their masculinity, and their manhood seems to be positively related to the number of concurrent sexual partners they have. Studies have shown that Latino men are more likely to have multiple partners than black or white men. Additionally, Latino men with more traditional gender role beliefs are more likely to engage in sexual coercion and less likely to feel comfortable communicating about sexual matters.[30]

Relationship Power

Imbalances of power within relationships frequently leave women exposed to risky sexual situations. As previously noted, in Latina/o relationships it is often the man who controls sexual and contraceptive decision making. Frequently, this position of power is maintained through the use of violence. This power dynamic not only limits Latina women's agency in their own lives but also increases their risk for acquiring HIV/AIDS and other STIs. Heterosexual relationships are the main source of HIV infection among Latina women, yet preventive campaigns that promote the use of condoms among Latina women have not been very successful, in part because of the lack of control Latina women have in their relationships. Latina women in abusive relationships reduce sexual risk by abstinence rather than by the use of condoms. Situations of power struggle may also explain those instances where women, as a way to show their love or support, practice unsafe sex with partners who have disclosed their seroprevalence. Not surprisingly, Latina women with higher levels of relationship power are more likely to report consistent condom use, although relationship power has been reported to be very low among Latina women. Therefore, a gender perspective should be part of any research aimed at reducing risky sexual behavior. It is also important to gain a better understanding of the dynamics of oppression and how they affect women's autonomy and their engagement in sexually risky behaviors.[31]

Recent studies on the effect of relationship power among Latinas have found different kinds of power (e.g., resource power that refers to level of education and employment and power that is related to commitment to the relationship and level of female decision making within the relationship) that affect their sexual practices; hence, the need to distinguish among them when addressing power imbalances among Latina/o couples. Further, studies have shown that Latina women feel more powerful in a relationship when they have economic independence (work outside the home, have money and education) and when they perceive themselves as physically attractive. However, no generalizations can be assumed since there is evidence that subgroup differences exist among Latina women in their sexual negotiation dynamics.[32]

Condom Use

National preventive campaigns to reduce HIV/AIDS and STIs have focused on behavioral changes to increase condom use among Latino men. As a result, a significant increase in condom use has been observed among Latinos who have multiple sexual partners; nevertheless, Latinos still show lower rates of condom use, especially condom use with their primary partners, compared to whites or blacks. Despite the efficacy of condom use in the prevention of HIV/AIDS and other STIs, Latina/os might also have other priorities. Gaining trust and social acceptability from their primary partners is very important among Latina/o couples, which is, however, a barrier to regular condom use. Similar attitudes toward the use of condoms—that it is too much trouble, that condoms turn off sexual feelings, that buying them creates feelings of discomfort and embarrassment—still pose major barriers to their use. On the positive side, some of the factors that facilitate regular condom use among Latino men are condom availability (e.g., carrying condoms), greater level of comfort in sexual situations, and level of condom use self-efficacy (a person's belief that he or she can use condoms).[33]

Literature on the Sexual Health of Lesbian and Bisexual Latinas

Lesbian and bisexual minority women face tremendous prejudice and discrimination and often violence both in society at large and within their communities of color, mainly owing to homophobic beliefs. In many Latina/o communities, "normal" gender role expectations and religion contribute to homophobic attitudes that severely affect all aspects of health among lesbian and bisexual Latina women. As with previous sections, only peer-reviewed articles were included in this section. Five articles were found that in some manner relate to the sexual health of Latina women who identified themselves as lesbians or bisexual women; three of them refer to levels of "outness" (i.e., the amount of disclosure about sexual orientation made to family members, heterosexual friends, lesbian/gay friends, and coworkers), and the remaining two refer to sexual health disadvantages among lesbians or bisexuals compared to heterosexual women.[34]

Level of outness, or being out, is associated with psychological stress among bisexual and lesbian women; however, using a national data set from the Lesbian

Wellness Survey on "being out/outness," Joseph F. Morris, Craig R. Waldo, and Esther D. Rothblum found that, unlike African Americans and Euro-Americans, Latinas' level of outness was not significantly associated with psychological stress. The authors also found that Euro-American and Latina women were more out than were African American women. Acculturation seems to be a factor related to level of outness. It has been reported that Latinas with low levels of acculturation are less likely to endorse the later stages of homosexual identity development; similarly, cultural values such as familism are barriers to disclosing sexual identity and sexual abuse. Lynn Rew et al. also found higher prevalence of reported history of sexual abuse and being tested or treated for HIV among gay and lesbian youths compared to heterosexual ones. The authors did not, however, provide racial or ethnic differences for these findings. Vickie M. Mays et al. examined the associations between sexual orientation and health disadvantages among a sample of Latina, African American, and Asian women and found that significantly more lesbian and bisexual women lacked a regular source of health care. Compared to estimates derived from heterosexual women of similar racial/ethnic backgrounds, rates of preventive care for conditions such as breast and cervical cancer, hypertension, and hypercholesterolemia were lower among lesbians and bisexual women.[35]

Literature on the Sexual Health of Older Latina/os

There is a dearth of research on older Latina/os' sexual health. Research on older Latino men has been mainly focused on erectile dysfunction, and although studies have found no racial or ethnic differences in rates of erectile dysfunction, they have found that increased likelihood of erectile dysfunction was related to moderate lower urinary tract symptoms, hypertension, and depression among Latina/os, to age and diabetes among whites, and to severe lower urinary tract symptoms among blacks. Among Mexican Americans, erectile dysfunction was more common among men suffering from diabetes.[36]

For older Latina women, a study using data from the Study of Women Across the Nation (SWAN)—a national study of midlife women conducted in seven U.S. cities (Los Angeles, Oakland, Chicago, Detroit, Pittsburgh, Newark, and Boston)—found no racial/ethnic differences in behaviors such as engaging in sex, getting emotional satisfaction, or physical pleasure; however, a higher proportion of Latina women reported having sexual intercourse and a lower proportion of Latina women reported masturbation compared to non-Latina white women.[37]

Conclusion

It is important to note that this review of literature on Latino/a sexual health was strategic rather than comprehensive. In general, we chose to address those areas that appeared to present the most important and immediate scientific opportunities. Therefore, although the issues brought up in this essay are certainly relevant for Latino/as' sexual health, they do not represent an exhaustive list, as we did not attempt in this chapter to provide a review of the extensive literature on adolescent sexual health. It is also important to note that this review was focused on peer-reviewed articles; we did not include books in our literature review process, so works like Rafael Díaz's book on Latino gay men and HIV and the recent publication by Gloria González-López on the sexual lives of Mexican immigrants in the United States are not included in this review.[38]

Although the Social Science Research Council Report *Sexuality Research in the United States: An Assessment of the Social and Behavioral Sciences* stated in 1995 that research on sexual behavior should be based on a framework of society and culture and be developmental in nature, nearly fifteen years later the lack of such a framework is still evident.[39] The need to address the gaping void that exists in research by incorporating the effects of contextual and cultural variables on the sexual health of racial and ethnic minority groups is evident. Research should especially consider (1) that, at present, there are no known biological or genetic factors that can account for the poorer sexual health outcomes—especially high rates of HIV/AIDS and STIs—of minority groups such as Latina/os when compared to white groups and (2) that previous studies on the social determinants of health have shown social factors, such as poverty, access to health care, discriminatory practices in health care settings, and quality of health care received, among others, to be associated with worse health outcomes of minority groups compared to whites.

Little is known about what and how the family and other institutions teach and influence sexual attitudes, norms, values, and behaviors that affect Latina/o adolescents' sexual behavior. For adolescents and adults, Latino/a sexual health research is still focused on reproduction, contraception, disease control, and sexual dysfunction. We found no studies on Hispanic sexual health that report on sexual well-being, and most of the studies have a disease framework. There is also a dearth of studies on the developmental, emotional, social, and cultural aspects of Latina/o sexual health.

A serious limitation is the medicalization of sexual dysfunction. Once sexual dysfunctions are considered solely as biological, aspects related to sociocultural factors are minimized. Regarding the sexual health of older Latino/as, for example, there is a lack of research on the effects of chronic health issues, such as diabetes and hypertension. Henry. A. Feldman et al. found these conditions to be associated with erectile dysfunction among older Latino men. Indeed, there has been no research on ethnic minority negotiation of any sexual dysfunction.[40]

Another limitation of the literature on sexual health is the manner in which sexual health is defined, as well as its specific application to ethnic minorities. As Weston M. Edwards and Eli Coleman point out, definitions of sexual health have emerged within the particular social and political context in each nation; however, within each nation's peculiarities, sexual health should be premised on such concepts as freedom from discrimination and violence, the importance of human rights, sexual responsibility, and sex as a positive and enriching aspect in a person's life. On these premises, sexual education could become more relevant and effective if it includes "accurate and appropriate knowledge, self-awareness, self-acceptance, internal congruence, intimacy, communication, sexual needs and desires, sexual function, responsibility, freedom to act, freedom from abuse and coercion, respect for other and community, self-esteem, freedom from illness or dysfunction, and sex as a positive and enriching force in one's life."[41]

Research on Latino/a sexual health is marked by a number of significant methodological limitations (among them are bias in national sampling, insufficient sample size to enable analysis of different Latina/o subgroups, and lack of contextual variables in national samples). Unfortunately, current survey data do not offer enough means to determine the causes of different sexual health outcomes (e.g., lack of data on different lifestyles, sexual networks, patterns of health care–seeking behavior, quality of services received).[42] Very much needed is research on the effects of oppression and discrimination (interpersonal and institutional) on Latina/o sexual health, with particular attention being given to such effects among gay, lesbian, bisexual, and transgender Latina/os. Similarly, sound research on issues of power and control in women's sexual realities as well as for Latina/os overall is still lacking.

Recommendations

A review of the literature suggests that, as with other fields of health, multilevel, multifaceted, and multidisciplinary approaches are needed to improve the sexual health of Hispanic communities. Critical needs are:

1. development of sexually transmitted infection surveillance and research tools that better capture Hispanics' heterogeneity, behavioral patterns, and sexual health care needs;
2. establishment of collaborative partnerships with communities to accurately identify and address the needs of their most vulnerable members;
3. targeting of high-risk groups and their networks by identifying contextual factors that surround their behaviors;
4. improving knowledge delivery venues that reach those at higher risk—for example, preventive campaigns that require open discussion about sexuality, sexual behaviors, gender roles, the influence of culture on communication, and negotiation within relationships; and
5. public funding for Hispanic men's sexual and reproductive health.

6

Latina/o Sex Policy

ELENA R. GUTIÉRREZ

It is difficult to identify social policies that do not directly or indirectly have an impact on our sexual lives. Sexuality, in its social, physical, and cultural meanings has relevance in some way for all Latinas and Latinos. As such, the social and governmental policies directly and indirectly related to Latina/o sexuality constitute a variety of community, state, and national initiatives. Beyond policies involving contraceptive use, family planning, sex education, abortion, and sex work restrictions, there are a myriad of issues that touch gay, lesbian and queer Latina/os in particular. The lack of access of these groups to marriage (in most states) and subsequent denial of certain of the civil rights and privileges that heterosexual couples experience are among the most obvious. In addition, critical social and political issues that on the surface appear to have little relation to sexuality but are immediately relevant today—such as immigration policy—also have significant repercussions for the lives of Latina/os and the resources (or lack thereof) that they can access to care for their sexual selves.

Despite the growing body of published research on topics relevant to Latina/o sexuality, academic consideration of how social policies influence the sexual lives of Latina/os or provide analyses of the types of policies that could benefit or protect their sexual practices, identities, and needs has only just begun. In the existing research focusing on these issues, scholars of sexuality often fail to extrapolate policy ramifications from their findings. That which does primarily reflects the priorities of available funding opportunities and the politics of grant making in the United States. As a result, policy-geared research tends to offer a medicalized or social problems approach that attempts to understand and change the sexual behaviors and practices of Latina/os and focuses on topics such as AIDS or teenage pregnancy. While the aforementioned issues are undoubtedly important for Latina/o communities, they have already received substantial coverage in this volume and therefore are not discussed further here.

One significant area that deserves increased attention outside of a social problems perspective is the reproductive and sexual health of Latina/os. This is arguably one of the most important policy areas that affects all Latina/os. Whatever their sexual practices and identities, all Latina/os face obstacles to receiving appropriate sexual and reproductive health care. Although some advocacy groups claim that there is a current crisis in Latina/o sexual and reproductive health care, the subject remains considerably underresearched.[1] Much of the existing scholarship available outside of academia has been conducted by nonprofit organizations dedicated to improving the reproductive and sexual health of Latina/os. In this chapter I discuss just a few topics from the spectrum of policies related to the sexual and reproductive lives of Latinas and Latinos. I begin by reviewing some of the predominant policies affecting gay and lesbian Latina/os; the remainder of the chapter concerns Latina sexual and reproductive health. Moreover, I aim to demonstrate how sexuality entangles with other policy arenas. In particular, as Eithne Luibhéid, Lionel Cantú Jr., and others have shown, the politics of migration has become a central policy arena offering significant repercussions for Latina/o sexual politics.[2]

The Social Context: U.S. Immigration Policy

The sexual and reproductive experiences of Latina/os are very much affected by the social context in which they live; namely, the contemporary political milieu and its attendant public policies. Today's anti-immigrant climate in the United States and globalization in the Western Hemisphere have direct consequences for the regulation of the sexuality of the nation's Latina/os in the twenty-first century. Immigration status and national legislation impacts Latina/o sexuality globally. Gays and lesbians from Latin America do seek asylum in the United States to escape the more stringent antigay climate in their home countries.[3]

Although social mores in the United States may be relatively more accepting of homosexuals, Latina/o homosexual individuals and couples continue to face discrimination that is explicitly and implicitly institutionalized in this country. This begins with discriminatory practices that deny the human and citizenship rights as they currently exist in the United States, such as the laws that prohibit same-sex marriage. Because most same-sex unions are not granted the same federal protections given to married heterosexual couples, same-sex partners, their children, and other family members do not enjoy basic civil rights.[4] Although the Commonwealth of Massachusetts offers legal, civil marriage of same-sex couples and several other states allow "civil unions" that offer the same rights and privileges as heterosexual marriage, gay and lesbian Latina/o couples in most other states do not experience these equal rights. One of the most significant areas of future policy research must be on the issue of access to marriage for gay and lesbian Latina/os and what factors could encourage Latina/o communities to rally for these rights. Moreover, we need to know more about what the repercussions are for same-sex couples and their families who cannot achieve these rights and privileges. While I do not want to overstate the role of social policy or context in regulating the sexual and reproductive practices and decisions of Latina/os, the social structures that surround their sexuality must be considered as a significant factor.

Existing studies suggest that gay and lesbian Latina/os suffer more from the inability to gain the rights of same-sex marriage than do persons from other racial and ethnic groups. A recently published national study of same-sex Latina/o couples, with sister studies in California and Florida, found significant differences in the social realities of Latina/o same-sex couples compared to others. Most notably, because Latina/o same-sex couples are more likely than other same-sex couples to have children, they risk a disadvantage in raising their families given the social discrimination they face. These households also demonstrated marked disadvantages in income, home ownership, and disability compared to other racial and ethnic groups included in the study.[5]

The repercussions of these circumstances on the lives of gay and lesbian Latina/os are heightened if either or both partners are undocumented. Those immigrants to the United States who are undocumented do not have access to many services because of their lack of citizenship status and the privileges that come with it. Jason Cianciotto also found that 51 percent of the men and women in same-sex couples in which both partners are Hispanic report that they are not U.S. citizens. One additional inequality is the inability of resident gay or lesbian Latina/os to sponsor their partners for citizenship. Efforts to eliminate the inequality that gay and lesbian domestic partners face by the lack of recognition of their families must continue to encourage legislators to propose initiatives that will grant gay and lesbian Latina/os the same rights as heterosexual couples. The proposed Uniting American Families Act (S 1278, formerly known as the Permanent Partners Immigration Act), introduced in Congress in 2005 in an attempt to add "permanent partner" to the federal Immigration and Nationality Act, failed to pass. Such legislation would have enabled same-sex domestic partners to be treated the same as opposite-sex married spouses for purposes of immigration rights and benefits.[6]

Although constitutional amendments intended to ban same-sex marriages and civil unions have been increasingly proposed at the state level, we have very little information on how Latinos respond to both efforts for and against endeavors to achieve greater equality for Latino same-sex couples. Increased research is needed to understand the opinions of Latinos on this issue so better advocacy and policy efforts can be designed that reflect their opinions. More research is also needed to measure and document the disproportionate challenges immigrant Latina/o same-sex couples and individuals face so that policymakers can develop better legislation and other initiatives to support them.

In sum, same-sex Latina/o couples are more seriously affected by their inability to marry than their white counterparts in multiple ways. While there is no research on this area, it is likely that queer Latina/os also face challenges when wanting to have children, as Latinoa/s in general face limits in gaining access to reproductive technologies.

Sex Trafficking and Sex Work

Rising rates of HIV. and AIDS among U.S. Latinos and in regions of Mexico and Central America that are sources of immigration to the United States are an indirect consequence of migration and labor policies that encourage the migration of men and not families. Research has only begun to explore male migrants' sexual risk behaviors, such as the resort to commercial sex workers, but suggests trends that deserve more attention. In a 2004 study of the prevalence and frequency of visits to commercial sex workers among 442 randomly selected Latino migrants in Durham, North Carolina, 28 percent of respondents reported seeking the services of a commercial sex worker during the previous year. Reported rates of condom use with commercial sex workers were high, but tended to fall where familiarity of the patron with a commercial sex worker increased. This rate is similar to that found among farmworkers in California and much higher than the 5 percent estimated to occur in Mexico. Among those visiting a commercial sex worker, the average number of visits in the previous year was 7.7. Of those who visited commercial sex workers, most men did so infrequently; half reported four or fewer visits within the year. The proportion of men reporting visits to commercial sex workers was 30 percent among Mexicans, 28 percent among Hondurans, 16 percent among Salvadorans, and 22 percent among other Latino men; the annual frequency of visits among those visiting commercial sex workers was 8.0, 7.3, 3.8, and 6.7, respectively.

We need to understand much more of the context in which migrant engagement in sex work occurs. A 2006 study of Mexican farmworkers found that both individual and environmental factors such as education, social and cultural isolation, long work hours, continued mobility, hazardous work conditions, and limited access to health care, together with sexual contact with sex workers, increased risks of sexually transmitted infections (STIs).[7] To inform policy development, research must go beyond looking at individual behavior to considering the social isolation and networks of immigrants.

Exposure to commercial sex workers poses a threat not only to migrants' own health but also to the health of those with whom they have sex. The cyclical nature of migration to the United States from Latin America, particularly from Mexico, suggests that large numbers of migrants are likely to return to their country of origin and engage in sexual contact with partners, possibly transmitting sexual disease. The fact that greater awareness of the risk for HIV infection is marginally related to fewer visits with commercial sex workers is pertinent to policy implementation.[8]

We are also concerned about the lack of protections surrounding the rights and health of Latina immigrants who engage in sex work. There is sufficient evidence to demonstrate that Latin American women are sometimes forced into sex work. The Rutherford Institute estimates that sex traffickers transport at least 18,000 captives into the United States each year, with the nation's southern border providing the main entry points for sex trafficking. Federal trafficking legislation has only been in place since 2000. While it is a positive development that the legislation provides stricter penalties for trafficking and gives victims a variety of benefits, including a special temporary visa for three years, medical and psychological counseling, and emergency shelter, victims must testify against their traffickers to ensure this assistance.[9]

Sex workers live under the daily threat of arrest, deportation, and violence. These dangers are compounded by the stigma, isolation, and invisibility associated with their work. These problems are even more severe for immigrants and for trafficked sex workers, most of whom fear deportation and already find it difficult to obtain mainstream employment. Because immigrant women are among the most disenfranchised in the United States, they are more likely to engage in sex work to guarantee their livelihood. Although this is a hard population to reach, increased research is needed to explore the phenomenon of sex work in the lives of immigrant women to help develop social policies and initiatives that can better support immigrant women and that will present them with other alternatives to gain a livelihood when they migrate.

Sexual and Reproductive Health

Latina/os face a variety of sexual and reproductive health circumstances that are impacted by their race, class, citizenship status, gender, and sexuality. Latina/os identify a large range of issues that fall under the rubric of sexual and reproductive rights. For Latinas, reproductive justice not only includes comprehensive, accessible, age-appropriate information about sexuality and reproductive control but also the right to the physical, emotional, spiritual, and economic means to parent (or not) children. In a "first-ever" report on Latinas and reproductive health, for example, the Latino Issues Forum conducted seven focus groups in Latina/o communities in California during an eight-month period. Although the findings were limited to certain regions of the state and the study was clearly biased toward heterosexuals, the participants identified several important problem areas related to sexuality and reproductive health:

1. a lack of education and information on sexual and reproductive health issues;
2. the need for open dialogue on these issues;
3. the need for more information and tools for parent-child discussions;
4. sexually transmitted diseases and HIV/AIDS;

5. limiting unwanted pregnancy, especially teenage pregnancy; and
6. reproductive health cancers.[10]

Migration similarly affects the sexual and reproductive health of hetero-sexual Latina/os. In a study conducted by the National Council of La Raza, participants in four focus groups across the nation cited immigration issues as one of the most significant factors deterring them from having a healthy sexual life. Immigrant women and men face many circumstances that hinder their access to sexual and reproductive health care information and services because of constant changes in national public health programs. Bureaucratic efforts to establish and verify citizenship status make immigrants hesitate to seek treatment, for fear that they will be deported. Moreover, the costs of health care make it unaffordable for many, particularly because a majority of female immigrants do not have insurance coverage. Latinas have a higher rate of being uninsured than women from any other racial or ethnic group. In 2002 43 percent of Latinos, 25 percent of whites, and 26 percent of low-income African Americans were uninsured across the nation.[11] In recent years state legislative efforts have severely limited health care and other publicly funded social services. As a result, immigrant women do not receive adequate reproductive health care, including cervical cancer and breast cancer screening and treatment, family planning services, HIV/AIDS testing and treatment, or accurate sex education. Many immigrants receive their health care at community clinics that provide free or low-cost reproductive health care. Because these community clinics are often government-funded, they are subject to policies requiring clients to document their citizenship, and Medicaid funding for treatment provided to undocumented immigrants is limited. Much more information about how these factors influence Latina/o sexual health is needed to develop policy that can enhance the resources available to these communities.

While Latin American countries are often believed to be more stringent in regard to reproductive politics, in the United States a number of social policies contemporarily work to impact the sexual and reproductive health of Latinas. For Latina/os to truly be able to realize sexual and reproductive justice, for example, they need access not only to comprehensive, age-appropriate information about sexuality and reproductive options at all stages of the life course but also to the physical, emotional, spiritual, and economic means to parent children. Thus adoption legislation, health care access, and childcare are all policy issues that could be considered important in relation to Latina/o sexuality. Academics and policy advocates agree that the reproductive and sexual health of Latina/os is in a dire state. The National Latina Institute for Reproductive Health states that "Latinas are facing a serious health care crisis that threatens to undermine the reproductive health and overall well-being of themselves, their families and their communities. Despite the growing number of uninsured Latinas and the significant health disparities they face, health policy makers have paid little attention to the reproductive health needs of Latinas. Against this backdrop, we are also witnessing an onslaught of attacks on the reproductive freedom of women in this country that will no doubt disproportionately impact Latinas."[12]

Moreover, although U.S. Latinas already account for one in every seven American women of reproductive age, Latina immigrants are less likely to receive adequate reproductive health care, including annual Pap smears, contraceptives, HIV treatment, and sex education. While we are beginning to collect more information about the actual health status of Latinas in relation to each of these issues, a better understanding of their comprehensive reproductive health experiences is needed.

Although epidemiological data are helpful in locating the primary areas of concern for Latina/o communities, the incidence of contraceptive behavior and disease contraction must be put in a much broader context. We need to know how Latina/os come to understand their reproductive and sexual behavior, attitudes, and health, where they learn to seek care, what their experiences are in health care facilities, and how they follow through with treatment. Moreover, a more complete picture of the sexual and reproductive health experiences and circumstances for individuals from their youth into their adulthood—a life span perspective—could be helpful in designing complementary policies that support women and men throughout their lifetime.

Socioeconomic Conditions and Challenges to Access

Uninsured Latinas often have no other recourse but to delay or forgo needed health care because they simply cannot afford to pay for such services. The uninsured, and particularly Latina immigrants, are more likely to delay treatment, to fail to fill prescriptions, or to go without important preventive medical procedures. This fact disproportionately determines their reproductive and sexual health. Cervical cancer, for instance, disproportionately affects Latinas, who have the second-highest rate of death from the disease after African American women. The rate of cervical cancer among Latinas is twice that of non-Latina white women, up to three times higher for Puerto Rican and Mexican American women. Yet Latinas' knowledge about human papillomavirus (HPV) and cervical cancer is very low. One study found that Latinas' fear of learning the results of a Pap test (or Pap smear) and their inability to communicate with their health care provider in Spanish are more likely to deter their seeking the screening than non-Latina respondents. Other studies have found that believing that the test would be painful and not knowing where to go to receive a Pap test were associated with never having the test.[13]

In general, Latinas are more likely than African American or non-Latina white women to delay health care appointments because of lack of transportation or child care, and they often report being dissatisfied with their visits to sexual and reproductive health care providers. Although it is a bit dated, one of the only studies actually to assess the experiences of Latinas found that only 51.5 percent felt comfortable at their most recent family planning clinic visit and even fewer reported that medical practitioners were concerned about their needs. The fact that most doctors are not Spanish speakers and do not have the requisite cultural knowledge to communicate sensitively and effectively with their Latina patients amplifies the many obstacles to accessing adequate health care. These factors are crucial to account for in the development of policy initiatives that can help increase Latinas' access to culturally proficient sexual and reproductive health treatment. Moreover, increased understanding of the variations that exist among Latinas is necessary as preliminary research has indicated that differences exist, not only among primary Latina/o subgroups but also in generation, education, and other social variables.[14]

One additional place where this significantly touches Latinas is access to prenatal care, which is an essential service to help women have healthy pregnancies. Latinas are less likely to receive prenatal care than women in most other ethnic groups. Historically, there have been initiatives to curb Latinas' access to prenatal care. For example, in 1997 California governor Pete Wilson issued regulations to eliminate prenatal care for more than 70,000 undocumented women in the state. For low-income Latinas and others who do not have health insurance coverage, prenatal care visits may provide an opportunity to obtain screenings for diseases and preventive care.[15] For some low-income Latinas, public funding may be the only viable source for prenatal care and other important health care services. However, federal policies increasingly limit prenatal care for undocumented immigrants. We do not yet have concrete data that help us understand how these existing social policies determine the sexual and reproductive decision making of Latina/os.

In the past decade, anti-immigrant efforts have had the unfortunate effect of further reducing access to needed health services.[16] In 1994 Proposition 187, a ballot initiative in California, proposed to bar undocumented children from public schools and turn away undocumented students from state colleges and universities. It also would have denied undocumented immigrants public benefits and social services, including prenatal and preventive care. While the proposition was passed by a majority of California voters, it was since opposed by immigrant advocates and was quickly deemed unconstitutional by a federal judge. Nevertheless, this proposition was part of a wave of assaults on immigrant communities in California and throughout the nation. Arizona has passed similar legislation, Proposition 200, that currently bans immigrants from receiving public health services in the state.

Welfare reform legislation enacted in the mid-1990s specifically affected the sexual and reproductive experiences of low-income and immigrant women. The federal Personal Responsibility and Work Opportunity and Reconciliation Act (PRWORA) of 1996 is the most restrictive welfare reform policy in the nation to date. Ostensibly legislation that would benefit low-income women, in practice these initiatives worked to deter out-of-wedlock births and to promote two-parent marriages and ultimately legislated particular types of sexual relations for low-income women. PRWORA included such requirements as family cap provisions, which deny women benefits for any of their children if they bear another child while on public assistance *except* if they agree to be sterilized or use other long-term methods of birth control. Under PRWORA "illegitimacy rewards" of $20 million were granted by the federal government to the top five states that prevent and reduce the number of out-of-wedlock births (with no increase in abortion rates) to end families' dependence on government assistance. Such provisions promote sexuality within monogamous, marriage-based relationships while undercutting nonmarital sexuality and out-of-wedlock childbearing. This legislation also reinforced the illegitimacy of nontraditional families such as many single-parent households or cohabiting same-sex couples by strictly defining marriage as the legal union of a man and a woman.[17]

Current welfare laws also limit options for sex education for low-income women, as they promote abstinence-only approaches, with sex (assumed to be heterosexual intercourse) being acceptable only after marriage. Through these measures, the government influences the personal reproductive choices of women as well as their sexual and reproductive behavior. These measures could be considered coercive for women by requiring them to use long-term or permanent methods that are not in their control. Such reforms severely infringe on a woman's right to make decisions regarding sexuality and procreation free from governmental interference and financial constraint. PRWORA also specifically affected immigrant women because previously available Medicaid benefits were limited to five years for those who immigrated after 1996. The result has been that women who fall under these circumstances experience limited access to family planning and prenatal care services. Together, welfare reform and immigration reform have severely curtailed the ability of low-income women, especially Latinas, to participate in safety-net programs such as Medicaid. A perhaps not unintended consequence of these initiatives is the regulation of the sexual and reproductive behavior of all low-income women, particularly undocumented Latina immigrants.

Research is needed that seeks to understand the actual effects that these measures have on the sexual and reproductive lives of Latinas and their partners. Latina/os' willingness to discuss sex and family planning is increasing. In separate studies conducted by the Latino Issues Forum and the National Council of La Raza each found a consensus among participants that there are both a desire and need to increase outreach and education about issues of reproduction and sexuality in the Latino community.[18]

Abortion

The current battle over abortion rights in the United States is a major area of policy discussion that greatly affects the sexual and reproductive lives of Latinas.

There is insufficient academic or advocacy research available on the decision making, attitudes, or experiences related to abortion of Latinas, particularly immigrants. However, existing research does suggest that Latinas, especially those who are not immigrants themselves, are more favorable toward abortion than commonly believed. Through analysis of data from the Latino National Political Survey, Bolks et al. found that there is no difference between the variables that influence the abortion attitudes of Mexican Americans, Puerto Ricans, and Cubans and those of other groups in the nation.[19] Moreover, although there is a slightly greater tendency of Latina/os to oppose abortion altogether, the distribution of their attitudes toward abortion reflects that of the general U.S. population. The results from this study also suggest some differences in the attitudes toward abortion among Latino groups, with Cuban Americans being significantly more likely than Mexican Americans to support abortion rights.[20]

Research has also determined that Latinas have abortion procedures in disproportionate numbers, and although their rates are lower than those of African American women, they are higher than those of non-Latina white women. There are, however, few studies that explore the circumstances and complexities of these higher rates of abortion and the ramifications for Latina women's lives. The available research evidence suggests that Latinas carrying unintended pregnancies face a number of obstacles to obtaining an abortion, including limited resources, language and cultural differences with providers and health care practitioners, and lack of information about abortion services.[21] High rates of poverty, coupled with limited public funding, make it difficult for many Latinas to access abortion. The Hyde Amendment (1976), which prohibits federal funding of abortion, means that many low-income women cannot afford abortion services. Even where Medicaid funds to pay for abortion services are available, there are often lengthy processes that must be followed that may prevent a woman from acquiring the means to pay for the abortion in a timely manner.

The situation for many Latinas is particularly precarious because, in addition to these barriers, some immigrants have lived in countries where abortion is illegal in most or all cases. Consequently, limited access and information, or misunderstanding about abortion laws in the United States, have led some Latina immigrants to use off-label prescription medications to self-induce abortions. There is growing documentation that Latinas are self-aborting with a variety of methods, perhaps because they are unaware that abortion is legal in the United States or because it is less expensive than other options. Some women obtain medication that induces abortion from Central or South America or at their local bodegas. For many years, Latina immigrants in New York City have purchased the ulcer-treating medication Misoprostol® in order to use it to induce abortions.[22] This practice is more common in Latin America, where abortion is restricted. Latina immigrants, especially young Latinas, need more and better information about preventing pregnancy and improved access to safe and affordable abortion services. Scholars, service providers, and advocates must continue to understand the significance of abortion in Latina lives in order to push for policy that meets their needs appropriately.

While poverty and lack of resources are obvious factors, the context and experiences of Latinas vis-à-vis abortion must be explored further in order to understand why, how, when, and where Latinas have abortions and their experiences at every level to begin to develop the conditions necessary to prescribe social policy. Latinas who want to have access to abortion have expressed the serious need for services that are confidential from family and friends.[23] Because it is largely assumed that Latinas do not have abortions or support pro-choice attitudes, they are often left out of policy discussions. Increased research is needed to gauge and analyze the various attitudes and practices among these communities.

Women Who Have Sex with Women

The amount of research on the specific reproductive health needs of Latina lesbians and bisexuals, as well as transgender individuals, is minuscule. What limited research exists has shown that such Latinas face multiple barriers to health care access, and they may be at higher risk for certain reproductive health problems. A recent study of self-identified lesbian and bisexual women of color living in Los Angeles, California, for example, revealed that Latina lesbians and bisexuals are less likely to have a regular source of care and have lower rates of preventive care and higher rates of health risk behaviors (among them, obesity and alcohol and tobacco use) than heterosexual Latinas. The higher rates of breast and cervical cancer among lesbian Latinas, compared to heterosexual Latinas, are also related to inadequate preventive care. One study found that only 67.9 percent of Latina lesbians reported having a Pap test in the previous two years, compared to 80.6 percent of Latina heterosexuals. Similarly, 66.2 percent of Latina lesbians reported receiving a clinical breast exam within the two years before the survey, compared to 75.7 percent of Latina heterosexuals.[24] Clearly for lesbian and queer women, additional structural and cultural challenges influence their reproductive and sexual health. Although these issues are further explored in other chapters of this volume, it is important to reiterate here that further research is sorely needed.

Research Priorities

The foregoing review demonstrates that we are in dire need of research on which to base comprehensive policies that will ensure sexual and reproductive health of Latina/o communities. Research is needed from a variety of disciplinary and interdisciplinary perspectives to allow for a thorough understanding of the various elements of Latina/o sexuality and the social context and existing policies that set the context. Consideration should be given to the sexual attitudes, practices, and needs of Latina/o communities and the factors that influence them. A better understanding of these subjects can make significant inroads in identifying the structural and cultural changes necessary to ensure better health care provision for Latinas and Latinos.

This will be no easy task, as research must be increased on a number of levels in order to gain a complex assessment that can effectively inform the development of social policies that benefit the sexual health of Latina/o communities. Large-scale quantitative data collection and analysis that allow for a general understanding of broad trends in the Latina/o population and also allow investigation into the subgroups of the community need to be improved. As of now, few studies, and in particular large-scale national samples, even account for Latina/o subgroups, and those that do, do not provide community-level data or account for the great diversity in Latina/o attitudes and experiences. As in the case of Latina/os' attitudes toward abortion, there are significant differences among attitudes and experiences of Latina/o subgroups, so large-scale data collection must better account for and enable assessment of these nuances. To develop effective policy, these data will have to be representative of the Latina/o population in the United States and account for regional, generational, citizenship, and the myraid other differences that exist within Latina/o communities.

Quantitative data analysis can only help us see the general contours of trends within Latina/o communities. We also need a more detailed understanding of the daily lived realities of Latina/os across the United States. Only qualitative, ethnographic, and local studies can provide the contextual and intimate information necessary to inform the design and implementation of programs that will truly have an impact on the sexual and reproductive lives of individuals and communities. Ideally, research should strive to be participatory and to include not just policymakers but community members and those who can help shape and implement the study and put the findings of the research into action.

Historical analysis can also contribute to the development of policy over time, and particular attention should be paid to how Latina/o communities have responded to previous policy efforts designed to alter their sexual and reproductive behaviors. Moreover, increased research is needed to demonstrate how discriminatory policies have impinged on their lives and how Latina/os have responded to previous legislative efforts. The study of sterilization abuse in Latina communities, for example, provides evidence of how formal and informal state policies directly led to the termination of Latinas' childbearing. However, it is also crucial to note that Latinas are not passive victims of such attempts, but active in the process of policy development and implementation.[25]

Longitudinal research will allow scholars and analysts to understand the range of issues surrounding sexuality across the life span and to shape the long-term outcomes of particular practices and policies. We know much about the sexual attitudes and contraceptive practices of Latina/o youth, primarily through research driven by the effort to eliminate teen pregnancy in this community, whereas we have much less information on the sexual and reproductive health attitudes, experiences, practices, and needs of adult Latina/os. Ultimately, a more comprehensive analysis of how Latina/os experience their sexuality over the life span and the ability to understand those attitudes, practices, and needs in a broad social context is necessary for the understanding of both how social policies currently impact the reproductive and sexual lives of Latina/os and how policy can be garnered to be more beneficial to their communities.

Conclusion

Beyond the needs of academic scholarship, a much greater effort must be made to foster research on the various issues related to Latino sexuality so that advocacy groups can begin to develop their agendas and policy recommendations based on solid information. Nongovernmental organizations that work to achieve rights to sexual and reproductive justice for Latina/os directly face a dearth of data regarding the reproductive and sexual health of this community. Their advocacy efforts are often stunted by the lack of information available upon which to design agendas. Further data collection on sexuality is essential to design community outreach and intervention strategies, as well as to institute legislation and policies that will benefit Latina/os. Research and advocacy must be designed and implemented to effect policy change at the federal, state, and local levels. The adoption of a social justice perspective allows for the integration of various policy arenas under one rubric with the aim of achieving the full range of options necessary to reach reproductive health equality for Latina/os, their families, and their communities.

7

Heterosexuality Exposed

Some Feminist Sociological Reflections on Heterosexual Sex and Romance in U.S. Latina/o Communities

GLORIA GONZÁLEZ-LÓPEZ

"Why aren't you in a relationship? Haven't you found the right man?" I have been asked these questions countless times by some of my relatives, some close friends on both sides of the U.S.-Mexico border, and a few self-identified progressive women and men colleagues studying gender and romantic relationships across disciplines. As I have spent extended periods of my adult life without a romantic partner, others have additionally inquired with a tone of sadness, "Don't you trust men? Are you divorced? Hmmm . . . Maybe you are, and I do not know about it! For a Mexican woman, isn't it kind of odd that you have never been married?" While engaging in these conversations with complete honesty, I have always enjoyed the endless curiosity both parties experience as these exchanges unfold. At the same time, these dialogues have transformed my persona into a kind of "Latina sex and romance Rorschach" that stimulates emotional reactions, opinions, and questions exploring Latin American cultures and societies; Mexican beliefs and practices with regard to love, dating, and sex; and what U.S. Latina/os may expect from their romantic exchanges.

My conversations with relatives and friends about my relationship history reflect in part some of the concerns the average person may eventually express if she or he were to engage in a dialogue with a childless, never-married Mexican immigrant woman who is already in her forties. And while to my various interlocutors I have at times identified myself as "historically heterosexual," they have rarely explored what I might mean by this expression as they lead the conversation back to heterosexual dating and marriage (at a certain age) as the avenue promising happiness, personal stability, and emotional well-being. In these dialogues, it is even more fascinating to observe that some who criticize social norms and regulations still do not escape from reproducing the very idealized expectations and stereotypes illustrated above and reproduced in contemporary society.

This essay offers some feminist sociological reflections with regard to the social and cultural ways in which U.S. Latina/o communities have reproduced and maintain heterosexuality as the norm controlling the sexual and romantic lives of their members. In this essay I present

1. a reflection of the dominant paradigms in the literature with regard to U.S. Latinas and their experiences of heterosexual love and sex;
2. an analysis of the ways in which coming-of-age passages represent social rituals of heterosexual initiation; and
3. an examination of the ways in which race relations and heterosexuality have interacted to promote both white racial and heterosexual supremacy in U.S. Latina/o communities.

Finally, I submit some reflections for future research and policy implications with regard to these populations' experiences of heterosexual love and sex.

Latina/o Cultures, Heterosexual Love, and Sex

In U.S. Latina/o popular and academic publications, different dimensions of heterosexual relationships have been examined from two contrasting and opposing perspectives. The first perspective is the oldest and traditional tendency in the literature. Machos, virgins, and whores; machismo and marianismo; Catholic guilt and religion; *familismo* and personalism; and acculturation (among other overused concepts and paradigms) all have become rigid and monolithic categories of analysis in this body of research and theory.[1] In these publications, a so-called Latino culture (or Hispanic culture) has similarly become an emblematic and problematic concept. In recent years, this concept has promoted a pan-Latina/o identity and inspired political organizing that is informed by identity politics in the United States.[2] When not used carefully, however, this concept has become a theoretical fiction that overlooks the heterogeneity and multiplicity of Latina/o cultures, and inter- and intragroup diversity of expressions, national and ethnic identities, and communities within both the United States and Latin America.[3] These concepts and paradigms have dominated the prolific literature in the behavioral sciences, epidemiology and public health disciplines, and scholarship on Latinas and Latinos and HIV/AIDS.

Culture-based concepts and paradigms were introduced decades ago in order to examine different aspects of the sexual experiences of these populations (assumed in general to be heterosexual) from—ironically—"culturally sensitive" perspectives. They have become highly respected, and in my first publication I could not escape from reproducing some of these ideas, which I revised and corrected later.[4] These analytical categories and concepts (frequently identified as "cultural factors") deserve equal analytical attention. In this essay, however, I focus on what I consider to be two of the most challenging paradigms: machismo and marianismo.[5] Machismo is frequently identified as an accentuated expression of masculinity in Latin American men, one that promotes sexist attitudes and behaviors. Machismo's heterosexual partner marianismo seems to be used less often (and at times it is not known) in Latin American academic circles examining the lives of women. As an idea, Evelyn Stevens coined this term in the early 1970s while arguing that women of Latin American origin internalize values represented by the Virgin Mary. As part of this process, women are trained to value self-sacrifice, pain, and suffering and to accept sexism as part of their experience. Based on this framework, the representation of the sex lives of Latinas is identified as follows: "Marianismo refers to Latino cultural expectations that include the spiritual and moral superiority of women, and encourage Latinas to be virginal, seductive, privately wise, publicly humble, fragile, and yet, provide the glue that holds the family together."[6]

Matthew C. Gutmann and I offer a critique with regard to this analytical pattern in the literature:

> If a Mexican man, for instance, is abusive and aggressive, he will be labeled a macho. If a Mexican woman quietly endures such an abusive relationship, her behavior is automatically examined within the *marianismo* paradigm. But if a white man and a white woman display similar behavior, they are seldom analyzed in so cavalier and simplistic a fashion. What is more, frequently these traits of machismo and *marianismo* are pegged in particular to working class men and women, as if those from the middle and upper strata were too sophisticated for their lives to be captured by such crude academic groupings. As theoretical categories, therefore, machismo and *marianismo* are not only culturally chauvinist but elitist as well. The machismo-*marianismo* paradigm represented an expression of the widespread intellectual colonial mentality in the behavioral and social sciences that remained dominant and unchallenged for far too long.[7]

Interestingly, research by Jeanette Rodríguez with Catholic Mexicanas shows that some of them may experience feelings of empowerment in their relationships with the Virgin of Guadalupe, an icon of Mexican national identity for many immigrants from Mexico. I myself have witnessed Mexican immigrant women carrying iconographic images or statuette replicas of the Virgin of Guadalupe while screaming, shouting, and protesting at immigrant rights rallies opposing Proposition 187 in 1994 in California and during the May 1, 2006, national boycotts and public demonstrations. Paradoxically, marianismo as a concept and a paradigm is still used across disciplines in order to explain many aspects associated with the disempowerment that U.S. Latinas may experience within their families and their relationships with men, as illustrated in the behavioral sciences, in the HIV/AIDS literature, and in cultural studies.[8]

Thus, the most serious concerns the use of these concepts represent for a critical understanding of Latina/os and their heterosexual relationships include

1. the theoretical fiction they promote,
2. the empirical inaccuracies they reflect,
3. the damaging stereotypical images and misrepresentations they portray, and
4. the racism and classism they reproduce.

In addition, an overemphasis on what have been identified as "cultural factors" risks neglecting socioeconomics, unique historical contexts, and other social forces shaping the personal and sex lives of these diverse groups. These paradigms are at risk of overlooking the historical, political, and socioeconomic forces shaping the lives of many adult women and men who have migrated from Latin American countries, those who have been colonized (such as Puerto Ricans), and the indigenous and mestizo populations with historical roots in the U.S. Southwest regions that once belonged to Mexico.[9]

The above concerns have been addressed in the second trend in the literature, which has emerged in the social sciences within the last ten to fifteen years. This body of knowledge argues that, even though cultural factors may become important to an examination of U.S. Latina/o groups' heterosexual lives, a more critical view across disciplines is necessary to develop comprehensive examinations of different aspects of their experiences of heterosexual sex and romance. Inspired and informed by social science scholarship, these research projects with U.S. Latina/o populations aim at exploring—beyond "culture"—the following areas, among other related topics: women's and men's experiences of heterosexual love within frameworks that examine gender relationships across generations and before and after migrating; initiation of heterosexual sex; desire and emotional dimensions of heterosexual sex and paradoxes of experiencing pleasure; contradictions and tensions between mothers and daughters with regard to premarital sex and virginity; socioeconomics, psychosexual development, and everyday life interactions and contexts; migration and sexual violence against women; women, Catholic religion, and sex; and heterosexuality in the context of migration, incorporation, and settlement processes.[10]

This essay is inspired by this emerging critical intellectual perspective in the field of Latina/o sexualities and by my training as a sociologist who studies gender and sexuality in Mexican populations. From an angle informed by feminism and sociology, I examine the ways in which heterosexuality has been socially constructed as the norm and the institution regulating the sex lives of these groups. However, I am challenged by the fact that critical examinations of U.S. Latina/os and heterosexuality across disciplines have not been able to document the complex heterogeneity and increasingly visible demographic presence of different Latina/o groups. While grappling with this demand, I hope to unmask some of the social forces that have created and perpetuated the idealized expectation of heterosexual love and sex across these communities and thereby expose Latina/o heterosexualities.[11]

Social Norms and Cultures of Heterosexuality
in U.S. Latina/o Communities

"Isn't heterosexuality the way it is supposed to be? Why do you have to say that it was a heterosexual love story?" a Mexican friend asked me with a frown of curiosity on her face during an informal conversation about what each of us had done over the weekend. I was explaining to her that I had rented and watched a few Latin American movies, one of which included a "heterosexual love story."

Heterosexuality as the norm that is taken for granted is not only well ingrained in the perceptions of love and romance of my good friend; it is the dominant belief defining mainstream ideologies in Western and Western-ized societies. The idea of heterosexual sex and romance as something that is "natural"—and thus automatically assumed and in no need of identifica-tion or examination as such—has produced groundbreaking examinations of heterosexuality as a political institution controlling women's lives, as well as contributions exploring and documenting historical and sociological analyses of heterosexuality.[12] These intellectual projects have inspired and informed my own work with self-identified heterosexual Mexican immigrant women and men and their sexual and romantic experiences within the context of immigration and socioeconomic and racial marginality in the city of Los Angeles.

As in all Western and Westernized societies, *heteronormativity* has estab-lished heterosexuality as the privileged expression of sexuality. Heteronormativ-ity refers to the norms and institutions, regulations and constraints that shape and control the sexualized feelings and emotions; desires and fantasies, beliefs, attitudes, and behaviors; and identities and everyday life interactions of people who live in a given social context in which heterosexuality has become estab-lished as the idealized and expected form of sexuality.[13] Within some Latina/o communities (mainly of Mexican origin), this regulatory framework has become better understood thanks to Chicana lesbian texts documenting romance, sex, family life, religion, cultural beliefs and practices, and different forms of social inequality (such as racism) as central to a grasp of heterosexuality as a social institution. Autobiographical/theoretical texts by Gloria E. Anzaldúa and Cherríe Moraga, Emma Pérez, and Carla Trujillo denounce the ways in which heteronormativity has become the social and cultural organizer of U.S. Latina women's sex lives, desires, and lust within social and cultural contexts and mainstream society.[14]

With its cultural roots in both pre-Hispanic and Spanish societies and throughout more than five hundred years, heterosexual love and sex became part of a project of nation-state building in very selective ways across Latin American soil, part of which now belongs to the United States. In pre-Hispanic Mexico, for instance, women and men who engaged in same-sex sexual activi-ties were the object of social condemnation; women who had sex with other women (known as "*patlache*") experienced social stigma and rejection. In colonial society, indigenous women and men were asked in confession about same-sex sexual activities as a sin that is committed "against nature [*pecado contra natura*]." And in sixteenth-century Nueva Galicia (a vast region of what is now western Mexico), many trials took place to prosecute women for engaging with other women in relationships that were identified as "*raras* [rare, odd, strange]."[15]

Although same-sex civil unions became legal in Mexico City (in late 2006) and the northern state of Coahuila (in early 2007), Catholic values and practices, patriarchal states and institutions, and hetero- and procreative-oriented popular cultures, values, practices, and belief systems remain strong. U.S. Latina/os with roots in Mexico and other Latin American nations have been socially and culturally exposed to a state- and church-sanctioned heteronormativity, a social process that situates heterosexuality as a social institution and the ideal form of sexual activity.

The Latin American immigrants who have been exposed to heteronormative values and practices are the potential parents of future generations of U.S. Latina/os; however, the sex lives of this younger generation being raised in the United States are shaped by a series of complex forces quite distinct from what these Latina/os experienced decades earlier in their places of origin.[16] *United* by common historical, cultural, social, linguistic, and socioeconomic roots, but *divided* by the historical and political uniqueness of each region and nation, each one of the Latina/o cultures that has emerged on U.S. soil invites a critical view of their sex lives—in this case, their heterosexual experiences. With this critical awareness, I examine some of the traditional practices that have been documented with regard to U.S. Latina/o youths, hoping this will spark new reflections and research. Next, I discuss the most relevant socially and culturally constructed heteronormative beliefs and practices of sexuality in these Latina/o communities and contexts.

Becoming Heterosexual: Sexualized Rites of Passage

Adolescent women and men coming to maturity in U.S. Latina/o communities go through their coming-of-age experiences within racialized, meaningful heteronormative traditions. Not all U.S. Latina/o groups follow these rituals, however, and not all Latin American countries uniformly reproduced them either. Even so, they have become cultural traditions in many U.S. Latina/o immigrant communities. *La quinceañera* (the fifteenth birthday celebration of an adolescent woman) is an emblematic illustration.[17] La quinceañera as a gendered and sexualized cultural rite of passage has been examined by social scientists.[18] Traditionally, the celebration includes a thanksgiving Mass or religious ceremony (originally Catholic but other Christians may have an equivalent religious service) and a formal ball. This involves a heterosexual protocol: the presence of the proud mother and father of the young woman, a court of fourteen maids of honor (*damas*) and their fourteen young male escorts (*chambelanes*), and an additional *chambelán* to accompany the actual quinceañera.

In this rite of passage, the adolescent girl symbolically becomes a young woman—*la joven* or *la señorita*.[19] In this expensive, gendered celebration, an adolescent Latina goes through a cultural and ethnic process of becoming a quasi woman—a quinceañera is not a woman yet.[20] With this understanding, she is socially initiated into heterosexuality as the norm of romance and dating. The idealized image of the quinceañera is the woman who is accompanied by a man who may be (or become) her boyfriend, and the same is potentially possible for each one her damas.[21]

Heterosexuality as the idealized social norm is celebrated and stimulated through this rite, but it also is repressed. Heterosexuality promotes paradoxes, contradictions, and double morality messages. In this romanticized arrangement, the event portrays a woman whose femininity is traditionally emphasized by being dressed up in pink and who is potentially ready to date and fall in love with a man (ideally—but not yet) and to get married (ideally—but not yet). In a sexualized ritual of potential courtship that resembles a wedding, she is expected to be a virgin or, in the most flexible scenario, to be knowledgeable of contraceptive methods that can protect her from potential pregnancy and its negative consequences.[22]

While this description presents the standard protocol, the real-life experiences of a quinceañera may vary. As illustrated in *Quinceañera* (a low-budget film produced and directed by Wash Westmoreland and Richard Glatzer in 2005), Magdalena is the pregnant quinceañera-to-be who learns it will be possible to have the emblematic celebration only after a gynecologist confirms for her father (via her mother) that an improbable sexual exchange got her pregnant without compromising her virtue as a virgin. Magdalena's uncle Carlos, a young gay man, eventually becomes the respectable family figure who accompanies his niece to her non-Catholic religious ceremony, and who voluntarily accepts responsibility for the financial future of Magdalena's child.

Although U.S. Latina/o communities and Spanish-speaking countries and societies are predominantly homophobic, humanized images of gay men such as Carlos are gradually becoming central in Spanish-speaking movies and telenovelas. The Mexican telenovela *La vida en el espejo* (1999) became popular for openly portraying the story of an upper-middle-class, well-educated young gay man. In contrast, lesbian women characters remain marginalized, devalued, objectified, hypersexualized, or simply invisible in these popular cultural productions.[23] To the best of my knowledge, Mexican telenovelas—aimed at female audiences— have never displayed lesbian romance as a central theme in their stories. As I walked out of the theater after watching *Quinceañera* with these reflections in mind, I thought about what the unthinkable would look like in real life, or on the small or big screen: a *lesbian* quinceañera. A provocative disruption to the heteronormative social function of the ritual would include fifteen couples of young women. A more fluid option includes a *queer* quinceañera, in which young women may freely have partners of their sexual orientation.

While young women take part in more public and romanticized rituals of heterosexuality (such as the quinceañera), young men often undergo more intimate and at times violent expressions of heterosexual initiation. For some young Latino men, social initiation into heterosexuality may involve (voluntary and involuntary) sexual contact with a woman. Research in the social sciences has examined this pattern in the experiences of adult Latin American immigrant men who report being forced during their early teens into sexual initiation with a sex worker—a stigmatized, objectified, devalued, and marginalized expression of womanhood. In this ritualized experience, the purpose is to initiate a young boy into a form of manhood that is patriarchal and heterosexual. The ritual emphasizes the importance of using sexuality in order to become a man: manhood is asserted and constructed through a ritual of coercive heterosexual sex. In this scenario, an older male relative takes a young boy (usually an adolescent) to a brothel to have his first sexual experience with a woman considerably older than the young man. In my research with Mexican immigrants, I have learned that men who have lived this kind of experience may associate these first sexual encounters with emotional responses of different intensity, including fear, anger, pain, confusion, and anxiety (see *Erotic Journeys*). This ritual of initiation into heterosexual manhood shows that in some patriarchal contexts, not only women but men as well are vulnerable to a social expectation of sexual availability (to older men and women) in order to reproduce heterosexuality in compulsory but also painful ways.[24]

Finally, the most perverse aspect of this practice is the fact that some parents and older brothers may use this ritual as a corrective measure against homosexuality.[25] And in extreme cases, heterosexual initiation under coercion as a homophobic practice has been used with women as well. While conducting an ongoing project in Mexico, I learned from a lesbian rights activist about the sexual violence some young lesbian women are exposed to within the family context. In one particular case, when the family of a lesbian woman learned about her sexual orientation, her parents hired a policeman to have sex with their daughter. By hiring a man who could "make her a real woman," the parents thought they could "fix" the sexual orientation of their daughter. With this hope in mind, the young woman's parents set up the sexual encounter. She resisted; the man raped her.

The extent to which these kinds of experiences are selectively reproduced or contested for younger generations of U.S. Latina/o youth should be part of a research agenda for scholars designing future research projects on these issues and concerns.

Racialized Heterosexualities: Heteroromance and Race

Empirical research on interracial heteroromance, dating, and marriage involving Latina/o populations is invisible in sexuality research. And even though thought-provoking awareness with regard to conducting empirical research on heterosexuality and privilege within contexts of racial difference is emerging, romance and race relationships are still limited to white and black interactions in sociological sexualities research.[26]

U.S. Latina/o heteronormativities are racialized—that is, race relations shape these groups' beliefs, practices, and experiences of heterosexuality as the ideal norm of sex and romance. The historical origins of these interactions, clashes, and reconciliations between both heteroromance and race are frequently associated with the colonial roots of Latin American nations. Race relations placed indigenous women in opposition to *mestizas* and also *españolas*, thus promoting a racist paradigm in which the latter (especially españolas) were identified with a higher social status.[27]

On the painful side, some indigenous women were raped and became impregnated by European conquistadores as part of a Catholic Church–sanctioned project of invasion and colonization. Spanish blood (which went hand and hand with higher class) also helped women from Spain to receive special protection in cases of rape. But racism and ethnocentric ideologies of cultural superiority placed both indigenous women and indigenous men in a devalued position in the social construction of sexual violence. These men were dehumanized and perceived as savages. From this perspective, as François Giraud convincingly argues, "the indigenous man is the only one that is a rapist because of his own indigenous nature. The indigenous woman, and even the wife of the indigenous man, sees that her word is devalued and therefore she cannot have a way to articulate a complaint." Giraud found that men who received more severe forms of punishment (including the death penalty) for rape were less frequently of Spanish blood than from such groups as mestizos, mulattoes, and indigenous people.[28]

Within but also beyond violent contexts, the first mestizas and mestizos were born from the indigenous and Spanish blood unions in the Americas, including that part of present U.S. territory that used to be Mexican soil. In countries where black women and men became part of these histories of colonization and racialized sexual interactions, mulattas and mulattoes were born. Migration from Asia, the Middle East, and other parts of Europe has further shaped these combinations selectively across nations and regions. In all of these processes, racism has created a "pigmentocracy," which has granted special social privileges to individuals with lighter skin.[29]

Thus, throughout history and within racist contexts, the limitless phenotype combinations that have emerged from the U.S. Southwest to Tierra del Fuego have created (in unique and local historical, economic, and political contexts) countless shades of skin colors, facial features, body types, Spanish accents and pronunciations, and linguistic expressions to distinguish these racialized identities. In the contemporary Spanish-speaking Americas, these racialized processes have been reproduced by, within, and through heteronormativity to fortify a form of privilege further reinforced by North American mainstream society: Eurocentric white supremacy.

The following anecdote, based on interracial love relationships I have personally witnessed more than once after migrating from Mexico to the U.S. Southwest in the mid-1980s, illustrates these dynamics. The story features a light-skinned Latina woman involved with an African American man, whom she later introduces to her family—the social institution regulating her sex life and romantic choices. She then becomes the target of "well-intentioned" comments of relatives and friends who meticulously evaluate every aspect of the romantic candidate in order to find out "sin tan siquiera el hombre vale la pena [is the man even worth it]." These scenes take place as relatives and friends advise her that, while dating and potentially marrying are important, to think about choosing a man good enough "para mejorar la raza [to improve the race]." Accordingly, if the same woman were to fall in love with a white man, she is less likely to be questioned about her romantic choice. Her love mate would be even more celebrated if he possessed the Western ideals of beauty or if his socioeconomic status (including education and material possessions) would help improve her current living conditions. In the former case, she would be "marrying down" racially, which is socially rejected and punished; in the latter scenario, she would be "marrying up" racially, which is socially accepted and celebrated.[30]

For a Latino man, interracial dating and romance are affected by racialized images of masculinity. A man may have the ethnic disadvantage, especially if his phenotype characteristics place him far from the quintessential expression of Westernized hegemonic masculinity—the idealized form of manhood in contemporary society. In order to "marry up" in terms of race, he needs to possess the cultural and social capital (such as a college education, high income, middle-class values, and the like) necessary to exchange and compensate for his racial marginality. One research project on Mexican American men found that marrying outside their ethnic group increased as these men's occupational status improved.[31]

In these and other potential scenarios, gender, race, and class relations intertwine and alternatively shape the experiences of heterosexual romance and marriage in Latina/o communities. The above illustrations may explain in part the findings of research projects on interracial marriage that indicate that U.S. Latinas marry white men more frequently than do their counterpart Latinos marry white women. Others have found that Latina/o populations with a history of African ancestry—and thus with darker skin, such as Puerto Ricans and Dominicans—are less likely to marry white people when compared to Latina/os of Cuban, Mexican, Central American, and South American origin.[32]

Interracial marriage research in the social sciences is mainly quantitative and based on "marital assimilation" perspectives, which identify Latina/o groups, assimilation, and their marriage (up) patterns with white populations.[33] The two examples I cite are clear-cut marriage down and up patterns. However, it is necessary to conduct qualitative research in order to explore the interactions, nuances, and complexities that emerge when one examines all the possible marital combinations between Latina/o populations, African Americans, Asian Americans, and other groups across and within a wide range of race, class, and phenotype diversity. Finally, it is especially crucial to examine these same dynamics when heterosexual romance takes place between U.S. Latina/o populations from different racial and national origins.

U.S. Latina/o heteronormativities within contexts of racialized identities that reinforce both heterosexuality and white supremacy have been reproduced and idealized through what Chrys Ingraham has called a "heterosexual imaginary." This concept refers to "a belief system that relies on romantic and sacred notions of heterosexuality in order to create and maintain the illusion of well-being."[34] This "heterosexual imaginary" has been dominant in Latin America and in U.S. Latina/o immigrant communities in the United States and other Westernized societies. Beyond these dominant sexual norms, some Mexicanas are going beyond the limits of heteronormativity in very creative ways. Recently, the linguistic imagination of Mexican women caught me by surprise.

Queering Heterosexuality: *Ser* versus *Estar* Heterosexual

"Y tú, ¿estás heterosexual? o ¿eres heterosexual?" a woman activist asked me during an animated personal conversation, part of my recent fieldwork in Mexico. *Estás* and *eres* come from stem verbs *estar* and *ser*, respectively, and while both mean "to be" in English, Spanish-speaking people use them selectively according to grammar rules that identify the temporary or permanent nature of the condition that is described in the sentence. My activist friend then explained that while she had been in heterosexual relationships in the past, she was in a lesbian relationship at present, and accordingly, she used the conjugation of *estar* in the first person while stating, "Ahora yo estoy lesbiana [Now, I am "temporarily" a lesbian]."

During the first twenty-six years of my life in Mexico, and later while visiting my family on a regular basis after migrating, this was the first time I was exposed to this creative pattern of language use, sexuality, and relationships. So in my conversations with other activists working on sexuality-related issues and themes, I asked about the emergence and prevalence of this pattern in contemporary Mexico. Some of these activists replied that, while this pattern is not widely used, some "liberated" women engage in this creative speech in order to explain the ways in which they can justify their blurring of the borders of heterosexuality.

These recent experiences became an invitation to reflect on the status of contemporary research on heterosexuality and U.S. Latinas. I thought of the ways in which Mexicanas use the unique nature of the Spanish language to conjugate their sex lives in "queer" ways that allow them to preserve some fluidity with regard to their desires, fantasies, behaviors, and identities. I wondered about other unknown ways in which women might be using language *to queer* heterosexuality within this contextualized fluidity. I revisited the publications in which lesbian Chicana writers have offered their *auto-historias* and cultural examinations of traditional texts to dissect heteronormativity and the problems that emerge with regard to the traditionally polarized categories of heterosexual versus homosexual. I kept thinking of the need to document the voices of self-identified heterosexual women who from their standpoint and real-life experiences are engaging in the many symbolic ways to go from "ser" to "estar" (and vice versa) in their fluid explorations of sexualized fantasies, desires, emotions, behaviors, relationships, and identities.[35]

Shortly after learning about the *ser* versus *estar* conjugation of romantic relationships in the life of my Mexican activist friend, I engaged in an interesting conversation with another colleague and friend in Mexico. He said, "Based on your research, what does a sexually emancipated Latina look like?" As I recalled the life experiences of the forty immigrant women I interviewed more than ten years ago in Los Angeles, I considered the sexual fears, emotional challenges, and moral discomfort that most of them expressed when relationships with men were discussed and also when lesbian sex was part of our conversations. Then I wondered what these informants would have to say about *ser* versus *estar* heterosexual and about my own self-identification as "historically heterosexual." After a long pause, the images of these women inspired what I finally told my friend, "Many of the self-identified heterosexual women who have confided their sex lives to me dream of becoming *mujeres libres*, free women who are able to overcome their fears and concerns while enjoying sex. They aspire to become 'happily heterosexual.' They dream of experiencing the sexual norm with joy and freedom."

Future Directions

In this chapter, I have offered some reflections about the traditional trends in the literature on heterosexuality and U.S. Latina/o communities, and I have established a dialogue with some of the critical views that have emerged in the literature. I have also examined two sociocultural rituals of heterosexual initiation and the ways in which racial relations and heteronormativity have become interwoven as dominant ideologies of heterosexual love and sex. Finally, I describe ethnographic research in the emerging field of sexuality research on heterosexuality and U.S. Latina/o populations as practically virginal; the following represent some of the areas that need future inquiry.[36]

Heterosexual Intimacies and Relationships

New research is challenging traditional views of Latina women, sex, and intimacy. However, a general assumption is that sex "is done" to women by men. In-depth explorations of what both women and men actually need and desire in these intimate exchanges are needed. Some questions come to mind. What does each expect from the other? How do they experience these interactions? What are the emotional and sexual challenges of heterosexual bonding experiences? What are the social forces that shape these dynamics and processes of erotic and emotional intimacy?

Desire

The erotic drives, sensations, emotions, feelings, impulses, fantasies, longings, and cravings that are at the core of the erotic have been creatively documented in the humanities and more recently in anthropology, but they desperately call for sociological research with U.S. Latina/o populations. How do women and men experience these emotional processes of the erotic? What forces selectively repress or stimulate these silent and unexplored journeys of pleasure? What are women's and men's actual fantasies and practices?

Beyond Borders of Heterosexual Desire, Behavior, and Identity

The literature on Latino gay men has documented and examined the experiences of self-identified heterosexual Latino men who engage in sexualized encounters with other men, but there is no empirical research with women who engage in similar behaviors. What are the dynamics for self-identified heterosexual women who engage in sexualized experiences and relationships with other women? What are the social forces that alternatively repress and stimulate same-sex sexual desire in these women's lives? How do these women perceive and negotiate their sexual identities?

Political Economies of Latina/o Heterosexualities

Some of the political economies of Mexican immigrants' experiences of heterosexual love and sex within large urban contexts have been documented.[37] However, more exploration is needed. How do other Mexicans redefine their sex lives within migration contexts that are rural? How do other Latina/o immigrant groups experience sex and love within the context of migration? What are the implications of emerging research projects for innovative methodologies that may inform public health and human rights issues and concerns?

Invisible Heterosexual Love and Sex

Heterosexual love as the norm is usually associated with young populations that are perceived as physically and mentally functional. Common assumptions and prejudices promote the idea that aging generations neither experience sexual desire nor fall in love. How do older and aging generations experience heterosexual relationships and sex? How do people with special needs and disabilities experience heterosexual desire and relationships? What are the challenges they encounter and the strategies they use as they explore sex and romance?

These are some of the most important issues to address as we design a research agenda on heterosexuality-related topics with U.S. Latina/o populations. And while most of the research that has been conducted on heterosexual relationships has informed important epidemiological and public health concerns, creative methodologies that are ethically informed are needed to address the above research questions and related concerns with regard to the human rights of Latina/os. What kind of methodologies could be used to establish a bridge between sexuality research and community-based activism? How can our sexuality research agendas be sensitive to and inclusive of the actual needs of immigrant communities and grassroots efforts on specific issues and concerns? What implications does this research have for establishing policy and laws to protect the human and immigrant rights of these populations? I trust that the reflections I offer in this essay will contribute in some way toward these collective goals of social justice and change.

8

Representations of Latina/o
Sexuality in Popular Culture

DEBORAH R. VARGAS

This chapter provides an overview of the ways in which various loci of popular culture constitute and stage representations of Latina/o sexuality in the U.S. context. Research on such representations proves significant knowledge to the construction of public policy because cultural production reinforces structural systems of inequality as much as it forms possibilities for contesting systems of structural oppression. Drawing from Latina/o and Chicana/o studies, among other disciplines and interdisciplinary fields, I provide a critical overview of literature addressing popular cultural forms with specific attention to the production of Latina/o subjectivities and representations of sexualities.

As a state-of-knowledge assessment, this review brings to bear information addressing the production, consumption, and reception of Latina/o sexuality and popular culture. I contend that the attention paid to representations of Latina/o sexuality in popular culture to date solidifies traditional heterosexual femininity and masculinity by paying less heed to both nonheteronormative subjectivities and queer readings of sexuality in popular culture. Moreover, within a U.S. context, there remains less critical attention to color and the ways race is central to the production of hegemonic masculinity and femininity among Latina/o representations.[1]

In this review of the literature—ranging from cinema, media, Latina/o and Chicana/o music to communications, sociology, and cultural studies—Latina/o sexuality is critically engaged by devoting particular attention to language, racialization, colonization, commodification, and class as constituted in the overdetermination of too often assumed heterosexuality. Analysis and debates on cinema, music, and television, most notably by Frances Aparicio, Frances Negrón-Muntaner, Rosa Linda Fregoso, Raquel Z. Rivera, Maria Herrera-Sobek, Michelle Habell-Pallan, and Chon Noriega, have critically considered the relationship between the representations of racialized subjects and power ranging from structural systems of oppression to individual agency. This type of analysis has contributed to understanding how popular depictions of Latina/o sexuality have produced, for the most part, a systematic discursive violence through extreme polarizations of either visible or invisible representations. As my critical recommendations for policy implications will address, representations of an assumed heteronormativity commonly produce overly simplistic assessments of the politics of consumption, audience reception, and production.[2] My review of the literature charts a discursive shift from sexuality to sexualities and from an unproblematized heteronormative gender toward multiple masculinities and femininities. In so doing, this review is organized around two key areas that have emerged in the literature: "stereotypes of (hetero)sexuality" and "color matters" (in the politics of Latina/o representations of sexuality); the literature review closes with examples of future directions for research, exemplified by key scholarship with attention to queer subjectivities and queer analysis. With these areas in mind, I address implications for future policy.

Historically, popular culture has provided both a space for the staging of politics and an arena for the reproduction of oppressive representations of Latina/os. Stuart Hall's often-noted call to analyze popular culture as a site of power makes political sense in terms of representations of Latina/o sexuality. It is fitting to recall Gloria Anzaldúa's claim that representations of Latina/o sexualities are inscribed by social structures, "carved and tattooed with the sharp needles of experience."[3] Popular culture proffers a "site where this struggle for and against a culture of the powerful is engaged: it is also the stake to be won or lost in that struggle. It is the arena of consent and resistance."[4] The literature I focus on denotes scholarship that has centered the politics of representation pertaining to Latina/o sexuality and studies of popular culture. Scores of books and articles as well as anthologies pertaining to Latina/os' production of and engagement with popular culture attests to both a burgeoning Latino public as well as an increase of disciplinary and interdisciplinary methodologies that form the field of Latina/o popular culture. There are multiple ways one may define Latina/o popular culture and, therefore, a range of possibilities of literature from which to draw from. This literature review examines a body of critical scholarship into how representations of Latina/o sexuality have been (re)produced, contested, re-imagined, and commodified, with specific attention to the popular culture venues of cinema, television, and music, with some attention to performance and public art.

Critical Analysis of the Issues: Representation as Stereotypes

As the twentieth century gave way to the new millennium, popular culture representations of Latina/o sexuality seemed omnipresent. From late-night talk shows, music videos, and movies to the popularity of sports stars utilizing media to become popular icons, our visual and sonic senses have been met with the booty-shaking moves of Selena, Ricky Martin, and Jennifer Lopez while even boxer Oscar De La Hoya took advantage of his suave sexy image and heavily Latina/o fan base to enter the popular arena of *ranchero* music.

Television and film scholarship has largely focused on stereotypical representations and the contestations of such representations. This is best exemplified by the assertion by mass communications scholars Clint Wilson, Felix Gutiérrez, and Lena M. Chao, who, in their book on racism, sexism, and the media, state that "any discussion of the portrayals of people of color in American entertainment must include the concept of stereotyping." In general, Latina/o visual culture studies have mapped the origins and historical placement of these representations as linked to structural systems of inequality, including immigration legislation and social welfare policies. Studies of Latina/o visual culture make clear that popular representations of racialized sexual subjects involve dialectical processes constituted by structural inequality and countermodes of self-empowerment. As such, research on stereotypical representations often influences public policy discourses—expressed in arenas ranging from policy agendas to newspaper editorial pages—that call for "positive" counterrepresentations. Yet feminist scholars argue that these "positive" representations typically are those that prioritize class, whiteness, and heterosexuality, which often results in equally problematic representations of Latina/os as normative citizen-subjects, especially those that reify the heteronormative family.[5] Moreover, according to Arlene Dávila, such "commercial representations of Latinidad" have resulted in "a recurrence of themes and corrective images that, while becoming tantamount to 'Latinidad,' have further constrained its representation, ironically bringing to the forefront the pervasiveness of racial hierarchies in the very constitution of corrective images."[6]

The relationship between visual technology and race proves key with regard to the production of racialized subjects. Visual media historically have had a close relationship to the production and circulation of racialized subjectivities. An oft-cited example in cinema scholarship addressing the interconnectedness between race and cinema in the United States is D. W. Griffith's *The Birth of a Nation*, released in 1915, and how its racist portrayals of African Americans in the post–Civil War South fueled justification for their continued social and legal oppression.[7] In general, representations of Latina/o masculinities and femininities in popular culture genres and venues are constituted by racialized discourses of conquest, imperialism, and colonization, consistently represented as either deviantly hypersexual or inhumanly desexual. Latina/o sexuality has been shaped by visual media productions that leave little room outside extremes of hypersexuality or nonthreatening, infantilized asexuality as exemplified, for example, by the figures of the buffoon and the domesticated mother.

One inescapable representation of Latino masculinity and sexuality is the "Latin lover," most notably and problematically associated with Rudolph Valentino. The fact that Valentino, an Italian immigrant, was represented as "Latin" serves to remind us of the range of ethnicities—from the Mexican actor Gilbert

Roland to the Italian Valentino—that fell within the racially charged Latin lover category in early cinema. In the early twentieth century, the term Latin was not synonymous with Latin American but encompassed both Europeans who spoke Latinate languages, such as Italians and Spaniards, and Latin Americans. As Clara E. Rodríguez argues, a key racialized shift occurs in the U.S. context when non-Hispanic European ethnics, such as Italians, assimilate into whiteness, leaving non-European ethnics to bear the brunt of the racist stereotypes of excess and deviant sexuality.[8]

For the most part, the Latin lover trope remained a dominant pathologization of Latino masculinity in order to maintain the masculinist hegemony of the great white hero as emblematized, for instance, in films starring John Wayne or Clint Eastwood. As Charles Ramírez-Berg maintains, "In order to prop the protagonist up, characters of cultural/ethnic/racial/class backgrounds different from the hero's are therefore generally assigned sundry, minor roles: villains, sidekicks, temptresses, the 'other man.'" From Ramón Novarro in the 1920s to Cesar Romero in the 1940s and Ricardo Montalbán and Fernando Lamas in the 1950s, Latino actors were typecast as Latin lovers, and found it difficult to establish their careers beyond the predictable suave sexuality hinting at danger and perhaps contagion. The Latin lover became the "possessor of a primal sexuality that made him capable of making a sensuous but dangerous—and clearly non-WASP—brand of love."[9]

The Latin lover stereotype has extended to other constructions of masculinity on television and in cinema as well, including figures like that of the boxer and *pachuco* or *cholo*. Boxing in particular has provided one of the most visible stages for performing Latino hypermasculinity as virile and physically dominant. Actual sports figures and fictional narratives of boxers exemplify the extension of the Latin lover figure. Showtime's *Resurrection Boulevard* features what Michelle A. Holling refers to as "el simpatico boxer"—a representation of Latino masculinity as sexually desirable, devoted to family, and advancing Latino culture within the framework of traditional American ideals. In television coverage of sport, there is no greater example of "el simpatico boxer" than "Golden Boy" Oscar De La Hoya. After garnering enormous attention as a sex symbol, De La Hoya attempted to transfer this representation to popular music, with his release of *Oscar De La Hoya* on EMI Latin in 2000. Instead of succumbing to the figure of thuggish boxer emblematized in the film *Rocky*, De La Hoya has succeeded in maintaining a suave sexual status, because he endorses boxing "as a means to a healthy and beautiful body." Ironically, De La Hoya's image has been represented as sexual, contrary to the animalistic nature often framing physically brute masculinity, such that his "pretty boy" masculinity leaves many male fans unsettled.[10]

For Latinas, representations of their sexuality have been dichotomized as virgin/whore or mother/prostitute—what Chicana feminist scholars refer to as "La Virgen/La Malinche" dichotomy. These polarized representations have their origins in the cinematic figures of the demure señoritas and spitfires of the 1920s and 1930s, respectively.[11] Once a stock figure in the genre of Western films, the equivalent of the Latin lover for Latinas has been the lusty, hot-tempered harlot, a character most widely associated with Lupe Vélez. Having starred in eight movies as the "Mexican spitfire" Carmelita Woods, Vélez herself was often described as "the hot baby of Hollywood" or "just a Mexican wild kitten" in publicity photo captions. In the following assertion, Ramírez-Berg notes that the harlot or spitfire is usually an unmarried woman with absence of a husband signifying her uncontrolled sexuality: "a slave to her passions, her conduct is simplistically attributed to her inherent nymphomania, innately lusting for a white male."[12] Katy Jurado best exemplifies this stereotype in her role as the home-wrecking other woman, Helen Ramirez, opposite Gary Cooper's Will Kane in *High Noon* (1952).

Historically for Latinas, those extreme representations as either hot-blooded spitfire or dutiful mother have reified dominant notions of ostensibly American subjectivity, citizenship, and family, especially in politically tense contexts. As feminist analyses of nationalism argue, notions of country, homeland, region, locality, and ethnicity are constructed through the racialization, sexualization, and genderization of female corporeality. In a U.S. context, then, representations of Latina sexuality as hot-blooded and excessive become the markers of what is morally wrong, set against the good morals and hegemonic U.S. citizenship values of non-Latino whites.[13]

More contemporary reproductions of Latinas have desexualized their gender constructions into that of mother or domestic worker. This strategy has been the result of what I contend is a resistance strategy to overly correct hegemonic hypersexual representations. As feminist analyses of Latina/o cultural representations demonstrate, there is a dual pressure based on U.S. nationalist and Chicano nationalist projects to represent Latina sexuality as domestic, virginal, and asexual.[14] Almost always in the background of movies that focus on heroic Latino characters looms the sacrificing mother. In fact, the role of mother and wife has been central to sustaining what Fregoso, referring to Lorena Oropeza's reading of "la raza," describes as the "Chicano familia romance" through the metaphoric chain of "la familia = la raza = the community = the Chicano nation."[15] In fact, the 1980s, commonly referred to as "the decade of the Hispanic," arguably mark "the beginning of positive long-term changes" in cinema representations of Latina/os.[16] However, the notion of positive Latina characters often resulted in a reification of Latina femininity as heteronormative mother or daughter. Notable examples include barely legible presence of the girlfriends in *Zoot Suit* (1981), the character of Ritchie Valens's mother in *La Bamba* (1987), the roles of wives and daughters in *Mi Familia* (1995) and *The Milagro Beanfield War* (1988), and even Gregory Nava's depiction of Selena in *Selena: The Movie* (1997).

Extremes of hyper- or asexuality have left Latinas in roles that represent little agency over their sexuality. "The Latina's sexual allure must somehow be negated. Generally, her character is sullied (she is made promiscuous and criminal, as is the case with the harlot stereotype) or ridiculed (portrayed as sexually 'easy' or simply silly and comical, as with the female buffoon)."[17] A combination of "spitfire" and comedic release, Carmen Miranda—born María do Carmen Miranda da Cunha in Portugal and raised in Brazil, and nicknamed the "lady in the tutti-frutti hat"—best exemplifies the representation of Latinas as sensually playful and sexually primitive.[18] Miranda was a key figure of Latina representation during the era of the Good Neighbor policy initiated by President Franklin Roosevelt that emphasized cooperation and trade with Latin America in order to maintain U.S. influence and deter any possible political, economic, and cultural invasion by Germany and its allies before and during World War II. Miranda's playful sexuality came to embody Latin America as a cultural and sexual playground. Miranda's excessive yet clownish femininity—marked by her platform shoes, energetic rhythmic dancing, and massive exotic head-dresses—represented a sexual subjectivity not threatening to white hegemonic femininity. In this historical context, Latinas and Latinos were represented as infantalized characters or by cheerful musical performances, such as those by Xavier Cugat and Desi Arnaz.[19]

Feminist scholarship's most crucial contribution to analyzing representations of Latina/o sexuality in popular culture may be the articulation of how the constructions of hypersexual and asexuality illuminate the combined systems of oppression that converge—within both Latino cultural productions and hegemonic American cultural production—resulting in the "many headed demon of oppression."[20] As such, literature addressing problematic repercussions and consequences of representational stereotypes of Latinas and Latinos nevertheless falls short of the fuller integration that can be gained from queer analysis, beyond the recognition of specifically homosexual, gay, and lesbian characters. Analysis of representations of Latina/o sexuality must also account for femininity and masculinity beyond often assumed links to heterosexuality.

Color Matters

A key issue with regard to the representations of Latina/o sexuality in popular culture is that of race, or more precisely, color. Following the popular mantra that social structural systems of power matter, *color* matters when it comes to the configuration of demonized, pathologized, and desexualized Latina/o representations. According to Ramírez-Berg, contemporary figures of hypersexual Latino masculinity like the gangster, drug runner, and inner-city urban homeboy—ruthlessly in pursuit of vulgar cravings for money, power, and sexual pleasure—have their origins in the *bandido* figure dating back to early "greaser" films such as *Bronco Billy and the Greaser* (1914).[21] The Mexican bandit—most often of dark skin—whose outlaw characteristics include deviant sexuality, made numerous appearances in films throughout the twentieth century, most notably in *The Magnificent Seven* (1960), *Pancho Villa* (1972), and *Bring Me the Head of Alfredo Garcia* (1974).[22] Moreover, representations of Latina/o sexuality as "exotic" often function through the figure of the primitive dark-skinned Other rooted in "tropicalism," as a "system of ideological fictions with which the dominant (Anglo and European) cultures trope Latin American and U.S. Latina/o identities and cultures."[23] Exotic sexuality has been represented in roles that reinforce a sense of sultry beauty rooted in some distant land, signified by the dark primitive Other.

Frances R. Aparicio and Susana Chávez-Silverman remind us that tropicalism has worked for decades to justify social, political, and ideological agendas of U.S. hegemony. Representations of Latina sexuality have become synonymous with exotic adventures south of the border, epitomized by María Móntez, born in Barahona, Dominican Republic, whose character roles in adventure epics were popular during the 1940s. During the 1950s and 1960s, dark-skinned Rita Moreno—the first Latina to win an Academy Award—consistently had to work against a publicity machine that subsumed her under such descriptors as "fiery love machine," "Puerto Rican firecracker," and "Rita the cheetah." Such descriptors were used in the popular press after her breakthrough role in the 1955 film *Untamed*.[24]

West Side Story, the cinematic vehicle for which Moreno is most remembered, offers one of the most obvious examples of the dualistic images of Puerto Rican women as Madonna (Natalie Wood's innocent, passive, and virginal character, Maria) or whore (Moreno's hot-blooded spitfire caricature, Anita). As with the ethnically European (specifically Russian) Wood, Dolores Del Rio's and Rita Hayworth's lighter skin color allowed their ethnicity to be read as "international exoticism," rather than as the fiery uncontainable sexuality of Moreno's Anita. As such, Del Rio's onscreen sexuality differs markedly: representationally, Del Rio is allowed a much more sexually refined elegance and glamour than stands as counter to unwieldy sexuality. Notably, Del Rio's skin tone afforded her a range of roles beyond the stock characters of servants and villains reserved for darker-skinned Latina/os. Géliga Vargas astutely notes that in regard to the politics of color and Puerto Rican representations in relation to a U.S. context, it is key to note the variation of island and off-island Puerto Ricans and the ways in which this difference affects class and race in the constructions of sexuality.[25]

Arguably the most mainstream recognized Puerto Rican woman in cinema since Rita Moreno is Rosie Pérez. In the early 1990s, Pérez became the next version of the Latina spitfire. Shorter, darker, and most recognizable by her Nuyorican Brooklyn accent, Pérez has expressed her distaste at being typecast as the "feisty, foul-mouthed, working-class Latina." Ana López's assessments of Lupe Vélez are informative in exploring contemporary figurations of Latinas such as Pérez. Similar to Lupe Vélez, Pérez's "beauty and sexual appeal [is] aggressive, flamboyant, and stridently ethnic." Just as with Vélez's midcentury spitfire roles, Pérez, too, has played roles characterized by savvy and aggressive qualities.

Thus, arguably Pérez's on- and off-camera representations denote possibilities of Latina agency by disidentifying with normative white middle-class standards of femininity.[26]

Unlike Jennifer Lopez, another Nuyorican actor, Pérez possesses dark skin, curly hair, and a heavy accent that cannot be readily de-ethnicized. Moreover, fair skin has garnered Lopez more ethnic mobility across a range of sexualities to which darker women do not have access, particularly, character roles that represent non-Latina white sexuality. Moreover, her sexuality is shaped by the ways her ethnicity collapses around the often urban working-class status of her character roles. "She is at once Latina because she is working class and working class because she is Latina."[27] Scholarship in popular culture studies has yet to offer a critical assessment of sexuality with regards to darker-skinned Latinas such as America Ferrera, Sara Ramírez, and Salma Hayek. Hayek's character roles in *Desperado* (1995) and *From Dusk Till Dawn* (1996) seem to have resulted in popular press references to her sexuality as "hot," as exemplified by the August 1999 London *Times* interview article on Hayek whose title was: "Hot, Hot, Hot."[28]

As commercial television began to emerge as a major mass medium in the late 1940s, representations of Latina/o seen on the big screen found a new public venue, arriving specifically with the romantic figure of "The Cisco Kid" in 1950. With regard to color, early character roles of Latina/os on television represented their sexuality in ways similar to cinematic representations. For instance, the 1957 television adventure *Zorro* was divided along class and race lines, with Spanish settlers set against the villains, buffoons, or backdrops of Mexican characters.[29]

Spanish-language talk shows and daily telenovelas beamed across the United States from countries throughout Latin America are key sites for analysis of Latina/o sexuality on television and the politics of color. The talk shows *El Show de Cristina* and *Laura en América*, which aired daily on the networks Univision and Telemundo, respectively, garnered huge ratings among Latinas in the United States from the mid-1990s into the early 2000s. The gossip show genre serves as an interlocutor that allows Latinas to work through issues of sexuality and cultural/ethnic identity by commenting on guest panelists and their anecdotes. In this way, the shows are simultaneously empowering and disempowering representations of sexuality that nonetheless create a platform for entering into social debates and private conversation about sexuality. Cristina Saralegui, host of *El Show de Cristina*, has been strongly criticized for airing issues of "promiscuity, homosexuality, and women's equality."[30] Laura Buzzo, founder of the *Laura en América* show has been equally criticized, especially in the Peruvian press, for her exploration of what are considered racy topics of sexuality and gender roles as well as for the ways in which she exposes Peruvian men's sexual affairs. In spite of these criticisms, there is no denying that, more so than with contemporary cinematic productions, representations and discussions of Latina/o sexuality—located in the dual language media homes of

English- and Spanish-language television viewers—manifest a daily platform for public debate. In fact, Viviana Rojas has noted that *El Show de Cristina* began to lose ratings until Saralegui integrated more topics on sexuality.

To be sure, there is an argument to be made that the exposure to topics such as homosexuality and extramarital affairs can be empowering to viewers (as in the case of queer Latina/os) who rarely or never see themselves represented in the media or who have little or no ability to confront a cheating spouse within the private, domestic realm (as in the case of many of the Latinas who appear on *Laura*). While *any* representation may be a positive accomplishment for some, there is a need to remain critical of the way in which race plays a central part in perpetuating the sexuality of some Latina/os as dysfunctional. It is key to note that although telenovelas and talk shows such as these may be filmed and broadcast in contexts where race is comprehended and defined differently, these figures play a key role in the production of Latina representations of sexuality in the Unite States. In the case of these talk shows, both hosts are light-skinned Latinas from privileged class backgrounds who do indeed include Latina guests who are darker skinned. Yet, when Laura invites women on the show for the purpose of saving them from abusive or adulterous husbands, almost always these guests are darker, indigenous Peruvians. The sexuality these Latinas represent is uncontained and chaotic, as demonstrated by the eventual highlight of the show, when the women begin beating each other over a man or joining forces in physically attacking the man himself. Hypersexual Latinas, such as those routinely invited to discuss such topics as prostitution or nonmonogamy, for instance, are usually darker as well. In general, scholarship on television contends that increased representations of Latinas has come at the expense of those of darker skin, thereby still upholding whiteness as hegemonic feminity.[31]

In terms of Latino masculinity, comic relief provided by the stock character of the buffoon has historically worked to retain the dominance of white masculinity while ameliorating the danger and deviance often attributed to dark-skinned masculinity. The desexualized clown figure has historical context in the character of Gordito in the *Cisco Kid* film series dating to the 1930s, precursor to the 1950s television series. While not always the darker skinned, Latino masculine figures become less threatening in comic relief. For example, Ricky Ricardo on *I Love Lucy*, played by Desi Arnaz, had fair skin, yet his heavy accent was the marker for Other masculinity that consistently reinforced hegemonic masculinity of the WASP (White Anglo-Saxon Protestant) American mainstream.[32]

More contemporary versions of comedic figures include Cheech Marin's character "Rudy" in the movie *Born in East L.A.* (1987), although feminist analysis of this character and the movie also acknowledge the space for subversive readings of comedic characters with respect to historical and political context of narrative and reception. There are times when the comedic Latino character subverts hegemonic whiteness through parody. Fregoso argues that "parodic elements" such as these "reflect a more significant symbolic elaboration of the contradiction of white American nativism." Although he theorizes about African American images in Hollywood cinema, Ed Guerrero's assertions about nonwhite masculine Others are applicable here because of how masculinities are relationally situated. Latino masculinity as comedic relief in roles such as Ricky Ricardo and Rudy are set in "corrective custody of a White lead or co-star and therefore in conformity with dominant White sensibilities" whether these sensibilities are represented by the hegemonic family or, in the case of Rudy, the nation-state.[33]

The character Chico Rodríguez in the 1970s hit comedy *Chico and the Man* is another prime example of a dark-skinned comedic representation during this unique historical moment in television for Latinos and blacks. The first U.S. television comedy series to feature a Latino as the lead character, *Chico and the Man* was first aired in 1974 in the context of "ghetto-centric" comedic programming that included *Sanford and Son* and *Good Times*. While Chico was not quite akin to the adolescent-acting bumbling staple buffoon figure best represented by Gordito, his masculinity nonetheless came to embody discursively the threat of brown East L.A. that was at the heart of "a good deal of the 'humor' derived from the racist insults that Ed Brown, the elderly garage owner played by Jack Albertson, directed at the surrounding Chicano community."[34]

The representation of dark-skinned masculinity in Chico's character came to symbolize "much of the country being overrun by dark-skinned Others," as portrayed through comedic tension between Chico and his grumpy white friend, Ed. Television representations of Latino masculinity were significant during the late 1960s and 1970s as Latinos, especially Chicanos and Puerto Ricans, became the objects of blame for rates of poverty and low educational attainment. Thematic content in such shows reflected social debate and racial tensions situated in public policy reports like the 1965 Moynihan Report, authored by Daniel Patrick Moynihan, which adopted the discourse of "culture of poverty" from Oscar Lewis's 1959 ethnography *Five Families: Mexican Case Studies in the Culture of Poverty*. The Moynihan Report, which focused on black families but extended especially to poor Mexican Americans and Puerto Ricans, attributed the economic and social conditions to dysfunctional family and sexuality rooted in a pathology of culture and home.[35]

In historical contexts of popular culture such as this, Latino sexuality represented through the body of the dark masculine Other becomes trapped between replicating heteronormative familial masculinity (as good U.S. citizens) and acting out the dysfunctional representation as an irresponsible drain on the state. Significantly, the only prime-time comedy series with a Latino in a lead role since *Chico and the Man* is *The George Lopez Show*, which premiered on ABC in 2002.[36] Lopez himself is one of the few darker-skinned Latinos with any degree of visibility in early-twenty-first-century popular culture. Future scholarship should pay attention to this comedic representation as it relates to the politics of color and Latino masculinity, especially in the contemporary period of hyper-surveillance of darker-skinned Others that buttresses discourses of "terrorism" and "threat" in the post-9/11 era.

The politics of color with regard to representations of Latino sexuality is key as well when it comes to constructions of family, particularly as this entails normative formations of U.S. citizenship. Television programs such as the 2002 Public Broadcasting System series *American Family* or the movie *Mi Familia* (1995) have served to offer "positive" representations of Latina/o sexuality, with darker-skinned Latina/os as central characters. In fact, it is the nostalgic rural indigenous history of Mexican peoples—as in the origins narrative of *Mi Familia*—that shifts the dark-skinned Latino subject from stereotypical representations of urban gangs and hypersexual single motherhood as Other to immigrant subject capable of assimilation.

Yet these positive representations of Latina/o sexuality tend to rely on reducing Latina sexuality to that of the dutiful, sacrificing mother figure. Too often, what results is a slippery slope toward reinforcing Latino sexuality as heteronormative, particularly as charted or fixed within the family unit, instead of a more broadly conceived representational rendering of the multiplicity of masculinities that constitute Latino sexualities. As noted earlier in this discussion on stereotypes, this move toward "positive" representation results in what Holling terms "inscribing Chicana/os into American consciousness."[37] Latina/o sexuality remains trapped by representations consistently measured against a racialized litmus test of American identity, reaffirmed always by hegemonic heterosexual white masculinity and femininity. As Holling reminds us, "brown masculinity" stands in stark contrast to white American masculinity, consistently attempting to abide by cultural expectations of hegemonic home and family.

Color matters with regard to representations of Latina/o sexuality in the arena of popular music as well. At the 1999 Grammy Awards show in Miami, millions of people across the country watched as Ricky Martin shook up the popular music stage. In a span of several minutes, his performance of "La copa de la vida" (The Cup of Life) marked a shift from popular culture precedents of darker deviant Latino-as-gangster masculinity to a sexy masculinity embodied by the gyrating yet less-threatening buttocks and hips of Ricky Martin, himself a popular icon who Negrón-Muntaner asserts represents the "white upper-class Islanders, or *blanquitos*."[38]

Particularly as regards cinema and music, Aparicio and Negrón-Muntaner have been most central in critically identifying the politics of color in analysis of representations of sexuality among Latinos and especially Latinas. Their scholarship interrogates the ways Latinas are reduced to the sexualized objects of the heterosexual male gaze throughout all aspects of music from song lyrics to performance. In her analysis of Jennifer Lopez as Selena—in the film *Selena* about the slain Tex-Mex singer—Negrón-Muntaner theorizes the ways in which the butt becomes the site of racialization as sexual excess for Lopez (and by extension the singer Selena herself). "A big *culo* upsets hegemonic (white) notions of beauty and good taste because it is a sign of the dark, incomprehensible excess of 'Latino' and other African diaspora cultures." Moreover, she continues, "a big Latin butt is an open air invitation to pleasures construed as illicit by WASP ideologies." Aparicio similarly asserts that the female butt, particularly through hypereroticization of the dark female body of the mulatta in Caribbean music, comes to signify rhythm, movement, and erotic pleasure. For example, the bolero "Tan Sabrosona" (1956) addresses the mulatta in lyrics that read: "mi negra no te molestes si te dicen sabrosona / por ese andar que tú tienes / tan tremendo y retozón [my black woman, don't get upset if they call you tasty / because of the way you walk / so tremendous and playful]." In this way, the dark Latina body represents a sexuality overexposed and hypervisible that "disrupts the ordered masculine political and national body."[39]

In fact, among Latino musical genres, sexuality has been given the most critical attention, in relation to historical transnational migrations of bolero music, and in particular to the ways in which skin color shapes representations of sexuality. It is the Latino bolero genre that most unambiguously formulates a discursive site of excessive desire and explicit sexuality. Most music historians trace the genre to the streets of Santiago de Cuba, where elements of Afro-Cuban rhythms were central. Arguably, however, the bolero gained its widest exposure in Mexico City, where it was transformed and urbanized by composers such as Agustín Lara. Much of this focus on sexuality pertains to the historical and social context in Mexico in which the bolero emerged, easily noted in the explicit sexuality Lara allegorized in his compositions, many of which are set in Mexican bordellos. As Adela Piñeda Franco explains, "Lara was defying social and moral codes, as well as musical patterns, through a lyrical homage to prostitutes and chorus girls through his urban musical style." Vanessa Knights concurs, arguing that "prostitutes and relationships outside the legal confines of marriage were particularly immortalized" in Lara's work. Lara brings inappropriate sexuality to the forefront through images of prostitutes or chorus girls marginalized by Mexican society and influenced by the Modernist movement.[40]

In our contemporary moment of popular culture, particularly in the arena of music, representations of Latina/o sexuality direct attention to the varied manifestations of racialized subjectivities within the panethnic formation of *Latinidad* in the U.S. public sphere. A critical scholarly contribution to the subjects of skin color and Latino identity formation is Yeidy M. Rivero's analysis of what she terms "the erasing of blackness" in the Puerto Rican comedy "Mi Familia." Ironically, *Mi Familia* was the first television comedy in Puerto Rico to have an all-black cast, yet, as Rivero earlier argued, the series still operates as a nonracial narrative. Negrón-Muntaner's analysis of the 1997 release of Puerto Rican Barbie (on the island of Puerto Rico) is yet another excellent example of how race, skin color, sexuality, and femininity converge at the site of Latina subjectivity formations. Whether it is skin color, the butt, or hair color and texture, the dialectical tension Aparicio and Chávez-Silverman articulate as "tropicalization"—as both the problematic tropes of Latinas/os by dominant U.S. culture and the possibilities of subaltern agency and counters to theses tropes— serves as a key theoretical foundation for the ways Latina/o sexuality will be represented in the decades to come.[41]

The politics of color and representation is thus at the center of much feminist analysis of Latina/o pop icons. For instance, analyses of Jennifer Lopez, the highest-paid musical and cinematic Latina artist in the United States, call attention to the ways in which her lighter skin tone has imparted her with access to a range of sexual subjectivities in ways a darker woman can not without risking negative consequences. Similarly and insightfully, Maria Elena Cepeda notes how Shakira (who once declared in a press release her "desire to seduce the U.S."), Lopez, and Christina Aguilera have grown thinner and blonder as they have moved up the ladder of success.[42] In fact, the documentary film *Corpus: A Home Movie for Selena* (1999) by Lourdes Portillo and scholarship by Deborah Paredez and Deborah R. Vargas stress the significance Selena's brown body had for young Latinas who rarely saw themselves reflected in popular culture representations of lighter-skinned Latinas in music.[43]

To be sure, even as these Latinas have grown thinner and blonder, it is important that future scholars remain attentive to the spirit of "tropicalization" that encourages explorations of how Latinas themselves rework dominant cultural tropes into transformative representations. Thus, there is an argument to be made that, although thinner and blonder, both Aguilera and Shakira have opened up public discussion about the contested notions of "Latina," through interviews in the popular press and their ever-changing representations. In general, the literature's attention to the politics of skin color and representations of Latina/o sexuality is significant because it highlights the ways in which hypersexuality and other sexualities often deemed "deviant" do not merely remain reduced to racist discourse within dominant U.S. culture. Representations of such sexualities may also be self-consciously manufactured stagings that mock hegemonic femininity and encourage debate, reflection, and critique about the politics of race and sexuality in Latino cultural productions. For example, we await future analysis critically assessing the politics of color and sexuality pertaining to movies such as *Bordertown*, starring Jennifer Lopez, and the murders of (most often) dark-skinned, poor, maquiladora workers in Ciudad Juárez, Mexico.

Future Directions: Multiple Femininities and Masculinities

As this review has demonstrated, representations of Latina/o sexuality in popular culture may be situated in two general areas of scholarship. I have reviewed scholarship that historicizes and analyzes the production of stereotypes that link to structural processes of inequality and thus the ways such racist representations have worked to reify oppressive social ideologies and political policy agendas. Review of this scholarship directs critical attention to the ways in which skin color (racialization) is key to the construction of Latina/o sexuality, particularly in relation to U.S. hegemonic constructions of white femininity and masculinity. In general, recommendations for future directions in scholarship include queer theoretical analyses that will complicate the constructions of femininity and masculinity beyond heteronormative sexual designations of female and male.[44] Scant explicit attention to multiple masculinities and femininities is evident in most of the literature. Lack of attention to multiple and ever-shifting sexualities works to the detriment of popular culture studies theorizing the politics of representation—specifically, in cinema, on television, and in music—insofar as such work ignores shifting contexts of meaning, production, and reception.

Whereas race has proved central to critical analysis of representations of Latina/os, the construction of "queer" or nonheteronormative sexualities as central to the racialization of ethnic bodies has been largely unincorporated in the literature, except when the subject of concern is specifically "lesbian" "gay," "bisexual," or "homosexual." Unless popular culture sites or subjects themselves are designated as "homosexual" the assumption of social science, cinema, and communications media scholarship in analyzing stereotypes such as the spitfire or Latin lover is a default heterosexuality. For example, there is much to be reconsidered about Latina femininity if analysis also moves away from the assumption that femininity is reduced to heterosexuality. Potentially fruitful future directions beyond the reinscription of heterosexual stereotypes may be found at the intersection of queer studies and feminist Latina/o studies.[45] The following discussion draws on what I contend are strong examples of where the future direction in scholarship addressing representations of Latina/o sexualities in popular culture is taking us. The literature reveals at least two overarching foci, scholarship addressing the visibility of gay and lesbian Latina/o subjects and the utilization of queer studies frameworks to analyze heterosexual representations in popular culture.

One area of scholarship that represents a key shift in popular culture studies to further disrupt the assumption of heterosexual femininities and masculinities is analysis informed by Latina/o queer studies. This scholarly area has been attentive to often-ignored gay and lesbian subjects and themes in past television decades as well as the contemporary era of increased gay and lesbian characters. This scholarship is a key future direction, especially as representations of Latina/o lesbians and gays seem to remain, thus far, in subordinate relationship to white gay and lesbian characters. A contemporary example of (in)visible Latina lesbians is the cable drama series *The L-Word*.

In his study on representations of gay Latinos on television, Horacio R. Ramírez argues that homosexuality on television has been extremely (in)visible. Homosexuals on talk shows, for instance, either appearing as drag queens or displaying hypereffeminate characteristics, are often the center of ridicule; on Spanish-language television homosexuality may also be referenced through subtle inside jokes or via double entendre in Spanish humor. Visibility of gay and lesbian subjects in this way, according to Ramírez, results in a disempowered enactment of "visibility without representation."[46] The political and social consequences of such polarizing representations in popular culture range from queer Latinos' disenfranchisement in political dialogues on same-sex marriage to disinvestment in health care education, particularly as this pertains to reproduction, adoption, and HIV/AIDS. Ironically, reducing the issue of HIV/AIDS to homosexuality in such public media stagings has resulted in limited attention to the increasing rates of infection among heterosexual Latinos and young Latinas.

Future scholarship on the representation of Latina/o sexualities in popular culture should look to analyses of sexuality addressing Latina/o queer art and performance. As Alicia Arrizón argues, sites of theatre and performance chart critical shifts not only from invisibility to representation, but, significantly, to *self*-representation. Performing artists and writers such as Marga Gómez, Alina Troyano, Cherríe Moraga, Luis Alfaro, Adelina Anthony, Nao Bustamante, and Monica Palacios have been key to establishing a queer Latina/o public performance sphere. Similarly, artists such as Yolanda López, Alma Lopez, and Ester Hernández have been important to constructing self-representations of Latina sexuality in their re-appropriations of the hegemonic religious representation of the iconic figure of the *Virgen de Guadalupe*. Scholarship on performance and art point to heterogeneous genders and sexualities, which scholars must remain aware of when considering the power and disempowerment cultural production makes possible. For instance, Mitchell Fitch's analysis of John Leguizamo's *Mambo Mouth* exemplifies how Latina/o queer theater is a critical space for reworking dominant fictions of the Latina/o Other. Certainly performance does not always result in transgressive representations of nonheteronormative sexualities; nonetheless, it has been a productive site for representing the nuanced interplay of systems of power and sexuality.[47] The arenas of art and performance have contributed significantly to the heterogeneous range of Latina/o sexualities through alternative engagements with heterosexual tropes of *mestizaje, familia,* and Catholicism.[48]

A second area of scholarship that is moving studies in popular culture in a direction disruptive of heterosexual femininities and masculinities is analysis of queer reception, consumption, and fandom of heterosexual narratives and popular culture icons.[49] Theoretical frameworks that have contributed key insights include Stuart Hall's cultural studies paradigm of encoding/decoding and José Muñoz's queer studies theorization of disidentifications. In other words, scholarship acknowledging multiple femininities and masculinities must also move beyond a mere accounting for the visibility of gay and lesbian Latina/os and thereby multiply situated reception. Instead, what have often been assumed as merely heterosexual stereotypical representations of the Latin lover or spitfire may also be registered as nonheterosexual, nonheteronormative, or queer. A significant example here is Negrón-Muntaner's analysis of queerness in the Broadway play (1957) and subsequent movie (1961) *West Side Story* through a historical analysis of the play's creation, thematics, and performances of social and sexual desires that center race and gender in the production of *boricua* subjectivities.[50]

There is also a rich queer analysis of Latino music. The bolero genre provides an excellent example of a more contemporary analysis that moves beyond sexual excess as merely a (hetero)sexually oppressive representation. As José Quiroga asserts, Olga Guillot, known simply as La Guillot, mastered the bolero of despair and Eros, "the song that produces the erotic charge of steamy sex under a red light bulb." Guillot's performative interpretations of boleros were unapologetically sexual, especially in her live performance as her hand typically "mov[ed] down to trace circles in front of her stomach, down to her sex." In this example, the performance of a bolero promotes its public staging to illuminate nonnormative sexuality: the dark, the homosexual, the illegitimate lovers all reside and thrive in the sound of the bolero.[51]

A more recent figure of analysis pertaining to representations of Latina sexuality is La Lupe. Born Lupe Yoli in Santiago de Cuba in 1936 and known as "the queen of Latin soul," La Lupe has been retrieved—by contemporary queer and feminist filmmakers and scholars—from the margins of sexual excess that had resulted in the elision of her performative and musical contributions. La Lupe's exaggerated sexuality on stage was framed by her desire to embody and inhabit the space of anger, longing, and desperation in song.[52] Her performances connected with publics whose social conditions and various subordinate positionalities could be rechanneled through passion and fervor. In fact, La Lupe is routinely cited as a prominent precursor to queer performative art. Queer analysis of the bolero supports that, more so than any other genre, the bolero has fortified a space where nonheteronormative representations and subjectivities of Latina/o sexualities not only reside but are assembled.[53] For example: "The use of the genre by gay men exposes the very marginalization given within borders staked out by society. Boleros allow gay men to deploy and suspend the borders implicit in the genre, and to re-motivate them according to their own wishes and desires. By placing themselves on the border, they refuse marginalization."[54]

This alliance between Latino gay men and Latina performers of bolero emerges, in part, from the emphasis on notions of mobility and freedom of movement, both in lyrics and in performance gestures, that subvert the gendered binary division of masculine as active and feminine as passive.[55] Bolero songs in the contemporary era, more than any other Latina music genre, have sonically delineated nonheteronormative modes of desire in Latina/o queer cinematic productions. Quiroga, in fact, maintains that Spanish director Pedro

Almodóvar should be credited with the comeback and rediscovery of La Lupe, specifically for his homoerotically charged films *Law of Desire* (1987) and *Women on the Verge of a Nervous Breakdown* (1989). Another example of the appropriation of boleros in queer cinema is the 1997 independent erotic short by Claudia Morgado Escanilla, *Sabor a Mi*.[56]

Recent feminist and queer scholarly attention to the hypermasculine scenes of punk and hip-hop music also reveal queer articulations of sexuality. Especially for young Chicanas, punk scenes have been places where queer sexualities and nonnormative notions of femininity have been encouraged, most evidently in sartorial style and live music performance. According to Michelle Habell-Pallán, singers like Alicia Armendariz Velásquez, Teresa Covarrubias, and Angela Vogel gave birth to a Chicana version of "do-it-yourself" grassroots feminist cultural production in the 1970s. In fact, self-representations of sexuality and gender were conscious strategies for rejecting the equation of femininity with victimization and passivity.[57] Critically historicizing participation of these Chicanas in punk—a music characterized by loud instrumental sound and vocals and extreme body movement on stage and in the audience—engenders representations of sexuality and femininity that counter the spatial and sonic gender norms characterizing appropriate or seemly femininity, such as that of the desexualized mother figure articulated in representational stereotypes of Latinas.

In stark contrast to the pachuco or cholo—iconic representations of "la raza"—the Chicana "chola" or "pachuca" character has not been a prominent Latina representation in a wide range of popular culture sites, except for cinema and some fiction. When the *chola* has appeared prominently, she has been cast as a criminally deviant female subjectivity such as in *Mi Vida Loca* (My Crazy Life) (1993). Feminist analysis of *Mi Vida Loca*, along with ethnographies and literary analysis of *cholos* and homegirls, offer key arguments for how this representation of Latina sexuality has come to justify racist/hegemonic/policing policies in social welfare and the judicial system. Future directions in scholarship should follow the lead of Marie Miranda's *Homegirls in the Public Sphere*, which takes to task cinematic and ethnographic products of Chicana sexuality that have reduced "homegirl" or "chola" figures to victims or deviants as a result of dysfunctional families.[58] Moreover, *The Woman in the Zoot Suit* by Catherine Ramírez offers unique analysis of pachucas that is informative to Chicana representations in popular culture. Ramírez's analysis draws attention to the pachuca as symbolic of "an aberrant femininity and sexuality (namely lesbian) during World War II."[59] Such directions in scholarship that centralize queer studies theories of Latina "female masculinity" would reveal more complicated analysis of Latina sexuality. For example, analysis of sexuality of Michelle Rodríguez's character Diana in *Girlfight* (2000) is better served by scholarship that moves beyond the too familiar trope of the street-tough chola, as a dysfunctional femininity that is the result of an abusive household and stress-ridden economic environment.[60] Similarly, the constructions of "female masculine" subjectivities, particularly in the emerging musical arena of "homo-hop" (self-identified gay and lesbian songwriters and rappers of hip-hop), represent another fruitful site for exploring Latina representations of sexuality that break with the heteronormative representations of masculinity in hip-hop music.[61]

Scholarship reviewed herein offers productive examples for future directions in analyses of representations of Latina/o sexualities across disciplinary confines of hetero- or homosexuality. Future directions of scholarship addressing the multiplicity of masculinities and femininities—not only in clearly defined gay or lesbian subjects—contribute analysis required to assess Latina/o representations of sexuality in an increasingly complex global era of consumption, reception, and desire. Whereas there has been critical intervention in unbuckling female from femininity and male from masculinity, much of this scholarship has been produced within feminist queer studies of performance and art. What has more rarely occurred in studies of Latina/o sexualities and popular representations is a conversation across social science disciplines such as political science, sociology, and communications with queer and feminist studies. Undeniably, there are feminist sociologists and feminist media scholars, yet more disciplinary boundaries remain to be dismantled in methodological approaches to sexuality beyond research questions that merely add "homosexual" ("gay" or "lesbian") subjects. In turn, fuller integration of queer studies into sociology, political science, and communications addressing gender and sexuality representations of Latina/os in popular culture is wanting.

Implications for Policy

At the turn of the new century, popular culture remains, to paraphrase Stuart Hall, a highly charged arena of consent and resistance for minority populations in the United States. In particular, public cultural production, especially of movies, music, television programs, public performance, and art—because of technological reach—is increasingly the sphere in which representations of Latina/o sexualities provide the main ideological frame by which to make sense of policies related to immigration, education, criminology, and health care, among others. Certainly, popular culture has had a close relationship to policy agendas in the United States, yet most often in terms of the media regulating offensive language, nudity, and copyright issues. For the most part, popular culture has not been the arena policymakers have turned to for political insight or for models addressing social inequality. This section addresses implications for policy by turning to an instance that initially may not seem policy oriented but yet offers an example of the ways Latina/o popular culture has much to offer future policy discussions related to representations of sexuality of Latina/o populations in a U.S. context.

Over the past decade artist Hector Silva has presented us with a popular culture canvass of transforming Latina/o sexualities. Silva's artwork of pencil-sketched masculine "homeboys" or cholo Latinos—complete with tattoos, khaki pants, and shaved heads—captures racialized gay men provocatively and amorously posed with each another. As such, Silva "queers the home boy aesthetic."[62] These sketches, circulating in spaces ranging from art galleries to gay bars, mark a number of productive critical disruptions to representations of Latino sexuality that rely on heteronormative models of hypersexualization and deviant sexuality. Silva's artwork challenges our comfort zone of assumed constructions of masculinity associated with "gay" or queer Latinos. Silva's artwork refigures love, eroticism, and nonheteronormative family through the homeboy figure—most often registered by such movies as *American Me* (1992)—and typically relegated solely to the trope of gang violence and criminality. No longer is cholo or homeboy masculinity exclusively the possession of heterosexual Latinos. No longer is the gay Latino subject seamlessly stitched to the hypereffeminate stereotype. Such representational disruptions epitomize directions for future scholarship but also bring to bear the power of popular culture representations on public policy agendas. A heterogeneous range of masculinities as depicted in such figures as the homo-homies of Silva or the reconsideration of the chola and homegirl challenge the heteronormative figures associated with constructions of family, parenting, and citizenship. Without such scholarship and cultural production (as that referenced here) there continues a sealing of reductive representations of masculinity to gayness or of heterosexual femininity to "motherhood." Such figures in popular culture continue to fail to produce insights for addressing civil rights and sociopolitical agendas of all Latinas/os. In short, Silva's artwork is an example of a cultural product that is an informative lens for future researchers analyzing the changing constructions of gender, sexuality, and Latino identity formation, particularly as these systems engage with other social structural systems of power and the policies created to address poverty, the rise of the prison industrial complex, and exploitation of immigrants in the United States.

Policy recommendations can no longer afford to be concerned with merely "cleaning up" the public media of undesirable elements of nonnormative sexuality like the homeboy or the hypersexualized Latina; for these representations may be figures of alternative citizenry and diverse constructions of "family" among Latina/o communities.[63] Policy agendas need to encompass multiple configurations of masculinities and femininities in order critically to assess the problematic investments inherent in normative constructions of Latino "family" and citizenship as these concepts apply to social services, welfare, and citizenship rights. As self-identifying lesbian, gay, bisexual, and transgender Latina/os —as well as the range of masculinities and femininities—become increasingly vocal and visible, so will constructions of family require more nuanced frameworks to examine gender and power in order to address policy issues such as health care, adoption, and marriage. As the literature attests, scholars and policy analysts must remain vigilant when it comes to representations of Latina/os as one unproblematic unit of analysis. Discourses that follow an assumed homogenous Latina/o "community" work against complex political agendas addressing institutions of religion, education, and health care.

Policy studies have generally considered race and class as the central organizing principles by which to address Latina/o social issues and political concerns. Concerns with gender and sexuality most often arise within discourses of single-motherhood and the welfare state of families with missing fathers. The arena of public policy too often considers popular culture venues as superficial reflections of what is wrong or right in society rather than as a stage where politics actually occurs.

Representations of family, criminality, and sexual deviance are not mere sideshows; they are central to discourses that frame policy arguments such as those justifying more prisons and fewer social welfare programs for single mothers. Equally as problematic are public discourses forging "positive" representations of familia narratives in movies or untenable icons such as Oscar De La Hoya's "Golden Boy" masculinity. Such normative representations are powerful, if ill-conceived, mechanisms for perpetuating Latina/os as assimilatable citizens; they do little to contest racist and sexist hierarchies of masculinity and femininity among Latina/os. Heterogeneous representations of Latina/o sexualities in popular culture need to be more seriously integrated in policy agendas addressing Latina/o poverty, illiteracy, educational attainment, and incarceration. In this way, more funding for independent cultural productions is critical as this arena often has presented the public with alternative ideologies and discourses of gender and sexuality not found in commercial venues.

As the earlier "Color Matters" section of this chapter attests, there needs to be increased and sustained attention to the integration of blackness in configurations of Latina/o identity in the United States. The social construction of whiteness becomes a very different system for analysis when it is assessed not only as the dominant U.S. cultural paradigm but also as an axis of power pertaining to Latina/o sexualities, especially in public representations. Lack of attention in public policy to blackness as well as to nonheterosexual representations of sexuality is sure to result in ineffective strategies to combat everything from hate crimes, sex trafficking of Latinas, and the disenfranchisement of alternative family formations.

9

Cultural Production of Knowledge on Latina/o Sexualities

JOSÉ QUIROGA AND MELANIE LÓPEZ FRANK

The artificial separation that existed between queer studies and racial/ethnic studies has been bridged in recent years by work from artists, critics, historians, sociologists, and other cultural producers. This separation had entailed, paradoxically, a normative narrative, with sexuality studies in the United States originating at a certain point (in the contemporary U.S. academy, this is normally placed in the late 1980s and early 1990s) and then developing by trying to incorporate other approaches that contested the new field's universalist assumptions, based as they were on demarcations and false distinctions. This narrative is, of course, simplified for the sake of expediency. But until very recently, this was the narrative engaged by traditional historiography on sexuality studies as the latter refused to come to terms with the relationship between colonialism and sexuality and with the differences between sexualities and racial or ethnic categories. In more recent years, these problematic linkages have been underscored by Latina/o writers and critics who have debunked some of the pieties that used the pursuit of human rights as cover for colonialism itself.[1] Principally, cultural production on Latina/os and their sexualities engages the question of overlapping identities as a way of avoiding essentialist readings of queer Latina/os. The fact that hybrid subjectivities have been theorized in many ways apart from each other does not do justice to the complexities of subjectivities themselves. There may be no unified subjectivity, just as there may be no unified sexuality, but it is clear that the separation between the race/ethnic dynamic and sexuality does a disservice to the complexities in understanding that necessarily must be present when dealing with how subjects may define themselves.

In this chapter, we provide an overview of the cultural production by Latina/os in relation to their sexualities , and we focus on key moments and conflicts that have allowed this field to be carved out by artists, activists, academics, and social researchers. Because critical work on and by Latina/os shows to what extent the pretense of historical objectivity serves as a cover for ideological attempts to engage systems of inclusion or exclusion, we also question the way in which the cultural production of Latina/os on sexualities complicates notions of identity, community, and the national frameworks from which an ethnic category such as Latina/o arises. We have attempted to move between history and critique, as we believe that cultural production on sexualities in general should question normative narratives on sexuality. As such, we think that all the different aspects pertaining to research on sexualities and Latina/os involve more than simply naming or discussing issues that relate to particularized subjects or to universalist assumptions. The different intersections through which cultural production and Latina/o sexualities move define cultural production, and the specificities involved in Latina/o sexualities as political, intellectual, and liberatory projects.

Even while separations delimiting fields of study have been addressed in recent years, essays on Latina/os and their sexualities have customarily started by setting up definitions, establishing normativities, and expressing what would or would not be included in the term Latina/o and the equally contentious term "sexualities." This has been the result, in part, of the perceived divide between Latin Americans and U.S. Latina/os and also of the conflicted relationship between colonialism and sexuality. The question of both male and female Latinos and their sexualities has often been subject to paternalistic and imperialist gestures by normative feminist and gay/lesbian movements in the United States and Europe. Many times these demands, ranging from "coming out of the closet" to "identity politics," have had the effect of insisting on the primacy of sexuality over ethnicity, and therefore at times they have sought to devalue Latina/o social and community links and networks by portraying the ethnic source community as repressive and patriarchal, while the target (or "broader") community of mainstream homosexuals is perceived as open and accommodating. This narrative often leads to an unchanging trajectory for the subject, who begins in confusion and ends in understanding, once again demonstrating an oversimplification. Much of the recent cultural production by Latina/os exploring and trying to understand their sexualities is devoted to nuancing these paradigms or responding forcefully to them—for their implicit or explicit disfiguring of ethnic communities and communities of color in the United States. The very term Latina/o sexualities can too easily be seen as the mark of an inflection of difference from the norm, while also gesturing toward a critique of essence, which leads to the always problematic idea(1) of essentialism. For this reason we use the possessive pronoun Latina/os and *their* sexualities in order to avoid the idea that there can even exist an inherent Latina/o sexuality feeding into the same overgeneralizing that defined studies and perceptions of Latina/os in the past.

As we understand it, the cultural production by Latina/os about their sexualities precisely questions aspects of normativity, ethnicity, nationality, inclusion, and definition. While all terms are open to critique, the cultural production on sexualities has also affirmed difference—or even identity as difference—strategically and situationally. An example of this can be found in the groundbreaking work of Gloria Anzaldúa as both an author and an editor, in which she brings forth not just the female, or queer, or Chicana perspective to the so-called culture wars but rather *her* voice and the voices of others—which are not a simplified exposition that explains what it is to *be* Latina/o or how one's sexuality determines this.[2]

To clarify our point better, we refer readers to comments recorded by Bernardo García. The participants in his study negotiate daily among and between different categories; both their Latino identities and their gay identities are important to them. For some, one identity and its maintenance are more important than the other, with the majority of the men participating more in the gay community than in their Latina/o communities. However, some men (the study did not include women) also reported that they would not separate their Latino identities from their gay identity, and thus García engaged the notion of "concentric circles" in order to discuss and understand these problems and decisions, as ways in which Latinos have to *negotiate* terms of inclusion when homosexualities are seen as "foreign" or "nontraditional" in terms of the Latina/o community itself.[3] These negotiations illustrate the continuous clashes and forms of difference in play within and around the terms that we are examining here.

In our research, the starting point for the cultural production of knowledge on Latina/os and their sexualities arises from activist work in the 1960s and 1970s. Latina/o artists, writers, and cultural producers all agree that this period produced the defining debates that have marked subsequent histories. Though certainly there was work done on these issues before that time, it is a convenient marker for notions of ethnic identification and the negotiation of sexualities. One of the most important features of activist work at that time went beyond the situationist context of agitating for social policy, and fostered the creation of those whom Antonio Gramsci called "organic intellectuals," who would be able to speak truth to power from the solidarity that obtains from belonging to the same class and background as those doing the protesting. Martin Duberman has accurately underscored the role of Latina/os and African Americans in the first Stonewall rebellion that began on June 28, 1969, and lasted for several days—particularly by focusing on Silvia Rivera's work. Very early on in the AIDS epidemic, as government inaction was evident in the response to the crisis, artist/activist collective organizations such as Gran Fury or ACT UP (AIDS Coalition To Unleash Power)—both founded in 1987—counted Latina/os among their members. In the 1980s, and as a result of work done in the 1970s, collective organizations were formed, such as the Audre Lorde Project in New York (brought together by Advocates of Gay Men of Color in 1994), with a mission to help communities of color that were not necessarily defining themselves as gay or lesbian.[4] By opting for more inclusive forms of social organization, these collectives actually operated in opposition to much of the governmental frameworks in which they found themselves, and they would set the stage for academic discourses and for the production of knowledge on Latina/os and their particular understanding of sexualities for years to come. Latina/os already had associations like the Puerto Rican Young Lords on the East Coast and in Chicago, and MEChA (Movimiento Estudiantil Chicano de Aztlán) in the Southwest.[5] They argued for Latina/o recognition, engaged in acts of civil disobedience, and forced their agendas to the center of political discourse. Latina/o participation in these early organizing efforts helped bring to the forefront the fact that the question of AIDS was bisected by ethnicities, class, and race. It reflected the varied sexual partnerships and commitments within the community, and it forcefully underscored that these alliances were a powerful reflection that the liberatory ways in which the community saw itself during the 1970s were not going to be lost with the onset of this terrible disease. More important, they allowed for effective treatment to reach the most vulnerable parts of the population, by keeping in check the notion of the identity of homosexuality by forcefully inscribing homosexuality as something that was beyond identity and was present in multiple sites. The HIV/AIDS sector, in fact, has been a center for the production of knowledge on Latina/os and their sexualities thanks to the work of Héctor Carrillo, Rafael Díaz, Manolo Guzmán, María Cecilia Zea, and Alex Carballo-Dieguez—all of whom effectively critiqued and nuanced our understanding of ethnicities and sexualities at this particular juncture.[6] They have worked, or collaborated, with other grassroots initiatives that have been both ethnic specific and pan-Latina/o, such as the Puerto Rican Initiative to Develop Empowerment, Gay Men of the Bronx, Latino Gay Men of New York, and others.

Present work on ethnicity, race, gender, and sexuality owes much to the fact that these issues came to the forefront in the 1970s via the feminist and homosexual struggles for recognition. Feminist, lesbian, and gay activists learned their lessons in civil disobedience from the civil rights movement, but they centralized questions of gender and sexuality while leaving aside issues relating to race and ethnicity, in order to reach broader sectors of the population that they defined as middle class and white. While first- and second-wave feminists developed an important critical discourse on patriarchy and oppression, they did not take into account other forms of political struggle that were particularly pertinent to African American or Latina women and to lesbians. Lesbians and feminists of color came together on their own to critique the feminist movement for its continued use of normative structures. Claims by gay and lesbian movements to represent ethnic or Latina/o communities were alienating to Latinas because of the former's insistence on gender and sexuality as defined by normative terms. The economic and political structures on which these organizations were forced to operate created difficult positionalities and strange bedfellows. In many ways, Latina/o organizations had to decide whether to incorporate themselves into the wider struggle for gay and lesbian rights or to seek to understand sexuality on their own terms. A turning point was the decision by LLEGO (Latino/a

Lesbian and Gay Organization) in the late 1990s to align itself with the Human Rights Campaign—an organization that had itself been criticized for pushing aside concerns by black and feminist grassroots organizers, by insisting on a very middle-class notion of political incorporation within structures of power in Washington. Ultimately, LLEGO lost its focus and its very reason for being, as a national Latina/o organization that brought together different grassroots organizing projects, for the sake of having a place at the table of majoritarian lesbian and gay organizations. Other grassroots efforts, such as the Audre Lorde Project, have been more successful in not diluting their mandate, while at the same time remaining inclusive in their outreach efforts, which puts them at the intersection of different communities. In addition, new social science research has allowed scholars to broaden notions of culture and sexuality in order to incorporate sites for the production of knowledge on Latina/os and their sexualities that had not been so readily available in the past. La Escuelita, Esta Noche, the Doo Wop, and Tempo, among other nightclubs and bars, were places where Latina/os found connection, politicization, sex, clarification, pride, identity, and affirmation. Latina/os learned (and are still learning) about ourselves and each other in these places. We both shaped and were shaped by these sites, which we used and still use to articulate and rearticulate our sexualities and our critical notions of what being Latina/o entails. These sites were important also because many of them welcomed gender, age, and class mixing, which influenced how knowledge about Latina/os and their sexualities were and still are shaped, by raising questions about class, age, and gender differences or similarities.

To this day, it seems, normative definitions of nationality collide with the question of sexual preference, while the issues surrounding the transnationalization of gay and lesbian politics are by no means resolved.[7] A vision of nationality as one that validates the uniqueness of culture ends up regulating, aestheticizing, and even globalizing ethnic differences without taking specificities into account. Nationalist myths are sexualized in ways that are oppressive, and this has been an important lesson learned from feminist Chicana lesbian scholars, above all with their treatment of La Malinche, aka La Chingada.

Perhaps the first book that illustrated a broadening of the academic universe by intellectuals who were not necessarily bound by the academy was *This Bridge Called My Back: Writings by Radical Women of Color* edited by Cherríe Moraga and Gloria Anzaldúa. It was first published in 1981 by Women of Color Press and has been reprinted multiple times. It essentially started what is now called "third-wave feminism"—which took into account the importance of class, race, and sexuality—and was able to put together a comprehensive account, in terms of race and class, of the intersections between ethnicity, feminism, and homophobia. The fourth (of six) sections, for example, is titled "Between the Lines: On Culture, Class, and Homophobia"; as with the other sections, it is filled with the prose and poetry of women of color. In this section, Cuban American Mirtha Quintanales makes two contributions, "I Come with No Illusions" and

"I Paid Very Hard for My Immigrant Ignorance," both of which take the form of a letter and deal with Quintanales's status as a Latina lesbian. Her first, and shorter, letter details her understanding that "human nature/culture" means variety and difference. In her second, which she addresses to fellow contributor Barbara Smith, an African American lesbian, Quintanales tries to understand her role and definition as a white "woman of color" and the different types of racism that one encounters in the United States. She questions the continued inability of people here to see shades of color and difference beyond the typical dichotomies that have been inscribed in U.S. history. In fact, this insistence on U.S. dichotomies of race as "universalized" identifies the problems that most studies of Latina/os or *Latinidad* encounter in the United States—how to explain the idea of diversity within an ethnic grouping. That is to say, Latina/os cannot all fit in this preconceived notion of the brown, Spanish-speaking, Catholic, and often sexually overdriven beings that seems to permeate the American psyche. In her second letter, Quintanales also underlines the importance of having contact with her Latina sisters, which does not necessarily supersede her connection to other lesbians of color but is an important connection that she cannot give up. Rosario Morales, a Nuyorican, writes in "The Other Heritage" about the need to pass in her daily life, to be "white" in the stores while ignoring the other heritage—"the ebony sheen to [her] life." It is through contact with black women in a poetry workshop that she can recapture what previously had been lost. Once again, these two writers underscore the problematic issues of race in Latina/o identity—as Anzaldúa's new mestiza, Latina/os contradict the usual U.S. definitions and divisions along the binary of black versus white. Perhaps it would be best to understand that as Latina/os "pass" between the different racial categories in play in the United States, so too do some of them negotiate and pass between the different divisions of sexuality.[8]

One interesting aspect of *This Bridge Called My Back* is the way it migrates from activist circles to the academy. The same could be said for Anzaldúa's considerable impact in Latina/o studies and feminism, by means of her *Borderlands/La Frontera: The New Mestiza* (1987), as well as her later edited collection, *Making Face, Making Soul: Haciendo Caras* (1990). In the 1980s, these collaborations between activists and academic work seemed promising, and they continued with interesting results throughout the decade. Among these, and aside from those mentioned before, we should also note the Centro Mariposa/Mariposa Women's Center, founded in 1977 in Orange, California, as well as Las Buenas Amigas (LBA), a group for lesbian Latinas of New York City, which was created on November 10, 1986. Activist work was also important in the growth of LLEGO, which turned into the first and only national lesbian and gay organization dedicated to Latina/os with offices in D.C., an impressive development for an organization initially formed on October 8, 1985, in Austin, Texas.

Before and after these cultural organizations gave particular impetus to Latina/os and their sexualities, important works had already tackled these issues in fiction and poetry. One of the first books to deal with the sex trade was John Rechy's *City of Night*, narrating in short vignettes and chapters the nightlife of Los Angeles. In other books, such as *The Sexual Outlaw*, Rechy dealt with similar topics.[9] An interesting study of Puerto Rican masculinity is the work of Luis Rafael Sanchez, particularly his novel *La Importancia de Llamarse Daniel Santos*, which deconstructs the sexual energy of the mythic Puerto Rican singer as well as his lyrics. In Puerto Rico, as well as in New York, Manuel Ramos Otero did exemplary work during the late 1960s and 1970s as one of the first on the island as well as in the Puerto Rican community in New York to tackle issues of homosexuality. His status as an iconoclast is evident in all of his work, from the stories in which two lovers in New York share news of a mythic land that is the real, but also invented, Puerto Rico in "El cuento de la mujer del mar" to his last book of poems, *Invitación al polvo*, where he juxtaposes the islands of Puerto Rico and Cuba to the discourse of exile and to the ravages of the body with AIDS. More recently, his work has been republished in collections such as *Tálamos y tumbas: Prosa y verso* and *Cuentos de buena tinta*.[10]

A similar situation obtained with the Cuban writer Reinaldo Arenas, particularly in his works published in Spanish in the United States. Never simply a dissident figure of the Cuban Revolution, Arenas was already well known in Latin America through his writings before he became instrumental in setting up *Mariel* magazine in New York, which he edited with Reinaldo García Ramos and Roberto Valero. *Mariel* became the most important Cuban magazine outside of Cuba and produced important issues—in particular one dedicated to homosexuality during the revolutionary process in the island. Ana María Simo and García Ramos contributed to that issue "Hablemos claro," their response to a debate registered in Lourdes Argüelles and B. Ruby Rich's "Homosexuality, Homophobia, and Revolution," published in two parts in *Signs*. This debate, concerning the repression of homosexuals in Cuba during the 1970s, had already become internationalized because of the movie *Conducta impropia* (1984), directed by Nestor Almendros and Orlando Jiménez Leal, which interviewed gay and lesbian Cuban exiles living in New York and Miami. *Mariel* reconstructed the Cuban canon both inside and outside the island, and though the gist of the work directly refers to Cuba's particular political situation, there is no attempt to sideline the question of sexuality or homosexuality in its analyses of the national tradition.[11]

Rechy, Sanchez, Ramos Otero, and Arenas were the first Latino writers in the 1960s and 1970s openly to address the question of homosexuality in their work. They never argued for a "separate but equal" sphere in terms of their homosexuality. They were (and are still) important figures in the canon of Latin American and U.S. Latina/o literature. Sexuality was never subsumed to the question of literature in their work, but at the same time they did not relegate it to secondary status. In this way, they managed openly to pass their homosexuality to a heteronormative reading public. Arenas became a gay writer only in the United

States and after his death, with the publication of his memoir, *Before Night Falls*, and the film of the same name by Julian Schnabel.[12] Recent research on their work underscores author positionalities while keeping in mind the way in which the market, since the 1990s in particular, created "gay and lesbian literature" as a category. On the one hand, Arenas's success underscored sexuality as a viable way of focusing on literature; but on the other hand, it separated canonical and heteronormative authors from those who belonged to the category of gay and lesbian. It is clear that while many writers have refused these categorizations, such compartmentalization has taken place because of the demands of the market, but also owing to these authors' understanding of what the reading public wants. It is interesting to recall also, in this context, Richard Rodriguez's disconcerting experience of finding his books at the bookstore shelved under "Hispanic" authors, a scene that he relates very early in *Hunger of Memory*. Obviously, the effect of the new classification is the defamiliarization of the known or the desired. With Arenas, the effect is different, as he is being particularized as queer, whereas Rodriguez is resisting being particularized as Hispanic and seeks a more universal status as an author.[13]

In the 1990s gay and lesbian Latina/os launched important thematic literary contributions that included fiction and poetry, as well as performance arts. An interesting writer in this regard is Jaime Manrique, whose *Latin Moon in Manhattan* narrates the story of Colombian migrants to New York City. Later on, in his *Eminent maricones*, Manrique tackled the historical legacies of Federico García Lorca, Manuel Puig, Reinaldo Arenas, and others, and in the collection *Bésame mucho* Manrique assembled poems and stories by a more recent generation of gay and lesbian Latina/o writers. Manrique's work decisively addresses the notion of a gay literary canon as well as gay history.[14]

In Achy Obejas's work, sexuality is joined to her Cuban American identity. From her first collection of stories, *We Came All the Way from Cuba So You Could Dress Like This?*, on to *Memory Mambo*, the question of sexuality is one more element in the sometimes humorous narratives of ethnic survival in a hostile medium. Obejas makes no apologies and offers no excuses as a lesbian and does not place her ethnic and sexual selves oppositionally—rather, they exist, as they should, as facets of her identity, not as deciding and ruling factors. In her more recent and ambitious novel, *Days of Awe*, she returns to her native land in order also to explore her Jewish roots.[15] This is a sprawling account of the retrieval of an ethnic memory of a subject that seeks to understand the complicating factors surrounding ethnicity, which are never as clear-cut as they are meant to be.

In the early 1990s a group of Latina/o playwrights and poets also came to grips with issues of sexuality in their work. Again, as with the examples noted above, these were not necessarily coming-out tales but rather nuanced and complicated works that tried to address Latina/os and sexuality by creating intersectional bonds with other minorities. Important figures in this regard are Ricardo Bracho, Jorge Cortiñas, and Caridad Svich. They developed by furthering examples of their mentors, such as Cherríe Moraga and the Cuban playwright María Irene Fornés, whose long and distinguished career in New York vanguard theater was also marked by her discussing questions of feminism and sexualities.[16] Moraga, in particular, has made important strides in allowing us to understand the pull of ethnicity even in the midst of feminist and homonormative insistence on understanding the issues from a gay and lesbian perspective. Straddling both these communities, Moraga ultimately sees more progressive work in terms of rescuing a freer notion of tradition, instead of the disfigured tradition that white lesbians and feminists present as Latin American or Latina.

Representations of the different Latina/o sexualities appeared in various literary productions during the 1990s. In her book *Chicana Falsa: And Other Stories of Death, Identity, and Oxnard*, Michele Serros reveals the "controversy" of being straight but being in a relationship with a white man. In the poem "White Owned," she is informed by a white woman that "Spaniards" steal white babies— and so she must question what will happen if she has a "beige baby" that people will think she stole. Other Latina writers have shown their female, and male, protagonists pursuing relationships with those outside the Latina/o community, to both good and bad ends. In terms of Latina/os and their sexualities, it is clear that a crossover potential exists. *The Dirty Girls Social Club* by Alisa Valdes-Rodriguez gained its author a near-$500,000 advance from St. Martin's Press and the moniker "Godmother of Chica Lit" from *Time* magazine (August 22, 2005), which also named her one of the twenty-five most influential Hispanics in the United States. In this first novel, Valdes-Rodriguez introduced the *sucias*: six different Latinas who attempt to cover the spectrum of *Latinidad* in the United States. Elizabeth, the "stunning black Latina" from Colombia, has a high-profile job as a morning television anchor and must hide her sexuality. She is secretly in love with her best friend, the Cuban American Sara, who is a proper Latina house-wife, but Jewish, and is of course being abused by her Cuban husband. Within the novel the other sucias also pursue relationships with Latino men, white men, African men, and others. This novel tries hard to cover all the bases but does end up glossing a bit too much. Valdes-Rodriguez's view of U.S. Latina/o life has found a diverse and willing audience. *Dirty Girls* has sold more than 350,000 copies and is in development to become a series on the Lifetime network. Her second book, *Playing with Boys*, has sold upwards of 130,000 hardcover copies. Once again, Valdes-Rodriguez takes a group of Latinas from various national ori-gins who have relations with Latina/os and non-Latina/os alike. *Make Him Look Good* and the Young Adult fiction *Haters* were both published in 2006, while more women's novels as well as works of Young Adult fiction are in the pipeline. Since *Dirty Girls* made its debut, similar works by Latina authors, like *Hot Tamara* by Mary Castillo, have found their way into bookstores. Michele Serros has also published a teen fiction novel, *Honey Blonde Chica*. Valdes-Rodriguez hesitates to take any credit. "These writers have always been there," she says. "It's just that the industry wasn't ready to publish them. They're ready now."[17]

The production of knowledge on Latina/os and their sexualities in academia starts with the advent of structuralism, deconstruction, and the postdeconstructive turn in the 1970s and early 1980s and was followed in the United States by the culture wars of the late 1980s and the 1990s, including the debate on what should be included in the canon that flourished with particular urgency in big state school systems like California's. Within these broader social debates, academic units were being changed, reclassified, or restructured to provide comprehensive programs for students who were not relating to the general requirements as a whole. In the broader context where knowledge and the academy met, questions of ethnicity and sexuality started coming to the fore. First, by the creation of gay and lesbian studies, queer studies, or sexuality studies programs, and then by the sheer force of discourses on sexuality during the 1990s in all realms of society. Given the previous fights over inclusion or exclusion in terms of women's studies and sexuality studies, gay and lesbian Latina/o scholars have had to engage on two fronts: first, in the normative, white-oriented discourse that was prevalent in women's studies and sexuality studies programs; and second, with the homophobia that is, regrettably, still present in Latina/o studies or Latin American studies and foreign-language programs. To this extent, the cultural production on Latina/os and the way in which they understand their sexualities does not stake out a field that is separate from those other normative fields, but rather seeks for points of commonality or difference—or both—between different theoretical domains. To paraphrase Chela Sandoval's brilliant *Methodology of the Oppressed*, racialized domains on the one hand allow for particularities to come to the foreground, but on the other hand are not allowed to radicalize the constitutive normativity of those same categories. In terms of academic disciplines, the production of knowledge on the ways in which Latina/os understand their sexualities has allowed for these compartmentalizing effects to be noted and critiqued, for they do not radicalize spheres of knowledge. One should take into account, of course, the present backlash against Latina feminists from the point of view of normative Chicano nationalist discourse in order to gain a perspective of the strong positions taken by nationalist Latino scholars when they see themselves attacked for their non-inclusive practices.[18]

This is why more recent cultural productions center on historical and social analyses that take into account the way in which Latina/os interact and intersect with other U.S. minoritarian discourses. Knowledge as to how forms of identity develop over time has been one of the main themes of more recent cultural work on Latina/o sexualities. Representing the present nexus of sexuality, ethnicity, and nationality, the works authored by Emilio Bejel, Josianna Arroyo, Alberto Sandoval, Carlos Decena, Arnaldo Cruz Malavé, Juana María Rodríguez, Alicia Gaspar de Alba, Ben Sifuentes-Jáuregui, Lawrence La Fountain-Stokes, Yolanda Martínez-San Miguel, Emma Pérez, and Rubén Ríos-Avila stand out as complicating the models that insist on a universal assumption of homosexual sameness, while at the same time focusing on the nuance given to homosexual identities by way of class, race, and nationality.[19]

There has been a wealth of cultural knowledge produced about Latina/os in media. Frances Negrón-Muntaner in *Boricua Pop* explores media representation and self-representation of Puerto Ricans on the island as well as in the diaspora. Licia Fiol Matta, whose groundbreaking book on Gabriela Mistral allowed us to understand the different positionalities of one of the most important Latin American poets, is now undertaking research on Puerto Rican female singers in the diaspora and on the intersections of diaspora, music, and sexuality. Frances Aparicio and Cándida Jáquez have uncovered the relationship between homophobia and sexism in traditional Caribbean music, noting in particular gender oppression and masculinist performance, while Juan Carlos Quintero-Herencia, in *La Máquina de la Salsa*, explores how the physicality of music underscores the different sexual positionalities possible in Caribbean music.[20]

Performance studies offer incisive and important accounts of Latina/os and their sexualities. José Muñoz nuances narratives of identity by exploring disidentification as a process that takes into account how minoritarian subjects define themselves. Incorporating, but also departing from, the work of Diana Fuss, Judith Butler, and others, Muñoz traces an important bridge: between Latina/o and specifically Cuban American performance, identities, and sexualities, to African American art, Pop Art, film, documentary, and visual culture. For critics such as Chon Noriega, Ana López, and Clara Rodriguez, among others, cultural production deploys, critiques, and comments on notions of gender and sexuality. Yvonne Yarbro-Bejarano's study on Chabela Vargas, for example, examines how this important Mexican singer employs her gender performance to destabilize normative visions of masculinity and femininity. For José Quiroga, the polemics surrounding Ricky Martin's sexuality and the U.S. media's insistence on his coming out paradoxically underscored the various publics and counterpublics that Martin appeals to within a network that is intergenerational and interethnic—networks that the artist does not seem ready to let go, over and beyond his almost coy insistence on the privacy of his sexuality. Negrón-Muntaner has been just as incisive with Jennifer Lopez, Martin, and Selena, who in turn is also the focus of explorations by Aparicio. All these critics share a renewed concentration on media as the source for many of our ideas about gender as a performative gesture repeated and redeployed by minoritarian subjects.[21]

Moving away from essentialist visions of gender and sexualities, many of these critics see the media as potential sites for playing with representation, in spite of their conservative tendencies. The progressive gesture in all these studies on representation belies an alternate countercurrent that may well be ahead of social policy. The media have a long history of portraying Latina/os as the exotic Other, the hot-blooded sexualized figure of desire. With the U.S. film industry located in California almost from the outset, Latina/os have maintained a presence throughout the history of motion pictures. Whether as Latin lovers, drug lords, maids, harlots, *bandidos*, and the like, Latina/os and their sexualities have been important in the industry. In recent film and television productions, we have seen increasing numbers of Latina/o actors and characters. Film has had an important role in terms of establishing queer Latina/o voices, with such films as *Latin Boys Go to Hell* (1997), directed by Ela Troyano or the seminal *Paris Is Burning* (1990), directed by Jennie Livingston. Most recently in the television series *Lost* (2004–), Jorge García's character Hugo "Hurley" Reyes has been for the most part completely desexualized; his two romantic interests have been shown more as innocent crushes than as anything more adult. By contrast, Michele Rodríguez, who with her first film, *Girlfight* (2000), became known as a "tough" Latina with a forceful personality and sexuality, was vilified by fans of *Lost* as the former cop Ana Lucia Cortez. She acted as the tough leader of the tail section and also employed her sexuality to achieve her ends. She was violently killed after one season on the show. Meanwhile, *Ugly Betty* (2006), the American version of the Colombian telenovela *Yo soy Betty, la fea* (1999), has allowed for the portrayal of a variety of sexualities within the Mexican family of the protagonist Betty Suarez. From her sister Hilda, a single mother, to her widower father, Ignacio, to her "pregay" nephew, Justin, and Betty herself as a not quite virginal young woman, the show allows, not for an essential Latina/o sexuality, but rather for a notion of plural sexualities that relate to and at the same time clash with each other. Although representation of Latina/os and their sexualities in the mainstream media must be qualified by the fact that it constitutes the gaze of an Other looking at "us," the growing presence of Latina/os at every stage of the production process in the big media conglomerates seems to promise new representations of sexualities that will further complicate what has to date been a facile picture of the ways in which the cultural production of Latina/o sexualities destabilizes the majoritarian normative ideologies.

The object of this examination of Latina/o cultural production on sexualities is not merely to set up policies that pertain to these populations, but rather to understand the ways in which representation may or may not lead to empowerment, or to allow for cultural life to be complicated and disturbed in myriad ways, as well as to enable future forms of cultural enrichment to take place. Latina/o cultural production as a whole has furnished strong critiques of majoritarian ideologies and sharp analyses of problematic social situations. Latina/o cultural production on sexualities may give us a different view of the Latina/o community, but it is also a sign that the community needs to understand itself in order to grow, as it comes into contact with other and different forms of social polity. While there has been much conceptual separation between Latina/os, minoritarian discourses and sexualities, there has also been much overlapping for the sake of political expediency. At this point, this overlapping reveals the way in which research should guide our understanding of subjectivities. The field that explores Latina/os and sexualities is rich in academic intersections, and there is the possibility that queer Latina/o cultural production may shift our understanding of minoritarian cultural production in general. We think there is a strategic multiplicity at play when we are dealing with the relationships between ethnic minorities and sexualities. Within a multicultural context rich in technological advances that at the same time allow for personal contact to take place without physical contact, subjects may be able to pass between different identity structures with relative ease. It seems clear that future cultural production relating to Latina/os and their sexualities will allow for more interesting interventions, as we continue debating the questions of subjectivity, media, technology, and culture in new and novel ways, in order to complicate further what by now seems a very restrictive sense of sexualities and ethnicities.

10

Where There's *Querer*

Knowledge Production and the
Praxis of HIV Prevention

GEORGE AYALA, JAIME CORTEZ, AND PATRICK "PATO" HEBERT

"Sorry I can't be what you want me to be.

Hate won't change me,

Hate won't change me."

–Byron Stingily, "Hate Won't Change Me"

"For a long time, I've thought that the purpose of activism and art, or at least of mine, is to make a world in which people are producers of meaning, not consumers, and writing this book I now see how this is connected to the politics of hope and to those revolutionary days that are the days of the creation of the world. Decentralization and direct democracy could, in one definition, be this politic in which people are producers, possessed of power and vision, in an unfinished world."

–Rebecca Solnit, *Hope in the Dark*

"And remember when I moved in you

And the holy dove was moving too

And every breath we drew was hallelujah?"

–Leonard Cohen, "Hallelujah"

In this chapter, we share the ways we synthesize community mobilization, creative production, and cultural studies in service of HIV prevention. Our work is grounded in a reverence for *querer*, the supple Spanish verb that simultaneously evokes multiple concepts. Querer is to love, to want, and even to wish. Our loved ones are our *queridos*, and these concepts form the most tender of greetings

in e-mails and old-fashioned letters, which open with the flourish "*Querido/a*
. . ." Querer can be used to express casual affection, deep love, intense passion
and magically raunchy desire—sometimes all at once. It is this multiplicity and
simultaneity that mark our work—our querer for one other, our communities,
and our shared commitment to wellness in a time of expanding plague.

All three of us are long-term cultural workers. We draw on decades of AIDS
work combined with disciplines as varied as education, psychology, visual art,
creative writing, performance, graphic design, research, grassroots organizing,
and community-based arts programming. Together, we have spent the last
four years seeking a kind of flexible synergy, honing our work in concert with
hundreds of community members, artists, writers, designers, clients, students,
social scientists, academics, public health officials, and AIDS service providers.
We believe relationships and social contexts are central to the production of
vibrant knowledge. Too often, we—academics, community workers, activists—
work in isolation. The danger of working alone is that the work can become
dehydrated because too little time is spent growing ideas within and through
relationships. We recognize these risks and therefore remember that community
cannot exist without meaningful connection and exchange. Knowledge grown in
playful, purposeful partnership with others is stronger, more lithe, and better
able to resonate across competing social terrains. Here we present a number of
examples of this cultural production of knowledge from the contested currents
of HIV prevention. We begin with a basic overview of our methodology and then
devote the bulk of the chapter to presenting case studies showing how knowledge is produced by queer communities of color that are deeply affected by the
AIDS pandemic. Throughout this process, we conceptualize knowledge not as a
passive, static object but rather as energy, a force, an elixir. We treat knowledge
as our connective tissue, from past to present to future, from self to Other, from
fear to courage.

The conduit for this now four-year effort is AIDS Project Los Angeles
(APLA). APLA has served the HIV/AIDS community in Los Angeles County for
nearly twenty-five years and has become the largest AIDS service organization
in California, with 125 employees and 1,500 volunteers. The projects described
here emanate from APLA's education department. Many of them were produced
in collaboration with the prevention department of Gay Men's Health Crisis
(GMHC), which is located in New York City. APLA began in 1982 with four
friends providing HIV services out of a home closet. Queer citizens and their
supporters were the first responders to the pandemic. Social fear, homophobia,
and severe government neglect ensured that this front line of community members felt little distinction between being activists and AIDS service providers.
Over time, the disease changed and spread, as did a growing network of AIDS
service organizations. Now more than twenty-five years into the pandemic,
APLA operates at a scale that some have referred to as "AIDS, Inc." With this
increased scale and attendant professionalization come tremendous resources

and opportunities. But there is also great risk that APLA's founding, community-based approach will be neglected in favor of more clinical and bureaucratic models. What happens when your community becomes your clients? How do we honor a range of constituent voices and still navigate the choppy waters of funding restrictions, public health mandates, shifting cultural norms, and an ever-changing client profile?

Over the last eight years of intense political repression, we tried to stay connected to the power of community-based knowledge by grounding our work in four key tenets: It is strengths-based, participatory, sex-positive, and critically self-reflexive. Exemplars of querer, these core values each deserve explication.

Being Strengths-Based

Our work is strengths-based because too often the communities most affected by HIV (queer, black or Latina/o, working class, poor) are pathologized—cast as passive victims or outright threats in the social landscape. A strengths-based approach is crucial because it instead values infected individuals and communities as key social actors who not only face dilemmas, uncertainties, and responsibilities but also possess considerable agency, brilliance, and creativity. We believe the efficacy of large-scale public health initiatives is compromised if the approach is simply top-down. This is especially true in the field of HIV/AIDS because the communities most affected by the disease have long and sometimes brutal histories of being on the receiving end of repressive policies imposed without consideration for the realities of community norms and needs. The campaigns we most want to carry out are those that identify, honor, galvanize, and nourish the knowledge that already exists in affected communities while deploying that knowledge in a coordinated and sustained fashion. Therefore, our initiatives are always participatory and evolving.

Being Participatory

Participation is imperfect, messy, and time-consuming. It is also deeply invigorating, inspiring, and necessary if we as AIDS service providers are to remain anchored in the realities of the communities we purport to serve. Participation and genuine reciprocity are critical modes of knowledge production and cultural exchange. This confluence enables the possibility of synergy and change. Our efforts attempt to engage multiple stakeholders as participants—co-producers, readers, outreach workers, models, critics. The conduit for participation is openness. For example, APLA hosts community forums where people can gather in auditoriums, or visit online, to offer their views on programs or issues of the day. Volunteer programs provide staff members an opportunity for formal and informal discussions with community members. Surveys folded into the pages of print material serve as another critical way of creating a feedback loop between APLA and its clients. Community planning groups and professional conferences are additional modes of knowledge exchange and partnership development.

Being Sex-Positive

In all of our work, we remain sex-positive. This does not mean we are uncritical of desire, disease, or power. We remain ready to engage questions of community sexual ethics. As we noted in the foreword to *Corpus II*, a publication that serves as one of our key prevention vehicles:

> *Corpus* is about the sex gay men have: how we feel about our sex; how we perform the beautifully broad range of masculinities and femininities inside our sex; and how we seek to experience and learn about our own sex and each other's bodies before, during and after our sex. Sometimes, our sex happens in irreverent celebration, communion and joy, and other times, in the silence of self-reflection or in the poetry of anonymous park sex. . . . *Corpus* stands as a fierce refusal to allow the sex and lives of gay men to be flattened, as is often and sadly the case in our efforts to prevent HIV transmission.

In *Corpus*, as in all of our work, we have remained committed to the most open and generous understanding of desire possible. We are proactive about creating representations that counter stigma, homophobia, misogyny, patriarchy, hatred, and social isolation by nurturing sexual self-determination and justice. Sexual repression by religious, state, cultural, or interpersonal strictures shuts down open communication about sexuality, thus fostering ever-greater risk for new infections and discrimination. For this reason, we believe sexual repression must be countered by sexual communication if we are to stem the spread of HIV. In short, we must address desire, not repress desire. This is particularly crucial in HIV prevention, where part of the charge must be to help people tap the potent knowledge of their own bodies as they learn to recognize the rhythms of their risk.

Being Critically Self-Reflexive and Finding Uncommon Ground

The three of us have deliberated the ethics of cultural production exhaustively, and at times exhaustingly. We disagree. We agree. Sometimes we hunker down at the periphery of ideas and stubbornly defend our positions. Sometimes we grow tired and just let others do it their way. Repeatedly, we are challenging one another and our partners with the fundamental questions of who gets to tell the story of HIV prevention and wellness and who gets to claim the authority of the storyteller? The questions are meaty and impossible for us to answer simply:

Is what we're doing really prevention? If so, is it effective enough? How do we know?

When does "keepin' it real" shut down our sense of possibility and optimism?

Where does tokenism end and genuine equity begin?

What should be translated into Spanish? Sez who? ¿y por qué?

When is ambiguity an invitation to explore ideas and when is it a dis- service to our readers?

What does it mean to spend this much time, energy, and treasure on putting out publications and imagery when there is a host of com- peting needs that APLA could serve?

To arrive at answers for these questions, we must continually find or cre- ate middle ground in the bleed between competing modes of knowing. In many ways, this process is a microcosmic example of Latina/o cultural synthesis. Again and again, we find that the most useful approach is the broadest, most syncretic and inclusive, a theoretical *mestizaje*, if you will, in which hybridity is privileged over didactic binaries. But this is about as essentialist as we get. If hybridity is something of a creed for our HIV-prevention efforts, it is always open to destabilizing and rejuvenating forces. This is perhaps what Latina/o diasporic experiences compel us to do: we must reckon ourselves with each other as a strategy for producing knowledge. Some HIV prevention practitioners retreat into Latina/o essentialisms as a source of fragile and fleeting power. We choose a different path in our work, one that disrupts comfortable race politics by problematizing them *and* decentering whiteness, thereby holding open a space for coexistence and multiple race, gender, and sexual orientation points of refer- ence. In trying to speak in unison, our "we" can be fraught with presumption, but "we" can also be buoyed by possibility.

The Context of Our Knowledge Production

In this intense reflexivity, our work aims to be mindful of the shifting social and cultural landscapes of people's lives. Risk does not happen in a vacuum, and our experience suggests that while official gatekeepers of what counts as knowledge may be ignorant or resistant to this reality, affected communities are all too aware. Therefore, APLA grounds its community-based work in a holis- tic approach that combines development of materials (journals, monographs, pamphlets, and palm cards) with a constellation of direct services (treatment adherence, a food bank, a dental clinic, mental health services, support groups, condom distribution, and outreach), applied research, and advocacy work. It is precisely in concert with its comprehensive programmatic cousins that the following portfolio of designs gains its greatest meaning. Yet in the interest of space, we focus solely on the production of print materials and creative discourse. The risk in this focused approach is that the knowledge featured here will be de-contextualized and flattened. It must be emphasized that the materials we created were part of a larger coordinated approach to HIV prevention and AIDS services. We feel strongly that meaningful social initiatives at the start of the twenty-first century must be layered, flexible, and informed. The stakes and challenges are too staggering for a singular or myopic approach. And when as service providers we make the mistake of feeling that we are needed—an egotistical need for power or importance—we remind ourselves that it is once again time to listen closely to and learn from others.

Following the Community's Lead

One example of community-based knowledge production is the now-common practice of sero-sorting. This sexual behavior has changed the way we talk about and approach HIV prevention. In 2005 GMHC in New York City spearheaded with APLA the production of a small outreach brochure called *What's Safe to You?* Produced on glossy stock and small enough to fit in your shirt pocket, the twenty-four-page brochure was designed for distribution in service centers and clinics as well as pride parades, bars, sex clubs, and public outreach. It targets young gay and bisexual men of color and features language and realities familiar to the community. Brian Toynes's design juxtaposes dynamic digital imagery with text crafted by Francisco Roque to be at once informed, authoritative, and familiar. One page shows two brown-skinned men toasting with drinks over coasters that read "positive." The quote reads: "I only sleep with POZ guys so I don't have to use condoms." The facing page features more thorough explication: "Some experts say that an increase in the number of gay and bisexual men who know their HIV-positive status and who search for HIV-positive partners might be contributing to the decrease in new HIV cases in San Francisco. The dating practice, which is called 'sero-sorting,' involves men choosing sex partners based on their common HIV serostatus. Studies have shown when people have knowledge of their serostatus, they take that knowledge and use it to protect their partners."

Sero-sorting has been a common sexual practice for a number of years but is only now beginning to be addressed explicitly in HIV-prevention research, programming, and materials. Gay men created an innovative (although far from fail-safe) approach to reducing risk, expanding their sexual possibilities, and destigmatizing HIV-positive status. This knowledge eventually led to research efforts whose findings suggest that this unprotected but safe(r) sexual practice might actually be helping to prevent the spread of HIV. This is counterintuitive to much all-or-nothing prevention dogma that circulated both officially (via public health efforts) and unofficially (via community norms) in the 1980s and

1990s. "Safe" and "protected" sexual practices are no longer necessarily synonymous. The terrain of desire and sexual practice has grown increasingly complex, and the knowledge generated in chat rooms and personal ads, monogamous relationships, and park trysts has filtered into the prevention departments of major AIDS service organizations, giving rise to new and unprecedented HIV-prevention strategies.

Elsewhere in *What's Safe to You?* a young black man wearing a baseball cap pulled low says, "When I fuck raw, I only do it as a top because I don't want to get HIV" (see fig. 1). Known in prevention vernacular as "strategic positioning," this is a common strategy used by men to reduce their risk for HIV infection. In the brochure, the facing-page explication notes: "A lot of men top to avoid HIV infection. While being a top is less risky, it's not risk free. HIV can enter the body through the dick and anytime you have unprotected sex you run the risk of getting or giving HIV as well as other STDs. . . . Check in with your partner before you top him. Even if you don't like to, using condoms should always be an option you give to him." Here a more nuanced suite of options and sexual decision making is encouraged. Community members have long told service providers that they are sick of being told what to do with their bodies. Despite this, they have simultaneously sought to protect themselves and share knowledge. Out of these exchanges between providers and clients (in focus groups, community forums, and counseling sessions) emerged a more flexible prevention practice that still endorses condoms while grounding the prophylactic option in the wider range of realities and scenarios that people face in their daily sexual lives. These materials in turn challenge public health dogma and conservative approaches that call for abstinence-only until marriage. In this way, community practices bump up against prevailing official discourse in a clash of cultural productions.

FIGURE 1 From *What's Safe to You?* Design by Francisco Roque and Brian Toynes. Courtesy of Gay Men's Health Crisis (GMHC) and AIDS Project Los Angeles (APLA).

A Body of Knowledge

While many of our materials are explicit in nature and targeted in scope, we also aim to address the fuller social context in which HIV risk occurs. One of our most successful endeavors has been the journal *Corpus*, now in its fourth year of publication. We chose the title "Corpus" because it simultaneously suggested a physical body and a body of knowledge, dovetailing with the theme of multiplicity that would run through each issue.

Querer for the lives and bodies of queer men is reflected both in *Corpus*'s content and in the process of its making. With five issues thus far, *Corpus* utilizes art, memoir, fiction, and poetry to convey salient issues related to HIV prevention and gay men's health. Published in a unique square format, *Corpus* is designed to live in people's lives. Its high production value is purposeful, utilizing heavy stock covers and glossy pages to reproduce the ideas and images in full splendor. At the outset, we wondered if community members and other stakeholders would retain copies after their initial perusing. We have been pleased to see that we bet on beauty and won. Again and again, we have heard of people leaving the publication on their coffee table to be shared with friends, in reception areas at clinics where demand is fierce, in classrooms as catalysts for heated discussions, and in outreach contexts where flyers and other prevention materials are often discarded as mere printed noise.

Corpus's relative shelf life is literally and figuratively by design. Readers keep *Corpus*, as they would a good book, long after other publications have been tossed out because it grapples with the emotions and stories of gay men's lives, something that seldom occurs in either official AIDS discourse or the general popular culture. Readers regularly express to us their great hunger to see this idiosyncratic yet collective knowledge *acknowledged*, reflected, amplified, and shared. *Corpus* runs in editions of 5,000 and is distributed nationally for free to AIDS service organizations, nightclubs, universities, support groups, research institutions, drop-in centers, libraries, and public health departments. Guest editors (ourselves included) and ever-changing contributors are asked to locate and generate unique content for each issue. The publication is asymmetrically bilingual, with the foreword, introduction, and two to four key pieces printed in Spanish for each issue.

The first issue of *Corpus*, in 2003, featured Joel Tan's poignant meditation on losing friends to the epidemic, working as a long-term AIDS service provider, and navigating unprotected sex in the context of a monogamous relationship. *Corpus I* also offers a moving, Spanglish personal essay by Pedro Bustos, who addresses the lessons of a migrant, sissified HIV-positive body that endures sexual abuse, border crossings and shifting social allegiances and finally armors up with muscles in preparation for a protracted battle with AIDS. Bustos writes: "The text of the history of how the migrant body of AIDS is changing us as it destroys us is yet to be written. It will not come from the keyboards of the intellectuals of the age of cyberspace; it will come from the bodies and trajectories of the millions of disenfranchised migrants whose porous bodies are no less permeable than the borders they continue to cross. And it will be written in contradictory form, in a language beyond grammar and with a different syntax." The syncopated contradictions of which Bustos writes are the very fiber of *Corpus*.

In the second issue, playwright and activist Ricardo Bracho takes to task the simplistic and sensationalistic notions of the "down-low" while offering humorous and on-point knowledge gleaned from his own experience and that of his carnal comrades: "This then is not based on something as petty as my singular experience, but what I know from being part of the collective of gay, queen, bangy cunt boys and men. . . . The following are some of the lessons I & I have learned while ridin sidesaddle thru thug life" (see fig. 2). Juxtaposed with Derek Jackson's staged narrative photography, Bracho lists life lessons for his tribe of "gay, queen, bangy cunt boys" whose sexual preferences include men who refuse such definitions. The lessons range from informal ethics to strategies for navigating social networks. Number 2 in the list reads: "You may initiate sex but never affection." Lesson number 11 recommends: "If he's someone who doesn't like condoms and you are someone who does and he is a persistent mofo, you will have to get used to falling asleep after him and waking before he does. Besides reducing one's chance of STI/HIV (re)infection you will get to see him in a moment of unarmored beauty. And that is a most beautiful thing." Finally, lesson number 12 reminds the reader in full sex-positive splendor: "Ridin sidesaddle does not preclude being buck wild." Bracho's lessons, which remind one of the dating guidelines often found in women's magazines like *Latina* and *Elle*, speak rather of same-sex strategies that are rich, nuanced, and seldom supported in polite HIV-prevention circles. The language is lithe and the theory organic sans-spermicides, but the purpose is deadly serious. Safe-sex messages and counterpathological poetry are woven into "big sister" tales of pleasure and survival.

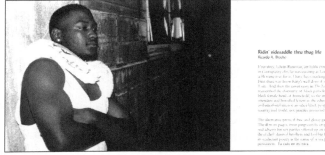

FIGURE 2 From *Corpus II*, no. 1. Photograph by Derek Jackson; text by Ricardo A. Bracho. Courtesy of APLA.

These themes are echoed elsewhere in *Corpus II*. The authors of this essay contributed a comic book spread that explored park sex among men and the body knowledge that emerges from these nocturnal liaisons. Entitled "Burning Bush," the spread utilizes the grainy green aesthetic of night vision digital photography, the technology first deployed in military surveillance (see fig. 3). Here the tool is used to represent the movements of men seeking pleasure with other men under night's cover. The images are presented in such a manner that it is not immediately clear whether the bodies are performing or actually caught in the act. Hovering somewhere between staging and documentation, the eerie green photographs cast a compelling illumination on the thoughts and occasional utterances of the so-called bush queens, who frequent outdoor settings for anonymous sex. As the viewer turns the pages, texts in distressed font read like a collective stream of consciousness: "Fuck me," "Hold me like I'm precious," "Condoms?" and "Make my life simple." A narrator's voice emerges in an effort to offer some sense of gravitas:

> years now
> the virus
> and us
> been negotiating
> pleasure
> power
> we have learned
> we are not deficient
> we have acquired animal genius
> wolf's nose for danger or dinner
> bear's sovereign aura of immunity.

Here the body is honored as a source of deep, primal, and evolving knowledge. Rather than be reduced to the risk and stigma of the human immunodeficiency virus, our park protagonists take on heightened powers of perception triggered by the confluence of danger, desire, doubt, and sexual surrender.

Corpus III also frontally addresses the power of presentation, which guest editor Laurence Padua theorizes under the rubric of pageantry. His notion of pageantry seeks to honor its interactive and reciprocal qualities. Pageantry is more than mere spectacle, more than simple consumption. It is an important site for knowledge production. And it is the creative celebration that ensues when we present/experience our multiple genders, voices, fashions, and cravings. We queers create our pageants while watching television and reading against the grain of the pop culture we help to generate. We code pageantry with our friends during two-way text messaging. We enact pageantry while inventing movements on dance floors and discovering sensations in sex clubs. We marvel at pageantry while watching our lovers get out of bed to go to the bathroom. We revel in the daily pageantry of breaking bread with our chosen families. In

FIGURE 3 From *Corpus II*, no. 1. Photograph and text by Jaime Cortez; designed with Pato Hebert.

Courtesy of APLA.

all this pageantry, we are using our sensory wisdom to express deeply embedded meanings. Teen Filipina transgender Tyra Kreuk reveals a series of digital self-portraits made in her bedroom late one night (see fig. 4). Presenting herself in a variety of attire, poses, and attitudes, she notes: "This work is titled 'Skin' because it's about expressing yourself and being comfortable in your own skin. . . . I have different sides of myself I want to express. That's why I have different images of me that came out from my own skin . . . I just brought those out and expressed them. I can be a personality and represent it in front of the camera. I'm that character, and at the same time, I'm still me." With its costuming and tableau-like posing, Kreuk's work is simultaneously a production in the theatrical sense, a production of knowledge of/for herself, and a production of the cultural knowledge of youth trans identity formation in 2005 (down to the pop-inflected particulars of her bedroom decor).

Official HIV-prevention efforts have failed to honor the complexity of gay men's lives, especially those who have survived HIV/AIDS for over two decades. Understanding this, author and scholar Robert Reid-Pharr edited *Corpus IV* with a focus on the ways that HIV shifts in meaning as gay men age. In his introduction he writes:

> Few seem to have noticed that both HIV disease and the persons dealing with HIV disease continue to develop and indeed to age. We do so, moreover, in the face of the conceit that everyone knows everything about HIV and its effects but in which many of us continue in our confusion and bewilderment. The truth of the matter is that we have remarkably limited information about how it is that one might thrive as a social

FIGURE 4 From *Corpus III*, no. 1. Photograph by Viet Le.
Courtesy of APLA and GMHC.

and sexual being affected by HIV and living in a body and a community
for that matter that constantly change and deteriorate regardless of the
grand wonders of medicine or the more mundane wonders of gyms and
nail salons. The result is that as we mature with and through HIV, many
of us become even more isolated in our struggles. It is in this way that
to live with HIV today involves a rather peculiar species of managed risk.
Not only must one ask how long the everyday magic of three-pronged
regimens will last but also how one might continue healthy development
within communities that seem so very uncomfortable with normal processes of maturation.

Reid-Pharr is not only critiquing an increasingly medicalized approach to
the *social* disease/dis-ease of HIV but also challenging any romanticized and
antiquated notion of a utopian gay community. He compiles a wide range of

FIGURE 5 From *Corpus II*, no. 1. Photograph by Jay Diaz.
Courtesy of APLA and GMHC.

writers who tackle these questions and produce knowledge from a broad continuum of vantage points. Science fiction legend Samuel Delaney contributes a personal essay titled "The Gamble," a meditation on twenty-five years of oral sex as safe sex. Viet Le's moving color photo series "Pictures of You" consists of more than twenty gay male subjects, mostly male nudes in their own domestic spaces, and explores masculinity, vulnerability, loss, race, sexuality, and the politics of desire.

Twenty-year-old Alex Osuna shares his conceptual photo essay entitled "Alex in Wonderland." The images are flush with references to death and resilience and chronicle a time when Osuna was working through the loss of his mother, grandfather, and uncle all within a month's time. Osuna notes:

> I went through many things. I went through low self-esteem, thoughts of prostitution and suicide. I was raped. I wanted people to have sex with me because I thought that would make me feel wanted. It was like chasing the white rabbit. I guess the rabbit was perfection. . . . If I hadn't stopped chasing the white rabbit, I probably would have died during that surreal month. If I hadn't realized my own power, my own beauty, I would have died with them. Sometimes I wonder, am I the disease or the cure? Am I making people feel better or worse with this work? But I like these pictures because of how they make me feel.

Corpus V was edited by video artist, activist, and media professor Alexandra Juhasz. The issue focuses on the relationship between women, gay men, and HIV and is seasoned with the textures of history and legacy. In her introduction, Juhasz writes:

FIGURE 6 From *Corpus III*, no. I. Photographs and text by Alex Osuna.
Courtesy of APLA and GMHC.

Those of us who suffered AIDS' early losses in the eighties and into the early nineties first found our love and anger to be rousing but later experienced our grief as private and debilitating. We retreated back to that place of secrecy, guilt, fear, and sadness. We stopped communicating, interacting, representing. Changes in the national and local, political and institutional climate around AIDS, coupled with an escalation of media about all things all the time, altered the conditions that supported our earlier activity and interactivity. It seemed hard to be heard, difficult to be productive, and impossible to be supported. But there are consequences to forgetting, and these are as visible as we had once made AIDS out to be. . . . Thus, I am equally moved by the contributions in this issue that claim responsibility for showing us what AIDS looks like today, and imagining what might be its healthier future. . . . *Corpus* survives in a landscape of didactic AIDS edutainment-of-displacement: representing as if another's burden, as if absent or concluded. *Corpus V* models how we might better represent today. Evidenced in this body of work is a politics of AIDS representation that is messy, interactive, and communal, a representation that dares to associate the places, people, and times that aren't supposed to go together.

The contributions to *Corpus V* are wide-ranging, from Sarah Schulman and Jim Hubbard's reflection on their years in ACT UP and the knowledge repository that is the video library of the ACT UP Oral History Project to graduate student Emily Roysdon's conceptual photographs that feature performances for the camera by herself wearing a mask of renowned (and deceased) artist and AIDS

FIGURE 7 From *Corpus IV*, no. 1. Photograph by Emily Roysdon.
Courtesy of APLA and GMHC.

activist David Wojnarowicz. Teen activist and baby dyke Tiffany Baires shares digital snapshots that comprise her ethnography of a Los Angeles park where men meet for public sex. Longtime scholar Cheryl Clarke drops science in her essay "Pomo Afro Homo Vexing of Black Macho in the Age of AIDS," while artist Monica Majoli paints luminous and nuanced images that depict S&M practices by gay men as a way to explore her own lesbian understanding of desire and the body. Finally, APLA staff member Monica Nuño convenes a roundtable of women to discuss the joys and challenges of being self-professed "fag hags." Entitled "The Fag Whisperers," the discussion examines the exchange of ideas and the mutual support possible as straight and bisexual women create knowledge in their friendships with gay men.

FIGURE 8 From *Corpus IV*, no. 1. Painting by Monica Majoli, *Hanging Rubberman #4*, 2002, watercolor and gouache on paper, 51 × 78 in. Courtesy of the artist and Gagosian Gallery.

Photo: Doug Parker Studio.

Comic Relief

As *Corpus* solidified itself as an HIV-prevention and wellness venture known nationwide, we shifted gears again, driving straight into the realm of comic books. In our devotion to language and images, we were excited about how comics might be an approachable medium for those who are uninterested in or unable to engage text-intensive publications. Using comics for social interventions is hardly a new idea. We have all seen the "Brush your teeth, kiddies!" type of public health comics before. Proscriptive and simplistic social intervention comics abounded, but what we had not yet seen and what we hungered for were comics invested in the questions of wellness within the context of complicated, contradictory queer lives.

Sexile/Sexilio is a bilingual English/Spanish graphic novel that addresses just such questions through telling the story of one Adela Vazquez, an unapologetic transgender "wild child" with a highly developed taste for sex and controlled substances. *Sexile* is an effort to encapsulate the fullness and contradiction of one extraordinary individual without trying to pathologize or lionize that person. It tells, as honestly as possible, the story of a body moving through some of the great Latina/o histories of the past half century: the Cuban Revolution, the Mariel boatlift, the advent of AIDS in immigrant communities, and the rise of transgender consciousness. Over the years, Adela used condoms and speed with equal regularity and fervor. In the comic book, she unapologetically discusses her history as a sex worker, calling herself "a great fuck, but a lousy ho."

FIGURE 9 From *Sexile/Sexilio*.
Drawing by Jaime Cortez;
design by Pato Hebert.

Courtesy of Jaime Cortez, APLA,.
and GMHC.

The process of creating *Sexile* was its own saga. For the better part of a year, we authors burned up the phone lines between rural Watsonville, California, and the APLA offices. The consultations were dense and at times complicated. How explicit could we be and still respect Adela's intimate life story, APLA's priorities, the authors' artistic integrity, and the needs of the eventual readers? How does the project stay on track when the process of researching, plotting, and especially drawing seems to swell with each passing month? What's the deadline? If an author is having a minimeltdown as an artist, what's the *real* deadline? Is that on Latina/o time? What's that supposed to mean? Do we include the part where Adela arrived in the United States and race politics here suddenly cast her as a "colored" person for the first time? Would that advance the HIV-prevention discourse? Can we possibly engage a prevention discourse without mentioning racialization? Are there even enough time and space to try? How would the executive directors of the two sponsoring agencies respond to such explicit and controversial content?

In spite of the intense communications back and forth, or perhaps because of these deliberations, *Sexile* has proven to be a great success. Positive feedback for the publication exceeded our hopes, with transgender people and nontransgender people alike responding to the courageous honesty, moral complexity, and salty humor of the main character. One high school boy in APLA's gay youth group had been struggling mightily to stay in school: he reported excitedly that he had read the book seven times. In courses at Stanford, UC Santa Cruz, and

FIGURE 10 From *Sexile*. Drawing, text, and design by Jaime Cortez.
Courtesy of Jaime Cortez, APLA, and GMHC.

UC Santa Barbara, *Sexile* was received with enthusiasm by both faculty and students alike. The comic book also took flight at hormone treatment centers and academic gender conferences. All 5,000 copies were gobbled up within eighteen months of its release, prompting exciting but challenging possibilities of second runs and reprints.

FIGURE II From *Turnover*.
Courtesy of APLA and GMHC.

Hot on the high heels of *Sexile*, we expanded the comic work into a different format. The compilation *Turnover* features the work of various artists discussing turning points in their lives. The range of comic formats was inspiring and a challenge to conventions in both the comic world and the AIDS-prevention world. We had traditional comics drawn in inks, but there were also photo-based comics, typographically based comics, digitally rendered comics, and of course, hybrids.

Turnover's content is no less a challenge to convention. For example, danger, doubt, desire, and determination combine most poignantly as the writer/artist team of Gary Gregerson and Colter Draper tell the story of one man's life journey through safe and unsafe sex. Their comic contribution details a history of sexual adventuring familiar to many middle-aged queer men, spanning a sexual history that begins at the dawn of the HIV era and leaps forward into a fanciful futuristic world. The very protagonist who would never think to have sex sans condom tells of going from the STD clinic with his HIV-negative results in hand, straight to a video porn booth to do it bareback. One of HIV prevention's greatest challenges is to address these seemingly contradictory impulses with strategies that are honest, accepting, and thoughtful. Querer compels us to do no less, for it reminds us to listen actively to the complex lives of gay men. Querer challenges us to be more concerned with social justice than judgment. Querer asks of us the fullness of intimacy.

As with *Corpus* and *Sexile*, our querer for the artists involved with *Turnover*, their work, and the process of creating the book led to a necessary and deeply time-intensive production schedule. During the editing process, when the artists would stop answering e-mails, the editor knew from experience that they were running behind production schedule. He called them and left messages. He reassured them that the most important thing was to communicate if they were withering under deadlines and to stay grounded in the steady progress of the work itself. Most contributors responded with their best work ever. But after holding up the entire publication for weeks with repeated extensions, one ten-page beauty of a comic had to be dropped. Its twelve-page story couldn't be told in ten, and, besides, the artist estimated she'd need several more weeks to finish the two concluding pages. Herding artists is perhaps not as physical as herding cats, but it's likely just as intensive. This, too, generated a certain kind of knowledge about the limits of community-based publishing with independent artists volunteering their time to a nonprofit HIV-prevention initiative. How much can a nonprofit give? How much should community members be asked to give? And when the elusive middle ground seems too far in the distance, what gives? Nearing the end of the fiscal year, and with a rare lump of dedicated publishing dollars, we reluctantly elected to publish *Turnover* without one of our favorite stories. But it is first on our list for future anthologies, should funding and opportunity arise.

Corpus, *Sexile*, and *Turnover* are all projects invested in combining as many voices, disciplines, and desires as possible in service of innovative HIV prevention. These community-based publishing projects aim to honor and disseminate the knowledge that resides in community members. These community members come from diverse ages, levels of education and publishing experience, HIV status, immigration status, and locations around the country. This strategic diversity allows our publications to draw from the immense creative and experiential wisdom that resonates from various concerned communities.

Pinche *Scraps* y *Critical* Cricas

In sharing these various forms of knowledge production, we should be careful not to suggest that culture must always be large scale and mass-produced to be of import. On the contrary, our cultural ventures aim simply to bring the intimacy of the handmade, bodily gestured, and interpersonally known into the public view for engagement. So our work never strays far from the power of the hand. Singer Erykah Badu calls herself an "analog girl in a digital world." We can relate. Our work often begins in the fragile, fierce, fabulous analog world of analogies and aspirations.

There is perhaps no better example of our approach to collaboratively producing print materials with the audience for which it is intended than the personal journals kept by members of our youth program. Simple school book journals purchased at the ninety-nine-cent store are given to our youngest

FIGURE 12 From personal journal of Enzo Ybarra.
Courtesy of APLA.

clients/community members/activists for their own unique expressions. These books then become sanctuaries rich with fantasy and metaphor. They are important sites for their knowledge production and exchange. Youth group meetings and HIV 101 sessions regularly feature the excited sharing of the week's latest pages. Amid giggles, blushes, boasts, and bonding, the youths share their

FIGURE 13 From Mpowerment archive.
Courtesy of APLA.

creations with each other: yearbook photos of "hot" straight guys; photo booth
stickers of best, best girlfriends; old family snapshots from Durango, Ponce, and
Pomona; tortured teen poetry and lists of important things to do. And if we
listen (and sometimes even when we don't!), the youths also share these knowledge repositories with us. Their cartoon characters become program mascots.
Their scrapbooks serve as formative research for social marketing campaigns.
And their understandings of gender, power, and desire are primary texts that
push the prevention envelope into the future. These "prevention" activities
don't fit neatly into any health department's "request for proposals" or Master
of Public Health curricula. But the nuanced knowledge of our youth is absolutely
essential to the AIDS industry's ability to stay ahead of the epidemic.

Querer Queriendo

We are not likely to see an end to AIDS in our lifetime. This knowledge is sobering, but it also inspires a deep passion and compassion for mutual self-care.
Self-care is at the heart of querer. Desire, like knowledge, can connect us more
closely to one another. Communication is crucial, and as our colleague Ray
Fernandez says, "We shouldn't put a condom on the conversation." When we
don't share our knowledge openly, loneliness, isolation, depression, and even
death ensue.

In the winter of 2005, we lost yet another colleague to AIDS. His number
is still in our cell phones. Our fingers unable to erase this simple reminder of
his powerful presence in our lives—we now dial his memory. His death went
unknown for weeks. His Hershey's chocolate sweetness had not been seen on
the dance floor. His outrageous fashion, swish, and cackle were missed. E-mails
and voice mails went unreturned. Finally word came that he had passed in a
hospice, alone, with no Los Angeles friends or Midwest biological family in the
know. Perhaps this was how he wanted it, alone, private, purposeful. But this
essay and our ongoing work are haunted by the gnawing sense that he chose
isolation in his final days not in peaceful, proactive fashion but out of fear,
afraid we would see him like that; afraid he would see us seeing him; afraid to
acknowledge that AIDS was not something of the past, but was in fact still all
too real, a necrophilic nest for the new millennium. Maybe not. Maybe in his

FIGURE 14 From Mpowerment archive.

Courtesy of APLA.

mind he died away from friends and family as one last generous act. We cannot ever know. But our unknowing produces in us the desire to ensure that nobody should feel they must face this disease alone. Uneasy and exhausted, yet hopeful and determined, we channel this information with the knowledge of his life, if not an understanding of his passing in our prevention practice. Knowing where there's querer and why it is important is crucial to stemming the spread of HIV. Our lives depend on it.

11

Religion/Spirituality, U.S. Latina/o Communities, and Sexuality Scholarship

A Thread of Current Works

SALVADOR VIDAL-ORTIZ

"In U.S., Hispanics Bring Catholicism to Its Feet," proclaimed the May 7, 2007, *Washington Post*.[1] Catholic churches are providing space and a different kind of religious experience to charismatic-influenced Catholicism, as practiced by U.S. Latina/os. The Pew Hispanic Center and the Pew Forum on Religion and Public Life collaboration in their most recent research on U.S. Latina/o populations (referred to below as the Pew Report) confirms it. Drawing from public opinion surveys of more than four thousand people, they conclude that Catholicism is supported in greater numbers by U.S. Latina/o populations, with a special emphasis on charismatic religious practice. Christian churches are adapting to Latina/o immigration as what the Pew Report calls "Ethnic Churches." Within these churches, sermons on abortion and homosexuality are often preached; abortion is the most discussed subject from the pulpit (about 60 percent), with homosexuality a close second in evangelical churches (58 percent), though less discussed in Catholic (37 percent) and mainline Protestant (42 percent) denominations. Immediately after reporting these findings, the Pew Report goes on to discuss immigration, successfully shifting the focus from sexuality and public debates on sex education, women's sexuality, and reproductive rights to the most popular notion about U.S. Latina/os—that of undocumented immigrants. In this chapter, I offer a queer reading implicit in such reporting. That is, while the media and current research illustrate high levels of religiosity among Latina/os in the United States, there is an erasure of Latina/os as sexual beings. U.S. policy and similar structural readings of Latina/os in U.S. society, however, tend to frame such populations as hypersexual and uncontrollably reproductive, traditionally Catholic and conservative, and afflicted by some perceived common "culture" that influences their discussions about sexuality and ascribes "sexual silence" to that culture.[2]

I will examine three aspects of U.S. Latina/o populations—the religious (and/or spiritual), Hispanic or Latina/o heritage, and sexuality—as illustrated and analyzed in social science literatures.[3] While most scholarship addresses only two of these three variables, my review shows how most of the social science literature is limited in its analysis and elaboration of the life circumstances of people who are religious/spiritual and of Latina/o or Hispanic heritage and their sexualities, including sexual orientations, sexual patterns, sexual behaviors, sexual groupings, and gender and sexual experiences.

The first part of the chapter considers the complexity of "Latina/os" as a group, as well as their interaction with religion, through a general discussion of three surveys on religion and Latina/os, followed by specific social science research that delves into such religious experiences. This section does not explicitly address sexuality—the literatures and studies examined do not center on it—but, rather, the complex relationship Latina/os have to religiosity in the United States. The second part of the chapter engages the literatures about sexuality and religiosity/spirituality, including limited discussions by Latino gay men and Latina lesbians as well as heterosexual women's relationship to institutional religion.[4] Here I show the various ways in which religion (more than spirituality) has influenced Latina/o sexualities and, equally important, how Latina/os reinvent, negotiate, resist, accept, reject, interpret, and internalize religious scriptures, and also how they respond to peer pressure and to the host culture (and its notions of what is acceptable in terms of religious ritual and worship at work, in certain neighborhoods, and at school). I conclude with some general directions for future research as well as register the implications for the linking of religion/spirituality and sexuality to U.S. Latina/o communities. These recommendations span the various data collection methods, the focus on less studied Latina/o populations, the sexuality and religiosity issues that need inquiry, and how to best address them.

Whom Do We Mean by Latina/o?
What Are Latina/os' Religions?

It is important to operationalize the various communities we lump together into the U.S. Latina/o population, in order to understand their religious practices. The heterogeneous group of Latina/os in U.S. society may incorporate people from currently colonized lands, fourth-generation Mexican Americans, South Americans (with their subdivisions within the continent), and places where Spanish, English, Spanglish, Guaraní, Portuguese, and Quechua are among the languages spoken. This complex notion of Latina/o heritage, often subsumed in a pan-Latino ethnicity, erases substantial differences not only among the countries represented under such an umbrella but also within each of the geographic places of origin. Moreover, it creates an idea of who

Latina/os are, irrespective of their heterogeneity. Religion is no exception to this general pattern.[5]

The "new" immigrants are broadening the diversity of religions in the United States.[6] The variety of non-Christian religious/spiritual traditions that some Latina/os adhere to include Buddhism, Judaism, and Islam, as well as Jehovah's Witness, Santería, and Wicca.[7] For instance, as of 2003, a Muslim Latina/o presence in the United States has become visible through the case of José Padilla, "the Puerto Rican Taliban," in the news after 9/11.[8] Protestantism is drawing large numbers of Latin Americans and U.S. Latina/os; in many instances, immigrants come to the United States with a religious view already distant from Catholicism.[9] Indeed, it becomes harder as more Latina/os come to the United States (or become more visible here) to sustain a claim of Hispanic or Latina/o groups as inherently Catholic, a claim (common in the United States) that often is contrasted to the nation's Protestant predominance. This perceived contrast has uneven results: Catholicism is used as a sign of Latin America's lack of development, because the Catholic (presumably "backward") Latin American religious traditions lag behind those of the United States. This backwardness is also reinforced through the sexual and reproductive rights mobilizing—often funded by "first world" countries and nongovernmental organizations and injected into Latin America. Latin American countries are thus imagined as inherently oppressive in their dealings regarding gender equity, reproductive rights, and nonheteronormative sexuality and sexual orientation. It follows that an assignment of cultural traits like machismo or homophobia and a quest for political asylum on the basis of sexual identity or gender identity/status are presumptively superimposed on people of Latina/o origin, regardless of local or "indigenous"-based responses to homophobia in Latin American countries. Some scholars have argued for a critique of these imposed cultural readings that exclusively frame the Latin American nations, and within them the institutions of family and religion, as oppressive in the lives of sexual and gender minority groups, because these frameworks make invisible the imperial tactics of liberation implicit in impositions of globalized sexualities.[10]

Because of the challenges that studying Latina/o communities pose and the simultaneous dearth of scholarship on Latina/o religiosity and sexuality, I first illustrate the general religious patterns of Latina/os in the United States through three large-scale surveys on religion, one that includes Latinos and two that focus on Hispanic/Latino populations specifically. I then engage the (mostly qualitative) social science studies that illustrate, in a more tangible sense, the religious experiences of U.S. Latina/o populations in a comparative perspective—in order to explore the kind of religious cultural practices that Latina/o immigrants from Central America observe, in relation to Mexican Americans, Puerto Ricans, Cubans, and non-"new" immigrants.

Religion and Latina/os: Three Large-Scale Studies

The American Religious Identification Survey

This 2001 study from the Graduate Center of the City University of New York, was conducted with more than fifty thousand respondents and a more detailed subset of seventeen thousand households. Participants were asked to define their religion with an open-ended question (e.g., What is your religion, if any?), as opposed to a list of options. This study also asked for the religion of the spouse/ partner, which was an innovation from previous studies. The study found that among the Hispanic population surveyed, about 57 percent identified as Catholics, and about 22 percent identified as Protestants. Of the rest, 5 percent stated other religions and 12 percent identified having no religion in their responses.[11] This study argues that immigrants have a very limited impact on the religious traditions in the United States overall—although because its focus is not on immigrants, this conclusion may be overstated.[12] The survey results indicate that gender is an important variable: women have higher rates of religiosity than men.[13] The findings do not place Hispanics/Latina/os as the most secular of the groups included in the study (Asians are the most secular; African Americans are the least, when the survey responses are weighted to a national sample); but neither are Latina/os the most religious. Latina/os' responses to being "somewhat religious" or "religious" (75 percent) lagged behind those of whites (77 percent) and blacks (81 percent). This large sampling study helps identify the place of U.S. Latina/os and Hispanics and their religiosity and gives an angle to compare Latina/os to other ethnoracial groups in the United States. The next two surveys considered focus specifically on Latina/o populations and their different religious practices.

The Hispanic Churches in American Public Life: Summary of Findings

This national survey covered more than twenty-three hundred Latina/os in the United States and Puerto Rico, combined with a mailed survey of close to five hundred leaders in Latina/o politics and civic and religious communities, and other sources (community profiles, scholarly articles, and added research). It offers a look not at religiosity but at the relationship between religious beliefs and affiliation and political views. The study finds that "Latinos tend to be morally and ethically conservative but politically and economically liberal," a fact that has invited both political parties to court the votes of U.S. Latina/o populations. The findings point out that, with few exceptions, Catholics and Protestants can join collaborative advocacy work on "key educational, moral, and political issues" even though they respect and keep separate their religious beliefs and affiliations. Latina/os comprised 70 percent of the study's total sample; Protestants were 23 percent, and respondents expressing either "no religious preference" or "other or world religion" constituted 6 percent and 1 percent, respectively.[14] These results are consistent with the numbers of the 2001 American Religious Identification Survey.[15] When studying the report closely, however, it is clear that the authors—Gastón Espinoza, Virgilio Elizondo, and Jesse Miranda—are invested in productively showing that there are variations not just among Protestants but also among Catholics; they do this especially when looking at "born-again" Catholics (more than a quarter of the Catholic sample) and, among them, the Catholics who identify as charismatic. Thus, our traditional understanding of Catholicism is complicated by the experiences of Latina/o immigrants (as the Pew Report, discussed next, also shows). In addition, this study reveals that Protestant Latina/os in the United States include a large group of evangelical and charismatic or "born again"/"spirit-filled" Protestants. These are no small numbers: "To put these findings in national perspective, there are now more Latino Protestants in the U.S. than Jews or Muslims or Episcopalians and Presbyterians combined."[16]

Latina/os' social engagement is linked to religiosity in this study. More Protestants reported feeling their religion provided day-to-day living guidance than did Catholics. Both Catholics and Protestants think that their religious leaders should be involved in public affairs and try to influence them—especially in matters linked to immigration. The respondents were clear that their churches did not ask them to be involved in political, social, or educational aspects of their communities. And when asking about political affiliation, even though U.S. Latina/os tend to be conservative on social issues, they tend to vote Democratic—though the authors of the report specify that these Latina/os are not tied to the Democratic Party. In fact, almost 40 percent of the Latina/os surveyed were categorized as politically independent. This allows them to vote for candidates on the basis of issues rather than party platforms. But there are some conservative postures, such as 70 percent supporting prayer in schools, while 58 percent are in favor of "the teaching of both creation and evolution in public schools." This study makes the linking of religiosity and politics a very complex matter; there is no easy answer to how U.S. Latina/o populations will respond to religious issues in combination with social matters such as sexuality.[17]

Changing Faiths: Latinos and the Transformation of American Religion

This most recent study by the Pew Hispanic Project and the Pew Forum on Religion and Public Life, referred to here as the Pew Report, covered more than four thousand telephone surveys as a representative national sample of U.S. Hispanics.[18] Unlike the studies discussed above, the Pew Report highlights how evangelical Latina/os are twice as likely to identify with the Republican Party. The study also concludes that more than two-thirds of Latina/os (68 percent) are Catholic; perhaps the smaller number of evangelicals in comparison to Catholics, plus the effect of immigration status among recent immigrants who might be evangelical, accounts for the four out of five Latina/os voting Democratic (as shown in the *Hispanic Churches in American Public Life* study).

It is in this study that we see some of the religious and geographic origin differences; Mexicans, for instance, are by far much more Catholic than their Puerto Rican counterparts, who tend to be evangelicals in larger numbers. Cubans tend to have the largest number of secular respondents. Furthermore, the study compares Latina/o populations to whites and blacks, thus offering intra- and interreligious affiliation comparisons. Pew researchers discussed six main religious traditions among Latina/os: Roman Catholicism, Evangelical Protestantism, Mainline Protestantism, Other Christians, Other Faiths, and Seculars. The study asked for both religious denomination and whether respondents identified as "born again" or "evangelical." Among the Catholic respondents, roughly two-thirds were foreign-born, more than half spoke Spanish as a primary language (55 percent), about two out of five did not graduate from high school, and about half of them have a household income of less than $30,000 per year. Evangelical Protestants and Mainline Protestants shared similar percentages; a majority were foreign-born but spoke English as a first language (a higher percentage of Evangelical Protestants than Mainline Protestants). The majority are high school graduates, and only three or four out of ten have a household income of less than $30,000 per year.[19]

The report is rich in demographic data beyond the scope of this chapter; suffice it to say that there are comparisons between first, second, and third generations as well as more details of country-specific religious traditions. A last point to make is that whereas Latina/os report religious affiliation percentages similar to other ethnoracial groups in the United States, the intensity of their religious beliefs appears to be higher. This has significant implications for the study of sexuality and gender equity.

Overall, the three reports indicate a strong connection on the part of Latina/os to religious traditions (Catholicism in particular) and also a renewal of charismatic and more evangelical traditions, intensity in daily prayer, having religious images at home, and the like. The variability of religious affiliation needs to be further explored in relation to sexuality, but for now, I move from large-scale studies of religion and Latina/os to social science studies of Latina/o religiosity.

Research on Latina/o Religiosity and Spirituality

In the United States, notions of the relationship between Catholicism and Latina/o populations are changing; as suggested above, the political-conservative assignment of Latina/os' views on social matters is shifting. Studies on religiosity and spirituality compare the two, not only to show how spirituality is becoming a common language to establish links between groups from disparate religious backgrounds, but also to indicate that both "religious" and "spiritual" have several popular (and possible) interpretations.[20] Notions of spirituality as private and personal or as a challenge to institutionally imposed regulations by the Church are often contrasted to religiousness.[21]

The study of religiosity and Latina/o populations is uneven. As with many other issues, Latina/o communities are either studied in the abstract through the use of Hispanic/Latina/o as the general category or studied from the baseline populations—Mexicans, Puerto Ricans, and Cubans—while overlooking others. In particular, Central American populations have often received little attention in terms of their religiosity and immigrant experience.[22] Milagros Peña has studied the impact of religion in the lives of Latina/o communities, most notably among women. In "Border Crossings," Peña forces theologians to see themselves as members of the community and their theologies as informed by such communities, and she compels sociologists (her audience) to think outside the "objective outsider" box of social science knowledge production. In an article on the Latina experience, she illustrates how Latinas have helped shape their religious practice. Focusing on methodological distinctions for studying the Latina communities, she offers a complex view of Latina religiosities—and how to study them. Not surprisingly, she urges scholars not to generalize among Chicanas/ Mexicanas, other large Latina groups in the United States, and all Latinas. This article in particular argues for the value and benefits, as well as limitations, of quantitative (survey) and qualitative (focus group interviewing) methods in studying these issues among Latinas.[23]

Peña also expands the notion of religion to that of "popular religious practice" in her 1998 article with Lisa Frehill. Based on pre–focus group questionnaires with Latin American women in eight U.S. cities, the authors asked about the types of religiosity these women (N = 106) experienced, including social, personal religiosity, and prayer frequency. They also asked about the Virgin Mary's image and its impact on their lives as religious women, as well as about cultural embeddedness—that is, by having the women complete surveys in English or Spanish, and subsequent assumptions of insertion and absortion in mainstream U.S. culture. The questions that were posed pertained to the Virgin Mary; their respondents were mostly Catholic (almost 70 percent) or Protestant (a little over 10 percent), and they primarily compared the two groups.[24] The majority of their respondents were Cuban, Mexican, or Puerto Rican (N = 75), thus their results mainly reflect the largest groups of Latinas in the United States. While this study does not focus on sexuality per se, some questions concerned the religious imposition of the rhythm method of contraception (and women's responses to such imposition), as well as some of the women's decisions to reject abuse in their marriages, and their perceptions of the role of marriage; therefore, the study can be of use in better understanding the relationship between religiosity and U.S. Latinas.

Sarah Stohlman conducted fieldwork among several Pentecostal churches in Los Angeles, focusing mostly on Salvadoran, Guatemalan, and Honduran populations. Noting the involvement of many immigrants in some of these churches and the everyday material struggles they faced, Stohlman discussed the variations of Pentecostalism throughout Los Angeles. Adherence to Protestantism is estimated to be at least three to five times higher among Central Americans than Mexicans, and the author illustrates how some of these immigrants arrived in the United States already adhering to a Protestant faith (the violence and war in the preceding decades in several Central American countries that spurred this migration might be a factor in the increasing numbers of Central American Protestants). A redefinition by immigrants of their religious system allows for a general maintenance of ethnic solidarity and also tends to prevent the adherents from assimilating into mainstream culture. Moreover, some of their healing practices, discussions about charity (which includes donations as well as sharing a place to live), and even the structuring of their religious practice is autonomous from other religious traditions (this dramatic difference is most relevant when Protestantism is compared to the top-down approach of Catholicism).[25]

Depending on the U.S. region one studies, as well as the religious denomination, there might be significant ethnoracial diversity or a lot of homogeneity.[26] Even in Stohlman's study, some of the religious spaces were not visible to the general population or did not have signs to designate them as a public Pentecostal space—matters of much importance to the study of religion.[27] Cecilia Menjívar compares Salvadoran populations (both Catholic and evangelical churches) in San Francisco, Washington, D.C., and Phoenix, Arizona.[28] Through a series of surveys and interviews with both Salvadoran immigrant laypeople and priests or pastors, she looks at the religious impact of non-Catholic churches, as manifested by Salvadorans either leaving the Catholic Church or reinvigorating their own congregations. Like Stohlman, Menjívar addresses the material and spiritual needs of these immigrants as well as their stories of war and violence (and the perceived conservatism of the Catholic Church in their countries of origin). The communitarian approach is offered in both of these articles as a way of showing a more mobilized religiosity.

Whereas the scarce social scientific literature addresses the relationship between (mostly) immigrant women and religion, there is variation in terms of the study of religion (Peña and Menjívar look at both Catholicism and Protestantism; Stohlman looks at Protestantism), as well as diversity in the United States (all look at religion in various U.S. cities). There are significant individual findings from this literature in terms of the value Latina women—and Latina/o immigrants—give to their religious affiliation. While much more research is needed, especially in other areas (sociology seems to dominate this literature), these publications offer us a general roadmap of women's impact on religion, as well as religious structures' impact on women and immigrants.

Latina/o Sexuality and Religion/Spirituality

Scholarship on religion and race in the United States often follows a black/white comparative framework, but Latina/os in U.S. society experience life not as mere "ethnic" populations but as racialized ones (meaning they are marked as racial "others" in spite of U.S. Census definitions of Hispanics/Latinos as "ethnic."[29] In addition, religion and sexuality scholarship that is devoid of immigrants' views ignores the ways these two variables—along with economic and other political needs—influence both the choice to immigrate (for those for whom it is a choice) and the psychological experience of migration.[30] Latina/o communities in the United States may embrace indigenous traditions that portray the body and the spirit as dual and oppositional. This sense, as the available literature demonstrates, has significant implications for the study of sexuality.[31] The following discussion explores factors such as immigration, sexual experiences, and religiosity among Latina lesbians, gay and bisexual Latino men, and heterosexual women.

Religion and Sexualities among Latina/os: A Handful of Writings on the Subject

In an earlier era, Olivia M. Espín published several works that touch on religion and Latinas and on immigrant Latinas and sexuality. In her *Latina Healers* (1996), Espín writes about *curanderas*, *espiritistas*, and *santeras* in relation to their immigrant and religious experiences, and about the empowering of women in their participation of these religious cultural practices (Curanderismo, Espiritismo, and Santería). *Latina Realities* (1997) argues for a psychological look at the study of immigration of Latina lesbians. In a refreshing, intersectional way, her work encompasses immigration, sexuality, and religion. However, lesbianism and religion do not often meet in her writings—or more specifically, sexuality studies do not connect to these women's lives as religious healers. For instance, in another essay, Espín discusses the impact of religion, especially the healing practices of *espiritismo* and Santería, in the lives of ten Latina (mostly Cuban) women. The women's sexuality is barely discussed, however, and when mentioned, it is simply presumed to be heterosexual. No direct mention of lesbian or bisexual women's involvement in healing is made available. Similarly, in "Issues of Identity in the Psychology of Latina Lesbians," Espín makes no explicit mention of any involvement in religion of the more than a dozen Latina lesbians interviewed.[32] Note that these essays were mostly written in the early or mid-1980s and reprinted in 1997; there are, in 2008, a few sources that address the intersection of religion, sexuality, and U.S. Latina/o communities, most of which were only published as articles or theses/dissertations from 2000 on (and which will be discussed briefly).

A significant contribution of Espín's writing is her discussion of machismo. Because much of her work centers on showing the power Latina women have (the literal power of healing and also the symbolic power of healing oneself), she incorporates a view in response to cultural assumptions such as machismo, as based on her research. Critical of this stereotype, Espín nonetheless establishes that it is a "Hispanic version of the myth of male superiority supported by most cultures."[33] With this claim, Espín not only makes the reader notice the impact such a cultural attribute may have on Latina women but also shatters the idea that this is inherently a Latino trait. Espín's research has proven to be key to the study of the intersection of the variables that are the focus of this chapter (Latina/os, sexuality, and religiosity/spirituality), even if she does not link them explicitly.

Espín's contributions help contextualize the next set of discussions, where in some instances machismo and images of Latina/o culture as oppressive are looked at uncritically, or redefined through their "positive" aspects, and in other instances these notions are challenged through the experiences of women themselves. Eric M. Rodriguez focuses on the study of gay, lesbian, and bisexual Christians. He is critical of studies that focus narrowly on Latina/o populations, calling these studies fragmented and challenging their small sampling strategies.[34] Although Rodriguez barely addresses the relationship between gay and lesbian Latina/os and religiosity, simply mentioning machismo and issues of acculturation, his dissertation attempts to analyze the different psychological and coping mechanisms in comparison between gay men and lesbians, and it should prove useful in long-term discussions about homosexuality and religion.

Rodriguez and Suzanne C. Ouellette explore the complexity of meanings for four gay Latino Christian men in the Metropolitan Community Church of New York (MCCNY), which is by no means a traditional Christian church (it is a hybrid denominationally, and it celebrates its homosexual members and same-sex relationships). The authors focus on gay men because previous studies show that men expressed "conflict between their homosexual and religious identities significantly more than did lesbians." Their main claim is the positive, nonheterosexist impact of MCCNY on the lives of the religious members and leaders (two of their four informants were deacons). Through their data, they show the positive impact of machismo's variant of a nurturing, feminine side (or as they say, the presence of a machismo "characterized by an androgynous or feminine orientation," or a "positive machismo"). Much of their discussion centers on the tension or conflict between their informants' acceptance of their own homosexuality and the difficulties others had with it. Specifically, Rodriguez and Ouellette discuss the history of these men who do not feel as positive about both their commitment to religion and their homosexuality. Gay sex in particular—the actual sexual act with another man—was a commonly described source for this discomfort. What becomes an intriguing yet unfounded aspect of their work is the claim of "close women" and "distant, familiar men" figures as affecting the study participants' notions of machismo or masculinity. The authors fall short of claiming that these men's experiences with a positive side of machismo can serve as a source for nonsexist and nonheterosexist attitudes: "What we have heard from the men in this study identifies MCCNY and religion as an important context for the crafting of a masculine identity that is not oppressively masculine." The expectation follows that because these men accept traits traditionally viewed as feminine (such as caring for the congregants, or selflessness), they have created a gay male masculinity that is not oppressive toward women, other men, or themselves. Regardless of this, their argument does show the affinity and clash these men felt in being gay, male, Latino and Christian. This is a significant finding that connects to other Latina/o religious people.[35]

In a similar fashion, but with a substantially different Latina population, in "*Confesiones de Mujer*," Gloria González-López argues that Catholic Mexican immigrant heterosexual women maneuver the *enseñanzas* (teachings, mandates) of the Church at the same time that they recognize the patriarchal, regulatory aspects of the institution. Thirty-two of the forty women she interviewed altered for themselves some of the regulations stipulated by the Catholic Church in order to accommodate their own sexual beliefs. The women had migrated from Jalisco and Mexico City to Los Angeles, which is where González-López talked with them. González-López uses a feminist sociological perspective in her analysis of these interviews, inserting women's positionality, their standpoint as immigrant Catholic straight women, and a sense of agency. Factors such as the women's sexual and reproductive health, their experience of gender oppression, practice of sexual abstinence, experience of sexual eroticism (sometimes through fantasies involving their priests), and their overall sexual activity with their male partners (including matters such as making anal sex an option) challenge in many ways traditional conceptions of sexual and reproductive mandates by the Catholic institution. Overall, the stress caused by the religious regulations and the women's actual choices in these matters becomes manageable through a generally agreeable sense of separating the religious components of their lives—more succinctly, their spiritual lives—from the sexual and reproductive ones (i.e., those pertaining to their bodies). Through this negotiation, women effectively bifurcate the spiritual and the sexual, by their clinging, if only temporarily, to the religious mores of the Church. In that sense, Rodriguez and Ouellette and González-López illustrate, albeit with different populations, the success of their subjects' negotiations that take place in a strictly religious (in these cases, basically Catholic or Protestant) framework, even when their religious institutions sometimes do not value or validate their sexuality, their sexual and reproductive choices, or their sexual activities.[36]

Nontraditional Religious Belief Systems among Latina/os: The Case of Santería

Regarding certain religious practices that are less written about, my work in particular links the relationship of forced migration and slavery in the development of Afro-Cuban religions like Santería and the gender and sexuality aspects within this religious cultural practice in its U.S. setting.[37] Santería survived the forced migration of slaves to Cuba in the eighteenth century, then developed further in the nineteenth century (as some argue, by fusing with Catholicism its Yoruba origins), and most recently migrated to the United States in the mid-twentieth century. In the United States, it is most noticeable for the animal sacrifice involved in some of its practices and for the "possession" or trance state of its practitioners—santeras and santeros—who attempt to communicate with and worship divinities from the spirit realm, sometimes in order to change the outcome of their own destiny. Estimates of at least a million Santería practitioners in the United States are common in relevant literature and the media. By conducting ethnography and interviews and maintaining long-term contact with U.S. informants, I explored the relationship of gender and sexuality to the Afro-Cuban religious tradition, where possession, labor and tasks, divination, and other nonritualistic aspects have gendered and sexualized implications. Practitioners' use of a Catholic saint to illustrate its Santería counterpart (for instance, Catholic Saint Barbara vis-à-vis Santería Changó) and the phenomenon of possession among men and women as "mounting" are but two of the ways in which gender and sexuality are intertwined, in a rather complex manner, in this religious cultural practice.[38]

In studying the relationship between ethnoracial minorities and sexual minorities, my work has challenged the notion of Santería as an inherently homophobic space. But, while in general Santería spaces bring higher numbers of self-identified gays and lesbians than other religions where worshiping is mixed (in terms of sexual orientation), Santería is in no way a haven for gays and lesbians—and significant tensions and negotiations occur. In Santería, sex education, acceptance of gay and lesbian practitioners, and discussions about sexuality are permissible and oftentimes happen on an everyday basis; people's religiosity and sense of spirituality is not challenged as strongly by their minoritized sexual orientation. Indeed, because different understandings of gender and sexuality are taking place in this religious cultural practice, it is quite possible that homosexuality is seen as a requisite for participating in certain roles. Gay men in particular have found a place in Santería as *oriatés*, or divination priests.[39] Understanding the uneven focus of studies on lesbian, bisexual, and transgender or transsexual religious people, especially in Santería, is still paramount. A significant finding in my research is of the assumption that all women and gay men encompass a category of people who can be mounted, thus ascribing in the process a sexual minority status to them all.[40]

In this review of the scarce literature that engages Latina/os, sexuality, and religiosity/spirituality, I have noted both traditional and nontraditional religious practices and discussed, in a limited fashion, the place of heterosexual women and gay men and lesbians in some of these religions. There is variability in terms of individuals' perceptions about their religious institution, their faith, and their spirituality and the venues where they practice religion—which fall within such diverse settings as a predominantly gay site (MCCNY), a generic heteronor-mative site (Catholic), and a pluralistic sexual orientation site (Santería). Based on these readings, additional research questions would be: Can sexuality and religion be merged in research with heterosexual (or same-sex) populations in aspects beyond the issue of marriage? What happens when marriage as an insti-tution becomes a religiously framed preferred sexual experience, yet the further into marriage, the more the religious aspects (especially around reproduction) take a back seat to everyday sexual experience? Similarly for gays and lesbians, what is the long-term impact of living through the current discourse around the demands that marriage as a holy institution be opened up to nonhetero-sexuals? Will gays and lesbians now getting married fall into patterns similar to heterosexual couples? Do only those married people who abide by the current guidelines of Christian scriptures experience a closer relationship between sexuality and religiosity/spirituality? What are the experiences, representations, cultural attributions, and general perceptions by (or of) heterosexual Latino men who are either religiously involved or spiritual? There are large gaps in the social science studies about all of these groups of people. What follows is the overall general sense of this literature's contribution, as well as potential steps to further this scholarship.

Conclusion

Clearly, we do not have a strong body of literature that explicitly links sexuality, religiosity/spirituality, and Latina/os in the United States. The available sources do reveal that Latina/os are diverse in spirituality and religious choices, even though a sizable majority are Catholics. Religiosity is more often studied, rela-tive to spirituality, in the literature reviewed here—especially in the surveys on policy and religious studies discussed early on. Also, and perhaps more impor-tant, the manner in which Latina/os incorporate their religious teachings and to what extent they negotiate the institutional teachings for more personal choices is evidenced in a few of the sources. A related point is the extent to which their religiosity informs political decisions: for Latina/os, religion revitalizes them and their political involvement in the United States, yet clearly immigrant Latina/os also reinvigorate the religious traditions as incoming practitioners.

The social science and policy reports reviewed here contribute an initial roadmap as to the relationship among religion/spirituality, sexuality, and U.S. Latina/o communities. Little research truly offers a connected analysis that threads these variables. The handful of work that does varies in approach, from qualitative research to survey analysis. What can be concluded from this limited scholarship is the urgency to fund and carry out empirical research (through one-on-one interviews, interactive settings such as focus groups, and ethnographic studies, as well as quantitative surveying) to fill the gaps in the literature.

Suggestions for Further Research

The following are general recommendations for future research and analysis on the scope and depth of sexuality, spirituality/religiosity, and U.S. Latino populations:

Diversify the Scope of Research

Other less discussed choices and experiences in Latina/o sexuality and religiosity scholarship may include understandings of monogamy and fidelity (by heterosexual men and women, as well as nonheterosexuals). Studies that not only confront the differing impacts of notions of "monogamy" and "fidelity" among Latina/os of all sexual orientations are needed, but as important, we need reports and research documenting, in a deeper way, the influence of religiosity (I am excluding spirituality from this suggestion) as a powerful social force in the lives of Latina/os from all nationalities—not just the larger groups of Latina/os—in the United States.

Similarly, there is a lack of research focusing specifically on heterosexual Latino males' relationship to spirituality. For instance, Marysol Asencio found that Puerto Rican Catholic male teenagers have an easier time negotiating themselves out of the religious strictures and mandates, in contrast to their Pentecostal counterparts, for whom failure to control themselves and their sexuality is interpreted as a sign of weakness and sinful behavior.[41] Other comparative studies should similarly investigate the relationship among various nationally based groups, by sexual orientation, gender and gender identity, and religious/ spiritual practice or orientation, and focus most exclusively on the religious aspect. (Asencio's work touches upon this aspect in passing.) When such studies focus on women, it will be important not to assume their heterosexuality and to inquire about how sexuality is a variable that influences their religious (and spiritual) experience as Latinas in the United States.

Advocacy for a National Database and
Other Broad Data Collection Strategies

Menjívar has stated that partly because the Census Bureau or the Immigration and Naturalization Service (now within the Department of Homeland Security) were not allowed to include questions about religion in their large-scale studies, it becomes very difficult to assess the post-1965 immigration groups coming to the United States. Longitudinal and large-scale studies focusing on religion/spirituality, sexuality, and U.S. Latina/os are needed. Perhaps studies that concentrate on quantitative sampling and opportunistic interviews or that combine quantitative and qualitative methods (such as that modeled by Peña) will continue to give more sense to the experience of U.S. Latina/o communities, as well as the institutional impact of the religious structures on their lives. Yet, even focus groups about religion and sexuality composed of Latina/o populations could prove to be a rich source of data analysis, offering both commonalities and discrepancies in terms of attitudes and beliefs and religious and/or sexual experiences.

Extend a More Balanced Research between Insiders and Outsiders

Studies and research that either resort to outsiders or at the very least problematize their inside status are needed, because otherwise, as stated by Menjívar, "the absence of a critical mass of immigrant social scientists contributes to the paucity of studies of religion among post-1965 immigrants." As Peña illustrates so well, finding indigenous researchers who care less about the status of objectivity in research than about the study of the nuances in Latina/o communities is imperative to further our understanding of Latina/o experience with religion and sexuality—from sexual regulation to sexual pleasure to reproductive health.[42]

To conclude, what would the study of religion, sexuality, and U.S. Latina/os look like outside of the scope of any of these areas? Can we imagine these studies being developed in fields like immigration studies, ethnoracial studies, multidisciplinary studies (American studies, area studies), or feminist studies? Can networks be developed to support the emergence of interdisciplinary scholarship across the fields of sexuality, religious and theological, and U.S. Latina/o studies? Answers to these questions are needed in order to both allocate the funds and resources to further such scholarship and mentor the scholars to produce such research.

12

Latina/o Sexualities in Motion

Latina/o Sexualities Research Agenda Project

SUSANA PEÑA

This chapter examines the existing literature on the relationship between Latina/o sexualities and migration. Drawing on literature in the social and behavioral sciences (and related disciplines), I examine studies that explicitly focus on Latino migration to the United States and sexuality. In addition, I draw on studies indirectly related to migration and sexuality that add important issues to our conversation. In general, the literature discussed in this chapter tackles the following questions:

- How does the state monitor, control, and categorize sexuality in the migration and naturalization process? How does this affect the sexuality of first-generation immigrant Latina/os?
- Does a sexual minority status or experience of sexual violence promote emigration?
- How do immigrant-generation and acculturation affect sexual practices and identities?
- How are sexual values, practices, and identities being communicated between generations of Latina/os?

Several recent edited collections focus explicitly on the intersection of sexuality with immigration, globalization, and transnationalism. The primarily humanities-centered *Queer Diasporas* was followed by the 2002 publication of *Queer Globalizations*. Preceded by a conference at the Center for Lesbian and Gay Studies of the City University of New York, *Queer Globalizations* draws on scholarship in the humanities, cultural studies, and social sciences to "identify both the opportunities and perils inherent in [global] transformations and their implication for queer cultures and lives." Contributors draw on geographically and racially diverse examples to illustrate the queer contradictions of globalizations. As the editors argue, globalization "despite its tendency to reduce the social and political significance of queer sexualities and culture to a commodity exchangeable in the marketplace—has also provided the struggle for queer rights with an expanded terrain for intervention." The 2005 collection *Queer Migrations* similarly combines papers from two conferences held at Bowling Green State University and at the University of California–Santa Cruz. This volume is particularly relevant to this essay because it squarely centers on immigration per se and a majority of its chapters focus on Latina/os. This collection examines both how immigration discourses monitor, control, and categorize sexuality and how lesbian, gay, bisexual, and transsexual (LGBT) immigrants of color create communities in the shadows of these policies. Published the same year, *Passing Lines* emerged out of a conference at the David Rockefeller Center of Latin American Studies at Harvard University. Defining as queer "anyone who does not conform, or who is understood as not conforming, to conventional sexual mores," the editors argue that "U.S. immigration law and practice have historically considered queer people as *problems* and have made our sexualities, desires, and 'lifestyles' into objects of interrogation, debate, censure, control, and exclusion." In addition to providing a strong foundation for the conceptual underpinnings of this essay, these collections and the university-supported academic conferences that inspired them indicate increasing scholarly attention to the study of Latina/o sexualities "in motion." In this chapter, I discuss the strengths of this emerging literature as well as some of the gaps that remain in the scholarship, ending with recommendations for future areas of study.[1]

Sex and Immigration Policy

Although the relationship between gender and immigration is now generally recognized, until fairly recently there was almost no acknowledgment that sexuality might bear on immigration. In her review of heteronormativity and immigration scholarship for *Gay and Lesbian Quarterly*, Eithne Luibhéid laments that the "study of sexuality and immigration remains marginalized, trivialized, depoliticized, or treated with hostility." By documenting and analyzing the ways sexuality has historically factored into immigration exclusion and naturalization policies, scholars such as Luibhéid, Margot Canaday, and Siobhan Somerville have been instrumental in demonstrating precisely why sexuality should be examined in immigration studies. I want to emphasize that this concerns sexuality in all its forms—not just the sexuality of stigmatized sexual groups. In a recent article, Martin F. Manalansan emphasizes that a focus on sexuality in migration research is particularly important because it makes visible the heteronormative assumptions about family, reproduction, and marriage that structure immigration policy and are reproduced in the scholarly literature.[2]

In *Entry Denied: Controlling Sexuality at the Border*, Luibhéid argues that the "U.S. immigration control system has served as a crucial site for the construction and regulation of sexual norms, identities, and behaviors since 1875." She examines the ways technologies of "examination" figure in immigration control mechanisms and argues that even when these examinations lead to "positive" results (such as admission to the United States), they still situate immigrants "within the larger relations of power to which they remained subjected after entry."[3]

Chapter 1 of *Entry Denied* provides a concise and inclusive overview of the ways in which sexuality and gender have been controlled by immigration policy. From Luibhéid's analysis it is clear that sex-related U.S. immigration policies affected homosexuals (or suspected homosexuals) and racialized heterosexuals alike, both of which groups were similarly interpreted as dangerous. In fact, historically, U.S. immigration control has surveilled a wide range of "peripheral sexual figures" including "the racialized prostitute, the amoral and despotic pimp, the fecund woman whose reproduction was uncontrolled, the gold-digging hussy intent on snaring an American husband, and the foreigner who threatened miscegenation."[4]

Although it would be impossible to outline all relevant immigration policies here, a few examples will provide a foundation for the rest of my discussion. Even before the immigration control system was federalized in 1891, normative notions of sexuality led to the definition of family as "a husband, a wife, and children born to the couple," the exclusion of women pregnant outside of marriage (who were deemed liable to become a public charge), and the exclusion of women believed to "directly threaten heteropatriarchy's dominance." In 1891 having committed a crime of moral turpitude became grounds for exclusion, and subsequently this criterion was used to bar people who had been convicted of "adultery, bigamy, rape, statutory rape, and sodomy." The 1917 medical exclusion of "persons with abnormal sexual instincts" was the precursor of the 1952 exclusion of those with "psychopathic personality." Beginning in 1952, homosexuals were classified under this category, and if thus identified by the state, they were issued Class A medical exclusions. Between 1965 and 1979 homosexuals were reclassified as "sexual deviates" and still subjected to Class A medical exclusions. In 1979 the surgeon general ordered the Public Health Service to stop issuing automatic Class A medical exclusions to homosexuals. The INS then reworked and reinstituted an exclusion policy. Beginning in 1980, only entering immigrants who made "an unsolicited, unambiguous oral or written admission of homosexuality" or those identified by "a third party [as homosexual] . . . without prompting or prior questioning" would be sent to a secondary inspection where they would be asked if they were homosexual. If they answered no, they would no longer be detained. If they answered yes, they would be "referred to an immigration judge for an exclusion proceeding." In 1990 explicit gay and lesbian exclusion was removed from the law, although good moral character remained a requirement for permanent residency.[5]

Luibhéid's analysis of Sara Harb Quiroz's case illustrates how homosexual exclusion functioned in practice. Quiroz was a Mexican immigrant and a U.S. permanent resident when she was detained upon reentering the United States after a regular trip across the El Paso–Ciudad Juárez border in 1960. Quiroz was apparently questioned about her sexuality because she "look[ed] like a lesbian." Quiroz was issued a Class A medical exclusion and ultimately deported. Rather than interrogate the historical record to identify whether Quiroz was "really" a "lesbian" and assume that "predefined lesbian or gay identities always existed," Luibhéid employs a Foucauldian analysis to demonstrate the ways in which the "immigration service, in conjunction with larger circuits of power and knowledge, established the boundaries of who and what counted as lesbian and then confined Quiroz within that definition." Through her discussion of the "inducement to speak" (and to respond to all INS officers' questions), "methods of interpretation," and the "medicalization of the effects of confession," Luibhéid identifies the technologies of surveillance, categorization, and social control then operative. One important insight that emerges out of Luibhéid's work is the importance not only of analyzing the outcomes of legal battles around immigration/sexuality but also of examining the ways that the processes of criminalization, surveillance, and policing themselves affect immigrant sexualities.[6]

In her historical analysis of the ways in which homosexual exclusion was applied in the mid-twentieth century, Canaday discusses two cases (among others) of Cubans who were eventually deported. She uses the cases of *United States of America v. Roberto Flores-Rodriguez* and *Ganduxe y Marino v. Murff* to show how the federal government adopted a "process by which two competing paradigms for understanding homosexuality (status and conduct) were consolidated into a single model in which homosexual identity could be deduced from homosexual acts." Both Luibhéid and Canaday provide textured accounts, drawn from legal immigration cases, of the impact of homosexual exclusion on individual Latina/o lives. Scholars of Latina/o sexualities need to know more, however, about the extent to which race, phenotype, and national origin might have affected the process and outcomes of these types of cases. For example, why did Canaday choose two Cuban men for analysis? Were immigrant Caribbean men especially targeted? Commenting on Canaday's article, Brad Epps, Keja Valens, and Bill Johnson González state that it should "come as no surprise" that of the cases Canaday examines, "those in which the immigrant came from Latin America and the Caribbean resulted in deportation, while those in which the immigrant came from Western Europe at times resulted in admittance." While their analysis appears convincing, further empirical data would strengthen, and perhaps complicate, their claims.[7]

During the 1980s and 1990s, HIV status (and the perceived sexual dangers associated with it) increasingly became a focus of U.S. immigration control agents. Discussing the differential processing of Cuban and Haitian immigrants, the editors of *Passing Lines* argue that, while intercepted Haitians were either returned to Haiti or automatically screened for HIV, Cubans were tested less systematically. After HIV was added to the list of dangerous contagious diseases that could deter legalization of status—from undocumented to permanent legal resident—applicants under the Immigration Reform and Control Act of 1986 were required to submit an HIV test as part of their application and were deemed "inadmissible" if that test showed they were HIV positive. Although HIV-positive applicants could apply for a waiver, Bettina M. Fernandez found that the majority of these waivers were denied. Because universal testing occurred during the period Fernandez discusses, one could argue that HIV testing did not discriminate against homosexuals. However, in his review of homosexual and HIV exclusion, Jorge L. Carro argues that the "grim reality for homosexual aliens is that AIDS provides an additional reason on which to base the exclusion of gay men. Despite superficial appearance of nondiscrimination, fear of AIDS may lead to the failure to revise current INS policies regarding immigration of homosexuals to comport with current medical understandings." By 1993 HIV-positive status had become grounds for exclusion of immigrants, tourists, short-term workers, and legal permanent residents, although this exclusion has already been informally used to exclude Haitians who had grounds for asylum claims.[8]

In the 1980s and early 1990s, U.S. immigration control also began considering asylum cases for gays and lesbians fearing persecution in their country of origin. The precedent came from the case of a Cuban homosexual man, Fidel Armando Toboso-Alfonso, who had entered the United States as part of the Mariel migration. After a cocaine conviction, Toboso-Alfonso's parole was revoked, and he entered "exclusion" proceedings that might have led to deportation or indefinite detention. When his case came up for appeal in 1990, he claimed asylum on the grounds that he faced persecution based on his membership in a "particular social group": homosexuals. Although technically Toboso-Alfonso was not granted asylum, his was the first case in which homosexuals were recognized as a particular social group. In 1993 and 1994, respectively, Brazilian Marcelo Tenorio and Mexican "Jose Garcia" were granted asylum based on the logic that as homosexuals they were members of a persecuted "particular social group." Later in 1994, the Toboso-Alfonso case was made precedent for other gay men and lesbians to claim asylum based on persecution for being homosexual. As Timothy J. Randazzo clarifies, although the Toboso-Alfonso case defined homosexuals as a "particular social group," in order to be granted asylum, immigrants also needed to prove "well-founded fear of persecution" ("generally understood to mean frequent or severe acts of abuse . . . perpetrated either by the government or by individuals the government is unable or unwilling to control") based on their membership in the "particular social group" (i.e., homosexuals) if they returned to their country of origin. The 2000 asylum case of Geovanni Hernandez-Montiel expanded the definition of particular social group to include "gay men with female sexual identities" and therefore facilitated further asylum cases of transgender individuals.[9]

Reflecting on his experiences as an expert witness in asylum cases of five Mexican-origin men, Lionel Cantú Jr. describes one irony of this new interpretation of asylum law. Although asylum (if granted) provides protection from deportation, making a successful claim requires that expert witnesses and clients assert that being gay was an immutable characteristic and "paint[] one's country in racialist, colonialist terms, while at the same time disavowing the United States' role in contributing to the oppressive conditions that one fled."[10]

Alisa Solomon's discussion of another asylum seeker, Christina Madrazo, points to a further aspect of the intersection of immigration and sexuality: the role of sexual violence in immigration control. Madrazo, a "transsexual transmigrant" from Mexico, was detained during asylum proceedings when two previous misdemeanor charges were discovered. During her detention at the Krome Detention Center, she was raped twice by a guard. Her reporting of these rapes led eventually to an investigation that revealed multiple occurrences of sexual misconduct at the detention facility. Sexual abuse as an element of border control is not limited to the Krome Detention Center. Luibhéid also discusses the rape of women on the U.S.-Mexico border by Border Patrol officials and the difficulty of prosecuting these cases.[11]

Immigration and welfare policy are also increasingly interlinked with the state placing more of the economic burden of supporting new immigrants on family networks. This trend can be seen in changes to policies regarding the affidavit of support in the Illegal Immigrant Reform and Immigrant Responsibility Act of 1996 (IIRIRA 96). IIRIRA 96 required that immigrant sponsors meet an income threshold (125 percent of the poverty level) and made the affidavits of support they must sign enforceable. These changes were specifically introduced in an effort to deny visas to anyone who might become a public charge. Welfare policies, by linking benefits to particular family structures, further affect immigrant gender and sexuality.

Post-9/11, immigration has become more highly politicized, with vigilante Minutemen policing the U.S.-Mexico border, ongoing plans for the erection of physical border blockades, and increasing challenges to the civil rights of immigrants. The intersection of sexuality with these immigration issues is not always apparent. Jessica Chapin's analysis of the 1993 Border Patrol initiative Operation Hold the Line is instructive in this regard.[12] Discussing a previous period of U.S. immigrant anxiety, she indicates that politicians and the media repeatedly demonstrated the "success" of a border blockade by pointing to the absence of transvestite prostitutes, or *vestidas*, in El Paso. Therefore, the rhetoric of ridding the city of the negative effects of "illegals" was gendered, sexualized, and represented by the multiply marginalized, undocumented, gender-transgressive sex workers. Chapin's analysis makes visible the connections between anti-immigrant actions and homophobic fears—connections often hidden from view. Given the current climate, careful attention to the ways in which anti-immigrant attitudes, state policies, and vigilante actions are interlinked with gender and sexuality is required.

Sexiles? Sexual Immigrants?
Does Sexuality Encourage People to Migrate?

Some scholars argue that Latin Americans who are seen as sexually transgressive in their home countries are more likely to emigrate than those who are not and that Latin Americans who have been victims of sexual violence might be more likely to emigrate than those who have not. For example, Lourdes Argüelles and Anne Rivero argue that factors such as the experience of "gender violence, enforced sex and gender roles, sexual orientation, sexual abuse and assault, or coerced motherhood" might contribute to a Latin American woman's decision to migrate.[13] Anecdotal evidence also suggests that Latin American gay men and lesbians are more likely to migrate than nonhomosexuals in order to escape sexual oppression in their home countries. In the following section, I review the scholarly discussion of this issue.

The terms sexile, *sexilio*, and *séxodo* have been used in a range of texts that imply that nonnormatively sexually identified Latin Americans are motivated to migrate because of their sexuality. I believe the first use of the term occurs in a Manolo Guzmán article in which he recounts his first entrance into the famed Latino gay club La Escuelita in New York City. He defines sexile in a footnote as "the exile of those who have had to leave their nation of origin on account of their sexual orientation." While this definition is fairly general, in the article itself Guzmán applies the term to the experiences of middle- and upper-class gay migrants. Rather than describe the regular patrons or performers in the club (who are more likely to be working class) this way, he employs sexile to describe a group of Puerto Ricans who had previously convinced him that he would not like this place. These "bourgeois sexiles," as he refers to them, created a distance between themselves and those they perhaps viewed as something like proletarian sex-immigrants. When they tried to dissuade Guzmán from going to the club, they placed him in their category—middle-class sexiles—as opposed to the other. He later refers to parting ideological ways with his "fellow sexiles," as he came to enjoy his weekly trips to La Escuelita.[14]

The graphic novel *Sexile/Sexilio* uses Guzmán's term as a title for the life story of Adela Vazquez, a transgender Cuban woman who left Cuba as part of the 1980 Mariel boatlift.[15] This particular migration of Cuban homosexuals and gender transgressive men and women is unique in that homosexuals *as a group* were *systematically* encouraged to emigrate by the state. In other cases (either of Cubans in a different period or of other national-origin groups), the emigration of homosexuals was not as directly facilitated and encouraged by the state. If the state does not explicitly "encourage" homosexuals to leave the country, can their departure be described as "sexile"? Scholars who use this term suggest the importance of other institutions, especially the family, in promoting this sexually driven emigration.

Several texts widely assume that sexuality is a central, if not the primary, reason gay, lesbian, and transgender Latin Americans migrate to the United States. David William Foster, for one, discusses the "homoerotic diaspora in Latin America" and argues that one of the factors promoting the "extensive migration of Latin Americans to the United States and Europe" is the "repression, oppression, and persecution" related to their "sexual identity." Although such exile is sometimes related to political projects, it may also represent "merely the quest for a new life space, far from hearth and home and the family nucleus, to pursue a life considered deviant by that nucleus." A 2001 article in the popular gay magazine *The Advocate* reiterates this assertion. The headline announces that immigrants from Latin America are "Coming to America to Be Gay." David Kirby argues that the motivations commonly associated with immigrants, such as better opportunity for jobs and education, also apply to gay and lesbian Latino immigrants, but that for them there is also an "added incentive." According to Kirby, this incentive plays a bigger role for middle- and upper-class Latinos. In other words, he argues that the immigration of middle- and upper-class homosexuals would be more likely to be motivated by sexuality, whereas the immigration of working-class homosexuals would be more likely to be motivated by economic factors.[16]

In a recent discussion of the "Puerto Rican queer diaspora," Lawrence La Fountain-Stokes laments that "sexuality and divergent gender expression and sexual orientation have only recently come to be acknowledged as causal factors in national (internal) and international (cross-border) migration." While reclaiming the abjection of AIDS Latina/o queer identities, Alberto Sandoval-Sánchez describes a "generation of Latino gay men that in a self-imposed s/exile migrated to the U.S. from the Caribbean and Latin America in search of independence and sex, satisfaction and love." Identifying as a member of this generation, he argues that "migration had provided him" freedom, "particularly the opportunity to articulate a gay identity shaped by a Latino consciousness."[17]

Scholars widely assert that homosexuality or nonnormative sexuality causes or promotes emigration from Latin American countries; however, few scholars have examined this claim empirically. One important contribution comes from Lionel Cantú, who illustrates the subtle variations in the ways in which sexuality can be related to migration. Although some of his Mexican-origin male respondents directly and explicitly identified the desire to escape sexual oppression as their primary motivation for migrating, others claimed economic and educational opportunities as their primary motivation. Cantú argues, however, that the "social inequalities of sexuality, like race and gender, are integrally linked to the economic structures of society" and that therefore "when immigrants, who are a sexual minority, say that they immigrated for financial reasons, part of the analysis must include sexuality." Homosexual relationships in the country of origin might also affect migration directly or indirectly. He adds that the sexual identity and gay perspective of those who did not claim explicitly to have moved because of their sexuality are, nonetheless, transformed by migration. Challenging many assumptions of Latino gay research, Cantú comments that at least one middle-class participant may have felt he could "be 'himself'" more in Guadalajara than in the United States, and Cantú tentatively attributes this to his class and occupational privilege in Mexico. Because sexuality and political economy intersect, sexual minority status shapes economic opportunity (in the case of the middle-class business owner whose upward mobility is impeded by heteronormative social expectations of his colleagues) and vice versa.[18]

In addition to complicating the assumptions embedded in the term sexile, Cantú's analysis points to the methodological difficulty in ascertaining *why* immigrants migrate, since responses collected after migration are necessarily influenced by identities, experiences, and social conditions that shift after and because of that migration. Luibhéid further illustrates this methodological complication. Drawing on Saskia Sassen's work, she argues that "immigrants move not primarily because of a cost-benefit differential that can be objectively assessed in advance but because unequal global relations—which involve economic exploitation, imperialism, and military interventionism—create linkages between countries that serve as bridges for migration."[19]

Drawing on literature on globalization and cultural hybridity, Héctor Carrillo defines sexual migration as "international migration that is motivated, fully or partially, by the sexuality of those who migrate, including motivations connected to sexual desires and pleasures, the pursuit of romantic relations with foreign partners, the exploration of new self-definitions of sexual identity, the need to distance oneself from experiences of discrimination or oppression caused by sexual difference, or the search for greater sexual equality and rights." Rather than analyze only how immigrant sexualities change after migration (as Gloria González-López does), he suggests that scholars use a "synthetic theoretical perspective" to analyze the "role sexuality itself plays as a force propelling transnational movement." In order to do this, he suggests scholars examine "the sexual and social situation of the immigrants prior to relocation, along the migration path, and after arrival and settlement, as well [as] during periods when the immigrants return to their home country."[20]

In his own analysis, Carrillo discusses sexual agency of migrants and sexual tourism. For example, he argues that sexual migration should be analyzed alongside sexual tourism because people moving from rich to poor countries are often perceived as sexual tourists, while those engaging in similar activities and desires moving from poor to rich countries are perceived as sexual migrants. Carrillo adds that it would be important to explore the "same kind of fantasies [that] may be prevalent among gay Mexican male tourists who travel to the U.S.—that these men are sex tourists in their own right when they travel to see for themselves gay urban centers in U.S. cities." It is important to note that the categories of "tourist" and "immigrant" are not only sociological but also categories employed by the state. The forms of regulation and surveillance used to monitor tourists are quite different from those used to monitor immigrants. How might these differences affect how people experience sexual fantasies? In general, Carrillo argues that we need to study whether "there are differences between sexual immigrants and other types of immigrants"; "how immigrants' sexual behavior changes as a result of relocation"; and "what happens to immigrants' sexualities and sexual behavior over time, in their back and forth movement between home and host countries, or when the definition of home shifts to include the host country as well."[21]

The questions raised in this section emerge out of scholarship about LGBT immigrants. These questions do not, however, apply only to LGBT immigrants. Might heterosexual immigrants pursuing a heteronormatively structured "American dream" also be considered sexiles? In what ways does heterosexual sexuality propel transnational movement? How does migration affect the sexual behavior or the sexual attitudes of heterosexuals? Increasingly, scholars of Latina/o sexuality are critically and productively analyzing the interconnections between heterosexual and nonheterosexual sexualities.

Sex after Migration: Challenging Culturalist Understandings of Latina/o Sexuality

There is also a debate about how immigration and levels of acculturation affect sexual health, gender inequalities, sexual identities, and sexual behaviors. While discussing "sexual migration," Carrillo interrogates the literature on this issue and critiques the way in which a common sense of "traditional" Latina/o culture is used simplistically to explain contradictory evidence. Some researchers who have found that recent immigrants have lower HIV risk than immigrants who have resided in the United States for longer periods of time argue that "recent immigrants are more sexually conservative or sexually modest, and thus that traditional sexual cultures are somewhat protective." When researchers have found the opposite—that recent immigrants have a higher HIV risk—they have "tend[ed] to blame machismo and traditional Latino sexual cultures, and then emphasize that more acculturated Latina/os might have lower risk because they have acquired more self-determination, self-assertiveness, and individuality (all characteristics that are imagined as being more prevalent in mainstream U.S. cultures)." Marysol Asencio highlights a similar discrepancy in the literature on the effect of acculturation on sexual health and gender inequalities. She states that "although most studies support the notion that Latino and Puerto Rican acculturation to U.S. mainland society creates 'positive' outcomes in terms of gender equity and power differentials, other studies have also noted areas where there have been negative effects," including poorer health, lower educational attainment, and lower educational aspirations for more-acculturated Latina/os, as opposed to less-acculturated Latina/os.[22]

Cantú explains the assumptions embedded in these culturalist arguments and their ramifications. He critiques the "manner in which 'culture' as a focal argument not only obscures other structural dimensions that shape Latino men's lives but also pathologizes our 'culture'" and identifies three ways in which cultural arguments function to obscure sociological analysis. First, they homogenize Latino cultures—that is, cultural arguments often assume that there is "a Latino culture"—which obscures differences of national origin, class, gender, sexuality, and regional differences among Latina/os. Second, cultural arguments tend to represent Latina/o cultures as tradition-bound systems that are fixed and static, and that represent a past from which the West has already evolved and progressed. Third, cultural arguments identify Latina/o culture as an exotic Other against which the unidentified Western norm can be positively compared.[23] Throughout his work, Cantú highlights the different effects of culturalist arguments. When using reductionist cultural arguments, scholars, even those who seek to improve the quality of life of gay Latino men, reproduce difference. Cultural explanations also serve to blame the victim. That is, in cultural reductionist arguments, "Latino culture," because it is *machista*, homophobic, patriarchal, and traditional, becomes the cause of the problems that Latino gay men face. One of the key limitations of a cultural reductionist argument is that the culture of the group under scrutiny becomes the cause of social ills, while structural issues that place that group in a subordinate position in relation to the dominant racial/class/gender group are obscured.

In order to avoid some of the shortcomings of a culturalist argument, Cantú proposes a materialist framework in which the "cultural" is understood not only as shifting and heterogeneous but also as cross-cutting with structural forces. Interested in both macro and micro social processes, Cantú proposes to "examine from a queer materialist perspective dimensions that shape the social relations of families of origin and families of choice and thus, the intimate context by which identity itself is shaped." He argues "for a theoretical move toward a *queer political economy* in order to understand the dynamics that shape 'the sexuality of migration' and the fluidity of identities in a global context." Whereas materialist studies foreground structural inequalities, they also sometimes depict the people who live amid those inequalities as simple victims, lacking agency. On the other hand, studies that focus on identities forefront the identification strategies and agency of individuals, while sometimes ignoring the structural forces that limit those identity "choices." By queering political economy, Cantú seeks to draw strength from both of these perspectives.[24]

Racialization of Sexuality:
Latina Female Sexuality as a Social Problem

Culturalist arguments have not only been used to explain the migration of homosexuals from "traditional" Latin America to the United States but have also colluded in the racialization of Latina female heterosexuality. In the United States, Latina sexuality has often been defined as a "problem." Social scientists, public health officials, and the popular press have defined Latinas as hyper-sexual, overly fertile, and bad mothers. Immigrant Latinas, in particular, are targeted as the bearers of this cultural problem. The culturalist underpinnings of this argument assume that Latinas emigrate from "traditional" countries with higher fertility, and that with acculturation in the United States their fertility will decrease. Studies that attempt to evaluate how migration affects fertility show contradictory evidence. Nancy S. Landale and Susan M. Hauan, for example, found that "first- and second-generation migrants to the U.S. mainland [metropolitan New York] face substantially higher risks of conceiving and bear-ing a first child before marriage than do nonmigrants in Puerto Rico."[25]

The presumed fertility of Latinas is one component of the "culture of pov-erty" used to explain the socioeconomic position of Latina/o families. Laura Briggs discusses the legacy of culture of poverty descriptions of Puerto Ricans. Successfully supplanting economic-based critiques of the causes of Puerto Rican socioeconomic conditions, the culture of poverty discourses, popularized in part by Oscar Lewis's best-selling book on Puerto Rican life, La Vida, "shifted the terrain of debate about poverty and colonialism from the economy to sex." Briggs argues that discourses characterizing Puerto Ricans as a "bizarre and gro-tesque" problem were "so effective and became so widespread [because] they were grounded in a narrative of family, sex, and reproduction." She argues that with the emergence of the concept of the culture of poverty, Puerto Ricans—and Puerto Rican women more specifically—were rearticulated as the cause of the ethnic group's socioeconomic position. The culture of poverty created a group, "the poor," that was defined not by "their relationship to labor or the means of production, but [by] a set of behaviors and their reproduction of children." These included those of hypersexual women, bad mothers, female-headed households, and "disorganized families." Briggs is interested in exploring the ways in which this discursive move is a precursor to the more recent representations of Afri-can American and Puerto Rican/Latina women as "welfare queens."[26] These discourses about the dangers of Latina childbearing also resonate with current anti-immigration debates where issues of family size, reproduction, and fertility are used to highlight the threat of Latino immigration and the need to control it. For the purposes of this review geared toward defining future agendas of social-behavioral scientists, it is important to emphasize the role that social scientists played in creating and circulating these discourses that associated Puerto Ricans with sexual deviance and identified that sexual deviance with the cause of their socioeconomic position.

While culture of poverty discourses "explained" and constructed the dan-gers of Latina sexuality, on the ground this sexuality was controlled in such concrete ways as coercive sterilization, which was used in both Puerto Rico and the mainland United States to control Latina fertility. The "bioethics of reproductive technologies" are complicated in the sense that reproductive freedom means quite different things to women who are positioned differently in terms of race, nationality, and immigration status. Iris Lopez places her discussion of sterilization decisions made by Puerto Rican women living in New York City in the context of sterilization abuses in the city as well as on the island. Drawing on intensive interviews with 128 Puerto Rican women conducted in the early 1980s, Lopez demonstrates that "women do actively seek to transform and improve their lives, and controlling their reproduction is one of the primary means of which they avail themselves to do so." However, "the constraints of their lives play an equally significant role in shaping their reproductive decisions and experiences." In her discussion of the sterilization of Mexican-origin women in Southern California, Elena Gutiérrez shows how language differences and presumed citizenship status systematically undermined the consent process and contributed to the coercive underpinning of Mexican immigrant women's fertility choices. The issue of coercive sterilization and reproductive rights illustrates the political complexities of thinking about immigrant female sexualities, because the same interventions could be seen as contributing to or eliminating females' reproductive control of their own bodies. These historical cases also illustrate how medical "solutions" were used to control social science "problems."[27]

In a groundbreaking study of the sex lives of Mexican immigrants, Gloria González-López challenges a range of preconceptions about Mexican and Mexican American sexuality—including the understanding of Latina sexuality as a problem. Drawing on open-ended interviews with first-generation Mexican immigrants in Southern California, she challenges acculturation and assimilation models that, according to her, define the parameters of HIV/AIDS-related studies. She challenges, for example, a model that presumes men and women in Mexico are enchained by a static, traditional culture and that upon migration to the "modern" United States, they challenge these oppressive gender and sexual norms. Rather, through women's narratives, González-López shows that in Mexican society there are "multiple femininities and heterosexualities." She employs the concept of "regional patriarchies" to provide a nuanced and multiple account of regional variations in the ways in which gender inequalities are structured. She therefore begins with a complex notion of patriarchies and women's varied responses to those patriarchies: "These experiences of femininity reveal tensions, contradictions, and fluidity that allow women to have sexual agency and pleasure but also to be exposed to forms of control and danger. As they migrate, women *continue* reinventing these gendered and sexualized processes in flux."[28]

In her discussion of men's and women's sex lives after migration, González-López emphasizes the different ways in which working outside the home affect women and men. For some women, "working full-time outside the home, earning a salary, and attaining financial autonomy or responsibility became part of their sexual emancipation." Some women expressed that after migration they were less likely to feel obligated "to have sex with a partner as a way to reciprocate for his being the family provider." For other women, migration represented "a strategy for coping with and escaping the combined effects of gender, class, and sexual abuse" in Mexico. In addition, she argues that sexual fears associated with "child sexual abuse, alcohol and drug use, gang activity in the community, and the fear of sexually transmitted diseases (i.e., HIV/AIDS) permeate the daily lives of these men and women." While connected to sexual fears in Mexico, this "culture of sexual fear migrates and begins to take new forms that are embedded in the new social and economic realities of immigrants." For example, working-class male day laborers experience "not only sexual harassment and coercion" at work but also temptations "into sexualized encounters for money" with white women and white gay men. González-López therefore challenges the assumption that immigration to the United States is consistently and unproblematically liberatory. Focusing on differences of gender and previous sexual histories, she explains how migration can be experienced both as sexually liberatory and as oppressive, sometimes simultaneously.[29]

Jennifer S. Hirsch also challenges the assumption that Latino immigrants are simply moving from a traditional culture to a modern and more liberatory one. Drawing on innovative ethnographic research in Atlanta, Georgia, as well as in Degollado and El Fuerte, Mexico, she argues that the "idea that women automatically benefit from migration draws on the assumption that they are moving from a society rigidly controlled by tradition and machismo to one of unlimited economic opportunity and gender equality." She argues instead that the "reasons for women's assorted successes and failures [in the Atlanta area] lie as much in women's individual courage to risk getting on a bus alone without being absolutely sure of the final destination as they do in material resources they bring with them (kin, papers, work experience)." Hirsch's transnational methodological approach highlights changing gender and sexual discourses in both Mexico and the United States and helps elucidate the complicated intersection between globalization and sexual ideologies and practices.[30]

Parents and Youths:
Intergenerational Conversations about Sex

Recent scholarship has focused on communication between Latina/o parents and their children about sex. The majority of this research has focused on relationships between mothers and daughters.[31] A notable exception is González-López's discussion of Latino fathers' views of their daughters' virginity. Some studies confirm the expectation that traditional Latina/o cultures have an adverse effect on both sex education and sexual health. In an analysis of in-depth interviews with twenty-two Latinas, for example, Marcela Raffaelli and Lenna L. Ontai found that there was a "low level of family communication regarding sexuality" and that "Latinas have limited romantic and sexual experience prior to leaving home." In "Good Girl or Flirt Girl?" Sandra L. Faulkner discusses the apparent persistence of traditional values even in the fairly new sexual scripts that emerged in interviews with thirty-one young Cuban American, Puerto Rican, and Dominican women, most of whom were "fairly well acculturated." These young Latinas defined a "flirt girl" as "the unmarried woman who is free and open about her sexual desires; she accepts 'straight-out' invitations for sex from men, has 'sex when she can,' sleeps and dates around, and 'allows her man to be with other women.'" Although the "flirt girl" apparently emerged through the interviews, few women seemed to identify with this role. Faulkner explains: "Women did not want to be seen as a whore, ho, slut, or flirt girl. Almost all the participants described feeling 'impure,' 'dirty,' and like 'sluts' for sexual activity they had engaged in previously. Many women regretted their sexual experience and wished they could reverse at least some past activity, particularly if they had been with a player, as that meant they were potential flirt girls."[32] The distancing from sexuality viewed as "promiscuous" and the shame associated with it seems to coincide with traditional understandings of Latina sexuality.

Other studies challenge the assumption that traditional Latina/o cultures negatively affect sex education and sexual health. In a study of study of low-income Latina mothers and daughters of Caribbean descent living in the Northeast United States, for example, M. Diane McKee and Alison Karasz found that all mothers and daughters believed "open communication" was crucial, something not commonly associated with the "traditional culture" model. Although the researchers acknowledge that this open communication, while valued, is "evidently difficult to achieve," they also identify successful strategies Latina mothers and daughters use. For example, they discuss a strategy used by "low-conflict dyads" where mothers attempted to build *confianza* with their daughters over the long term and "established a pattern of communication, including about reproductive health, from an early age." They found that both the mothers and daughters in these dyads "emphasized the friendly, egalitarian nature of their relationships." In another study, Erum Nadeem, Laura Romo, and Marian Sigman interviewed pregnant Latina adolescents and analyzed videotaped conversations between them and their mothers. They found that age and religiosity "were not associated with explicit or implicit maternal communication," and they concluded that "these trends raise questions about the extent to which traditional values in Latino culture inhibit discussion of contraceptive use among women living in the U.S., including perceived ideals [such] as sexual silence and religious beliefs." Interestingly, they also found that "explicit maternal communication made a greater impact on girls from Spanish-speaking families" as opposed to girls from English-speaking families where the explicitness of the message did not have an impact. They suggest one possible interpretation: that "Spanish-speaking mothers and daughters are generally more comfortable with explicit discussion about contraceptive use, which made it easier for these adolescents to communicate in explicit terms with . . . research assistants."[33]

Possibly reflecting an internalization of messages about the dangers of Latina sexuality, a study of white, black, and Latina girls' discussion of *Seventeen* magazine found that working-class Latina girls, unlike the middle-class white girls, "expressed an awareness of the dangers of their sexuality; for example, the possibility of becoming pregnant or being physically abused." In addition, the Latinas "talked about parents' and school personnel's lack of trust in them and fear of girls' sexual activity."[34]

In general, there is less scholarly literature on youth sexuality than adult sexuality. In the field of Latina/o sexuality, the literature on youth often relied on an assumption that Latino (and especially Latina) sexuality was a problem that needed to be controlled. More recent studies move away from this assumption and are better able to examine the ways in which narratives of sexual problems, dangers, and threats are constructed and how these narratives are internalized by young women and men.

Where Are Latina Lesbians?

The literature on the ways in which migration influences Latina lesbian sexuality is much more limited than the literature that examines its impact on either Latina heterosexuality or Latino gay male sexuality. Olivia Espín's work is an important contribution to this scholarship. In one article, she explores the similarities between "coming out" as a lesbian and migrating internationally. She argues, for example, that "many women who identified as lesbian before the migration have to learn to be lesbian in their new cultural context." Such Latina immigrants not only may have to assimilate to new definitions of lesbian, but they may also have to acculturate as a minority in the United States. In an analysis of immigrant lesbian life narratives, she adds that "for most women, issues of sexuality are usually not part of the conscious decision to migrate." In the life narratives, she found that lesbian immigrants said it was easier for them to talk about sexual topics in English. Some explained that "they could not have had such discussions in their first language because they did not know the vocabulary or were not used to talking about sexuality in their native language.[35]

In an interesting analysis of two Latinas' construction of gender/sexuality, Patricia Zavella discusses the life story of María, who fell in love with Josefina, one of her classmates in Mexico. After their relationship was discovered by María's parents, her father beat her and she eventually went to live with Josefina's family. In Mexico, María says she was masculine-identified and investigated the possibility of having sex-reassignment surgery. After moving to the United States in 1986, she "experienced a new awareness of racism and found more openness regarding sexuality." She underwent what Zavella describes as a "profound transformation," during which she "came out of the closet herself and began accepting herself as female." This transformation affected her physical form. Whereas María states that before she "'looked like a boy,'" she now, in Zavella's words, "became more curvaceous, and changed from androgynous-looking to having a female body type."[36]

These studies raise interesting questions about Latina lesbian sexuality and identity and how culture is related to migration. Further research in this area is definitely needed.

Questions and Directions for Future Research

I began this essay with reference to a set of interdisciplinary edited collections that focus on queer migrations. The focus on globalization and transnationalism in these collections challenges scholars to analyze the political economy of sexuality, to avoid binary constructions of here versus there, to not see national cultures as neatly bounded, and to think about the dynamic relationship between nation-states and the back-and-forth movement not only of people but also of cultures, capital, and commodities across geopolitical borders. The centering of a queer analysis that highlights the construction of heteronormativity also challenges scholars to think simultaneously about the relationship between stigmatized heterosexualities (e.g., Latinas imagined to be problematically fertile), homosexualities, and other forms of sexuality.

These challenges are beginning to be addressed in the social and behavioral sciences. For example, recent studies examine sexuality in a transnational context. The question of how sexuality (including nonnormative sexual identity, experience of sexual abuse, and transgressive female sexual practices) influences immigration is an important one. It is not clear, however, that asking immigrants in the United States why they migrated is the only or best way to answer this question. Recent transnational studies that entail research in both countries of origin and destination are promising, especially because they allow us to think about groups of people who do migrate, those who do not migrate (nonmigrants), and the relationship between these two groups.[37] These transnational studies have their own methodological limitations. How to study the impact of sexuality on migration is, therefore, still an open question—one that invites creative and multiple methodological strategies.

Studies about lesbian and gay Latina/o sexualities conducted in the United States, and not transnationally, have mostly been conducted in particular geographic areas in the United States: New York City, San Francisco, and Los Angeles. Although I would like to see more research on other urban areas with high Latina/o concentrations, including Miami and Chicago, the need for information about sexual practices in nonurban settings is more pressing. It would be important to see how immigrants' (sex) lives are differently affected in areas where there are fewer resources and social networks for immigrants.

There has been varied research on Latina female sexuality with emphasis on girls, relationships between immigrant parents and U.S.-born daughters (and more rarely, sons), and how adult women's sexuality is influenced by migration. More recent research does not assume that female sexuality is a problem (as in the "Hispanic teenage pregnancy" approach) and challenges the simplistic assumption that immigrants to the United States move from traditional (that is, oppressive) Latin American cultures to a modern (progressive) U.S. culture. This research, however, almost exclusively focuses on heterosexual Latinas. Research on Latina lesbians in the social and behavioral sciences is extremely limited. This is especially obvious given the relative wealth of literature in the humanities written by and about Latina lesbians. The centrality (even if token) of some of these Latina lesbian texts in women's studies, LGBT studies, and queer studies (I am thinking here of such works as *This Bridge Called My Back* and *Borderlands*) has not translated into empirical studies of Latina lesbian sexuality in the social and behavioral sciences.[38] Some unanswered questions of particular interest are: How do the experiences of Latina lesbians and Latino gay men differ? What social spaces do they share? If sexuality does influence gay men's decision to migrate, does it affect lesbians in the same way? My preliminary observations in South Florida suggest that Latina lesbian cultures are much less commercialized than Latino gay male cultures and are also much less visible. If this is the case in South Florida, is it also true in other urban areas with concentrations of Latina/os and LGBT-identified people? If so, how does less commodification of sexuality and distance from commercial spaces affect Latina lesbian sexual identities, practices, and cultures?

Particular immigrant populations originating from the Caribbean and Latin America have traditionally not been defined as Latina/o when the country of origin is not Spanish-speaking and the primary colonial history is not Spanish. These populations include Haitians and Brazilians. Although I am convinced of the importance of historical distinctions between Haiti and Brazil on the one hand and the Spanish-speaking countries of Latin America and the Caribbean on the other, the fact is that studies of these two particular populations fall between different areas of study recognized in the United States: Latina/o studies, Latin American studies, and African American studies. Even "Black Atlantic" definitions tend to privilege English-speaking black Caribbeans. Therefore, the definitions of these fields result in a lack of adequate research on Brazilians and Haitians. Given that the Ford Foundation sponsored two boards on Latina/o sexualities and on black sexualities, I think we are particularly well suited to consider how to challenge this research deficiency and point to where these studies could be intellectually placed. In terms of the study of Latina/o immigration and sexuality, both of these cases are particularly interesting. Haitian Americans, in addition to originating from a nation that shares an island with the Dominican Republic, have had immigration streams parallel to Cuban Americans but with notably different receptions and outcomes. In addition, immigration exclusion related to HIV was practiced on the bodies of Haitians, who were associated from the beginning with AIDS infection. However, we know very little about Haitian American sexualities. Social scientists do seem to know a lot about transgressive sexuality in Brazil, with recent work analyzing the exotic gaze of the Western world on Brazil as a sexual site.[39] Despite significant Brazilian immigration to the United States, however, very little work has been done on this U.S.-based population. In terms of sexuality, it would be interesting to examine to what extent immigrants must negotiate an exoticized notion of Brazilian sexuality and how this varies according to class and phenotype.

Finally, in the last ten years, there has been a national conversation about immigration policy that has been interlinked with debates about welfare and terrorism. These debates recycle some familiar tropes of Latina/o sexuality. The highly fertile Latina with many children, for example, was a recurring figure used to prove the immigrant "threat," the "drain" on welfare, and the challenge to certain family values. This trope has a direct relation to Latina/o sexualities. Further research is needed to unpack the ways in which heavily reduced social services, anti-immigrant attitudes, and continuing socioeconomic challenges facing Latina/o populations will affect Latina/o sexualities.

13

Latinas, Sex Work, and Trafficking in the United States

AMALIA L. CABEZAS WITH DOLORES ORTIZ AND SONIA VALENCIA

Even though the popular media in the United States often depict Latinas as sex workers, there is little research on the experiences of Latinas working in the sex trade. Only a few small-scale studies examine Latinas engaged in "street" prostitution. National, regional, or local studies that specifically investigate the lives and working conditions of Latinas in the sex industries are nearly nonexistent. In this essay we offer a brief overview of the research available on Latinas whose work is providing commercial sexual services in the United States. We also examine recent U.S. policies pertaining to the traffic in women for forced prostitution. We have divided the chapter into two parts because trafficking into forced prostitution and sex work may have little in common. While there may be varying degrees of abuse and exploitation in commercial sex, it is important to distinguish between diverse working conditions of the sex industries and the slavery-like practices that are characteristic of trafficking and involuntary servitude. Both trafficking in women and sex work involve a wide range of multifaceted policy and legal issues. There is a spectrum of practices that exist between trafficking and sex work, with girls forced into involuntary sexual servitude at one end, and women exercising some degree of agency at the other end.[1] We wish to emphasize that trafficking encompasses different and specific elements and has other characteristics that are not necessarily present in commercial sex work. The conflation of these two often leads to confusion and ultimately to harmful policies that violate the rights of people who work in the sex industries. We analyze working conditions by focusing on the immigrant's documentation status as a factor determinative of the level of vulnerability that she may experience in selling sexual services.

Latinas and Sex Work

The sex industries incorporate many types of businesses, some of which operate legally, others illegally, and still others in gray areas of the law. Some new forms of commodified sexuality, such as telephone sex and cybersex, are legal and highly lucrative. These exist alongside older forms of commercialized sex, such as brothels and street prostitution, that continue to be subject to criminal prosecution.[2] The diversity of types of activities, working conditions, health and safety issues, occupational practices, and levels of legality vary according to the sector of the sex trade and local laws. For example, indoor forms of prostitution, such as massage parlors, offer workers more protection from arrest and sexual violence as well as working conditions more conducive to the practice of safer sex. Nevertheless, whether in legal businesses or in the underground economy, sex workers constitute a stigmatized and often an invisible workforce.

There are many different venues for commercial sex, and Latinas can be found working in such diverse settings as massage parlors, escort services, telephone sex lines, exotic dancing, cybersex, and other forms of sexualized entertainment, where they experience inconsistent working conditions and differing levels of legality. Segmentation is one of the characteristics of the sex industries, with specialized niches catering to particular sexual tastes and population demographics. Certain sectors of the sex trade provide only fantasies or role-playing, with no physical sexual intimacy. For instance, telephone sex work and stripping offer indoor working conditions without the exchange of bodily fluids.[3] Both cybersex and telephone sex also offer a degree of anonymity and relatively flexible working schedules.

Practices and conditions vary widely in the sex industries, and a woman's cultural capital plays an important role in determining her work options. As in other labor markets that are segmented by English-language skills, citizenship status, age, nationality, and race or skin color, the participation of Latinas in the sex trade is configured by these dynamics as well. From the general research on the sex trade, we conclude that racial/ethnic stratification figures prominently in the occupational status of the worker, as do English-language-skills and immigration status. Latinas with citizenship or documented status, higher socioeconomic levels, and more cultural capital have greater income potential in the better-paid and less dangerous forms of sex work in the United States than do recent immigrants, particularly those who are undocumented. For women without proper immigration authorization, the illegality of sex work, compounded by their undocumented status, places them in a position of vulnerability and isolation, and the constant threat of deportation hinders their ability to seek social support or remedy for any injustices they face. Consequently, the type of work that is available to undocumented immigrant women exposes them to greater risks, including exploitative and abusive working conditions and greater vulnerability to HIV/AIDS. This is one area that needs further exploration in investigations and research projects. Comparisons between Latinas with citizenship and undocumented migrants could provide important findings for social policy and advocacy.

There is a dearth of research into the lives of Latinas who work in commercial sex businesses. The information that is available is limited and further complicated by the categories used in the study of commercial sex. Some of the existing research relies on the notion of "prostitute" that, as Gail Peterson notes, attaches immensely diverse meanings to the category. Often what represents the prostitute is the image of a woman standing on a street corner with stiletto heels and a miniskirt. Thus, the picture that emerges from studies of prostitution often relies on stereotypes and static notions of identity and practices that obscure behaviors that are far more complicated and nuanced. In unpacking the category of prostitute, Peterson notes that it is based more on "symbolic and legal representations of the bad woman or whore than upon a set of characteristics within a population of persons." In other words, researchers are not investigating similar sexual-economic interactions in the lives of those not branded as prostitutes. The prostitute label becomes fixed on already marginal populations such as runaway teenagers, streetwalkers, gender outlaws, racialized women, women in prison, and drug addicts. Moreover, by solidifying activities and fixing identities under the rubric of "prostitute," investigations often miss the ways in which sex-for-money exchanges are part of many other relationships. Sex work and other forms of sexual-economic exchanges are often temporary and typically are combined with other forms of labor to supplement inadequate income; they are not a full-time, long-term career for most people. Thus, the category of prostitute may obfuscate more than reveal.[4]

Furthermore, it is common in the study of sex work to treat women involved in the sex industry as vectors of disease. For many studies, the main objective is to identify women as potential carriers of venereal disease and create interventions that mitigate their role in the transmission of infections. The concern is with the health and well-being of the client. There is little interest in improving the lives and working conditions of women working in the sex industries.

Finally, studies of sex work that employ pan-ethnic categories for racial/ethnic identities (such as "Hispanic" or "Latina") can at times obscure the particularities of experiences rooted in differences in race and ethnicity, culture, socioeconomic class, country of origin, immigration and legal status, language skills, and levels of acculturation. While pan-ethnic groupings can facilitate comparative analysis and the formation of policy, it is important that we remain attentive to when and where salient differences operate.[5]

Despite the lack of large-scale studies that focus on the experiences of Latinas in the sex trade, we can nevertheless surmise some commonalities about their participation from the research that is available. Most of the existing research has been conducted on women working in street-level prostitution, and we know very little about other sectors of sex work. Indeed, there are no major studies or publications that investigate and document the participation of Latinas in other segments of commercialized sex such as escort agencies, massage parlors, telephone sex, cybersex, exotic dancing, and stripping. Historical studies have documented the participation of Mexican and Latin American women in sexual labor in Louisiana, California, and Texas.[6] The lives and conditions of people working in the many diverse forms of commodified sex, in general, remain invisible and relatively underexplored. We also need a better understanding of the kinds of vulnerabilities to exploitation that undocumented women face. Nevertheless, anecdotal evidence and newspaper accounts do document the participation of Latinas in all key segments of commercialized sex.

Street-Level Sex Work

The fear of HIV/AIDS during the 1980s and 1990s, along with the War on Drugs, created funding opportunities that generated several studies focused on the selling of sexual services by Latinas on the streets. Generally, these studies reveal that Latinas working the streets have low levels of educational attainment and lack job skills, training, and other economic options for survival, which, when combined with high levels of poverty and social disenfranchisement, make for bleak lives and futures. For those who suffer from drug addiction, exposure to street violence, coupled with the demands of a drug habit, place them at risk for HIV infection. Recent studies in major cities such as Chicago, Los Angeles, and New York indicate that the majority of sex workers on the streets are women of color.[7]

Studies focusing on street-level sex work continue to be the primary sources of information on Latina sex workers. This is an expanding area of research that documents one of the most dangerous segments of the sex trade, where women are exposed to high levels of violence, arrest, and chaos. Street-level sex workers have difficult lives, marked by extreme poverty, homelessness, and drug addiction. They are exposed to rape, extortion, and other forms of violence, including ill-treatment and sexual abuse from the police. They also experience high levels of violence and stigma from clients, business owners, and other members of society. Numerous newspaper accounts from throughout the country indicate that the police are particularly violent and abusive toward such sex workers. Police have been implicated in cases of rape, robbery, and extortion involving women working the streets. It appears that street-level sex work is the most dangerous and harmful segment of the sex trade.[8]

Apartment Brothels, Massage Parlors, Strip Clubs, and Cantinas

Indoor commodified sex tends to be safer and to provide women with more control over their clients and working conditions. Some investigations and newspaper accounts reveal that Latinas work in illegal underground brothels found in residential apartments that cater to working-class Latino populations. For example, Sherry Deren et al. (1996) document Latinas (Dominican women) working in New York apartment-brothels in which women receive relatively more protection from police harassment and customer violence and where they can better safeguard their health than working the streets. Reports from other cities indicate that residential brothels are sometimes managed by women and that the majority of the clientele are immigrant Latinos and migrant farmworkers. Recent newspaper accounts report that the women found working in these brothels are from Honduras, the Dominican Republic, Colombia, Mexico, and El Salvador. In one case, women were traveling in vans on the weekend from New York and New Jersey to provide sexual services to Latinos in Washington, D.C. However, except for a few high-profile cases, we know very little about the circumstances and extent of these practices.[9] It does appear, however, that the women working in these settings are recent arrivals, subject to police raids, arrest, and deportation.

Latinas also can be found working as strippers and exotic dancers in venues that cater to Latino customers. These two occupations sell sexualized entertainment and do not necessarily involve direct sex-for-money exchanges. In other words, sexual intimacy may not be present at all. There is also a market on the Internet for the sale of racial and ethnic-specific escorts, exotic dancers, and strippers in various large cities across the nation. Some of the women use this work to help finance their education. Others appreciate the lucrative earnings and flexible schedules. While the working hours are flexible in these occupations, they tend to be long, and the workers, who operate as independent contractors, do not have job security.[10] Owing to the age-sensitive nature of this segment of the sex market, with many of the women stopping well before they are forty, most dancers must plan early on for other career options.

Latinas and other women of color who work in venues not targeted toward a Latino clientele face racial discrimination from both management and customers. There is a bias in favor of white women in strip and exotic dancing clubs, which enforce "informal quotas on the number of women of color hired" and performing on stage. The number of women of color offered more profitable performances at strip clubs is also limited and controlled.[11]

In Los Angeles and Houston, Mexican and Central American women also work as *cantineras*, in legitimate businesses such as cantinas (beer joints) or bars, where they sell high-priced beers and dance with Latino customers. As dance hall hostesses, selling sex is not part of their formal job, but they may supplement their earnings by selling sexual services on the side.[12] In California, others work in massage parlors, chiropractic offices, and aromatherapy and shampoo spas, where sex-for-sale services are often thinly veiled. We know very little about these businesses except that they cater primarily to immigrant Latino laborers.

Latinas are relegated to the most dangerous, least remunerated, most stigmatized, and criminalized sector of the sex trade.[13] Racism and socioeconomic class preclude many Latinas from better-paying and safer jobs in the sex businesses. Social stigma, the legal ambiguity of some segments of the sex trade, and political agendas hinder the study of sex work. With the exception of street-level prostitution, there is an absence of investigations that provide information on the working conditions, hours and rates of pay, experiences, job satisfaction, and health and safety issues of Latinas in the sex trade. Again, more studies are needed to examine these issues.

Trafficking in Women

Few areas are as sensitive as the issue of trafficking in women for forced prostitution, yet we have many sensationalist reports and few scholarly investigations. The intersection of two areas fraught with political tension—sex and immigration—and the illegality of immigrant smuggling and some forms of sex work push the practices and conditions of Latina sex workers further into an underground world that is difficult to access and investigate. In this section we address issues concerning the current antitrafficking campaign in the United States. We argue that, in the new antitrafficking legislation, the conflation of sex work with forced labor or slavery-like conditions creates interventions and approaches that are based more on discourses of sexual morality and xenophobia than on empirical evidence. We provide a brief, and incomplete, overview into the efficacy of the Trafficking Victims Protection Act (TVPA) and suggest further areas for research.

At the end of the twentieth century, as at the beginning, sex trafficking was a hot topic of debate, with feminists, nongovernmental and multilateral organizations, as well as European and North American governments generating a frenzy of attention to this issue. At the beginning of the twentieth century, trafficking in women was referred to as "white slavery," and the concern centered on European working-class women migrating alone to the Americas, South Africa, and Asia. The discourse of white slavery portrayed its victims as white, virginal, innocent, and naive women who were lured into brothels and forced against their will into selling sex in faraway places. Contemporary historians and other scholars have argued that the idea of white slavery was mainly social in origin, operating more as proxy for discussion of the endemic issues of prostitution, women's poverty, and injustices around class and gender, with few documented cases of true sexual slavery. Rather, historians contend that the idea of white slavery contained the anxieties produced by women's independence, mobility, and sexual self-determination. At the beginning of the twenty-first century many of the same fears are in place, with the exception that now the victim has a brown face.[14]

International trafficking in persons for the purpose of sex became a priority for the Bush administration. This was one of the few issues where the administration was able to elicit support from both the Christian Right and feminist organizations. One explanation for such unity on the issue is its urgent emotional appeal. Certainly, conditions of slavery-like practices in any type of work, sex work included, cannot be tolerated, but the nature of the problem and approaches to it are disputed.

Figures detailing the scope of trafficking for forced prostitution are often contradictory and based on unreliable estimation methods. For example, while the U.S. government initially estimated that up to 50,000 people were being trafficked into the United States every year, this figure was reduced to between 14,500 to 17,500. Of these trafficked persons, 80 percent are estimated to be women, and 70 percent of those women are trafficked for commercial sex. The U.S. government estimates that 3,500–5,500 victims in all labor sectors originated in Latin American countries.[15] Although these numbers are used to suggest epidemic levels, the evidence does not support these claims.

Even the U.S. government is uncertain about its own estimates. The Government Accountability Office (GAO) has produced a report on the need for better data and methods in antitrafficking efforts and research in which it states: "The accuracy of the estimates is in doubt because of methodological weaknesses, gaps in data, and numerical discrepancies. The U.S. government has not yet established an effective method for (estimation)." In questioning the numbers, critics have also pointed to exaggerated stories that lack substantial evidence. For example, when a 2004 *New York Times Magazine* cover story entitled "The Girls Next Door" voyeuristically detailed sexual slavery of Mexican women lured into the United States, controversy erupted among journalists representing a variety of publications over the legitimacy and sensationalism of the story, which painted a picture of an epidemic (more than 10,000 victims) but used only two real cases.[16]

Although there are no solid estimates of the number of persons trafficked into the United States for forced prostitution, large-scale instances of labor trafficking have consistently been documented and researched. Historically, there is more evidence of trafficking into agricultural, domestic services, and manufacturing (sweatshops) than into sex work. Why are these areas less important than sex work? Why have they not been worthy of the same kind of attention and moral outrage? Given the current anti-immigrant political climate, does the issue of trafficking serve as an excuse to round up and deport more unauthorized migrants? Whose interests are being served by the new attention to trafficking? What is the impact on the women concerned? Does the TVPA help to combat abuse and improve conditions for the women involved? These questions remain unanswered.

In the late 1990s, international antitrafficking protocols at the United Nations repositioned the debate, effectively unlinking traffic in women from prostitution. The new UN language and protocols reflect a concern with organized criminal activities across national borders. Instead of focusing exclusively on the trafficking of women into the international sex trade, as the 1949 UN Convention for the Suppression of Traffic in Persons and the Exploitation of

Prostitution of Others had done, the new understanding reflected in the 2000 UN Optional Protocol to Prevent, Suppress, and Punish Trafficking in Persons, Especially Women and Children encompassed a broader range of industries and practices, not just commercial sex.[17] As Kamala Kempadoo (2005) points out, the new paradigm emerged out of the advocacy efforts of feminists, researchers, and community organizers concerned with the plight of migrant workers and sex workers in the global capitalist economy. However, the new global governance approach does not adequately reflect the human rights and social justice concerns that advocates fought for and instead focuses on controlling immigration and crime and on prosecution, while not necessarily protecting migrants from the exploitative working conditions that they encounter when they leave their home countries seeking work.

The intensified international concern with trafficking was also echoed in the U.S. with the TVPA of 2000. The trajectory of antitrafficking legislation dates back to the Clinton administration, when two bills to combat sex trafficking were first introduced. The Bush administration, with the support of both the religious Right and some feminist organizations, took a tough stand on combating trafficking in the United States that resulted in a revised TVPA that deemphasizes the broader labor concerns of earlier versions.[18] Although political efforts were united around combating all forms of trafficking and slavery, the Bush administration has focused on trafficking for the purposes of sexual slavery, depicting all forms of prostitution as "inherently harmful and dehumanizing." In essence, the Bush administration conflates all forms of prostitution with sex trafficking, a position that activists and scholars argue is harmful and violates the human rights of people working in the sex industries. The TVPA is designed to combat all forms of trafficking by aggressively prosecuting traffickers and assisting those that meet the stringent requirements to become "certified" victims. The regulations are complex and have changed since the TVPA 2000 was originally proposed. Victims must meet the definition of a "victim of a severe form of trafficking," be willing to assist with the investigation and prosecution of trafficking cases, and demonstrate they will suffer extreme hardship and harm if removed from the United States. Since the emphasis of the law centers on prosecuting traffickers, it does not adequately protect victims who are unable or unwilling to testify against their traffickers. The requirement to testify against their captors is an especially unreasonable and potentially harmful measure given that many people fear personal retaliation and for the safety of their families back home.[19]

If victims are either found by or notify authorities about their situation, they may receive some federally funded or administered benefits and services and can apply to become a "certified" victims of trafficking; upon approval each will receive a "victim certification letter" and can obtain more services and the opportunity to apply for a new T-Visa. This visa permits qualified "victims of severe trafficking" to remain in the United States legally and apply for residency status. In fiscal year 2005, 230 certifications were issued to victims in nineteen states. The countries of origin the certified victims reported included Bolivia, Colombia, Ecuador, El Salvador, Guatemala, Mexico, Paraguay, and Peru. The annual Trafficking in Persons Report for 2008 states that in the 2007 fiscal year, 303 persons were certified; 33 of these were minors. Mexico accounted for 9.6 percent of the letters and Peru 10.0 percent. However, the Department of Justice 2006 report does not provide information about gender or the type of trafficking involved, and it indicates that many cases of trafficking in persons involve both labor and sex elements. As the GAO report notes, owing to the lack of coordination between government agencies, the government is "unable to provide an account of the age, gender, type of exploitation suffered, and origin and destination of trafficking victims into the U.S."[20] Consequently, it is difficult to determine from the information available, and the lack of specifics, the extent of trafficking for forced prostitution.

Another area of concern is the new T-Visa. The T-Visa was expected to be a huge success in combating trafficking because it allowed people who would otherwise be deported to avoid the dangers of returning to the location and conditions from which they were originally trafficked. Not many people have applied for T-Visas, however, and the approval rate for the T-Visa applications is very low. In 2004 302 people applied for T-Visas and only 136 were approved. In 2005 229 applied, and 112 were approved.[21] By June 2006 650 T-Visas in total had been issued. The Trafficking in Persons Report for 2008 states that in the 2007 fiscal year, 279 T-Visas were approved for victims of trafficking and 261 T-Visas were issued to immediate family members of trafficking victims. The dismal application and approval rates are likely owing to the rigid process and what some claim are dehumanizing requirements.

Several scholars have analyzed the effectiveness of the TVPA in providing assistance and support services to victims. It has also been claimed that the TVPA reforms have been antiprostitute and anti–sex work in their implementation, rather than antitrafficking across all labor sectors. Additionally, the focus has been on policing, which interferes with providing health and rights-based services to migrant or trafficked sex workers. Furthermore, scholars, activists, and sex worker organizations all contend that a crude approach that links all migration for sex work with "trafficking" impedes efforts to improve the work situation of sex workers and migrants and creates obstacles in providing the health and social services they need.[22]

There is very little unambiguous information about Latinas being trafficked for purposes of sexual exploitation. The U.S. Immigration and Customs Enforcement lauds its prosecution of two cases of sex trafficking that resulted in the conviction of small, three-to-five-person trafficking rings. In these cases, the men lured young Mexican girls into forced prostitution in the United States. However, studies conducted in western Europe with migrant sex workers from Asia, Latin America, and the Caribbean depict a wide array of situations and complex realities that cannot easily be reduced to conventional and highly emotive depictions of passive and ignorant victims. We lack accounts from victims of trafficking or more nuanced understandings of how Latina immigrants negotiate what is an increasingly dangerous entry into the United States. We need to hear from Latinas themselves how they cope and how we can best represent their interests.[23]

Research from the Caribbean and Latin America indicates that women seeking to migrate are not easily duped or deceived and are aware that most job offers are in the sex industry. Given that the TVPA provides a narrow definition and application of the law, which excludes anyone "who consented to some aspect of his or her transportation or employment," it is possible that many Latinas are as vulnerable to trafficking into forced prostitution and lack resources and remedies now as they did before the passage of the TVPA.[24]

Finally, there is sufficient evidence to indicate that the continuing militarization of the U.S.-Mexico border, free trade agreements, more restrictive immigration policies, and the widening inequalities in global wealth propagated by neoliberal policy mandates by the World Bank and the International Monetary Fund have made Latinas more vulnerable to exploitative practices and degrading treatment in many industries and forms of labor, not just sex work.[25] In essence, the underlying causes of trafficking need to be addressed in more systematic ways than the current UN protocol and the TVPA have done. This can redirect the debate to recognize that migrants need rights, to travel and work, and that their interests need to take center stage in programs and policies. Putting the interests of powerful groups first, whether those of the nation-state or employers, will continue to perpetuate the harmful conditions that migrants and sex workers face.

Conclusion

In this chapter we have surveyed issues pertinent to Latinas employed in sex work. As we have stressed throughout, there is a dire need for research projects that address the diverse forms of commodified sexuality and the conditions of Latinas in these various settings. We need more information about the lives of Latinas who make a living in the sex trade, and we need to understand the commercial practices and working conditions, including how migrants are positioned in the sex sector.

We have also surveyed some of the main concerns surrounding the antitrafficking campaign in the United States. While we have emphasized the need to distinguish sex work that is voluntarily undertaken from involuntary forms of servitude, in both sex work and trafficking the full legal protection of labor laws for all workers is required to safeguard against exploitative working practices. Until labor protections can be granted to all workers, regardless of immigration status or type of work, abusive practices will continue to take place with impunity.

14

Latina *Lesbianas, BiMujeres,* and Trans Identities

Charting Courses in the Social Sciences

LUZ CALVO AND CATRIÓNA RUEDA ESQUIBEL

This essay reviews the research on Latina lesbians, an understudied population in the social sciences. Migdalia Reyes explains, "Historically, most research and treatment has focused on men, with some recent attention to African American and Latino men. Because of the AIDS epidemic, some attention has recently been given to exploring the treatment needs of gay males. Yet Latina lesbians are one of the least researched population groups."[1] Interestingly, despite the paucity of empirical studies on this population, there is a rich body of Latina lesbian creative work circulating at film festivals, poetry readings, and comedy shows and in short stories, anthologies, theater, performance art, and a significant number of novels. This creative production has inspired an equally rich body of critical work on Latina lesbian culture and identity.[2] In this article, we continue the detective work begun by Esquibel in her search for Chicana lesbian fiction, which culminated in the publication of *With Her Machete in Her Hand: Reading Chicana Lesbians*. In seeking out references to queer Latinas and WSW (women who have sex with women) in social science research, we have found several sources of interest. Although few take queer Latinas as their sole object of study, nevertheless we find subjects that are recognizable as queer Latinas or WSW.[3] Some of the themes that emerge from the literature include formations of identity, both gender and sexual, the culture of silence, and the social context of violence. We will address these issues in order, before turning to our assessment of the field and potential areas of future research. Our reading of this emerging field requires that we address the contested nature of the identities "Latina lesbian," "Latina WSW," and "queer Latina." A pivotal moment in the formation of an imagined community of Latina lesbians was the publication by Juanita Ramos (Díaz) of *Compañeras: Latina Lesbians* (1987), a collection of creative works and oral histories that produced an imagined community of Latina lesbians, linked the disparate experiences of New York Puerto Rican lesbians, Bay area Chicana lesbians, Cuban lesbians in Miami—rural with urban, middle class with working class, older with younger. The emergence of this volume was inextricably tied to women of color publishing and activism in the 1980s, especially the publication of Cherríe Moraga and Gloria Anzaldúa's *This Bridge Called My Back: Writings by Radical Women of Color* (1981), which prominently features Latina lesbian voices. The rhetorical force of these two volumes (among others) was to create connections, real and imagined, between lesbians of color living across the United States and to produce new "coalitional" identities, such as "Latina lesbians" and "women of color." These identities, however, were not simply produced through the publication of texts; rather, they were profoundly influenced by the civil rights, women's rights, and gay liberation movements and their concomitant difficulties in dealing simultaneously with issues of race, gender, and sexuality. Yolanda Retter and Juana María Rodríguez have documented the history of queer Latina social and political organizations in the post–civil rights era.[4]

The formation of these organizations and the surge in publications (mostly from small feminist presses) were simultaneous and synergistic occurrences: members of Latina lesbian organizations hosted Latina lesbian authors for readings and talks; in some cases, the authors themselves belonged to the organizations. The years following the publication of *Compañeras* have seen an explosion of cultural production by, for, and about queer Latinas.[5] The emergence of queer activism and queer theory has led to a critical engagement with previously entrenched lesbian feminist versions of identity. Rigid dichotomies—such as between male and female, heterosexual and homosexual—have given way to an ever-growing multiplicity of identity formations, gendered bodies, and fluid desires. Bisexual Latina activists, who had hitherto been asked to work silently under the banner of "Latina lesbian," have challenged their erasure and exclusion. In claiming their place, they are also claiming their history, for many Latina lesbian organizations were founded with the help of bisexual *mujeres*. Gender-queer lesbians are demonstrating connections between contemporary "trans" identities and historical "butches." Reflecting these changes, in 2006 the Lesbian Caucus of the National Association of Chicano and Chicana Studies changed its name to the Lesbian, BiMujeres, and Trans Caucus. Thus, "Latina lesbian" must be used with caution for it may, in some contexts, signify mostly as a series of exclusions: not allowing bisexual, not allowing transgender. For the purpose of this article, we have adopted the terms queer Latina and Latina WSW to begin to account for the variation in the ways the word lesbian is claimed and contested by Latina women and transgender-identified individuals. We recognize that "queer" and "WSW" are historically situated in a post-HIV era. We trace the emergence of "queer" to activism and not to theory. In particular, we acknowledge the role of Queer Nation, a 1990s street activist group, for its work on the ground and in communities. Its activism shifted the terms of identity formation for many members of the lesbian, gay, bisexual, transgender (LGBT) community, breaking down previously existing dichotomies and challenging the policing of desire found in some versions of lesbian feminism and gay assimilationism. Queer Nation was a direct offshoot of the AIDS activist group, ACT UP. Many people belonged to both groups simultaneously. The history of "queer of color" participation in this 1990s activism remains an untold story, but it is clear that queer activism and queer theory have led to revisions of previously entrenched lesbian identities.

Identity as a Social Formation

Early social scientific scholarship on Latina lesbians focused on the concept of identity. For example, in her discussion of psychotherapy with Latina lesbians, Olivia Espín interprets Latina lesbian identity as "stigmatized": "the dilemma for Latina lesbians is how to integrate who they are culturally, racially, and religiously with their identity as lesbians and women." Espín frames her project with the models of ethnic identity formation from Donald R. Atkinson, George Morten, and Derald Wing Sue and of lesbian identity formation from Vivienne Cass, both of which posit development whereby an initially conflicted subject comes to a position of acceptance and synthesis.[6] These models posit an ideal end point (in this case, Latina lesbian) but do not account for the subtle and not-so-subtle ways that queer Latina identity has changed, depending on the decade, locality, political context, community formation, cultural production, and so forth. Not only are *individual* queer Latinas always involved in a process of "becoming," so are queer Latina communities. Thus, the end point of any process of coming to identity will always be shifting. Rather than stable or fixed, queer Latina identities are continuously in formation, being contested, and reformulating themselves. Despite this theoretical limitation, Espín's project provides an interesting data set of queer Latina subjects. Her data come from questionnaires completed by sixteen Cuban lesbians living in the United States. Espín focuses attention on whether her respondents identified more with the Cuban community or more with the Anglo lesbian community. Espín finds, "It is impossible to determine that one aspect of the identity of these Cuban lesbians is more important for them than the other." It seems that her respondents rejected the framing of their identity in either-or terms. One informant puts it this way, "Eating black beans and rice while speaking in Spanish with other Latina lesbians makes those beans taste like heaven!" However, Espín's respondents report that because of racism in the lesbian community and heterosexism in the Cuban community, there were few spaces that allowed them to embrace both identities at once.[7] This research echoes Hilda Hidalgo and Elia Hidalgo-Christensen's research, which documents the homophobia of the Puerto Rican community. Hidalgo and Hidalgo-Christensen base their analysis on twenty-six interviews with Puerto Rican "gay women" and 264 questionnaires received from Puerto Rican respondents. Their data demonstrate that "Puerto Rican homosexuals living in the U.S. experience a triple prejudice and oppression: the Anglo community oppresses them for being gay and Puerto Rican; the Puerto Rican community oppresses them for being gay." Both of these studies pose the question of queer Latina identity primarily in terms of its location at the intersection of two oppressed (per Hidalgo and Hidalgo-Christensen) or stigmatized (per Espín) communities. This "intersectional" position is understood primarily as a challenge to the queer Latina subject who must find her ground by negotiating various cultural systems and structural inequalities. While we do not discount the challenges posed by racist and homophobic prejudice and violence, we recognize that being positioned at the border of hegemonic racial and sexual identities also presents critical openings for political practice, community formation, and resistant identifications. The potential of this borderlands space between queer and Latina/o is evident in the work of the late Gloria Anzaldúa. In her revolutionary treatise, *Borderlands/La Frontera: The New Mestiza*, Anzaldúa writes: "The work of *mestiza* consciousness is to break down the subject-object duality that keeps [*la mestiza*] a prisoner and to show in the flesh and through the images in her work how duality is transcended. The answer to the problem between the white race and the colored, between males and females, lies in healing the split that originates in the very foundation of our lives, our culture, our languages, our thoughts." Rodríguez argues that "queer" operates similarly to Anzaldúa's mestiza consciousness, "breaking down . . . categories, questioning definitions and giving them new meaning, moving through spaces of understanding and dissension, working through the critical practice of 'refusing explication.'" Thus, static or fixed notions of Latina lesbian identities are likely to overlook or misread the wide variety of ways that individual queer Latina subjects negotiate nonnormative sexualities, identities, and practices.[8]

A new ("post-*Borderlands*") generation of scholarship is represented by the work of Anita Tijerina Revilla. In her dissertation, Revilla undertook a qualitative study of the UCLA student organization Raza Womyn. This group defines itself as "united in the spirit of a collective movement to achieve sexual, political, educational, cultural, social, and self-determination." Revilla analyzes this group based on a five-year ethnographic study, using participant observation, surveys, document examination, focus group interviews, and in-depth interviews. Of particular interest is Revilla's approach to the analysis of sexual identity among group members. Using open-ended questions that allowed for a significant variety of responses, Revilla reports that the women in the group identified as follows: Queer 9, Bisexual 5, Two-Spirited 1, Lesbian 4, Tortillera 4, Heterosexual 17, "Presumed heterosexual, but I don't like to identify" 1, and "Heterosexual, but not by choice" 1. Revilla's study, focusing on the years 1999–2004, reveals a multiplicity of sexual identities, which exceed both the traditional binary of straight/lesbian and the tripartite straight/lesbian/bisexual. In thinking about the list of possible sexual identity formations generated by her subjects, we find value to this kind of localized understanding of sexual identity in Latina contexts, where well-designed qualitative research—such as Revilla's—allows for nuanced and complexly situated sexual identities to emerge as objects of study and knowledge. It is clear from the women's responses that they were contesting both heteronormative and lesbian-normative constructions of identity. Local conditions, including the historical context of the late 1990s, the university environment, values of *indigenísmo* (in the claiming of "Two Spirit") and trans-nationalism (in the use of *tortillera*), and the mutual support afforded by the organization all provided the conditions that produced this particular constellation of identities. In short, Revilla's study provides an excellent case history of the social construction of queer Latina identities. It is important to note that Revilla's study predates the expansion of gender identifications available to non-normatively gendered queer Latinas.[9]

A similar study conducted today with this demographic would have to find a way to include transgender identifications. One such example of inclusion can be found in the poster for Tongue 2 Tongue: Provoking Critical Dialogues among Queer Women of Color, a conference held September 7–9, 2007, in Los Angeles. The poster announces, "Tongue 2 Tongue explicitly acknowledges and honors transgender and gender queer experiences of womanhood which have historically been silenced in women-oriented spaces. All are invited to participate." Here we see that current formations of identity in queer Latina communities are challenging gender-specific language. The announcement, while asserting a woman of color identity, simultaneously gestures to the fact that part of the target audience may no longer identify as "women."

Another approach that deals with the problem of language and the inability of the term Latina lesbian adequately to name the population being studied is that of Sana Loue and Nancy Méndez, which identifies Latina WSW as its focus. We are interested in the ways that the category WSW provides insight into those who may exceed or reject the identity of lesbian. Loue and Méndez's research summary sets forth the stakes of their project: "These women's stories challenge both the lesbian and the Latino communities to reexamine how and why they claim individuals as their own and they similarly challenge professional communities, including HIV educators, health researchers, and medical care providers, to develop effective HIV prevention programs and counseling approaches that facilitate patient/client self-disclosure and consider cultural and contextual barriers to both self-disclosure and the provision of services." In their analysis, however, Loue and Méndez do not seem willing to completely question the category lesbian. Their article provides the story of three women: "Maria," who has had relationships with women but is conflicted about her sexuality because of her religion; "Ann," who identifies as butch and has two girlfriends but is not out to her family because they have shown themselves to be homophobic and antigay; and "Lydia," who identifies as "*alegre* or gay" and who previously had serious relationships with women when she lived far from her family, but who, now that she lives close to her family, is in a relationship with a man. The authors conclude: "The reluctance of these women to self-identify as lesbian may be attributable to cultural and community expectations of women, concomitant constraints on their behavior, whether heterosexual or lesbian, and the women's fears of potential consequences should they violate the set mandated behavior scripts." Loue and Méndez find that "sex with men is a highly stigmatizing behavior within lesbian communities and woman-woman sex may be equally marginalized within Latino communities." Here, the binary Latino/lesbian precludes other possibilities of identification. For example, the article does not mention the possibility of bisexuality or of a fluid sexuality that might change over the course of a lifetime. "Lydia's" culturally specific term *alegre* is not pursued or analyzed within the study. Nor do the researchers recognize that these three women are already "violat[ing] the set mandated behavior scripts." Overall, the analysis suffers from not allowing for the fact that there are multiple ways that WSW might identify and that these identities are fluid, contextual, and local. Instead, the authors seem to believe that having a stronger lesbian identity would afford these women a stronger sense of themselves. Loue and Méndez conclude: "Although their mental illness cannot be attributed to the precariousness of the self-situated-ness, one must ask whether their liminal status between communities and their awareness of their own marginalization may contribute to their inability to progress to more improved health status and a healthier lifestyle."[10] Left unquestioned, then, is the social construct of exclusive and fixed notions of Latina and lesbian identities. Some subjects actively resist researchers' attempts to consolidate identities.

Tonda L. Hughes et al., in their 2006 study of alcohol use among lesbians, note that in preliminary telephone interviews, their subjects were asked whether they identified as "lesbian, bisexual, heterosexual, transgender, or something else." Subjects who indicated bisexual, heterosexual, or transgender were excluded from the study. However, during the study interview, thirteen unruly subjects identified themselves as bisexual (eleven), queer (one), and refuse label (one). According to the researchers, "These women were compared with the rest of the sample on demographic characteristics other than sexual orientation. Because no statistically significant differences were found, they were included in the analyses reported here." The study, therefore, initially defined "lesbian" as exclusive of bisexual and transgender; the researchers later capitulated to include some bisexual and other queer women, but their study would have been more consistent had they accepted a more-inclusive definition from the beginning.[11]

Vernon Rosario proposes a radical notion of identity in his contextual analysis of an MTF (male-to-female) Latina who has sex with men titled "*¡Qué Joto Bonita!*" We find his approach to be so helpful that we offer it here as a model for future research on queer Latina and WSW populations. Rosario bases his research on a case history of Frances, a "39-year-old Mexican-American, who presents herself in the clinic in casual, loose-fitting clothes." Frances challenges set notions of either gay or transgender categories. The title of Rosario's article—based on a catcall she received from some Latino construction workers, "¡Qué joto bonita!" (What a pretty girl is that gay boy)—points to the challenge to gender that Frances presents just in her everyday activities. She lived for many years as a gay man, but "he never felt that he totally fit into the gay identity." At one point, he started to frequent gay Latino nightclubs in L.A., with their drag shows of lip-synced impersonations of Latina pop stars. As a result of this experience, he began to explore cross-dressing and eventually identified as transgender, undertaking hormone therapy. At the time of the article, Frances was a sex worker, making her living as a she-male. Rosario finds Frances to be an example of the changes in transgender identity that have occurred in the past decade: "Transsexuals have come out of the closet and been more honest about the complexity of their erotic and gender experiences and desires." Rosario's research succeeds because it listens to the experiences of someone who does not quite fit the preexisting categories. He points to the need to rework the categories themselves to account for the complexity of subjects like Frances.[12] We call for the same kind of critical interrogation of the category Latina lesbian.

Methodology: *Sitios y Lenguas*

Emma Pérez directs our attention to the erasure of lesbian of color subjectivity from dominant discourses, including Chicano, white feminist, and colonizer scholarship. She writes: "We have been spoken about, written about, spoken at but never spoken with or listened to. Language comes from above to inflict us with little Western-white—colonizer ideology. We speak our history to each other now, just as our ancestors used oral tradition. A tradition which is minimized." Pérez proposes that scholarship be attuned to Latina lesbian "*sitios y lenguas,*" which she interprets as "sites and discourses." In a similar vein, historian Yolanda Leyva introduces the theme of "listening to the silences" as a methodology in the study of queer Latinas:

> I looked out my window and saw her, Norma García—sixty years old with a still-trim body, a man's haircut, and jeans. I had heard all about her. I knew the story of how forty years earlier she loved a woman named Dora. Everyone knew. *Pero nadie decía nada. . . .* That day I started to think about silences in a different way. I stopped imagining silence as the absence of something. Rather I started to listen for what silences held within them. For lesbianas Latinas, silence has been an enigma, a survival strategy, a wall which confines us, the space that protects us.

Leyva's article is rich with the oral histories of queer Latinas, including "La Sylvia," "Norma," "Charlie," "Susana," and "Alicia." After careful consideration of their stories, Leyva comes to the realization that "silence has its own contour, its own texture. We cannot dismiss the silences of earlier generations as simply a reaction to fear. Rather than dismiss it, we must explore it, must always attempt to understand it. . . . This is not, however a call to continue the silence nor to justify it." What Leyva argues, then, is that we must recognize the role of silence—like the margins of the text—as a space in which queer Latina histories are written, perhaps in an invisible ink that we must hold up to the light to read.[13]

The theme of listening to silences and being attuned to queer Latina "sitios y lenguas" is echoed in the work of Lourdes Argüelles and Anne Rivero in their study of Latina immigrant and refugee women. While their study does not focus exclusively on lesbian immigrants, they do find WSW and lesbian-identified women among their informants. The inspiration for the project arose from Argüelles's teaching experience at the Claremont Colleges, where some twenty students, including Latinos, "had recently begun working as interns in public agencies and had a number of recent Latina immigrant and refugee women in their caseload." Argüelles is stunned by the "common misbeliefs and generaliza-tions . . . about transnational dynamics of Third World women" that her students parrot back to her, despite their training and education in ethnic studies and immigration research. Argüelles encourages her students, rather than continue making generalizations about their clients, to start thinking about their lives dif-ferently, to listen for "issues of gender violence, enforced sex and gender roles, sexual orientation, sexual abuse and assault or coerced motherhood"; to specu-late "about whether or not issues of same-sex erotic attraction or orientation" contribute to women's decisions to emigrate; and to envision "the possibility that for some women transnational migration may have been one more strategy for managing or escaping from gender and sexual abuse and victimization"—that is, the women are "involved in an ongoing struggle to reconstruct the rigid and confining gender roles received in their culture of origin."[14]

Much of the data collected for Argüelles and Rivero's study comes from interviews of Mexican, Cuban, Salvadoran, and Guatemalan women conducted after community education events, lectures, or information sessions on HIV transmission and risk issues. By locating themselves in the community and in the midst of "community education" campaigns, in one case at a Laundro-mat, Argüelles and Rivero gained access to the immigrant women who would stay behind and discuss their own experiences and reasons for migration. The women disclosed childhood sexual abuse or adult rape and parental disap-proval of homoerotic tendencies, which led the parents to tell their daughters to go to the United States. In some cases, it seems that there was the suggestion of a better life for queer women in the United States; in other cases, that the women were overwhelmed by the negative reaction, or even physical abuse, that followed their identification and were forced to run away to seek some relief. Argüelles and Rivero make the important point that mental health practitio-ners, social workers, and immigration officers are unable to hear the diversity and complexity of the women's stories; instead, their training blinds them to hosts of possibilities. Argüelles and Rivero argue that researchers must, as Leyva instructs, "listen to the silences" and recognize that in patterns of absence there is a suggestion that a different story is possible. Through this kind of critical listening, Argüelles and Rivero find stories that do not fully conform to hegemonic ideas about immigration. For example, not all of the women's stories conform to a "better life in the United States" model, as some women report that immigration officers in the United States raped them with impunity, just as other women had experienced in their countries of origin. Argüelles and Rivero lay important groundwork for future research on queer Latinas and WSW, discussing the way their interactions with the women in the study prompted them to reassess their earlier work on migration. They emphasize the need to create safe spaces in which women can disclose their histories, in their own "sitios y lenguas": "We have learned that to listen we must quiet the mind of its internal chatter and preconceived notions and allow the space necessary for the words of these women, in whatever form their stories may emerge."[15]

Violence as Context in the Lives of Queer Latinas

Existing research on queer Latinas and WSW demonstrates the prevalence of violence: violence and abuse in families, state violence, and street violence. Much of this research situates the violence experienced by queer Latinas within the violence experienced by Latinas as a whole. Patricia Zavella's study of Chicana/Mexicana sexuality, which examines the cultural scripts of sexuality shared by Mexicanas and U.S. Chicanas, for instance, finds violence and silence as themes that cross national borders: by historicizing these women's experiences, we see the transnational nature of discourse and practice that links second-generation Chicanas and Mexicana immigrants regarding sexuality. The pervasiveness of themes of silence and violence are clear. Zavella notes that, as girls, many of the women in her study had experiences of sexual molestation or of negativity from parents for showing a curiosity about or interest in sex. She interprets these experiences as contributing to negative self-image and the difficulty these women have in "taking charge of their own desires—sexual or otherwise."[16]

In the study we discussed earlier, Loue and Méndez find that of the eight Puerto Rican WSW with severe mental illness, "many of them have experienced abuse in their relationships with men, as children and later as adults. . . . . For some of these women, the abuse that they have suffered in their relations with men led them to conclude that intimate relationships are best pursued with women." The women's own declaration—that they turned to women because of negative experiences with men—point to a familiar perception about lesbianism: that women become lesbians as a result of male violence or sexual abuse. Loue and Méndez note that this perception is not borne out by research on broader samples of lesbians; for example, Hidalgo and Hidalgo-Christensen find that "contrary to popular belief, past experiences with men did not seem to be significant in determining the female homosexual identity. The women did not express negative attitudes toward heterosexual sex: they just recognized that this was not how they wanted to express their sexuality. A significant number of Puerto Rican gay women had had heterosexual experiences and had chosen a homosexual relationship. This, they [Hidalgo and Hidalgo-Christensen] point out, was in contrast with the predominant attitude of Puerto Rican heterosexuals, who expressed negative attitudes toward homosexuality without having had any direct experience." With regard to the issue of violence, Loue and Méndez note that their particular group of WSW may have been at even higher risk for violence than other populations of Latina WSW: "Although disturbing, the level of violence that we see in the lives of these women is not surprising. Existing research indicates that severely mentally ill women may be at increased risk for partner violence, perhaps resulting from impaired judgment, poor reality testing, and difficulties associated with planning that comprise many mental illness diagnoses." While the population studied by Loue and Méndez may be at higher risk of violence, other research points to the disturbing levels of violence in the lives of queer Latinas across mental health status.[17]

Current work on women of color and violence, such as *The Color of Violence: The INCITE! Anthology,* points to the need to expand our conceptualization of violence. While recognizing that interpersonal violence (in families, relationships, and workplaces) is a serious concern, *INCITE!* demonstrates the need for research into the effects of state violence, including war, police brutality, prison violence, and abuse by border control or immigration officers. Argüelles and Rivero demonstrate the interconnectedness of interpersonal violence and state violence in the lives of Latina immigrant women, including lesbians. One of their informants, "Chini," from El Salvador, relates a story of violence in her family of origin: "I know my parents knew I was different because I was always falling in love with some woman they knew. So when I was 17 they told me to come to the U.S. and to send money back to them. My sisters were not permitted to come, but then they were not beaten up as often as I was. We all were beaten though." Similarly, "Mila," from Tijuana, described how the discovery of her homoerotic attachment led to violence and sexual abuse: "When I was 14 they found me kissing my best girlfriend. It was a pretty deep kiss. So they beat me up, and then they took me to this priest. He fondled me and wanted to go all the way. My father wanted me to get married immediately and have a baby so I could get cured. I ran away and crossed the border. I was 15." The act of immigrating itself, especially traveling as "women alone," marked these women out for further violence: "Upon arriving in the border towns unaccompanied by men, the violence and abuse that they had to endure was of a more public nature than that which they had experienced earlier in their lives." Argüelles and Rivero find that, often, Latinas leave their home countries in order to escape violence only to find themselves subjected to further violence in their movement north, or in their new environments in the United States.[18]

Butch/Femme in Latina Contexts

In their analysis, Argüelles and Rivero argue that women may assume a "masculine attire and mannerisms" as a strategy to protect themselves from violence: "Chini has found that dressing like a male seems to make her more intimidating even for those people who know that she is a woman. . . . 'Others who know I am a woman think that maybe I can defend myself like a man so they are less likely to try something. When they try I'll be ready for them.'" In a similar vein, Matu Feliciano, featured in Debra A. Wilson's video *Butch Mystique*, argues that in the 1930s and 1940s, lesbians took on butch or masculine personas as a survival strategy: "The reason was, if you were with a woman, and you didn't know how to kick ass, you were going to get your ass kicked. And that's one of the reasons why butches took on this strong, kick-ass attitude, because of what was going on back then. They were getting threatened, murdered, jumped on, all of that. And so they disguised themselves to look like men for that reason." The production of butch identity—as a survival strategy, as an erotic position, and as a gender identity—has been explored in some detail in the essays and cultural work by queer Latinas. Cherríe Moraga explains: "The classic extreme-butch stereotype is the woman who sexually refuses another woman to touch her." In this conversation between Moraga and Amber Hollibaugh, Moraga explores the meaning of "butchness" in relation to feminism, which she argues judges butch/femme dynamics as mimicking heterosexuality.[19]

More recently, Butchlalis de Panochtitlán (a butch Latina lesbian performance group based in Los Angeles) has used its performances to explore the nuances and diversity of butch identification, addressing such issues as butch bottoms, S/M sexuality, and emotional attachments of butch-identified Latinas. In some of their most powerful work, Butchlalis de Panochtitlán depicts dramatic readings of vignettes in the life of Los Angeles–area butch Latinas from previous eras. Butch identity features prominently in cultural representations of queer Latinas, sometimes at the expense of femme identity. In lesbian culture in general, there is often a conflation of butch with visible lesbian. The construction of the masculine woman as the real lesbian is tied to the sexology of the late nineteenth and early twentieth centuries, which put forth the "invert." Lesbians were thus men in women's bodies and showed a predilection for masculine attire and pursuits. Teresa de Lauretis has argued that masculine attire functions not primarily from a desire to be a man, but rather as a fetish to indicate the lesbian's desire for other women. The figure of the womanly lesbian, or femme, consistently confounded the sexologists, who proposed that she was, in fact, an appropriately gendered and therefore submissive woman who was easily led astray by the more domineering masculine woman. The womanly lesbians were therefore perceived as more "curable," needing only further and more gender-appropriate persuasion.[20]

Femme lesbians are commonly conflated with bisexual women, particularly as the latter are frequently excoriated for merely "playing at" lesbianism. Writings by queer Latina femmes, such as tatiana de la tierra, Karla Rosales, and Teresa Mendoza, are prominently featured in the zines *Esto no tiene nombre*, *ConMoción*, *Tongues*, and *Jota*. Femme Latina characters are represented in cultural productions, as in Margo Rivera-Weiss's film *¿Tienes Hambre?* (2005) and the performance art of Adelina Anthony and "Ms. Cherry Galette" (María Cristina Rángel). Critical study and theorization of femme identities is scarce, although Juana María Rodríguez and Stacy Macias are among those examining and articulating this area of scholarship. The complexities of queer Latina gender identifications can confound researchers. Zavella relates the story of María Luisa Pérez, a lesbian from Puebla, Mexico. Her gender identification there had always been male. Zavella describes María's male gender identification growing up in Mexico: "María then began a period where she perceived herself as 'the most popular boy,' when she had 'a heap of admiring girls.' She began a process of sexual exploration and play (*juego sexual*) only with women and usually with more than one. In a classic Mexican sense, María was solidifying her sense of herself as male and predator." Here, Zavella uses "predator" not in the homophobic sense in which lesbians are depicted as "preying upon" girls and women, but through María's adult lens of feminism, which criticizes her earlier claiming of male sexual prerogatives. Zavella relates: "Talking about her behavior over two decades later, María was embarrassed about her past mimicry of . . . the negative male qualities of jealousy, infidelity, and possessiveness toward her girlfriends. . . . 'I was a *macho cabrón*.'" According to Zavella, María defined herself as transsexual and began looking into sex-reassignment surgery. When a nine-year relationship ended, she relocated to Santa Cruz, California. Becoming part of Santa Cruz's lesbian feminist community brought about changes in her identity; with the active support of one lover, María came out of the closet herself and began accepting herself as female: "She's very beautiful and she made me realize that if women were with me, it wasn't because I appeared to be a man or I was pretending to be a man. No, it was because I was a *woman*. So I confronted that. Now I say 'Yeah, I'm a woman and I love women.'" This reconciliation with herself even had a dramatic effect on her body. "Before, I was less femme, I didn't have large breasts. I looked like a boy." She gained weight, became more curvaceous, and changed from androgynous-looking to a more female body type. "Because of the comfort of being accepted, I have learned to cope. And my body changed after I accepted that I was a woman. I think it was psychosomatic." Zavella's own evaluation, following María's discussion of her new identity, demonstrates that Zavella and Pérez do not share the same definitions of gender. María describes herself as now much more femme than in Mexico, while Zavella describes her appearance thus: "María now wears pants, oxford shirts, and short hair; from a distance *she appears gender-neutral*." María's account is especially important because it shows how sexuality and gender identification can change through space and context.[21]

Conclusion: Directions for Future Research

Qualitative research on queer Latinas is sparse, based on relatively small sets of data. In addition, some of this research is already quite dated. Respectful and socially engaged research on this population is urgently needed. We conclude by calling for studies that

> develop a language for talking about queer Latina identities—this research should be attuned to the diversity of identities claimed by queer Latinas and the specific terms and words that this population uses;

> approach their subjects without rigid notions of identity—lesbian-normativity and lesbian feminism are as likely to skew results as are homophobia and heterosexism;

> are situated historically, geographically, and in terms of class/educational levels of the subjects—queer Latina identities are often formed in local sites: bars, social networks, community organizations, and interactions with social service agencies;

> analyze local productions of queer Latina identity within national and transnational economics, politics, and cultures;

> examine the role of violence, both interpersonal and state-sanctioned, in the life of queer Latinas;

> include working-class, queer Latina identities, issues, and sites, such as the social networks and negotiations of gender and sexual identity among undocumented workers or recent immigrants; and

> examine health and medical issues, in particular health disparities in care and treatment.

15

Latina/o Transpopulations

MARCIA OCHOA

This essay attempts to review the existing literature on the subject of Latina/o transpopulations to describe trends in both the dynamics of these populations and published work on them, as well as to identify knowledge gaps and directions for future research. After more than twelve years of experience with the trans-Latina/o communities of San Francisco, as well as my own research on transgender existence in Latin America, I believed there to be a small but growing number of publications in various media documenting the lives of U.S. Latina/o transgender individuals and populations. I now realize that there are two substantial gaps on the face of this literature: first, no published monograph exists that focuses exclusively on any Latina/o transpopulation; second, there is a dearth of written and other archival forms of cultural production by trans-Latina/os themselves. The only two published autobiographical works of Latina/o trans persons I have located are *A Low Life in High Heels: The Holly Woodlawn Story* and Max Wolf Valerio's recently published memoir of his transition from female to male (Valerio is Latino and Native American).[1]

In this essay, "trans" is a category that encompasses many terms used to describe living, dressing, or identifying—or some or all of these—as a member of a gender with which a person was not assigned at birth. This includes transsexual, transgender, and transvestite forms of social and personal identity.[2] This essay includes a consideration of both female-to-male (FTM) and male-to-female (MTF) trans individuals. I consider trans a broad category when looking at representations of people who lived in other times and within gender systems not overdetermined by Western binarism. As such, I want to be clear that my use of trans is not intended to claim any particular existence as part of a unitary project of trans identity; rather, I understand trans to be composed of many different forms of gendering, embodiment, and power relations. This review will draw from my empirical and personal experience of U.S. Latina/o trans people and communities, as well as an extensive literature search in humanities, social sciences, public health, and film and video.³ First, I discuss the concept of transpopulation and how it applies to the topic of this chapter. Then, I review some of the dynamics of these populations, and finally, I discuss trends and gaps in the literature on Latina/o transpopulations.

Transpopulations

I once assumed the term "transpopulation" meant populations of trans people in the context of sexuality studies of U.S. Latina/os. After all, the field of population genetics uses the same term to refer to massive projects of migration (of genes, humans, and other organisms). Because this was the primary context in which this term had been used, I questioned what we stood to gain by understanding U.S. trans-Latina/os' experience through the notion of populations. I have chosen to engage the term transpopulation in this essay. Although I remain skeptical about the term's usefulness outside this academic context, I can think of a few reasons why the concept of populations might be useful here. First, as an empirical category, populations provide a bit of distance between the researcher and the subject of study. (I imagine a biologist standing in a marsh, studying flocks of birds.) This may be advantageous in that we are looking for general trends and expect diversity within populations. As such, the concept of populations allows us to keep the basic unit of analysis—whether that is individual experience, social networks, "community," or group behavior—an open question. It is reminiscent of the public health and policy literature on HIV/ AIDS that identifies "behavior risk population" rather than relying on identification or self-representation. It is through this shift that we get a category such as "men who have sex with men" (MSM), to describe a wide range of behaviors and identities.⁴ Employing the term populations may also serve to signal some of this public health literature as well as literature and policy on the migration of Latin Americans to the United States.

Finally, the term populations allows us to think outside of community and identification. Community and identity are tried-and-true rubrics of racial/ ethnic experience in the United States as well as lesbian, gay, bisexual, transgender, queer, and intersex (LGBTQI) experiences. These categories, while they mobilize collective forms of resistance and expression, provide only one model for social formations created around cultural or social characteristics and also produce categories of resistance that privilege unity and can erase difference. Treatments of Latina/o trans *communities* or Latina/o trans *identities* would look a bit different from this chapter, as they would likely contain an emphasis on the cultural production and self-expression of communities or individuals who promote trans identity. They would also run the risk of unifying trans experiences or social formations.

In San Francisco, the staff of the El/La Transgender Latina HIV Prevention Program and I noted the difficulty of organizing transgender Latinas in San

Francisco through a community-building model.[5] Instead, we focused our HIV-prevention interventions on individual needs and risk reduction. Recent focus groups have revealed a desire for a space to produce collective identity and vision, particularly in the form of a discussion group that meets regularly. My scholarly work has focused on MTF existence, and my personal experience of FTM uses of community and identity has shown these to be quite different. Latina/o FTM uses of community and identity notions are well illustrated in Karla Eva Rosales's documentary *Mind If I Call You Sir?* (2004).[6] As a proponent and firm believer in the community-building model, I had to let go of my attachment to community as a useful form of transgender Latina collectivity and be open to the forms of collectivity that are produced organically by trans-Latinas. This was the first step in supporting trans organizing on its own terms. Although I remain a bit uneasy with the analytical distance created by the notion of populations, I do appreciate its usefulness in helping us take trans experience and trans collectivity on its own terms. Ultimately, the goal is to make visible the plethora of categories and forms of social organization in the diverse groups of people who make up what we call in this collection "Latina/o transpopulations."

Population Dynamics and Histories

Where and how might we find populations of U.S. Latina/o trans people? In discussing general trends in the formation of U.S. Latina/o populations, I keep an eye on the documentation that exists about transpopulations within these trends. I then consider the dynamics of "queer migrations" and how these two factors might combine to produce Latina/o transpopulations.[7]

U.S. Latina/o Populations

By way of a brief history of the Latin American presence in the United States, I explore below some key moments in the constitution of these populations and the places where they originate.[8] This overview, although broad, signals where we might begin to look for the tracks of trans people in the formation of U.S. Latino populations, acknowledging that trans people may have been present in any of these periods and places. The Spanish colonial presence in North America produced populations throughout what are now Texas, California, and the U.S. Southwest, extending as far north as the Pacific Northwest and east into what is now the Midwest. Populations of Spaniards and Mexican mestizos appropriated the territories and labor of northern Native American societies in the colonial project through the establishment of pueblos, missions, and presidios. These settlements produced regional mestizo identities: Tejanos, Hispanos (in New Mexico), and Californios. As early as the colonial period, Spanish chroniclers noted the existence of individuals and social classes in indigenous societies that did not conform to Spanish gender norms during this era.[9] The ways that Spanish and mestizo colonizers used gender and sexuality as tools in the colonial project shaped cultural attitudes about gender variance and sexual behavior. Much of the literature concerning "Two-Spirit" people in colonial Spanish America centers on Native American societies in what are now Arizona and New Mexico.[10]

After the 1848 Treaty of Guadalupe Hidalgo (which, with the Gadsden Purchase in 1853, completed the present U.S.-Mexico border), the border "crossed" populations of Tejanos, Californios, and Hispanos, and they become racialized through U.S. Anglo racial formations. During the period of expansionism, the United States continued its project of Manifest Destiny, moving into the Caribbean and the Pacific to acquire Puerto Rico, Cuba, Hawaii, Guam, and the Philippines in 1898. Routes of migration between the Caribbean islands and the U.S. mainland were established in the years before the Spanish-American War by communities of laborers and expatriates. New York, Tampa, and Key West are sites where enclaves of transnational Cuban and Puerto Rican communities began to form, the first such communities in the United States. Though there seems to be no documentation of transpopulations in these communities during this period, they suggest someplace to start looking for traces of trans people. Recent research notes the existence of transvested Mexican Americans, both MTF and FTM, in this time period in San Francisco.[11]

The next period to consider is that between the end of the nineteenth century and World War II. Rubén G. Rumbaut characterizes this period as one of capitalist development in Latin America and increasing labor migration of both Mexicans and Puerto Ricans. The government of Porfirio Díaz in Mexico created what Rumbaut calls a "landless peasantry"; campesinos were recruited and transported to the U.S. labor market via rail lines, resulting in Mexican settlement in Texas, California, the Southwest, and midwestern industrial cities such as Chicago and Detroit. The literature tends to focus on the colonial, post–World War II, and contemporary periods, rather than on this period. Anthropological accounts of Two-Spirit people in the Southwest are the only representations I have found resembling trans people in relation to a U.S. Latina/o population. While it would be inaccurate to describe early-twentieth-century southwestern Two-Spirit individuals as part of Latina/o transpopulations, since they are Native American, I mention them here to suggest that there does exist documentation of gender diversity in this time period and in these locations.[12] The shift in power from Spanish to Anglo colonial systems involved the employment of two kinds of surveillance that would help make these individuals (and possibly other trans people) visible: anthropology and criminology. This would suggest an avenue of research for the historical documentation of transpopulations.

After World War II, U.S. expansionism took different forms, characterized by internal migration, cultural imperialism, and interventionist foreign policies in Latin America as well as other parts of the world. Migration dynamics shifted as well, partially in response to this project. Internal migration, including the movement of people between Puerto Rico and the mainland and the migration of diverse groups of people within the borders of the United States to major metropolitan areas or their suburbs, expanded. Queer migration to urban enclaves begins during this period. Puerto Rican migration to New York and other enclaves also continued. Cuban migration increased during the 1960s as a result of U.S. policies that granted political refugee status to Cubans fleeing the socialist revolution. Many settled in Miami, although Cuban Americans also settled in Los Angeles, Chicago, and New York, among other places. Cuban migration continued through the 1990s, though affected by marked differences in class as well as attendant changes in U.S. policy toward refugees.[13]

In this period, the Mariel boatlift deserves special attention in a study of Latina/o transpopulations. The Mariel boatlift of 1980 and the Balsero "crisis" of the 1990s produced segments of the U.S. Cuban population that were not as connected with existing kin and social networks in the United States as the migrations of the 1960s Camarioca boatlift and "Freedom Flights." In 1985 B. Ruby Rich and Lourdes Argüelles pointed out the need for additional research on the place of lesbians, gay men, and transgender women in the Mariel emigration. Susana Peña's 2002 dissertation, "Visibility and Silence: Cuban-American Gay Male Culture in Miami (Florida)," begins to answer this question. Peña, who carried out her research in Miami, collapses transgender (MTF) Marielitas into the category of gay men for the purposes of her dissertation, preferring to focus on performativity and public visibility rather than on transgender experience. Peña's thoughtful study of Cuban American gay men includes mentions of "drag queens" and "*locas*," but although transgender Marielitas have been documented elsewhere, Peña's analytical lens, like those of many other researchers, keeps MTF Marielitas in the category "gay." I argue that this practice makes trans experience invisible. Peña recognizes Marielitas as part of her social world but places them in the category of gay men:

> After Mariel, queens or transvestites became a common presence in my neighborhood, doing something I had never seen before: wearing women's clothes . . . during the day! I remember how 'obviously gay' men became a regular fixture at department stores, both as clients and employees, their mannerisms and talk marking them as 'other' even if they did not wear women's attire. My grandmother, who worked at a women's clothing store, would regularly report that yet another man had insisted on trying on a dress in the dressing room.[14]

In addition to the Puerto Rican and Cuban migrations, the postwar era also saw increased migration from Mexico to many parts of the United States beyond previously established enclaves, as well as Central American migrations from El Salvador, Guatemala, Nicaragua, and Honduras in the wake of civil wars and U.S. interventions in the latter half of the twentieth century. Immigration from South America, primarily Colombia, Ecuador, and Peru, also rose, with increasing proportions of immigrants arriving between 1970 and 2000. Through long historical processes, Latina/o populations have developed throughout the United States. Currently, the largest concentrations of these populations are in New York and Los Angeles, with significant urban ethnic enclaves in Chicago, Miami, Houston, and San Francisco.[15] This overview suggests some starting points from which we may begin to identify trans people and populations in U.S. Latino settlements and migrations.

Queer Migrations

U.S.-based queer populations from Latin America inhabit the intersection of two migrations; at the same time, they are not necessarily determined by them. John D'Emilio's model for gay and lesbian migration and settlement in San Francisco, for example, does not necessarily explain the ways in which *vestidas*, lesbians, and gay men congregate in a farmworker community two hours south of San Francisco. To understand this community, we would need also to attend to the forms of public visibility and sexuality produced in Mexican societies and how these are negotiated in the context of transnational migration circuits. Horacio Roque Ramírez's work on Latina/o LGBT communities and their representation in Spanish-language media provides a good introduction to the dynamics of these communities around the country.[16]

Migrations within the national borders of the United States in the post–World War II era led to the formation of "gay enclaves" in many cities. Trans people have participated in the formation of these communities, despite the transphobia many face from these same communities, as well as the ways that gay enclaves become less central to the experiences of transgender and trans-sexual people who enter heterosexual relationships. While it is difficult to quantify these enclaves so that we might see them as part of the larger dynamics of migration and immigration in the United States, I have attempted to find some basis for my common-sense understanding of where these communities and populations are located. Despite its limitations in accuracy and measurement of queer populations, the 2000 U.S. Census, for the first time, attempted to measure the incidence of cohabiting same-sex couples. The census results match my own anecdotal understanding of where to find queer enclaves in the United States. Several of these areas coincide with urban areas of Latina/o population. These are logical places to look for trans people and transpopulations, but rural and suburban migration and settlement patterns will consequently be overlooked.[17]

My estimations of likely sites of trans-Latina/o population through these broad outlines are intended to suggest possibility, as well as to point out the limitations of our current ways of understanding (im)migration patterns and the place of particular experiences within them. Much of the work on trans-Latina/os is either so particularized that it is not generalizable or so generalized as to make trans lives invisible; therefore, I seek to embed trans experience in local, national, and transnational processes while still maintaining a focus on the richness of everyday responses to major social forces. I turn now to an overview of the representations of Latina/o transpopulations in the literature.

Representations of Latina/o Trans People and Transpopulations

As objects of study, trans people have held more interest when encountered in Latin America than among U.S. Latina/o populations. Academic attention to Latin American transpopulations has taken the form of ethnographic or socio-logical studies and has resulted in several monographs specifically focused on small social networks of male-to-female Latin Americans in urban settings.[18] It is possible that such monographs are not appropriate to the project of represent-ing trans-Latina/o existence in the United States or that U.S. populations are not as accessible to investigators as the more publicly visible MTF social networks in certain Latin American cities. Certainly, the conditions of visibility for trans people—Latina/o or not—are different in the United States from those in Latin American contexts, owing to differences in the configuration of public and urban spaces, the prevailing forms of homo- and transphobia, and the regulation of public space and behavior in general. In addition to these factors, it is clear that the conditions of visibility—or even intelligibility—for (FTM) trans-Latinos are notably different from those of (MTF) trans-Latinas in either context. Social networks seem to have very different functions for transgender women than they have for transgender men in both Latin American and U.S. Latina/o contexts.[19]

Lack of visibility and ambiguous practices of categorization are obstacles to the study of both transpopulations and U.S. Latina/os. As a result, the litera-ture on Latina/o transpopulations is marked either by a focus on highly visible individuals (such as Holly Woodlawn and Sylvia Rivera) or by nearly invisible mentions within larger projects (such as the miscategorization of trans-Latinas as MSM in HIV-prevention risk assessments, or mentions of trans people within the larger Latina/o LGBT community, or historical studies). I am not aware of any ethnographic or historical projects whose sole focus is some aspect of a Latina/o transpopulation. This is not, however, the case for video documen-tary. Direct attention to the lives and experiences of transgender Latinas and Latinos in these videos suggests a greater sense of legitimacy for trans-Latina/o subjects in nonacademic contexts. Several scholars of queer *Latinidad*, including José Esteban Muñoz, Horacio Roque Ramírez, Juana María Rodríguez, Lawrence La Fountain-Stokes, and Lionel Cantú, Jr. (see below), have begun to challenge this question of academic legitimacy by recognizing the presence of U.S. trans-Latina/os as integral to projects of queer Latina/o cultural expression, commu-nity building, and organizing.[20]

I now turn to a discussion of the trends and gaps in the literature through a set of four categories:

1. work that focuses exclusively on the lives and social worlds of Latina/o trans people themselves;
2. approaches that include trans people within a larger project of LGBT history or the history of sexuality;
3. descriptions of Latina/o trans people (usually MTF) in HIV surveillance and prevention as well as other health policy issues; and
4. ethnographic, oral history, and cultural studies approaches to queer Latinidad, which includes trans-Latina/os in accounts of queer communities.

I avoid generalizing or defining characteristics of trans-Latina/o experience or populations because it is more important at this point to map the landscape for future directions in research. In the conclusion, I will suggest some of the questions that might guide this research.

Rather than privileging any one of these four approaches, each of which has its advantages and disadvantages, as the most appropriate for representing Latina/o transpopulations, I suggest that we might use all of these approaches together to fully appreciate the complexity of Latina/o transgender experience and to develop inclusive policies and practices. As a cautionary tale, I point to the controversy around Northwestern University psychology professor J. Michael Bailey's monograph *The Man Who Would Be Queen*. Bailey's controversial attempts to explain gender-bending and cross-dressing "scientifically" relied in large part on interviews and observations he made with transgender women in the Chicago area. In 2003 Anjelica Kieltyka, a transsexual woman who had unknowingly participated in Bailey's research, brought a complaint against him for failing to secure informed consent before treating her as a research subject. Although Bailey's research on the subject of transsexuality has been discredited and does not accurately describe the lives of the trans women—some Latinas—about whom he wrote, the book does indicate the presence of trans-Latinas in Chicago, centering on several bars.[21] I find it worth mentioning the presence of these women in Bailey's book to signal the way that the invisibility of trans-Latina/os in the literature creates opportunities for someone like Bailey to co-opt their stories for his own ends.

While work that focuses exclusively on the lives and social worlds of trans-Latina/os is the exception in the literature reviewed here, there have been some important attempts to document their lives. Visual media, specifically video and graphic novels, have been the media of choice for these representations; oral history has been the primary research method. Jaime Cortez's stunning graphic novel depicting the life of transgender Marielita and San Francisco community activist Adela Vazquez is based on hours of oral history interviews and discussions. *Sexile/Sexilio*, produced as an HIV-prevention project by the Institute for Gay Men's Health and AIDS Project Los Angeles, tells the story of Vazquez's childhood in postrevolutionary Cuba and her experience of the Mariel boatlift, AIDS, drugs, and sex work in Los Angeles and San Francisco. Vazquez tells of vibrant communities in Miami, L.A., and San Francisco.[22]

Susan Aikin and Carlos Aparicio's memorable videos *The Salt Mines* and *The Transformation* document the everyday survival of a community of homeless transgender Latina immigrants from Puerto Rico, Colombia, Cuba (also Marielitas), and the Dominican Republic to New York City. Valentín Aguirre's video *Wanted Alive: Teresita la Campesina* (1997) and film *¡Viva 16!* (1994), coedited with Augie Robles, document the presence of transgender Latinas, drag queens, and vestidas in 1990s San Francisco. Singing legend Teresita la Campesina (Alberta Nevares), pillar of San Francisco's Mission District, is featured in the 1997 video and recounts her life in San Francisco and rural California. Roque Ramírez, who participated in the filming of *Wanted Alive*, published his thoughtful account of his oral history research with Teresita as part of his dissertation (2001), and as a chapter in Antoinette Burton's *Archive Stories* in 2005. Karla Rosales produced an important video dialogue between butch Latinas and transgender Latinos in San Francisco, focusing on two central figures: butch Chicana club promoter and activist Diane Félix and transgender Latino community worker Prado Y. Gómez. Rosales traces the ways both Félix and Gómez inhabit their genders and negotiate their lives as gender-nonconforming Latina/os in the Mission District. I am currently unaware of any similar documentary projects with trans-Latina/os in Los Angeles or other parts of the United States. Another recent addition to this list of representations is a 2006 Lifetime movie based on the case of Gwen Araujo, a teenager from Newark, California (in the Bay Area), who was murdered after it was revealed at a party that her anatomical sex was male. Araujo's murder catalyzed the transgender movement in the Bay Area and the rest of the United States and led to greater visibility for the issues faced by young transgender people of color. Max Valerio's autobiography records both his New Mexican and Native American heritage and the multicultural transgender communities of the San Francisco area. Holly Woodlawn's autobiography, *A Low Life in High Heels*, is the earliest work I have found that documents trans-Latina experience and community. Although her autobiography certainly has different stakes from many of the other representations in this category, Woodlawn records her scene in 1960s New York City, after she ran away from home in Hialeah, Florida, at age fourteen. Woodlawn is Puerto Rican, but this is not the primary focus of her memoir, which is more concerned with the Warhol scene in the 1970s and 1980s and the invention of Woodlawn's celebrity in New York.[23]

The second category I have outlined incorporates various forms of trans existence into larger projects of LGBT history or the history of sexuality as they relate to Latina/o populations. I have briefly discussed several of these authors above. Of particular interest is the case of Babe Bean/Jack Garland. Although Garland's cross-dressing and passing as a man in late-twentieth-century San Francisco has interested historians, little attention has been paid to Garland's

Mexican origin—s/he was born into a wealthy gold rush–era Anglo-Mexican San Francisco family, the daughter of a Mexican consul.[24] Clare Sears records other cases of Mexican cross-dressing in this time period in her survey of cross-dressing law in San Francisco from 1860 to 1900.[25] The historical approach does not suggest the existence of particular populations, but rather social contexts in which Latinas and Latinos emerge as individual instances of cross-dressing. Despite the problems with assigning both Latina/o and trans designations to reports of Native Americans who inhabited gender categories not falling into Western binaries (*berdache*, Two-Spirit, and others), I refer to the literature on colonial "third genders" here to encourage those interested in working on the history of Latina/o transpopulations to attend to the long and complex processes that have produced them. I earlier pointed to two distinct colonial moments: that of the Spanish occupation of North America and the nineteenth- and twentieth-century U.S. western expansionist project. Each of these moments produced different forms of sexuality and different conditions of visibility for trans existence. Debates in this literature include the meaning of active/passive and masculine/feminine dichotomies and the politics of recuperation for these figures.[26]

A third category where we can trace the existence of and production of knowledge about Latina/o transpopulations is in the literature on health policy issues, particularly HIV. Transgender (FTM) Latinos are virtually absent from this literature, although the TRANS-project at the University of California–San Francisco's Center for AIDS Prevention Studies has included FTMs in its investigations of health outcomes for transgender people of color. To my knowledge, the FTM studies were still in the data-gathering and analysis stage when this article was completed.[27]

There has been a tendency in this literature to collapse trans MTFs into the category "men who have sex with men" (MSM), although more recent work insists on the distinction between transgender Latinas and MSMs, as well as the importance of the "MST" category to describe the male sexual partners of transgender women. The relative newness and instability of trans categories may be one factor in the reduced visibility of transpopulations considered as such in the literature and may lead to their incorporation into other collectivities, particularly that of gay men or MSM. Often, trans-Latinas in particular are considered part of *el ambiente*, a social world to which many Latino gay men also feel they belong. One contribution of health policy studies is simply to signal possible sites of el ambiente, which themselves point to the potential existence of associated transpopulations.

Rafael Díaz, George Ayala, and Edward Bein carried out their probability sample of Latino gay men in New York, Miami, and Los Angeles and were able to recruit some three hundred participants in each city. Díaz has also worked closely with HIV-prevention projects in San Francisco. Jesús Ramirez-Valles included transgender Latinas in a respondent-driven sampling study on community involvement and HIV risk in both Chicago and San Francisco.[28]

The conventions of trans invisibility make it difficult to identify Latina/o transpopulations in larger projects. Héctor Carrillo's innovative work on sexual migration from Mexico to California, for example, discusses his observations of a beauty pageant "where men dressed as women represent the Mexican states of origin of each male participant." Based on my own work on beauty in Venezuela and my experience of transgender Mexicana communities in San Francisco and Los Angeles, I would be very surprised not to find *any* vestida- or trans-identified participants of such a beauty pageant. Carrillo does not provide information about the identification of these participants; however, his brief narration of the event suggests that his attention to gay men rather than trans-Latinas might make this population invisible. Transgender populations are also not specifically considered in a recent review on public health for Mexican migrants in California for the purposes of planning primary HIV-prevention and treatment-access policy. Given that transgender Latinas have demonstrated increased seroprevalence rates, their omission from such policy studies implies serious consequences in terms of the availability of services and treatment.[29]

Research programs that focus on transpopulations in general have been generating important findings on transphobia, violence, and health issues affecting trans people. Many of these projects explicitly target trans-Latinas for inclusion. UCSF's TRANS-project has produced seroprevalence, risk-behavior, and transphobia rates among transgender people of color, including Latinas. The Los Angeles Transgender Health Study has also investigated these questions, with a significant portion (49 percent) of study participants who are Latina. National Development and Research Institutes, Inc. is currently carrying out a similar study on treatment and services for transgender people in the New York metropolitan area, although I have not located any publications resulting from this study that pertain to Latina/o transpopulations. Rita Melendez has conducted research among HIV-positive transgendered people in New York, Los Angeles, San Francisco, and Milwaukee through the National Institute of Mental Health's Healthy Living Project.[30]

The final category of approaches I have identified for this literature include ethnographic, oral history, and cultural studies approaches to queer Latinidad, which include trans-Latinas and trans-Latinos in accounts of queer communities. Introduced by Juana María Rodríguez in her book *Queer Latinidad*, this concept comprehends the formation of identities, subjectivities, and communities related to antiheteronormative sexualities and genders in the cultures emerging from Iberian colonization in the Americas. There is an element of queer Latinidad that involves the adoration of divas, including trans-Latinas. La Fountain-Stokes's and Roque Ramírez's meditations on the lives of two divas are thoughtful representations of the lives of trans-Latinas and the impression their lives have made on communities: Lady Catiria in New York and Teresita la Campesina in San Francisco, respectively. Carlos Decena's work on transnational Dominican communities in Washington Heights (in New York City) and

Santo Domingo straddles the worlds of health policy and queer Latinidad. While Decena's publications do not directly address trans-Latina/os, they provide context for the Dominican ambiente. José Esteban Muñoz's work on queer of color performance also does not consider the question of trans-Latina/o existence directly but provides a framework for interpreting the role of the imaginary (what he calls "worldmaking") in the survival of queer Latina/o subjects. Salvador Vidal-Ortiz's 2005 dissertation on Santería in the New York metropolitan area employs a similar "queer of color critique" and also considers transgendering and transsexuality through their absences in Santería practice. Vidal-Ortiz interviews several queer *Santera/os* and notes that the cases he has encountered of transsexual participation exclusively refer to MTF transsexuals.[31]

Conclusion

In this review, I have drawn from a broad range of literatures to approximate an idea of how we might find Latina/o transpopulations embedded in various social, cultural, and historical contexts. Because they are easily overlooked, a cross-disciplinary approach is key to producing analytical visibility for Latina/o transpopulations and understanding them in their specific conditions of possibility. Although there is a growing body of work that addresses Latina/o transpopulations, such work is heavily weighted in favor of trans-Latina visibility, to the near exclusion of FTM Latinos. Major gaps exist, and more work is certainly required, as evidenced by the lack of dedicated monographs concerning these populations and by the virtual nonexistence of cultural production by trans-Latina/os in permanent form.

Having identified a trend toward invisibility in the way researchers approach Latina/o transpopulations, I suggest that researchers avoid practices that promote this invisibility. Researchers should make note of all gender categories that exist in a given social formation and avoid the tendency to see gender as a binary system anchored to the categories "men" and "women." Attempting to fit such categories as stud, *macha*, *vestida*, *loca*, and muscle queen into man or woman erases the distinctiveness of these experiences. David Valentine and Sel Wahng modeled this empirical approach to gender in their contributions to the 2004 GLQ Forum, "Thinking Sex/Thinking Gender."[32]

Studies of risk behavior that focus on the category MSM may collapse trans-Latina/o respondents into this category through their data collection strategies. Such studies should be reviewed at the level of data collection and analysis to parse out potential subsets of trans respondents. While it may be impossible to find these markers in data that have been previously gathered, I encourage future researchers who employ the MSM category to include categories of trans experience in their data-gathering strategies. For example, public health departments collecting HIV-prevention and care data can ensure the visibility of trans people by (1) including flexible gender identification coding (FTM/

MFT/Genderqueer and the like); and (2) respecting the gender and sexuality *reported* by informants, while also allowing for categories of *observed* gender and sexuality.[33]

I have traced the formation of U.S. Latina/o populations, as well as sexual migration, as two sites where we might begin to identify Latina/o trans people and transpopulations. Finally, I have categorized the existing literature into four distinct areas: documentary work on Latina/o trans people in various media; historical projects that incorporate trans figures; health policy literature; and queer Latinidad approaches. Each of these areas has something to contribute to the terms of visibility and survival of Latina/o transpopulations. It is my hope that this review will help us synthesize these approaches and put them in more direct dialogue with each other for the benefit of Latina/o trans people.

16

Boundaries and Bisexuality

Reframing the Discourse on Latina/o Bisexualities

MIGUEL MUÑOZ-LABOY AND CARMEN YON LEAU

Sonia and I talked all the time in our breaks. She was one of the cashiers. It was 24-hour taqueria restaurant. . . . One day I was pissed off at my sister [where Jorge was living] and Sonya invited me to a house party. I got there and there was really no party. It was just her husband, an acquaintance, the kids, Sonya and I. While the kids were playing in the room and Sonia's husband was drinking with his friend, Sonia and I went to surf on the internet. Somehow we end up looking at pornography and laughing like crazy. Her husband's friend left and the kids were in the room. Sonia's husband sat next to us. Sonia then went to the room and told the kids to go to sleep and close their door. "Shall we take the party to the pool [aboveground pool in the back yard]?" Sonia asked. I was kind of suspicious, we went to the pool and I started drinking. They convinced me to get into the pool. Soon we were all in our underwear in the water. Sonia kissed me. Her husband started massaging my back. We went to the room. They asked me to blow him and eat her. I did so. They asked me to do her. I refused. It was too weird. The guy wanted to do me. I said no. I don't know what the hell I was doing there. They started fucking while caressing me. He came fast and Sonia was furious because her husband came too quickly and I would not fuck her. I did not need this craziness. They started fighting so I left and slept on the sofa. The next day it was really weird. I did not think of Sonia as sexual, I just needed a friend. That day I left San Antonio without anything but my money. I took the Greyhound and ended up in Miami.[1]

What may look like a "threesome," in this case a couple looking for a third sexual partner, in fact represents an episode in the bisexual history of a young Mexican man who came to the United States less than three years before this event. "Jorge," the young man who told us the above account, got to San Antonio

243

by taking the Greyhound bus (after three failed attempts to cross the Mexico-U.S. border by foot). Sonia, who is also Mexican, knew that Jorge enjoyed having sex with men and women. In conversations between Jorge and Sonia, he became aware of her sexual desire for women, together with her frustration about never having a chance to act on it.

How we make sense of this episode will depend greatly on the interpretive framework we bring to it. In this essay we argue that the dominant framework for understanding Latina/o bisexualities in the United States has been historically influenced by the fields of psychology and public health. Using this framework, our attention focuses on Jorge's sexual risk behaviors, situational risk factors in Sonia's house, the relational deficiencies between Sonia and her husband, and the like.

To begin with, we will discuss psychological and public health approaches to Latina/o bisexualities in their different formulations. Two approaches that we examine have in common a pathologization of Latino bisexuality and in fact were part of the same interpretive framework but were formulated in relation to studies with a different focus of interest. Based on social and cultural studies of masculinities with Latin American and Latino straight men, one approach explains Latino bisexuality as a result of an insecure masculinity or a covert homosexuality as Latino bisexual practices do not correspond with an expected bisexual identity. This approach overlooks these men's definition of themselves as heterosexuals under a different cultural logic regarding their sexualities, related to their gender identities and practices. A second approach, framed by the AIDS epidemic and focused on bisexual men as an epidemiological bridge population, follows the same pathologizing perspective and assumes a series of emotional and identity malfunctions of Latino bisexuals. A third approach, termed "technical bisexuality," tends to reduce bisexuality to a response to structural factors or lack of heterosexual outlets, dismissing in this way the subjects' sexual agency, the fluidity of their sexual desires, and the cultural and social contexts shaping the experiential meanings and forms of their sexual practices. These three approaches have in common a reductionist view of Latina/o bisexualities that makes invisible the complex interplay between an individual's sexual desires and affectivity and the broader social and cultural contexts in which a person is embedded. Moreover, these approaches do not include Latina bisexualities. Latina bisexual women have remained a practically invisible population in the lenses of sexuality studies and public health.

In the second part of the chapter, we propose an agenda for future research on Latina/o bisexualities that aims to overcome the limitations of individual- and risk-oriented approaches. The thematic agenda is presented together with conceptual approaches mostly rooted in the frameworks of anthropology, sociology, gay and lesbian studies, or feminist studies, which at the same time inform the formulation of these areas of inquiry. These approaches have in common overcoming a dualistic view of the relation between individual and society and exploring the interplay between both. Although we are aware of the partial character of this agenda, we think that it can cover what has been made invisible by previous approaches to Latina/o bisexualities and may even contribute to their reformulation. Major themes of the agenda developed in this chapter are grouped as follows: sexual and gender cultures shaping Latina/o bisexualities; "bisexual markets" and structural limitations and opportunities organizing sexual partnering; sexual relations and sexual behavior; sexual rights, politics, and public policies; and Latina bisexualities.

In addressing the gender and sexual cultures of Latina/o bisexuals, we advocate for a nonmonolithic and nonstatic view of Latina/o cultures. Moreover, we recommend a comprehensive view of Latina/o bisexualities, including the study of cultural norms shaping sexual desire, affectivity, and gender and sexual identities. For a dynamic study of Latina/os' sexual and gender cultures shaping bisexualities, we found the notion of "ethnic boundaries" relevant. This concept was used for the first time by the social anthropologist Frederick Barth to denominate the cultural content that the actors themselves consider significant as signals of membership and difference even in situations of interethnic contact and interdependence. Barth's approach expresses a shift from cultural anthropology frameworks defining ethnicity in terms of ascriptive cultural traits pertaining to ethnic groups, to a more ecological and structural analysis of ethnicity.[2] Framing the study of Latina/o bisexuals' cultures in this way can help researchers avoid confounding the effects of Latinos' cultural traditions with the ways in which new social and cultural contexts lead to changes or tensions in cultural norms and patterns of behavior.

The second theme, focusing on Latina/o bisexual "markets" and structural factors shaping sexual behavior and sexual partnering among Latina/os, attempts to respond to the need to reframe individual-oriented approaches to Latina/os' sexual behavior. The notion of "sex market" has been used by the sociologist Edward O. Laumann and colleagues to study patterns of sexual partnering and sexual behavior among Chicago adults. These authors propose a sex market model to understand how the search for a partner is spatially, culturally, and socially bounded. Contrary to the economic notion of autonomous markets, the explanatory value of the "sex market" approach is on the local social and cultural structures limiting sexual choices and options.[3]

The third larger theme of our agenda—sexual rights, politics, and policies—attempts to raise initial exploratory questions related to the politically unexplored domain of Latina/o bisexualities. Broadly discussed from the 1990s, these notions are part of conceptual and political debates historically linked with gay, lesbian, and feminist (more clearly in the case of sexual rights) scholarship and politics. A fundamental potential contribution of approaches based on sexual rights and sexual citizenship is uncovering significant relationships between

Latina/o bisexuals' personal sex lives and the public realm of state policies and politics, law and normative institutions, and civil society.

Finally, we emphasize the need to include Latina bisexualities (generally unseen or unacknowledged in the literature until now) and a gender approach in the research about Latina/o bisexualities. Including gender as an analytical category will allow exploration of both individuals' identities and forms of social organization of sexual cultures and practices. Likewise, a comprehensive study about Latina/o bisexualities requires analyzing the complex intersections between bisexual identities or practices, gender, and other relevant sources of identity and social divisions (such as class and race) in the case of both women and men.

Is Latina/o Bisexuality a Sexual Problem?

Bisexuality has been defined as a psychosexual malfunction since the turn of the twentieth century, characterized as an intermediate state between heterosexuality and homosexuality, where homosexual desires are repressed and identity is disconnected from behavior or bisexual self-identification, preventing the development of a positive homosexual identity.[4] The American sexual revolution, the second wave of the feminist movement, the strong formation of the gay and lesbian rights movements, the incorporation of social sciences and humanities in the theorization and systematic study of sexuality, among other factors from the late 1960s to the early 1980s, facilitated a paradigm shift to conceptually and empirically contest the assumption of bisexuality as a malfunction.

From the mid-1980s to the most recent seminal volumes on bisexuality (among them, Paula Rodriguez-Rust's *Bisexuality in the United States* and Beth Firestein's *Bisexuality: The Psychology and Politics of an Invisible Minority*), several studies have found no evidence of psychopathology or psychological maladjustment. Moreover, these researchers have found that bisexual individuals are characterized by high self-esteem, self-confidence, and autonomy; a positive self-concept independent of social norms; and high assertiveness and cognitive flexibility. Bisexual identity has been demonstrated to be a viable sexual identity, with a separate developmental pathway distinct from that characteristic of a homosexual identity, yet such scholars as Ronald Fox caution us from defining "a bisexual identity" and argue in favor of understanding bisexuality as an intricate phenomenon with manifestations that are linked by complex psychosocial and cultural processes.[5] However, theorization and scholarly research on bisexuality across ethnic or racial groups other than white Anglos have been limited. Thus, we argue that the study of Latina/o bisexualities in the United States has continued to be under the paradigm of bisexuality as a psychosexual malfunction until today. This paradigm has characterized the ways we design our studies and has deeply influenced our current understandings of Latina/o bisexualities in the United States.

The Active/Passive Bisexual Malfunction

The breakthrough findings by scholars on Latin American masculinity, from the late 1960s to early 1990s, documented that many self-identified heterosexual, straight men who were married to women or had girlfriends would also engage in anal intercourse with other men, but their sexual orientation would not be threatened so long as they remained the penetrative, insertive, active partner during the sexual encounter. This finding is found in studies in Latin America, as well as among Latinos who migrated to the United States. Although the vast majority of these studies do not pathologize bisexual behavior—and present a

---

TABLE 16.1

Bisexual Typologies

1. *Transitional bisexuality* is the stage of bisexual self-identification and identity in the process of coming out as gay or lesbian or a step in the process of coming out as bisexual.

2. *Historical bisexuality* is experienced by individuals whose sexual lives are currently heterosexual or homosexual, but who have experienced both same- and opposite-gender sexual attractions or behavior in the past.

3. *Sequential bisexuality* refers to individuals who have had relationships with women and with men, but with only one person during a particular period of time.

4. *Concurrent bisexuality* refers to individuals who have relationships with both men and women during the same period of time.

5. *Defense bisexuality* occurs when a person may be hiding a homosexual orientation, exploring homosexuality, or in transition to a gay or lesbian identity.

6. *Married bisexuality* refers to individuals who are married and engage in homosexual behavior away from their family environments.

7. *Ritual bisexuality* occurs when homosexual behavior is prescribed for some or all members of a society.

8. *Equal bisexuality* refers to people whose sexual attraction or partner selection is not based on gender.

9. *Latin bisexuality* refers to male individuals who take only the insertor role in anal or oral sex with another male and consider themselves heterosexuals.

10. *Experimental bisexuality* occurs when homosexual behavior may be circumstantial, taking place once or a few times.

11. *Secondary bisexuality* occurs when there are no heterosexual outlets.

Source: Based on Ronald Fox, "Bisexual Identities," in *Lesbian, Gay, and Bisexual Identities over Lifespan*, ed. A. R. D'Augelli and C. J. Patterson (New York: Oxford University Press, 1995).

comprehensive understanding of the social and cultural context of this practice—an underlying assumption has been that the active/passive rationale for
bisexual behavior responds to a need to prove hegemonic norms of masculinity
in specific contexts or is a strategy for protecting the self from stigma associated
with homosexual identification. Many Latino men—straight, gay, or bisexual—
live in constant processes of attempting to "prove" their masculinity to themselves or to others. However, the active/passive finding unintentionally serves
as the core element in examining Latino male bisexuality (see the definition
of "Latin bisexuality" in table 16.1). One consequence is the generalized view of
bisexual men as having "flawed, insecure masculinities" or simply as "closeted
gay men," reminding us of the identity-behavior disconnect.[7] Latina bisexuality
has not been characterized as any psychosexual malfunction since, as far as we
were able to discover, it was not examined in the literature until the mid-1990s
in the context of the AIDS epidemic. The silence around Latina bisexualities
is astonishing, and believe this subject should be one of the first priorities in
sexuality and ethnic studies. References to Latina bisexual activists are found in
the literature, yet Latina bisexuality remains unexplored in the context of social
movements' literature.[8]

Medicalization of Latina/o Bisexualities

The emergence of the AIDS epidemic solidified the processes that led to the medicalization of Latina/o bisexualities. The progress in sexual rights of the late 1970s
and early 1980s was undermined by a shift toward depoliticizing the examination
of sexuality and gender. This shift was designed to counteract the spread of AIDS
and understand modes of transmission; sexuality became sexual behavior, and
individuals were defined by their behavior or by risk groups. This change was
particularly salient for Latino bisexuals and, more recently, for Latina bisexuals.
Bisexuals as a "bridge" population and technical bisexuality (this term refers to
bisexual behavior in contexts where there is a lack of a heterosexual outlet, similar to secondary bisexuality) are the predominant frameworks for understanding
Latina/o bisexualities.

HIV infections among Latinas are frequently attributed to the bisexual
behavior of their male partners. This was true at the beginning of the AIDS
epidemic and is still the case years later. For example, recent evidence indicates
that ethnic minority men who have sex with men and women (MSMW), specifically Latinos and African Americans, have a significantly higher prevalence of
HIV infection than men who have sex exclusively with men (MSM) or men who
have sex exclusively with women (MSW). Recent rates of new HIV infections
among Latina women have also increased dramatically when compared to other
ethnic subgroups of women. For more than a decade, researchers have suggested
that Latina and African American women are more likely than non-Latina white
women to become infected with HIV by bisexually active male partners.[9] This
situation has brought into question the role of bisexual behavior in the overall

transmission of HIV among ethnic minorities in the United States, particularly for the female partner in male-to-female sexual interactions.

However, scientific evidence substantiating bisexually active men as an epidemiological "bridge" is still inconclusive. A comprehensive review of research findings on this topic concluded that focusing on rates of unprotected sex or HIV sero-positivity alone is not reasonable evidence to estimate HIV transmission from bisexual men to their female partners.[10] Important and unexplored research questions related to bisexually active men remain: the risks that they might pose to their female partners; how bisexually active Latino men experience and express their sexual desires; and what interpersonal and contextual factors put bisexually active men and their female and male partners at risk for HIV.

Behavioral studies based on convenience samples suggest that behaviorally bisexual men use condoms inconsistently with male and female partners, seldom disclose their bisexuality, and are more likely than exclusively homosexual men to report multiple HIV-risk behaviors. Furthermore, most prevalence studies on bisexual men have shown that they have lower rates of HIV/AIDS than gay men and injecting drug users. However, this should not be interpreted as claiming that bisexual men are at lower risk for HIV. In fact, in places like New York City, bisexual men seem to become HIV seropositive at a faster rate than any other group. The findings of a blind HIV-sero-conversion study conducted with 2,023 patients of STI clinics between 1993 and 1995 suggests that bisexual men become HIV seropositive at a higher rate (5.2/100 person-years) than men who have sex exclusively with men (3.3/100 person-years) and injecting drug users (3.0/100 person-years). Caution must be used when interpreting prevalence and incidence data on bisexual men because these individuals might be systematically excluded or underrepresented in HIV/AIDS studies because of the possible stigma of participating in studies related to HIV, as well as marginalized from the venues where these studies do their sampling. Thus, interpretations of bisexual behavior based on prevalence or incidence studies could produce misinformed generalizations that can cause further stigma.[11]

The underlying assumptions about Latino bisexuals as a bridge population are as follows:

1. they are assumed to be self-identified straight men who have sexual encounters with other men out of "lust," with limited emotional-relational involvement;
2. they are assumed to be men who do not want to identify as gay or bisexual but have sexual and affective relationships with both male and female partners (originally labeled MSM and recently labeled MSMW); and
3. their bisexuality assumed to respond to internalized homophobia and structured heterosexist social environments and networks.

Let us compare these assumptions with the very limited research on Latina bisexuals as a bridge population. In the literature, most studies on female bisexuality among Latinas focus on lesbian Latinas who have sex with men as a result of rape or coercion or sex work.[12] Although many identify as lesbians, the term WSWM (women who have sex with women and with men) is common in the current public health discourse. Under this public health model, these Latinas' bisexuality is "technical," a response to structural factors such as gender oppression, economic exclusion, and heterosexism. Thus, the focal point of health studies on Latina WSWM is not the protection of the female partners (as is the case with heterosexual female partners of Latino bisexual men); rather, the aim is to develop protections for Latina WSWM themselves.

Because the bisexual bridge framework is rooted in the epidemiology of illness, it prevents our asking questions and generating comprehensive understandings of Latina/o bisexualities. Medicalizing Latina/o bisexualities leaves us with a reductionist-technical bisexual framework in which sexual actors' lack of agency as well as subjectivities, fluidity, and cultural and social contexts are eliminated from the bisexual act.

Traditionally, technical bisexuality refers to bisexual behavior in contexts where there is a lack of a heterosexual outlet, similar to secondary bisexuality, as illustrated in table 16.2. Prisons and the jail system are prime examples. Women having sex with other women in female penitentiaries or men with other men while imprisoned is common, including the formation of arranged sexual partnerships.[13] The coercive nature of many of these same-sex encounters and relationships, the use of rape or gang rape as a tool of submission or survival, and institutional silence with regard to HIV/STI prevention (e.g., no access to condoms) pose interesting challenges for research attempting to examine bisexuality beyond the reductionist-technical framework—that is, in terms of bisexual desire, emotional connectedness in the prison environment, and transformations in sexual scripts through the imprisonment period, among others.

The type of sex work in which individuals have bisexual relations with other people primarily for money, drugs, or other economic benefits, but not out of

TABLE 16.2

Combining a Sexual Rights Approach with Sexual Markets

	Bisexual Markets	
Bisexual Rights Framework	Relational Citizenship	Transactional Social justice
Legal Context	Marital-family laws	Sexual laws
Political Context	Social policy	Public health policy
Collective Action	Social mobilization	Social solidarity

internal sexual desire, can be interpreted as a form of technical bisexuality. We must be careful, however, because a large number of individuals have sex with other people without any sexual desires toward the person (such as cases of hypoactive sexual desire or sex for reproductive purposes only). Is that "sex work" or is that a "technical sexual encounter"? One can argue that the commodification of the sexual body or the bisexual encounter makes it technical. Studies in sex work economies that include Latina/o bisexuals often focus on identifying the scripts and symbols of the sexual trade, the political-macro structural factors shaping these economies, or the behavioral HIV/STI risk factors associated with bisexual sex work.[14] In spite of the important contributions of these studies, the focus on transactional sexuality frequently masks meaningful attention to the bisexuality (as opposed to the trade activities) of the social actors.

Because of class inequities and economic exclusion, a significant number of the people participating in transactional sexual economies are Latina/os. For similar structural reasons, Latinos are overrepresented among inmates nationwide.[15] The disproportional rates of HIV infections, AIDS-related deaths, STIs, and unintended pregnancy among Latinas testify to the public health failure in these communities and, not surprisingly, have perpetuated and privileged the technical-reductionist approach to Latina/o sexualities, bisexuality in particular. It is in this way that public health approaches to Latina/o bisexualities fuel bisexual stigma more broadly in society (such as the racialized demonization of African American and Latino bisexual men in national TV talk shows).[16]

How can we think about the study of Latina/o bisexualities beyond the narrow focus on risk behavior? Have we studied the sexuality of bisexual Latinas not involved in transactional sexual economies? How is bisexual experimentation experienced by heterosexual Latinas? How do Latina/o families where one or both parents are bisexual negotiate societal pressures for monogamy and heterosexual conformance? What roles do social class, nationality, ethnicity, generation/length of time living in the United States and the social class/ethnic background of partners play in the ability to configure a bisexual Latina/o family? For bisexual Latinas or Latinos who maintain their sexualities in secrecy, how do they cope with balancing the need for emotional connectedness with the family and having a sexual life that may be sanctioned by their own families? These are among the many questions that we cannot fully answer because of the privilege that the medical-reductionist framework has dominated the discourse on Latina/o bisexualities.

Agenda and Suggestions for Future Research

As most of the extant literature about bisexuality reviewed above has been shaped by epidemiological and psychological frameworks, in terms of both limitations and contributions, we consider that the crux of a research agenda about Latina/o bisexualities is to build on more comprehensive and multidimensional approaches with a particular emphasis on social, cultural, and political issues that have not been studied yet. In this way, research themes or questions of this agenda and relevant conceptual frameworks will be presented together and interdependently. Major themes of the agenda developed in this chapter have been framed using nonessentialist and comprehensive approaches about bisexuality; broader social theories about sexuality, gender, and sexual rights; and available research that addresses sexual identities and practices in different countries of Latin America as well as in Latina/o communities in the United States.[17] Owing to the nature of the proposed approaches and research questions, this agenda might indicate quantitative and ethnographic research (scarce in the available literature) or the combination, where convenient, of quantitative and qualitative methodologies.

Latina/o Bisexualities and Sexual and Gender Cultures: Beyond a Single Focus

Bisexuality has been viewed historically as individual behaviors and practices in the border between heterosexuality and homosexuality, from a Western dichotomous paradigm of sexuality reinforcing the heterosexual/homosexual binary.[18] However, the organization of sexuality in several Latin American societies differs from this paradigm, particularly in the ways that sexual categories intersect with gender role–based identities, as in the gendered notions of activity and passivity. Studies of Latina/os in the United States have also highlighted the inadequacy of Anglo categories to understand Latina/o sexual desires, practice, and identities.[19]

Instead of assuming a bifurcated sexual boundary (heterosexual/homosexual) defining Latina/o bisexual identities and practices, we argue in favor of exploring the particularities, complexities, and dynamism of social boundaries relevant for organizing Latina/os' sexualities, considering that it is a constitutive and not isolated dimension of their lives. The notion of social boundaries refers to dividing lines organizing collective identities and structuring social relations and hierarchies.

17

Revisiting *Activos* and *Pasivos*

Toward New Cartographies of Latino/ Latin American Male Same-Sex Desire

SALVADOR VIDAL-ORTIZ, CARLOS DECENA,
HÉCTOR CARRILLO, AND TOMÁS ALMAGUER

The publication of this volume provides an overdue opportunity to rethink social science debates about Latino same-sex male sexualities. Given the expertise of members of the advisory board for the Latina/o Sexualities project, we undertook this discussion in the form of a roundtable conversation. Taking Tomás Almaguer's article "Chicano Men" as a point of departure, and considering the subsequent direction of research on U.S. Latino and Latin American same-sex male sexualities, three scholars joined Almaguer in an in-depth discussion about the foundations of his article and its impact on the current scholarship—including that of the three scholars. Thus, we four men—a Mexican (Héctor Carrillo), a Chicano (Almaguer), a Dominican (Carlos Decena), and a Puerto Rican (Salvador Vidal-Ortiz)—produced the dialogue presented here about the state of Latino same-sex male sexuality research.[1] We prepared for this conversation through a series of e-mail exchanges in which ideas as well as notes and articles were shared. What follows is based on the transcript from this conversation (edited for clarity and argument flow).

We open our conversation by revisiting and also problematizing the "*activo/ pasivo*" dichotomy and its preeminence in scholarly work on Latino gay and bisexual men. We first offer some background to the activo/pasivo model. As will be detailed in the discussion below, some of the earliest work from the 1970s and the 1990s on homosexuality among Mexican men in the United States and Mexico made explicit use of this framework of homoerotic roles and relationships. The effeminate pasivo and masculinized activo are two sides of one coin in these literatures—one constructed as an active male inserter (or insertor), and the other as a passive female receptor. This masculine inserter/feminine receptor equation defines and provides the homoerotic currency transacted between highly gendered sexual protagonists. We begin the conversation with the 1950s text of Octavio Paz on Mexican masculinity, which includes a graphic

253

description of "male passivity" as a reference to the Mexican male homosexual and which still influences understandings of the way that homosexuality is given specific meaning among Mexican men and how it is intimately negotiated and sexually transacted.[2] Central to Paz's work is the way that circum-Mediterranean constructions of male honor and female shame provide the foundational gender binary that structures and ignites hierarchical heterosexual and homosexual relationships in Mexico. The masculinized activo retains his cultural sense of male honor by performing the inserter role in sexual relationships with women or other men. He remains a "man" or "hombre" in a homosexual context because he is not "feminized" by passively submitting to being anally penetrated. The pasivo, who submits to sexual penetration, is constructed as sexually passive, as women tend to be seen as in heterosexual relationships.

In our conversation, however, the binary pasivo/activo that Paz's work inspired in subsequent research on Latino and Latin American male homosexuality constitutes a point of departure. Without discounting its valence in today's Latino and Latin American imagination and interpretations of male sexualities and homosexualities, we seek to locate it as one among a more diverse set of options available in Latino sexual and homosexual worlds of the early twenty-first century.

CARLOS DECENA: I read a big portion of Laberinto de la soledad [Labyrinth of Solitude] because I figured I had to go back to that initial conversation, given your text, Tomás. I bring that piece in [Laberinto] to put it on the table when the time is appropriate. Maybe we could identify some theme areas that we are interested in initiating a more focused conversation on. For example, I'm interested in travel. I'm interested in the idea of how these theories travel. And I think that this comes from a very old conversation that Salvador and I have had over the years about how activo/pasivo has been circulating in various venues and texts.

HÉCTOR CARRILLO: I like that idea, Carlos, and I think we should also talk more generally about the place of activo/pasivo in the larger universe of Latino and Latin American male homosexualities. Where does the pasivo/activo fit in current understandings of Latino homosexualities? Does it fit or not? If it does, what is its place?

DECENA: I can start by responding to your piece, Tomás, and start addressing Héctor's initial question about where it fits and how it fits. What's at stake in this particular configuration of desire, and the various theoretical elaborations of it, is attempting to discern what certain sexual and other practices mean for differently situated social actors. The whole cultural inscription of these practices is really what is at stake in the work of Lancaster and Carrier.[3] In my view, what is really interesting about the activo/pasivo, just having taken a look at el Laberinto, is how all of these other things that play an important role in *Laberinto* don't quite make it into the discussion of activo/ pasivo. And so, for example, views about national identity and inscriptions of masculinity that are everything about enclosure rather than opening. They are the constitution of the Mexican *macho* as a closed body, as a closed entity. And the idea of opening in the context of either being anally recep- tive or being open in other ways as a kind of betrayal and a foundational betrayal in Mexican national ideology. What happens with the discussion in Carrier and in Lancaster is that those issues may play a role to some degree, but it is as if there is a lifting of sexual practices from all of these other con- texts in which they also are meaningful, aligned with these ideas of opening and closing, be it masculinity, be it national identity, or some other aspect. I wanted to go back to Paz because I had the feeling that there was a sense of incompleteness to the discussion. And it's an incompleteness that I only see fulfilled or addressed fully or well in the work of Héctor, where actually those issues come back in meaningful ways.[4]

TOMÁS ALMAGUER: That is a really fascinating way of repositioning the entire activo/pasivo issue, Carlos, and what is at stake in taking up this controver- sial question. Héctor, do you want to respond here?

CARRILLO: I think that's a very good start in terms of beginning to spell out in historical terms where some of these ideas come from, these understand- ings. I agree with you, Carlos, that there is a certain oversimplification in the construction of the activo/pasivo model that requires us to go back and examine the original thinking—in terms of the larger system of sexualities and gender—that gave origin to the conceptualization of gendered catego- ries of homosexuality in Latin America. That way we can begin to under- stand more deeply what place gendered homosexualities may still occupy within the universe of interpretation of homosexualities in Mexico and Latin America, and certainly also among Latinos in the United States. And I would say that part of the problem has been a kind of oversimplification that seems to have taken hold of the scholarly work in the last few decades. By this I mean that there is little room for considering the complexities of interpretation and categorization in relation to sexual identities and forms of self-identification.

We constantly seem to need to have an either-or. I mean by this that there is a tendency to think that Latino men either identify as gay—with all the implications about expected versatility in sexual roles and an emphasis on role equality—or they are trapped in a more traditional pasivo/activo model that prevents self-identification as gay in more contemporary (read "American") terms. In reality, however, the interpretations that men make appear to be so much more complex.

Several scholars have detected and analyzed interpretations of sexual identities in various Latin American countries. In my own work I analyze homosexual identities borrowing García Canclini's concept of cultural hybridization, but before me Richard Parker in Brazil discussed it in terms of the coexistence and overlapping of different systems of categorization, and in a recent book chapter Roberto Strongman talks about it in terms of cultural syncretism.[5] All of this scholarly work points to a complicated history that has led to the coexistence of "more traditional" views of gender and masculinity with emerging notions of gayness and homosexuality (that may be global or local, or both). Following after what you are saying, Carlos, I would tend to think of activo/pasivo as describing one part of a larger picture but an incomplete part if we don't pay attention to everything else.

SALVADOR VIDAL-ORTIZ: Part of what both of you have said made me think of recent work in Mexico that talks about the whole idea of sexual silence and how, just like what you said, Héctor, in that work you can see how there are aspects of sexual silence, but one cannot make this overarching assessment that Mexican culture is, all in all, driven by sexual silence. And so looking at the nuances and peeling those layers off, I think it's a really good way of thinking about it, or maybe there are other images: maybe thinking about what one sees through glasses, and the lenses as a noticeable artifact between what one sees and what one sees it through. So the activo/pasivo could be the very language that people may use if they use that language to articulate interactions. But it is important to note that there is more behind that initial set of terms, which is not articulated through activo/pasivo. So it's both—the activo/pasivo is not the only model we can use to explain cultural differences, and that is a part that I would love to hear us, at some point, talk about. But this conversation is also about recognizing that, in a way, this term acts as shorthand—like secretaries when they write in shorthand, to capture more information faster. It is shorthand for something else that is more complex. And that the oppositional model of the activo/pasivo was taken literally in the last couple of decades, but perhaps can be explained in ways that move beyond the simple negotiation that presumes that Western, Anglo cultures *are not* and Mexican/Latin American *are* based on the activo/pasivo model. I was also thinking of various colleagues that are conducting research in Latin America and how, in their research, they see how this language of activo/pasivo is used on the ground. So while we are having these conversations about these kinds of negotiations, and whether scholars saying this are Anglo or Latino (and whether one thing has anything to do with another), there are ways in which it is moving beyond the populations and the uses that we have articulated previously.

ALMAGUER: Salvador, I'm not sure I am clear about what you are saying about the expansion in usage of the terms activo and pasivo. Are you saying that these ideas are circulating in such a way that they are now being embraced by people on the ground?

VIDAL-ORTIZ: Absolutely. That some people are saying, "I know what I want to do in bed, do you know what you want to do in bed? So, I identify my sexual desires in this particular way." And they use the categories to ask each other out.

ALMAGUER: I guess my question would be, is this primarily the traveling or recirculation of an idea that is now being embraced, or does it, in fact, reflect something that might be more inherent in the constructions of gender and sexuality in their own upbringing and the personal meanings of these categories? In other words, do the categories of activo and pasivo have deep resonance and personal meaning due to their socialization in Mexican culture, or reflect circulating ideas that they are drawing upon to make sense of things in their intimate personal lives? Is this a matter of an underlying cultural template that shapes or structures their sexuality or the circulation of these sexual categories that they have embraced to make sense of their sexual desires and erotic role preferences?

DECENA: Tomás, if I may respond to that and go back to Salvador. Some of the work that you're mentioning, Salvador, suggests the adoption of the terms, perhaps the re-signification of the terms in a very different context. What that suggests to me is that there is a largely ideological component to the utilization of activo/pasivo that we have yet to really talk about in the scholarship, period, not just in this context. And this is what I mean, if you think of ideology in the Althusserian sense of imagined relationship to the conditions that make their reality possible in the first place.[6] And you think of the fact that despite how much one may discard or retire the idea of activo/pasivo, people use the opposition to talk about themselves, to talk about other people, and it surfaces in everyday forms of interaction and forms of labeling or categorizing, that people use just to get through their daily lives and to get through their daily beds. When I heard Salvador, I thought, what has been wrong about the scholarship has largely been that people have taken too literally the idea that one is either an activo or a pasivo and haven't really thought more about, metaphorically, what exactly does this mean when you say that to somebody else, and how does using that language position people vis-à-vis one another. Because we all know that things get more complicated when you're rolling around in bed, if we're going to use the Cherríe Moraga/Amber Hollibaugh notion of sexuality, sexual activity, and desire.[7] It gets more complicated and people go through different periods of time when they want to do something, or they want to do something else; people commit themselves to being versatile. I think what is largely absent in the discussion of activo/pasivo are the ideological components of the gendered meanings that these categories have; that these meanings are not just given, that they are a product of relations of inequality that are both imagined and because they are imagined they are recalled, they are real or realized in the context of people's interactions.

CARRILLO: I mostly agree with you. I like what you are saying in relation to this because I think it brings up another very fundamental aspect of the need to distinguish between activo/pasivo as essential categories of sexual/gender identity and a more contemporary use of the terms to refer to particular sexual role preferences in terms of what specific sexual partners want to do during sex, which are two different things. I would argue that the latter does not necessarily essentialize or fix men's identity (so a man can identify as gay in very contemporary terms, and perhaps even believe in role "versatility" as a clear possibility within such an identity, and also use the terms pasivo and activo to refer to his sexual role preferences). But people sometimes want to think that pasivo/activo, as identity categories (even meaning gay- and nongay-identified), are still the only options available to homosexual men in Latin America. And so, in my work in Mexico I have argued that increasingly activo and pasivo may be thought of locally in terms that are not completely different from top and bottom in the United States, or other kinds of binary pairs that suggest to sexual partners who will be doing what in bed, without necessarily defining one sexual partner as gay and the other as nongay.

ALMAGUER: Let me follow up on that, because I think that's a really wonderful point, Héctor. One of the things that seems to be a central part of what you said just now has to do with the particular ways in which gender and sexual categories (identities, roles, relationships) are constructed in these different cultural contexts. They seem to almost always be predicated on some type of inherently problematic binary (male/female, masculine/feminine, activo/pasivo, virgin/whore, what have you) that has some kind of deep resonance and cultural meaning in various Latina/o cultures. And so what is interesting about that is that those particular gendered constructions fuel and give personal meaning, not just to sexual identities and to erotic role preferences but, I suspect, to the very nature of sexual desire. There is something about homosexual desire that requires or seems to invoke some sense of transgression and the eroticization of difference that typically gets constructed in a very gendered way around the mapping of male/female bodies, masculine/feminine dispositions, and the signaling of certain kinds of gendered messages and meanings for people that fuel or ignite and ultimately structure sexual desire.

I guess my own way of thinking about it is that homosexuality has cross-culturally and historically been structured in fundamentally different ways and that the activo/pasivo kind of relationship that we are talking about, in its most simple way, reflects just one of the particular modalities and ways in which same-sex desire has been given cultural meaning. The erotic poetics of difference, however starkly polarized or fluid in form, seems to function in a very deep personal way for how people come to sexually define themselves and what they sexually desire. And it is here that I always come back to Steven Epstein's important work on sexual identity issues.[8] He argues that sexuality ultimately involves three distinct or core realms: what we want (sexual object choice), what we want to do (sexual aim), and who we say we are (sexual identity). So there is a way in which it's really fundamentally about what we want, what we want to do with that object of desire, and what particular name or sexual category we come to embrace that is so fundamentally important to this entire discussion.

VIDAL-ORTIZ: Part of what I was hoping we would get to are some of the pieces that in some way influenced or motivated your writing, Tomás. Because I was thinking about the writings by Moraga, I was thinking about "What We're Rollin' around in Bed With" and then the very embodied experiences of butchness and femmeness that are articulated in similar writings, that might have had an impact on how—my sense is that they did have an impact—on how you wrote the Chicano cartography. So part of what I would like to do is to explore what the questions are: around desire, when they are articulated in this kind of embodiment that equals a certain security about femmeness, about letting herself go, which was Hollibaugh's position, and then how Moraga "picks that up"—the negotiation, the care, the relationship between those two people, those two experiences that help articulate each other's. If we wanted to, we could look at what I think are some of the foundational elements of that article, or those arguments that have very rarely been picked up by scholars who have looked at it.

ALMAGUER: Yeah, please go forward. It sounds fascinating. Do you want to add to that, Salvador, and push on this issue?

VIDAL-ORTIZ: Yes. I was thinking about the ways in which Moraga and Hollibaugh make this almost clear distinction between the security of the femmeness and the ambivalence of the butchness, which, to me, could be taken in a lot of different ways that have little to do with Chicano or Latino experience, that have a lot to do with just masculinities, the supposed vulnerabilities of masculinities in masculinities studies vis-à-vis the more firm identities of being femme, which are much more politicized. I was also thinking about how, in Moraga's writings, there is a relationship of ambivalence—racially, and of belonging, or of the crossing, and there is a parallel from that to the sexuality discussion.[9]

DECENA: Just to follow up with you, Salvador, on what you just said now. So there is one possible formulation of the earlier discussion of sexuality, the one that Tomás outlined, who we are, what we want, and what was the other thing, Tomás?

ALMAGUER: What we want, what we want to do, and who we say we are, basically.

DECENA: Right. It just seems to me that part of what you may be thinking, Salvador, is that the ambivalence of the butch versus the relative security, for

lack of a better word, of the femme, suggests that there is a kind of tenu-
ousness of, in one's grip, on any one of these things—who we are, what we
want, and what we, how we see ourselves. To me actually, sexuality, and this
is where I think I see it somewhat differently, and I don't know exactly what
that difference is, but to me the part of what goes on with activo/pasivo is
that a lot of people have taken it as proxy for different identitarian formation. And it has become increasingly clear in the more recent work that it
does mean something to people. For example, I work with Dominican gay
men, and the whole view of the activo/pasivo appears in a very specific context.[10] What is idealized for many of them is actually versatility. It's not being
a top or a bottom. It's actually being both. It was a small sample, and you
can't really make these claims universally, but what the reliance on activo/
pasivo and reliance on the positionality of the top signals to them in other
Latino men, and in Dominican men specifically, is backwardness. The bedroom became a site where, apart from having sex, you are actually assessing
who is really a modern subject and who is not. And a modern subject is a
subject who does both, who is versatile. That is not being versatile all the
time, but who presents himself as somebody who is capable of engaging
in both. Who one is, just because of the ambivalence of that being that is
reflected through an exchange, is very unstable. Activo/pasivo signals the
total impossibility of ever completely embodying any one of those positions,
let alone what it means to actually be the top and feel like you have to be in
a somewhat defensive position about that particular role. That ambivalence
that Salvador points to suggests to me that a lot of what gets transacted
through sexual relations, and this configuration of desire in particular,
exceeds those three categories that Tomás mentioned earlier. I just wanted
to put that out there as an alternative way of viewing it.

ALMAGUER: Yes, I think that you've identified the dramaturgical aspect of all of
this, and after all, we are fundamentally talking about how sexual dramas
get transacted between sexual actors or protagonists. I think that John H.
Gagnon and William Simon's work on sexual scripts is important because
we always seem to be working with a script that implicitly or explicitly
guides our interactions with others.[11] The degrees of fluidity and versatility that we bring to these matters is partially what is at stake here. In this
regard, some individuals are simply more rigidly typecast than others and
have deep erotic investments in a particular role. Others may bring more
range and versatility to their erotic encounters with others.

CARRILLO: I liked your use of the word unstable, Carlos, to refer to activo/pasivo.
And with Mexican participants in my research, I have found something
similar in relation to the emphasis on versatility, at the same time that
activo/pasivo roles can exist by choice within people's self-understanding as
"versatile." But this does not deny that there are cases where activo/pasivo

shows up as marking actual differences in terms of self-identification, signifying who is thought of to be a man and who is not. Considering the instability of the categories, and also the variations, is important in order to understand the complicated arrangements that exist within contemporary Latino homosexualities. Activo and pasivo, as sexual roles, can happen in the context of sexual equality, and they can happen in the context of strong inequality. Latino homosexualities can take so many different forms that pinpointing just one exclusive model, say activo/pasivo, as defining all Latin American homosexuality is clearly impossible. And in that sense I would argue that this idea of singling out the activo/pasivo model as *the* Latino model of homosexuality is very problematic.

And I would agree in that sense with Strongman that the insistence on attaching activo/pasivo to Latino homosexualities may reflect a kind of exoticism that for some reason continues to have power in work by American scholars.[12] It seems surprising to me that despite all efforts to try to provide more nuance for understanding more deeply these complicated forms of categorization in Mexico, since my book came out I have seen a number of instances where I am being referenced or quoted exclusively in relation to the activo/pasivo model. It is as if that were the only thing that my book argued in relation to male homosexualities in Mexico, when my goal was precisely to problematize the idea that activo/pasivo is the only currently available way in which homosexual identities are organized and conceptualized in Mexico. I think that is something that we should examine. Why is it that there is such a tremendous insistence on the part of scholars to identify the activo/pasivo as the only form of male homosexuality that would be available in a place like Mexico, when everything points to something much more complex?

VIDAL-ORTIZ: There is a particular need for "difference" that I think motivates doing that. Making the term "Latino," which is so problematic in terms of pan-ethnicity and so many other ways (just empirically thinking about it), but that it reifies the difference that Lionel Cantú talked about, how it creates this clear boundary between the two and so it is almost self-referential—that which I am not is what you are.[13] So I think that the issue that I have with arguments like Strongman's is that in demanding or in critiquing that difference, in establishing that difference that academics and popular readers make, they essentialize this, and it solidifies a sense of Latin American culture, which I think is also problematic. So we fall in a trap either way.

DECENA: Can you elaborate a little bit? You mean in reference to the secrecy/disclosure proposal by Strongman?

VIDAL-ORTIZ: Yes. I think the argument Strongman puts forth creates this solid, unified oppositional sense . . .

DECENA: Yes.

VIDAL-ORTIZ: . . . of what Latino or Latin American is, as a response to demand that we don't use the activo/pasivo model. So it is unmaking some things, but it is reifying others. And so we are never out of the trap because then we can always say, "Well, there is Humphrey's research [on "Westerners" or "United Staters"] and, you know, this is happening in the U.S. and in first world countries, too."[14] I guess maybe the question of race or racial difference—or how we conceptualize those differences—gets essentialized in these sexuality readings "south of the border." Especially given the general U.S. scholarship's lack of critical lens about Latina/os as racialized, not simply ethnicized, and the investment in U.S. Latina/os as an ethnic, not racial, group of people.[15]

CARRILLO: I agree with you, Salvador. In reading the book chapter by Strongman, I felt the same: that somehow he was trying to get us out of one trap but perhaps inadvertently getting us into another trap. And it made me reflect on what I see as a fundamental problem in some of the scholarly analysis of Mexican sexualities that may be the bottom line: the assumption that sexual cultures in places like Mexico are essentially static. This combined with a strong emphasis on difference. And then the analysis leaves out the notion that sexual cultures are always in flux and motion, that change is happening, and that the change, instead of creating simplicity, creates complexity. I think that is part of the problem because then, if we are not going to talk about pasivo/activo, the proposed solution is that instead we are going to talk about disclosure/secrecy or other dichotomies, and each becomes the new dichotomy that defines all Latino homosexualities. Instead, I would argue that we need to consider simultaneously activo/pasivo, disclosure/secrecy, gender-based/object choice categorizations, and globalization/locality, all at the same time and as part of the same thing.

DECENA: . . . to think about this particular form of racialization that seems to be effected through the invocation of terms like activo/pasivo. If you look at it somewhat genealogically and go back to Octavio Paz, which is why I wanted to talk about this idea of travel, is that it becomes—part of what Paz is trying to do in el *Laberinto* is to define what it is to be Mexican.

ALMAGUER: Exactly.

DECENA: And this is a Mexican doing it, Mexican in Paris actually, defining *Mexicanidad* in Paris. Now what is really interesting to me is the way that activo/pasivo gets lifted by North Americans, many anthropologists, and so on. The need for difference, to me, seems to always go back to anal sex. It seems to be going, . . . I was thinking, in a somewhat glib way, that it is a little bit like the sphincter, the sphincter becomes the prism for modernity or lack thereof. There is this anal fixation that to me actually explains why people reading Héctor's book will go directly to the section where the activo/pasivo thing is talked about. I am thinking of the work of a researcher who found in his quantitative research with different Latino groups that one of the key differences between Dominicans, Puerto Ricans, Colombians, and Mexicans was that Mexicans liked to take it up the ass more than the other groups. And so there is an interesting kind of fixation with this particular sexual act. And I don't know if there is room for a psychoanalytic reading of this expectation because something is going on and it continues to go on in the scholarship. I am not quite sure how to get out of it unless we actually try to figure out or articulate explicitly what may be going on.

ALMAGUER: Well, if I can respond. I think here is where I keep coming back to Paz. I keep coming back to the way in which these troubling binaries of male honor/female shame, masculinity/femininity, activo/pasivo, etc., all have such particular resonance for Mexicans and Mexican culture. Now in a general kind of way, in reading Strongman, one of the things that he argues is that Caribbean Latino cultures have far more syncretic religious traditions—Santería, Candomblé, and Vodou—that do not invoke the same kind of rigid polarities and binaries. He suggests that among Caribbean Latinos, where the African diaspora has been most prevalent and prominent, that this syncretism is in fact very profound. But I honestly do not see that in Mexican culture and specifically among working-class Chicanos, where those categories and binaries continue to have such strong resonance. I have no problem with the attribution of this being a premodern phenomenon, because this does speak to the tenacity with which it is often held by these sexual actors. It provides the cultural template or normative ideals of manhood and womanhood that hold deep cultural and personal meaning for the way ethnic Mexicans map their gendered and sexual world. But let me quickly add that saying this does not belie the fact that something quite different might be happening in the real world and in the bedroom. And no one is denying that reality or that real fluidity or hybridity exists on the ground. People both incorporate and contest these cultural prescriptions in different ways; with different sexual partners, at different times, and in different places that make the idealized activo/pasivo construction a problematic but also a very real point of departure in the lives of Mexican men and women.

DECENA: But what gets lifted, if I may respond quickly to this, what gets lifted out of both the work of Paz and the work of Héctor, which is partly about modernization in the Mexican context, are the paradigms of sexual practice severed from this larger context. Activo/pasivo in Paz is about Mexican men in general. And I think that there is a larger landscape that keeps on being forgotten when people simply lift the paradigm. I am agreeing with you, Tomás. I am saying that I find it really curious, and that maybe at some point we want to think about what are some of the elements of the activo/pasivo that move, and what are the elements that don't move, that travel. Because clearly some of what is traveling in Héctor's work are the very specific, almost atomized, discussions severed from their larger context.

CARRILLO: I think also that part of the problem, in relation to what you are referring to, Carlos, in terms of what travels and what does not, is the assumption (based on the emphasis on difference to which Salvador was referring) that Mexicans cannot be gay in the way that we understand gayness in the U.S., which basically denies very important historical processes in Mexico. The history of sexuality in Mexico over the past century just gets wiped out in the assertion that Mexicans think exclusively in pasivo/activo terms, and thus Mexicans cannot be gay.

VIDAL-ORTIZ: I wanted to pitch in because the idea of adding the discussion of anal penetration and the issues that that may bring may be very well linkable to that earlier discussion I was trying to bring into this one about Moraga, because, even with all the problematics of activo/pasivo, I wonder: could that model, for a second, help us to think about power differently? And that is where I thought that the Moraga and Hollibaugh article and the idea of "letting yourself go" makes us rethink the notion of power. To me, there is a significant aspect to notions of power there: that the activo/pasivo tends to be looked at seriously as something that has everything to do with the power of the "man" that represents the nonpenetrated, the nonfeminine, the nongay. And in that sense it really misses out, it misrepresents the space of the so-called pasivo and the pleasures and the desire there. And in that sense, what I think it does is that it brings in, in some interesting ways, psychoanalysis, because it makes me think of the whole idea of the "man/nonman" that Don Kulick dealt with in Brazil and Manolo Guzmán deals with, and the whole idea that in a sexual event a "man" may be having sex with a "nonman."[16] Is it possible for people to actually understand themselves in these identificatory categories? It's very possible that this is rarely explored. So think about that as one variation of what could come out of the activo/pasivo, even as we problematize it. I think it's very important. And the other piece that I think is important is when you look at, for instance, Manolo's book, in his psychoanalytic readings, I think there is a way in which Mexicans cannot be gay if you use "gay hegemony" the way in which Manolo is discussing it.[17] So if one wants to push the envelope, yes, gay Mexican men can organize, and they can have a gay identity. But I think there is a reading that is both racial and sexual that makes gayness so hegemonically centered on whiteness in these arguments, and I think that is an interesting aspect to look at as well. So could one have an understanding that, yes, people on the ground, in their real lives, can actually identify as gay and can organize around that identity, but that the problematics of gay men and how that has been constituted are very, very context-specific and that are very, very racial-specific (if we use racial as another code that represents a more complex national or ethnoracial experience)?

CARRILLO: Salvador, I see where you are coming from, and I agree. But there are two ways of seeing gay, right? One is seeing gay as just exclusively a North American or European construct, and another way is seeing gay in connection to contemporary homosexualities in the way that they emerge in different sites around the world and become reconstituted to reflect local conditions. So, from the second perspective I would say yes, of course, Mexicans can be gay for a couple of reasons: one, because people in Mexico are calling themselves gay to begin with, and two, because if we don't understand Mexican gay as necessarily meaning exactly the same as American gay, then we begin to see the kind of nuance that allows us to make a connection between globalization and locality. We can then account for the wonderful interplay that allows for local forms of contemporary homosexuality or gayness to emerge, and without necessarily having to follow "hegemonic" models. And indeed the word gay is now officially part of the Spanish language, as it was accepted some time ago by the Real Academia Española de la Lengua (Royal Academy of the Spanish Language) in Spain.

VIDAL-ORTIZ: Yes, I follow you. I was not disagreeing with that. I think that the challenge is whether one can argue that, in this process of globalization, whether Mexican or Cuban or Puerto Rican or some other Latin American sexualities can ever become *that* gay.

CARRILLO: Right, like the American one.

VIDAL-ORTIZ: Right. And so to me it opens up an interesting tension because I am not suggesting one of them is Latin American and the other one is not. But to look at the origins of the gay hegemonic arguments of Guzmán is to think about how gay hegemony is constituted through both sexuality and race in very unique ways that I think push us to think about it differently. So I'm not denying the on-the-ground opportunity. But I kind of find energy and movement in that argument of pushing the envelope and asking: could one person that is nonhegemonic (race- or class-based), be, or achieve, that level of *gayness*? So I find it a really interesting way of integrating both racial and sexual discourses.

DECENA: The same could be said of activo/pasivo. If we go back to activo/pasivo and what Tomás said earlier about the dichotomy having a very clear valence among working-class Chicanos, and I would suspect other working-class populations. I mean, there is the class aspect here that we have not addressed explicitly. What may be going on are at least two processes that I can think of. One of them is the way in which the terminology circulates in what Manolo Guzmán has called "expert discourse"[18]—where the anthropologists who go to Latin America, Carrier and all these other people, and the more contemporary people, Héctor and Don Kulick, people like that—that's one thing. And there are examples in a lot of different Latin American countries. Here I am also thinking of Carlos Cáceres and other people who have been doing the work in those countries.[19] There is this expert discourse about what activo/pasivo is supposed to be. And then there is the practice and the ways in which these constructs obtain meaning from everyday, not just everyday sexual practice, but everyday interaction about sexual practice, because people talk about what they do. I mean all of those things are different instantiations of practice that tell us a lot, but tell us very little in the end. Because you never know. I mean, you know, part of the thrill of showing up to an apartment where you think you're going to find a top is that you flip the top, you know. I mean, you know, there are people for whom this is a turn-on, desire obtains from that form of transgression. If we were going to go back to something Tomás said earlier about homosexuality and transgression and desire and transgression, then part of the reason why we need difference is precisely so that we can flip it. Or part of the kind of the ideological work of difference, of creating those others, is so that we can actually kind of undo that difference in the context of sexual exchange. There are those layers, the activo/pasivo in the expert discourse, and then activo/pasivo in what people say and activo/pasivo in what people do.

ALMAGUER: Could I chime in here? Here's where I keep, in my very old-fashioned way, I keep coming back to Sigmund Freud's foundational work and the three essays on sexuality in particular where he talks about sexual object choice, and sexual aim.[20] And, yes, I think that we want a particular object, but what's important is what we want to do to that object and that typically invoke some kind of possession, penetration, or engulfment, and some sense of transgressing eroticized lines of difference. And whether it's capture, seduction, or whatever one's particular erotic investments and sexual repertoire; there is that dimension of erotic desire that continues to function through stark binaries and polarities. And that eroticization of difference and its transgression is not just a gendered phenomenon. Here I think of work like Gilbert Herdt's research on the Sambia in New Guinea and David Halperin's on transgenerational constructions of homosexuality in Greek culture where difference is age-defined among sexual protagonists.[21] I guess what I am trying to say is that there is something about the way in which objects of desire are defined or constructed that is central to our discussion of the activo/pasivo framework.

VIDAL-ORTIZ: To add to that, I was thinking about the differences in the activo/ pasivo model in terms of how one reads the desire off each other, each other's bodies, each other's energy, and other markers. How people interpret activo/pasivo when they read each other and read the desire for each other and when they enact it in sexual activity. And if I may be a little anecdotal and offer too much information, I just remember a story, it is certainly not about me, but it includes me. When I was eighteen, I would hang out in San Juan with a bunch of friends; I used to call it *"apartamento loca."* It was six queens, and we would all get up in the morning and make dresses up with the sheets, and some of us would put pumps on, and we would be *pateando* (you know, queening out) all morning. We had a group of people that had very distinctive gender roles among ourselves. And, if you think about a scale of masculinity and femininity, there was one of the guys who was the most effeminate of all of us who was a hairdresser, who was talked about in the female all the time, and was not trans-identified—this was in 1988 when transgender was not as articulated in '"gay and lesbian" community-based discourse. And what is interesting to me is how he had encoded his gender presentation and behavior to represent his desire, but how that was transformed. He actually met a *bugarrón* in San Juan in like the touristy Condado gay hotel area—just think of San Juan, Puerto Rico, and the Atlantic Beach Hotel and the whole area of Condado where the *bugarrones* work. So my friend engaged in a sexual and romantic relationship with this man for over a year, probably more (I am not sure how long, since we lost contact at some point in the 1990s).[22] And I remember talking with him six months into the relationship—it was a very gendered relationship by all means. If you looked at them, and my mother or my friends would say "OK, ahi va la mujer y ese es el hombre" [there is the man and there is the woman]. I mean, it was just that distinctive. And six months into the relationship I was asking about their sexual activity. And the very feminine guy was like, "Well, you can't make assumptions about what we do in bed. I've flipped him many, many times. That's why he stays with me." (He told me some of their sexual experience and sex life as well.) And so to have that be articulated from the experience of someone that is socially, supposedly socially, and many times actually socially stigmatized because of his gender presentation, because of his demeanor, the way he dresses, the way he walks, but at the same time realize that that plays into a whole construct of femme power. Even if he never used those terms (femme power or even activo/pasivo), which to me is really important because it uses the experience of activo/pasivo, but it moves from that, it absolutely moves from that. So it is interesting to see both of those things operate at the same time.

DECENA: Let me offer another example, that of the movie *Princesa*, which is about a Brazilian transgender prostitute in Italy.[23] When her boyfriend finds out that "Fernanda" has a penis, he gets very upset, but eventually they start having a relationship. And there is a really important moment in that movie, which is the moment when the guy, the heterosexual guy's love for Fernanda, the transgender woman, the love is such that it destabilizes his own heterosexuality and Fernanda's idea of what he is supposed to be. And so there is a moment in the movie, when they are bed, when this guy opens himself up to the idea of her penetrating him. And Fernanda flips out. She flips out. She kicks him out of there. She, and this is very consistent with the work of Kulick, and there are a number of meanings to the moment. Part of the meaning is about, "I'm expecting you to be a real man," which means a heterosexual man. And you're not a real man, you're really a *viado* [homosexual], and therefore you're really not what I want. But also Fernanda is someone who is commodifying her penis. And so part of what is going on in that exchange is that her boyfriend, by offering to bottom for her, he is literally bringing into the intimacy space what, in Fernanda's view, belongs on the market, because this is what she sells. She sells her penis to her clients. Now one of the things that Salvador has been talking about is gender. And it seems to me that one way to move forward with the pasivo/activo, or problematize it, or bring more nuance and richness to it, is to figure out a way to bring women into the equation somehow. I don't just mean feminized men. But I mean the actual role or the actual meanings that attach to female bodies or femininity without completely getting women out of the picture. And this is what I mean. It seems to me that part of the problem with formulations, like the man/nonman formulation, is that in the case of Kulick, he actually uses it or suggests that there is the potential, generalized ability of the application of the man/nonman paradigm to include women as nonmen. So he, there are a few moments in that article where he makes statements to the effect that it is really not the difference between men and women but the difference between men and nonmen. But there are women in the mix. And I think it becomes potentially very problematic to create this; it is a patriarchal enough construction to get rid of women altogether in its analysis. Or to not bring the fact of sexual difference or the construction of sexual difference into the equation somehow. So I think another place to move the discussion, or to extend it, might be into the context of transgender subjectivities and also the larger context of hegemonic patriarchal relations within which clearly activo/pasivo gains a lot of its power and meaning.

VIDAL-ORTIZ: I have a few thoughts, Tomás. I was actually just thinking about how there is a similarity to what you are describing in Kulick's work and what I have found in my own research in looking at Santería, that gay men and women of all sexual orientations tend to be lumped together as those who are most willingly able to be possessed.[24] So that there is that man/nonman creation established there, to a certain extent. And it happens through the kind of service they do, the figure of the women in the kitchen and "professions" assigned to women and gay men. So that possession as labor becomes something where nonheterosexual men, or in many instances, gay-identified men and women, are lumped together. It makes me think about the ways in which I want to highlight how women are in the process subsumed, I am not sure if to say they are erased, but collapsed with gay men, as perhaps a kind of sexual minority—which is part of where I am taking my research next. So I don't know, because Kulick was probably not looking at nontranssexual women, so I don't know how that applies to [his work].

DECENA: It may be a rhetorical problem, though, the men/nonmen thing. I'm troubled by the nonmen part. You know what I mean? Like it's not that what you are saying, what I think you are saying, makes sense. The structural location of women and non- and gay men in the context of Santería, like that location, that structural location being similar. I think that it is important to show what that location looks like.

VIDAL-ORTIZ: Is the problem the term—what you are referring to—the nonman?

DECENA: Yeah, I just have a problem with the term because it seems to me that the analysis that uses that term does something that is not exactly what we want to do. And because it's, you know, because there is more going on here, it may be simply my having a quibble with the language, but I think it is important. I do not know how other people feel about that. We could move on to other things, but on the other hand, Salvador, you are absolutely right in thinking that it is similar. You know, what to call it becomes a slightly different question.

ALMAGUER: Can I ask you all a question that is related to this? I'm just wondering about the relationship between constructions of, say, butch-femme in the forties and in the fifties among white and black women, between the *berdache*, or "Two-Spirit," individuals and their Native American sexual partners, and "fairies" and "trade" or the working-class, Italian Catholic men in George Chauncey's book.[25] The latter, for example, are also heavily invested in what parallels or seems to be activo/pasivo relationships in contradistinction to the sexuality of the WASP men who principally forged the kind of egalitarian modern gay identity that he talks about in his book. I guess I am wondering if there is any relationship between the activo/pasivo that we've been talking about and historical constructions of butch-femme among women and trade/fairy categories among white working-class immigrant men in this country? Do they have something that is inherently similar in the way that these erotic identities work, or are they qualitatively different? Are they all polarized, gendered mappings of homosexual desire and relationships that are part of this whole conversation in some very fundamental way? But maybe I am asking the wrong question.

DECENA: I was going to say, right off the bat, that butch-femme, simply because we're talking about women and men, the butch-femme dynamic will most probably operate on a different register, even though there may be some similarities precisely because we are talking about women and same-sex desire and configurations of gender. And the hierarchal relationships between men and women has traditionally been that; hierarchical. So I would think some of those, there may be similarities, but there is that difference to account for.

ALMAGUER: Okay.

CARRILLO: To me, Tomás, your question raises a larger question: Whether we are facing an either-or or whether part of the problem is that we have not done enough work to understand the complexities of how sexuality is organized within what we think of as American white gay communities. In referring to those communities we tend to assume that everything is gay, versatile, etc., but things may be more complex there, too. To me, the question is less whether these are the same or different and more what is it that we would need to do to understand more deeply the variations and diversity that exist within the so-called hegemonic or gay model. What are we missing in relation to its own complexity? My guess is that if we focused on that, we would find a kind of complexity within American gay that would make the activo/pasivo look less foreign or exotic, if you wish.

VIDAL-ORTIZ: I wonder if part of it is that, I think, the invisibility of acknowledging whiteness is precisely what has given it so much hegemony and so much control over certain definitions, like gay, that impact us all—labeled white or not. But I was reminded, when Tomás was speaking, and now that I heard you, Héctor, I was reminded of this notion, which is an ideal type and he acknowledges it, but José Muñoz's "Feeling Brown" and the idea of white as lacking and Latino, or brownness, as excess.[26] That is very productive because he makes this clear move about, and he says, "I'm not, I am sure that what the reader is thinking is like, you know, the hot and spicy Latino lover and I'm not referring to that, although I know that that comes up in our thinking," but that there is—when you think about race and class without essentializing them—could it be that there is some excess about the berdache and the butch-femme and the working-class understandings? Because that is somewhat excessive to what seems to be normal, what seems to be normative, what *seems* to be how *most* people operate. That maybe there is a similarity between all of those things that Tomás listed. Because they are, they seem to be, excessive and, as such, noticed or noticeable.

DECENA: But I would say that they are excessive in different ways. And so the reason, to add to what you are saying, Salvador, so one of the problems I think that we face as scholars doing this work is the balkanization that happens in academic work. For example, if we were really to think across different categories and practices, we will need to take into account more seriously in a comparative perspective the work on butch-femme, the work on transgender individuals. And a lot of the scholarship that we have discussed today, that we all are very familiar with because this is where we work, is scholarship centered on gay men, or mostly same-sex-identified male bodies. Part of what lies ahead in terms of finding the ways to extend the paradigm to really show how complex it is or how it manifests itself in different ways and to get at these dynamics may be through comparative works that do not deface the differences but rather attempt to speak through the differences to enrich the scholarship and the lines of communication.

ALMAGUER: That's a wonderful way of putting it.

CARRILLO: Yeah, I agree.

ALMAGUER: Well, there is also something about this conversation that leads me back to, aside from the central issue that we are talking about, the kind of tensions that we carry as social scientists trying to generalize about things and look for identifiable patterns and make broad, sweeping kinds of generalizations about what we are finding. That often rubs up against (excuse the metaphor) the specific localities we study and the need to be mindful of time, place, and context in the specificity of what we are looking at. And so in some ways the tensions and the differences in what we are talking about reflect some of these underlying tensions over generalizability and specificity that we face as academics trying to make some sense and find a logic and coherence to our understanding of these very complex issues.

CARRILLO: Yeah, very much.

VIDAL-ORTIZ: I'm wondering, just based on what you last said, Tomás, and something that was discussed earlier about Mexican—a Mexican and a Caribbean—relationship to either rigidity of roles or more fluid gender expression, there is a caution that stuck with me in terms of not developing a typology. I find it really engaging both to think within and to interrogate what "Latino" and "Latin American" mean and how these things may be different given the context, given the history. I wonder if at the same time it is part of that loop where we would fall into thinking of Caribbean as less activo/pasivo or less rigid in terms of gender, or more fluid. And so while I was the one that said "I think it is very problematic to think of Latin America and use the activo/pasivo model," I wonder if it is just within the structure that we operate in academia and the ways we think and write about these things that then we will end up creating a typology, for instance: "this is how the Caribbeans respond, or how Central Americans respond, or how people in South America respond" and to be cautious about that kind of reading, too.

ALMAGUER: Well, it does to me because of what I was hearing or reading in the Strongman article. He was contesting the use of the activo/pasivo framework to make sense of Latin American constructions of homosexuality or homosexualities. He suggested that the syncretic cultures of Caribbean Latinos seem to disrupt or contest the inherent binary in that model and express how those polarities or dichotomies are being transgressed in an important way. So I can certainly see where one could make a convincing case that this may be true among Caribbean Latinos who embrace syncretic religious practices such as Santería. But that does not necessarily belie the fact that this may not be the case for Mexican Catholics, where those lines of difference remain sharply drawn and continue to have deep resonance. I think that Patricia Zavella's and perhaps Gloria González-López's work both seem to strongly suggest this.[27] In any case, we are in fact talking about various constructions of homosexuality and about a pan-Latino population that makes it difficult to generalize about these things in the first place. So I can see where we also need to carefully unpack what we mean by both Latino and homosexuality and that involves talking about differences in nationality as well as class and gender as well as the religious issue that Strongman brings to our attention.

CARRILLO: I would also go back to something that we discussed at the beginning of today, which Carlos put squarely on the table and which I think is very important: the need for us to talk about Latino activo/pasivo or any understandings of homosexuality in Latin America and the Caribbean in a larger context of cultural and social change. And the need to constantly try to provide a more nuanced perspective of how different forms of understanding refer to specific historical moments, to the cultural context, to globalization, to locality, to all of these issues together, so as to avoid the kind of traps that we talked about earlier in the conversation today.

ALMAGUER: Okay. Other concluding thoughts here?

DECENA: I guess just to reemphasize that . . . we are at the point where the scholarship has developed enough for, and I can see it in the work of Gloria [González-López], for example.[28] Part of what lies ahead is being more hard-nosed about creating these linkages to the larger structures, be it through the discussion of the larger context or simply, you know, people don't live in gay ghettos in every part of whatever community we are going to be. I mean if we are looking at Latina/o communities and we are looking at Latina/o communities in the U.S. or Latin Americans, same-gender-loving people tend to be situated in places where there is a lot of overlap with a lot of other populations. We need to think about how to account for that heterogeneity while at the same time remaining focused on the groups that we are talking about. And in that sense I think that, for example, when I think of things like the figure of *la loca* in Dominican culture. There's a Dominican channel here in New York, and there is a guy named Zoilo who plays *la loca*. I mean he is a guy with a beer gut and a moustache who wears a blouse and who does all kinds of crazy things on TV. And there is something about that figure that makes it intelligible, not just to gay men, who may have a very ambivalent relationship with it but who often will laugh at Zoilo along with their straight counterparts, right? And there is this funny thing about what this theme, which I kind of witness a lot here in New York, suggests about the way these categories, the category of *la loca* becomes intelligible, not just because it's intelligible to gay men. It's a stereotype and it circulates, but because it is intelligible within gay male and other cultural contexts where people interact with one another. So I think part of the next step, some of the next steps, have to do precisely with figuring out a way to avoid the myopia of just looking at gay men as gay men or just looking at transgender people precisely because we know that there is this other context. This is something that Salvador is doing, it is something that Héctor is doing, and I think it needs to be done in the scholarship to move us forward.[29]

18

Retiring Behavioral Risk, Disease, and Deficit Models

Sexual Health Frameworks for Latino Gay Men and Other Men Who Enjoy Sex with Men

GEORGE AYALA

The HIV/AIDS epidemic has had an inordinate and constraining influence on contemporary ideas about gay Latino male sexual health. For example, sexual health is often and simply understood as the personal capacity to achieve abstinence before marriage, monogamy, the absence of sexually transmitted diseases (STIs), including HIV, and/or the consistent, correct, motivated use of condoms during sex.[1] From a public health perspective, deviation from any one of these would be cause for concern and reason to intervene. This view of sexual heath has been codified by public policy, research, and practice.[2] Scrutinizing gay Latino male sexual practices through this lens results in narrow understandings of sexual health. In the closing chapter of *Framing the Sexual Subject*, Carlos Cáceres eloquently underscores this point: "An overly superficial focus on sexual practices as defined by medical and behavioral science categories, rather than as understood and enacted by the individuals concerned, will inevitably lead to naive formulations of behavior change and to associated problems for intervention and program development. Further, to map human practices in terms of endless biomedical categories is likely to reinforce the construction of a medicalized body, its parts symbolically defined not only in relation to normal and abnormal (sexual practices), but also in regard to AIDS behavioral risk."[3]

Ironically, the HIV/AIDS industry has been conspicuously silent about many aspects of gay sexuality. This silence has retarded our conversations about sexual health by excluding examinations of gender, pleasure, satisfaction, and desire.[4] Yes, there is good epidemiological counting of same-sex behavior among men—we regularly ask gay men to report how often they use condoms during anal sex, with how many sex partners, of which gender, in what positions in a given window of time, as if this would teach us how to reduce the risk for STIs. Obsessive sex counting, however, yields only an impoverished understanding of what gay men think and feel when they have sex. In the end, we learn little about gender, pleasure, satisfaction, and desire, the place each occupies in the lives of gay men, and the meaning we bring to each. This essay challenges disease, deficit, and risk paradigms to hold open the possibility of new conceptual frameworks predicated on notions of sexual health. In doing so, it briefly reviews and critiques research on sexually transmitted disease with a focus on HIV/AIDS, calls for a more nuanced understanding of sexual health that is informed by but not dependent on disease frameworks, and offers some specific suggestions for possible sexual health domains that might inspire future directions in public health research and practice tailored to the needs of gay Latino men.

The sexual health of gay Latino men must be understood in the context of contemporary interpersonal, sexual, and social realities that these men must navigate on a day-to-day basis. These realities involve substance use, violence, sexual assault, homelessness, social isolation, and other social factors that are constantly at play in most sexual exchanges between men. In fact, the concurrence of STIs, such as syphilis and HIV, with depression, anxiety, anger, low self-esteem, histories of childhood sexual abuse, and substance abuse among gay men, including gay Latino men, has been documented repeatedly by researchers for nearly two decades.[5]

Few issues underscore the importance of understanding disease risk in its interpersonal, sexual, or social context more poignantly than gay men's use of the Internet to find sexual partners. Internet sex-seeking resulting in sexual liaisons or "hookups" made via chat rooms or personal ads has been associated with high-risk sexual behavior among some gay men.[6] For example, behavioral studies indicate that gay men who seek sex online were significantly more likely to report using methamphetamine, receiving money or drugs for sex, and meeting partners in bathhouses, bars, parks, and circuit parties than those who seek sex elsewhere.[7] In addition, gay men surfing the Internet for sex tend to be younger, more likely to have an STI, and have more sex partners, anal sex, unprotected anal sex, and sex with people known to be infected with HIV.[8] However, more recent data attribute declines in new HIV infections among gay men in San Francisco in part to gay men's use of the Internet to sero-sort.[9] Sero-sorting refers to the practice of seeking sex partners that are of the same HIV-sero-status as oneself, as a strategy for minimizing the risk for HIV exposure or transmission.

Other qualitative research studies reveal that many gay Latino men enjoy the convenience of Internet sex-seeking and many prefer the Internet to bars or clubs because it is easier to manage the risk for rejection in social contexts where race-based norms of physical attractiveness exist, which many men, especially Latino men, find oppressive. Internet sex-seeking is also less expensive than going out and is unapologetically sexual, which some gay men find liberating given the social stigma associated with homosexuality.[10] More research designed to understand the Internet as a "social space" for Latino gay men is needed.

Relationships represent yet another key, albeit understudied, context within which sexual risk and health could be better understood. This is especially so given the highly individualistic nature of STI-prevention research and practice. Multiple HIV/AIDS-prevention studies indicate that gay men are less likely to practice safe sex with close, regular relationship partners compared with sexual partners perceived as casual.[11] This is of particular concern for sero-discordant couples and couples who are unaware of each other's sero-status. There is some evidence to suggest that, among sero-discordant Latino gay couples, anal sex without condoms is more likely to occur.[12] Misinformation, lack of social support (partner, family, friends), experiences of social discrimination (i.e., heterosexism), and deficits in communication and negotiation skills specific to relationships can create unique barriers to safer sexual practices for gay couples.[13] For example, when communication is impaired as a result of unexpressed fears about HIV transmission, potential illness, relationship instability, loss, uncertainty about the future, or the desire to protect each other against some or all of these concerns, many aspects of the relationship that are important for sustaining gay couples' sexual health can be negatively affected. In addition, key emotional issues between gay sero-discordant couples, when left unaddressed, can compromise the couple's capacity to guard against HIV exposure.[14] Addressing these issues and legitimizing the emotional and intimacy needs of gay men in relationships may be critical to promoting sexual health in gay men.[15]

Gay Latino men and other gay men of color have and continue to shoulder a disproportionate disease burden when it comes to STIs, including HIV.[16] While race itself is not a risk factor for sexually transmitted diseases, social and economic factors including homophobia, high rates of poverty, unemployment, racism, gender violence, and lack of access to quality health care (including health education) act as barriers to sexual health for many gay men in general.[17] Other major barriers to sexual health for many Latino gay men include stigma, isolation, alienation from heterosexual Latino communities, and marginalization by the larger mainstream white gay communities.[18]

Effectively addressing disparities in sexually transmitted diseases requires that we scrutinize disease paradigms for their potential to pathologize. HIV-prevention research and practice, for instance, have at times resulted in problematic and reductionist characterizations of Latino gay male sexual behavior, limiting our ability to leverage personal, social, or community assets in the interest of research into or promotion of sexual health. Latino gay men's sexual behavior is often described as "risky"—resulting from diminished self-worth, social disconnection, and deficits in requisite skills for negotiating "safer" sex.[19] Indeed, Latino gay men have at times been portrayed as incomplete—the passive targets of social oppression, especially homophobia, sexual silence, and family ostracism.[20] While Latino gay men are the targets of systematic social oppression and discrimination, the emotional and erotic pleasure aspects of gay men's sexual decision making and the social nature of sexual exchange are rarely considered. [21] Although important and more nuanced works in the area of Latino male sexuality exist, they seldom get applied to public health policy and practice and even more rarely receive ongoing research support.[22] Public health practitioners and researchers alike are left with the question How should we conceptualize sexual health for Latino gay men, in the context of sexual health disparities and the dominance of disease paradigms?

Recent concern about a possible resurgence of new HIV infections, as evidenced by contemporary media attention given to crystal methamphetamine use, unabated syphilis outbreaks in large urban centers, and multidrug-resistant HIV, bring added urgency to this question.[23] But as public debate and media hype continue, Latino gay men and other men of color who have and enjoy sex with other men see less and less salience in contemporary sexual health campaigns as those programs are singularly focused on HIV/AIDS, become watered-down, and fail to address the subjective experiences of gay men in visible, sex-positive, and affirming ways.[24] With this sociopolitical environment as backdrop, sexual health campaigns at their worst aim to scare, shame, or blame gay men into changing their sexual behavior. Reflections of today's general culture of fear, these simplistic and overly generic prevention campaigns may be behind what is often referred to as "HIV-prevention fatigue" or "HIV/AIDS burnout," because gay men become turned off by messages that have little to do with their sexual health.[25]

Complicating matters is the dearth of research on lesbian, gay, bisexual, and transgender populations in general and on Latino gay men in particular. For example, Maria Cecilia Zea, Nadine Jernewall, and José Toro-Alfonso examined empirical literature published over a ten-year period (1992–2002) and found that fewer than 1 percent of the 14,482 empirical articles issued by American Psychological Association journals included lesbian, gay, or bisexual samples, and of those, only 6 (0.04 percent) focused on people of color. Reviewing HIV/AIDS literature focused on behavioral and psychological factors, Zea and colleagues found 1,674 empirical articles, of which 299 (18 percent) contained gay or bisexual male samples, and of those 47 (3 percent) sampled gay and bisexual men of color.[26] This is disconcerting, given that at the end of 2005, gay men of color and gay Latino men represented 50 percent and 18 percent of gay men living with HIV/AIDS, respectively.[27] Since then there have been some notable publications on Latina/o gays and lesbians that highlight coping as a mediator of social discrimination and aspects of psychological well-being.[28]

In 2004 the Institute for Gay Men's Health, a former program of two of the oldest and largest AIDS service organizations in the United States, AIDS Project Los Angeles (APLA) and Gay Men's Health Crisis (GMHC) in New York City, produced *Holding Open Space*. This monograph reports the proceedings of a meeting convened to discuss disturbingly high HIV seroprevalence estimates among gay men of color. During the meeting, the group of researchers and community-based providers who gathered grappled with gender, pleasure, satisfaction, and desire, while raising important questions about the roles sex and sexuality play in framing alternative responses to HIV prevention and the sexual health needs of gay men of color: "Is there such a thing as 'Black Sex,' 'Latino Sex,' 'Native Sex,' or 'Asian Sex'? What about 'Thug Sex,' 'Bi Sex,' 'Hot Sex,' 'Kinky Sex,' 'Pussy Sex'? Is there a local understanding of these ideas? How have these ideas changed over time in communities? How do community members act on their beliefs about sex [in relationship to the risk for HIV]?"[29] *Holding Open Space* goes on to suggest a set of guiding principles in prevention work with gay men of color, concluding that:

1. Prevention work should be rooted in the language of love, social connectedness, intimacy, and sex rather than in terms of risk and deficits.
2. Researchers and prevention practitioners should take a more situational and contextual approach to understanding risk and sexual health.
3. Pleasure, gender, satisfaction, and desire are key aspects for an understanding of sex and sexuality among gay men of color and therefore in formulating more meaningful research and programmatic responses.

Although the focus of *Holding Open Space* was on HIV prevention, the book's recommendations nevertheless give us a solid starting point for framing important parameters of sexual health for gay Latino men and all gay men. We need conceptual frameworks for Latino gay male sexual health that move beyond debate and media hype and that abandon preoccupations with individual risk behavior, disease, and deficits. Such frameworks have the potential to underscore more clearly how social and cultural contexts can come to influence sexual health and why gender, pleasure, satisfaction, and desire represent legitimate and critical foci for future sexual health research and practice.

Epilogue

Rethinking the Maps Where "Latina/o" and "Sexuality" Meet

CARLOS DECENA

I am usually surprised and curious about the bits of information maps miss or get wrong. There is the odd intersection or street name that Mapquest, AAA maps, and even Google Earth do not account for—a wrinkle in the positivist empiricism of maps that I delight in, even though it can make arriving at one's destination a gamble or, as one might say, echoing an expression U.S. East Coast Latinas and Latinos use to talk about difficulty: "*un yogurt.*"[1] The key lesson I have learned, living and dealing with maps and other empirical renditions of the world around me, is to have a healthy skepticism toward them. Like other forms of representation, maps do not offer a window into a real world. They are historically situated, cultural expressions that allow their viewers to conceptualize and navigate reality in specific, limited ways. Maps assure us of epistemological certainty. Unless our sense of direction betrays us, maps will get us where we are going, or so we think. When we bump into those creases in the landscape they do not account for, however, the anxiety we feel obtains from the rift between representation and reality. That we usually work our way back into the assurances offered by named streets and intersections does not erase the possibility that we may get lost again.

The essays in this collection provide several maps of knowledge about something called, provisionally and strategically, "Latina/o Sexualities." My task in this epilogue is to comment on the geographies of knowledge these essays produce collectively. Institutional, social, and political conditions shape the unevenness of the scholarship that exists, the problematic nature of representations of the populations most researched, and the neglect of otherwise important areas, themes, and populations in the literature.

That a collective project of this kind can be imagined, funded, and carried out at all points to massive demographic changes in the U.S. population, political mobilization, and struggles that have opened up institutional spaces, and to the growing recognition that current ways of imagining and studying these populations and issues will not get us very far in this new century. The growing numbers of Latina/os in the United States has been remarked on in the introduction and in many of the foregoing essays. Twenty years ago, a project of this kind would have instead been easily named "*Hispanic* Sexualities"; the currency and legitimacy of the term "Latina/o" reflects accomplishments of the last fifteen years or so. In the mid-1980s, dealing with the ravages various populations were suffering from the HIV/AIDS epidemic was one of the most pressing social and political issues referenced by the term "sexuality," as were the struggles to give academic and social legitimacy to lesbian and gay lives. And perhaps naming the project "Latina/o *Sexualities*" as we do here would have rendered it problematic twenty years ago, given the concentration of the epidemic among specific populations, not to mention criminal governmental neglect and the urgency to create spaces of institutional legitimacy for gay and lesbian studies as a fledgling field of inquiry.

Clearly, the growing sophistication, interactions, and changing political horizons of ethnic studies (Chicana/o, Puerto Rican, and Latino/a), sexuality studies (gay and lesbian studies, queer studies, and the political and intellectual challenges to these fields from intellectuals interested in transsexuality, bisexuality, heterosexuality, and the like), and feminist studies (whether in its mainstream form or in terms of third world feminism) have helped make this collection of essays possible. The contributions, while being individually shaped by the disciplinary or interdisciplinary orientation of the writers are best appreciated as emerging from previous intellectual dialogues and struggles as well as political and intellectual engagement.

Many of the essays point out a paucity of empirical research in the specific area in which they concentrate. Together, they demonstrate that certain areas of research are attractive precisely because of their viability and legitimacy in the eyes of private and government funders. The price of invisibility is that, at least in the health and behavioral sciences, some bodies and erotic attachments do not represent social or health "problems" that need representation and solution. By way of contrast, the price of visibility is the overabundance of frames of representation and paradigms that obscure more than reveal the complexities of lived experience.

As documented by several of the authors in this collection, the populations currently least studied in the literature include but are not limited to Latina lesbians, Latino male heterosexuals, and aging Latina/os. By contrast, representations of gay, bisexual, and other Latino males identified with same-sex behavior predominate. Issues that need to be addressed but that are generally relegated to the margins of the scholarship include sexuality across the life course for all Latinas and Latinos, class difference and sexuality, racial formation and Latina/o sexuality, and pleasure. Issues emphasized throughout the current behavioral and social science literature are the specificities of Latina/o "culture" and paradigms of risk-behavior identification.

I will limit my comments to three "invisibilities" and their attendant "visibilities," specifically: Latina lesbian invisibility versus hypervisible gay, bisexual, and MSM-identified men; the invisibility of racial formation and Latina/o sexuality versus the predominance of "culturalist" paradigms to interpret Latina/os and sex; and the invisibility of pleasure versus dominant risk framings of sexuality. While other invisibilities and visibilities pointed out above and throughout the essays deserve attention, the three I comment on here hint at larger and urgent political questions to studies of U.S. Latina/os and of sexualities and to the intellectual projects in which those fields come together.

Latina Lesbian Invisibility versus the Visibilities of Same-Sex Behavior among Latino Men

Women who self-identify as Latinas and as lesbians have made invaluable contributions to intellectual and social movements currently identified as feminist, queer, and ethnic nationalist throughout the last decades of the twentieth century in U.S. history. It is terribly ironic that, though figures such as Cherríe Moraga and Gloria Anzaldúa are noted critics of U.S. white supremacy, the various permutations of patriarchy (including ethnic nationalist ones), identitarian essentialisms, and the relationship of positionalities to the production of knowledge, there is a scanty archive of social science scholarship on Latina lesbians, as Luz Calvo and Catrióna Rueda Esquibel point out in their contribution to this collection. It is even more ironic that there is so little research, given how important their contributions have been to the creation of spaces where Latinas and other women of color of diverse sexual and gender orientations can talk about and work through their understandings of sexual desires, gender expressions, and agency. Calvo and Esquibel astutely argue that the work of Juanita Ramos (Díaz)—the landmark *Compañeras: Latina Lesbians* (1987)—presents readers with the conjunction of Latina and lesbian as a contested and multipronged identitarian project.[2] But the explosion of cultural production and cultural studies work spawned by *Compañeras* together with highly visible artists (such as Carmelita Tropicana and Marga Gómez) have been echoed only by a trickle of social-scientific publications that are often marred, as these authors explain, by small samples, outdatedness, and inflexible readings of identity.

The relative invisibility of women who love and have sex with other women in social scientific literature on Latinas in the United States can be explained partly by the difficulty of supporting scholars interested in these topics when so much of the empirical work undertaken and supported focuses on populations considered social problems, as many of the essays in this collection argue. Part of the issue also stems from fundamental epistemological challenges to empirical inquiry posed by attempts to document the multiple and heterogeneous bodies, desires, and identifications that may (or may not) coalesce around the term Latina lesbian. How do we "listen to silences," as Calvo and Esquibel—echoing work by Yolanda Leyva published in 1998—suggest we do methodologically?[3] Any project anchored in traditional notions of identitarian visibility or essentialism will not do. But how do we imagine alternatives when one of the great successes of organizing in the United States in the last decades has been to open institutional and philanthropic spaces that now require some version of bureaucratized identity politics to channel resources?

The invisibility of Latina lesbians to public health authorities and other behavioral and social scientists is nothing to celebrate. Nevertheless, a dose of the bite, humor, sophistication, self-reflexivity, and edginess of cultural production on the sexualities of Latina women who love and have sex with other women—and their vibrant links to feminist, lesbian, and queer social movement organizing—would benefit well-funded but often problematic scholarship on same-sex male erotic attachments, identities, and behaviors. To be fair, there is much edginess, sophistication, and political bite in some cultural critiques concerned with male same-sex desires, identities, practices, and forms of belonging among Latinos. But the HIV/AIDS crisis and its attendant mappings of risk tend to overwhelm the intellectual horizons of many a social and behavioral scientist. The structures established to support this work—at the level of government— foster scholarship that focuses on solving the problem represented by these populations. Cultural producers such as the team of George Ayala, Jaime Cortez, and Patrick Hebert have used some of these resources to develop extraordinary artifacts like *Sexilio* that have a life useful but not limited to the promotion of safer sex. Unfortunately, this work is not the most visible, and the dominant narrative of Latino same-sex male desires, identities, and attachments is one of behavioral risk, as Ayala puts it in his essay in this collection, or of psychosexual malfunction, as Miguel Muñoz-Laboy and Carmen Yon Leau state in their contribution. Sex counting and assessments of the amount of risk in a given population tell us very little about how people experience and enjoy the practices they engage in. It also tells us little about what these desires, identities, and behaviors mean to them.

Sex-negativity rears its ugly head often throughout much of the scholarship on Latina/o sexualities. However, critics and researchers have much to learn from the invisibilities and visibilities present in the available literatures. More research is needed, but the contributions to this volume teach us that revising and reformulating our epistemological premises and frameworks will be crucial to new developments in the study of the sexualities of Latinos and Latinas.

No Race and Too Much Culture?

Race is a shockingly absent theme in the behavioral and social science literature on Latina/o sexualities. This is particularly striking because, despite local, regional, and national variations in racial formation, the processes through which Latina/os recognize themselves and are recognized by others as U.S.

minorities involve interactions and historico-political relations with Anglo whites, African Americans, Native Americans, and other groups.

Coalition building among feminists of color in the United States to think about oppressions at the meeting points of gender, race, class, nation, and sexuality have been important for past and ongoing efforts to undo the damage done to studies of sexuality by the marginalization of race and to studies of race by the marginalization of sexuality, as José Quiroga and Melanie López Frank point out. Nevertheless, the overwhelming visibility of light-skinned Latina/os in the United States, as well as the historical and ongoing hypervisibility of European-looking Latina/os and Latin Americans in English-, Portuguese-, and Spanish-language U.S.-based and transnational Latina/o mass media (television and print) suggest the urgency of a critique of U.S. mainstream, U.S. Latina/o, and Latin American white supremacy. As the contribution of Deborah Vargas points out (as well as the work of Arlene Dávila), more critical attention needs to be paid to the racialization of U.S. Latinos and Latinas in U.S. mass media and to the complicity of Latina/o media workers themselves in reworking and subverting stereotypical portrayals of these populations as well as reproducing normative heterosexuality, traditional family values, and racial hierarchies that privilege whiteness.[4]

Gloria González-López's essay, "Heterosexuality Exposed," notes that although interracial relationships are barely visible in the social and behavioral scholarship, anecdotal evidence supports the claim that the reproduction of normative heterosexuality within U.S. Latina/o communities is connected with the reproduction of white supremacy within these populations. How this connection is enacted is an empirical and theoretical question worth asking, but it is clear that Latin American and U.S. ideologies of *blanqueamiento, mestizaje,* and the "one-drop" rule are under increased pressure and transculturation by the growth of interracial mixing in the United States and by the bewildering complexities and heterogeneities of racial, sexual, and class politics throughout U.S. society at large and within communities of color. These dynamics, which include how Latinos and Latinas themselves look at one another through complexly racialized lenses, have begun to be studied by Ana Ramos-Zayas, and Nicholas De Genova, among other scholars. A more explicit connection of racialization and same-sex desire in interracial relationships is captured insightfully and poignantly by Salvador Vidal-Ortiz.[5]

Several essays in this volume point out that culture, not race, brings together the plethora of models and approaches used for the construction of Latino/a sexualities in the United States—what Susana Peña calls "culturalist understandings of Latina/o sexuality." The "traditionalist" reading of Latin American cultures that Latina/o immigrants "carry" with them to the United States—machismo, *marianismo, familismo,* and *simpatía;* the supposed hyperfertile Latina female body; or the virgin/whore, honor/shame, and *activo/pasivo* dichotomies—are critiqued and complicated to varying degrees by many of the

contributors to this collection and in many of their publications, by the participants in the transcribed conversation, and by several Latino/a studies scholars
of sexuality such as Lionel Cantú, Marysol Asencio, and Laura Briggs, among
others. Peña's essay effectively situates discussions about Latina/o (sexual)
migration, acculturation, and immigrant parent-children communication in the
United States within a long-historical view that takes into account the continuing importance of culture of poverty arguments for the construction of Latina/o
sexualities as social problems.[6]

Intellectual and activist apologists of culture as a key marker of Latina/o difference abound, partly because it is through the circulation and reproduction of
these racialized narratives that they open up spaces and legitimate themselves
as representatives of U.S. Latino/a communities in the media, the academy, and
health and social activism.[7] As the conversation of Salvador Vidal-Ortiz, Tomás
Almaguer, Héctor Carrillo, and Carlos Decena also suggests—that culturalist
interpretations of *Latinidades* abound in U.S. Latino/a communities themselves—
retiring these frameworks will not be helpful. We need to understand how they
function, what political and cultural work they do, and how Latinos and Latinas
reproduce and transform them in daily life.

Why So Much Risk and So Little Pleasure?

Sexy sounds, images, conversations? One need look no further than U.S.-based
English- and Spanish-language Latina/o print, television, music, radio, film and
any other media to see that bacchanalian, anarchic, and exhilarating sexual
desires, sexual identifications, and practices are barely beneath the surface
and often quite central to the plots, the *chismes* (gossip), the *sin vergüensuras*
on display.[8] The raucous, raunchy humor of the New York–based *El Vacilón de
la Mañana* radio show; the parade of impossibly hot bodies on the Telemundo's
telenovelas and series like *Decisiones* and Telefutura's *Así es la vida*; music videos
by Shakira, Paulina Rubio, Gloria Trevi, and Aventura—all of these and many
other cultural workers and artifacts suggest that intellectuals in the social
and behavioral sciences interested in thinking through the meeting points
of "Latina/o" and "sexuality" in the United States in a sex-positive way have
plenty of material to study. Of particular interest to social critics interested in
the views, stories, and behaviors of average Latinos and Latinas are shows like
Cristina, *Caso Cerrado*, and *¿Quién tiene la razón?*—all U.S.-based programs that
feature a wide range of views, sexual proclivities, and conflicts. Many of the cultural producers who create these programs espouse traditional sexual politics
and render pathological any alternatives to patriarchal genders and sexualities.
But alternatives to normative heterosexuality, homosexuality, masculinity, and
femininity are sometimes presented sympathetically. Most crucially, these cultural expressions—together with more explicitly politicized work emerging from
feminist and queer social movements or from alternative media—teach us that

sex is messy, playful, dramatic, traumatic, energizing, spiritual, funny, funky, boring, hilarious, raunchy, kinky.

The contrast of the vibrancy of cultural production and cultural critiques of Latina/o sexualities to the risk and deficit foci in the social and behavioral sciences reveals that insofar as much of this research and the structures that support it are concerned, Latinos and Latinas are a disaster waiting to happen—if it has not happened already. Granted, there needs to be a concern with the possible effects of sex—STI transmission, unwanted pregnancies (especially for teens), and so forth. But as Laura Romo, Erum Nadeem, and Claudia Kouyoumdjian explain, there are relatively few data, in the communications between parents and adolescents about sex, about the positive aspects of sexuality—though the scanty archive of scholarship suggests that teens and their parents (particularly their mothers) do communicate about sexuality. Sexual health research on U.S. Latina/os, as Sandra Arévalo, Mariana Gerena, and Hortensia Amaro argue, is consistent with U.S. definitions of sexual health in its focus on specific problems: reproduction, sexually transmitted disease control, and sexual dysfunction; they found no research on sexual well-being. Finally, Sonya Grant Arreola shows that the dominant tenor of research on Latino/a sexuality and childhood is the prevention of early sexual initiation and sexual abuse, resulting in the absence of any work exploring the possibility that childhood sexual life can be positive and that children are capable of sexual pleasure and agency. Although these three essays draw attention to the problem represented by sex-negativity in the very frameworks that anchor much of this scholarship, the need to come up with more sex-positive ways to research sex appears often throughout most of the other essays. George Ayala puts it succinctly in his very title, "Retiring Behavioral Risk, Disease, and Deficit Models: Sexual Health Frameworks for Latino Gay Men and Other Men Who Enjoy Sex with Men." Like the men Ayala references in his title, all social and behavioral science research on Latina/o sexualities would benefit from recognizing that sex is not only trouble. It can be and often is a source of intense pleasures, affirmation, and joy in the lives of Latinos and Latinas. We need to theorize pleasure, empowerment, taking control, taking the lead, in ways that highlight the agency of Latina/os. We must remember that sexuality is one of the passions people pursue for a sense of health, well-being, collaboration, trust, and play.[9]

Beyond "Latina/o Sexualities"?

Changing from the production of knowledge on Latina/o sexualities for the purposes of social engineering, individual discipline, and population control to a sex-positive agenda will require all of the ingenuity and creativity academic researchers and intellectual activists aligned with the social and behavioral sciences can muster. This is especially true given that funding structures tend to change much more slowly than the realities that need to be better understood and appreciated. Rendering visible specific collectivities, desires, experiences, and lives will not be enough in itself. What is needed is continued critical engagement with existing paradigms in addition to the formulation of new, more elastic ones that represent sensitively the complexities, contradictions, joys, and pains of lived sexual experience.

As objects of knowledge, the categories "Latina/o" and "sexualities"—in "Latina/o sexualities" or "Latina/os and their sexualities" (the phrase José Quiroga and Melanie López Frank suggest we use)—require more critical engagement. Latina/o communities can be generationally, ethnically, and racially heterogeneous; they can emerge in relation, tension, and interaction of varying degrees to other populations, local infrastructures, and power hierarchies.

Future efforts may result in more accurate representations of these realities. But as a critical map user with an erratic sense of direction, I know that the topographies of knowledge that will face us will always present a wrinkle or two worth savoring. One can also learn a thing or two from misreading maps and even from getting lost. Social and behavioral science literatures on the sexualities of Latina/os would benefit from a stronger awareness of themselves *as representations* of the world they interpret. But these are not interpretations and representations that live only in obscure journals and in nooks and crannies of libraries, for the imagined terrains charted by this collection illustrate the production and reproduction of particular issues, agendas, research questions, and recommendations and the neglect of others across diverse intellectual locations. What needs to be addressed and how it should be addressed will vary and be the source of disagreement. But this collective effort offers an appreciation of the strengths of existing inquiry points to the issues that remain unexplored, and calls us to join in the conversation.

NOTES

INTRODUCTION

1. Racialization is the process by which racial identities are produced and imposed on individuals based on phenotype, class, and socioeconomic status. Latinas and Latinos are often subject to different and conflicting racial formation systems as they experience one in their countries of origin and another in the United States. For a discussion of the racialization of Latinas and Latinos in the United States, specifically Puerto Ricans, see: Salvador Vidal-Ortiz, "On Being a White Person of Color: Using Autoethnography to Understand Puerto Rican's Racialization," *Qualitative Sociology* 27 (2004): 179–203.

2. For examples of how Latinas have been racialized, exoticized, and polarized as either virgins or whores, see Maxine Baca-Zinn, "Social Science Theorizing for Latino Families in the Age of Diversity," in *Understanding Latino Families: Scholarship, Policy and Practice*, ed. Ruth E. Zambrana, Douglas S. Massey, and Sally Alonzo Bell (Thousand Oaks, Calif.: Sage Publications, 1995). Baca-Zinn, "Mexican American Women in the Social Sciences," *Signs* 8 (1995): 259–272. Patricia Zavella, "Playing with Fire: The Gendered Construction of Chicana/Mexicana Sexuality," in *The Gender/Sexuality Reader: Culture, History, Political Economy*, ed. Roger Lancaster and Micaela di Leonardo (New York: Routledge, 1997). Patricia Zavella, "Talkin' Sex: Chicanas and Mexicanas Theorize about Silences and Sexual Pleasures," in *Chicana Feminisms: A Critical Reader*, ed. Gabriela Arredondo, Aida Hurtado, Norma Klahn, and Olga Nájera-Ramirez (Durham: Duke University Press, 2003). Rosa Linda Fregoso, *MeXicana Encounters: The Making of Social Identities on the Borderlands* (Berkeley: University of California Press, 2003). Clara E. Rodriguez, ed., *Latino Looks: Images of Latinas and Latinos in the U.S. Media* (Boulder, Colo.: Westview Press, 1997).

3. Patricia Hill Collins, *Black Sexual Politics: African Americans, Gender, and the New Racism* (New York: Routledge, 2004), 27.

4. Frances Negrón-Muntaner, *Boricua Pop: Puerto Ricans and the Latinization of American Culture* (New York: NYU Press, 2004).

5. A. Rolando Andrade, "Machismo: A Universal Malady," *Journal of American Culture* 15 (1992): 33–41. Yolanda DeYoung and Edward F. Ziegler, "Machismo in Two Cultures: Relation to Punitive Child-Rearing Practices," *American Journal of Orthopsychiatry* 64 (1994): 386–395. Alfredo Mirande, *Hombres y Machos: Masculinity in Latino Culture* (Boulder, Colo.: Westview Press, 1997). Rafael L. Ramírez, *What It Means to Be a Man: Reflections on Puerto Rican Masculinity* (New Brunswick, N.J.: Rutgers University Press, 1999).

6. For a complete analysis of the representations of Latina/o sexualities in popular culture, see Chapter 8 of this volume. Also for an analysis of how the sexualities of black men are represented in popular culture, see Collins, *Black Sexual Politics*.

7. See http://rickymartinfoundation.org.

8. U.S. Bureau of the Census, "The Hispanic Population in the United States: Popula-tion Characteristics" (Washington, D.C.: U.S. Department of Commerce, 2000). U.S. Bureau of the Census, "The Hispanic Population: Census 2000 Brief" (Washington, D.C.: U.S. Department of Commerce, 2000).

9. Marysol W. Asencio, *Sex and Sexuality among New York's Puerto Rican Youth* (Boulder, Colo.: Lynne Rienner Publishers, 2002). Ruth E. Zambrana, ed., *Understanding Latino Families: Scholarship, Policy, and Practice* (Thousand Oaks, Calif.: Sage Publications, 1995). Vicki Ruiz, "*Morena/o, Blanca/o y Café con Leche*: Racial Constructions in Chicana/o Historiography," *Mexican Studies* 20 (2004): 343–359. Margarita B. Melville, "Hispanics: Race, Class, or Ethnicity?" *Journal of Ethnic Studies* 16 (1988): 67–83.

10. In the last couple of decades, the following have participated in the debates about the meaning and usage of these terms: Marilyn Aguirre-Molina and Carlos Molina, "Latino Populations: Who Are They?" in *Latino Health in the U.S.: A Growing Chal-lenge*, ed. Aguirre-Molina and Molina (Washington D.C.: American Public Health Association, 1994); Geoffrey Fox, *Hispanic Nation: Culture, Politics, and the Construction of Identity* (Tucson: University of Arizona Press, 1996); David E. Hayes-Bautista and Jorge Chapa, "Latino Terminology: Conceptual Bases for Standardized Terminology," *American Journal of Public Health* 77 (1987): 61–68; Melville, "Hispanics: Race, Class or Ethnicity?"; Rogelio Saenz, *Latinos and the Changing Face of America* (New York: Rus-sell Sage Foundation and Population Reference Bureau, 2004); Fernando M. Treviño, "Standardized Terminology for Hispanic Populations," *American Journal of Public Health* 77 (1987): 69–72; Alfred Yankauer, "Hispanic/Latino—What's in a Name?" *American Journal of Public Health* 77 (1987): 15–17; and Lillian Comas-Diaz, "Hispan-ics, Latinos, or Americanos: The Evolution of Identity," *Cultural Diversity and Ethnic Minority Psychology* 7 (2001): 115–120.

11. Elizabeth M. Grieco and Rachel C. Cassidy, "Overview of Race and Hispanic Origin: Cen-sus 2000 Brief C2KBR/01–1," U.S. Bureau of the Census (Washington, D.C.: U.S. Depart-ment of Commerce, 2001). Roberto R Ramirez and G. Patricia de la Cruz, "The Hispanic Population in the United States: March 2002," *Current Population Reports*, P20–545, U.S. Bureau of the Census (Washington, D.C.: U.S. Department of Commerce, 2002).

12. Michael Jones-Correa and David L. Leal, "Becoming Hispanic: Secondary Pan-Ethnic Identification among Latin American-Origin Populations in the United States," *His-panic Journal of Behavioral Sciences* 18 (1996): 214–254.

13. Angelo Falcón, Marilyn Aguirre-Molina, and Carlos W. Molina, "Latino Health Policy: Beyond Demographic Determinism," in *Health Issues in the Latino Community*, ed. Aguirre-Molina, Molina, and Ruth E. Zambrana (New York: Jossey-Bass, 2001), 7.

14. Betsy Guzmán, "The Hispanic Population: Census 2000 Brief, C2KBR/01–3" U.S. Bureau of the Census (Washington, D.C.: U.S. Department of Commerce, 2001). Alex Meneses Miyashita, "Census Data for '04 Provide Much New Detail on Hispanic Status," *His-panic Weekly Report*, February 26, 2007, 6. Melissa Therrien and Roberto R. Ramirez, "The Hispanic Population in the United States: March 2000," *Current Population Reports*, P20–535, U.S. Bureau of the Census (Washington, D.C.: U.S. Department of Commerce, 2000).

15. Therrien and Ramirez, "Hispanic Population in the United States."

16. Merrill Singer et al., "SIDA: The Economic, Social, and Cultural Context of AIDS among Latinos," *Medical Anthropology Quarterly* 4 (1990): 72–114. Guzmán, "The Hispanic Population." Therrien and Ramirez, "The Hispanic Population in the United States." Roberto Ramirez, "We the People: Hispanics in the United States: Census 2000

Special Report" (Washington, D.C.: U.S. Department of Commerce, 2004). Aida L. Giachello, "The Reproductive Years: The Health of Latinas," in *Health Issues in the Latino Community*, ed. Aguirre-Molina, Molina, and Zambrana.

17. Matthew C. Gutmann et al., eds., *Perspectives on Las Americas: A Reader in Culture, History, and Representation* (Oxford: Blackwell Publishers, 2003). John A. Garcia, "Latino Studies and Political Science: Politics and Power Perspectives for Latino Communities and Its Impact on the Discipline," Julian Samora Research Institute (JSRI) Occasional Paper no. 34, Latino Studies series (East Lansing: Michigan State University, 1997).

18. Michael W. Wiederman, Carri Maynard, and Amelia Fretz, "Ethnicity in 25 Years of Published Sexuality Research: 1971–1995," *Journal of Sex Research* 33 (1996): 339–343.

19. Juan Flores, "Latino Studies: New Contexts, New Concepts," *Harvard Educational Review* 67 (1997): 208–221.

20. Judith Butler, *Gender Trouble: Feminism and the Subversion of Identity* (New York: Routledge, 1990). Lillian Faderman, *Odd Girls and Twilight Lovers: A History of Lesbian Life in Twentieth-Century America* (New York: Penguin Press, 1991). Rosemary Hennessy, *Profit and Pleasure: Sexual Identities in Late Capitalism* (New York: Routledge, 2000). Carole S. Vance, ed., *Pleasure and Dangers: Exploring Female Sexuality* (Boston: Routledge and Kegan Paul, 1984).

21. Olivia M. Espín, *Latina Realities: Essays on Healing, Migration, and Sexuality* (Boulder, Colo.: Westview Press, 1997). Cherríe Moraga and Gloria Anzaldúa, *This Bridge Called My Back: Writings by Radical Women of Color* (New York: Women of Color Press, 1983).

22. Steven Seidman, *Queer Theory Sociology* (Malden, Mass.: Blackwell Publishing, 1996). Eithne Luibhéid, *Entry Denied: Controlling Sexuality at the Border* (Minneapolis: University of Minnesota Press, 2002). Luibhéid and Lionel Cantú Jr., eds., *Queer Migrations: Sexuality, U.S. Citizenship, and Border Crossings* (Minneapolis: University of Minnesota Press, 2005). Salvador Vidal-Ortiz, "Queering Sexuality and Doing Gender: Transgender Men's Identification with Gender and Sexuality," *Gender Sexualities* 6 (2002): 181–233.

23. Héctor Carrillo, *The Night Is Young: Sexuality in Mexico in the Times of AIDS* (Chicago: University of Chicago Press, 2002). Xochitl Castañeda and Patricia Zavella, "Changing Constructions of Sexuality and Risk: Migrant Mexican Women Farmworkers in California," *Journal of Latin American Anthropology* 8 (2003): 126–151. Carlos Decena, "Tacit Subjects," *Gay and Lesbian Quarterly* 14 (2008): 339–359.

24. Gloria González-López, *Erotic Journeys: Mexican Immigrants and Their Sex Lives* (Berkeley: University of California Press, 2005).

25. Chrys Ingraham coined the term "heterosexual imaginary" to describe the ideologies that prevent feminists from analyzing heterosexuality as a social construction and to critique the ways in which it has been institutionalized in our society. Ingraham, "The Heterosexual Imaginary: Feminist Sociology and Theories of Gender," in *Queer Theory/Sociology* (Malden, Mass.: Blackwell Publishing, 1996).

26. Vilma Ortiz, "The Diversity of Latino Families," in *Understanding Latino Families*, ed. Zambrana. Roberto Rodriguez, "Chicano Studies: As America's Latino Diaspora Evolves, So Does the Field," *Black Issues of Higher Education* 17 (2000): 26–31.

CHAPTER 1   A HISTORY OF LATINA/O SEXUALITIES

1. Throughout this essay I use the term Latina/o, indicating both females and males. When specifically referring to males or to females exclusively, I make that gender distinction clear in the text.

2. José Vasconcelos, *The Cosmic Race: A Bilingual Edition* (Baltimore: Johns Hopkins University Press, 1979). Suzanne Bost, *Mulattas and Mestizas: Representing Mixed Identities in the Americas, 1850–2000* (Athens: University of Georgia Press, 2003). Marilyn Grace Miller, *Rise and Fall of the Cosmic Race: The Cult of Mestizaje in Latin America* (Austin: University of Texas Press, 2004). Herman Lee Bennett, *Africans in Colonial Mexico: Absolutism, Christianity, and Afro-Creole Consciousness, 1570–1640* (Bloomington: Indiana University Press, 2003). Sandra Gunning, Tera Hunter, and Michele Mitchell, *Dialogues of Dispersal: Gender, Sexuality, and African Diaspora* (Malden, Mass.: Wiley-Blackwell Press, 2004).

3. Joan Corminas, *Diccionario crítico etimológico castellano e hispánico* (Madrid: Gredos, 1980), 7:235–236. Michel Foucault, *The History of Sexuality*, vol. 1: *An Introduction* (London: Vintage Press, 1979), 3.

4. Stephen Gudeman, "The Compadrazgo as a Reflection of the Natural and Spiritual Person," *Proceedings of the Royal Anthropological Institute of Great Britain and Ireland* (London: Royal Anthropological Institute of Great Britain and Ireland, 1971): 45–72, esp. 49.

5. Ramón A Gutiérrez, *When Jesus Came, the Corn Mothers Went Away: Marriage, Sexuality, and Power in New Mexico, 1500–1846* (Stanford: Stanford University Press, 1991), esp. 242.

6. Clemente de Ledesma, *Confesionario del despertador de noticias de los Santos Sacramentos*; quotation on 336. Asunción Lavrin, ed., *Sexuality and Marriage in Colonial Latin America* (Lincoln: University of Nebraska Press, 1989), 72–80.

7. Alonso de Herrera, *Espejo de la perfecta casada* (Granada, Spain: Imp. por Andres de Santiago Palomino, 1636); quotation on 139–140.

8. Tomás Sánchez, *De sancto matrimonii sacramento* (Antwerp: Mart. Nutium, 1607); quotation on 37–38.

9. Gutiérrez, *When Jesus Came*, 215.

10. Judith Brown, *Immodest Acts: The Life of a Lesbian Nun in Renaissance Italy* (Oxford: Oxford University Press, 1986). Lee Penyak, "Criminal Sexuality in Central Mexico, 1750–1850" (Ph.D. diss., University of Connecticut, 1993), 290.

11. Bartolomé de Alva, *A Guide to Confession Large and Small in the Mexican Language (1634)* (Norman: University of Oklahoma Press, 1999); quotations on 105. Zeb Tortorici, "'Heran Todos Putos': Sodomitical Subcultures and Disordered Desire in Early Colonial Mexico," *Ethnohistory* 54 (2007): 35–67; quotations on 10, 1.

12. Alva, *Guide to Confession*, 105. Mary Elizabeth Perry, *Gender and Disorder in Early Modern Seville* (Princeton: Princeton University Press, 1990), 125.

13. Francisco Guerra, *The Pre-Columbian Mind: A Study into the Aberrant Nature of Sexual Drives, Drugs Affecting Behavior, and Attitude towards Life and Death, with a Survey of Psychotherapy in Pre-Columbian America* (London: Academic Press, 1971). Ramón Gutiérrez, "Must We Deracinate Indians to Find Gay Roots?" *Out/Look* 1 (1989): 61–67. Geoffrey Kimball, "Aztec Homosexuality: The Textual Evidence," *Journal of Homosexuality* 26 (1993): 7–24. Richard C. Trexler, *Sex and Conquest: Gendered Violence, Political Order, and the European Conquest of the Americas* (Ithaca, N.Y.: Cornell University Press, 1995). Pete Sigal, "The *Culoni*, the *Patlache*, and the Abominable Sin: Homosexuality in Early Colonial Nahua Society," *Hispanic American Historical Review* 85 (2005): 555–594. Sigal, *From Moon Goddesses to Virgins: The Colonization of Yucatecan Maya Sexual Desire* (Austin: University of Texas Press, 2000). Sigal, ed., *Infamous Desire: Male Homosexuality in Colonial Latin America* (Chicago: University of Chicago Press, 2003). Sigal, "The Politicization of Pederasty among Colonial Yucatecan Maya," *Journal of*

the History of Sexuality 8 (1997): 1–24. Sigal, "Queer Nahuatl: Sahagún's Faggots and Sodomites, Lesbians and Hermaphrodites," *Ethnohistory* 54 (2007): 9–34. Tortorici, "Heran Todos Putos.'" Geoffrey Spurling, "Under Investigation for the Abominable Sin: Damián de Morales Stands Accused of Attempting to Seduce Antón de Tierra de Congo," in *Colonial Lives: Documents on Latin American History, 1550–1850*, ed. Richard Boyer and Geoffrey Spurling (New York: Oxford University Press, 2000). Gutiérrez, *When Jesus Came*. Serge Gruzinski, "The Ashes of Desire: Homosexuality in Mid-Seventeenth-Century New Spain," in *Infamous Desire*, ed. Sigal. David Higgs, "Tales of Two Carmelites: Inquisitorial Narratives from Portugal and Brazil," in *Infamous Desire*, ed. Sigal. Luis Mott, "Crypto-Sodomites in Colonial Brazil," in *Infamous Desire*, ed. Sigal; De Freitas Lessa quotation on 188–189.

14. Alva, *Guide to Confession*, 105–109.

15. Mariana de San Miguel, quoted in Jacqueline Holler, "'More Sin Than the Queen of England': Mariana de San Miguel before the Mexican Inquisition," in *Women in the Inquisition: Spain and the New World*, ed. Mary E. Giles (Baltimore: Johns Hopkins University Press, 1999), 224. Nora Jaffary, *False Mystics: Deviant Orthodoxy in Colonial Mexico* (Lincoln: University of Nebraska Press, 2004).

16. *Tercero Cathecismo y Exposición de la Doctrina Cristiana* (1585); quotation on 81. Brian T. McCormack, "Conjugal Violence, Sex, Sin, and Murder in the Mission Communities of Alta California," *Journal of the History of Sexuality* 18 (2007), 26. Gutiérrez, *When Jesus Came*.

17. On punishments see Ward Stavig, "Political 'Abomination' and Private Reservation: The Nefarious Sin, Homosexuality, and Cultural Values in Colonial Peru," in *Infamous Desire*, ed. Sigal, 142–144; and Tortorici, "'Heran Todos Putos.'" Trexler, *Sex and Conquest*. Gruzinski, "Ashes of Desire."

18. Gutiérrez, *When Jesus Came*, 238. Albert L. Hurtado, *Intimate Frontiers: Sex, Gender, and Culture in Old California* (Albuquerque: University of New Mexico Press, 1999).

19. Juan de Zumárraga, *Doctrina breve muy provechosa* (1543), fol. h v. Gabino Carta, *Práctica de confessores: Práctica de administrar los sacramentos, en especial el de la penitancia* (1653).

20. Solange Alberro, ed., *La actividad del Santo Oficio de la Inquisición en la Nueva España, 1571–1700* (Mexico City: Instituto Nacional de Antropologia e Historia, 1982). Richard E. Greenleaf, *The Mexican Inquisition of the Sixteenth Century* (Albuquerque: University of New Mexico Press, 1969). Henry Kamen, *Inquisition and Society in Spain in the Sixteenth and Seventeenth Centuries* (Bloomington: Indiana University Press, 1985), and "Notas sobre brujería y sexualidad y la Inquisición," in *Inquisición española: Mentalidad inquisitorial*, ed. Angel Alcalá (Barcelona: Ariel, 1984).

21. Serge Gruzinski, "*Confesión, alianza y sexualidad entre los indios de Nueva España*," in *El placer de pecar y el afán de normar*, ed. Seminario de Historia de Mentalidades (Mexico City: Editorial J. Mortiz, 1988). Guerra, *Pre-Columbian Mind*. Mariana Hidalgo, *La Vida Amorosa en el México Antiguo* (Mexico City: Editorial Diana, 1979). Alfredo López Austin, *Cuerpo humano e ideologia: Las concepciones de los antiguos nahuas*, 2 vols. (Mexico City: Universidad Nacional Autonoma de Mexico, Instituto de Investigaciones Antropologicas, 1980). María Isabel Morgan, *Sexualidad y sociedad en los Aztecas* (Toluca, Mex.: Mexico Universidad Autónoma del Estado de México, 1983). Noemí Quezada, *Amor y Magia Amorosa entre los Aztecas* (Mexico City: Universidad Nacional. Autónoma de México, 1975).

22. Nicolás de Chavez, quoted in Gutiérrez, *When Jesus Came*, 73.

23. Magnus Mörner, *Race Mixture in the History of Latin America* (Boston: Little, Brown, 1967). Karen Vieira Powers, *Women in the Crucible of Conquest: The Gendered Genesis of Spanish American Society, 1500–1600* (Albuquerque: University of New Mexico Press, 2005). Gutiérrez, *When Jesus Came*; quotation on 51.

24. Gutiérrez, *When Jesus Came*, 210.

25. Ibid., 51.

26. Carmen Castañeda, "La Memoria de las Niñas Violadas," *Encuentro* 2 (1984): 41–56. C. Castañeda, *Violacíon, estupro y sexualidad: Nueva Galicia, 1790–1821* (Guadalajara, Mex.: Editorial Hexagono, 1989). François Giraud, "Viol e société coloniale: Les Cas de la Nouvelle-Espagne au XVIII siècle," *Annales: Economies, Sociétés, Civilasations* 41 (1986): 625–637.

27. Josefina Muriel, *Los Recogimientos de Mujeres: Respuesta a una Problematica Social Novohispana* (Mexico City: Universidad Nacional Autónoma de México, Instituto de Investigaciones Históricas, 1974).

28. Will Roscoe, *The Zuni Man-Woman* (Albuquerque: University of New Mexico Press, 1991), and Roscoe, *Changing Ones: Third and Fourth Genders in Native North America* (New York: Palgrave Macmillan, 1998). Charles Callender and Lee Kochems, "The North American Berdache," *Current Anthropology* 24 (1983): 443–470. Gutiérrez, "Must We Deracinate Indians to Find Gay Roots?" Harriet Whitehead, "The Bow and the Burden Strap: A New Look at Institutionalized Homosexuality in Native North America," in *Sexual Meanings: The Cultural Construction of Gender and Sexuality*, ed. Sherry B. Ortner and Harriet Whitehead (Cambridge: Cambridge University Press, 1981). Walter Williams, *The Spirit and the Flesh: Sexual Diversity in American Indian Culture* (Boston: Beacon Press, 1986).

29. Sigal, "Politicization of Pederasty." Sigal, *From Moon Goddesses to Virgins*. Sigal, "Queer Nahuatl." Trexler, *Sex and Conquest*. Gutiérrez, "Must We Deracinate Indians to Find Gay Roots?" and Gutiérrez, "Warfare, Homosexuality, and Gender Status Among American Indian Men in the Southwest," in *Long Before Stonewall*, ed. Tom Foster (New York: New York University Press, 2007).

30. David Herlihy, "Family," *American Historical Review* 96 (1991): 2–35.

31. Dolores Enciso, "Bigamos en el Siglo XVIII," in *Familia y Sexualidad en la Nueva España*, ed. Seminario de Historia de Mentalidades (Mexico City: Fondo de Cultura Económica, 1982). Richard E. Boyer, *Lives of Bigamists: Marriage, Family and Community in Colonial Mexico* (Albuquerque: University of New Mexico Press, 1995).

32. Silvia M. Arrom, *La Mujer Mexicana ante el Divorcio Ecclesiástico* (Mexico City: Secretaría de Educación Pública, Dirección General de Divulgación, 1976).

33. Marcelo Carmagnani, "Demografía y Sociedad: La Estructura Social de los Centros Mineros del Norte de México, 1600–1720," *Historia Mexicana* 21 (1972): 419–459. David J. Robinson, *Studies in Spanish American Population History* (Boulder, Colo.: Westview Press, 1981).

34. Ann Twinam, "Honor, Sexuality, and Illegitimacy in Colonial Spanish America," in *Sexuality and Marriage*, ed. Lavrin. Ann Twinam, *Public Lives, Private Secrets: Gender, Honor, Sexuality and Illegitimacy in Colonial Spanish America* (Stanford: Stanford University Press, 1999).

35. Silvia M. Arrom, "Cambios en la Condición Juridical de la Mujer Mexicana en el Siglo XIX," in *Memoria del Congreso de Historia del Derecho Mexicano* (Mexico City: Universidad Nacional Autonoma de Mexico, Instituto de Investigaciones Juridicas, 1981). Arrom, *La Mujer Mexicana*. Silvia M. Arrom, *The Women of Mexico City, 1790–1858* (Stanford: Stanford University Press, 1985).

36. Gutiérrez, *When Jesus Came*, 328–329.

37. Louis Dumont, *From Mandeville to Marx: The Genesis and Triumph of Economic Ideology* (Chicago: University of Chicago Press, 1977).

38. *Familia y Sexualidad en la Nueva España*, ed. Seminario de Historia de Mentalidades. Matthew C. Gutmann, *The Meanings of Macho: Being a Man in Mexico City* (Berkeley: University of California Press, 1996). Carrillo, *The Night Is Young*.

39. Christine Hunefeldt, *Liberalism in the Bedroom: Quarreling Spouses in Nineteenth-Century Lima* (University Park: Pennsylvania State University Press, 2000).

40. Jeffrey Weeks, *Sexuality* (London: Ellis Horwood Ltd. and Tavistock Publications, 1986), 12–16.

41. Robert Buffington, *Criminal and Citizen in Modern Mexico* (Lincoln: University of Nebraska Press, 2000). Pablo Piccato, *City of Suspects: Crime in Mexico City, 1900–1931* (Durham: Duke University Press, 2001). Robert McKee Irwin, Edward McCaughan, and Michelle Rocío Nasser, eds., *The Famous 41: Sexuality and Social Control in Mexico, 1901* (New York: Palgrave Macmillan, 2003). James Naylor Green, *Beyond Carnival: Male Homosexuality in Twentieth-Century Brazil* (Chicago: University of Chicago Press, 1999). Jorge Salessi, *Médicos Maleantes y Maricas: Hygiene, Criminología en la Construcción de la Nación Argentina* (Rosario, Argentina: Beatriz Viterbo Editora, 1995).

42. Jorge Salessi, "The Argentine Dissemination of Homosexuality, 1890–1914," in *¿Entiendes? Queer Readings, Hispanic Writings*, ed. Emilie L. Bergmann and Paul Julian Smith (Durham: Duke University Press, 1995), 75. Green, *Beyond Carnival.*

43. Gómez, quoted in Salessi, "Argentine Dissemination of Homosexuality," 80.

44. Piccato, *City of Suspects.* Buffington, *Criminal and Citizen in Modern Mexico.* Robert McKee Irwin, *Mexican Masculinities* (Minneapolis: University of Minnesota Press, 2003).

45. Simon Le Vay, *Queer Science: The Use and Abuse of Research into Homosexuality* (Cambridge: MIT Press, 1996), 1–12.

CHAPTER 2   MAKING SEX MATTER

Acknowledgments: The author would like to thank Marysol Asencio, Ramón Gutiérrez, Beth McLaughlin, Horacio Roque Ramírez, Anne Theriault, and an anonymous reader of the manuscript for their helpful comments and suggestions.

1. Horacio Roque Ramírez, "'That's My Place!': Negotiating Racial, Sexual, and Gender Politics in San Francisco's Gay Latino Alliance, 1975–1983," *Journal of the History of Sexuality* 12 (2003): 224–258. George Lipsitz, "World Cities and World Beat: Low-Wage Labor and Transnational Culture," *Pacific Historical Review* 68 (1999): 213–231.

2. David G. Gutiérrez, *The Columbia History of Latinos in the United States since 1960* (New York: Columbia University Press, 2004); quotations on 4–5.

3. Lawrence La Fountain-Stokes, "1898 and the History of a Queer Puerto Rican Century: Gay Lives, Island Debates, and Diasporic Experience," *Centro Journal* 11 (1999): 91–110, and "Sylvia Rivera's Talk at LGMNY, June 2001," *Centro Journal* 14 (2007): 117–123. Jennifer Nelson, *Women of Color and the Reproductive Rights Movement* (New York: New York University Press, 2003). Susana Peña, "Visibility and Silence: Mariel and Cuban American Gay Male Experience and Representation," in *Queer Migrations: Sexuality, U.S. Citizenship, and Border Crossings*, ed. Eithne Luibhéid and Lionel Cantú Jr. (Minneapolis: University of Minnesota Press, 2005). Roque Ramírez, "'That's My Place!'"; Horacio Roque Ramírez, "Claiming Queer Citizenship: Gay Latino (Im)Migrant Acts

in San Francisco," in *Queer Migrations*, ed. Luibhéid and Cantú; and "A Living Archive of Desire: Teresita la Campesina and the Embodiment of Queer Latino Community Histories," in *Archive Stories: Facts, Fictions, and the Writing of History*, ed. Antoinette Burton (Durham: Duke University Press, 2005), 111–135.

4. Julia Pérez, quoted in *Compañeras: Latina Lesbians*, ed. Juanita Ramos (Díaz) (New York: M. E. Sharpe, 1987), 20.

5. Roque Ramírez, "Living Archive of Desire"; quotations on 114.

6. La Fountain-Stokes, "Sylvia Rivera's Talk at LGMNY"; quotation on 117.

7. Eileen J. Suárez Findlay, *Imposing Decency: The Politics of Sexuality and Race in Puerto Rico, 1870–1920* (Durham: Duke University Press, 1999); quotation on 81.

8. José Flores Ramos, "Virgins, Whores, and Martyrs: Prostitution in the Colony, 1898–1919," in *Puerto Rican Women's History*, ed. Félix V. Matos-Rodríguez and Linda C. Delgado (New York: M. E. Sharpe, 1998), 83–104.

9. Laura Briggs, *Reproducing Empire: Race, Sex, Science, and U.S. Imperialism in Puerto Rico* (Berkeley: University of California Press, 2002); quotations on 23, 73.

10. Francisco A. Rosales, *Pobre Raza: Violence, Justice, and Mobilization among México Lindo Immigrants, 1900–1936* (Austin: University of Texas Press, 1999); quotations on 68.

11. Pablo Mitchell, *Coyote Nation: Sexuality, Race, and Conquest in Modernizing New Mexico, 1880–1920* (Chicago: University of Chicago Press, 2005).

12. Mark Wild, *Street Meeting: Multiethnic Neighborhoods in Early Twentieth-Century Los Angeles* (Berkeley: University of California Press, 2005).

13. Elizabeth R. Escobedo, "The Pachuca Panic: Sexual and Cultural Battlegrounds in World War II Los Angeles," *Western Historical Quarterly* 38 (2007): 133–156. Vicki Ruíz, *From Out of the Shadows: Mexican Women in Twentieth-Century America* (New York: Oxford University Press, 1998).

14. Rosa Linda Fregoso, *meXicana Encounters: The Making of Social Identities on the Borderlands* (Berkeley, CA: University of California Press, 2003); quotations on 133, 113.

15. Gustavo Pérez Firmat, *Life on the Hyphen: The Cuban-American Way* (Austin: University of Texas Press, 1994); quotation on 76.

16. José Limón, *Dancing with the Devil: Society and Cultural Poetics in Mexican-American South Texas* (Madison: University of Wisconsin Press, 1994).

17. Frances Negrón-Muntaner, *Boricua Pop: Puerto Ricans and American Culture* (New York: New York University Press, 2004); quotation on 69.

18. Emma Pérez, *The Decolonial Imaginary: Writing Chicanas into History* (Bloomington: Indiana University Press, 1999).

19. John D'Emilio and Estelle B. Freedman, *Intimate Matters: A History of Sexuality in America* (Chicago: University of Chicago Press, 1997), 198–200, 255, 315.

20. Jennifer Terry, *An American Obsession: Science, Medicine, and Homosexuality in Modern Society* (Chicago: University of Chicago Press, 1999). Kevin J. Mumford, *Interzones: Black/White Sex Districts in Chicago and New York in the Early Twentieth Century* (New York: Columbia University Press, 1997); quotation on 56.

21. Johanna Schoen, *Choice and Coercion: Birth Control, Sterilization, and Abortion in Public Health and Welfare* (Chapel Hill: University of North Carolina Press, 2005); quotations on 213, 202, 209.

22. Stephen Robertson, *Crimes against Children : Sexual Violence and Legal Culture in New York City, 1880–1960* (Chapel Hill: University of North Carolina Press, 2005), 295, 184; quotation on 295n31.

23. Ibid., 34, 166, 170.

24. Mary Odem, *Delinquent Daughters: Protecting and Policing Adolescent Female Sexuality in the United States, 1885–1920* (Chapel Hill: University of North Carolina Press, 1995), 51.

25. Ann R. Gabbert, "Prostitution and Moral Reform in the Borderlands: El Paso, 1890–1920," *Journal of the History of Sexuality* 12 (2003): 575–604, esp. 591. The Mann Act was one of several pieces of U.S. legislation passed in the early twentieth century aimed at preventing prostitution and other forms of commercial sex across the nation. The act focused on the transportation of women across state lines for "immoral purposes," and according to D'Emilio and Freedman, *Intimate Matters*, "the Justice Department obtained almost twenty-two hundred convictions for trafficking in women" in the first eight years after its passage (210).

26. Eithne Luibhéid, *Entry Denied: Controlling Sexuality at the Border* (Minneapolis: University of Minnesota Press, 2002); quotations on 78.

27. Luibhéid and Cantú, *Queer Migrations*. Siobhan Somerville, "Sexual Aliens and the Racialized State: A Queer Reading of the 1952 U.S. Immigration and Nationality Act," in *Queer Migrations*, ed. Luibhéid and Cantú; quotations on 76, 83.

28. Nan Alamilla Boyd, *Wide Open Town: A History of Queer San Francisco to 1965* (Berkeley: University of California Press, 2003); quotations on 60, 54–55.

29. Lillian Faderman and Stuart Timmons, *Gay L. A.: A History of Sexual Outlaws, Power Politics, and Lipstick Lesbians* (New York: Basic Books, 2006); quotations on 1, 89, 80. Joanne Meyerowitz, *How Sex Changed: A History of Transsexuality in the United States* (Cambridge: Harvard University Press, 2002), 239.

30. Rochella Thorpe, "'A House Where Queers Go': African-American Lesbian Nightlife in Detroit, 1940–1975," in *Inventing Lesbian Cultures in America*, ed. Ellen Lewin (Boston: Beacon Press, 1996), 40–61. Carroll Smith-Rosenberg, *Disorderly Conduct: Visions of Gender in Victorian America* (New York: Oxford University Press, 1986). Elizabeth Lapofsky Kennedy and Madeline D. Davis, *Boots of Leather, Slippers of Gold: The History of a Lesbian Community* (New York: Routledge, 1993). Lisa Duggan, *Sapphic Slashers: Sex, Violence, and American Modernity* (Durham: Duke University Press, 2000).

31. George Chauncey, *Gay New York: Gender, Urban Culture, and the Making of the Gay Male World, 1890–1940* (New York: Basic Books, 1994). David K. Johnson, "The Kids of Fairytown: Gay Male Culture on Chicago's Near North Side in the 1930s," in *Creating a Place for Ourselves: Lesbian, Gay, and Bisexual Community Histories*, ed. Brett Beemyn (New York: Routledge, 1997). Allen Drexel, "Before Paris Burned: Race, Class, and Male Homosexuality on the Chicago South Side, 1935–1960," in *Creating a Place for Ourselves*, ed. Beemyn. Peter Boag, *Same-Sex Affairs: Constructing and Controlling Homosexuality in the Pacific Northwest* (Berkeley: University of California Press, 2003).

CHAPTER 3   LATINA/O CHILDHOOD SEXUALITY

1. The Latina/o population grew 3.3 percent from July 1, 2004, to July 1, 2005, and as of July 1, 2005, totaled 42.7 million. U.S. Census Bureau, December 11, 2006, http://www.census.gov/Press-Release/www/releases/archives/population/006808.html.

2. John Bancroft, ed., *Sexual Development in Childhood*, Kinsey Institute series (Bloomington: Indiana University Press, 2003), 484. J. DeLamater and W. N. Friedrich, "Human Sexual Development," Special Issue: Promoting Sexual Health and Responsible Sexual Behavior, *Journal of Sex Research* 39 (2002.): 10–14.

3. A. K. Driscoll et al., "Adolescent Latino Reproductive Health: A Review of the Literature," Special Issue: Adolescent Reproductive Health, *Hispanic Journal of Behavioral Sciences* 23 (2001): 255–326. S. L. Faulkner, "Good Girl or Flirt Girl? Latinas' Definitions of Sex and Sexual Relationships," *Hispanic Journal of Behavioral Sciences* 25 (2003): 174–200. Marcella Raffaelli and Lenna L. Ontai, "'She's 16 years old and there's boys calling over to the house': An Exploratory Study of Sexual Socialization in Latino Families," *Culture, Health, and Sexuality* 3 (2001): 295–310. D. M. Upchurch et al., "Sociocultural Contexts of Time to First Sex among Hispanic Adolescents," *Journal of Marriage and the Family* 63 (2001): 1158–1169. A. M. Villarruel, "Cultural Influences on the Sexual Attitudes, Beliefs, and Norms of Young Latina Adolescents," *Journal of the Society of Pediatric Nurses* 3 (1998): 69–79. A. M. Villarruel et al., *"La Uniendo de Fronteras:* Collaboration to Develop HIV-Prevention Strategies for Mexican and Latino Youth," *Journal of Transcultural Nursing* 14 (2003): 193–206.

4. R. H. DuRant et al., "Contraceptive Behavior among Sexually Active Hispanic Adolescents," *Journal of Adolescent Health Care* 11 (1990): 490–496. C. S. Scott et al., "Hispanic and Black American Adolescents' Beliefs Relating to Sexuality and Contraception," *Adolescence* 23 (1988): 667–688. A. Thornton and D. Camburn, "Religious Participation and Adolescent Sexual Behavior and Attitudes. *Journal of Marriage and the Family* 51 (1989): 641–653.

5. Marysol W. Asencio, *Sex and Sexuality among New York's Puerto Rican Youth* (Boulder, Colo.: Lynne Rienner Publishers, 2002). Héctor Carrillo, *The Night Is Young: Sexuality in Mexico in the Times of AIDS* (Chicago: University of Chicago Press, 2002), 352.

6. G. Marin and B. VanOss Marin, "Research with Hispanic Populations," *Applied Social Research Methods Series* 23 (1991). F. Sabogal et al., "Hispanic Familism and Acculturation: What Changes and What Doesn't?" *Hispanic Journal of Behavioral Sciences* 9 (1987): 397–412.

7. A. M. Padilla and T. L. Baird, "Mexican-American Adolescent Sexuality and Sexual Knowledge: An Exploratory Study," *Hispanic Journal of Behavioral Sciences* 13 (1991): 95–104. Driscoll et al., "Adolescent Latino Reproductive Health." Upchurch et al., "Sociocultural Contexts." Villarruel, "Cultural Influences." W. W. Westhoff, D. R. Holcomb, and R. J. McDermott, "Establishing Health Status Indicators by Surveying Youth Risk Behaviors of High School Students in the Dominican Republic," *International Quarterly of Community Health Education* 16 (1996): 91–104.

8. D. de Anda, R. M. Becerra, and E. P. Fielder, "Sexuality, Pregnancy, and Motherhood among Mexican-American Adolescents," *Journal of Adolescent Research*, Special Issue: Adolescent Sexual Behavior, 3 (1988): 403–411. P. B. Smith, L. McGill, and R. B. Wait, "Hispanic Adolescent Conception and Contraception Profiles: A Comparison," *Journal of Adolescent Health Care* 8 (1987): 352–355. P. B. Smith and M. L. Weinman, "Cultural Implications for Public Health Policy for Pregnant Hispanic Adolescents," *Health Values: Journal of Health Behavior, Education, and Promotion* 19 (1995): 3–9. B. C. Hodges et al., "Gender and Ethnic Differences in Adolescents' Attitudes toward Condom Use," *Journal of School Health* 62 (1992): 103–106.

9. Y. O. Mayo and R. P. Resnick, "The Impact of Machismo on Hispanic Women," *Journal of Women and Social Work* 11 (1996): 257–277. Olivia M. Espín, *Women Crossing Boundaries: A Psychology of Immigration and Transformations of Sexuality* (Florence, Ky.: Taylor and Frances/Routledge, 1999), 194. A. Santiago-Rivera, "Latino Values and Family Transitions: Practical Considerations for Counseling," *Counseling and Human Development* 35 (2003): 1–12. G. Bacigalupe, "Family Violence in Chile: Political and Legal Dimensions in a Period of Democratic Transition," *Violence Against Women* 6 (2000): 427–448.

10. E. Morales, "Gender Roles among Latino Gay and Bisexual Men: Implications for Family and Couple Relationships," in *Lesbians and Gays in Couples and Families: A Handbook for Therapists*, ed. J. Laird and R. Green (San Francisco: Jossey-Bass, 1996), 272–927. C. J. Falicov, *Latino Families in Therapy: A Guide to Multicultural Practice*, Guilford Family Therapy series (New York: Guilford Press, 1998), 198.

11. G. González-López, "Fathering Latina Sexualities: Mexican Men and the Virginity of Their Daughters," *Journal of Marriage and the Family* 66 (2004): 1118–1130.

12. S. Lopez-Baez, "Marianismo," in *Key Words in Multicultural Interventions: A Dictionary*, ed. J. Mio et al. (Westport, Conn.: Greenwood, 1999), 183.

13. William Simon and John H. Gagnon, "A Sexual Scripts Approach," in *Theories of Human Sexuality*, ed. J. Geer and W. O'Donahue (New York: Plenum, 1987), 363–383. C. A. Gomez and B. VanOss Marin, "Gender, Culture, and Power: Barriers to HIV-Prevention Strategies for Women," *Journal of Sex Research* 33 (1996): 355–362.

14. Asencio, *Sex and Sexuality*, 195. Driscoll et al., "Adolescent Latino Reproductive Health." Faulkner, "Good Girl or Flirt Girl?" Hodges et al., "Gender and Ethnic Differences." M. Hovell et al., "Family Influences on Latino and Anglo Adolescents' Sexual Behavior," *Journal of Marriage and the Family* 56 (1994): 973–986. Padilla and Baird, "Mexican-American Adolescent Sexuality." K. H. Beck and C. J. Bargman, "Investigating Hispanic Adolescent Involvement with Alcohol: A Focus Group Interview Approach," *Health Education Research* 8 (1993): 151–158.

15. Sonya Arreola, "Childhood Sexual Abuse and HIV among Latino Gay Men: The Price of Sexual Silence during the AIDS Epidemic," in *Sexual Inequalities and Social Justice*, ed. N. Teunis (Berkeley: University of California Press, 2006). K. F. Darabi et al., *Sexual Activity and Childbearing among Young Hispanics in the U.S.: An Annotated Bibliography* (New York: Greenwood Press, 1987), 6–8. B. VanOss Marin and C. A. Gomez, "Latino Culture and Sex: Implications for HIV Prevention," in *Psychological Interventions and Research with Latino Populations*, ed. J. Garcia and M. Zea (Boston: Allyn and Bacon Press, 1997), 73–93. Jorge G. Garcia and Maria Cecilia Zea, *Psychological Interventions and Research with Latino Populations* (Boston: Allyn and Bacon, 1997). Gomez and VanOss Marin, "Gender, Culture, and Power." Rafael M. Díaz, "Latino Gay Men and HIV: Culture, Sexuality, and Risk Behavior," *Cultural Diversity and Ethnic Minority Psychology* 5 (1999): 292–293. Laura F. Romo et al., "A Longitudinal Study of Maternal Messages about Dating and Sexuality and Their Influence on Latino Adolescents," *Journal of Adolescent Health* 31 (2002): 59–69.

16. DeLamater and Friedrich, "Human Sexual Development."

17. William Masters, Virginia E. Johnson, and R. C. Kolodny, *Human Sexuality* (Boston: Little, Brown, 1982). F. M. Martinson, *The Sexual Life of Children* (Westport, Conn.: Begin and Garvey, 1994).

18. M. Reynolds, D. Herbenick, and J. Bancroft, "The Nature of Childhood Sexual Experience: Two Studies 50 Years Apart," in *Sexual Development in Childhood*, ed. Bancroft. J. Bancroft, D. Herbenick, and M. Reynolds, "Masturbation as a Marker of Sexual Development," in *Sexual Development in Childhood*, ed. Bancroft. J. M. Tanner, ed., "Puberty," *Advances in Reproductive Physiology*, vol. 2, ed. A. McLaren (New York: Academic Press, 1967). DeLamater and Friedrich, "Human Sexual Development." J. R. Udry, "Biological Predispositions and Social Control in Adolescent Sexual Behavior," *American Sociological Review* 53 (1988): 709–722.

19. Reynolds, Herbenick, and Bancroft, "Nature of Childhood Sexual Experience."

20. L. Fontes, *Sexual Abuse in Nine North American Cultures: Treatment and Prevention* (Thousand Oaks, Calif.: Sage Publications, 1995).

21. P. A. Hulme, "Retrospective Measurement of Childhood Sexual Abuse: A Review of Instruments," *Child Maltreatment* 9 (2004): 201–217. G. E. Wyatt and S. D. Peters, "Methodological Considerations in Research on the Prevalence of Child Sexual Abuse," *Child Abuse and Neglect* 10 (1986): 241–251.

22. Wyatt and Peters, "Prevalence of Child Sexual Abuse." G. A. Kercher and M. McShane, "The Prevalence of Child Sexual Abuse Victimization in an Adult Sample of Texas Residents," *Child Abuse and Neglect* 8 (1984): 495–501. O. Tzeng and H. Schwarzin, "Gender and Race Differences in Child Sexual Abuse Correlates," *International Journal of Intercultural Relations* 14 (1990): 135–161.

23. K. J. Lindholm and R. Willey, "Ethnic Differences in Child Abuse and Sexual Abuse," *Hispanic Journal of Behavioral Sciences* 8 (1986): 111–125. J. M. Siegel et al., "The Prevalence of Childhood Sexual Assault: The Los Angeles Epidemiologic Catchment Area Project," *American Journal of Epidemiology* 126 (1987): 1141–1153. M. C. Kenny and A. G. McEachern, "Racial, Ethnic, and Cultural Factors of Childhood Sexual Abuse: A Selected Review of the Literature," *Clinical Psychology Review* 20 (2000): 905–922.

24. D. F. Duncan, "Prevalence of Sexual Assault Victimization among Heterosexual and Gay/Lesbian University Students," *Psychological Reports* 66 (1990): 65–66. K. F. Balsam, E. D. Rothblum, T. P. Beauchaine, "Victimization over the Life Span: A Comparison of Lesbian, Gay, Bisexual, and Heterosexual Siblings," *Journal of Consulting and Clinical Psychology* 73 (2005): 477–487.

25. S. Jinich et al., "Childhood Sexual Abuse and HIV Risk-Taking Behavior among Gay and Bisexual Men," *AIDS and Behavior* 2 (1998): 41–51. J. P. Paul et al., "Understanding Childhood Sexual Abuse as a Predictor of Sexual Risk-Taking among Men Who Have Sex with Men: The Urban Men's Health Study," *Child Abuse and Neglect* 25 (2001): 557–584. A. Carballo-Dieguez and C. Dolezal, "Association between History of Childhood Sexual Abuse and Adult HIV-Risk Sexual Behavior in Puerto Rican Men Who Have Sex with Men," *Child Abuse and Neglect* 19 (1995): 595–605.

26. W. G. Watkins and A. Bentovim, "The Sexual Abuse of Male Children and Adolescents: A Review of Current Research," *Journal of Child Psychology and Psychiatry and Allied Disciplines* 33 (1992): 197–248. A. W. Baker and S. P. Duncan, "Child Sexual Abuse: A Study of Prevalence in Great Britain," *Child Abuse and Neglect* 9 (1985): 457–467. M. Schwartz, "Negative Impact of Sexual Abuse on Adult Male Gender: Issues and Strategies of Intervention," *Child and Adolescent Social Work Journal* 11 (1994): 179–194. R. M. Cunningham et al., "The Association of Physical and Sexual Abuse with HIV Risk Behaviors in Adolescence and Young Adulthood: Implications for Public Health," *Child Abuse and Neglect* 18 (1994): 233–245. P. Cameron et al., "Child Molestation and Homosexuality," *Psychological Reports* 58 (1986): 327–237. R. L. Johnson and D. K. Shrier, "Sexual Victimization of Boys: Experience at an Adolescent Medicine Clinic," *Journal of Adolescent Health Care* 6 (1985): 372–376. Carballo-Dieguez and Dolezal, "Childhood Sexual Abuse and Adult HIV-Risk." W. C. Holmes, "Association between a History of Childhood Sexual Abuse and Subsequent Adolescent Psychoactive Substance Use Disorder in a Sample of HIV Seropostive Men," *Journal of Adolescent Health* 20 (1997): 414–419. W. R. Lenderking et al., "Childhood Sexual Abuse among Homosexual Men: Prevalence and Association with Unsafe Sex," *Journal of General Internal Medicine* 12 (1997): 250–253. G. Remafedi, J. A. Farrow, and R. W. Deisher, "Risk Factors for Attempted Suicide in Gay and Bisexual Youth," *Pediatrics* 87 (1991): 869–875. Jinich et al., "Childhood Sexual Abuse." Sonya Arreola et al., "Higher Prevalence of Childhood Sexual Abuse among Latino Men Who Have Sex with Men than Non-Latino Men Who Have Sex with Men: Data from the Urban Men's Health Study," *Child Abuse and Neglect* 29 (2005): 285–290. P. A. Moisan, K. Sanders-Phillips, and P. M.

Moisan, "Ethnic Differences in Circumstances of Abuse and Symptoms of Depression and Anger among Sexually Abused Black and Latino Boys," *Child Abuse and Neglect* 21 (1997): 473–488. Lindholm and Willey, "Ethnic Differences."

27. A. Browne and D. Finkelhor, "Impact of Child Sexual Abuse: A Review of the Literature," *Psychological Bulletin* 99 (1986): 66–77. M. D. Everson et al., "Maternal Support Following Disclosure of Incest," *American Journal of Orthopsychiatry* 59 (1989): 197–207. L. Pierce and R. Pierce, "Race as a Factor in the Sexual Abuse of Children," *Social Work Research and Abstracts* 20 (1984): 9–14. K. Sanders-Phillips et al., "Ethnic Differences in Psychological Functioning among Black and Latino Sexually Abused Girls," *Child Abuse and Neglect* 19 (1995): 691–706. K. Rao, R. J. DiClemente, and L. Ponton, "Child Sexual Abuse of Asians Compared with Other Populations," *Journal of the American Academy of Child and Adolescent Psychiatry* 31 (1992): 880–886. Siegel et al., "Prevalence of Childhood Sexual Assault." L. Fontes, "Disclosures of Sexual Abuse by Puerto Rican Children: Oppression and Cultural Barriers," *Journal of Child Sexual Abuse* 2 (1993): 21–35.

28. G. J. Romero et al., "Prevalence and Circumstances of Child Sexual Abuse among Latina Women," *Hispanic Journal of Behavioral Sciences*, Special Issue: The Psychology of Latina Women, 21 (1999): 351–365. F. E. Mennen, "Sexual Abuse in Latina Girls: Their Functioning and a Comparison with White and African American Girls," *Hispanic Journal of Behavioral Sciences* 16 (1994): 475–486; and "The Relationship of Race/Ethnicity to Symptoms in Childhood Sexual Abuse," *Child Abuse and Neglect* 19 (1995): 115–124. Siegel et al., "Prevalence of Childhood Sexual Assault." Fontes, "Disclosures of Sexual Abuse."

29. Romero et al., "Child Sexual Abuse among Latina Women." D. S. Derezotes and L. R. Snowden, "Cultural Factors in the Intervention of Child Maltreatment," *Child and Adolescent Social Work Journal* 7 (1990): 161–115. Siegel et al., "Prevalence of Childhood Sexual Assault."

30. Mennen, "Sexual Abuse in Latina Girls." G. E. Wyatt, "The Sexual Abuse of Afro-American and White-American Women in Childhood," *Child Abuse and Neglect* 9 (1985): 507–519. G. E. Wyatt et al., "Sexual Abuse," in *Handbook of Women's Sexual and Reproductive Health: Issues in Women's Health*, ed. G. M. Wingood and R. J. DiClemente (New York: Kluwer Academic/Plenum, 2002), 195–216. G. E. Wyatt et al., "Does a History of Trauma Contribute to HIV Risk for Women of Color? Implications for Prevention and Policy," *American Journal of Public Health* 92 (2002): 660–665. Siegel et al., "Prevalence of Childhood Sexual Assault." Kathy Sanders-Phillips et al., "Ethnic Differences in Psychological Functioning among Black and Latino Sexually Abused Girls," *Child Abuse and Neglect* 19 (1995): 691–706. J. V. Becker and M. S. Kaplan, "Rape Victims: Issues, Theories, and Treatment," *Annual Review of Sex Research* 2 (1991): 267–292. Romero et al., "Child Sexual Abuse among Latina Women."

31. K. B. Morrow and G. T. Sorell, "Factors Affecting Self-Esteem, Depression, and Negative Behaviors in Sexually Abused Female Adolescents," *Journal of Marriage and the Family* 51 (1989): 677–686. J. Steel et al., "Psychological Sequelae of Childhood Sexual Abuse: Abuse-Related Characteristics, Coping Strategies, and Attributional Style," *Child Abuse and Neglect* 28 (2004): 785–801. Romero et al., "Child Sexual Abuse among Latina Women." J. A. Arroyo, T. L. Simpson, and A. S. Aragon, "Childhood Sexual Abuse among Hispanic and Non-Hispanic White College Women," *Hispanic Journal of Behavioral Sciences* 19 (1997): 57–68. C. Feiring, D. L. Coates, and L. S. Taska, "Ethnic Status, Stigmatization, Support, and Symptoms Development Following Sexual Abuse," *Journal of Interpersonal Violence* 16 (2001): 1307–1329. D. S. Katerndahl et al., "Differences in Childhood Sexual Abuse Experience between Adult Hispanic and

Anglo Women in a Primary Care Setting," *Journal of Child Sexual Abuse* 14 (2005): 85–95. Arreola et al., "Higher Prevalence of Childhood Sexual Abuse." Mennen, "Sexual Abuse in Latina Girls." G. E. Wyatt, "The Aftermath of Child Sexual Abuse of African American and White American Women: The Victim's Experience," *Journal of Family Violence* 5 (1990): 61–81.

32. W. C. Holmes and G. B. Slap, "Sexual Abuse of Boys: Definition, Prevalence, Correlates, Sequelae, and Management," *Journal of the American Medical Association* 280 (1998): 1855–1862.

33. C. Cinq-Mars et al., "Sexual At-Risk Behaviors of Sexually Abused Adolescent Girls," *Journal of Child Sexual Abuse* 12 (2003): 1–18. Jinich et al., "Childhood Sexual Abuse." Carballo-Dieguez and Dolezal, "Childhood Sexual Abuse and Adult HIV-Risk." L. Nieves-Rosa, A. Carballo-Diéguez, and C. Dolezal, "Domestic Abuse and HIV-Risk Behavior in Latin American Men Who Have Sex with Men in New York City," *Journal of Lesbian and Gay Social Services* 11 (2001): 77–90. L. J. Koenig et al., eds., *From Child Sexual Abuse to Adult Sexual Risk: Trauma, Revictimization, and Intervention* (Washington, D.C.: American Psychological Association, 2004).

34. D. A. Neumann et al., "The Long-Term Sequelae of Childhood Sexual Abuse in Women: A Meta-Analytic Review," *Child Maltreatment: Journal of the American Professional Society on the Abuse of Children* 1 (1996): 6–16. R. T. Mulder et al., "Relationship between Dissociation, Childhood Sexual Abuse, Childhood Physical Abuse, and Mental Illness in a General Population Sample," *American Journal of Psychiatry* 155 (1998): 806–811. L. Briggs and P. R. Joyce, "What Determines Post-Traumatic Stress Disorder Symptomatology for Survivors of Childhood Sexual Abuse?" *Child Abuse and Neglect* 21 (1997): 575–582. J. A. Chu, "Psychological Defense Styles and Childhood Sexual Abuse," *American Journal of Psychiatry* 157 (2000): 1707. D. M. Johnson, J. L. Pike, and K. M. Chard, "Factors Predicting PTSD, Depression, and Dissociative Severity in Female Treatment-Seeking Childhood Sexual Abuse Survivors," *Child Abuse and Neglect* 25 (2001): 179–198. E. J. Ozer et al., "Predictors of Post-Traumatic Stress Disorder and Symptoms in Adults: A Meta-Analysis," *Psychological Bulletin* 129 (2003): 52–73.

35. Alan Guttmacher Institute, *Sex and America's Teenagers* (New York, 1994). Alan Guttmacher Institute, "U.S. Teen Pregnancy Statistics: National and State Trends and Trends by Race and Ethnicity," September 2006, http://www.guttmacher.org/pubs/2006/09/12/USTPstats.pdf. S. K. Henshaw, "Unintended Pregnancy in the United States," *Family Planning Perspectives* 30 (1998): 24–29, 46.

36. Hulme, "Retrospective Measurement of Childhood Sexual Abuse." M. Roosa et al., "Measurement of Women's Child Sexual Abuse Experiences: An Empirical Demonstration of the Impact of Choice of Measure on Estimates of Incidence Rates and of Relationships with Pathology," *Journal of Sex Research* 35 (1998): 225–233. K. A. Moore et al., *Adolescent Sex, Contraception, and Childbearing: A Review of Recent Research* (Washington, D.C.: Child Trends, 1995). J. S. Santelli et al., "The Association of Sexual Behaviors with Socioeconomic Status, Family Structure, and Race/Ethnicity among U.S. Adolescents," *American Journal of Public Health* 90 (2000): 1582–1588.

37. J. A. Martin, M. M. Park, and P. D. Sutton, "Births: Preliminary Data for 2001," *National Vital Statistics Report* 50 (2002): 1–20. K. Pittman and G. Adams, *Teenage Pregnancy: An Advocate's Guide to the Numbers* (Washington, D.C.: Children's Defense Fund, 1988). Centers for Disease Control and Prevention, "Youth Risk Behavior Surveillance—United States, 1999" (Atlanta, 2000). J. S. Santelli et al., "Adolescent Sexual Behavior: Estimates and Trends from Four Nationally Representative Surveys," *Family Planning Perspectives* 32 (2000): 156–165, 194.

38. S. J. Ventura et al., "Trends in Pregnancies and Pregnancy Rates by Outcome: Estimates for the United States, 1976–96," *Vital Health Statistics* 21 (2000): 1–47. C. Brindis et al., "The Associations between Immigrant Status and Risk-Behavior Patterns in Latino Adolescents," *Journal of Adolescent Health* 17 (1995): 99–105.

39. H. Balcazar, G. Peterson, and J. A. Cobas, "Acculturation and Health-Related Risk Behaviors among Mexican-American Pregnant Youth," *American Journal of Health Behavior* 20 (1996): 425–433. J. A. Epstein, G. J. Botvin, and T. Diaz, "Linguistic Acculturation and Gender Effects on Smoking among Hispanic Youth," *Preventive Medicine: An International Journal Devoted to Practice and Theory* 27 (1998): 583–589. A. G. Gil, E. F. Wagner, and W. A. Vega, "Acculturation, Familism, and Alcohol Use among Latino Adolescent Males: Longitudinal Relations," *Journal of Community Psychology* 28 (2000): 443–458. C. S. Aneshensel et al., "Onset of Fertility-Related Events during Adolescence: A Prospective Comparison of Mexican American and Non-Hispanic White Females," *American Journal of Public Health* 80 (1990): 959–963. C. S. Aneshensel, E. P. Fielder, and R. M. Becerra, "Fertility and Fertility-Related Behavior among Mexican-American and Non-Hispanic White Female Adolescents," *Journal of Health and Social Behavior* 30 (1989): 56–76. B. VanOss Marin, C. A. Gomez, and N. Hearst, "Multiple Heterosexual Partners and Condom Use among Hispanics and Non-Hispanic Whites," *Family Planning Perspectives* 25 (1993): 170–174. B. VanOss Marin et al., "Acculturation and Gender Differences in Sexual Attitudes and Behaviors: Hispanic vs. Non-Hispanic White Unmarried Adults," *American Journal of Public Health* 83 (1993): 1759–1761.

40. Centers for Disease Control and Prevention, "Youth Risk Behavior Surveillance—United States, 1999" (Atlanta, 2000). T. R. Raine et al., "Sociodemographic Correlates of Virginity in Seventh-Grade Black and Latino Students," *Journal of Adolescent Health* 24 (1999): 304–312. D. M. Upchurch et al., "Gender and Ethnic Differences in the Timing of First Sexual Intercourse," *Family Planning Perspectives* 30 (1998): 121–127. J. W. Gibson and J. Kempf, "Attitudinal Predictors of Sexual Activity in Hispanic Adolescent Females," *Journal of Adolescent Research* 5 (1990): 414–430.

41. P. I. Erickson, "Cultural Factors Affecting the Negotiation of First Sexual Intercourse among Latina Adolescent Mothers," *International Quarterly of Community Health Education* 18 (1998): 121–137.

42. C. P. Kaplan, P. I. Erickson, and M. A. Juarez-Reyes, "Acculturation, Gender Role Orientation, and Reproductive Risk-Taking Behavior among Latina Adolescent Family Planning Clients," *Journal of Adolescent Research* 17 (2002): 103–121.

43. B. VanOss Marin et al., "Older Boyfriends and Girlfriends Increase Risk of Sexual Initiation in Young Adolescents," *Journal of Adolescent Health* 27 (2000): 409–418. R. L. Paikoff et al., "Parenting, Parent-Child Relationships, and Sexual Possibility Situations among Urban African American Preadolescents: Preliminary Findings and Implications for HIV Prevention," *Journal of Family Psychology* 1 (1997): 11–22. A. L. Coker et al., "Correlates and Consequences of Early Initiation of Sexual Intercourse," *Journal of School Health* 64 (1994): 372–377.

44. S. C. Carvajal et al., "Psychosocial Predictors of Delay of First Sexual Intercourse by Adolescents," *Health Psychology* 18 (1999): 443–452.

45. M. Fishbein and I. Ajzen, *Belief, Attitude, Intention, and Behavior: An Introduction to Theory and Research* (Reading, Mass.: Addison-Wesley, 1975). I. Ajzen, *Attitudes, Personality, and Behavior* (Chicago: Dorsey Press, 1988). Albert Bandura, *Social Foundations of Thought and Action: A Social Cognitive Theory* (Englewood Cliffs, N.J.: Prentice-Hall, 1986), and *Self-Efficacy: The Exercise of Control* (New York: W. H. Freeman, 1997).

46. Icek Ajzen, "The Theory of Planned Behavior," *Organizational Behavior and Human Decision Processes* 50 (1991): 179–211. Bandura, *Self-Efficacy.* Fishbein and Ajzen, *Belief, Attitude, Intention, and Behavior.* Bandura, *Social Foundations of Thought and Action.* D. Flannery, D. Rowe, and B. Gulley, "Impact of Pubertal Status, Timing, and Age on Adolescent Sexual Experience and Delinquency," *Journal of Adolescent Research* 8 (1993): 21–40. E. A. Smith, J. R. Udry, and N. M. Morris, "Pubertal Development and Friends: A Biosocial Explanation of Adolescent Sexual Behavior," *Journal of Health and Social Behavior* 26 (1985): 183–192. L. B. Whitbeck, R. L. Simmons, and M. Kao, "The Effects of Divorced Mothers' Dating Behaviors and Sexual Attitudes on the Sexual Attitudes and Behaviors of Their Adolescent Children," *Journal of Marriage and Family* 56 (1994): 615–621. C. T. Halpern et al., "Testosterone and Pubertal Development as Predictors of Sexual Activity: A Panel Analysis of Adolescent Males," *Psychosomatic Medicine* 55 (1993): 436–447.

47. C. T. Pedlow and M. P. Carey, "Developmentally Appropriate Sexual Risk Reduction Interventions for Adolescents: Rationale, Review of Interventions, and Recommendations for Research and Practice," *Annals of Behavioral Medicine* 27 (2004): 172–184.

48. T. G. M. Sandfort and J. Rademakers, *Childhood Sexuality: Normal Sexual Behavior and Development* (Binghamton, N.Y.: Haworth Press, 2000), 136.

CHAPTER 4   LATINA/O PARENT-ADOLESCENT
COMMUNICATION ABOUT SEXUALITY

Acknowledgments: Funding for this essay was provided in part by a William T. Grant Scholar's award to Dr. Romo.

1. B. E. Hamilton et al., "Births: Preliminary Data for 2004," *National Vital Statistics Reports* 54 (2005): 1–18.

2. R. Dutra, K. S. Miller, and R. Forehand, "The Process and Content of Sexual Communication with Adolescents in Two-Parent Families: Associations with Sexual Risk-Taking Behavior," *AIDS and Behavior* 3 (1999): 59–66. M. Hovell et al., "Family Influences on Latino and Anglo Adolescents' Sexual Behavior," *Journal of Marriage and the Family* 56 (1994): 973–986. M. K. Hutchinson et al., "The Role of Mother-Daughter Sexual Risk Communication in Reducing Sexual Risk Behaviors among Urban Adolescent Females: A Prospective Study," *Journal of Adolescent Health* 33 (2003): 98–107. K. S. Miller and D. J. Whitaker, "Predictors of Mother-Adolescent Discussions about Condoms: Implications for Providers Who Serve Youth," *Pediatrics* 108 (2001): 1–7. E. Terry and J. Manlove, "Trends in Sexual Activity and Contraceptive Use among Teens," *Child Trends Research Brief,* http://www.childtrends.org/Files//Child_Trends-2000_01_01_RB_Teentrends.pdf. P. East et al., "Positive Adolescent Sexuality as Evident in Consistent and Reliable Contraceptive Use: A Study of Sexually Active Latino and Non-Latino Youths' Contraceptive Behavior," *Sexuality Research and Social Policy: Journal of NSRC* 2 (2005): 42–53.

3. J. Brooks-Gunn and R. L. Paikoff, "'Sex Is a Gamble, Kissing Is a Game': Adolescent Sexuality and Health Promotion," in *Promoting the Health of Adolescents: New Directions for the Twenty-First Century,* ed. S. G. Millstein, A. C. Petersen, and E. O. Nightingale (New York: Oxford University Press, 1993), 180–208. L. Steinberg, *Adolescence,* 7th ed. (New York: Oxford University Press, 2005). D. L.Tolman, M. I. Striepe, and T. Harmon, "Gender Matters: Constructing a Model of Adolescent Sexual Health," *Journal of Sex Research, Special Issue: Gender and Sexuality* 40 (2003): 4–12.

4. B. L. Guzmán, E. Arruda, and A. L. Feria, "Los Papas, la Familia y la Sexualidad," in *Latina Girls: Voices of Adolescent Strength in the United States,* ed. J. Denner, and B. L. Guzmán

(New York: New York University Press, 2006), 29–43. M. K. Hutchinson, "The Influence of Sexual Risk Communication between Parents and Daughters on Sexual Risk Behaviors," *Family Relations: Interdisciplinary Journal of Applied Family Studies* 51 (2002): 238–247. L. Pick and P. Palos, "Impact of the Family on the Sex Lives of Adolescents," *Adolescence* 30 (1995): 667–675. M. Raffaelli and S. Green, "Parent-Adolescent Communication about Sex: Retrospective Reports by Latino College Students," *Journal of Marriage and the Family* 65 (2003): 474–481.

5. Dutra, Miller, and Forehand, "Process and Content of Sexual Communication."

6. R. M. Becerra and D. de Anda, "Pregnancy and Motherhood among Mexican American Adolescents," *Health and Social Work* 9 (1984): 106–123. L. H. Zayas and F. Solari, "Early Childhood Socialization in Hispanic Families: Context, Culture, and Practice Implications," *Professional Psychology: Research and Practice* 25 (1994): 200–206.

7. R. R. Ramirez, G. P. de la Cruz, and U.S. Bureau of the Census, *The Hispanic Population in the United States: March 2002* (Washington, D.C.: U.S. Department of Commerce, 2003).

8. L. Meneses et al., "Racial/Ethnic Differences in Mother-Daughter Communication about Sex," *Journal of Adolescent Health* 39 (2006): 128–131.

9. B. VanOss Marin, "HIV Prevention in the Hispanic Community: Sex, Culture, and Empowerment," *Journal of Transcultural Nursing* 14 (2003): 186–192. B. VanOss Marin and C. A. Gomez, "Latino Culture and Sex: Implications for HIV Prevention," in *Psychological Interventions and Research with Latino Populations*, ed. J. Garcia and M. Zea (Boston: Allyn and Bacon Press, 1997), 73–93.

10. L. F. O'Sullivan, H. F. L. Meyer-Bahlburg, and B. X. Watkins, "Mother-Daughter Communication about Sex among Urban African American and Latino Families," *Journal of Adolescent Research* 16 (2001): 269–292.

11. O'Sullivan, Meyer-Bahlburg, and Watkins, "Mother-Daughter Communication about Sex."

12. Guzmán, Arruda, and Feria, "Los Papas, la Familia y la Sexualidad."

13. O'Sullivan, Meyer-Bahlburg, and Watkins, "Mother-Daughter Communication about Sex."

14. V. Guilamo-Ramos et al., "Parental Expertise, Trustworthiness, and Accessibility: Parent-Adolescent Communication and Adolescent Risk Behavior," *Journal of Marriage and the Family* 68 (2006): 1229–1246.

15. K. S. Miller and D. J Whitaker, "Predictors of Mother-Adolescent Discussions about Condoms: Implications for Providers Who Serve Youth," *Pediatrics* 108 (2001). Laura F. Romo et al., "Determinants of Mother-Adolescent Communication about Sex in Latino Families," *Adolescent and Family Health* 2 (2001): 72–82.

16. M. D. McKee and A. Karasz, "'You have to give her that confidence': Conversations about Sex in Hispanic Mother-Daughter Dyads," *Journal of Adolescent Research* 21 (2006): 158–184.

17. K. S. Miller, R. Forehand, and B. A. Kotchick, "Adolescent Sexual Behavior in Two Ethnic Minority Samples: The Role of Family Variables," *Journal of Marriage and the Family* 61 (1999): 85–98. M. C. Vélez-Pastrana, R. A. González-Rodríguez, and A. Borges-Hernández, "Family Functioning and Early Onset of Sexual Intercourse in Latino Adolescents," *Adolescence* 40 (2005): 777–791.

18. Guilamo-Ramos et al., "Parental Expertise, Trustworthiness, and Accessibility." McKee and Karasz, "You have to give her that confidence."

19. Dutra, Miller, and Forehand, "Process and Content of Sexual Communication." Hutchinson et al., "Mother-Daughter Sexual Risk Communication." East et al., "Positive Adolescent Sexuality."

20. C. Adolph et al., "Pregnancy among Hispanic Teenagers: Is Good Parental Communication a Deterrent?" *Contraception* 51 (1995): 303–306. L. M. Baumeister, E. Flores, and B. VanOss Marin, "Sex Information Given to Latina Adolescents by Parents," *Health Education Research* 10 (1995): 233–239.

21. Dutra, Miller, and Forehand, "Process and Content of Sexual Communication."

22. B. L. Halpern-Felsher et al., "Adolescents' Self-Efficacy to Communicate about Sex: Its Role in Condom Attitudes, Commitment, and Use," *Adolescence* 39 (2004): 443–456.

23. R. Ancheta, C. Hynes, and L. A. Shrier, "Reproductive Health Education and Sexual Risk Taking among High Risk Female Adolescents and Young Adults," *Journal of Pediatric and Adolescent Gynecology* 18 (2005): 105–111. Baumeister, Flores, and Marin, "Sex Information Given to Latina Adolescents." M. E. Cruz, Claudia Kouyoumdjian, and Laura Romo, "College Women's Retrospective Accounts of Communication with Their Immigrant and U.S.-Born Asian and Latina Mothers about Sexual Health Topics," poster presented at Society for Prevention Research, San Antonio, 2006. Dutra, Miller, and Forehand, "Process and Content of Sexual Communication." Hutchinson et al., "Mother-Daughter Sexual Risk Communication." Marcella Raffaelli and Lenna L. Ontai, "'She's 16 years old and there's boys calling over to the house': An Exploratory Study of Sexual Socialization in Latino Families," *Culture, Health, and Sexuality* 3 (2001): 295–310. Raffaelli and Green, "Parent-Adolescent Communication about Sex."

24. O'Sullivan, Meyer-Bahlburg, and Watkins, "Mother-Daughter Communication about Sex." Patricia Zavella, "Talkin' Sex: Chicanas and Mexicanas Theorize about Silences and Sexual Pleasures," in *Chicana Feminisms: A Critical Reader*, ed. Gabriela Arredondo, Aida Hurtado, Norma Klahn, and Olga Nájera-Ramírez (Durham: Duke University Press, 2003). Olivia M. Espín, *Women Crossing Boundaries: A Psychology of Immigration and Transformations of Sexuality* (New York: Routledge Press, 1999). A. M. Villarruel, " Cultural Influences on the Ssexual Attitudes, Beliefs, and Norms of Young Latina Adolescents," *Journal of the Society of Pediatric Nurses* (1998): 69–79. Raffaelli and Ontai, "She's 16 years old." Espín, *Women Crossing Boundaries*.

25. Villarruel, "Cultural Influences."

26 . A. E. Norris and K. Ford, "Beliefs about Condoms and Accessibility of Condom Intentions in Hispanic and African American Youth," *Hispanic Journal of Behavioral Sciences* 14 (1992): 373–382. A. M. Padilla and T. L. Baird, "Mexican-American Adolescent Sexuality and Sexual Knowledge: An Exploratory Study," *Hispanic Journal of Behavioral Sciences* 13 (1991): 95–104.

27. Erum Nadeem, Laura Romo, and Marian Sigman, "Knowledge about Condoms among Low-Income Pregnant Latina Adolescents in Relation to Explicit Maternal Discussion of Contraceptives," *Journal of Adolescent Health* 39 (2006): 9–15.

28. Raffaelli and Green, "Parent-Adolescent Communication about Sex." Laura Romo et al., "A Longitudinal Study of Maternal Messages about Dating and Sexuality and Their Influence on Latino Adolescents," *Journal of Adolescent Health* 31 (2002): 59–69.

29. Guilamo-Ramos et al., "Parental Expertise, Trustworthiness, and Accessibility." Guzmán, Arruda, and Feria, "Los papas, la familia y la sexualidad." Villarruel, "Cultural Influences."

30. Guilamo-Ramos et al., "Content and Process of Mother-Adolescent Communication."

31. Zavella, "Talkin' Sex." Gloria González-López, *Erotic Journeys: Mexican Immigrants and Their Sex Lives* (Berkeley: University of California Press, 2005).

32. Hovell et al., "Family Influences on Adolescents' Sexual Behavior." N. K. Rucibwa et al., "Exploring Family Factors and Sexual Behaviors in a Group of Black and Hispanic Adolescent Males," *American Journal of Health Behavior* 27 (2003): 63–74.

33. B. Kotchick, K. Miller, and R. Forehand, "Adolescent Sexual Risk Taking in Single Parent Ethnic Minority Families," *Journal of Family Psychology* 13 (1999): 93–102. S. W. Liebowitz, D. C. Castellano, and I. Cuellar, "Factors That Predict Sexual Behaviors among Young Mexican American Adolescents: An Exploratory Study," *Hispanic Journal of Behavioral Sciences* 21 (1999): 470–479.

34. A. M. Villarruel et al., "Predictors of Sexual Intercourse and Condom Use Intentions among Spanish-Dominant Latino Youth: A Test of the Planned Behavior Theory," *Nursing Research* 53 (2004): 172–181.

35. M. L. Gilliam et al., "Interpersonal and Personal Factors Influencing Sexual Debut among Mexican-American Young Women in the United States," *Journal of Adolescent Health* 41 (2007): 495–503.

36. A. M. Teitelman, S. J. Ratcliffe, and J. A. Cedarman, "Parent-Adolescent Communication about Sexual Pressure, Maternal Norms about Relationship Power, and STI/HIV Protective Behaviors of Minority Urban Girls," *Journal of American Psychiatry Nurses Association* 14 (2008): 50–60.

37. Romo et al., "Maternal Messages about Dating and Sexuality."

38. F. S. Christopher, D. C. Johnson, and M. W. Roosa, "Family, Individual, and Social Correlates of Early Hispanic Adolescent Sexual Expression," *Journal of Sex Research* 30 (1993): 54–61. A. M. Fasula and K. S. Miller, "African-American and Hispanic Adolescents' Intentions to Delay First Intercourse: Parental Communication as a Buffer for Sexually Active Peers," *Journal of Adolescent Health* 38 (2006): 193–200.

39. M. Hyams, "*La Escuela*: Young Latina Women Negotiating Identities in School," in *Latina Girls*, ed. Denner and Guzmán. Guilamo-Ramos et al., "Parental Expertise, Trustworthiness, and Accessibility." McKee and Karasz, "You have to give her that confidence." O'Sullivan, Meyer-Bahlburg, and Watkins, "Mother-Daughter Communication about Sex."

40. Laura Romo et al., "Promoting Values of Education in Latino Mother-Adolescent Discussions about Conflict and Sexuality," in *Latina Girls*, ed. Denner and Guzmán.

41. A. Gallegos-Castillo, "La Casa: Negotiating Family Cultural Practices, Constructing Identities," in *Latina Girls*, ed. Denner and Guzmán. Aida Hurtado, *Voicing Chicana Feminisms: Young Women Speak Out on Sexuality and Identity* (New York: New York University Press, 2003). J. Ayala, "*Confianza, Consejos,* and Contradictions: Gender and Sexuality Lessons between Latina Adolescent Daughters and Mothers," in *Latina Girls*, ed. Denner and Guzmán.

42. Villarruel, "Cultural Influences."

43. O'Sullivan, Meyer-Bahlburg, and Watkins, "Mother-Daughter Communication about Sex."

44. Y. G. Flores-Ortiz, *Theorizing Justice in Chicano Families*, JSRI Occasional Paper no. 43, Latino Studies series (East Lansing: Michigan State University, 2000).

45. M. L. Gilliam et al., " Interpersonal and Personal Factors Influencing Sexual Debut among Mexican-American Young women in the United States," *Journal of Adolescent Health* 40 (2007): 495–503.

46. Liebowitz, Castellano, and Cuellar, "Factors That Predict Sexual Behaviors." Baumeister, Flores, and Marin, "Sex Information Given to Latina Adolescents."

47. A. M. Villarruel et al., "Predictors of Sexual Intercourse and Condom Use Intentions among Spanish-Dominant Latino Youth: A Test of the Planned Behavior Theory," *Nursing Research* 53 (2004): 172–181.

48. East et al., "Positive Adolescent Sexuality." J. B. Unger, G. B. Molina, and L. Teran, "Perceived Consequences of Teenage Childbearing among Adolescent Girls in an Urban Sample," *Journal of Adolescent Health* 26 (2000): 205–212.

49. O'Sullivan, Meyer-Bahlburg, and Watkins, "Mother-Daughter Communication about Sex."

50. McKee and Karasz, "You have to give her that confidence." Raffaelli and Ontai, "She's 16 years old." Espín, *Women Crossing Boundaries.*

51. Espín, *Women Crossing Boundaries*

52. McKee and Karasz, "You have to give her that confidence."

53. Guilamo-Ramos et al., "Parental Expertise, Trustworthiness, and Accessibility."

54. Romo et al., "Maternal Messages about Dating and Sexuality."

55. O'Sullivan, Meyer-Bahlburg, and Watkins, "Mother-Daughter Communication about Sex." Laura Romo et al., "Mexican-American Adolescents' Responsiveness to Their Mothers' Questions about Dating and Sexuality," *Journal of Applied Developmental Psychology* 25 (2004): 501–522.

56. M. Kerr et al., "Family Involvement, Problem and Prosocial Behavior Outcomes of Latino Youth," *American Journal of Health Behavior* 27 (2003, supplement): 55–65.

57. E. A. Borawski et al., "Parental Monitoring, Negotiated Unsupervised Time, and Parental Trust: The Role of Perceived Parenting Practices in Adolescent Health Risk Behaviors," *Journal of Adolescent Health* 33 (2003): 60–70.

58. Vélez-Pastrana, González-Rodríguez, and Borges-Hernández, "Early Onset of Sexual Intercourse."

59. McKee and Karasz, "You have to give her that confidence." Raffaelli and Ontai, "She's 16 years old." Romo et al., "Mexican-American Adolescents' Responsiveness." Villarruel, "Cultural Influences."

60. Hovell et al., "Family Influences on Adolescents' Sexual Behavior." Borawski et al., "Parental Monitoring and Parental Trust."

61. M. Raffaelli and L. L. Ontai, "Gender Socialization in Latino/a Families: Results from Two Retrospective Studies," *Sex Roles* 50 (2004): 287–299. Ayala, "*Confianza, Consejos,* and Contradictions." Gallegos-Castillo, "La Casa."

62. McKee and Karasz, "You have to give her that confidence." Guilamo-Ramos et al., "Parental Expertise, Trustworthiness, and Accessibility."

63. Ayala, "*Confianza, Consejos,* and Contradictions." Gallegos-Castillo, "La Casa."

64. Hovell et al., "Family Influences on Adolescents' Sexual Behavior."

65. Villarruel, "Cultural Influences."

66. Romo et al., "Mexican-American Adolescents' Responsiveness."

67. T. Leventhal and J. Brooks-Gunn, "The Neighborhoods They Live In: The Effects of Neighborhood Residence on Child and Adolescent Outcomes," *Psychological Bulletin* 126 (2000): 309–337.

68. M. C. LaSala, "Parental Influence, Gay Youths, and Safer Sex," *Health and Social Work* 32 (2007): 49–55.

69. M. J. Rotheram-Borus, J. Hunter, and M. Rosario, "Suicidal Behavior and Gay-Related Stress among Gay and Bisexual Male Adolescents," *Journal of Adolescent Research* 9 (1994): 498–508.

70. M. E. Eisenberg and M. D. Resnick, "Suicidality among Gay, Lesbian, and Bisexual Youth: The Role of Protective Factors," *Journal of Adolescent Health* 39 (2006): 662–668. A. R. D'Augelli and S. L. Hershberger, "Lesbian, Gay, and Bisexual Youth in Community Settings: Personal Challenges and Mental Health Problems," *American Journal of Community Psychology* 21 (1994): 421–448.

71. Zavella, "Playing with Fire." B. S. Newman and P. G. Muzzonigro, "The Effects of Traditional Family Values on the Coming Out Process of Gay Male Adolescents," *Adolescence* 28 (1992): 213–226.

72. Newman and Muzzonigro, "Effects of Traditional Family Values."

73. Héctor Carrillo, *The Night Is Young: Sexuality in Mexico in the Times of AIDS* (Chicago: University of Chicago Press, 2002). M. C. LaSala, "Lesbians, Gay Men, and Their Parents: Family Therapy for the Coming-Out Crisis," *Family Process* 39 (2000): 67–81.

74. Hurtado, *Voicing Chicana Feminisms.*

75. LaSala, "Lesbians, Gay Men, and Their Parents."

76. Carrillo, *The Night Is Young.* Espín, *Women Crossing Boundaries.* Zavella, "Playing with Fire." Hurtado, *Voicing Chicana Feminisms.*

77. Carrillo, *The Night Is Young*

78. Hurtado, *Voicing Chicana Feminisms.*

79. Quote by Latina mother (Migdalia Santiago) is from Parents, Families and Friends of Lesbians and Gays Organization (PFLAG), "From My Perspective," http://community.pflag.org/Page.aspx?pid=468.

80. Quotation from *De Colores—Lesbian and Gay Latinos: Stories of Strength, Family, and Love,* documentary film (San Francisco: EyeBite Productions, 2001): D. Mosbacher, executive producer; P. Barbosa, producer/director; and G. Lenoir, director.

81. Rafael M. Díaz, *Latino Gay Men and HIV: Culture Sexuality and Risk Behavior* (New York: Routledge, 1998).

82. D'Augelli and Hershberger, "Lesbian, Gay, and Bisexual Youth." R. Garofalo, B. Mustanski, and G. Donenberg, "Parents Know and Parents Matter: Is It Time to Develop Family-Based HIV Prevention Programs for Young Men Who Have Sex with Men?" *Journal of Adolescent Health* 43 (2008): 201–204.

83. Carrillo, *The Night Is Young.*

84. Adolph et al., "Pregnancy among Hispanic Teenagers." Baumeister, Flores, and Marin, "Sex Information Given to Latina Adolescents."

85. J. M. Contreras et al., *A Conceptual Model of the Determinants of Parenting among Latina Adolescent Mothers* (Westport, Conn.: Greenwood, 2002). Nadeem, Romo, and Sigman, "Knowledge about Condoms among Latina Adolescents." Erum Nadeem and Laura Romo, "Low-Income Latina Mothers' Expectations for their Daughters' Autonomy and Interdependence," *Journal of Research on Adolescence* 18 (2008): 215–238.

86. M. B. Adams et al., "Acculturation as a Predictor of the Onset of Sexual Intercourse among Hispanic and White Teens," *Archives of Pediatric and Adolescent Medicine* 159 (2005): 261–265. Gilliam et al., "Factors Influencing Sexual Debut." V. Guilamo-Ramos et al., "Acculturation-Related Variables, Sexual Initiation, and Subsequent Sexual Behavior among Puerto Rican, Mexican, and Cuban Youth," *Health Psychology* 24 (2005): 88–95.

87. Raffaelli and Ontai, "She's 16 years old."

CHAPTER 5　　SEXUAL HEALTH OF LATINA/O
POPULATIONS IN THE UNITED STATES

Acknowledgments: The authors wish to thank Mariana Gerena for her assistance with earlier drafts of this manuscript.

1. U.S. Bureau of the Census, "2000 Census of Population, Public Law 94–171 Redistricting Data File" (updated every ten years), http://factfinder.census.gov.

2. World Health Organization, "Defining Sexual Health: Report of a Technical Consultation on Sexual Health, 28–31 January 2002," Sexual Health Document series, Special Programme of Research, Development and Research Training in Human Reproduction (Geneva, 2006); quotation on 5.

3. A. Giami, "Sexual Health: The Emergence, Development, and Diversity of a Concept," *Annual Review of Sex Research* 13 (2002): 1–35. *The Surgeon General's Call to Action to Promote Sexual Health and Responsible Sexual Behavior,* ed. Eli Coleman, Janet Shibley, and Michael W. Ross (Washington, D.C.: U.S. Department of Health and Human Services, Office of the Surgeon General, 2001), 1–29.

4. Hortensia Amaro et al., "Cultural Influences on Women's Sexual Health," in *Women's Sexual and Reproductive Health: Social, Psychological and Public Health Perspectives,* ed. R. J. DiClemente and G. M. Wingood (New York: Plenum, 2001), 71–92. H. Amaro, A. Raj, and E. Reed, "Women's Sexual Health: The Need for Feminist Analyses in Public Health in the Decade of Behavior," *Psychology of Women Quarterly* 25 (2001): 324–334. Centers for Disease Control and Prevention, "STD Surveillance, 2005: National Profile," http://www.cdc.gov/std/stats/toc2005.htm. A. A. Adimora and V. J. Schoenbach, "Social Context, Sexual Networks, and Racial Disparities in Rates of Sexually Transmitted Infections," *Social Context and Sexual Networks* 191 (2005): 115–122.

5. G. Herdt, "Sexual Development, Social Oppression, and Local Culture," *Sexuality Research and Social Policy* 1 (2004): 39–62. A. M. Gonzales and G. Rolison, "Social Oppression and Attitudes toward Sexual Practices," *Journal of Black Studies* 35 (2005): 715–729.

6. Amaro et al., "Cultural Influences on Women's Sexual Health." Amaro, Raj, and Reed, "Women's Sexual Health."

7. Herdt, "Sexual Development, Social Oppression, Local Culture."

8. J. Zenilman, "Ethnicity and Sexually Transmitted Infections: A Review Article," *Sexually Transmitted Diseases* 11 (1999): 47–52. Adimora and Schoenbach, "Rates of Sexually Transmitted Infections." Centers for Disease Control and Prevention, "Sexually Transmitted Disease Surveillance 2005: National Profile" (Atlanta: U.S. Department of Health and Human Services, November 2006), 1–44.

9. D. Wulf, "In Their Own Right: Addressing the Sexual and Reproductive Health Needs of American Men" (New York: Alan Guttmacher Institute, 2002), 88.

10. Ibid. Nancy Hendrix, Suneet Chauhan, and John Morrison, "Sterilization and Its Consequences," *Obstetrical and Gynecological Survey* 54, no. 12 (1999): 766.

11. P. M. Harrison and A. Beck, "Prisoners in 2005," http://www.ojp.usdoj.gov/bjs/pubalp2.htm#Prisoners (November 2006). P. M. Harrison and A. Beck, "Prisoner and Jail Inmates at Midyear, 2005," http://www.ojp.usdoj.gov/bjs/pubalp2.htm#Prisoners (May 2006). U.S. Bureau of the Census, "Census Bureau Releases Population Estimates by Race, Hispanic Origin, and Age for States and Counties," *News,* August 4, 2006, http://www.census.gov/Press-Release/www/releases/archives/population/. Wulf, "In Their Own Right." Adimora and Schoenbach, "Rates of Sexually Transmitted Infections."

12. Agency for Healthcare Research and Quality, "National Healthcare Disparities Report [NHDR], 2006" (Rockville, Md.), http://www. ahrq.gov/qual/nhdr06/nhdr06.htm. N. Krieger, "Discrimination and Health," in *Social Epidemiology*, ed. L. Berkman and I. Kawachi (New York: Oxford University Press, 2000), 36–75. Adimora and Schoenbach, "Rates of Sexually Transmitted Infections."

13. Centers for Disease Control and Prevention, "Youth Risk Behavior Surveillance—United States, 2007: Surveillance Summaries," *Morbidity and Mortality Weekly Report* (June 6, 2008): 57 (No. SS-4).

14. Ibid.

15. Centers for Disease Control and Prevention, "Proportion of AIDS Cases and Population among Young Adults13 to 19 Years of Age, by Race/Ethnicity Diagnosed in 2006—33 States," slide 1 in *HIV/AIDS Surveillance in Adolescents and Young Adults (through 2006)*, http://www.cdc.gov/hiv/topics/surveillance/resources/slides/adolescents/index.htm. B. E. Hamilton et al., "Preliminary Births for 2004: National Center for Health Statistics" (Hyattsville, Md., 2004), http://www.cdc.gov/nchs/products/pubs/pubd/hestats/ prelim_births/prelim_births04.htm. B. E. Hamilton et al., "Births: Preliminary Data for 2005," released November 21, 2006, http://www.cdc.gov/nchs/data/hestat/prelim-births05_tables.pdf.

16. G. N. Holmbeck et al., "Cognitive Development, Egocentrism, Self-Esteem, and Adolescent Contraceptive Knowledge, Attitudes, and Behavior," *Journal of Youth and Adolescence* 23 (1994): 169–193. J. M. Zweig, S. D. Phillips, and L. D. Lindberg, "Predicting Adolescent Profiles of Risk: Looking Beyond Demographics," *Journal of Adolescent Health* 31 (2002): 343–353. A. K. Driscoll et al., "Adolescent Latino Reproductive Health: A Review of the Literature," Special Issue: Adolescent Reproductive Health, *Hispanic Journal of Behavioral Sciences* 23 (2001): 255–326. A. M. Gloria, J. Castellanos, and V. Orozco, "Perceived Educational Barriers, Cultural Fit, Coping Responses, and Psychological Well-Being of Latina Undergraduates," *Hispanic Journal of Behavioral Sciences* 27 (2005): 161–183. S. Valentine, "Self-Esteem, Cultural Identity, and Generation Status as Determinants of Hispanic Acculturation," *Hispanic Journal of Behavioral Sciences* 23 (2001): 459–468. P. R. Portes and M. F. Zady, "Self-Esteem in the Adaptation of Spanish-Speaking Adolescents: The Role of Immigration, Family Conflict, and Depression," *Hispanic Journal of Behavioral Sciences* 24 (2002): 296–318.

17. Patricia Goodson, Eric R. Buhi, and Sarah C. Dunsmore, "Self-Esteem and Adolescent Sexual Behaviors, Attitudes, and Intentions: A Systematic Review," *Journal of Adolescent Health* 38 (2006): 310–319. L. S. Zabin, "Addressing Adolescent Sexual Behavior and Childbearing: Self-Esteem or Social Change?" *Women's Health Issues* 42 (1994): 92–97.

18. L. O'Sullivan et al., "Mother-Daughter Communication about Sexuality in a Clinical Sample of Hispanic Adolescent Girls," *Hispanic Journal of Behavioral Sciences* 21 (1999): 447–469. L. L. Meschke, S. Bartholomai, and S. R. Zentall, "Adolescent Sexuality and Parent-Adolescent Processes: Promoting Healthy Teen Choices," *Family Relations* 49 (2000): 143. K. S. Miller, "Patterns of Condom Use among Adolescents: The Impact of Mother-Adolescent Communication," *American Journal Public Health* 88 (1998):1542–1544. D. M. Shoop and P. Davidson, "AIDS and Adolescents: The Relation of Parent and Partner Communication to Adolescent Condom Use," *Journal Adolescence* 17 (1994): 137–148. D. Hotzman and R. Rubinson, "Parent and Peer Communication Effects on AIDS-Related Behavior among U.S. High School Students," *Family Planning Perspectives* 6 (1995): 235–240. B. L. Guzman et al., "Let's Talk about Sex: How Comfortable Discussions about Sex Impact Teen Sexual Behavior," *Journal of Health and Community* 8 (2003): 583–598.

19. Laura F. Romo et al., "A Longitudinal Study of Maternal Messages about Dating and Sexuality and Their Influence on Latino Adolescents," *Journal of Adolescent Health* 31 (2002): 59–69. L. F. O'Sullivan, H. F. L. Meyer-Bahlburg, and B. X. Watkins, "Mother-Daughter Communication about Sex among Urban African American and Latino Families," *Journal of Adolescent Research* 16 (2001): 269–292. C. Adolph et al., "Pregnancy among Hispanic Teenagers: Is Good Parental Communication a Deterrent?" *Contraception* 51 (1995): 303–306.

20. K. Ford and A. Norris, "Urban Hispanic Adolescents and Young Adults: Relationship of Acculturation to Sexual Behavior," *Journal of Sex Research* 30 (1993): 316–323. G. Prado et al., "The Prevention of HIV Transmission in Hispanic Adolescents," *Drug and Alcohol Dependency* 84 (2006): S43–53. A. M. Minnis and N. S. Padian, "Reproductive Health Differences among Latin American and U.S.-Born Young Women," *Journal of Urban Health* 78 (2001): 627–637. L. Rojas-Guyler, N. Ellis, and S. Sanders, "Acculturation, Health Protective Sexual Communication, and HIV/AIDS Risk Behavior among Hispanic Women in a Large Midwestern City," *Health Education and Behavior* 32 (2005): 767–779.

21. Barbara VanOss Marin, "HIV Prevention in the Hispanic Community: Sex, Culture, and Empowerment," *Journal of Transcultural Nursing* 14 (2003): 186–192. A. M. Villarruel, "Cultural Influences on the Sexual Attitudes, Beliefs, and Norms of Young Latina Adolescents," *Journal of the Society of Pediatric Nurses* 3 (1998): 69–79.

22. Centers for Disease Control and Prevention, "STD Surveillance, 2005."

23. Centers for Disease Control and Prevention, *HIV/AIDS Surveillance Report, 2005* (Atlanta, 2006). J. Murphy, G. Mueller, and S. Whitman, "Epidemiology of AIDS among Hispanics in Chicago," *Journal of Acquired Immune Deficiency Syndromes and Human Retroviral* 11 (1996): 83–87.

24. Marin, "HIV Prevention in the Hispanic Community." Merrill C. Singer et al., "Syndemics, Sex in the City: Understanding Sexually Transmitted Diseases in Social and Cultural Context," *Social Science and Medicine* 63 (2006): 2010–2021.

25. R. E. Zambrana et al., "Latinas and HIV/AIDS Risk Factors: Implications for Harm Reduction Strategies," *American Journal of Public Health* 94 (2004): 1152–1158. S. J. Henderson et al., "Older Women and HIV: How Much Do They Know and Where Are They Getting Their Information?" *Journal of American Geriatric Society* 52 (2004): 1549–1553. M. A. Johnson, A. R. Gotthoffer, and K. A. Lauffer, "The Sexual and Reproductive Health Content of African American and Latino Magazines," *Howard Journal of Communications* 10 (1999): 169–187. S. D. Rhodes et al., "Preventing HIV Infection among Young Immigrant Latino Men: Results from Focus Groups Using Community-Based Participatory Research," *Journal of the National Medical Association* 98 (2006): 564–573. C. H. Bradner, L. Ku, and L. D. Lindberg, "Older, but Not Wiser: How Men Get Information about AIDS and Sexually Transmitted Diseases after High School," *Family Planning Perspectives* 32 (2000): 33–38. G. G. Urizar and M. A. Winkleby, "AIDS Knowledge among Latinos: Findings from a Community and Agricultural Labor Camp Survey," *Hispanic Journal of Behavioral Sciences* 25 (2003): 295–311.

26. E. J. Essien, A. F. Meshack, and M. W. Ross, "Misperceptions about HIV Transmission among Heterosexual African-American and Latino Men and Women," *Journal of the National Medical Association* 94 (2002): 304–308. Bradner, Ku, and Lindberg, "Older, but Not Wiser." L. Romo, A. B. Berenson, and Z. H. Wu, "The Role of Misconceptions on Latino Women's Acceptance of Emergency Contraceptive Pills," *Contraception* 69 (2004): 227–235. C. H. Browner and H. M. Preloran, "Interpreting Low-Income Latinas' Amniocentesis Refusals," *Hispanic Journal of Behavioral Sciences* 22 (2000): 346–368.

R. Otero-Sabogal et al., "Access and Attitudinal Factors Related to Breast and Cervical Cancer Rescreenings: Why Are Latinas Still Underscreened?" *Health Education and Behavior* 30 (2003): 337–359. Wulf, "In Their Own Right." A. F. Abraido-Lanza, M. T. Chao, and M. D. Gammon, "Breast and Cervical Cancer Screening among Latinas and Non-Latina Whites," *American Journal of Public Health* 8 (2004): 1393–1398. M. A. Rodriguez, L. M. Ward, and E. J. Perez-Stable, "Breast and Cervical Cancer Screening: Impact of Health Insurance Status, Ethnicity, and Nativity of Latinas," *Annals of Family Medicine* 3 (2005): 235–241.

27. Liany Arroyo and L. Amparo Pinzón, *Entre Parejas: An Exploration of Latino Perspectives Regarding Family Planning and Contraception*, Conference ed. (Washington, D.C.: National Council of La Raza, 2006). D. Castañeda, "The Close Relationship Context and HIV/AIDS Risk Reduction among Mexican Americans," *Sex Roles* 42 (2000): 551–580. Barbara VanOss Marin et al., "Self-Efficacy to Use Condoms in Unmarried Latino Adults," *American Journal of Community Psychology* 26 (2006): 53–71.

28. J. S. Hirsch et al., "The Social Constructions of Sexuality: Marital Infidelity and Sexually Transmitted Disease–HIV Risk in a Mexican Migrant Community," *American Journal of Public Health* 92 (2002): 1227–1237. D. M. Castañeda and B. E. Collins, "The Effects of Gender, Ethnicity, and a Close Relationship Theme on Perceptions of Persons Introducing a Condom," *Sex Roles* 39 (1998): 369–390. Yolanda R. Dávila, "The Social Construction and Conceptualization of Sexual Health among Mexican American Women," *Research and Theory for Nursing Practice: An International Journal* 18 (2005): 357–368. S. T. Bird et al., "Getting Your Partner to Use Condoms: Interviews with Men and Women at Risk of HIV/STDs," *Journal of Sex Research* 38 (2001): 233–240.

29. Jennifer J. Frost and Anne K. Driscoll, "Sexual and Reproductive Health of U.S. Latinas: A Literature Review," *Guttmacher Institute Occasional Report*, No. 19 (2006). S. M. Harvey et al., "Relationship Power, Decision Making, and Sexual Relations: An Exploratory Study with Couples of Mexican Origin," *Journal of Sex Research, Sex Roles* 42 (2002): 7–8.

30. B. VanOss Marin, C. A. Gomez, and N. Hearst, "Multiple Heterosexual Partners and Condom Use among Hispanics and Non-Hispanic Whites," *Family Planning Perspectives* 25 (1993): 170–174. F. Sabogal, B. Faigeles, and J. A. Catania, "Multiple Sexual Partners among Hispanics in High-Risk Cities," *Family Planning Perspectives* 25 (1993): 257–262. Barbara VanOss Marin et al., "Condom Use in Unmarried Latino Men: A Test of Cultural Constructs," *Health Psychology* 16 (1997): 458–467.

31. Frost and Driscoll, "Sexual and Reproductive Health." M. I. Torres et al., "Focused Female Condom Education and Trial: Comparison of Young African American and Puerto Rican Women's Assessments," *International Quarterly of Community Health Education* 18 (1998): 49–68. H. Amaro, "Love, Sex, and Power: Considering Women's Realities in HIV Prevention," *American Psychologist* 50 (1995): 437–447. Amaro, Raj, and Reed, "Women's Sexual Health." L. A. Smith, "Partner Influence on Noncondom Use: Gender and Ethnic Differences," *Journal of Sex Research* 40 (2003): 346–350. A. Suarez-Al-Adam, M. Raffaelli, and A. O'Leary, "Influence of Abuse and Partner Hypermasculinity on the Sexual Behavior of Latinas," *AIDS Education and Prevention* 12 (2000): 263–274. G. M. Marks, P. J. Cantero, and J. M. Simoni, "Is Acculturation Associated with Sexual Risk Behaviors? An Investigation of HIV-Positive Latino Men and Women," *AIDS Care* 10 (1998): 283–295. J. Pulerwitz et al., "Relationship Power, Condom Use, and HIV Risk among Women in the USA," *AIDS Care* 14 (2002): 789–800. H. Amaro and A. Raj, "On the Margin: The Realities of Power and Women's HIV Risk Reduction Strategies," *Journal of Sex Roles* 42 (2000): 723–749.

32. J. Saul et al., "Heterosexual Risk for HIV among Puerto Rican Women: Does Power Influence Self-Protective Behavior?" *AIDS and Behavior* 4 (2000): 361–371. Harvey et al., "Relationship Power, Decision Making, Sexual Relations." V. E. Gil, "Empowerment Rhetoric, Sexual Negotiation, and Latinas' AIDS Risk: Research Implications for Prevention Health Education," in *Sexual and Reproductive Health Promotion in Latino Populations: Parteras, Promotoras y Poetas*, ed. M. I. Torres and G. P. Cernada (Amityville, N.Y.: Baywood Publishing, 2003), 45–62.

33. J. A. Catania et al., "Risk Factors for HIV and Other Sexually Transmitted Diseases and Prevention Practices among US Heterosexual Adults: Changes from 1990 to 1992," *American Journal of Public Health* 85 (1995): 1492–1499. G. E. Ibanez, "Condom Use at Last Sex among Unmarried Hispanic Men: An Event Analysis," *AIDS and Behavior* 9 (2005): 433–441. Alexi San Doval, Richard Duran, and Lydia O'Donnell, "Barriers to Condom Use in Primary and Nonprimary Relationships among Hispanic STD Clinic Patients," *Hispanic Journal of Behavioral Sciences* 17 (1995): 385–397. S. M. Noar, P. J. Morokoff, and L. L. Harlow, "Condom Influence Strategies in a Community Sample of Ethnically Diverse Man and Women," *Journal of Applied Social Psychology* 34 (2004): 1730–1751. L. O'Donnell et al., "STD Prevention and the Challenge of Gender and Cultural Diversity: Knowledge, Attitudes, and Risk Behaviors among Black and Hispanic Inner-City STD Clinic Patients," *Sexually Transmitted Diseases* 21 (1994): 137–148. Barbara VanOss Marin, Cynthia A. Gomez, and Jeanne M. Tschann, "Condom Use among Hispanic Men with Secondary Female Sexual Partners," *Public Health Reports* 108 (1993): 742–750. Marin et al., "Condom Use in Unmarried Latino Men."

34. G. W. Harper and M. Schneider, "Oppression and Discrimination among Lesbian, Gay, Bisexual, and Transgender People and Communities: A Challenge for Community Psychology," *American Journal of Community Psychology* 31 (2003): 243–252. N. A. Nabors et al., "Multiple Minority Group Oppression: Divided We Stand?" *Journal of Gay and Lesbian Medical Association* 5 (2004): 101–105. Marin, "HIV Prevention in the Hispanic Community."

35. Joseph F. Morris, Craig R. Waldo, and Esther D. Rothblum, "A Model of Predictors and Outcomes of Outness among Lesbian and Bisexual Women," *American Journal of Orthopsychiatry* 71 (2001): 61–71. M. A. Alquijay, "The Relationships among Self-Esteem, Acculturation, and Lesbian Identity Formation in Latina Lesbians," in *Ethnic and Cultural Diversity among Lesbians and Gay Men*, ed. B. Greene (Newbury Park, Calif.: Sage Publications, 1997), 249–265. M. DeVidas, "Childhood Sexual Abuse and Domestic Violence: A Support Group for Latino Gay Men and Lesbians," *Journal of Gay and Lesbian Social Services* 30 (1999): 51–61. Lynn Rew et al., "Sexual Health Risks and Protective Resources in Gay, Lesbian, Bisexual, and Heterosexual Homeless Youth," *Journal of Specialists in Pediatric Nursing* 10 (2005): 11–19. Vickie M. Mays et al., "Heterogeneity of Health Disparities among African American, Hispanic, and Asian American Women: Unrecognized Influences of Sexual Orientation," *American Journal of Public Health* 92 (2002): 632–639.

36. Edward O. Laumann et al., "Prevalence and Correlates of Erectile Dysfunction by Race and Ethnicity among Men Aged 40 or Older in the United States: From the Male Attitudes Regarding Sexual Health Survey," *Journal of Sexual Medicine* 4 (2006): 57–65. John Zweifler, Adriana Padilla, and Sean Schafer, 1998. "Barriers to Recognition of Erectile Dysfunction among Diabetic Mexican-American Men," *Journal of the American Board of Family Practice* 11 (1998): 259–263.

37. Edward O. Laumann et al., "A Political History of the National Sex Survey of Adults," *Family Planning Perspectives* 26 (1994): 34–38. V. S. Cain et al., "Sexual Functioning and

Practices in a Multi-Ethnic Study of Midlife Women: Baseline Results from SWAN," *Journal of Sex Research* 40 (2003): 266–276.

38. See Rafael Díaz's book *Latino Gay Men and HIV: Culture, Sexuality and Risk Behavior* (New York: Routledge, 1998) and Gloria González-López's recent publication *Erotic Journeys: Mexican Immigrants and Their Sex Lives* (Berkeley: University of California Press, 2005).

39. D. di Mauro, *Sexuality Research in the United States: An Assessment of the Social and Behavioral Sciences* (New York: Social Science Research Council, 1995).

40. L. J. Lewis, "Models of Genetic Counseling and Their Effects on Multicultural Genetic Counseling," *Journal of Genetic Counseling* 11 (2002): 193–212. E. Kaschak and L. Tiefer, *A New View of Women's Sexual Problems* (Binghamton, N.Y.: Haworth Press, 2001). Henry. A. Feldman et al., "Impotence and Its Medical and Psychosocial Correlates: Results of the Massachusetts Male Aging Study," *Journal of Urology* 151 (1994): 54–61. L. J. Lewis, "Examining Sexual Health Discourses in a Racial/Ethnic Context," *Archives of Sexual Behavior* 33 (2004): 223–234.

41. Weston M. Edwards and Eli Coleman, "Defining Sexual Health: A Descriptive Overview," *Archives of Sexual Behavior* 33 (2004): 189–195; quotation on 192.

42. K. Fenton, A. M. Johnson, and A. Nicoll, "Race, Ethnicity, and Sexual Health," *British Medical Journal* (editorials), 314 (1997): 1703.

CHAPTER 6   LATINA/O SEX POLICY

1. A. L. Giachello, "The Reproductive Years: The Health of Latinas," in *Latina Health in the United States: A Public Health Reader*, ed. M. Molina-Aguirre and C. W. Molina (San Francisco: Jossey-Bass, 2003), 77–131.

2. National Latina Institute for Reproductive Health, *A National Latina Agenda for Reproductive Justice* (New York, 2005). California Latinas for Reproductive Justice, *Promoting a New Policy Framework for Latinas' Reproductive Health, Rights, and Justice* (Los Angeles, 2006). Eithne Luibhéid and Lionel Cantú Jr., eds., *Queer Migrations: Sexuality, U.S. Citizenship, and Border Crossings* (Minneapolis: University of Minnesota Press, 2005).

3. L. Cantú, with E. Luibhéid and A. M. Stern, "Well-Founded Fear: Political Asylum and the Boundaries of Sexual Identity in the U.S.-Mexico Borderlands," in *Queer Migrations*, ed. Luibhéid and Cantú, 61–74. Gloria González-López, *Erotic Journeys: Mexican Immigrants and Their Sex Lives* (Berkeley: University of California Press, 2005). Patricia Zavella, "Playing with Fire: The Gendered Construction of Chicana/Mexicana Sexuality," in *The Gender/Sexuality Reader: Culture, History, Political Economy*, ed. Roger Lancaster and Micaela di Leonardo (New York: Routledge, 1997). Olivia M. Espín, "Cultural and Historical Influences on Sexuality in Hispanic/Latin Women," in *Pleasure and Danger: Exploring Female Sexuality*, ed. Carole S. Vance (Boston: Routledge and Kegan Paul, 1984), 149–164. Espín, "'Race,' Racism, and Sexuality in the Life Narratives of Immigrant Women," *Feminism and Psychology* 5 (1995): 223–238. Espín, *Latina Realities: Essays on Healing, Migration, and Sexuality* (Boulder, Colo.: Westview Press, 1997). Luibhéid and Cantú, *Queer Migrations*.

4. Human Rights Watch, *Family, Unvalued: Discrimination, Denial, and the Fate of Binational Same-Sex Couples under U.S. Law* (New York, 2006).

5. J. Cianciotto, *Hispanic and Latino Same-Sex Couple Households in the United States: A Report from the 2000 Census* (New York: National Gay and Lesbian Task Force Policy Institute and National Latino/a Coalition for Justice, 2005).

6.   Ibid., 7.

7.   Y. Apostolopoulos et al., "STI/HIV Risks for Mexican Migrant Laborers: Exploratory Ethnographies," *Journal of Immigration and Minority Health* 8 (2006): 291–302.

8.   E. Parrado, C. A. Flippen, and C. McQuiston, "Use of Commercial Sex Workers among Hispanic Migrants in North Carolina: Implications for the Spread of HIV," *Perspectives in Sexual and Reproductive Health* 36 (2004): 150–156.

9.   J. W. Whitehead, *Sex Trafficking: The Real Immigration Problem* (Charlottesville, Va.: Rutherford Institute, 2006).

10. Elena R. Gutiérrez, "'We Will No Longer Be Silent or Invisible': Latinas Organizing for Reproductive Justice," in *Undivided Rights: Women of Color Organize for Reproductive Justice*, ed. J. Silliman et al. (Cambridge, Mass.: South End Press, 2004), 215–239. Latino Issues Forum, *Our Health, Our Rights: Reproductive Justice for Latinas in California* (San Francisco, 2003).

11. Liany Arroyo and L. Amparo Pinzón, *Entre Parejas: An Exploration of Latino Perspectives Regarding Family Planning and Contraception* (Washington, D.C.: National Council of La Raza, 2006). Jennifer J. Frost and Anne K. Driscoll, "Sexual and Reproductive Health of U.S. Latinas: A Literature Review," *Guttmacher Institute Occasional Report*, No. 19 (2006).

12. National Latina Institute for Reproductive Health, *The Reproductive Health of Latina Immigrants* (New York, 2005), 1.

13. T. Shiffner and L. P. Buki, "Latina College Students' Sexual Health Beliefs about Human Papilloma Virus Infection," *Cultural Diversity and Ethnic Minority Psychology* 12 (2006): 687–696. M. G. del Carmen et al., "Demographic, Risk Factor, and Knowledge Differences between Latinas and Non-Latinas Referred to Colposcopy," *Gynecologic Oncology* 104 (2007): 70–76. T. Byrd et al., "Cervical Cancer Screening Beliefs among Young Hispanic Women," *Preventative Medicine* 38 (2004): 192–197.

14. Kaiser Family Foundation, *Racial and Ethnic Disparities in Women's Health Coverage and Access to Care* (Menlo Park, Calif., 2004). Jacqueline Darroch Forrest and Jennifer J. Frost, "The Family Planning Attitudes and Experiences of Low-Income Women," *Family Planning Perspectives* 28 (1996): 246–255. C. Velez, "Sexual Behavior among Puerto Rican Adolescents," *Puerto Rican Health Sciences Journal* 19 (2000): 69–76. M. Raffaelli, B. L. Zamboanga, and G. Carlo, "Acculturation Status and Sexuality among Female Cuban American College Students," *Journal of American College Health* 54 (2005): 7–13. B. Ortiz-Torres, I. Serrano-Garcia, and N. Torres-Burgos, "Subverting Culture: Promoting HIV/AIDS Prevention among Puerto Rican and Dominican Women," *American Journal of Community Psychology* 28 (2000): 859–881.

15. National Latina Institute for Reproductive Health, *Reproductive Health of Latina Immigrants*.

16. Elena R. Gutiérrez, *Fertile Matters: The Politics of Mexican Origin Women's Reproduction* (Austin: University of Texas Press, 2008).

17. Elena R. Gutiérrez, *National Welfare Reform: An Analysis of Its Impact on Latinas* (Oakland, Calif.: National Latina Health Organization, 1995). Colorado Organization for Latina Opportunity and Reproductive Rights, *The Impact of Welfare Reform on Latina Reproductive Health* (Denver, 2003).

18. Latino Issues Forum, *Our Health, Our Rights*. Arroyo and Pinzón, *Entre Parejas*.

19. C. P. Kaplan et al., "Young Latinas and Abortion: The Role of Cultural Factors, Reproductive Behavior, and Alternative Roles to Motherhood," *Health Care for Women International* 22 (2001): 667–689. Sean M. Bolks et al., "Core Beliefs and Abortion Attitudes: A Look at Latinos," *Social Science Quarterly* 81 (2000): 253–260.

20. Bolks et al., "Core Beliefs and Abortion Attitudes." B. Pesquera and D. Segura, "'It's Her Body, It's Definitely Her Right': Chicanas/Latinas and Abortion," *Voces: A Journal of Latina Studies* 2 (1998): 103–127.

21. R. Jones, J. Darroch, and S. Henshaw, "Patterns in Socioeconomic Characteristics of Women Obtaining Abortions in 2000–2001," *Perspectives on Sexual and Reproductive Health* 34 (2002): 226–235. Bolks et al., "Core Beliefs and Abortion Attitudes."

22. Silliman et al., *Undivided Rights.* National Latina Institute for Reproductive Health, *Reproductive Health of Latina Immigrants.*

23. J. P. Peterman, *Telling Their Stories: Puerto Rican Women and Abortion* (Boulder, Colo.: Westview Press, 1996). Latino Issues Forum, *Our Health, Our Rights.*

24. Mays et al., "Heterogeneity of Health Disparities."

25. Gutiérrez, *Fertile Matters.*

CHAPTER 7   HETEROSEXUALITY EXPOSED

1. For in-depth theoretical critiques of both machismo and marianismo, see Gloria R. González-López and Matthew C. Gutmann, "Machismo," in *New Dictionary of the History of Ideas* (New York: Charles Scribner's Sons, 2005), 4:1328–1330; and Gloria González-López, *Erotic Journeys: Mexican Immigrants and Their Sex Lives* (Berkeley: University of California Press, 2005). See also Tracy Bachrach Ehlers, "Debunking *Marianismo*: Economic Vulnerability and Survival Strategies among Guatemalan Wives," *Ethnology* 30 (1991): 1–16.

2. For sociological reflections on "Latino culture" as a concept and a paradigm, see Gloria González-López and Salvador Vidal-Ortiz, "Latinas and Latinos, Sexuality, and Society: A Critical Sociological Perspective," in *Latinas/os in the United States: Changing the Face of America*, ed. Havidán Rodríguez, Rogelio Sáenz, and Cecilia Menjívar (New York: Springer, 2008).

3. Examples abound in behavioral and epidemiological journals dedicated to examining the lives of these Latino groups. See González-López, *Erotic Journeys*, and "Heterosexual *Fronteras*: Immigrant *Mexicanos*, Sexual Vulnerabilities, and Survival," *Sexuality Research and Social Policy* 3 (2006): 67–81, for a comprehensive discussion of these concerns and a list of references with regard to these images of Latinas and Latinos portrayed in the literature.

4. In an essay entitled *"De madres a hijas"* (2003), I introduced the concept of "regional patriarchies" to examine the ways in which patriarchy is reproduced in nonuniform ways in Mexican territory, and I suggested that *"machismos regionales"* could be used as a pseudonym for such a concept. In my book, *Erotic Journeys*, I corrected this conceptualization, and I no longer use the latter.

5. See Matthew C. Gutmann, *The Meanings of Macho: Being a Man in Mexico City* (Berkeley: University of California Press, 1996).

6. Miguel A. Pérez and Helda L. Pinzón, "Latino Perspectives on Sexuality," in *The International Encyclopedia of Sexuality*, ed. Robert T. Francouer (New York: Continuum, 1997), 1423–1436; quotation on 1427.

7. González-López and Gutmann, "Machismo," 1329.

8. Jeanette Rodríguez, *Our Lady of Guadalupe: Faith and Empowerment among Mexican-American Women* (Austin: University of Texas Press, 1994). Marie L. Talashek et al., "The Context of Risky Behaviors for Latino Youth," *Journal of Transcultural Nursing* 15 (2004): 131–138. Catrióna Rueda Esquibel, *With Her Machete in Her Hand: Reading*

Chicana Lesbians (Austin: University of Texas Press, 2006), 27, 154. In *Sexuality, Society, and Feminism*, ed. Cheryl Brown Travis and Jacquelyn W. White (Washington, D.C.: American Psychological Association, 2000), Pamela T. Reid and Vanessa M. Bing incorporate marianismo as a "concept based on the Catholic cult of the Virgin Mary, which dictates that when women become mothers, then and only then do they attain the status of Madonna, and in so doing they are expected to deny themselves in favor of their children and husbands" (158). For in-depth theoretical critiques of both machismo and marianismo, see González-López and Gutmann, "Machismo," and González-López, *Erotic Journeys*. See also Ehlers, "Debunking *Marianismo*."

9. Gloria Anzaldúa, *Borderlands/La Frontera: The New Mestiza* (San Francisco: Aunt Lute Books, 1987).

10. Maxine Baca-Zinn, "Mexican American Women in Social Sciences," and "Chicano Men and Masculinity," in *Men's Lives*, 5th ed., ed. Michael S. Kimmel and Michael A. Messner (Boston: Allyn and Bacon, 2001), 24–32. Gutmann, *Meanings of Macho*. Marysol W. Asencio, *Sex and Sexuality among New York's Puerto Rican Youths* (Boulder, Colo.: Lynne Rienner Publishers, 2002). Xóchitl Castañeda and Patricia Zavella, "Changing Constructions of Sexuality and Risk: Migrant Mexican Women Farmworkers in California," *Journal of Latin American Anthropology* 8 (2003): 126–151. Lorena García, "Beyond the Latina Virgin/Whore Dichotomy: Investigating Latina Adolescent Sexual Subjectivity" (Ph.D. diss., University of California–Santa Barbara, 2006). Gloria González-López, "Fathering Latina Sexualities: Mexican Men and the Virginity of Their Daughters," *Journal of Marriage and the Family* 66 (2004): 1118–1130; *Erotic Journeys*; "Heterosexual Fronteras"; "Catholic Church and Sacred Morality in the Sex Lives of Mexican Immigrant Women," in *Sexual Inequalities and Social Justice*, ed. Niels F. Teunis and Gilbert Herdt (Berkeley: University of California Press, 2007), 148–173; and "*Nunca he dejado de tener terror*: Sexual Violence in the Lives of Mexican Immigrant Women," in *Women and Migration in the U.S.-Mexico Borderlands: A Reader*, ed. Denise A. Segura and Patricia Zavella (Durham: Duke University Press, 2007), 224–246. Jennifer S. Hirsch, "*En el norte la mujer manda*: Gender, Generation, and Geography in a Mexican Transnational Community," *American Behavioral Scientist* 42 (1999): 1332–1349; and *A Courtship after Marriage: Sexuality and Love in Mexican Transnational Families* (Berkeley: University of California Press, 2003). Lourdes Argüelles and Anne M. Rivero, "Gender/Sexual Orientation, Violence, and Transnational Migration: Conversations with Some Latinas We Think We Know," *Urban Anthropology* 22 (1993): 259–275. Patricia Zavella, "Playing with Fire: The Gendered Construction of Chicana/Mexicana Sexuality," in *The Gender/ Sexuality Reader: Culture, History, Political Economy*, ed. Roger Lancaster and Micaela di Leonardo (New York: Routledge, 1997); and "Talkin' Sex: Chicanas and Mexicanas Theorize about Silences and Sexual Pleasures," in *Chicana Feminisms: A Critical Reader*, ed. Gabriela Arredondo, Aida Hurtado, Norma Klahn, and Olga Nájera-Ramirez (Durham: Duke University Press, 2003); Patricia Zavella and Xochitl Castañeda, "Sexuality and Risks: Young Mexican Women Negotiate Gendered Discourse about Virginity and Disease," *Latino Studies* 3 (2005): 226–245.

11. González-López and Vidal-Ortiz, "Latinas and Latinos, Sexuality, and Society."

12. Adrienne Rich, "Compulsory Heterosexuality and Lesbian Existence," *Signs* 5 (1980): 631–660. Lynne Segal, *Straight Sex: Rethinking the Politics of Pleasure* (Berkeley: University of California Press, 1994). Jonathan Ned Katz, *The Invention of Heterosexuality* (New York: Dutton, 1995). Chrys Ingraham, "The Heterosexual Imaginary: Feminist Sociology and Theories of Gender," *Sociological Theory* 12 (1994): 203–219; *White Weddings: Romancing Heterosexuality in Popular Culture* (New York: Routledge, 1999); and *Thinking Straight: The Promise, the Power, and the Paradox of Heterosexuality* (New York:

Routledge, 2005). Michael A Messner, "Studying Up on Sex," *Sociology of Sport Journal* 13 (1996): 221–237.

13. Rich, "Compulsory Heterosexuality and Lesbian Existence." Michael Warner, "Introduction: Fear of a Queer Planet," *Social Text* 9 (1991): 3–17. In this essay, heteronormativity refers to this process, and the plural form heteronormativities considers the multiple ways in which this process is potentially expressed in these communities; I use both concepts interchangeably.

14. Anzaldúa, *Borderlands/La Frontera*. Cherríe Moraga and Gloria Anzaldúa, *This Bridge Called My Back: Writings by Radical Women of Color* (New York: Women of Color Press, 1983). Emma Pérez, *Gulf Dreams* (Berkeley: Third Women Press, 1996), and *The Decolonial Imaginary*. Carla Trujillo, ed., *Chicana Lesbians: The Girls Our Mothers Warned Us About* (Berkeley: University of California Press, 1991). For an extensive analysis of the literature on Chicana lesbians and a genealogy of Chicana lesbian writings, see Esquibel, *With Her Machete in Her Hand*.

15. For a discussion on the concept of "patlache," see Rosemary A. Joyce, *Gender and Power in Prehispanic Mesoamerica* (Austin: University of Texas Press, 2000), 160, 161. Serge Gruzinski, *"Confesión, alianza y sexualidad entre los indios de Nueva España,"* in *El placer de pecar y el afán de normar*, ed. Seminario de Historia de Mentalidades (Mexico City: Editorial J. Mortiz, 1988); 1988 quotation on 185. C. Castañeda, *Violacíon, estupro y sexualidad: Nueva Galicia, 1790–1821* (Guadalajara, Mex.: Editorial Hexagono, 1989), 52–53. In *Erotic Journeys*, 18–36, I examine in more depth the historical and social origins of heterosexual norms and regulations shaping the sex and romantic lives of women and men migrating from Mexico.

16. Gloria González-López, *"De madres a hijas*: Gendered Lessons on Virginity across Generations of Mexican Immigrant Women," in *Gender and U.S. Migration: Contemporary Trends*, ed. Pierrette Hondagneu-Sotelo (Berkeley: University of California Press, 2003), 217–240. González-López, "Fathering Latina Sexualities." Aida Hurtado, *Voicing Chicana Feminisms: Young Women Speak Out on Sexuality and Identity* (New York: New York University Press, 2003).

17. While growing up in Mexico and based on my ongoing research and frequent trips to different urbanized areas of the country, I have noticed that quinceañeras are class specific, with more apparent prevalence in popular sectors. In the United States, I have observed that Mexican American families celebrate this across socioeconomic differences.

18. Karen Mary Davalos, *"La Quinceañera*: Making Gender and Ethnic Identities," in *Velvet Barrios: Popular Culture and Chicana/o Sexualities*, ed. Alicia Gaspar de Alba (New York: Palgrave Macmillan, 2003), 141–162. This ritual has also caught the attention of Mexican telenovela producers and U.S. independent filmmakers. The Mexican telenovela *Quinceañera* had high ratings when it was first aired in 1987; it was written by the late Cuban writer René Muñoz and produced by Mexican telenovela entrepreneur Carla Estrada.

19. Though *señorita* as a concept has multiple meanings, it may be used to identify an adolescent girl who is perceived as a young woman. In Mexican American contexts, it may also refer to a young girl when she gets her period, or a woman who has never been married. Calling a woman "señorita" implies that she is not married (or a *señora*), and thus, the moral interpretation is that she is a virgin. I offer additional reflections with regard to the social and moral meanings of this concept in *Erotic Journeys*, 249.

20. This ritualized process becomes more complicated as it involves not only coming of age but also preparing a young adolescent to embrace womanhood in ethnic or culturally

specific ways—as a Mexicana, or Cubana, or *puertorriqueña*, or Dominicana—or in any other option within an array of national and ethnic/racial possibilities. See Davalos, "*La Quinceañera*," for an informative feminist anthropological examination of these and other cultural, religious, and gendered aspects of this rite of passage in Mexican American communities.

21. The highly expensive event requires a rehearsal in which the members of the "court" meet to practice and master the dance. Friendship, closeness, bonding, camaraderie, flirting, rivalry, and competition, among other kinds of exchanges, emerge among participants as part of the process.

22. In "Fathering Latina Sexualities," I discuss the ways in which twenty Mexican immigrant fathers educating their daughters in the United States perceive the virginity of their daughters. The most serious concern these men have as fathers is fear of their daughters' becoming pregnant. Their concern generally has nothing to do with a sexual morality they associate with "traditions of the past." Instead, their main concern is that pregnancy out of wedlock would affect the possibilities of the young woman completing her education and achieving the dream these men have as fathers for their daughters: attending college and obtaining a degree.

23. For some reflections on telenovelas and representation of women and men in contemporary Mexican society, see Héctor Carrillo, *The Night Is Young: Sexuality in Mexico in the Times of AIDS* (Chicago: University of Chicago Press, 2002); and "Neither *Machos* nor *Maricones*: Masculinity and Emerging Male Homosexual Identities in Mexico," in *Changing Men and Masculinities in Latin America*, ed. Matthew C. Gutmann (Durham: Duke University Press, 2003), 351–369.

24. Rafael M. Díaz, *Latino Gay Men and HIV: Culture Sexuality and Risk Behavior* (New York: Routledge, 1998); González-López, *Erotic Journeys*, 62–97; Pérez and Pinzón, "Latino Perspectives on Sexuality." Rich, "Compulsory Heterosexuality and Lesbian Existence."

25. Héctor Carrillo, "Cultural Change, Hybridity, and Male Homosexuality in Mexico Culture," *Health and Sexuality* 1 (1999): 223–238. Genaro Castro-Vázquez, "Masculinity and Condom Use among Mexican Teenagers: The Escuela Nacional Preparatoria No. 1's Case," *Gender and Education* 12 (2000): 479–492.

26. Amy C. Steinbugler, "Visibility as Privilege and Danger: Heterosexual and Same-Sex Interracial Intimacy in the 21st Century," *Sexualities* 8 (2005): 425–443.

27. Antonia I. Castañeda, "Sexual Violence in the Politics of Conquest," in *Building with Our Hands: New Directions in Chicana Studies*, ed. Adela de la Torre and Beatríz M. Pesquera (Berkeley: University of California Press, 1993), 15–33.

28. Ibid. C. Castañeda, *Violación, estupro y sexualidad*, 152. François Giraud, "*La reacción social ante la violación: Del discurso a la práctica (Nueva España, siglo XVIII)*," in *El placer de pecar y el afán de normar*, ed. Seminario de Historia de las Mentalidades (Mexico City: Editorial J. Mortiz, 1988), 341, 337.

29. Ramón A. Gutiérrez, *When Jesus Came, the Corn Mothers Went Away: Marriage, Sexuality, and Power in New Mexico, 1500–1846* (Stanford: Stanford University Press, 1991). Rachel F. Moran, *Interracial Intimacy: The Regulation of Race and Romance* (Chicago: University of Chicago Press, 2001), 50.

30. For a list of publications discussing the ways in which the family institution shapes the sex lives of Latino groups, Mexicans in particular, see *Erotic Journeys*, 31.

31. Robert W. Connell, *Gender and Power: Society, the Person, and Sexual Politics* (Stanford: Stanford University Press, 1987). Zhenchao Qian, "Breaking the Racial Barriers:

Variations in Interracial Marriage between 1980 and 1990," *Demography* 34 (1997): 263–276. Robert M. Jiobu, *Ethnicity and Assimilation* (Albany: SUNY Press, 1988), 153.

32. Greta A Gilbertson, Joseph P. Fitzpatrick, and Lijun Yang, "Hispanic Intermarriage in New York City: New Evidence from 1991," *International Migration Review* 30 (1996): 445–459. Even though class shapes the experiences of heterosexual romance in unique ways, in this essay I focus more on race relations and alternatively reflect on class, which also represents an important dimension of social life and deserves special attention in future examinations of the social organization of heterosexuality. In *Erotic Journeys*, 122, I discuss some of these reflections especially within the context of youth, dating, and family control.

33. For examples of this pattern in the sociological literature, see Qian, "Breaking the Racial Barriers"; Zhenchao Qian and Daniel T. Lichter, "Measuring Marital Assimilation: Intermarriage among Natives and Immigrants," *Social Science Research* 30 (2001): 289–312; and Zhenchao Qian, "Race and Social Distance: Intermarriage with Non-Latino Whites," *Race and Society* 5 (2002): 33–47.

34. Ingraham, *White Weddings*, 16.

35. Esquibel, *With Her Machete in Her Hand*.

36. Research on some of these topics has been conducted using quantitative methodologies, which are informative but overlook the nuances and complexities of these exchanges.

37. My own work with Mexican populations is an attempt to fill this gap in the literature.

CHAPTER 8   REPRESENTATIONS OF LATINA/O
SEXUALITY IN POPULAR CULTURE

1. See Arlene M. Dávila, *Latino Spin: Public Image and the Whitewashing of Race* (New York: New York University Press, 2008).

2. Chon Noriega, ed., *Chicanos and Film: Representation and Resistance* (Minneapolis: University of Minnesota Press, 1992). Noriega, "Citizen Chicano: The Trials and Titillations of Ethnicity in American Cinema, 1935–1962," in *Latin Looks: Images of Latinas and Latinos in the U.S. Media*, ed. C. E. Rodríguez (Boulder, Colo.: Westview Press, 1997), 85–103. Noriega, *Shot in America: Television, the State, and the Rise of Chicano Cinema* (Minneapolis: University of Minnesota Press, 2000). Frances Negrón-Muntaner, *Boricua Pop: Puerto Ricans and American Culture* (New York: New York University Press, 2004). Rosa Linda Fregoso, *The Bronze Screen: Chicana and Chicano Film Culture* (Minneapolis: University of Minnesota Press, 1993). Fregoso, *meXicana Encounters: The Making of Social Identities on the Borderlands* (Berkeley, CA: University of California Press, 2003). Frances Aparicio, *Listening to Salsa: Gender, Latin Popular Music, and Puerto Rican Cultures* (Middletown, Conn.: Wesleyan University Press, 1998). Aparicio, "Jennifer as Selena: Rethinking *Latinidad* in Media and Popular Culture," *Latino Studies* 1 (2003): 90–105. M. Warner, *Fear of a Queer Planet: Queer Politics and Social Theory* (Minneapolis: University of Minnesota Press, 1993).

3. N. Alarcón, " *Traddutora, Traditora*: A Paradigmatic Figure of Chicana Feminism," *Cultural Critique* 13 (1989): 57–87. F. R. Aparicio and S. Chávez-Silverman, *Tropicalizations: Transcultural Representations of Latinidad* (Hanover, N.H.: Dartmouth College, 1997). Fregoso, *MeXicana Encounters*. Negrón-Muntaner, *Boricua Pop*. V. Rojas, "The Gender of *Latinidad*: Latinas Speak about Hispanic Television," *Communication Review* 7 (2004): 125–153. Anzaldúa, *Making Face, Making Soul,* Haciendo

Caras: *Critical Perspectives of Women of Color* (San Francisco: Aunt Lute Books, 1990); quotation on xv.

4. Stuart Hall, "Notes on Deconstructing the 'Popular,'" in *People's History and Socialist Theory*, ed. R. Samuel (New York: Routledge, 1981); quotation on 239.

5. C. Wilson, C. F. Gutiérrez, and L. M. Chao, *Racism, Sexism, and the Media: The Rise of Class Communication in Multicultural America* (Thousand Oaks, Calif.: Sage Publications, 2003); quotation on 65. Fregoso, *Bronze Screen*. Noriega, "Citizen Chicano." Arlene M. Dávila, *Latinos, Inc.: The Marketing and Making of a People* (Berkeley: University of California Press, 2001).

6. Dávila, *Latinos, Inc.*

7. C. Pieraccini and D. L. Alligood, *Color Television: Fifty Years of African American and Latino Images on Prime-Time Television* (Dubuque, Iowa: Kendall/Hunt Publishing Co., 2005). M. Rogin, "The Sword Became a Flashing Vision: D. W. Griffith's *The Birth of a Nation*," *Representations* 9 (1985): 150–195. F. T. Rony, *The Third Eye: Race, Cinema, and Ethnographic Spectacle* (Durham: Duke University Press, 1996). The following quote by historian John Hope Franklin that appears at the beginning of *The Birth of a Nation* stresses the link between the power of cinema, representation, and race: "As an eloquent statement of the position of most white southerners using a new and increasingly influential media of communication and as an instrument that deliberately and successfully undertook to use propaganda as history, the influence of *A* [sic] *Birth of a Nation* on the current view of reconstruction has been greater than any other single force."

8. F. J. Berumen, *The Chicano/Hispanic Image in American Film* (New York: Vantage Press, 1995). Rodríguez, *Latin Looks*. C. E. Rodríguez, *Heroes, Lovers, and Others: The Story of Latinos in Hollywood* (Washington, D.C.: Smithsonian Books, 2004).

9. Fregoso, *MeXicana Encounters*. C. Ramírez-Berg, *Latino Images in Film* (Austin: University of Texas Press, 2002); quotations on 67, 76. Rodríguez, *Heroes, Lovers, and Others*. Berumen, *Chicano/Hispanic Image in American Film*.

10. Fregoso, *Bronze Screen*. Noriega, "Citizen Chicano." M. A. Holling, " *El simpatico* Boxer: Underpinning Chicano Masculinity with a Rhetoric of *Familia* in *Resurrection Blvd*," *Western Journal of Communications* 70 (2006): 91–115. G. Rodriguez, "Boxing and Masculinity: The History and (Her)story of Oscar De La Hoya," in *Latino/a Popular Culture*, ed. M. Habell-Pallán and M. Romero (New York: New York University Press, 2002); De La Hoya quotation on 257. F. P. Delgado, "Golden but Not Brown: Oscar De La Hoya and the Complications of Culture, Manhood, and Boxing," *International Journal of the History of Sport* 22 (2005): 196–211.

11. Alarcón, "*Traddutora, Traditora.*" R. Alcalá, "A Chicana Hagiography for the Twenty-First Century: Ana Castillo's Locas Santas," in *Velvet Barrios: Popular Culture and Chicana/o Sexualities*, ed. Alicia Gaspar de Alba (New York: Palgrave Macmillan, 2003), 3–16. A. Del Castillo, "Malintzín Tenepal: A Preliminary Look into a New Perspective," in *Chicana Feminist Thought: The Basic Historical Writings*, ed. A. García (New York: Routledge, 1997), 122–125. Catrióna Rueda Esquibel, *With Her Machete in Her Hand: Reading Chicana Lesbians* (Austin: University of Texas Press, 2006). C. List, *Chicano Images: Refiguring Ethnicity in Mainstream Film* (New York: Garland Publishing, 1996). Berumen, *Chicano/Hispanic Image in American Film*.

12. On Lupe Vélez see Fregoso, *MeXicana Encounters*. José Limon, *American Encounters: Greater Mexico, the United States, and the Erotics of Culture* (Boston: Beacon Press, 1998). Harlot quotation in Ramírez-Berg, *Latino Images in Film*, 71. Rodríguez, *Heroes, Lovers, and Others*; quotation on. 68. V. Sturtevant, "Spitfire: Lupe Vélez and the Ambivalent Pleasures of Ethnic Masquerade," *Velvet Light Trap* 55 (2005): 19–32.

13. C. Mohanty, L. Torrres, and A. Russo, *Third World Women and the Politics of Feminism* (Bloomington: Indiana University Press, 1991). Caren Kaplan, Norma Alarcón, and Minoo Moallem, *Between Women and Nation: Nationalisms, Transnational Feminsims, and the State* (Durham: Duke University Press, 1999). Fregoso, *MeXicana Encounters*. Rodríguez, *Heroes, Lovers, and Others*.

14. C. E. Cortés, "Chicanas in Film: History of an Image," in *Latin Looks*, ed. Rodríguez, 121–141. Fregoso, *Bronze Screen*. R. S. Lichter and D. R. Amundson, "Distorted Reality: Hispanic Characters in TV Entertainment," in *Latin Looks*, ed. Rodríguez, 57–72. Noriega, *Chicanos and Film*. Alarcón, "*Traddutora, Traditora.*" Angie Chabram-Dernersesian, "And, Yes . . . the Earth Did Part: On the Splitting of Chicana Subjectivity," in *Building with Our Hands*, ed. Adela de la Torre and Beatríz Pesquera (Berkeley: University of California Press, 1993), 34–56. Del Castillo, "Malintzín Tenepal." L. A. Flores and M. A. Holling, "*Las Familias y Las Latinas*: Mediated Representations of Gender Roles," in *Mediated Woman: Representations in Popular Culture*, ed. M. Meyers (Cresskill, N.J.: Hampton Press, 1999), 339–354. C. Ramirez, "Crimes of Fashion: The Pachuca and Chicana Style Politics," *Meridians: Feminism, Race, Transnationalism* 2 (2002): 1–35.

15. Fregoso, *MeXicana Encounters*, 74.

16. Berumen, *Chicano/Hispanic Image in American Film*, 190.

17. Ramírez-Berg, *Latino Images in Film*, 73.

18. Rodríguez, *Heroes, Lovers, and Others*. Christine List, *Chicano Images: Refiguring Ethnicity in Mainstream Film* (New York: Garland Publishing, 1996).

19. A. López, "Are All Latins from Manhattan? Hollywood, Ethnography, and Cultural Colonialism," in *Unspeakable Images: Ethnicity and the American Cinema*, ed. L. D. Friedman (Champaign: University of Illinois Press, 1991). Wilson, Gutiérrez, and Chao, *Racism, Sexism, and the Media*. Rodríguez, *Heroes, Lovers, and Others*.

20. Fregoso, "Chicana Film Practices: Confronting the Many Headed Demon of Oppression," in *Chicanos and Film*, ed. Noriega.

21. Ramírez-Berg, *Latino Images in Film*, 68.

22. Ibid. Rodríguez, *Heroes, Lovers, and Others*.

23. Aparicio and Chávez-Silverman, *Tropicalizations*, 1.

24. Ibid. Rodríguez, *Heroes, Lovers, and Others*; Rita Moreno quotations on 119.

25. Rodríguez, *Heroes, Lovers, and Others*, 69, 59. J. Géliga Vargas, "Who Is the Puerto Rican Woman and How Is She? Shall Hollywood Respond?" in *Mediated Woman*, ed. Meyers, 111–132.

26. Peter Applebome, "Trying to Shake a Stereotype but Keep On Being Rosie Pérez," *New York Times*, February 14, 1999, xx. López, "Are All Latins from Manhattan?"; quotation on 412. Vargas, "Who Is the Puerto Rican Woman?" A. N. Valdivia, *A Latina in the Land of Hollywood and Other Essays on Media Culture* (University of Arizona Press: Tucson, 2000). Rodríguez, *Heroes, Lovers, and Others*.

27. Valdivia, *Latina in Hollywood*; quotation on 97.

28. Vargas, "Who Is the Puerto Rican Woman?" A. N. Valdivia, "Stereotype or Transgression? Rosie Pérez in Hollywood Film," *Sociological Quarterly* 39 (1998): 393–408. Rodríguez, *Heroes, Lovers, and Others*; *Times* headline on 219.

29. F. Subervi-Vélez et al., "Mass Communication and Hispanics," in *Handbook of Hispanic Cultures in the United States*, ed. N. Kanelos (Houston: Arté Público Press, 1994), 304–357. Wilson, Gutiérrez, and Chao, *Racism, Sexism, and the Media*.

30. Dávila, *Latinos, Inc.* Rojas, "Gender of *Latinidad*," 130.

31. Rojas, "Gender of *Latinidad*." Suberví-Vélez et al., "Mass Communication and Hispanics." Noriega, *Shot in America*. Dávila, *Latinos, Inc.* A. Dávila, "Talking Back: Spanish Media and U.S. Latinidad," in *Latino/a Popular Culture*, ed. Habell-Pallán and Romero, 25–37.

32. Ramírez-Berg, *Latino Images in Film*.

33. Fregoso, *Bronze Screen*; quotation on 56. E. Guerrero, "The Black Image in Protective Custody," in *Black American Cinema*, ed. M. Diawara (New York: Routledge, 1993); quotation on 237.

34. G. Oguss, "Whose Barrio Is It? *Chico and the Man* and the Integrated Ghetto Shows of the 1970s," *Television and New Media* 6 (2005): 3–21; quotation on 6.

35. Oguss, "Whose Barrio Is It?"; quotation on 7. Daniel Patrick Moynihan, *The Negro Family: The Case for National Action [The Moynihan Report]* (Washington, D.C.: U.S. Department of Labor, Office of Policy, Planning, and Research, 1965). Oscar Lewis, *Five Families: Mexican Case Studies in the Culture of Poverty* (Washington, D.C.: New American Library Mentor Book, 1959). Noriega, *Shot in America*. Pieraccini and Alligood, *Color Television*.

36. Noriega, *Shot in America*.

37. Fregoso, *Bronze Screen*. Flores and Holling, "*Las Familias y Las Latinas*. Holling, "*El simpatico* Boxer"; quotation on 91.

38. M. E. Cepeda, "Columbus Effect(s): Chronology and Crossover in the Latin(o) Music 'Boom,'" *Discourse* 23, no. 1 (Winter 2001): 63–81. Cepeda, "*Mucho Loco* for Ricky Martin; or the Politics of Chronology, Crossover, and Language within the Latin(o) Music 'Boom,'" in *Global Pop, Local Language*, ed. H. Berger and H. T. Carroll (Jackson: University of Mississippi Press: 2003), 113–130. I. M. Guzmán and A. N. Valdivia, "Brain, Brow, and Booty: Latina Iconicity in U.S. Popular Culture," *Communication Review* 7 (2004): 205–221. Negrón-Muntaner, *Boricua Pop*; quotation on 247.

39. Negrón-Muntaner, *Boricua Pop*, 237. Aparicio, *Listening to Salsa*; quotations on 143, 144.

40. Aparicio, *Listening to Salsa*; M. Pedalty, "The Bolero: The Birth, Life, and Decline of Mexican Modernity," *Latin American Music Review* 20 (1999): 30–58. C. Monsiváis, *Mexican Postcards* (New York: Verso Press, 1997). A. Piñeda Franco, "The Cuban Bolero and Its Transculturation to Mexico: The Case of Agustín Lara," *Studies in Latin American Popular Culture* 15 (1996): 120–130; quotation on 123. V. Knights, "Tears and Screams: Performances of Pleasure and Pain in the Bolero," in *Queering the Pitch*, ed. S. Whiteley, and J. Rycenga (New York: Routledge, 2006); quotation on 85.

41. Y. M. Rivero, "Erasing Blackness: The Media Construction of 'Race' in *Mi Familia*, the First Puerto Rican Situation Comedy with a Black Family," *Media, Culture, and Society* 24, no.4 (2002): 481–497. Y. M. Rivero, *Tuning Out Blackness: Race and Nation in the History of Puerto Rican Television* (Durham: Duke University Press, 2005). Negrón-Muntaner, *Boricua Pop*. Aparicio and Chávez-Silverman, *Tropicalizations*.

42. Aparicio, "Jennifer as Selena." Guzmán and Valdivia, "Brain, Brow, and Booty." Cepeda, "*Mucho Loco* for Ricky Martin"; quotation on 222.

43. See Deborah Paredez, *Selenidad: Selena, Latinos, and the Performance of Memory* (Durham: Duke University Press, 2009); Deborah R. Vargas, "*Cruzando Frontejas*: Remapping Selena's Tejano Music Crossover," in *The Chicana/o Cultural Studies Reader*, ed. Angie Chabram-Dernersesian (New York: Routledge, 2006), 314–323.

44. Warner, *Fear of a Queer Planet*. José Esteban Muñoz, *Disidentifications: Queers of Color and the Performance of Politics* (Minneapolis: University of Minnesota Press, 1999). Juana

María Rodríguez, *Queer Latinidad: Identity Practices, Discursive Spaces* (New York: New York University Press, 2003). Negrón-Muntaner, *Boricua Pop.*

45. Yvonne Yarbro-Bejarano, "Crossing the Border with Chabela Vargas: A Chicana Femme's Tribute," in *Sex and Sexuality in Latin America*, ed. D. Balderston and D. J. Guy (New York: New York University Press, 1997), 33–43. Muñoz, *Disidentifications.* José Quiroga, *Tropics of Desire: Interventions from Queer Latino America* (New York: New York University Press, 2000). Susana Peña, "*Pájaration* and Transculturation: Language and Meaning in Miami's Cuban American Gay Worlds," in *Speaking in Queer Tongues: Globalization and Gay Language*, ed. W. Leap and T. Boellstorff (Urbana: University of Illinois Press, 2004). Negrón-Muntaner, *Boricua Pop.*

46. H. R. Ramírez, *A Language of (In)Visibility: Latina and Latino LGBT Images in Spanish-Language Television and Print Media* (New York: GLAAD Gay and Lesbian Alliance Against Defamation Center for the Study of Media and Society, 2004); quotation on 77.

47. Mitchell Fitch, "Queer Representations in Latino Theatre," *Latin American Theatre Review* 31, no. 2 (Spring 1998): 67–78.

48. A. Arrizón, *Latina Performance: Traversing the Stage* (Bloomington: Indiana University Press, 1999). M. Habell-Pallán, *Loca Motion: The Travels of Chicana and Latina Popular Culture* (New York: New York University Press, 2005). M. T. Marrero, "Out of the Fringe: Desire and Homosexuality in the 1990s Latino Theatre," in *Velvet Barrios*, ed. Gaspar de Alba, 283–294. Muñoz, *Disidentifications.* Quiroga, *Tropics of Desire.* Yarbro-Bejarano, *The Wounded Heart: Writings by Cherríe Moraga* (Austin: University of Texas Press, 2001). Luz Calvo, "Art Comes for the Archbishop: The Semiotics of Contemporary Chicana Feminism and the Work of Alma Lopez," *Meridians: Feminism, Race, Transnationalism* 5 (2004): 201–224. A. Arrizón, *Queering Mestizaje: Transculturation and Performance* (Ann Arbor: University of Michigan Press, 2006).

49. See Deborah R. Vargas, "Selena: Sounding a Transnational Latina/o Queer Imaginary," *English Language Notes* 45, no. 2 (Fall/Winter 2007).

50. Stuart Hall, "Encoding/Decoding," in Hall et al., *Culture, Media, Language* (London: Hutchinson, 1980), 128–138. Muñoz, *Disidentifications.* Negrón-Muntaner, *Boricua Pop.*

51. Quiroga, *Tropics of Desire*; quotations on 145, 146. Aparicio, *Listening to Salsa.* Aparicio and W. Valentín-Escobar, "Memorializing La Lupe and Lavoe: Singing Vulgarity, Transnationalism, and Gender," *Centro Journal* 16 (2004): 78–101. Knights, "Tears and Screams."

52. See *La Lupe Queen of Latin Soul*, directed by Ela Troyano (New York: Troyano Inc., 2008). See also Alexandra Vasquez and Ela Troyano, eds., *La Yiyiyi: Impacts of La Lupe* (Durham: Duke University Press, forthcoming).

53. Quiroga, *Tropics of Desire.* Aparicio and Valentín-Escobar, "Memorializing La Lupe and Lavoe." Muñoz, *Disidentifications.*

54. Quiroga, *Tropics of Desire*; quotation on 162.

55. Knights, "Tears and Screams," 85.

56. Quiroga, *Tropics of Desire.* V. Knights, "Queer Pleasures: The Bolero, Camp, and Almodóvar," in *Changing Tunes: The Use of Pre-existing Music in Film*, ed. P. Powrie, and R. Stilwell (Aldershot, U.K.: Ashgate, 2006), 91–104. Knights, "Tears and Screams."

57. Habell-Pallán, *Loca Motion*; quotation on 149.

58. Marie "Keta" Miranda, *Homegirls in the Public Sphere* (Austin: University of Texas Press, 2003).

59. Catherine Ramírez, *The Woman in the Zoot Suit* (Durham: Duke University Press, 2009), 20.

60. "Más Macha: The New Latina Action Hero," in *Action and Adventure Cinema*, ed. Yvonne Tasker (London: Routledge, 2004), 186–200.

61. J. Moore, *Going Down to the Barrio: Homeboys and Homegirls in Change* (Philadelphia: Temple University Press, 1991). M. Brown, *Gang Nation: Delinquent Citizens in Puerto Rican, Chicano, and Chicana Narratives* (Minneapolis: University of Minnesota Press, 2002). Fregoso, *MeXicana Encounters*. K. Miranda, *Homegirls in the Public Sphere* (Austin: University of Texas Press, 2003). J. Halberstam, *Female Masculinity* (Durham: Duke University Press, 1998). R. Kelly, "Hip Hop Chicano: A Separate but Parallel Story," in *It's Not about a Salary: Rap, Race, and Resistance in Los Angeles*, ed. B. Cross (New York: Verso, 1993), 65–75. Kelly, "Aztlan Underground," in *It's Not about a Salary*, ed. Cross, 265–266. R. Z. Rivera, "Hip Hop and New York Puerto Ricans," in *Latino/a Popular Culture*, ed. Habell-Pallán and Romero. Raquel Z. Rivera, *New York Ricans from the Hip Hop Zone* (New York: Palgrave, 2003).

62. R. T. Rodriguez, "Queering the Homeboy Aesthetic," *Aztlan: A Journal of Chicano Studies* 31 (2006): 127.

63. See Richard T. Rodriguez, *Next of Kin: The Family in Chicana/o Cultural Politics* (Durham: Duke University Press, 2009).

CHAPTER 9   CULTURAL PRODUCTION OF
KNOWLEDGE ON LATINA/O SEXUALITIES

1. An exemplary essay on this relationship can be found in Lawrence La Fountain-Stokes, "1898 and the History of a Queer Puerto Rican Century: Gay Lives, Island Debates, and Diasporic Experience," *Centro Journal* 11 (1999): 91–110. See also José Quiroga, "Latino Cultures, Imperial Sexualities," in *Tropics of Desire: Interventions from Queer Latino America* (New York: New York University Press, 2000). From a different but related angle, see Jasbir Puar, "Circuits of Queer Mobility, Tourism, Travel and Globalization," *Gay and Lesbian Quarterly* 8 (2002): 101–137. Also see M. Jacqui Alexander, "Not Just (Any) *Body* Can Be a Citizen: The Politics of Law, Sexuality, and Postcoloniality in Trinidad and Tobago and the Bahamas," *Feminist Review* 48 (1994): 5–22.

2. Cherríe Moraga and Gloria Anzaldúa, *This Bridge Called My Back: Writings by Radical Women of Color* (New York: Women of Color Press, 1983); Anzaldúa, *Borderlands/La Frontera: The New Mestiza* (San Francisco: Aunt Lute Books, 1987). Anzaldúa, *Making Face, Making Soul,* Haciendo Caras: *Critical Perspectives of Women of Color* (San Francisco: Aunt Lute Books, 1990). Haciendo Caras: *Critical Perspectives of Women of Color* (San Francisco: Aunt Lute Books, 1990).

3. Bernardo García, *The Development of a Latino Gay Identity* (New York: Routledge, 1998); quotation on 109.

4. Martin Duberman, ed., *Queer Representations: Reading Lives, Reading Cultures* (New York, 1997). George Chauncey, in *Gay New York: Gender, Urban Culture, and the Making of the Gay Male World, 1890–1940* (New York: Basic Books, 1994), does not include many Latino organizational structures in his study. In fact, Chauncey only refers to Puerto Ricans (the only Latinos mentioned) twice, once on p. 53 as merely "ethnic" and thus an Other in relation to the gay Other (he is discussing permissible shirt colors and the fact that chartreuse was seen as Latin, or worse, Negro), and on p. 141 in regard to the New York Society for the Prevention of Cruelty to Children and its persecution of sodomy, which only occurred in the ethnic barrios—once again black and Puerto Ricans were the majority persecuted.

5. For questions dealing with Latinos as a whole, see Suzanne Oboler, *Ethnic Labels, Latino Lives: Identity and the Politics of Representation in the United States* (Minneapolis: University of Minnesota Press, 1995), esp. chap. 3. Oboler states:

> Members also organized both a women's caucus and a men's caucus in which each group discussed sexism, homophobia, and machismo in their lives and relationships. Pablo Guzmán writes of the party's acceptance of the notion of "women's oppression" put forth by the women's movement but adds, "Since I'm talking about sexism, the second thing that made perhaps a greater impact on us was when we first heard about Gay Liberation. That's a whole other trip, because we found out it's a lot quicker for people to accept the fact that sisters should be in the front of the struggle, than saying that we're going to have gay people in the party." He goes on to explain that "from the time you were a kid your folks told you the worst thing you could be was gay." In his family, he was told that if he were to "turn out gay," he would be "disinherited, beat up, kicked out—and my father was *big*, you know, and fear . . . kept me from being gay. . . . When you think about fear keeping you from being anything, you realize there must be something wrong with it." Noting that he did not "turn out gay," Guzmán nevertheless emphasized that "the Gay Liberation struggle has shown us how to complete ourselves, so we've been able to accept this, and understand this." (55)

This is the only citation of "gay" in the book, which is one of the key texts in Latino/a Studies.

6. Héctor Carrillo, *The Night Is Young: Sexuality in Mexico in the Times of AIDS* (Chicago: University of Chicago Press, 2002). Rafael M. Díaz and George Ayala, "Social Discrimination and Health: The Case of Latino Gay Men and HIV Risk" (New York: Policy Institute of the National Gay and Lesbian Task Force, 2001). Manolo Guzmán, *Gay Hegemony/Latino Homosexualities* (New York: Routledge, 2006). María Cecilia Zea et al., "Asking and Telling: Communication about HIV Status among Latino HIV-Positive Gay Men," *AIDS and Behavior*, 7 (2003): 143–152. Alex Carballo-Diéguez and Curtis Dolezal, "HIV Risk Behaviors and Obstacles to Condom Use among Puerto Rican Men in New York City Who Have Sex with Men," *American Journal of Public Health* 86 (1996): 1619–1622.

7. Martin F. Manalansan, "In the Shadows of Stonewall: Examining Gay Transnational Politics and the Diasporic Dilemma," in *The Politics of Culture in the Shadow of Capital*, ed. Lisa Lowe and David Lloyd (Durham: Duke University Press, 1997), 485–503.

8. See Mirtha Quintanales, "I Come with No Illusions" and "I Paid Very Hard for My Immigrant Ignorance," in *This Bridge Called My Back*, ed. Moraga and Anzaldúa, 148–149, 150–156. Rosario Morales, "The Other Heritage," in *This Bridge Called My Back*, ed. Moraga and Anzaldúa, 107–108.

9. John Rechy, *City of Night* (New York: Grove Press, 1963), and *The Sexual Outlaw* (New York: Grove Press, 1977).

10. Luis Rafael Sanchez, *La Importancia de Llamarse Daniel Santos* (Hanover, N.H.: Ediciones El Norte, 1988). Manuel Ramos Otero, *El Cuento de la Mujer del Mar* (Río Piedras, P.R.: Ediciones Huracán, 1991), *Invitación al Polvo* (Río Piedras, P.R.: Plaza Mayor, 1991), *Tálamos y Tumbas, Prosa y Verso* (Guadalajara, Mex.: Universidad de Guadalajara, 1988), and *Cuentos de Buena Tinta* (San Juan: Instituto de Estudios Puertorriquenos, 1992).

11. Ana María Simo and Reinaldo García Ramos, "Hablando claro," *Mariel, revista de literatura y arte* 2 (1984): 9–10. Lourdes Argüelles and B. Ruby Rich, "Homosexuality,

Homophobia, and Revolution: Notes toward an Understanding of the Cuban Lesbian and Gay Male Experience," *Signs* 9 (1984): 683–699, 10 (1985): 120–136.

12. Studies on these and other Latin American writers, as well as on masculinity and sexuality in Latino America, can be found notably in Benigno Sifuentes-Jáuregui, *Transvestism, Masculinity, and Latin American Literature: Genders Share Flesh* (New York: Palgrave Macmillan, 2002). An interesting study of the way in which Arenas became classified and internationalized as a gay writer can be found in Jacqueline Loss, *Cosmopolitanisms and Latin America: Against the Destiny of Place* (New York: Palgrave Macmillan, 2005).

13. Richard Rodriguez, *Hunger of Memory: The Education of Richard Rodriguez* (Boston: Bantam Books, 1983).

14. Jaime Manrique, *Latin Moon in Manhattan* (New York: St. Martin's Press, 1992), *Eminent Maricones* (Madison: University of Wisconsin Press, 2002), and *Bésame Mucho* (New York: Painted Leaf Press, 1999).

15. Achy Obejas, *We Came All the Way from Cuba So You Could Dress Like This?* (Pittsburgh: Cleis Press, 1994), *Memory Mambo* (Pittsburgh: Cleis Press,1996), and *Days of Awe* (New York: Ballantine Books, 2002).

16. Ricardo Bracho's plays include *The Sweetest Hangover*, *A to B*, *Querido*, and *Mexican Psychotic*. Jorge Ignacio Cortiñas's works include the plays *Look! a Latino*, *Sleepwalkers*, *Tight Embrace*, and *Blind Mouth Singing*. Caridad Svich's plays include *Any Place but Here*, *Alchemy of Desire/Dead-Man's Blues*, *Iphigenia . . . a Rave Fable*, *Fugitive Pieces*, *The Tropic of X*, *Lucinda Caval*, *Magnificent Waste*, *Prodigal Kiss*, *Thrush*, *Luna Park*, and *Twelve Ophelias*. María Irene Fornés's plays include *Fefu and Her Friends*, *Sarita*, *Lolita in the Garden*, *Mud*, *Lovers and Keepers*, *Terra Icognita*, *Hunger*, *Balseros* (Rafters), and *Letters from Cuba*.

17. Michele Serros, *Chicana Falsa, and Other Stories of Death, Identity, and Oxnard* (New York: Riverhead Books, 1993). Alisa Valdes-Rodriguez, *The Dirty Girls Social Club* (New York: St. Martin's Press, 2003), *Playing with Boys* (New York: St. Martin's Griffin, 2005), *Make Him Look Good* (New York: St. Martin's Griffin, 2007), and *Haters* (Boston: Little, Brown, 2008). Mary Castillo, *Hot Tamara* (New York: Avon Trade, 2005). Michele Serros, *Honey Blonde Chica* (New York: Simon and Schuster, 2006).

18. Chela Sandoval, *Methodology of the Oppressed* (Minneapolis: University of Minnesota Press, 2000). Similar debates took place in the 1960s, when students and faculty seeking a more specifically political meaning to their work lobbied for ethnic studies programs. See, for example, Ignacio M. García, "Juncture in the Road: Chicano Studies since 'El plan de Santa Barbara,'" in *Chicanas/Chicanos at the Crossroads: Social, Economic, and Political Change*, ed. David R. Maciel and Isidro D. Ortíz (Tucson: University of Arizona Press, 1996), 181–203, esp. the following observations: "The lesbian Chicana scholars have even gone as far as promoting the idea that homosexuality is an integral part of Chicano culture. . . . It is even more likely that these scholars will further alienate themselves with their gender politics, which, unlike the politics of the Chicano Movement, are not based on what the predominantly working-class community thinks. The academy has become the only world for some of these scholars, because they have redefined the concept of community" (190).

19. See also Emilio Bejel, "*Fresa y chocolate o la salida de la guarida*," *Casa de las Americas* 35 (1994): 10–22. Alicia Gaspar de Alba, ed., *Velvet Barrios: Popular Culture and Chicana/o Sexualities* (New York: Palgrave Macmillan, 2003); and "Tortillerismo: Work by Chicana Lesbians," *Signs* 18 (1993): 956–963. Emma Pérez, "Sexuality and Discourse: Notes from a Chicana Survivor, in *Chicana Lesbians: The Girls Our Mothers Warned Us About*, ed. Carla Trujillo (Berkeley: University of California Press, 1991).

20. Frances Negrón-Muntaner, *Boricua Pop: Puerto Ricans and American Culture* (New York: New York University Press, 2004). Licia Fiol Matta, *A Queer Mother for the Nation: The State and Gabriela Mistral* (Minneapolis: University of Minnesota Press, 2002). Frances Aparicio and Cándida Jáquez, with María Elena Cepeda, eds., *Musical Migrations*, vol 1: *Transnationalism and Cultural Hybridity in Latin/o America* (New York: Macmillan, 2003). Juan Carlos Quintero-Herencia, *La máquina de la salsa* (San Juan: Ediciones Vértigo, 2005).

21. José Esteban Muñoz, *Disidentifications: Queers of Color and the Performance of Politics* (Minneapolis: University of Minnesota Press, 1999). Chon Noriega and Ana M. López, eds., *The Ethnic Eye: Latino Media Arts* (Minneapolis: University of Minnesota Press, 1996). Alina Troyano, with Ela Troyano and Uzi Parnes, *I, Carmelita Tropicana: Performing between Cultures* (Boston: Beacon Press, 2000). C. E. Rodríguez, *Heroes, Lovers, and Others: The Story of Latinos in Hollywood* (Washington, D.C.: Smithsonian Books, 2004). Quiroga, *Tropics of Desire*.

CHAPTER 10   WHERE THERE'S *QUERER*

Acknowledgments: Special thanks to Tony Powell and Christopher N. Ferreria for first introducing us to the music.

CHAPTER 11   RELIGION/SPIRITUALITY, U.S. LATINA/O COMMUNITIES, AND SEXUALITY SCHOLARSHIP

Acknowledgments: Many thanks to Gloria González-López for inspiring me to write this chapter. I particularly wish to thank Marysol Asencio and Anne Theriault for their continuous support, suggestions for reading and related material, and patience. My acknowledgment also goes to Chanda Cook, a research assistant whose research skills helped me find significant sources to delineate the contours of this chapter. A last word of appreciation goes to Eric M. Rodriguez, for his publications, and for the "push" to get further immersed into these literatures.

1. Anthony Faiola, "In U.S., Hispanics Bring Catholicism to Its Feet: The Church Offers Livelier Services for a Growing Constituency of Charismatics," *Washington Post*, May 7, 2007, http://www.washingtonpost.com.

2. The Pew Hispanic Center and the Pew Forum on Religion and Public Life, "Changing Faiths: Latinos and the Transformation of American Religion," April 25, 2007, http://pewforum.org/surveys/hispanic/. Gloria González-López and Salvador Vidal-Ortiz, "Latinas and Latinos, Sexuality, and Society: A Critical Sociological Perspective," in *Latino/as in the United States: Changing the Face of América*, ed. Rodríguez et al. (New York: Springer, 2008), 308–322. Vidal-Ortiz, "Sexuality Discussions in *Santería*: A Case Study of Religion and Sexuality," *Sexuality Research and Social Policy* 3 (2006): 52–66. For purposes of this chapter, the term sexuality includes sexual reproduction and sexual health; I refer to gender and women's issues as part of sexuality, since so much of the literature refers to the reproductive or (sometimes) oppressive status of women. Similarly, the use of gender includes both gender identity and expression (as in the case of transgender and transsexual topics) as well as its more traditional use of linking sex and gender.

3. Throughout this chapter, I use the category religion as institutionally based, and spirituality as a state of being, a belief system that may be independent of religion, or as an everyday life experience potentially tied to cultural markers. An important distinction made in the main text and in these notes is the use of social sciences

versus other literatures (e.g., humanities based, religious studies). Throughout the essay, I discuss the main articles, chapters, or books that address the relationship of any of these three variables to each other in the social sciences; yet some auto-biographical or literature-based discussions from a humanities-based posture are introduced through endnotes. While I have challenged the notion of social scientific knowledge production through an exclusion of the self and one's autobiography in my autoethnographic work, and I believe interdisciplinarity is essential to grasping the complexity of issues brought together in the study of religion/spirituality, sexu-ality, and Latina/os, this essay foregrounds the social science literatures as a way of maintaining focus. For more on this point, see Vidal-Ortiz, "On Being a White Person of Color: Using Autoethnography to Understand Puerto Rican's Racialization," *Quali-tative Sociology* 27 (2004): 179–203.

4. I have not found a lot of literature addressing the intersection between Latino hetero-sexual men and spirituality/religiosity. This gap is discussed in the conclusion as one area that requires further attention.

5. For readings on Latina/os' impact on U.S. religion, as well as popular religion for Latina/os, see Ana María Díaz-Stevens and Anthony M. Stevens-Arroyo, *Recognizing the Latino Resurgence in U.S. Religion: The Emmaus Paradigm* (Boulder, Colo.: Westview Press, 1998), and Stevens-Arroyo and Díaz-Stevens, eds., *An Enduring Flame: Studies on Latino Popular Religiosity* (New York: Bildner Center Books, 1994).

6. Helen R. Ebaugh, "Religion and the New Immigrants," in *Handbook of the Sociology of Religion*, ed. Michele Dillon (New York: Cambridge University Press, 2003), 225–239. "New" immigrants here refers to the post-1965 wave of immigrants, who were pri-marily Asian and Latin American.

7. Indeed, Latina/os do not always practice one form of religious tradition, as illustrated in Thomas A. Tweed, *Our Lady of the Exile: Diasporic Religion at a Cuban Catholic Shrine in Miami* (New York: Oxford University Press, 1997).

8. For a general description of worthiness and Puerto Ricans and a particular discussion of the general media image of Padilla, see Ana Y. Ramos-Zayas, "Delinquent Citizen-ship, National Performances: Racialization, Surveillance, and the Politics of 'Wor-thiness' in Puerto Rican Chicago," *Latino Studies* 2 (2004): 26–44. Also see Harvard University's "Pluralism Project" and its reprint of Abbas Barzegar's article from *High Plains Applied Anthropologist*, http://www.pluralism.org/research/profiles/.

9. Sarah Stohlman, "At Yesenia's House: Central American Immigrant Pentecostalism, Congressional Homophily, and Religious Innovation in Los Angeles," *Qualitative Soci-ology* 30 (2007): 61–80. Vidal-Ortiz, "Religion and Sexuality in Latin American/U.S. Cultural Systems and the Practice of *Santería*," paper presented at the 99th annual meeting, American Sociological Association, San Francisco, 2004.

10. Lionel Cantú, "A Place Called Home: A Queer Political Economy of Mexican Immigrant Men's Family Experiences," in *Queer Families, Queer Politics: Challenging Culture and the State*, ed. Mary Bernstein and Renate Reimann (New York: Columbia University Press, 2001), 112–136. Manolo Guzmán, *Gay Hegemony/Latino Homosexualities* (New York: Routledge, 2006).

11. Barry A. Kosmin, Egon Mayer, and Ariela Keysar, "American Religious Identification Survey," The Graduate Center, City University of New York, http://www.gc.cuny.edu/faculty/research_briefs/aris/aris_part_two.htm; quotation on 8.

12. For a different perspective, see also the discussion of the two survey reports that follow. For academic references that show the impact of migration on religious practice and "host" religious sites, see Peter Casarella and Raúl Gómez, eds., *El*

Cuerpo de Cristo: The Hispanic Presence in the U.S. Catholic Church (New York: Cross-road Publishing, 1998); Ana María Díaz-Stevens, *Oxcart Catholicism on Fifth Avenue: The Impact of Puerto Rican Migration upon the Archdiocese of New York* (Notre Dame, Ind.: University of Notre Dame Press, 1993); and Anthony M. Stevens-Arroyo, *Prophets Denied Honor: An Anthology on the Hispano Church of the United States* (Maryknoll, N.Y.: Orbis Books, 1980). On religion on the U.S.-Mexico border, see Luis D. León, *La Llorona's Children: Religion, Life, and Death in the U.S.-Mexican Borderlands* (Berkeley: University of California Press, 2004); and Jeannette Rodriguez, *Our Virgen de la Guadalupe: Faith and Empowerment among Mexican-American Women* (Austin: University of Texas Press, 1994).

13. For writings about women in Catholicism specifically, refer to Ana María Díaz-Stevens, "Latinas and the Church," in *Hispanic Catholic Culture in the U.S.: Issues and Concerns*, ed. Jay P. Dolan and Allan Figueroa Deck (Notre Dame, Ind.: University of Notre Dame Press, 1994), 240–277.

14. Gastón Espinoza, Virgilio Elizondo, and Jesse Miranda, "The Hispanic Churches in American Public Life: Summary of Findings"; quotations on 11–12, 12, 16, http://latinostudies.nd.edu/pubs/pubs/HispChurchesEnglish.

15. Kosmin, Mayer, and Keysar, "American Religious Identification Survey."

16. Espinoza, Elizondo, and Miranda, "Hispanic Churches in American Public Life," 16. Note that the authors edited *Latino Religions and Civic Activism in the United States* (New York: Oxford University Press, 2005), the goal of which was to "initiate a critical discussion about the impact of Latino religions on political, civic, and social action" (5) in the United States.

17. Espinoza, Elizondo, and Miranda, "Hispanic Churches in American Public Life," 19, 21.

18. Pew Hispanic Center and Pew Forum on Religion and Public Life, "Changing Faiths."

19. Ibid.; quotation of respondents' self-descriptions on 8, statistics on education and income on 11–12.

20. Laurel Zwissler, "Spiritual, but Religious: 'Spirituality' among Religiously Motivated Feminist Activists," *Culture and Religion* 8 (2007): 51–69. Wade Clark Roof, "Religion and Spirituality: Toward an Integrated Analysis," in *Handbook of the Sociology of Religion*, ed. Dillon, 137–148.

21. Zwissler, "Spiritual, but Religious." In separating the spiritual from the religious and making it common language across populations, activists in social justice movements in one case (discussed by Zwissler) linked themselves to other activists of religious belief systems different from their own. In doing so, they distinguished themselves from more conservative members of their religious congregations and at the same time spoke to or engaged with them, attempting to alter their conservative position on certain matters.

22. Cecilia Menjívar, "Religion and Immigration in Comparative Perspective: Catholic and Evangelical Salvadorans in San Francisco, Washington, D.C., and Phoenix," *Sociology of Religion* 64 (2003): 21–45. Stohlman, "At Yesenia's House."

23. Milagros Peña, "Border Crossings: Sociological Analysis and the Latina and Latino Religious Experience," *Journal of Hispanic/Latino Theology* 4 (1997): 13–27. M. Peña, "Devising a Study on Religion and the Latina Experience," *Social Compass* 49 (2002): 281–294.

24. M. Peña, "Border Crossings." M. Peña, "Religion and the Latina Experience." M. Peña and Lisa M. Frehill, "Latina Religious Practice: Analyzing Cultural Dimensions in Measures of Sociology," *Journal of the Scientific Study of Religion* 37 (1998): 620–635.

About 9 percent were of some other religion, and the other 11 percent reported no religious affiliation.

25. Stohlman, "At Yesenia's House." This ethnography shows a particular situation of a presumably unacceptable arrangement of a female and two male roommates who share a studio in Los Angeles. The author asked about the morality involved in such an arrangement, only to be told that these are part of the teachings of God, and also that the pastor was supportive of helping one's neighbor. Whether there is a sexual subtext unavailable to the reader is only secondary to the religious (as within their Pentecostal group) and larger social (i.e., in Los Angeles or in the United States) arrangement of (presumably) heterosexual men and women living together, but not sharing a sexual, intimate life.

26. In "How Monochromatic Is Church Membership? Racial-Ethnic Diversity in Religious Community," *Sociology of Religion* 64 (2003): 65–85, Kevin D. Dougherty also stresses this point, as he looks at five different denominations and their white/black/Latino shared presence. While most are generally diverse ethnically and racially speaking, there is some correlation between crossing class lines, yet remaining within a racial group. Moreover, of all the denominations, Southern Baptist is the one with the most homogeneity, ethnoracially speaking.

27. Stohlman, "At Yesenia's House."

28. Menjívar, "Religion and Immigration in Comparative Perspective."

29. See Bonnie Urciuoli, *Exposing Prejudice: Puerto Rican Experiences of Language, Race, and Class* (Boulder, Colo.: Westview Press, 1996), Vidal-Ortiz, "On Being a White Person of Color."

30. Olivia M. Espín, *Women Crossing Boundaries: A Psychology of Immigration and Transformations of Sexuality* (Florence, Ky.: Taylor and Frances/Routledge, 1999).

31. Most recent sexuality research in U.S. scholarship (not specific to Latina/o populations) produces sexuality as spiritual and earthlike, as linked to nature, or as a division of body and spirit that needs to be linked, as in Loraine Hutchins, "Erotic Rites: A Cultural Analysis of Contemporary U.S. Sacred Sexuality Traditions and Trends" (Ph.D. diss., Union Institute, Cincinnati, 2001), and Martha J. Horn, "Sexual Orientation and Embodied Spirituality as Predictors of Personal Well-Being and Health Practices" (Ph.D. diss., Loyola College in Maryland, 2005). These works aside, oftentimes a reduction of sexuality to the earth is a reduction to women as closer to the earth (as those birthing the world), and sometimes it is to indigenous and other racialized groups of people. A "return to nature" of both spirituality and sexuality takes on the form of indigenous peoples, women, and to a lesser degree, African-descendant peoples—where primitive becomes closer to nature, and thus, go(o)d. Ironically, the colonization of lands and cultures was enacted in order to save those impacted, disrobing them of their tribal and animalistic cultures and making their groups erupt into modernization and assimilation. For a significant challenge to this duality, see Sylvia Marcos, "Beyond Binary Categories: Mesoamerican Religious Sexuality," in *Religion and Sexuality in Cross-Cultural Perspective*, ed. Stephen Ellingson and M. Christian Green (New York: Routledge, 2002), 111–135.

32. Olivia Espín, "Spiritual Power in the Mundane World: Hispanic Female Healers in Urban U.S. Communities," in Espín, *Latina Realities: Essays on Healing, Migration, and Sexuality* (Boulder, Colo.: Westview Press, 1997). Espín, "Issues of Identity in the Psychology of Latina Lesbians," in Espín, *Latina Healers: Lives of Power and Tradition* (Encino, Calif.: Floricanto Press, 1996).

33. Espín, *Latina Realities*; quotation on 89.

34. A related critique of limited scope or specificity can be made of Eric M. Rodriguez's work ("At the Intersection of Church and Gay: Religion, Spirituality, Conflict, and Integration in Gay, Lesbian, and Bisexual People of Faith" [Ph.D. diss., City University of New York, 2006], 4, 43) as he focuses on homosexualities, not broader sexualities, in religious practice. While his previous work (Eric M. Rodriguez and Suzanne C. Ouellette, "Religion and Masculinity in Latino Gay Lives," in *Gay Masculinities*, ed. Peter Nardi [Thousand Oaks, Calif.: Sage Publications, 2000], 101–129) addresses gay religious Latino men and is based on the stories of four men, in his most recent work, Rodriguez distances himself from that qualitative approach and moves into a statistical analysis (of secondary data) of gay Christians.

35. Rodriguez and Ouellette, "Religion and Masculinity in Latino Gay Lives"; quotations on 106, 124, 125, 126. The chapter poses a set of methodological limitations: (*a*) the focus of the 40 interviews from which these four were extracted were not about machismo and masculinity; (*b*) content analysis was used to better understand the use of words such as *men, masculinity, man, macho*, and *father*; (*c*) Latino men in this religious context are the only ones associated with machismo literatures, and while it may potentially reinforce the popular and academic relationship between machismo and Latino men as a relationship that excludes other ethnoracial men, or women, from machismo, it delves into the relationship of masculinity for Latino men in religious contexts and thus serves further scholarship.

36. Gloria González-López, "*Confesiones de Mujer*: The Catholic Church and Sacred Morality in the Sex Lives of Mexican Immigrant Women," in *Sexual Inequalities and Social Justice*, ed. Niels F. Teunis and Gilbert Herdt (Berkeley: University of California Press, 2007), 148–173. Although her book *Erotic Journeys* also addresses religion, this article is more directly related to my review.

37. Salvador Vidal-Ortiz, "Sexuality and Gender in *Santería*: LGBT Identities at the Crossroads of Religious Practices and Beliefs," in *Gay Religion*, ed. Scott Thumma and Edward R. Gray (Walnut Creek, Calif.: AltaMira Press, 2005), 115–137. Vidal-Ortiz, "Sexuality Discussions in *Santería*." Worthy of mention in this regard are the works by Mary Ann Clark, Randy Conner, and Roberto Strongman. Clark, *Where Men Are Wives and Mothers Rule: Santería Ritual Practices and Their Gender Implications* (Gainesville: University Press of Florida, 2005), focuses on women and feminism in Santería and has little to do with sexuality among *Santería* practitioners, although she develops a feminist analysis of Santería spaces to challenge the perception of such spaces as male centered and powerful. Conner, *Queering Creole Spiritual Traditions: Lesbian, Gay, Bisexual, and Transgender Participation in African-Inspired Traditions in the Americas* (New York: Harrington Park Press, 2004), develops work among LGBT populations that practice Creole traditions, but the traditions he studies are not exclusively Latina/o or Afro-Latina/o, nor are the populations exclusively (or predominantly) U.S. Latina/o populations. In "Syncretic Religion and Dissident Sexuality" (in *Queer Globalizations: Citizenship and the Afterlife of Colonialism*, ed. Arnaldo Cruz-Malavé and Martin F. Manalansan [New York: New York University Press, 2002], 176–192), Strongman writes about the syncretic religious aspects of Santería and Candomblé but does not devote much space to Latina/o communities in particular.

38. Morris Kennedy, "*Santeria* Faith Much-Practiced in Tampa," *Tampa Tribune*, January 1, 2000, 9. Vidal-Ortiz, "Sexuality and Gender in *Santería*." The mere fact that a full paragraph is required to describe Santería while introducing Catholicism or the MCCNY church takes only a sentence (if that much) delineates the marginality of the former as a religion.

39. Vidal-Ortiz, "Sexuality Discussions in *Santería*." Vidal-Ortiz, "'The Puerto Rican Way Is More Tolerant': Constructions and Uses of Homophobia among *Santeria* Practitioners across Ethno-Racial and National Identification," *Sexualities* 11 (2008): 476–495. Vidal-Ortiz, "Sexuality and Gender in *Santería*." Clark, in *Where Men Are Wives and Mothers Rule*, argues that the *babalawo*, a "higher" priest than the *oriaté* (which like the oriaté requires a male practitioner but, unlike the oriaté, is restricted to heterosexual men), is no longer as central to the religious cultural practice and that Santería is a female-dominant space, owing to the fact that women constitute more than half of its practitioners and take on leadership roles, as well as tasks and centrality both in possession and even in general animal sacrifice. Practitioners in my study often referred to Santería houses as oriaté led—where sometimes a babalawo is not utilized anymore. Thus, there is a very changing set of cultural values as to who "rules" and guides in Santería, which may show productive arrangements in the coming decades. For those interested in comparative work, relate Clark's readings of Santería to Espín's (*Latina Healers*, 1996) work with *curanderas/espiritistas/santeras* and Díaz-Stevens's ("Latinas and the Church," 1994) work on women's roles in the Catholic tradition.

40. I have made this argument in a book in progress, tentatively titled "An Instrument of the *Orishas*: Racialized Sexual Minorities in *Santería*."

41. Marysol W. Asencio, *Sex and Sexuality among New York's Puerto Rican Youth* (Boulder, Colo.: Lynne Rienner Publishers, 2002).

42. Menjívar, "Introduction: Public Religion and Immigration across National Contexts," *American Behavioral Scientist* 49 (2006): 1447–1454. Ebaugh, "Religion and the New Immigrants."

CHAPTER 12   LATINA/O SEXUALITIES IN MOTION

1. Cindy Patton and Benigno Sánchez-Eppler, *Queer Diasporas* (Durham: Duke University Press, 2000). Cruz-Malavé and Manalansan, eds., *Queer Globalizations: Citizenship and the Afterlife of Colonialism* (New York: New York University Press, 2002); quotations on 3, 2. Eithne Luibhéid and Lionel Cantú Jr., eds., *Queer Migrations: Sexuality, U.S. Citizenship, and Border Crossings* (Minneapolis: University of Minnesota Press, 2005). Brad Epps, Keja Valens, and Bill Johnson González, eds., *Passing Lines: Sexuality and Immigration* (Cambridge: Harvard University, David Rockefeller Center for Latin American Studies, 2005); quotations on 7.

2. Eithne Luibhéid, "Thinking Sex/Thinking Gender: Heteronormativity and Immigration Scholarship, a Call for Change," *Gay and Lesbian Quarterly* 10 (2004): 227–233; quotation on 227. Luibhéid, *Entry Denied: Controlling Sexuality at the Border* (Minneapolis: University of Minnesota Press, 2002). Margot Canaday, "Who Is a Homosexual? The Consolidation of Sexual Identities in Mid-Twentieth-Century American Immigration Law," *Law and Social Inquiry* 28 (2003): 351–386. Siobhan Somerville, "Sexual Aliens and the Racialized State: A Queer Reading of the 1952 U.S. Immigration and Nationality Act," in *Queer Migrations*, ed. Luibhéid and Cantú. Martin F. Manalansan, "Queer Intersections: Sexuality and Gender in Migration Studies," *International Migration Review* 40 (2006): 224–249.

3. Luibhéid, *Entry Denied*; quotations on x, xvi.

4. Ibid., xv.

5. Ibid.; quotations on 3, 5, 9, 78.

6. Ibid.; quotations on 95, 87.

7. Canaday, "Who Is a Homosexual?"; quotation on 351. Epps, Valens, and Johnson González, *Passing Lines*; quotation on 8.

8. Epps, Valens, and Johnson González, in *Passing Lines*; quotation on 16. B. M. Fernandez, "HIV Exclusion of Immigrants under the Immigration Reform and Control Act of 1986," *La Raza Law Journal* 5 (1992): 65–107. Jorge L. Carro, "From Constitutional Psychopathic Inferiority to AIDS: What Is the Future for Homosexual Aliens?" *Yale Law and Policy Review* 7 (1989): 51–78; quotation on 77. Luibhéid, *Entry Denied*.

9. Timothy J. Randazzo, "Social and Legal Barriers: Sexual Orientation and Asylum in the United States," in *Queer Migrations*, ed. Luibhéid and Cantú, 30–60; quotations on 35, 37. Juana María Rodríguez, "The Subject on Trial: Reading *in re Tenorio* as Transnational Narrative," in *Queer Latinidad: Identity Practices, Discursive Spaces* (New York: New York University Press, 2003), 84–113. *Geovanni Hernandez-Montiel v. Immigration and Naturalization Service*, U.S. Court of Appeals, 9th Circuit (August 24, 2000), *International Journal of Refugee Law* 12, (2001): 608–625. Jason Cox, "Redefining Gender: *Hernandez-Montiel v. INS*," *Houston Journal of International Law* 24 (2001): 187–207. Michael G. Daugherty, "The Ninth Circuit, the BIA, and the INS: The Shifting State of the Particular Social Group Definition in the Ninth Circuit and Its Impact on Pending and Future Cases," *Brandeis Law Journal* 41 (2003): 631–658. "Immigration Law—Asylum—Ninth Circuit Holds That Persecuted Homosexual Mexican Man with a Female Sexual Identity Qualifies for Asylum under Particular Social Group Standard.—*Hernandez-Monteil v. INS*, 225 f.3d 1084 (9th cir., 2000)," *Harvard Law Review* 114 (2001): 2569–2575.

10. Lionel Cantú, with Eithne Luibhéid and Alexandra M. Stern, "Well-Founded Fear: Political Asylum and the Boundaries of Sexual Identity in the U.S.-Mexico Borderlands," in *Queer Migrations*, ed. Luibhéid and Cantú, 61–74; quotation on 61–62. Tracy J. Davis, "Opening the Doors of Immigration: Sexual Orientation and Asylum in the United States," *Human Rights Brief: A Legal Resource for the International Human Rights Community* 6 (1999). Katharine M. Donato et al., "A Glass Half Full? Gender in Migration Studies," *International Migration Review* 40 (2006): 3–26.

11. Alisa Solomon, "Trans/migrant: Christina Madrazo's All-American Story," in *Queer Migrations*, ed. Luibhéid and Cantú, 3–29. Luibhéid, *Entry Denied*, chap. 5.

12. Jessica Chapin, "Closing America's 'Back Door,'" *Gay and Lesbian Quarterly* 4 (1998): 403–422.

13. Lourdes Argüelles and Anne Rivero, "Violence, Migration, and Compassionate Practice: Conversations with Some Latinas We Think We Know," in *Racism in the Lives of Women: Testimony, Theory, and Guides to Antiracist Practice*, ed. Jeanne Adelman and Gloria M. Enguídanos (New York: Haworth Press, 1995), 149–160; quotation on 149.

14. Pedro B. Aguilar, "Sexilio," *Corpus* I (Spring 2003): 47–52. Jaime Cortez, *Sexile/Sexilio* (Los Angeles: Institute for Gay Men's Health, 2004). Manolo Guzmán, "'Pa' la Escuelita con Mucho Cuida'o y por la Orillita': A Journey through the Contested Terrains of the Nation and Sexual Orientation," in *Puerto Rican Jam: Essays on Culture and Politics*, ed. Frances Negrón-Muntaner and Ramón Grosfoguel (Minneapolis: University of Minnesota Press, 1997), 209–228; quotation on 227. Alberto Sandoval-Sánchez, "Politicizing Abjection: In the Manner of a Prologue for the Articulation of AIDS Latino Queer Identities," *American Literary History* 17 (2005): 542–549.

15. Cortez, *Sexile/Sexilio*.

16. David William Foster, "The Homoerotic Diaspora in Latin America," *Latin American Perspectives* 29 (2002): 163–189; quotations on 165. David Kirby, "Coming to America to Be Gay," *The Advocate* 834 (2001): 29.

17. Lawrence La Fountain-Stokes, "Cultures of the Puerto Rican Queer Diaspora," in *Passing Lines*, ed. Epps, Valens, and Johnson González, 275–309; quotation on 276. Sandoval-Sánchez, "Politicizing Abjection"; quotations on 542, 543.

18. Lionel Cantú, "A Place Called Home: A Queer Political Economy of Mexican Immigrant Men's Family Experiences," in *Queer Families, Queer Politics: Challenging Culture and the State*, ed. Mary Bernstein and Renate Reimann (New York: Columbia University Press, 2001), 112–136; quotation on 122. Cantú, "Entre Hombres/Between Men: Latino Masculinities and Homosexualities," in *Gay Masculinities*, ed. Peter Nardi (Thousand Oaks, Calif.: Sage Publications, 2000), 224–246.

19. Luibhéid, "Thinking Sex/Thinking Gender"; quotation on 228. Saskia Sassen, "Why Migration?" *NACLA Report on the Americas* (1992), 26.

20. Héctor Carrillo, "Sexual Migration, Cross-Cultural Sexual Encounters, and Sexual Health," *Sexuality Research and Social Policy* 1 (2004): 58–70; quotations on 59. See Gloria González-López, *Erotic Journeys: Mexican Immigrants and Their Sex Lives* (Berkeley: University of California Press, 2005).

21. Carrillo, "Sexual Migration"; quotations on 68. See also Gisela Fosado, "Gay Sex Tourism, Ambiguity, and Transnational Love in Havana," in *Cuba Transnational*, ed. Damián J. Fernández (Gainesville: University Press of Florida, 2005), 61–78.

22. Ibid.; quotation on 67. Marysol W. Asencio, *Sex and Sexuality among New York's Puerto Rican Youths* (Boulder, Colo.: Lynne Rienner Publishers, 2002); quotation on 29.

23. Cantú, "Entre Hombres/Between Men"; quotation on 225.

24. Cantú, "A Place Called Home," 113 (emphasis in original).

25. Nancy S. Landale and Susan M. Hauan, "Migration and Premarital Childbearing among Puerto Rican Women," *Demography* 33 (1996): 429–442; quotation on 429.

26. Laura Briggs, "*La Vida*, Moynihan, and Other Libels: Migration, Social Science, and the Making of the Puerto Rican Welfare Queen," *Centro Journal* 14 (2002); quotations on 87, 76, 84.

27. Adaljiza Sosa Riddell, "Bioethics of Reproductive Technologies: Impacts and Implications for Latinas," in *Chicana Critical Issues*, ed. Norma Alarcón et al. (Berkeley: Third Women Press, 1993), 183–196. Iris Lopez, "Agency and Constraint: Sterilization and Reproductive Freedom among Puerto Rican Women in NYC," in *Situated Lives*, ed. Louise Lamphere, Helena Ragone, and Patricia Zavella (New York: Routledge, 1997), 157–174; quotation on 157. Elena R. Gutiérrez, "Policing Pregnant Pilgrims: Situating the Sterilization Abuse of Mexican-Origin Women in Los Angeles County," in *Women, Health, and Nation*, ed. Georgina Feldberg, Molly Ladd-Taylor, and Kathryn McPherson (Montreal: McGill-Queens University Press, 2003).

28. Gónzalez-López, *Erotic Journeys*; quotation on 4–5 (emphasis added).

29. Ibid.; quotations on 187, 203, 231, 206.

30. Jennifer S. Hirsch, *A Courtship after Marriage: Sexuality and Love in Mexican Transnational Families* (Los Angeles: University of California Press, 2003); quotations on 267.

31. González-López, *Erotic Journeys*. D. M. McKee and A. Karasz, "'You have to give her that confidence': Conversations about Sex in Hispanic Mother-Daughter Dyads," *Journal of Adolescent Research* 21 (2006): 158–184. Erum Nadeem, Laura Romo, and Marian Sigman, "Knowledge about Condoms among Low-Income Pregnant Latina Adolescents in Relation to Explicit Maternal Discussion of Contraceptives," *Journal of Adolescent Health* 39 (2006): 9–15. Lucia F. O'Sullivan et al., "Mother-Daughter Communication about Sexuality in a Clinical Sample of Hispanic Adolescent Girls," *Hispanic Journal of Behavioral Sciences* 21 (1999): 447–469. Marcella Raffaelli and Lenna L. Ontai, "'She's

16 years old and there's boys calling over to the house': An Exploratory Study of Sexual Socialization in Latino Families," *Culture, Health, and Sexuality* 3 (2001): 295–310. Laura Romo et al., "Mexican-American Adolescents' Responsiveness to Their Mothers' Questions about Dating and Sexuality," *Journal of Applied Developmental Psychology* 25 (2004): 501–522. Gloria González-López, "Fathering Latina Sexualities: Mexican Men and the Virginity of Their Daughters," *Journal of Marriage and the Family* 66 (2004): 1118–1130.

32. Raffaelli and Ontai, "She's 16 years old"; quotation on 306–307. S. L. Faulkner, "Good Girl or Flirt Girl? Latinas' Definitions of Sex and Sexual Relationships," *Hispanic Journal of Behavioral Sciences* 25 (2003): 174–200; quotations on 174, 192. Gloria González-López, "*De Madres a Hijas*: Gendered Lessons on Virginity across Generations of Mexican Immigrant Women," in *Gender and U.S. Immigration: Contemporary Trends*, ed. Pierette Hondagneu-Sotelo (Berkeley: University of California Press, 2003), 217–240.

33. McKee and Karasz, "You have to give her that confidence"; quotations on 177. Nadeem, Romo, and Sigman, "Knowledge about Condoms among Latina Adolescents"; quotations on 119n14.

34. Elaine Bell Kaplan and Leslie Cole, "'I want to read stuff on boys': White, Latina, and Black Girls Reading *Seventeen* Magazine and Encountering Adolescence," *Adolescence* 38 (2003): 141.

35. Olivia M. Espín, "Issues of Identity in the Psychology of Latina Lesbians," in *Lesbian Psychologies: Explorations and Challenges*, ed. Boston Lesbian Psychologies Collective (Urbana: University of Illinois Press, 1987). Espín, "Tribe," in Espín, *Latina Realities: Essays on Healing, Migration, and Sexuality* (Boulder, Colo.: Westview Press, 1997); quotations on 190, 192. "Crossing Borders and Boundaries: The Life Narratives of Immigrant Lesbians," in *Ethnic and Cultural Diversity among Lesbians and Gay Men*, ed. Beverly Greene (Thousand Oaks, Calif.: Sage Publications, 1997), 191–215.

36. Patricia Zavella, "Playing with Fire: The Gendered Construction of Chicana/Mexicana Sexuality," in *The Gender/Sexuality Reader: Culture, History, Political Economy*, ed. Roger Lancaster and Micaela di Leonardo (New York: Routledge, 1997); quotations on 403–404.

37. Hirsch, *Courtship after Marriage*. David J Bellis, *Hotel Ritz: Comparing Mexican and U.S. Street Prostitutes: Factors in HIV/AIDS Transmission* (New York: Haworth Press, 2003).

38. Cherríe Moraga and Gloria Anzaldúa, *This Bridge Called My Back: Writings by Radical Women of Color* (New York: Women of Color Press, 1983). Anzaldúa, *Borderlands/La Frontera: The New Mestiza* (San Francisco: Aunt Lute Books, 1987).

39. See James Naylor Green, *Beyond Carnival: Male Homosexuality in Twentieth-Century Brazil* (Chicago: University of Chicago Press, 1999). Don Kulick, *Travesti: Sex, Gender, and Culture among Brazilian Transgendered Prostitutes* (Chicago: University of Chicago Press, 1998).

CHAPTER 13   LATINAS, SEX WORK, AND TRAFFICKING IN THE UNITED STATES

Acknowledgments: We appreciate the helpful comments from two reviewers on an earlier version of this article. We are particularly grateful to Carole Vance for guidance and suggestions and to Montreece Payton, David A. Martinez, Mathew Marquez, and Marlene Felix for research assistance.

1. Kate Butcher, "Confusion between Prostitution and Sex Trafficking," *The Lancet*, June 7, 2003. For an overview of Latina sex workers in the United States, see Amalia L.

Cabezas, "Sex Workers," in *Oxford Latino/Latina Encyclopedia*, ed. Deena J. González and Suzanne Oboler (Oxford: Oxford University Press, 2005).

2. For information about laws that regulate sexually explicit materials in cyberspace, see C. J. Portenelli and C. W. Meade, "Censorship and the Internet: No Easy Answers," *SIECUS Report* 27 (1998): 4–8. Only licensed brothels can operate legally in ten (mostly rural) counties in Nevada. Brothels are regulated by local governments and the Nevada State Department of Health. For a discussion of brothels in the Nevada economy, see Kathryn Hausbeck and Barbara G. Brents, "Inside Nevada's Brothel Industry," in *Sex for Sale: Prostitution, Pornography, and the Sex Industry*, ed. Ronald Weitzer (New York: Routledge, 2000), 217–241.

3. Stripping and telephone sex work provide spatial separation of customer and provider. For further discussion of telephone sex work, see Grant Jewell Rich and Kathleen Guidroz, "Smart Girls Who Like Sex: Telephone Sex Workers," in *Sex for Sale*, ed. Weitzer, 35–48. In *G-Strings and Sympathy: Strip Club Regulars and Male Desire* (Durham: Duke University Press, 2002), Katherine Frank emphasizes that sexual intimacy did not take place in the clubs where she worked and conducted research in the South. Certainly, many other sex acts performed with a condom do not involve the exchange of bodily fluids.

4. Gail Peterson, "The Category 'Prostitute' in Scientific Inquiry," *Journal of Sex Research* 27 (1990): 397–407, esp. 399; quotation on 398. Amalia Cabezas, "Between Love and Money: Sex, Tourism, and Citizenship in Cuba and the Dominican Republic," *Signs* 29 (2004): 987–1015. Kamala Kempadoo and Jo Doezema, eds., *Global Sex Workers: Rights, Resistance, and Redefinition* (New York: Routledge, 1998). Sherry Deren et al., "HIV Risk Behaviors among Dominican Brothel and Street Prostitutes in New York City," *AIDS Education and Prevention* 8 (1996): 444–456.

5. For a study that is attentive to cultural and geographic differences, see Deren et al., "Dominican Brothel and Street Prostitutes."

6. For examinations of the participation of Mexican and Latin American women in sexual commerce in Louisiana, California, and Texas, see Marion Goldman, *Gold Diggers and Silver Miners: Prostitution and Social Life on the Comstock Lode* (Ann Arbor: University of Michigan Press, 1981). Gordon H. Frost, *The Gentlemen's Club: The Story of Prostitution in El Paso* (El Paso: Mangan, 1983). Thomas C. Mackey, *Red Lights Out: A Legal History of Prostitution, Disorderly Houses, and Vice Districts, 1870–1917* (New York: Garland, 1987). Richard F. Selcer, "Forth Worth and the Fraternity of Strange Women," *Southwestern Historical Quarterly* 96 (1992): 55–86. David C. Humphrey, "Prostitution in Texas: From the 1830s to the 1960s," *East Texas Historical Journal* 33 (1995): 27–43. Ann R. Gabbert, "Prostitution and Moral Reform in the Borderlands: El Paso, 1890–1920," *Journal of the History of Sexuality* 12 (2003): 575–604.

7. Nancy Romero-Daza, Margaret Weeks, and Merrill Singer, "Much More than HIV! The Reality of Life on the Streets for Drug-Using Sex Workers in Inner-City Hartford," *International Quarterly of Community Health Education* 18 (1998–99): 107–119. A. Hyamathi and R. Vasquez, "Impact of Poverty, Homelessness, and Drugs on Hispanic Women at Risk of HIV Infection," *Hispanic Journal of Behavioral Science* 11 (1989): 299–314. For a study of street-based prostitutes in Los Angeles, see David E. Kanouse et al., *Drawing a Probability Sample of Female Prostitutes in Los Angeles County* (Santa Monica, Calif.: Rand Corporation, 1999); for Chicago, see Jody Raphael and Deborah L. Shapiro, *Sisters Speak Out: The Lives and Needs of Prostituted Women in Chicago* (Chicago: Center for Impact Research, 2002), and Claudine O'Leary and Olivia Howard, *The Prostitution of Women and Girls in Metropolitan Chicago: A Preliminary Report* (Chicago:

Center for Impact Research, 2001). For New York City, see Juhu Thurkal and Melissa Ditmore, "Revolving Door: An Analysis of Street-Based Prostitution in New York City," Sex Workers Project, Urban Justice Center, 2003, http://www.urbanjustice.org/pdf/publications/.

8. See Deren et al., "Dominican Brothel and Street Prostitutes"; Marcia Hood-Brown, "Trading for a Place: Poor Women and Prostitution," *Journal of Poverty* 2 (1998): 13–33; J. Raul Magaña, "Sex, Drugs, and HIV: An Ethnographic Approach," *Social Science Medicine* 33 (1999): 5–9; Nancy Romero-Daza, Margaret Weeks, and Merrill Singer, "'Nobody Gives a Damn if I Live or Die': Violence, Drugs, and Street-Level Prostitution in Inner-City Hartford, Connecticut," *Medical Anthropology* 22 (2003): 233–259; Lori E. Dorfman, Pamela A. Derish, and Judith B. Cohen, "Hey, Girlfriend: An Evaluation of AIDS Prevention among Women in the Sex Industry," *Health Education Quarterly* 19 (1992): 25–40; Romero-Daza, Weeks, and Singer, "Much More than HIV!"; Lisa Maher, *Sexed Work: Gender, Race, and Resistance in a Brooklyn Drug Market* (New York: Clarendon Press of Oxford University Press, 1997); and Thurkal and Ditmore, "Revolving Door."

9. Deren et al., "Dominican Brothel and Street Prostitutes." Associated Press, "10 Men Charged With Running Memphis Brothel," October 25, 2006. Associated Press, "Police: Brothel at Ala. Trailer Park Grossed 800K Annually," February 28, 2007. Ernesto Londono, "Police in Area Targeting Brothels," *Washington Post*, January 20, 2006. Christine MacDonald, "2 Are No-Shows on Pimp Charges; Police Operation Targets Brothels," *Boston Globe*, January 15, 2006. Wayne Parry, "Arrests Highlight Scope of Human Trafficking," *Philadelphia Inquirer*, May 3, 2006. C. J. Vogel, "X-Rated," *Washingtonian*, November 2005. Maria Cramer and Christine MacDonald, "Police Seek to Stop Surge in Prostitution: Advocates Fearful for Women: Most Are Immigrants," *Boston Globe*, January 28, 2006. Steven Kreytak, "Plea Sheds Light on Immigrant Brothels," *Austin American-Statesman*, February 10, 2007.

10. "Independent contractor" is a legal term for a person who is hired to perform a job but is not an employee; the independent contractor is not entitled to the same labor and employee protections as an employee. For further discussion with regards to women of color, see Siobhan Brooks, "Exotic Dancing and Unionizing: The Challenge of Feminist and Antiracist Organizing at the Lusty Lady Theater," in *Feminism and Antiracism: International Struggles for Justice*, ed. France Twine Winddance and Kathleen M. Blee (New York: New York University Press, 2001), 59–70.

11. Wendy Chapkis, "Power and Control in the Commercial Sex Trade," in *Sex for Sale*, ed. Weitzer; quotation on 187. Brooks, "Exotic Dancing and Unionizing." Frank, *G-Strings and Sympathy.*

12. Armida Ayala, Joseph Carrier, and J. Raul Magaña, "The Underground World of Latina Sex Workers in *Cantinas*," in *AIDS Crossing Borders: The Spread of HIV among Migrant Latinos*, ed. Shiraz Mishra, Ross F. Conner, and J. Raul Magaña (Boulder, Colo.: Westview Press, 1996).

13. Elizabeth Bernstein, "Economies of Desire: Sexual Commerce and Post-Industrial Culture" (Ph.D. diss., University of California–Berkeley, 2001). Chapkis, "Power and Control." Kempadoo and Doezema, *Global Sex Workers.*

14. Donna J. Guy, *Sex and Danger in Buenos Aires: Prostitution, Family, and Nation in Argentina* (Lincoln: University of Nebraska Press, 1991). Jo Doezema, "Loose Women or Lost Women? The Re-Emergence of the Myth of White Slavery in Contemporary Discourses of Trafficking in Women," *Gender Issues* 18 (2000): 23–50. Judith R. Walkowitz, "Male Vice and Feminist Virtue: Feminism and the Politics of Prostitution in Nineteenth-Century Britain," *History Workshop Journal* 13 (1982): 79–93.

15. U.S. Department of Justice, "Assessment of U.S. Government Activities to Combat Trafficking in Persons," 2004, http://www.usdoj.gov/ag/annualreports/tr2005/assessmentofustipactivities. In *Trafficking in Women and Children: The U.S. and International Response*, Congressional Research Service Report 98–649C (Washington, D.C.: Library of Congress, 2000), Francis T. Maki and Grace Park estimate that more than 100,000 women and children are trafficked yearly for sexual exploitation from Latin America to the global market.

16. U.S. Government Accountability Office (GAO), "Human Trafficking: Better Data, Reporting, and Strategy Needed to Enhance U.S. Antitrafficking Efforts Abroad," Report to the Chairman, Committee on the Judiciary, and the Chairman, Committee on International Relations, House of Representatives (Washington, D.C., 2006); quotation on 3, http://www.gao.gov/new.items/d06825.pdf. Peter Landesman, "The Girls Next Door," *New York Times Magazine*, January 25, 2004. See also Jack Schafer's coverage, http://www.slate.com/id/2094502/.

17. Kamala Kempadoo, "Introduction: From Moral Panic to Global Justice: Changing Perspectives on Trafficking," in *Trafficking and Prostitution Reconsidered: New Perspectives on Migration, Sex Work, and Human Rights*, ed. Kempadoo (Boulder, Colo.: Paradigm Publishers, 2005). The new UN protocol contains an extensive list of practices that constitute trafficking, including "threat or use of force or coercion: kidnapping, fraud, and deception" and even the abuse of power and vulnerability of the victim; see http://www.uncjin.org/Documents/Conventions/dcatoc/final_documents_2/convention_%20traff_eng.pdf. See also Jennifer M. Chacón, "Misery and Myopia: Understanding the Failures of U.S. Efforts to Stop Human Trafficking," *Fordham Law Review* 74 (2006); quotation on 3.

18. When Congress enacted the TVPA in 2000, it also established the President's Interagency Task Force to Monitor and Combat Trafficking in Persons. The TVPA was reauthorized in 2003 and 2005: U.S. GAO, "Human Trafficking." For the political trajectory of the TVPA, see Gretchen Soderlund, "Running from the Rescuers: New U.S. Crusades against Sex Trafficking and the Rhetoric of Abolition," *NWSA Journal* 17 (2005): 64–87; Lisa Katayama, "Sex Trafficking: Zero Tolerance," *Mother Jones*, May 4, 2005; http://www.motherjones.com/news/dailymojo/2005/05/sex_trafficking.html, and Debbie Nathan, "Oversexed," *The Nation*, August 29, 2005, http://www.thenation.com/doc/20050829/nathan. According to the TVPA 2000, sex trafficking refers to the "recruitment, harboring, transportation, provision, or obtaining of a person for the purpose of a commercial sex act." The TVPA does not provide services to victims unless acts of sex trafficking meet the criteria of "severe forms of trafficking in persons." "Severe forms of trafficking in persons" means (*a*) sex trafficking in which a commercial sex act is induced by force, fraud, or coercion or in which the person induced to perform such act has not attained 18 years of age; or (*b*) the recruitment, harboring, transportation, provision, or obtaining of a person for labor or services, through the use of force, fraud, or coercion for the purpose of subjection to involuntary servitude, peonage, debt bondage, or slavery.

19. U.S. Department of State, "Trafficking in Persons Report," 2005; quotation on 19, http://www.state.gov/documents/organization/47255.pdf. Alice Miller, "Human Trafficking and American Policy," *SIPA News*, Columbia University, January 2007: 25–26, http://www.sipa.columbia.edu/about_sipa/sipa_publications/sipa_news/sipanewsf06.pdf. Joanna Busza, "Sex Work and Migration: The Dangers of Oversimplification—a Case Study of Vietnamese Women in Cambodia," *Health and Human Rights* 7 (2004): 231–250. Wendy Chapkis, "Soft Glove, Punishing Fist: The Trafficking Victims Protection Act of 2000," in *Regulating Sex: The Politics of Intimacy and Identity*, ed. Elizabeth

Bernstein and Laurie Schaffner (New York: Routledge, 2005), 51–65. In "Misery and Myopia," 20, Chacón details various situations in which victims cannot meet these requirements because of the traumatic events they have suffered.

20. U.S. GAO, "Human Trafficking"; quotation on 23. Department of Justice, "Assessment of U.S. Government Activities to Combat Trafficking in Persons," September 2006, http://www.usdoj.gov/ag/annualreports/tr2005/assessmentofustipactivities.pdf. Office to Monitor and Combat Trafficking in Persons, U.S. State Department, "Trafficking in Persons Report, 2008," http://www.state.gov/g/tip/rls/tiprpt/2008/.

21. Department of Justice, "Government Activities to Combat Trafficking in Persons," 10, indicates that some approvals are from prior fiscal years' filings and that some applicants have been denied twice.

22. Chapkis, "Soft Glove, Punishing Fist." Butcher, "Confusion between Prostitution and Sex Trafficking." Busza, "Sex Work and Migration." Sealing Cheng, "Interrogating the Absence of HIV/AIDS Prevention for Migrant Sex Workers in South Korea," *Health and Human Rights* 7 (2004): 231–249. Laura Agustín, "Migrants in the Mistress's House: Other Voices in the 'Trafficking' Debate," *Social Politics* 12 (2005): 96–117.

23. Agustín, "Migrants in the Mistress's House." Susanne Thorbeck and Bandana Pattanaik, *Transnational Prostitution: Changing Global Patterns* (New York: Zed Books, 2002). Marjan Wijers and Lin Lap-Chew, *Trafficking in Women: Forced Labour and Slavery-Like Practices in Marriage, Domestic Labour, and Prostitution* (Utrecht, The Netherlands: Foundation Against Trafficking in Women, 1998). Denise Brennan, "Methodological Challenges in Research with Trafficked Persons: Tales from the Field," *International Migration* 43 (2005): 35–54. See also the Immigration and Customs Enforcement news Web site, http://www.ice.gov/pi/news/factsheets/humantraffic_071404.htm.

24. Agustín, "Migrants in the Mistress's House." Wijers and Lap-Chew, *Trafficking in Women.* Chacón, "Misery and Myopia"; quotation on 18.

25. Amalia Cabezas, Ellen Reese, and Marguerite Waller, eds., *The Wages of Empire: Neoliberal Policies, Repression, and Women's Poverty* (Boulder, Colo.: Paradigm Publishers, 2007).

CHAPTER 14   LATINA *LESBIANAS, BIMUJERES,* AND TRANS IDENTITIES

1. M. Reyes, "Latina Lesbians and Alcohol and Other Drugs: Social Work Implications," *Alcoholism Treatment Quarterly* 16 (1998): 179–192; quotation on 180.

2. Yvonne Yarbro-Bejarano, "The Wounded Heart: Writings on Cherríe Moraga," in *Chicana Matters*, ed. A. Castañeda and D. González (Austin: University of Texas Press, 2001). Catrióna Rueda Esquibel, *With Her Machete in Her Hand: Reading Chicana Lesbians* (Austin: University of Texas Press, 2006). M. P. Brady, *Extinct Lands, Temporal Geographies: Chicana Literature and the Urgency of Space* (Durham: Duke University Press, 2002). Deborah Vargas, "Bidi Bidi Bom Bom: Selena and Tejano Music in the Making of Tejas," in *Latino/a Popular Culture*, ed. M. Habell-Pallán and M. Romero (New York: New York University Press, 2002), 117–126. Vargas, "*Cruzando Frontejas*: Mapping Selena's Tejano Music 'Crossover,'" in *Chicana Traditions: Continuity and Change*, ed. N. Cantú and O. Nájera-Ramírez (Urbana: University of Illinois Press, 2002), 224–236. E. Hernández, "Chronotope of Desire: Emma Pérez's Gulf Dreams," in *Chicana Feminisms, A Critical Reader*, ed. G. F. Arredondo et al. (Durham: Duke University Press, 2003), 155–178. T. López-Craig, "The Role of Carmelita Tropicana in the Performance Art of Alina Troyano," *Journal of Lesbian Studies* 7 (2003): 47–56. Luz Calvo, "Art Comes for the Archbishop: Contemporary Chicana Feminist Struggle,"

Meridians: Feminism, Race, Transnationalism 5 (2004): 201–224. S. K. Soto, "Cherríe Moraga's Going Brown: "Reading Like a Queer," *Gay and Lesbian Quarterly* 11 (2005): 237–263. A. Arrizon, *Queering* Mestizaje: *Transculturation and Performance* (Ann Arbor: University of Michigan Press, 2006).

3. See, in particular, the work of H. Hidalgo and E. Hidalgo-Christensen, "The Puerto Rican Cultural Response to Female Homosexuality," in *The Puerto Rican Woman*, ed. E. Acosta-Belen and E. Hidalgo-Christensen (New York: Praeger, 1979), 110–123. O. M. Espín, "Cultural and Historical Influences on Sexuality," in *Pleasure and Danger: Exploring Female Sexuality*, ed. Carole S. Vance (Boston: Routledge and Kegan Paul, 1984), 149–164. Espín, "Crossing Borders and Boundaries: The Life Narratives of Immigrant Lesbians," *Division* 44 (1995): 18–27. Espín, *Latina Realities: Essays on Healing, Migration, and Sexuality* (Boulder, Colo.: Westview Press, 1997). Espín, *Women Crossing Boundaries: A Psychology of Immigration and Transformations of Sexuality* (Florence, Ky.: Taylor and Frances/Routledge, 1999). Y. Retter Vargas, "Lesbians," in *Oxford Encyclopedia of Latinos and Latinas in the United States*, ed. Suzanna Oboler and D. J. González (Oxford: Oxford University Press, 2005), 545–549. Y. G. Retter, "Identity Development of Lifelong vs. Catalyzed Latina Lesbians" (M.A. thesis, University of California–Los Angeles, 1987). Yolanda Retter, "On the Side of Angels: Lesbian Activism in Los Angeles, 1979–1990" (Ph.D. diss., University of New Mexico, 1999). Lourdes Argüelles and Anne M. Rivero, "Gender/Sexual Orientation, Violence, and Transnational Migration: Conversations with Some Latinas We Think We Know," *Urban Anthropology* 22 (1993): 259–275. J. M. Martinez, "Radical Ambiguities and the Chicana Lesbian: Body Topographies on Contested Lands," in *Spoils of War: Women of Color, Cultures and Revolutions*, ed. T. D. Sharply-Whiting and Renee T. White (Lanham, Md.: Rowman and Littlefield, 1997), 127–150. Martinez, "Speaking as a Chicana: Tracing Cultural Heritage through Silence and Betrayal," in *Speaking Chicana: Power, Voice, and Identity*, ed. D. L. Galindo and M. D. Gonzalez-Velásquez (Tucson: University of Arizona Press, 1999), 59–84. Yolanda Leyva, "Listening to the Silences in Latina/Chicana Lesbian History," in *Living Chicana Theory*, ed. Carla Trujillo (Berkeley: Third Woman Press, 1998), 429–434. Patricia Zavella, "Playing with Fire: The Gendered Construction of Chicana/Mexicana Sexuality," in *The Gender/ Sexuality Reader: Culture, History, Political Economy*, ed. Roger Lancaster and Micaela di Leonardo (New York: Routledge, 1997); and "Talkin' Sex: Chicanas and Mexicanas Theorize about Silences and Sexual Pleasures," in *Chicana Feminisms: A Critical Reader*, ed. Gabriela Arredondo, Aida Hurtado, Norma Klahn, and Olga Nájera-Ramirez (Durham: Duke University Press, 2003). Y. G. Flores-Ortiz, "Voices from the Couch: The Co-Creation of a Chicana Psychology," in *Living Chicana Theory*, ed. Trujillo, 102–122. Reyes, "Latina Lesbians and Alcohol." P. E. Stevens, "The Experiences of Lesbians of Color in Health Care Encounters: Narrative Insights for Improving Access and Quality," *Journal of Lesbian Studies* 2 (1998): 77–94. C. Cruz, "Toward an Epistemology of a Brown Body," *International Journal of Qualitative Studies in Education* 14 (2001): 657–669. Aida Hurtado, *Voicing Chicana Feminisms: Young Women Speak Out on Sexuality and Identity* (New York: New York University Press, 2003). Anita Tijerina Revilla, "Raza Womyn Re-Constructing Revolution: Exploring the Intersections of Race, Class, Gender, and Sexuality in the Lives of Chicana/Latina Student Activists" (Ph.D. diss., University of California–Los Angeles, 2004). S. Loue and N. Méndez, "I Don't Know Who I Am: Severely Mentally Ill Latina WSW Navigating Differentness," *Journal of Lesbian Studies* 10 (2006): 249–266.

4. Juanita Ramos (Díaz), ed., *Compañeras: Latina Lesbians* (New York: M. E. Sharpe, 1987). Cherríe Moraga and Gloria Anzaldúa, *This Bridge Called My Back: Writings by Radical*

Women of Color (New York: Women of Color Press, 1983). Retter, "On the Side of Angels." Retter Vargas, "Lesbians." Juana María Rodríguez, *Queer Latinidad: Identity Practices, Discursive Spaces* (New York: New York University Press, 2003).

5. It would be an enormous task (and quite beyond the purview of this brief article) to document the entirety of Latina lesbian cultural production that emerged in this time period, but we point the reader to a few important figures in queer Latina culture: Butchlalis de Panochtitlán (performance group), Alicia Gaspar de Alba (novelist), Marga Gomez (comedian), Felicia Luna Lemus (novelist), Cherríe Moraga (playwright and essayist), Emma Pérez (novelist), tatiana de la tierra (poet and editor of *Esto No Tiene Nombre*), and Ela Troyano (performance artist and filmmaker). For a bibliography of queer Latina fiction (1971–2000), see Esquibel, *With Her Machete in Her Hand*, 183–190.

6. Espín, *Latina Realities*, 97. D. R. Atkinson, G. Morten, and D. W. Sue, *Counseling American Minorities* (Dubuque, Iowa: W. C. Brown Co., 1979). Vivienne C. Cass, "Homosexual Identity Formation: A Theoretical Model," *Journal of Homosexuality* 4 (1979): 219–235.

7. Espín, *Latina Realities*; quotations on 107.

8. Hidalgo and Hidalgo-Christensen, "Puerto Rican Cultural Response"; quotation on 121. Gloria Anzaldúa, *Borderlands/La Frontera: The New Mestiza* (San Francisco: Aunt Lute Books, 1987); quotation on 102. Rodríguez, *Queer Latinidad*; quotation on 24.

9. Revilla, "Raza Womyn Re-Constructing Revolution," 2, 87.

10. Loue and Méndez, "I Don't Know Who I Am"; quotations on 250, 260.

11. T. L. Hughes et al., "Age and Racial/Ethnic Differences in Drinking and Drinking-Related Problems in a Community Sample of Lesbians," *Journal of Studies on Alcohol* 67 (2006): 579–590; quotations on 581.

12. V. Rosario, "'*Qué Joto Bonita!*': Transgender Negotiations of Sex and Ethnicity," *Journal of Gay and Lesbian Psychotherapy* 8 (2004): 89–97, esp. 91–92; quotations on 93, 91.

13. Emma Pérez, "Sexuality and Discourse: Notes from a Chicana Survivor," in *Chicana Lesbians: The Girls Our Mothers Warned Us About*, ed. Carla Trujillo (Berkeley: University of California Press, 1991), 159–184; quotation on 175. Leyva, "Listening to the Silences"; quotations on 429, 432.

14. Argüelles and Rivero, "Gender/Sexual Orientation Violence"; quotations on 260, 261.

15. Ibid.; quotations on 260, 273.

16. Zavella, "Talkin' Sex"; quotation on 247.

17. Loue and Méndez, "I Don't Know Who I Am"; quotations on 250–251, 253. Hidalgo and Hidalgo-Christensen, "Puerto Rican Cultural Response," 115.

18. INCITE! Women of Color Against Violence, *Color of Violence: The INCITE! Anthology* (Cambridge, Mass., 2006). Argüelles and Rivero, "Gender/Sexual Orientation Violence"; quotations on 263 ("Chini," "Mila"), 264.

19. Argüelles and Rivero, "Gender/Sexual Orientation Violence"; quotation on 268–269. Debra A. Wilson, director, *Butch Mystique*, documentary film (Moyo Entertainment, 2003). Amber Hollibaugh and Cherríe Moraga, "What We're Rollin' around in Bed With: Sexual Silences in Feminism," in *Powers of Desire*, ed. Ann Snitow, Christine Stansell, and Sharon Thompson (New York: New Feminist Library, 1983), 400.

20. Raquel Gutierrez and Claudia Rodriguez, Butchlalis de Panochtitlán (in performance), La Peña Cultural Center, Berkeley, Calif., March 10, 2007. Teresa de Lauretis, *The Practice of Love: Lesbian Sexuality and Perverse Desire* (Bloomington: Indiana University Press, 1994).

21. Rodríguez, *Queer Latinidad.* Juana María Rodríguez, "Femme Gestures: Fragments from a Sexual Archive," paper presented at annual meeting of the American Studies Association, Oakland, 2006. Stacy Macias, "Femme Ontology: Queer Femininities and the Politics of Race On-line," paper presented at annual meeting of the American Studies Association, Oakland, 2006. Zavella, "Playing with Fire"; quotations on 399, 400, 404 (emphasis added).

CHAPTER 15   LATINA/O TRANSPOPULATIONS

1. Holly Woodlawn and J. Copeland, *A Low Life in High Heels: The Holly Woodlawn Story* (New York: St. Martin's Press, 1991). Lou Reed fans might realize that she is the "Holly from Miami, F-L-A." that he sings about in "Walk on the Wild Side." Max Wolf Valerio, *The Testosterone Files: My Hormonal and Social Transformation from FEMALE to MALE* (Emeryville, Calif.: Seal Press, 2006).

2. I focus particularly on transsexual, transgender, transvestite, *travesti*, and *vestida* experiences, which require social recognition as a member of a gender to which one was not assigned at birth, rather than those experiences, particularly some transvestite experiences (including my own) that do not require persona, pronoun, or name changes.

3. I recognize, however, that owing to the instability of categories used to identify these populations in the literature, an exhaustive bibliography is elusive; I welcome revisions and additions to this bibliography.

4. See Horacio N. Roque Ramírez, "Communities of Desire: Memory and History from Queer Latinas and Latinos in the San Francisco Bay Area, 1960s–1990s," unpublished manuscript, for documentation of the emergence of this category through the efforts of gay men of color to create the conditions of legibility for their own existence in the early 1990s. It is important to note that the category MSM has been used to eclipse the presence of trans-Latinas, in both research and policy work, by counting trans women as "men who have sex with men."

5. Mobilization Against AIDS International (MAAI), "Monitoring Report: El/La Transgender Latina Program of Mobilization Against AIDS International" (San Francisco, 2006).

6. Karla Rosales and Manolo Guzmán, *Mind If I Call You Sir? A Discussion between Latina Butches and Female-to-Male Transgendered Latinos*, video recording (San Francisco: StickyGirl Productions, 2004).

7. See Eithne Luibhéid and Lionel Cantú Jr., eds., *Queer Migrations: Sexuality, U.S. Citizenship, and Border Crossings* (Minneapolis: University of Minnesota Press, 2005).

8. I follow the periodization suggested in an overview by Rubén G. Rumbaut, "The Americans: Latin American and Caribbean Peoples in the United States," in *Perspectives on Las Américas: A Reader in Culture, History, and Representation*, ed. Matthew C. Gutmann (London: Blackwell, 2003): the Spanish colonial presence in North America (ca. 1560 to 1848); U.S. expansion and nation formation (1803–98); pre–World War II (1898–1944) and post–World War II (1944–present). These periods account for both settled populations and migrations.

9. In "Homosexuality, Homophobia, and Revolution: Notes toward an Understanding of the Cuban Lesbian and Gay Male Experience," pt. 2, *Signs* 11 (1985): 120–136, B. Ruby Rich and Lourdes Argüelles make a similar argument about Cuban sexuality with respect to U.S. imperialism in prerevolutionary Cuba. For these cases in the colonial and expansionist periods, see Pete Sigal, ed., *Infamous Desire: Male Homosexuality in*

Colonial Latin America (Chicago: University of Chicago Press, 2003); Richard C. Trexler, *Sex and Conquest: Gendered Violence, Political Order, and the European Conquest of the Americas* (Ithaca, N.Y.: Cornell University Press, 1995); Ramón Gutiérrez, "Must We Deracinate Indians to Find Gay Roots?" *Out/Look* 1 (1989): 61–67; Walter Williams, "The Abominable Sin: The Spanish Campaign against 'Sodomy' and Its Results in Modern Latin America," in *The Spirit and the Flesh: Sexual Diversity in American Indian Culture*, ed. Williams (Boston: Beacon Press, 1986); and Will Roscoe, *The Zuni Man-Woman* (Albuquerque: University of New Mexico Press, 1991), and *Changing Ones: Third and Fourth Genders in Native North America* (New York: Palgrave Macmillan, 1998). For an example of this type of account at Zuñi, see Elsie Clews Parsons, "The Zuñi La'mana," *American Anthropologist* 18 (1916): 521–528.

10. These reports have been the subject of much speculation about "LGBT history," the meanings of indigenous gender categories, and the possibilities of transgender existence. While there are serious questions as to whether berdache or "Two-Spirit" people can or should be read as transgender, these cases do represent alternate formations of gender in the colonial system that precedes the establishment of U.S. Latina/o populations. I argue that they are part of the analytical field "trans" as I have established its usage in this essay.

11. Nancy Mirabal, "*De aqui, de alla*: Race, Empire, and Nation in the Making of Cuban Migrant Communities in New York and Tampa, 1823–1924" (Ph.D. diss., University of Michigan, 2000). Clare Sears, "'A Dress Not Belonging to His or Her Sex': Cross-Dressing Law in San Francisco, 1860–1900" (Ph.D. diss., University of California–Santa Cruz, 2005).

12. Rumbaut," The Americans." On "Two-Spirit" people see Sigal, *Infamous Desire*, and Roscoe, *Zuni Man-Woman*.

13. Between 1930 and 1950, the mainland Puerto Rican population grew nearly six times, from 53,000 to 301,000. By 1960, it had grown to 888,000; Rumbaut, "The Americans," 96, 97. John D'Emilio, "Gay Politics and Community in San Francisco since World War II," in *Hidden from History: Reclaiming the Gay and Lesbian Past*, ed. Martin Duberman, Martha Vicinus, and George Chauncey Jr. (New York: New American Library, 1989).

14. In "Race and Place in the Adaptation of Mariel Exiles," *International Migration Review* 35 (2001): 450, Emily H. Skop characterizes the waves of twentieth-century Cuban migration to the United States as: "Golden Exiles (1960–1964), Freedom Flight refugees (1965–1974), and Mariels (1980)." The Mariel boatlift included Cubans who had been criminalized or pathologized—among these, lesbians, gay men, and transgender women. Peña, "Visibility and Silence"; quotation on 32. See also Peña's article by this title in *Queer Migrations*, ed. Luibhéid and Cantú. I am not aware of any references in Peña's or anyone else's work to FTM Marielitos. Lourdes Argüelles and B. Ruby Rich, "Homosexuality, Homophobia, and Revolution: Notes toward an Understanding of the Cuban Lesbian and Gay Male Experience," *Signs* 9 (1984): 683–699, 10 (1985): 120–136. Jaime Cortez, *Sexile/Sexilio* (Los Angeles: Institute for Gay Men's Health, 2004).

15. Rumbaut, "The Americans," 99. The 2000 Census reports the following cities as the sites of the largest Latina/o populations, by group—Mexican: Los Angeles, Chicago, Houston, San Antonio, and Phoenix; Puerto Rican: New York, Chicago, and Philadelphia; Cuban: Hialeah, Miami, New York, Tampa, and Los Angeles; Central American: Los Angeles, New York, Houston, Miami, and San Francisco; and South American: New York, Los Angeles, Chicago, and Miami. See U.S. Bureau of the Census, "The

Hispanic Population: Census 2000 Brief" (Washington, D.C.: U.S. Department of Commerce, 2001).

16. D'Emilio, "Gay Politics and Community." Carter Wilson, "Queen of Hearts: Dancing 'til Dawn in the Artichoke Capital of the World," *Out/Look* 5 (1992): 48–53. Horacio Roque Ramírez, *A Language of (In)Visibility: Latina and Latino LGBT Images in Spanish-Language Television and Print News Media* (New York: Gay and Lesbian Alliance Against Defamation, Center for the Study of Media and Society, 2003). Roque Ramírez, "Latina/Latino Americans," in *glbtq: An Encyclopedia of Gay, Lesbian, Bisexual, Transgender and Queer Culture*, ed. C. J. Summers (Chicago: glbtq, Inc., 2005), http://www.glbtq.com/social-sciences/latina_latino_americans.html.

17. Luibhéid and Cantú, *Queer Migrations*, xxix. The top ten metropolitan statistical areas for same-sex cohabitation are: New York, Los Angeles, San Francisco, Washington, D.C., Chicago, Boston, Philadelphia, Dallas, and Atlanta. Miami comes in at eleventth. This is based on a simple analysis I ran from U.S. Bureau of the Census, "Census 2000: Summary File 1 (SF 1) 100-Percent Data, Table PCT 14 Unmarried-Partner Households by Sex of Partners" (Washington, D.C.: U.S. Department of Commerce, 2000). The existence of cohabiting same-sex couples does not, however, even remotely begin to pinpoint where trans people, much less trans Latina/os, live. First, trans people may often not be visible as part of this subset, even if they are cohabiting with a partner who appears to be of the same sex as they are. Heterosexually oriented trans people will not be legible to this analysis. And, of course, this approach does not include people who are not cohabiting with a partner.

18. Don Kulick, *Travesti: Sex, Gender, and Culture among Brazilian Transgendered Prostitutes* (Chicago: University of Chicago Press, 1998). Marcia Ochoa, "Queen for a Day: *Transformistas*, Misses, and Mass Media in Venezuela" (Ph.D. diss., Stanford University, 2006). Annick Prieur, *Mema's House, Mexico City: On Transvestites, Queens, and Machos* (Chicago: University of Chicago Press, 1998). J. Schifter, *From Toads to Queens: Transvestism in a Latin American Setting* (New York: Harrington Park Press, 1999).

19. The trans Latin American men whom I have encountered in Venezuela approached me through clinical or academic settings, not at clubs, in neighborhoods, or on the street, as was the case with *transformistas*, the trans women with whom I worked in Venezuela. They tell me of their extreme isolation and desire to make contact with other trans men around the world. In the U.S. Latino context, the trans-Latinos I have met also talk about isolation, but there have been important efforts by these trans men (initially through the organization FTM International, which lists affiliates in Mexico, Brazil, and Argentina) to develop social networks to fight isolation. See the international chapter listings at http://www.ftmi.org/8.htm.

20. Sylvia Rivera, one of the key figures of the Stonewall rebellion in New York in 1969, has had a long history of activism around issues faced by queer, trans, and people of color. Lawrence La Fountain-Stokes, "*Translocas* and *Transmachos*: Trans Diasporic Puerto Rican Drag," unpublished manuscript, 2005. Eric Marcus, "The Drag Queen—Rey 'Sylvia Lee' Rivera," in *Making History: The Struggle for Gay and Lesbian Equal Rights, 1945–1990* (New York: HarperCollins, 1992). Benjamin Heim Shepard, "Amanda Milan and the Rebirth of the Street Trans Action Revolutionaries," in *From ACT UP to the WTO: Urban Protest and Community Organizing in the Era of Globalization*, ed. B. H. Shepard and R. Hayduk (London: Verso, 2002), 156–163. "Queer *Latinidad*" was coined by Juana María Rodríguez, in *Queer Latinidad*.

21. Michael Bailey, *The Man Who Would Be Queen: The Science of Gender-Bending and Transsexualism* (Washington, D.C.: Joseph Henry Press, 2003). Lynn Conway's "Investigation

into the Publication of J. Michael Bailey's Book on Transsexualism by the National Academies" (2003–2006) painstakingly documents every step of the response to Bailey's book and the complaints that have been filed against him. Conway has asserted that it was precisely these women's marginality that Bailey sought out in his research subjects so that he could produce claims about them without their interference. Conway's informal account is available at http://ai.eecs.umich.edu/people/conway/TS/LynnsReviewOfBaileysBook.html. In "Transsexual 'Subjects' Complain about Professor's Research Methods," *Chronicle of Higher Education*, July 25, 2003, Robin Wilson also reported on the complaints.

22. Cortez, *Sexile/Sexilio.*

23. Susan Aikin and Carlos Aparicio, *The Salt Mines*, video recording (New York: Third World Newsreel, 1990), and *The Transformation*, video recording (New York: Starfish Productions, 1995). Valentín Aguirre, producer, video recording, *Wanted Alive: Teresita la Campesina* (San Francisco: La Tina, 1997), and, with Augie Robles, *¡Viva 16!*, video recording (San Francisco: 21st Century Aztlán, 1994). Horacio Roque Ramírez, "A Living Archive of Desire: Teresita la Campesina and the Embodiment of Queer Latino Community Histories," in *Archive Stories: Facts, Fictions, and the Writing of History*, ed. Antoinette Burton (Durham: Duke University Press, 2005). Rosales and Guzmán, *Mind If I Call You Sir?* Agnieszka Holland and Shelley Evans, *A Girl Like Me: The Gwen Araujo Story*, television broadcast (USA Lifetime, 2006). Valerio, *Testosterone Files.*

24. San Francisco Lesbian and Gay Historical Project, 1989.

25. Sears, "A Dress Not Belonging."

26. Gutiérrez, "Must We Deracinate Indians?" Roscoe, *Zuni Man-Woman* and *Changing Ones.* Sigal, *Infamous Desire.* Trexler, *Sex and Conquest.* Walter Williams, *The Spirit and the Flesh: Sexual Diversity in American Indian Culture* (Boston: Beacon Press, 1986).

27. The TRANS-Project, in addition to producing data about social and health outcomes, provided substance-abuse and HIV-prevention services to trans Latinas, including workshops, support groups, and counseling.

28. Rafael Díaz, George Ayala, and Edward Bein, "Sexual Risk as an Outcome of Social Oppression: Data from a Probability Sample of Latino Gay Men in Three U.S. Cities," *Cultural Diversity and Ethnic Minority Psychology* 10 (2004): 255–267. Jesús Ramirez-Valles, "The Protective Effects of Community Involvement for HIV-Risk Behavior: A Conceptual Framework," *Health Education Research* 17 (2002): 389–403. Ramirez-Valles et al., "From Networks to Populations: The Development and Application of Respondent-Driven Sampling among IDUs and Latino Gay Men," *AIDS and Behavior* 9 (2005): 387–402.

29. Héctor Carrillo, "Sexual Migration, Cross-Cultural Sexual Encounters, and Sexual Health," *Sexuality Research and Social Policy: Journal of NSRC* 1 (2004): 58–70. Ochoa, "Queen for a Day." Stephen F. Morin et al., "Policy Perspectives on Public Health for Mexican Migrants in California," *Journal of Acquired Immune Deficiency Syndrome* (2004): 252–259. In "HIV Risk Behaviors among Male-to-Female Transgender Persons of Color in San Francisco," *American Journal of Public Health* 94 (2004): 1193–1199, Tooru Nemoto et al. report seroprevalence among San Francisco transgender Latinas at 26–29 percent.

30. Nemoto et al., "HIV Risk Behaviors." Eiko Sugano, Tooru Nemoto, and Don Operario, "The Impact of Exposure to Transphobia on HIV Risk Behavior in a Sample of Transgendered Women of Color in San Francisco," *AIDS and Behavior* 10 (2006): 217–225. California Collaborations in HIV Prevention Research Dissemination Project,

"Module 2: The Los Angeles Transgender Health Study" (n.d.), http://chrp.ucop. edu/resources/dissemination_project/guidance.pdf . Cathy J. Reback et al., "Making Collaboration Work: Key Components of Practice/Research Partnerships," *Journal of Drug Issues* 32 (2002): 837–848. Cathy J. Reback and Emilia L. Lombardi, "HIV Risk Behaviors of Male-to-Female Transgenders in a Community-Based Harm Reduction Program," *Transgender and HIV: Risks, Prevention, and Care* 31 (2001): 59–68. Cathy J. Reback and Paul A. Simon, "The Los Angeles Transgender Health Study: Creating a Research and Community Collaboration," in *Preventing AIDS: Community-Science Collaborations*, ed. C. J. Reback, et al. (New York, Routledge, 2004), 115–131. Adam J. Heintz and Rita M. Melendez, "Intimate Partner Violence and HIV/STD Risk among Lesbian, Gay, Bisexual, and Transgender Individuals," *Journal of Interpersonal Violence* 21 (2006): 193–208. Rita M. Melendez et al., "Health and Health Care among Male-to-Female Transgender Persons Who Are HIV Positive," *American Journal of Public Health* 96 (2006): 1034–1037.

31. Lawrence La Fountain-Stokes, "Adoring Lady Catiria: Consumption, Expenditure, and Puerto Rican Trans Performance in New York," *XXV International Congress of the Latin American Studies Association*, 2004. Roque Ramírez, "Living Archive of Desire." Carlos Decena, "Notorious HIV: The Media Spectacle of Nushawn Williams," *GLQ: A Journal of Lesbian and Gay Studies* 11 (2005): 635–637. Sherry Deren et al., "Research Challenges to the Study of HIV/AIDS among Migrant and Immigrant Hispanic Populations in the United States," *Journal of Urban Health* 82 (2005): iii13–iii25. Michele Shedlin, Carlos Ulises Decena, and Denise Oliver-Velez, "Initial Acculturation and HIV Risk among New Hispanic Immigrants," *Journal of the National Medical Association* 97 (2005): 32S–37S. Michele Shedlin et al., "Immigration and HIV/AIDS in the New York Metropolitan Area," *Journal of Urban Health* 83 (2006): 43–58. José Esteban Muñoz, *Disidentifications: Queers of Color and the Performance of Politics* (Minneapolis: University of Minnesota Press, 1999). Salvador Vidal-Ortiz, "'Sexuality' and 'Gender,' in *Santería*: Towards a Queer of Color Critique in the Study of Religion" (Ph.D. diss., City University of New York, 2005).

32. Annamarie Jagose and Don Kulick, "The GLQ Forum: Thinking Sex/Thinking Gender," *Gay and Lesbian Quarterly* 10 (2004): 211–313.

33. At El/La, many of our trans-Latina participants report "female" gender and "straight" sexuality in our intake forms. While we obviously respect the categories they choose, we also record observed gender and sexuality, where we can clarify that these participants are transgender women who, if not for this observation, would be included in statistics on heterosexual women born women. Adding an additional category of observation allows us to respect both ways of seeing.

CHAPTER 16   BOUNDARIES AND BISEXUALITY

1. Segment from life history interview with "Jorge," a pseudonym for a research participant in the study "The Social Context and Organization of Sexual Risk among Mexican Immigrant Men to New York City, 2005–2007," principal investigator: Miguel Muñoz-Laboy, Ph.D. This study was funded by the National Institute of Childhood Health and Human Development (NICHD 3 R01 HD04172404 S1), and approved by the Columbia University Institutional Review Board, Protocol No. IRB-AAAB6847.

2. Frederick Barth, *Ethnic Groups and Boundaries: The Social Organization of Culture Difference* (Boston: Little, Brown, 1969). This move in anthropology was fueled by ethnographic studies in urban and changing settings, particularly by the work of urban anthropologists in Africa.

3. Edward O. Laumann et al., eds., *The Sexual Organization of the City* (Chicago: University of Chicago Press, 2004); quotation on 8.

4. M. Hirschfeld, *Sexual Anomalies and Perversions* (New York: Francis Aldor, 1938).

5. Ronald Fox, "Bisexual Identities," in *Lesbian, Gay, and Bisexual Identities over Lifespan*, ed. A. R. D'Augelli and C. J. Patterson (New York: Oxford University Press, 1995), 24–47. Paula Rodriguez-Rust, ed., *Bisexuality in the United States: A Social Science Reader* (New York: Columbia University Press, 2000). Ruth Firestein, *Bisexuality: The Psychology and Politics of an Invisible Minority* (Newbury Park, Calif.: Sage Publications, 1996). Ronald Fox, "Bisexuality in Perspective: A Review of Theory and Research," in Firestein, *Bisexuality*.

6. P. Aggleton, *Bisexualities and AIDS: International Perspectives* (Bristol, Pa.: Taylor and Francis, 1996). Tomás Almaguer, "Chicano Men: A Cartography of Homosexual Identity and Behavior," in *The Lesbian and Gay Studies Reader*, ed. H. Abelove, M. A. Barale, and D. Halperin (New York: Routledge, 1993), 255–270. C. Cáceres, "Male Bisexuality in Peru and the Prevention of AIDS," in *Bisexualities and AIDS*, ed. Aggleton. Joseph Carrier, *De los otros: Intimacy and Homosexuality among Mexican Men* (New York: Columbia University Press, 1995). Rafael M. Díaz, *Latino Gay Men and HIV: Culture Sexuality and Risk Behavior* (New York: Routledge, 1998). Richard Parker, *Bodies, Pleasures, and Passions: Sexual Culture in Contemporary Brazil* (Boston: Beacon Press, 1991). A. De Moya and R. Garcia, "AIDS and the Enigma of Bisexuality in the Dominican Republic," in *Bisexualities and AIDS*, ed. Aggleton. A. L. Liguori, M. Gonzalez-Block, and P. Aggleton, "Bisexuality and HIV/AIDS in Mexico," in *Bisexualities and AIDS*, ed. Aggleton. Rafael L. Ramírez, *What It Means to Be a Man: Reflections on Puerto Rican Masculinity* (New Brunswick, N.J.: Rutgers University Press, 1999). J. Schifter, *Public Sex in a Latin Society* (New York: Haworth Press, 2000). C. Taylor, "*El Ambiente*: Male Homosexual Social Life in Mexico City" (Ph.D. diss., University of California–Berkeley, 1978).

7. See, for example, Miguel Muñoz-Laboy and B. Dodge, "Bisexual Practices: Patterns, Meanings, and Implications for HIV/STI Prevention among Bisexually Active Latino Men and Their Partners," *Journal of Bisexuality* 5 (2005): 81–100.

8. C. Hemmings, *Bisexual Spaces: A Geography of Sexuality and Gender* (New York: Routledge, 2002).

9. R. Brooks et al., "HIV and AIDS among Men of Color Who Have Sex with Men and Men of Color Who Have Sex with Men and Women: An Epidemiological Profile," *AIDS Education and Prevention* 15 (2003): 1–6. S. Y. Chu et al., "AIDS in Bisexual Men in the United States: Epidemiology and Transmission to Women," *American Journal of Public Health* 82 (1992): 220–224. T. Diaz et al., "Sociodemographic and HIV Risk Behaviors of Bisexual Men with AIDS: Results from a Multistate Interview Project," *AIDS* 7 (1993): 1227–1232. S. Maguen, "Bisexuality," in *Encyclopedia of AIDS: A Social, Political, Cultural, and Scientific Record of the HIV Epidemic*, ed. R. Smith (Chicago: Penguin Group, 1998).

10. Rodriguez-Rust, *Bisexuality in the United States*.

11. L. Doll and C. Beeker, "Male Bisexual Behavior and HIV Risk in the United States: Synthesis of Research with Implications for Behavioral Interventions," *Guildford Press* 3 (1996): 205–227. New York City Department of Health, "HIV/AIDS Surveillance Report. December 2000."

12. E. Arend, "The Politics of Invisibility: Homophobia and Low-Income HIV-Positive Women Who Have Sex with Women," *Journal of Homosexuality* 49 (2005): 97–122. R. Young and I. Meyer, "The Trouble with 'MSM' and 'WSM': Erasure of the Sexual-Minority Person in Public Health Discourse," *American Journal of Public Health* 95

(2005): 164–168. R. Young et al., "Women Injection Drug Users Who Have Sex with Women Exhibit Increased HIV Infection and Risk Behaviors," *Journal of Drug Issues* 30 (2000): 499–524. G. Bauer and S. Welles, "Beyond Assumptions of Negligible Risk: Sexually Transmitted Diseases and Women Who Have Sex with Women," *American Journal of Public Health* 91 (2001): 1282–1286.

13. L. Solursh, D. Solursh, and C. Meyer, "Is There Sex after the Prison Door Slams Shut?" *Medicine and Law* 12 (1993): 439–443. M. Comfort et al., "'You Can't Do Nothing in This Damn Place': Sex and Intimacy among Couples with an Incarcerated Male Partner," *Journal of Sex Research* 42 (2005): 3–12. D. Seal and A. Ehrhardt, "Masculinity and Urban Men: Perceived Scripts for Courtship, Romantic, and Sexual Interactions with Women," *Culture, Health and Sexuality* 5 (2003): 295–319.

14. Margarita Burgos et al., "Assessing the Interrelationships of STIs, Substance Abuse, and Depression among Street-Based Female Adolescent Sex Workers in Puerto Rico: Implications for Community Health," in *Sexual and Reproductive Health Promotion in Latino Populations: Parteras, Promotoras y Poetas*, ed. M. I. Torres and G. P. Cernada (Amityville, N.Y.: Baywood Publishing, 2003), 135–146. Michele Shedlin and Sherry Deren, "Cultural Factors Influencing HIV Risk Behavior among Dominicans in New York City," *Journal of Ethnicity in Substance Abuse* 1 (2002): 71–95. Nancy Romero-Daza, Margaret Weeks, and Merrill Singer, "Much More than HIV! The Reality of Life on the Streets for Drug-Using Sex Workers in Inner-City Hartford," *International Quarterly of Community Health Education* 18 (1998–99): 107–119. Sherry Deren et al., "HIV Risk Behaviors among Dominican Brothel and Street Prostitutes in New York City," *AIDS Education and Prevention* 8 (1996): 444–456. Deren et al., "Dominican, Mexican, and Puerto Rican Prostitutes: Drug Use and Sexual Behaviors," *Hispanic Journal of Behavioral Sciences* 19 (1997): 202–213. Adeline Nyamathi and Rose Vasquez, "Impact of Poverty, Homelessness, and Drugs on Hispanic Women at Risk for HIV Infection," in *Hispanic Psychology: Critical Issues in Theory and Research*, ed. Amado Padilla (Thousand Oaks, Calif.: Sage Publications, 1995), 213–227. Mark Padilla, *Caribbean Pleasure Industry: Tourism, Sexuality, and AIDS in the Dominican Republic* (Chicago: University of Chicago Press, 2007).

15. More than one hundred thousand (111,900) Latina/os were incarcerated (i.e., more than 15 percent of the imprisoned population) in the United States, on July 1, 2005, as reported in May 2006 by the Bureau of Justice Statistics. The incarceration rates for Latinos and Latinas were the second highest after African Americans, followed by whites in the United States. For males, the incarceration rates per 100,000 residents by ethnic group were African American, 4,682; Latinos, 1,856; and whites, 709. For females per 100,000 residents by ethnic group, the incarceration rates were African American, 347; Latinas, 144; and whites, 88.

16. For example, the *Oprah Winfrey Show*: "A Secret Sex World: Living on the 'Down Low.'"

17. Paula Rodriguez-Rust, "Coming Out in the Age of Social Constructionism: Sexual Identity Formation among Lesbian and Bisexual Women," *Gender and Society* 7 (1993): 50–77. Rodriguez-Rust, "Managing Multiple Identities: Diversity among Bisexual Men and Women," in *Bisexuality*, ed. Firestein, 53–83. Rodriguez-Rust, "Who Are We and Where Do We Go from Here? Conceptualizing Bisexuality," in *Closer to Home: Bisexuality and Feminism*, ed. E. R. Weise (Seattle: Seal Press, 1992), 281–310. Fox, "Bisexual Identities."

18. A. P. MacDonald, "Bisexuality: Some Comments on Research and Theory," *Journal of Homosexuality* 6 (1981): 21–35. J. Paul, "Bisexuality: Reassessing Our Paradigms of Sexuality," in *Bisexuality in the United States*, ed. Rodriguez-Rust. M. Bradford, "The

Bisexual Experience: Living in a Dichotomus Culture," in *Current Research on Bisexuality*, ed. Ronald Fox (Binghamton, N.Y.: Harrington Park Press, 2004).

19. This is depicted, for Mexico, in the case studies of Carrier, *De los otros*, and Liguori, Gonzalez-Block, and Aggleton, "Bisexuality and HIV/AIDS in Mexico"; for Nicaragua, R. Lancaster, "Subject Honour and Object Shame: The Construction of Male Homosexuality and Stigma in Nicaragua," *Ethnology* 27 (1988): 111–125; for Peru, Cáceres, "Male Bisexuality in Peru"; for Dominican Republic, De Moya and Garcia, "AIDS and the Enigma of Bisexuality"; and for Brazil, Richard Parker, "Bisexuality and HIV/AIDS in Brazil," in *Bisexualities and AIDS*, ed. Aggleton. See also Manolo Guzmán, *Gay Hegemony/Latino Homosexualities* (New York: Routledge, 2006); Gloria González-López, *Erotic Journeys: Mexican Immigrants and Their Sex Lives* (Berkeley: University of California Press, 2005); Marysol W. Asencio, *Sex and Sexuality among New York's Puerto Rican Youth* (Boulder, Colo.: Lynne Rienner Publishers, 2002); Ana Maria Alonso and Maria Teresa Koreck, "Silences: 'Hispanics,' AIDS, and Sexual Practices," *Differences* 1 (1989): 110–125; Almaguer, "Chicano Men"; Miguel Muñoz-Laboy, "Beyond 'MSM': Sexual Desire among Bisexually Active Latino Men in New York City," *Sexualities* 7 (2004): 55–80; and Muñoz-Laboy, "The Organization of Sexuality of Bisexually Active Latino Men in New York City" (Ph.D. diss., Columbia University; 2001).

CHAPTER 17   REVISITING *ACTIVOS* AND *PASIVOS*

1. Tomás Almaguer, "Chicano Men: A Cartography of Homosexual Identity and Behavior," first published in *differences: A Journal of Feminist Cultural Studies* 3 (1991): 2; reprinted in in *The Lesbian and Gay Studies Reader*, ed. H. Abelove, M. A. Barale, and D. Halperin (New York: Routledge, 1993).

2. Octavio Paz, *Labyrinth of Solitude [Laberinto de la soledad]: Life and Thought in Mexico* (New York: Grove Press, 1961).

3. Roger. N. Lancaster. *Life Is Hard: Machismo, Danger, and the Intimacy of Power in Nicaragua* (Berkeley: University of California Press, 1992). Joseph Carrier, *De los otros: Intimacy and Homosexuality among Mexican Men* (New York: Columbia University Press, 1995).

4. Héctor Carrillo, *The Night Is Young: Sexuality in Mexico in the Times of AIDS* (Chicago: University of Chicago Press, 2002). Carrillo, "Cultural Change, Hybridity, and Male Homosexuality in Mexico," *Culture, Health, and Sexuality* 1 (1999): 223–238.

5. Richard Parker, *Bodies, Pleasures, and Passions: Sexual Culture in Contemporary Brazil* (Boston: Beacon Press, 1991). Parker, *Beneath the Equator: Cultures of Desire, Male Homosexuality, and Emerging Gay Communities in Brazil* (New York: Routledge, 1999). Néstor García Canclini, *Hybrid Cultures: Strategies for Entering and Leaving Modernity* (Minneapolis: University of Minnesota Press, 1995). Roberto Strongman, "Syncretic Religion and Dissident Sexuality," in *Queer Globalizations: Citizenship and the Afterlife of Colonialism*, ed. Arnaldo Cruz-Malavé and Martin F. Manalansan (New York: New York University Press, 2002).

6. Louis Althusser, "Ideology and Ideological State Apparatuses: Notes towards an Investigation," *Lenin and Philosophy and Other Essays by Louis Althusser* (New York: Monthly Review Press, 1971), 127–186.

7. Amber Hollibaugh and Cherríe Moraga, "What We're Rollin' around in Bed With: Sexual Silences in Feminism," *Heresies* 12 (1981), reprinted in *My Dangerous Desires: A Queer Girl Dreaming Her Way Home* (Durham: Duke University Press, 2000).

8. Steven Epstein, "Gay Politics, Ethnic Identity: The Limits of Social Constructionism," *Socialist Review* 17 (1987): 9–50.

9. For more on Cherríe Moraga's linking of racial and sexual discussions, see, e.g., "La Güera," in *Loving in the War Years: Lo Que Nunca Pasó Por Sus Labios* (Boston: South End Press, 1983), 50–59.

10. Carlos Ulises Decena, "Queering the Heights: Dominican Transnational Identities and Male Homosexuality in New York City" (Ph.D. diss., New York University, 2004).

11. William Simon and John H. Gagnon, "A Sexual Scripts Approach," in *Theories of Human Sexuality*, ed. J. Geer and W. O'Donahue (New York: Plenum, 1987), 363–383.

12. Strongman's chapter ("Syncretic Religion") referred to here and earlier makes a few important arguments in our discussion. Strongman engages U.S. anthropologists' portrayal of Latin American sexualities, critiquing the power between informant and researcher. He also portrays specific religious spaces as symbolic images of cultural hybridity in Latin America. Instead of an activo/pasivo framework, Strongman proposes a secrecy/disclosure paradigm, where sexual dissidence has significant space in Latin American societies, though not political presence through sexual identification.

13. Lionel Cantú, *The Sexuality of Migration: Border Crossings in Mexican Immigrant Men*, ed. Nancy A. Naples and Salvador Vidal-Ortiz (New York: New York University Press, 2009).

14. Laud Humphrey, *Tearoom Trade: Impersonal Sex in Public Places* (Chicago: Aldine, 1970).

15. See esp. Bonnie Urciuoli, *Exposing Prejudice: Puerto Rican Experiences of Language, Race, and Class* (Boulder, Colo.: Westview Press, 1996).

16. Don Kulick, *Travesti: Sex, Gender, and Culture among Brazilian Transgendered Prostitutes* (Chicago: University of Chicago Press, 1998). Manolo Guzmán, "*'Pa' la Escuelita con Mucho Cuida'o y por la Orillita'*: A Journey through the Contested Terrains of the Nation and Sexual Orientation," in *Puerto Rican Jam: Essays on Culture and Politics*, ed. Frances Negrón-Muntaner and Ramón Grosfoguel (Minneapolis: University of Minnesota Press, 1997).

17. Manolo Guzmán, *Gay Hegemony/Latino Homosexualities* (New York: Routledge, 2006).

18. Decena refers here to expert discourse in terms of anthropologists writing about Latina/o sexualities and homosexualities; Guzmán's discussion of the "analysis of expert discourse" points to scholars' "belief in the racial innocence of gayness, a belief in its total independence from racial matters," one that "also plagues the study of ethnic homosexualities" (in ibid., 1, 2).

19. Carlos Cáceres, *Secreto a voces—Homoerotismo masculino en Lima: Culturas, identidades y salud sexual* (Lima: Universidad Peruana Cayetano Heredia/REDESS Jovenes, 2000). Jacobo Schifter, *Latino Truck Driver Trade: Sex and HIV in Central America* (Binghamton, N.Y.: Haworth Hispanic/Latino Press, 2001).

20. S. Freud, *Three Essays on the Theory of Sexuality* (New York: Basic Books, 2000 [1962]).

21. Gilbert Herdt, *The Sambia: Ritual and Gender in New Guinea* (Belmont, Calif.: Wadsworth, 1987). David Halperin, *One Hundred Years of Homosexuality* (New York: Routledge, 1989).

22. *Bugarrones* often charge for sexual encounters with self-identified gay men, and the popular perception is that they act as activos in the sexual encounter. In "*Pa' la Escuelita*," 217, Guzmán discusses the *bugarrón* as a "partial sexual identity" and states that Puerto Rican bugarrones, "like Mexican *mayates*, articulate their sexuality within a sexual economy where sexual activity with another man does not necessarily constitute a homosexual identity or act."

23. *Princesa* (London: Parallax Pictures, 2001), Henrique Goldman, director.

24. Salvador Vidal-Ortiz, "'Sexuality' and 'Gender,' in *Santería*: Towards a Queer of Color Critique in the Study of Religion" (Ph.D. diss., City University of New York, 2005).

25. George Chauncey, *Gay New York: Gender, Urban Culture, and the Making of the Gay Male World, 1890–1940* (New York: Basic Books, 1994).

26. José Esteban Muñoz, "Feeling Brown: Ethnicity and Affect in Ricardo Bracho's *The Sweetest Hangover (and Other STDs)*," *Theatre Journal* 52 (2000): 67–79.

27. Patricia Zavella, *Women's Work and Chicano Families: Cannery Workers of the Santa Clara Valley* (Ithaca, N.Y.: Cornell University Press, 1987). Gloria González-López, *Erotic Journeys: Mexican Immigrants and Their Sex Lives* (Berkeley: University of California Press, 2005).

28. González-López, *Erotic Journeys*.

29. Salvador Vidal-Ortiz, "Sexuality and Gender in *Santería*: LGBT Identities at the Crossroads of Religious Practices and Beliefs," in *Gay Religion*, ed. Scott Thumma and Edward Gray (Walnut Creek, Calif.: AltaMira Press, 2005), 115–137. Carrillo, *The Night Is Young*.

CHAPTER 18   RETIRING BEHAVIORAL RISK, DISEASE, AND DEFICIT MODELS

1. U.S. Agency for International Development, "The 'ABCs' of HIV Prevention: Report of a USAID Technical Meeting on Behavior Change Approaches to Primary Prevention of HIV/AIDS," Population, Health, and Nutrition Information Project (Washington, D.C., 2003).

2. Centers for Disease Control and Prevention, "2008 Compendium of HIV Prevention Interventions," HIV/AIDS Prevention Research Synthesis Project (Atlanta, 2008).

3. Carlos Cáceres, "Afterword: The Production of Knowledge on Sexuality in the AIDS Era: Some Issues, Opportunities, and Challenges," in *Framing the Sexual Subject: The Politics of Gender, Sexuality and Power*, ed. Richard Parker, Regina Maria Barbosa, and Peter Aggleton (Berkeley: University of California Press, 2000).

4. Manolo Guzmán, *Gay Hegemony/Latino Homosexualities* (New York: Routledge, 2006).

5. Ibid. Ron S. Gold and Michael J. Skinner, "Situational Factors and Thought Processes Associated with Unprotected Intercourse in Young Gay Men," *AIDS* 6 (1992): 1021–1030. M. Boulton et al., "Gay Men's Accounts of Unsafe Sex," *AIDS Care* 7 (1995). 619–630. W. R. Lenderking et al., "Childhood Sexual Abuse among Homosexual Men: Prevalence and Association with Unsafe Sex," *Journal of General Internal Medicine* 12 (1997): 250–253. S. Jinich et al., "Childhood Sexual Abuse and HIV Risk-Taking Behavior among Gay and Bisexual Men," *AIDS and Behavior* 2 (1998): 41–51. R. Stall et al., "Alcohol Use, Drug Use, and Alcohol Related Problems among Men Who Have Sex with Men," *Urban Men's Health Study* 96 (2001): 1589–1601. P. N. Halkitis, J. T. Parsons, and M. J. Stirratt, "A Double Epidemic: Crystal Methamphetamine Drug Use in Relation to HIV Transmission among Gay Men," *Journal of Homosexuality* 41 (2001): 17–35. R. Stall et al., "Association of Co-occurring Psychosocial Health Problems and Increased Vulnerability to HIV/AIDS among Urban Men Who Have Sex with Men," *American Journal of Public Health* 93 (2003): 939–942. T. Bingham, "Special Analysis: Los Angeles Men's Survey, Los Angeles County Department of Health Services," HIV Epidemiology Program, 2004. I. M. Fernandez et al., "High Rates of Club Drug Use and Risky Sexual Practices among Hispanic Men Who Have Sex with Men in Miami, Florida," *Substance Use and Misuse* 40 (2005): 1347–1362. Sonya Arreola, "Childhood Sexual Abuse and HIV among Latino Gay Men: The Price of Sexual Silence during the AIDS Epidemic," in *Sexual Inequalities and Social Justice*, ed. N. Teunis (Berkeley: University of California Press, 2006).

6. Centers for Disease Control and Prevention, "Increases in HIV Diagnoses—29 States, 1999–2002," *Morbidity and Mortality Weekly Report* 52 (2003): 1145–1148. S. S. Bull and M. McFarlane, "Soliciting Sex on the Internet: What Are the Risks for Sexually Transmitted Diseases and HIV?" *Sexually Transmitted Diseases* 27 (2000): 545–550. P. N. Halkitis and J. T. Parsons, "Intentional Unsafe Sex (Barebacking) among HIV-Positive Gay Men Who Seek Sexual Partners on the Internet," *AIDS Care* 15 (2003): 367–378.

7. A. Mettey et al., "Associations between Internet Sex Seeking and STI Associated Risk Behaviors among Men Who Have Sex with Men," *Sexually Transmitted Infections* 79 (2003): 466–468. E. G. Benotsch, S. Kalichman, and M. Cage, "Men Who Have Met Sex Partners via the Internet: Prevalence, Predictors, and Implications for HIV Prevention," *Archives of Sexual Behavior* 31 (2002): 177–183. A. A. Kim, C. Kent, and W. McFarland, "Cruising the Internet Highway," *Journal of Acquired Immune Deficiency Syndrome* 28 (2001): 89–93.

8. J. Elford, G. Bolding, and L. Sherr, "Seeking Sex on the Internet and Sexual Risk Behavior among Gay Men Using London Gyms," *AIDS* (England) 15 (2001): 1409–1415. Bull and McFarlane, "Soliciting Sex on the Internet."

9. Kaiser Family Foundation, "HIV-Positive MSM Finding Partners through 'Sero-Sorting' Might Be Contributing to Decline in HIV Incidence in San Francisco," 2005, www.kaisernetwork.org/daily-reports/rep-index.

10. George Ayala, T. A. Bingham, and D. Rivas, unpublished qualitative findings from an epidemiological study of Latino men who have sex with men in Los Angeles, 2004, funded by the Centers for Disease Control and Prevention.

11. S. J. Misovich, J. D. Fisher, and W. A. Fisher, "Close Relationships and Elevated HIV-Risk Behavior: Evidence and Possible Underlying Psychological Processes," *Review of General Psychology* 1 (1997): 72–107. Rafael Díaz and George Ayala, *Social Discrimination and Health: The Case of Latino Gay Men and HIV* (New York: National Gay and Lesbian Task Force, 2001).

12. R. H. Remien et al., "Factors Associated with HIV Sexual Risk Behavior in Male Couples of Mixed HIV Status," *Journal of Psychology and Human Sexuality* 13 (2001): 31–48.

13. R. B. Hays et al., "Unprotected Sex and HIV Risk-Taking among Young Gay Men within Boyfriend Relationships," *AIDS Education and Prevention* 9 (1997): 314, 329. S. M. Haas, "Social Support as Relationship Maintenance in Gay Male Couples Coping with HIV or AIDS," *Journal of Social and Personal Relationships* 19 (2002): 87–111. G. M. Powell-Cope, "Heterosexism and Gay Couples with HIV Infection," *Western Journal of Nursing Research* 20 (1998): 478–496.

14. N. L. Beckerman, S. Letteney, and K. Lorber, "Key Emotional Issues for Couples of Mixed HIV Status," *Social Work in Health Care* 31 (2000): 25–42.

15. R. H. Remien, A. Carballo-Dieguez, and G. Wagner, "Intimacy and Sexual Risk Behavior in Sero-Discordant Male Couples," *AIDS Care* 7 (1995): 429–439.

16. Centers for Disease Control and Prevention, "Trends in Primary and Secondary Syphilis and HIV Infections in Men Who Have Sex with Men—San Francisco and Los Angeles, California, 1998–2002," *Morbidity and Mortality Weekly Report* 53 (2003): 574–578. Centers for Disease Control and Prevention, *HIV/AIDS Surveillance Report, 2006* (Atlanta, 2008), 18. U.S. Department of Health and Human Services, Centers for Disease Control and Prevention: 5–55, http://www.cdc.gov/hiv/topics/surveillance/resources/reports/.

17. I. H. Meyer, "Minority Stress and Mental Health in Gay Men," *Journal of Health and Social Behavior* 36 (1995): 35–56. J. Stokes and J. Peterson, "Homophobia, Self-Esteem, and Risk for HIV among African American Men Who Have Sex with Men," *AIDS Education*

and Prevention 10 (1998): 278–292. Rafael Díaz and George Ayala, "The Impact of Homophobia, Poverty, and Racism on the Mental Health of Latino Gay and Bisexual Men: Findings from a Probability Sample in Three U.S. Cities," *American Journal of Public Health* 91 (2001): 927–932. D. Malebranche, "Black Men Who Have Sex with Men and the HIV Epidemic: Next Steps for Public Health," *American Journal of Public Health* 93 (2003): 862–864. G. A. Millett et al., "Greater Risk for HIV Infection of Black Men Who Have Sex With Men: A Critical Literature Review," *American Journal of Public Health* 96 (2006): 1007–1019.

18. Rafael Díaz, George Ayala, and Edward Bein, "Sexual Risk as an Outcome of Social Oppression: Data from a Probability Sample of Latino Gay Men in Three Cities," *Cultural Diversity and Ethnic Minority Psychology* 10 (2004): 255–267.

19. J. D. Fisher and W. A. Fisher, "Theoretical Approaches to Individual-Level Change in HIV Risk Behavior," in *Handbook of HIV Prevention*, ed. J. L. Peterson and R. J. DiClemente (New York: Kluwer Academic/Plenum, 2000), 3–48.

20. Rafael M. Díaz, *Latino Gay Men and HIV: Culture Sexuality and Risk Behavior* (New York: Routledge, 1998).

21. V. M. Mays, S. D. Cochran, and A. Zamudio, "HIV-Prevention Research: Are We Meeting the Needs of African American Men Who Have Sex with Men?" *Journal of Black Psychology* 30 (2004): 78–103.

22. Héctor Carrillo, *The Night Is Young: Sexuality in Mexico in the Times of AIDS* (Chicago: University of Chicago Press, 2002). Guzmán, *Gay Hegemony/Latino Homosexualities.*

23. Centers for Disease Control and Prevention, "Internet Use and Early Syphilis Infection among Men Who Have Sex with Men—San Francisco, California, 1999–2003," *Morbidity and Mortality Weekly Report* 52 (2003): 1229–1232. Centers for Disease Control and Prevention, "Syphilis and HIV Infections." Halkitis, Parsons, and Stirratt, "Double Epidemic." Fernandez et al., "Club Drug Use and Risky Sexual Practices." S. M. Smith, "New York City HIV Superbug: Fear or Fear Not?" *Retrovirology* 2 (2005): 14, http://www.pubmedcentral.nih.gov/articlerender.

24. S. Aral, "Elimination and Reintroduction of Sexually Transmitted Disease: Lessons to Be Learned?" *American Journal of Public Health* 89 (1999): 995–997.

25. W. Odets, "AIDS Education and Harm Reduction Approaches for the 21st Century," *AIDS Public Policy Journal* 9 (1994): 1–15. J. Gallagher, "Risky Business," *Advocate*, March 17, 1998, 46–48.

26. María Cecília Zea, Nadine Jernewall, and José Toro-Alfonso, "Lesbian, Gay, and Bisexual Psychology and Ethnic Minority Issues over the Last 10 Years," in *Providing a Voice for Ethnic Minority Issues in Psychology*, Special Section of the Office of Ethnic Minority Affairs Communique, American Psychological Association, March 2003, iv–vi.

27. Centers for Disease Control and Prevention, *HIV/AIDS Surveillance Report, 2006* (Atlanta, 2008), 18. U.S. Department of Health and Human Services, Centers for Disease Control and Prevention: 5–55, http://www.cdc.gov/hiv/topics/surveillance/resources/reports/.

28. Gary W. Harper, Nadine Jernewall, and María Cecília Zea,, "Giving Voice to Emerging Science and Theory for Lesbian, Gay, and Bisexual People of Color," *Cultural Diversity and Ethnic Minority Psychology* 10 (2004): 187–199. P. J. Poppen et al., "Sero-Status Disclosure, Sero-Concordance, Partner Relationship, and Unprotected Anal Intercourse among HIV-Positive Latino MSM," *AIDS Education and Prevention* 17 (2005): 228–238. Cecilia Zea et al., "Disclosure of HIV Status and Psychological Well-Being among Latino Gay and Bisexual Men," *AIDS and Behavior* 9 (2005): 15–26.

29. G. Ayala, C. Husted, and A. Spieldenner, *Holding Open Space: Re-tooling and Re-imagining HIV Prevention for Gay and Bisexual Men of Color* (New York: Institute for Gay Men's Health, 2004), http://www.apla.org/publications/publications.html.

EPILOGUE

1. The delightful expression "Me hace la vida un yogurt" (She/He makes my life into a yogurt) appears often in US-based Spanish-language talk shows out of Miami. When uttered, it is accompanied by the vexation of the complaining party. In these cases, the host of the show is recruited to help resolve the conflict between the feuding parties. It is hard not be charmed by the metaphoric work that yogurt is supposed to do when invoked, except for the fact that, as many an avid yogurt eater might attest, the messiness of yogurt can be quite delicious—as can be the experience of watching these programs.

2. Cherríe Moraga and Gloria Anzaldúa, *This Bridge Called My Back: Writings by Radical Women of Color* (New York: Women of Color Press, 1983). Juanita Ramos (Díaz), ed., *Compañeras: Latina Lesbians* (New York: M. E. Sharpe, 1987). See Chapter 14.

3. Yolanda Leyva, "Listening to the Silences in Latina/Chicana Lesbian History," in *Living Chicana Theory*, ed. Carla Trujillo (Berkeley: Third Women Press, 1998), 429–434.

4. Arlene M. Dávila, *Latinos, Inc.: The Marketing and Making of a People* (Berkeley: University of California Press, 2001).

5. See Chapter 7. Ana Y. Ramos-Zayas, *National Performances: The Politics of Class, Race, and Space in Puerto Rican Chicago* (Chicago: University of Chicago Press, 2003). Ramos-Zayas, "Becoming American, Becoming Black? Urban Competency, Racialized Spaces, and the Politics of Citizenship among Brazilian and Puerto Rican Youth in Newark," *Identities* 14 (2007): 85–109. Nicholas De Genova, *Working the Boundaries: Race, Space, and "Illegality" in Mexican Chicago* (Durham: Duke University Press, 2005). De Genova and Ramos-Zayas, *Latino Crossings: Mexicans, Puerto Ricans, and the Politics of Race and Citizenship* (New York: Routledge, 2003). Salvador Vidal-Ortiz, "On Being a White Person of Color: Using Autoethnography to Understand Puerto Rican's Racialization," *Qualitative Sociology* 27 (2004): 179–203.

6. See Chapters 12, 10. Lionel Cantú, "Border Crossings: Mexican Men and the Sexuality of Migration" (Ph.D. diss., University of California–Irvine, 1999). Cantú, "*De Ambiente*: Queer Tourism and the Shifting Boundaries of Mexican Male Sexualities," *Gay and Lesbian Quarterly* 8 (2002): 139–166. Cantú, "A Place Called Home: A Queer Political Economy of Mexican Immigrant Men's Family Experiences," in *Queer Families, Queer Politics: Challenging Culture and the State*, ed. Mary Bernstein and Renate Reimann (New York: Columbia University Press, 2001). Marysol W. Asencio, *Sex and Sexuality among New York's Puerto Rican Youth* (Boulder, Colo.: Lynne Rienner Publishers, 2002). Laura Briggs, *Reproducing Empire: Race, Sex, Science, and U.S. Imperialism in Puerto Rico* (Berkeley: University of California Press, 2002).

7. Dávila, *Latinos, Inc.* Vilma Santiago-Irizarry, *Medicalizing Ethnicity: The Construction of Latino Identity in Psychiatric Settings* (Ithaca, N.Y.: Cornell University Press, 2001).

8. *Vergüenza* means "shame" and *sin vergüensura* means "shameless," roughly speaking.

9. Patricia Zavella, personal communication, April 15, 2008.

CONTRIBUTORS

KATIE ACOSTA is an assistant professor at Tulane. She received her doctoral degree from the University of Connecticut. Her master's thesis, "Invisible Immigrants: Exploring the Lives of Gays and Lesbians from Latin America," analyzes the legal experiences of Latino gay and lesbian immigrants and binational couples. Her interests include immigration, sexuality, Latina/o studies, and gender. Her article "'Everything Would Be Solved If Only We Could Marry': Queers, Marriage, and Immigration Policy" was accepted for publication as part of an edited series entitled At the Interface/Probing the Boundaries, which explores sex and sexualities.

TOMÁS ALMAGUER is a professor of ethnic studies and former dean of the College of Ethnic Studies at San Francisco State University. He currently teaches courses for the Ethnic Studies, Raza Studies, History, and Sociology Departments on that campus. He is author of *Racial Fault Lines: The Historical Origins of White Supremacy in California* (Berkeley: University of California Press, 1994) and the widely reprinted article "Chicano Men: A Cartography of Homosexual Identity and Behavior." He is completing a book project on the life histories of Chicano gay men in the Bay Area for the University of California Press.

HORTENSIA AMARO is Distinguished Professor of Health Sciences in Bouvé College of Health Sciences, Northeastern University, and director of the Institute on Urban Health Research. Amaro's work focuses on improving the connections between public health research and public health practice. Her research has resulted in more than 100 scientific publications on epidemiological and community-based studies of alcohol and drug use among adolescents and adults; the effectiveness of HIV/AIDS-prevention programs; substance abuse and mental health treatment among Latina and African American women; reentry programs for incarcerated men of color; and screening and brief intervention on alcohol and drug use in college populations.

SANDRA ARÉVALO is a research scientist at the Institute on Urban Health Research at Northeastern University, where she oversees a number of research studies on alcohol and drug use interventions for women of color. Arévalo is also a doctoral student in the Department of Sociology at Northeastern University and recipient of the Summer Science Research Fellowship from the National Hispanic Science Network. Arévalo has four publications in peer-reviewed journals and three book-report chapters in the areas of substance abuse treatment, health of incarcerated men, sexual and intimate violence, and sexual health. Arévalo received her MA in sociology from Northeastern University and her BA in psychology from the University of Massachusetts–Boston.

SONYA GRANT ARREOLA is a psychologist and epidemiologist by training with a long history of working in clinical and research settings. Currently, Arreola is the scientific director of Legacy, an initiative within the HIV Vaccine Trials Network intending to develop and conduct research aimed at increasing participation of underrepresented populations in HIV-prevention research.

MARYSOL ASENCIO is associate professor of Human Development and Family Studies and Puerto Rican and Latino Studies at the University of Connecticut. She is author of *Sex and Sexuality among New York's Puerto Rican Youth*. She is currently working on a series of articles as well as a book based on her three-year ethnographic study of migrant Puerto Rican sexual minorities. She was a 2003 Social Science Research Council–Sexuality Research postdoctoral fellow. She serves on the international editorial board of *Sexuality Research and Social Policy*.

GEORGE AYALA, PsyD, works as a research psychologist/public health analyst at RTI International's Urban Health Program in San Francisco, California, and serves as the executive officer of the Global Forum on MSM and HIV. Dr. Ayala is the former director of education at AIDS Project Los Angeles (APLA), where he managed HIV prevention; technical assistance; community-based research; and print, video, and Web-based media programs for six years. While at APLA, Dr. Ayala created and/or produced a series of provocative community-based publications that explore the intersections between race, gender, sex, and HIV. He has worked in the nonprofit HIV/AIDS sector supervising large and interdisciplinary teams of professionals for 18 years. Dr. Ayala's work in the HIV/AIDS sector includes international collaborations with nongovernmental agencies in Canada, India, South Africa, Honduras, Australia, Mexico, and China. A clinical psychologist by training, Dr. Ayala has also conducted HIV prevention research since 1996. His research mainly focuses on understanding the mechanisms through which social discrimination impacts health. Dr. Ayala continues to serve as a part-time consultant with APLA.

AMALIA L. CABEZAS is an associate professor of women's studies at the University of California–Riverside. Her areas of interest include Latina/o and Caribbean studies, tourism, sexualities and gender; and women's labor. Her book *Economies of Desire: Tourism and Sex in Cuba and the Dominican Republic* has been published by Temple University Press. In addition to various journal articles, she coedited *Wages of Empire: Neoliberal Policies, Repression, and Women's Poverty* (Boulder, Colo.: Paradigm Publishers, 2007).

LUZ CALVO is an assistant professor of ethnic studies at California State University–East Bay. She received her PhD in the history of consciousness at the University of California–Santa Cruz. Her dissertation was entitled "Border Fantasies: Sexual Anxieties and Political Passions in the Mexico-U.S. Borderlands." She has published essays on Chicano/a art, photography, and film.

HÉCTOR CARRILLO is associate professor of sociology and gender studies at Northwestern University. His current work examines the intersections between migration, sexuality, and health. He has recently completed a large ethnographic study of sexuality and HIV risk among Mexican gay and bisexual male immigrants in San Diego. His book, *The Night Is Young: Sexuality in Mexico in the Time of AIDS* (University of Chicago Press, 2002), received the Ruth Benedict Prize from the American Anthropological Association. He serves as associate editor for the journal *Sexuality Research and Social Policy.*

JAIME CORTEZ is an artist and cultural worker. He is the founding editor of *Corpus* magazine and the groundbreaking anthology *Virgins, Guerrillas, and Locas.* Cortez's work appears in numerous anthologies and journals, and his radio essays have been included on KQED's Perspectives series. His writing is anthologized in numerous collections including *Besame Mucho, 2sexE,* and *Queer PAPI Porn.* He is the author of a graphic novel, *Sexile/Sexilio* (Los Angeles: Institute for Gay Men's Health, 2004).

CARLOS DECENA is an interdisciplinary social scientist, writer, and cultural critic. He teaches in the departments of Women's and Gender Studies and Latino and Hispanic Caribbean Studies at Rutgers University. His work has appeared in the *Journal of the National Medical Association, Social Text* (a special issue titled "The Border Next Door," which he coedited with Margaret Gray), *Papeles de Población, AIDS Care,* the *Journal of Urban Health,* and *GLQ.* His book *Tacit Subjects: Dominican Transnational Identities and Male Homosexuality in New York City* is forthcoming from Duke University Press.

CATRIÓNA RUEDA ESQUIBEL is an alumna of the History of Consciousness Program and the Women of Color Research Cluster. An assistant professor in the College of Ethnic Studies, San Francisco State University, she is author of *With Her Machete in Her Hand: Reading Chicana Lesbians* (Austin: University of Texas Press, 2006). She is currently editing an anthology of queer Chicana fiction and, with Luz Calvo, is working on a project on twenty-first-century Queer Latinas.

MELANIE LÓPEZ FRANK is a PhD candidate at Emory University in Atlanta, Georgia, in the Department of Spanish and Portuguese. Her areas of interest are U.S. Latino/a studies, contemporary literature of the pan-Caribbean and the diaspora, as well as the politics and problems of identity—specifically, representations of identities in various media (film, music, literature).

GLORIA GONZÁLEZ-LÓPEZ is an associate professor in the Department of Sociology at the University of Texas at Austin. She conducts sexuality research with Mexican immigrants and teaches graduate and undergraduate courses on sexuality, gender and society, Latinas/Chicanas and sex, men and masculinity, and qualitative methods and sexuality research. Her book *Erotic Journeys: Mexican Immigrants and Their Sex Lives* was published by the University of California Press in 2005. She is currently conducting sociological research on the sexual and romantic histories and life experiences of adult incest survivors born and raised in the largest urbanized areas in Mexico.

ELENA R. GUTIÉRREZ is an associate professor of gender and women's studies and Latin American and Latino studies at the University of Illinois–Chicago. She authored *Undivided Rights: Women of Color Organizing for Reproductive Justice* with Jael Silliman, Marlene Gerber Fried, and Loretta Ross (Boston: South End Press, 2004); her book *Fertile Matters: The Politics of Mexican Origin Women's Reproduction* has been newly released by the University of Texas Press.

RAMÓN GUTIÉRREZ is the Preston and Sterling Morton Distinguished Service Professor of History at the University of Chicago. He is author of *When Jesus Came the Corn Mothers Went Away: Marriage, Sexuality, and Power in New Mexico, 1500–1846* (Stanford: Stanford University Press, 1991). He is currently working on "The Fire of the Ire of God: the Religious and Political Thought of Reies López Tijerina."

PATRICK "PATO" HEBERT is an artist, educator, and cultural worker based in Los Angeles. He is associate director of education at AIDS Project Los Angeles (APLA) and teaches in the Photography and Imaging Department at Art Center College of Design. His art has been featured at El Mueso de las Artes in Guadalajara, Longwood Arts in the Bronx, the Oakland Museum of California, Galería de la Raza in San Francisco, Voz Alta in San Diego, and the Japanese American National Museum in L.A. His writing has appeared in the *Journal of Visual Culture* and *disClosure*, and his images can be seen in the premiere issue of the journal *Encyclopedia*.

CLAUDIA KOUYOUMDJIAN is a doctoral student in the Department of Education at the University of California–Santa Barbara. Her research focuses on adolescent development, specifically sexuality, achievement motivation, ethnic minority family processes, and culture, gender, and health socialization.

PABLO MITCHELL is an associate professor of history at Oberlin College. He is the author of *Coyote Nation: Sexuality, Race, and Conquest in Modernizing New Mexico, 1880–1920* (Chicago: University of Chicago Press, 2005), which was awarded the 2007 Ray Allen Billington Award from the Organization of American Historians. His next book project, "West of Sex: Mexican Americans, Sex Crimes, and the Birth of the Modern West," examines significant features of Mexican American sexuality around the turn of the twentieth century through the use of sexual offense cases from California, New Mexico, and Texas.

MIGUEL MUÑOZ-LABOY is an associate professor of social-medical sciences at Columbia University, Mailman School of Public Health. His published work includes "Beyond 'MSM': Sexual Desire among Bisexually Active Latino Men in New York City" in *Sexualities*; "Bi-Sexual Practices: Patterns, Meanings, and Implications for HIV/STI Prevention among Bisexually Active Latino Men and Their Partners," with B. Dodge, in *Journal of Bisexuality*; "Bisexual Latino Men and HIV and Sexually Transmitted Infections Risk: An Exploratory Analysis," with B. Dodge, in *American Journal of Public Health*; and "Familism, Sexual Regulation, and Risk among Bisexual Latino Men," in *Archives of Sexual Behavior*.

ERUM NADEEM is a postdoctoral fellow at the University of California–Los Angeles. She has collaborated with the Public Health Foundation Enterprises WIC program to evaluate their services for teen parents and to study how Latina/o families adapt to adolescent pregnancy by examining videotaped mother-adolescent dialogues about motherhood, dating/sex, and family conflict.

MARCIA OCHOA is assistant professor of community studies at the University of California–Santa Cruz. Her book *Queen for a Day: Transformistas, Misses, and Mass Media in Venezuela* is under contract with Duke University Press. Her field research explores the strategic use of beauty and femininity by beauty pageant contestants and transgender women. She currently supervises the El/La Transgender Latina HIV Prevention Program, which promotes the health and survival of transgender Latina immigrants in San Francisco's Mission District. Ochoa has done extensive work on HIV prevention media campaigns, media literacy, and human rights for Latin American transgender people in Venezuela and the United States.

DOLORES ORTIZ is a graduate student in sociology at University of California–Riverside. Her current project is "A Queer Analysis of Breastfeeding in Public: Energy, Production, and Consumption." Her past research has included projects on Chicana heterosexuality, Latina teenage parenting, and risky sexual behaviors in at-risk youth populations. Her essay "The War at Home: A Chicana Mama Speaks Out" was published in *Semana de la Mujer Journal*, and reprinted in *Nuestra Cosa*.

SUSANA PEÑA is an associate professor in the Department of Ethnic Studies at Bowling Green State University. Peña's publications include "'Obvious' Gays and the State Gaze: Cuban Gay Visibility and U.S. Immigration Policy during the 1980 Mariel Boatlift," forthcoming in the *Journal of the History of Sexuality*, and "Visibility and Silence: Mariel and Cuban American Gay Male Experience and Representation," in *Queer Migrations: Sexuality, U.S. Citizenship, and Border Crossings* (Minneapolis: University of Minnesota Press, 2005), edited by Eithne Luibhéid and Lionel Cantú Jr. She received a postdoctoral fellowship from the Social Science Research Council's Sexuality Research Fellowship Program to conduct research for her forthcoming book, "*Oye Loca*: The Making of Cuban American Gay Miami."

JOSÉ QUIROGA is a professor of Spanish at Emory College, Emory University. He is the author of *Cuban Palimpsests* (Minneapolis: University of Minnesota Press, 2005) and, in collaboration with Daniel Balderston, *Sexualidades en disputa* (Buenos Aires: Ricardo Rojas, 2005). In addition, he has published *Tropics of Desire: Interventions from Queer Latino America* (New York: New York University Press, 2001) and *Understanding Octavio Paz* (Columbia: University of South Carolina Press, 2000).

LAURA F. ROMO is an associate professor at the Gervitz Graduate School of Education at the University of California–Santa Barbara. Her publications include "Promoting Values of Education in Latino Mother-Adolescent Discussions about Conflict and Sexuality Issues," with Claudia Kouyoumdjian, Erum Nadeem, and Marian Sigman, in *Latina Girls: Voices of Adolescent Strength in the U.S.* (New York: New York University Press, 2006); "The Role of Misconceptions on Latino Women's Acceptance of Emergency Contraceptive Pills," with A. B. Berenson and Z. H. Wu, in *Contraception*; and "Mexican-American Adolescent Responsiveness to Their Mothers' Questions about Dating and Sexuality," with Nadeem, T. K. Au, and Sigman, in *Journal of Applied Developmental Psychology*.

DEBORAH R. VARGAS is an assistant professor in the Department of Chicano/Latino Studies at the University of California–Irvine. Her publications include "*Cruzando Frontejas*: Remapping Selena's Tejano Music Crossover," reprinted in *The Chicana/o Cultural Studies Reader* (New York: Routledge Press, 2006), edited by Angie Chabram-Dernersesian, and "Rosita Fernandez: La Rosa de San Antonio," in *Frontiers: A Journal of Women's Studies* (2003). Vargas is the recipient of a 2007–2008 Ford Foundation Postdoctoral Fellowship at the UCLA Chicano Studies Research Center. She is revising her manuscript "Decolonial Divas: Gender, Sexuality, and Nation in the Making of Texas-Mexian-American Music."

SONIA VALENCIA is a graduate of the University of California–Riverside, with Bachelor of Arts degrees in English and women's studies. She will be pursuing a doctoral degree in cultural studies.

SALVADOR VIDAL-ORTIZ is an assistant professor in the Department of Sociology at American University, Washington, D.C. His research interests include Puerto Rican and Latina/o studies, race and ethnic studies, racialization, sex/gender/sexuality, transgender and transsexual studies, and queer theory. Vidal-Ortiz is also interested in feminist-based writings and women of color theorizing from personal experience, personal narratives, and autoethnography. He is working on a book manuscript that addresses the term "sexual minorities" in Santería, the Afro-Cuban religion, as practiced in the United States.

CARMEN YON LEAU is a PhD student in sociomedical sciences at Columbia University. Her published work includes *Género y sexualidad: Una mirada de los y las adolescentes de cinco barrios de Lima* (Gender and Sexuality: A View of Adolescents from Five Neighborhoods of Lima, 1998); and "Sistemas explicativos sobre el cuerpo y la salud e intervenciones en salud reproductiva" (Explanatory Systems about Body and Health and Reproductive Health Interventions), in C. Cáceres et al., eds., *La salud como un derecho ciudadano: Perspectivas y propuestas desde América Latina* (2003).

INDEX

ABC (television network), 126
abduction, rape, 22
abortion, 43, 98–100. *See also* contraception
abstinence, 49, 69, 98, 183, 274
acculturation: adolescent sexuality, 57–58; cultural challenges to sexuality, 197; heterosexual love and sex, 104–106; literature on, 81, 87
activism: feminist, 43; HIV/AIDS, 7, 139–141, 151–172, 219; queer, 218–219; student, 6
activo/pasivo paradigm, 10, 247–248, 253–273, 283–284, 350n12
ACT UP (AIDS Coalition To Unleash Power), 139, 163, 219; Oral History Project, 163; youth program, 169–171
adolescents. *See* Latina/o youths
adoption, issues of, 131, 136
adultery, 21–22, 30
The Advocate (magazine), 195
African Americans: biological mixing, 13; childhood sexual abuse, 53; incarceration rates, 348n15; as slaves, 19, 27; youths and sexual behavior, 78–79
Aguilera, Christina, 129
Aguirre, Valentín, 238
AIDS. *See* HIV/AIDS
AIDS Coalition To Unleash Power. *See* ACT UP
AIDS, Inc. *See* AIDS Project Los Angeles
AIDS Project Los Angeles (APLA), 151–172, 238, 277
Aikin, Susan, 238
Alba, Alicia Gaspar de, 146, 341n5
Albertson, Jack, 126
alcohol use, 57, 275
Alfaro, Luis, 131
Almaguer, Tomás, 253–273, 284
Almendros, Nestor, 143
Amodóvar, Pedro, 132–133
Alva, Bartolomé de, 18–19
Amaro, Hortensia, 285
American Family (television documentary), 127
American History and Life (database), 38
American Me (movie), 135
An American Obsession (Terry), 43
American Psychological Association, 277
American Religious Identification Survey, 176–177
amniocentesis, 84
anger, 275
Anthony, Adelina, 131, 228

anxiety, 275
Anzaldúa, Gloria E.: cultural production of knowledge, 139; "new mestiza" identity, 142, 220; on sexual norms and cultures, 107; on social structures, 118; third-wave feminism, 141; on White supremacy, 281; women of color publishing and activism, 218
Aparicio, Carlos, 238
Aparicio, Frances, 117, 123, 127–128, 129, 147
APLA. *See* AIDS Project Los Angeles
Araujo, Gwen, 238
Archive Stories (Burton), 238
Arenas, Reinaldo, 143, 144
Arévalo, Sandra, 285
Argentina, social deviants, 34
Argüelles, Lourdes, 143, 224–225, 226, 234
Arnaz, Desi, 42, 122, 125
arranged marriage. *See* marriage: arranged
Arreola, Sonya Grant, 285
Arrizón, Alicia, 131
Arroyo, Josianna, 146
Arroyo, Liani, 84
artist/activism. *See* activism
Asencio, Marysol, 186, 197, 284
Así es la vida (television program), 284
Atkinson, Donald R., 219
Atlanta, Georgia, 201
Audre Lorde Project, 139
Aventura, 284
Ayala, George, *162*, 239, 282, 285

Babe Bean. *See* Garland, Jack
Badu, Erykah, 169
Bailey, J. Michael, 237
Bailey, Martin, 44
Baires, Tiffany, 164
Ball, Lucille, 42
Balsero "crisis," 234
La Bamba (movie), 121
Bana, Juan, 44
Banderas, Antonio, 1
Barbie doll, 128
Barbosa, P., 72
Barth, Frederick, 245
Before Night Falls (Arenas), 144
Bein, Edward, 239
Bejel, Emilio, 146
berdache, 27–28, 37, 239, 269, 343n10
Bésame mucho (Manrique), 144
bestiality, 20